PATRICIA M. ANDERSON
Quinnipiac College

LEONARD G. RUBIN
Marketing Consultant
Management Institute of the
School of Continuing Education
New York University

MARKETING COMMUNICATIONS

PRENTICE-HALL, Englewood Cliffs, New Jersey 07632

Library of Congress Cataloging-in-Publication Data

ANDERSON, PATRICIA M. (date)
Marketing communications.

Includes bibliographies and index.
1. Communication in marketing. I. Rubin, Leonard G.
II. Title.
HF5415.123.A53 1986 659 85-19258
ISBN 0-13-557091-3

Editorial/production supervision
and interior design: **Joan Foley**
Cover design: **Ben Santora**
Manufacturing buyer: **Ed O'Dougherty**

Printed in the United States of America

10 9 8 7 6 5 4 3 2 1

ISBN 0-13-557091-3 01

Prentice-Hall International (UK) Limited, *London*
Prentice-Hall of Australia Pty. Limited, *Sydney*
Prentice-Hall Canada Inc., *Toronto*
Prentice-Hall Hispanoamericana, S.A., *Mexico*
Prentice-Hall of India Private Limited, *New Delhi*
Prentice-Hall of Japan, Inc., *Tokyo*
Prentice-Hall of Southeast Asia Pte. Ltd., *Singapore*
Editora Prentice-Hall do Brasil, Ltda., *Rio de Janeiro*
Whitehall Books Limited, *Wellington, New Zealand*

To G. Ernest, Russell, and Carol Anderson;
Ruth H. and the late Warren L. Mottram

P. A.

To Caryl Lee and Eric Fisher;
Albert and Cissy Haas

L. R.

To Russell, from mom,
Patricia M. Anderson

CONTENTS

PART TWO *Advertising*

PREFACE

There are numerous books on the subject of marketing. There are also many volumes on communications. While books about advertising and sales promotion do exist, they generally do not cover all elements of the marketing communications mix. There are few books about marketing communications that look at the subject from the point of view of the *retailer-manufacturer relationship*. The retail store is the key link in the marketing channel, obtaining manufacturers' products and getting them into the hands of consumers. This volume focuses on the manufacturers' and retailers' respective roles in marketing communications to the consumer. Every day, in thousands of retail stores, consumers vote with their dollars, deciding who are the successful marketers.

Almost all products that are marketed through retailers have at least two parties speaking to consumers: the retailer and the manufacturer. When distribution channels are longer, wholesalers and/or various sales agents might also communicate to consumers. These marketers tell consumers about themselves and the products via advertising, special promotions, public relations, publicity, personal selling, and displays. Marketing managers at various levels need to coordinate these communications efforts internally and among the various channels of distribution so that there is a consistent message. This book is about developing and managing these *marketing communications.*

Beginning with communications models and ending with marketing philosophy and strategic planning, this book takes a management approach to planning, organization, and control. Background chapter in Part I and integrative chapters in Part IV are included to augment the marketing communications chapters in Parts II and III. Marketing managers and others involved in marketing need to understand the competitive environment, research and information systems, and the relationship among manufacturers, retailers, and consumers as well as marketing communications and techniques. They must plan, implement, and evaluate advertising, sales promotion, and other communications efforts. They do not need to learn how to make layouts, draw, photograph, or write copy. However, they should be able to judge these elements in terms of effectiveness and consistency in the entire marketing picture.

This text also deals with the use of vendors' cooperative funding and other aids for advertising and promoting manufactured products at the retail level. Experience has indicated that there is a lack of understanding in this area. Both retailers and manufacturers can benefit from understanding the best roles for each in the marketing communications task.

The examples and exhibits in this book represent many types of firms and situations. Each can be taken as a prototype to consider for use in another type of firm or situation. While some examples and exhibits are more suitable for large operations, and others more suitable for small operations, the basic concept may suggest ideas that a creative person can adapt.

The chapters may be read in any order. However, the background chapters in Part I and those covering operational problems in Parts II and III should be read before going on to the chapters in Part IV. In this way, readers can get the greatest benefit from the integrative material contained in Part IV.

The authors write from their own experience in the academic and business worlds, as well as drawing from the experiences of others. Included in the book are relevant theories, research, and references. In the world of business, there have been periods of differing emphasis over the years. Production has been emphasized when goods are in short supply; finance has been emphasized when financial problems are paramount. Presently, and for the coming years, we are in the age of marketing.

ACKNOWLEDGMENTS

The authors enthusiastically thank the many persons and firms cited throughout the book for their help and ideas. Special thanks go to Elaine

Barker, owner of The Creative Needle; Dale Gibson of the Rochester Institute of Technology and his Spring 1984 sales promotion students; Henry R. Hoke of the Direct Marketing Association; Ronald Janoff of New York University's School of Continuing Education and Editorial Board, *Journal of Direct Marketing*; Carolyn Kennedy, marketing manager of the Worcester Center Galleria; Mina Lussier, owner of the Shoe Bin; Alfred P. Sloan, Jr., of the Fashion Institute of Technology; Robert D. Wilcox, retail sales representative of Armstrong International Industries, Inc.; Clark University MBA students Rhonda Avrith, Peter Galvin, Leslie Grimm, Matthew Hendel, Mary Beth Queenan, and Michael Resnick, and undergraduate interns Julia Breslof, Jeff Jones, Joy Le Blanc, and Karen Milke; and the Prentice-Hall reviewers who took time to read and comment on several drafts: Elsie S. Hebert, Louisiana State University; Jacquelene Robeck, University of Massachusetts at Amherst; Dorothy S. Rogers, New Hampshire College; Gilbert Seligman, Dutchess Community College; and Lee S. Wenthe, University of Georgia.

We also appreciate the helpful materials provided by B Altman & Co.; Bloomingdale's; the Celanese Fibers Corporation; the Direct Marketing Educational Foundation and its president, Richard L. Montesi; Lord & Taylor; Macy's; the National Retail Merchants Association and its vice president and director of sales promotion, John Murphy; Alfred Eisenpreis and his associates at the Newspaper Advertising Bureau; the Radio Bureau of Advertising and its vice president, Joyce Reed; the Television Bureau of Advertising; radio station WTTT in Amherst, Massachusetts; and Zayre Corporation and its marketing vice president, William Wendt.

PART ONE

Introduction and Overview

Marketing is at its best when the customer chooses to buy.
Communication is at its best when it is factual and tells the truth—L. Rubin

1

INTRODUCTION TO MARKETING COMMUNICATIONS

INTRODUCTION

Welcome to the exciting world of marketing communications, where something new is happening every hour of every day of every week, month, and year! Manufacturers and retailers of products and services must use marketing communications tools: advertising, promotion, personal selling, visual merchandising, and publicity, so that consumers will notice, desire, and purchase merchandise. Marketing communications involve aspects of theater or show-biz, psychology, media, research, marketing, and just plain good business sense. Meeting the marketing communications challenge draws on many talents and abilities. It requires artistic creativity, awareness, and scientific discipline. Both manufacturers and retailers benefit when each understands how the other communicates about products they both want to sell.

MARKETING AND COMMUNICATIONS

Past and Present Approaches to Marketing Communications

The old approach was simple: make or buy products and sell them at a profit. For hundreds of years, free space was available to all merchants, including farmers, at public market areas in their towns. In many parts of the world, this is still true. First on foot, and then later with pushcarts and wagons, merchants brought merchandise to their customers. This selling method was uncomplicated. Expenses were little more than the cost of the cart and horse, and the feeding and housing of peddler and animal.

Successful merchants of yesteryear were expert judges of what merchandise was likely to sell. They were also good at pricing and promoting this merchandise to produce sales and profits. As shown in Exhibit 1-1, early print advertising consisted mainly of telling customers what merchandise was available. In some cases, early special promotions included serving refreshments. For example, in 1818, Brooks Brothers served a draught of rum or sherry with the sale of men's accessories.[1]

Information about what customers want and need helps manufacturers and retailers predict sales. As enterprises grew in size and entrepreneurs were no longer in direct contact with their customers, new means of gathering data evolved. Information about consumers became available through sophisticated marketing research techniques used by the U.S. Census, private research firms, and businesses' own sources. Marketers could use this information to describe their targets first in demographic terms (age, sex, income, occupation) and, later, in terms of lifestyles and personalities.

Such information enabled marketers to determine how to tell customers about available merchandise, to remind them about a particular brand or store, and to persuade them to buy merchandise of that brand or at that store. The print ad in Exhibit 1-2 is directed at a special target—parents of young children—and invites readers to send for a circular with full descriptions.

The Marketing Approach to Communications Strategy

The new, 1985 American Marketing Association definition of marketing is "the process of planning and executing the conception, pricing, promotion, and distribution of ideas, goods, and services to create exchanges that satisfy individual and organizational objectives." Marketing strategy includes developing *goals* and allocating resources to achieve these goals in the *long run*. In order to measure whether the goals have been met, these goals must be operationally defined. Examples of operational goals are: (1) to earn at least X% on net worth in period Q; (2) to achieve gross

EXHIBIT 1-1 **Early Print Advertising (1733, 1748, 1784) Stated What Merchandise and Services Were Available**

Source: New York Public Library, New York, NY. Size of 1784 original, 16 × 32″ poster.

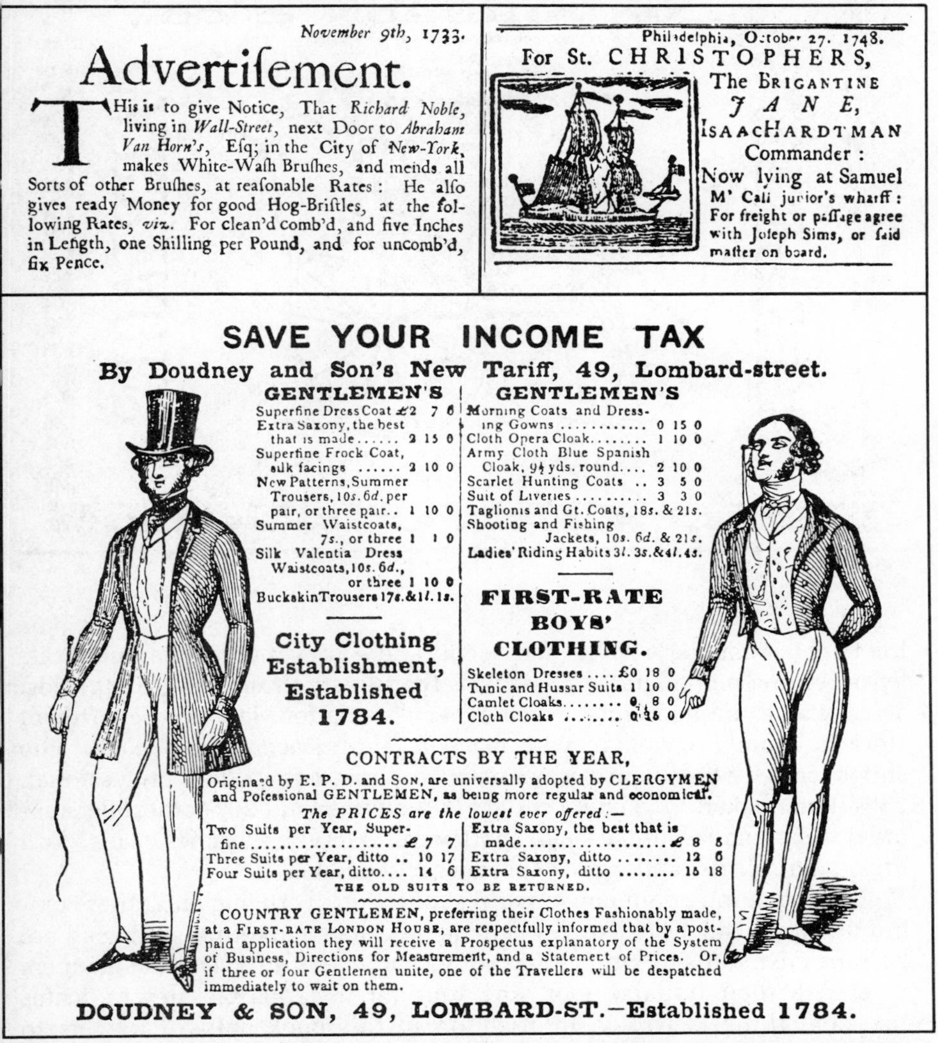
November 9th, 1733.
Advertiſement.
THis is to give Notice, That Richard Noble, living in Wall-Street, next Door to Abraham Van Horn's, Eſq; in the City of New-York, makes White-Waſh Bruſhes, and mends all Sorts of other Bruſhes, at reaſonable Rates: He alſo gives ready Money for good Hog-Briſtles, at the following Rates, viz. For clean'd comb'd, and five Inches in Length, one Shilling per Pound, and for uncomb'd, ſix Pence.
Philadelphia, October 27. 1748.
For St. CHRISTOPHERS,
The BRIGANTINE
JANE,
ISAAC HARDTMAN
Commander:
Now lying at Samuel M' Call junior's wharff: For freight or paſſage agree with Joſeph Sims, or ſaid maſter on board.
SAVE YOUR INCOME TAX
By Doudney and Son's New Tariff, 49, Lombard-street.
GENTLEMEN'S
Superfine Dress Coat £2 7 6
Extra Saxony, the best that is made...... 2 15 0
Superfine Frock Coat, silk facings 2 10 0
New Patterns, Summer Trousers, 10s. 6d. per pair, or three pair.. 1 10 0
Summer Waistcoats, 7s., or three 1 1 0
Silk Valentia Dress Waistcoats, 10s. 6d., or three 1 10 0
Buckskin Trousers 17s. & 1l. 1s.
GENTLEMEN'S
Morning Coats and Dressing Gowns 0 15 0
Cloth Opera Cloak........ 1 10 0
Army Cloth Blue Spanish Cloak, 9½ yds. round.... 2 10 0
Scarlet Hunting Coats .. 3 5 0
Suit of Liveries 3 3 0
Taglionis and Gt. Coats, 18s. & 21s.
Shooting and Fishing Jackets, 10s. 6d. & 21s.
Ladies' Riding Habits 3l. 3s. & 4l. 4s.
City Clothing Establishment, Established 1784.
FIRST-RATE BOYS' CLOTHING.
Skeleton Dresses £0 18 0
Tunic and Hussar Suits 1 10 0
Camlet Cloaks........ 0 8 0
Cloth Cloaks 0 15 0
CONTRACTS BY THE YEAR,
Originated by E. P. D. and SON, are universally adopted by CLERGYMEN and Pofessional GENTLEMEN, as being more regular and economical.
The PRICES are the lowest ever offered:—
Two Suits per Year, Superfine £7 7
Three Suits per Year, ditto .. 10 17
Four Suits per Year, ditto.... 14 6
Extra Saxony, the best that is made.................... £8 5
Extra Saxony, ditto 12 6
Extra Saxony, ditto 15 18
THE OLD SUITS TO BE RETURNED.
COUNTRY GENTLEMEN, preferring their Clothes Fashionably made, at a FIRST-RATE LONDON HOUSE, are respectfully informed that by a post-paid application they will receive a Prospectus explanatory of the System of Business, Directions for Measurement, and a Statement of Prices. Or, if three or four Gentlemen unite, one of the Travellers will be despatched immediately to wait on them.
DOUDNEY & SON, 49, LOMBARD-ST.—Established 1784.

sales of $Y in year R; (3) to attain a market share of Z% by date S; (4) to increase this year's dollar sales by W% over last year's sales.[2]

The marketing approach calls for a definition of a firm's character and personality and for a clear description of its relationship with its customers, whether stores or consumers. The firm must likewise describe these customers. According to the marketing concept, the marketer learns

EXHIBIT 1-2 **Illustrated Print Ad for a Special Market Segment (circa 1840)**
Source: New York Public Library, New York, NY.

the target consumer's wants and needs, and achieves organizational goals by providing merchandise or services that satisfy those wants and needs. To take an example in retail, the target customer for Mervyn's department store is usually a woman with a mean family income of $20,000 who shops for her whole family. Customers' occupations are 25% professional, 25% homemakers, 15% blue collar, 15% clerical and 20% other. Because many customers want casual sportswear, Mervyn's carries jeans, knit tops, sport shirts, and men's sportswear separates.[3]

Information about consumer response to advertising and other communications can be used to evaluate whether marketing strategies are helping customers to satisfy their wants and needs. In a sense, consumers vote with their dollars; poor voter turnout in terms of sales indicates that something is wrong. Information in this book helps marketers to plan marketing communications and then evaluate the effectiveness of various tools, like advertising.

Firms can use the marketing concept to zero in on the consumer. Thus merchants can select from a wide assortment of merchandise the items that will satisfy their target customers. In recent years, the marketing concept has been incorporated into the communications mix. An essential aspect of strategic planning in marketing communications is to integrate communications tools with each other and with the rest of the marketing mix to work toward predetermined goals. From small, owner-operated manufacturing or retail units to large national corporations, the familiar saying applies: the merchandise should go out and the customers return—not the reverse.

After identifying customers' perceptions, attitudes, and lifestyles, firms can more effectively use such strategic marketing communications tools as advertising, promotion, publicity, public relations, visual merchandising, and personal selling. These tools communicate what is available for sale at what prices, where and when it is available, and why customers should buy it.

Firms that best understand current marketing concepts and know how to use marketing communications effectively are usually the most successful, because their strategies are based on expertise and research rather than on guesses and luck. Expertise-based strategies adjust with changing times. Profitable sales based only on luck can change to losses in bad times.

Marketing communications strategy can be effective in many different types of business. For example, manufacturers of many consumer products realize that consumers must buy these products from retailers, either in stores or from catalogs. Some manufacturers have their own stores to build image and to control display and personnel.[4] The recent development of computers and information systems has increased information about consumer decisions and also has increased the use of manufacturers' and retailers' catalogs and other direct marketing communications.

The Place of Communications in Marketing

Marketing in its largest sense includes the creation, pricing, and distribution of products and services, as well as the communications covered in this book. Retailers make many sales transactions from which both stores and manufacturers must profit. Manufacturers use marketing communications to pre-sell brand names and images, first to sell to the retailer and then to help retailers sell the branded merchandise. To do this, manufacturers need to understand retail marketing communications fully.[5]

Marketing communications inform, persuade and remind customers about products, services and images. Marketing communications techniques enable manufacturers and retailers to establish and change images, generate sales, and send messages to customers, stockholders, employees, and the firm's various other publics. Sales volume and profits stem from marketers' ability to communicate effectively with customers, suppliers, and other relevant groups.

TYPES OF MARKETERS AND MARKETING COMMUNICATIONS TOOLS

A Brief Definition of Communications Tools

Marketing communications terminology is not standardized. General consensus is lacking for a number of definitions. Introductory definitions are provided here, to be expanded in later chapters.

Communication with markets is a two-way process that involves both receiving information from marketing research and communicating messages to customers and others. This book uses the term *marketing communications* to encompass advertising, special promotions, publicity/public relations, visual merchandising, and personal selling. Others prefer the term *promotion* to express this concept.[6]

Some manufacturers of packaged grocery products use the terms *promotion* or *sales promotion* to refer to such efforts as offering discounts, conducting sweepstakes, and the issuing of temporary coupons, to create interest in purchasing a product. Retailers often define *sales promotion* to mean "communications other than advertising, publicity, visual merchandising, and personal selling"; that is, to include such devices as, demonstrations, free samples, coupons, special store promotions like sales and special entertainment events on regular or irregular schedules.[7] Exhibit 1-3 shows a direct-mail invitation to a special store promotion conducted by a Boston specialty store.

Advertising is any paid form of nonpersonal presentation of ideas, goods, or services by an identified sponsor. Exhibit 1-4 shows a prize-winning print ad for brand-name fragrances of several vendors. Because advertising is probably the most important marketing communications tool, particularly for retailers, Part Two of this book explains up-to-date approaches to advertising.[8]

Visual merchandising refers to how merchandise is presented for sale by a store. It includes interior and exterior displays, signs, merchandise, and props. Exhibit 1-5 shows excerpts from a newspaper article about an interior display for a specialty chain store in a shopping center. This test display was designed to change the store image from "ordinary" to "upscale." Effective visual merchandising is essential for retailers. Often given little space in marketing and advertising texts, visual merchandising must be understood so that it can be coordinated with other marketing efforts. Vendors are often involved in visual merchandising through providing signs and point-of-purchase (POP) display materials. Because effectiveness of visual merchandising depends in part on the appropriateness of the POP materials for the task, and the extent to which retailers use them, manufacturers should be aware of how visual merchandising works at the retail level.[9]

EXHIBIT 1-3 Direct-Mail Invitation to Special Store Promotion Event

Source: Used with permission of Alan Bilzerian, who has stores in Boston and Worcester, MA. The Boston store is no longer at the address on this invitation because it has moved to a larger space at 34 Newbury St. Size of original, 4 × 6″.

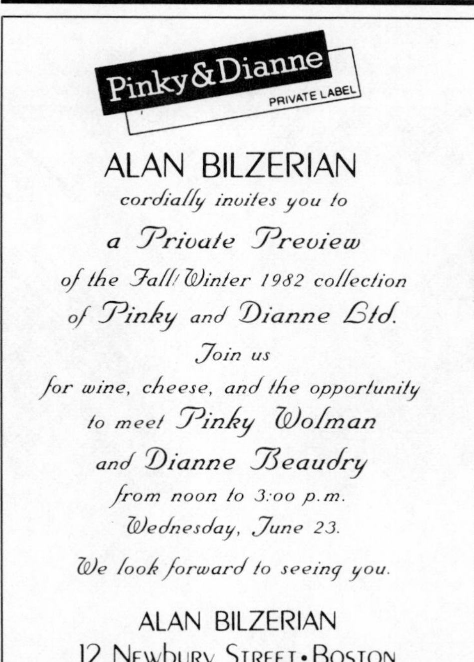

Personal selling is an oral presentation by a salesperson in a conversation with one or more customers. In previous years, the personal selling encounter often took place with customers on one side of a counter and salespersons on the other side, as in Exhibit 1-6. In recent times, many salesperson–customer interactions no longer take place over a counter, and the high cost of personal selling relative to other marketing communication costs has resulted in relatively fewer retail salespersons and more pre-selling by manufacturers. In self-service stores and self-service areas of larger stores, interactions of customers with *any employees*—even stock clerks and managers—can have a positive or negative effect on sales. Therefore, personnel concerns are addressed in this book under personal selling.[10]

EXHIBIT 1-4 Recent Department Store Ad, Winner of Athena Award in Contest of Newspaper Advertising Bureau

Source: Used with permission of Filene's in Boston, MA. See "DDB, Filene's Win Two Athena Awards," *Advertising Age*, 54 (September 12, 1983), p. 86.

EXHIBIT 1-5 In-Store Display Designed to Change Store Image
Source: C. Schmitt, "Thom McAn Takes a Step to New Look," *The Evening Gazette*, Worcester, MA (February 24, 1984), p. 16. Photo by Stephen T. Lanava. Size of original, 5½ × 7″.

...

Gone are tightly bunched, traditional racks of shoes. Instead, shoes sit on neat, cleanly-designed counters.

The store is brightly-lit, decorated in attractive neutral colors and matural wood finish. The shoes themselves—particularly in women's styles—are flashier and more trendy.

...

In marketers' parlance, Thom McAn's move is a textbook example of "repositioning." The company wants to put itself in a new range of the shoe-market spectrum catering to different customers and clientele.

A division of Melville Corp. with annual sales reported about $450 million, the company plans to spend $12 million a year for each of the next three years to upgrade about 900 of its 1,150 stores to reflect the new image, said Federman.

"We positioned ourselves more in the upper end of the market, but we've still maintained price" or raised them only slightly, said Paul Abbruzzese, the company's district manager. "We're still retaining most of our customers."

...

Publicity and *public relations*, like advertising, involve mass communications, but the communication appears in news or editorials printed or broadcast. Publicity and public relations can be used to increase the public's awareness of and change attitudes about products, services, and business firms themselves.[11] The photograph and text in Exhibit 1-5 appeared in a newspaper. Editorial or news managers decide whether press releases sent them by marketers are newsworthy enough to be printed or broadcast. Media managers also control editing of the press releases and reporting of news about firms and products.

Retailer Types and the Communications Mix

There are many types of retail institutions. Exhibit 1-7 lists some of the retail types and Standard Industrial Classification (SIC) codes of the U.S. Department of Commerce. Each retail type has its own code. For example,

EXHIBIT 1-6 Circa 1860–80, Personal Selling Took Place with Customer on One Side of a Counter and Salespersons on the Other. Illustration Is of Piece Goods Department of Retail Store.

Source: Leonard Rubin, *The World of Fashion* (San Francisco: Canfield, 1976), p. 180.

apparel and accessories stores, which are establishments engaged primarily in selling new clothing and related articles, are in SIC major group classification 56. SIC code 56 includes men's and women's clothing stores, custom tailors, tailor shops, corset and lingerie shops, and furriers, but not the apparel and accessories divisions of department and general merchandise stores. This two-digit code (56) is a broader classification than the three-digit code (566) for shoe stores and the four-digit code (5661) for men's shoe stores. The SIC classification system is useful for obtaining comparable statistics in Census data and related literature.[12] The *Predicast F&S Index-United States* is a guide to periodical literature in which the subject index is organized by SIC categories, and the alphabetical index is arranged by company name.

Department stores (SIC four-digit subgroup 5311) are establishments that employ 25 or more persons and have combined sales of soft goods and apparel representing at least 20% of total sales. These stores must sell minimum amounts of: (1) furnishings, appliances, radios and TV sets; (2) a general line of apparel; and (3) household linens and dry goods. SIC 5311 includes mass merchandisers such as Sears and J.C. Penney. Discount stores like Caldor, K mart, and Zayre are "discount variety stores" in SIC five-digit group 53312.[13]

EXHIBIT 1-7 Store Types by Standard Industrial Classification

Source: U.S. Office of Management and Budget, Statistical Policy Division, *Standard Industrial Classification Manual* (Washington DC: U.S. Government Printing Office), pp. 260–276. *Note:* These classifications are revised infrequently. See also the *F&S Index*, note 13, and current issues of the *Editor & Publisher Market Guide*.

Lumber, Hardware

(Building Materials, Hardware, Garden Supply, and Mobile Home Dealers)

Lumber and other building materials dealers (5211)

Paint, glass, and wallpaper stores (5231)

Hardware stores (5251)

Retail nurseries, lawn and garden supply stores (5261)

Mobile home dealers (5271)

General Merchandise

Department stores (5311)

Variety stores (5331)

Miscellaneous general merchandise stores (5399)

Food

Grocery stores (5411)

Freezer and locker meat provisioners (5422)

Meat markets (5423 PT.)

Fish (seafood) markets (5423 PT.)

Fruit stores and vegetable markets (5431)

Candy, nut, and confectionery stores (5441)

Dairy products stores (5451)

Retail bakeries—baking and selling (5462)

Retail bakeries—selling only (5463)

Miscellaneous food stores (5499)

Automotive Dealers

Dealers with domestic car franchise only (5511 PT.)

Dealers with imported car franchise only (5511 PT.)

Dealers with domestic, import car franchises (5511 PT.)

Used car dealers (5521)

Tire, battery, and accessory dealers (5531 PT.)

Other auto and home supply stores (5531 PT.)

Boat dealers (5511)

Recreational and utility trailer dealers (5561)

Motorcycle dealers (5571)

Automotive dealers, n.e.c. (5599)

Gasoline Service Stations

Gasoline service stations (5541)

Apparel and Accessories

Men's and boy's clothing and furnishings stores (5561)

Women's ready-to-wear stores (5621)

Millinery stores (5631 PT.)

Corset and lingerie stores (5631 PT.)

Other women's accessory, specialty stores (5631 PT.)

Children's and infants' wear stores (5641)

Family clothing stores (5651)

Men's shoe stores (5661 PT.)

Women's shoe stores (5661 PT.)

Children's and juveniles' shoe stores (5661 PT.)

Family shoe stores (5661 PT.)

Furriers and fur shops (5681)

Miscellaneous apparel and accessory store (5699)

Furniture, Home Furnishings, and Equipment

Furniture stores (5712)

Floor coverings stores (5713)

Drapery, curtain, and upholstery stores (5714)

Miscellaneous home furnishings stores (5719)

EXHIBIT 1-7 (continued)

Household appliance stores (5722)
Radio and television stores (5732)
Record shops (5733 PT.)
Musical instrument stores (5733 PT.)

Eating and Drinking Places

Restaurants and lunchrooms (5812 PT.)
Social caterers (5812 PT.)
Cafeterias (5812 PT.)
Refreshment places (5812 PT.)
Contract feeding (5812 PT.)
Ice Cream, frozen custard stands (5812 PT.)
Drinking places (alcoholic beverages) (5813)

Drug Stores

Drug stores (5912 PT.)
Proprietary stores (5912 PT.)

Miscellaneous Retail

Liquor stores (5921)
Used merchandise stores (5931)
General line sporting goods stores (5941 PT.)
Specialty line sporting goods stores (5941 PT.)
Book stores (5942)
Stationery stores (5943)
Jewelry stores (5944)
Hobby, toy, and game shops (5945)
Camera and photographic supply stores (5946)
Gift, novelty, and souvenir shops (5947)
Luggage and leather goods stores (5948)
Sewing and needlework stores and piece goods stores (5949)
General merchandise, n.e.c.—mail order (5961 PT.)
Other mail-order houses (5961 PT.)
Automatic merchandising machine operators (5962)
Furniture, home furnishings, equipment—direct selling (5963 PT.)
Mobile food service—direct selling (5963 PT.)
Other direct selling (5963 PT.)
Fuel and ice dealers, n.e.c. (5982)
Fuel oil dealers (5983)
Liquefied petroleum gas (bottled gas) dealers (5984)
Florists (5992)
Cigar stores and stands (5993)
News dealers and newsstands (5994)
Pet shops (5999)
Typewriter stores (5999 PT.)
Optical goods stores (5999 PT.)
Other retail stores, n.e.c. (5999 PT.)

Please note that **Miscellaneous Retail Stores** are not included in the Tables of Estimated Retail Sales.

Various types of retailers place different emphases on particular components of their communications mixes. For example, both supermarkets and small independent retailers with only one retail outlet tend to benefit from local print and radio broadcast advertising and from visual merchandising. National manufacturers, chain retailers, and franchisers that serve a geographically large market are able to use national television advertising effectively. Discount stores can reduce media costs by using tabloid preprints which they can distribute in several ways, including through newspapers. Specialty stores, department stores, catalog showrooms, and national chains like Sears and J.C. Penney often use catalogs and other direct-mail instruments.[14] Non-store retailers also use catalogs, as well as magazine and television advertisements.

Marketing managers in shopping centers collect, assist with, and organize retail tenants' advertisements for newspapers, tabloids, and the broadcast media. They also plan special events to attract traffic to the centers and hence into the stores. Neighborhood strip shopping centers and convenience stores, which tend to have a relatively regular local clientele, can emphasize displays. Sometimes a group of strip shopping centers owned by one developer will hire a marketing manager to assist tenant retailers with marketing communications. Smaller independent stores in towns and small cities sometimes form "downtown councils" to coordinate marketing communications.

MANAGING MARKETING COMMUNICATIONS

A Marketing Communications Model

Five elements are included in a communications model: the message sender, the message target, the message itself, the medium (vehicle of delivery), and the results (feedback, including *noise*—anything that distorts the message).[15] Here is one retail example: A retailer decides to send a message about a store or merchandise. The message is put into an advertisement by the retailer, by an advertising agency, or by a media representative. A media vehicle, such as radio, television, newspaper, or magazine, carries the message. Actual and potential customers can either pay attention to the message or ignore it. The extent to which the message is distorted depends on how clearly it was presented. Using language familiar to the target facilitates comprehension. Exhibit 1-8 has a diagram of a communications model.

After receiving the message, the consumer can either (1) ignore what it communicates, (2) contact the advertiser or competitors to find out more about the merchandise, or (3) purchase merchandise from the advertiser or from a competitor. The advertiser who sent the message uses feedback from customer comments and purchase activity to plan later communications. Noise may be caused by the advertiser's misunderstanding the target consumer's needs and language. The weather, other unpredictable events, and competitors' actions can also interfere with consumers receiving and acting on advertising messages.[16]

The prevailing idea in this communications model is stimulus-response. A percentage of consumers is expected to respond to the advertising stimulus. However, not all consumers are passive respondents to advertising

EXHIBIT 1-8 **A Simplified Communications Model**

Note: See David A. Aaker and John G. Meyers, Advertising Management, 2nd Ed., © 1982, p. 234. Adapted by permission of Prentice-Hall, Inc., Englewood Cliffs, N.J. Also, see other advertising or consumer behavior texts for more-detailed diagrams of the communications model.

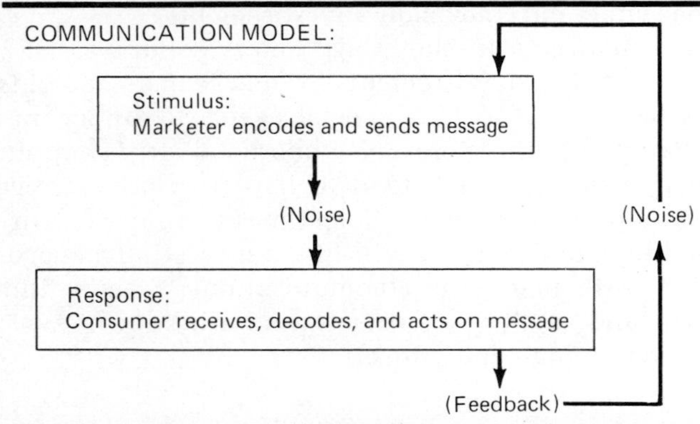

stimuli. Some consumers *actively* seek out information in advertisements in order to buy merchandise. Others actively enjoy the entertainment and information in ads whether or not they buy the advertised items. Even owning an advertised item might stimulate interest in an advertisement; that is, the stimulus is owning the merchandise, and the response is paying attention to the ad.

This newer method of looking at the communications process is based on information-processing theory. Faced with an overwhelming amount of information, consumers first decide whether a new ad is of any interest and whether it is comprehensible. If the information in the ad passes these tests, consumers then try to analyze, organize, and use the information by integrating it with their existing ideas and rules for making decisions. The experience of processing this new information can change the consumers' existing predispositions and rules.[17] Exhibit 1-9 illustrates this information processing.

The Marketing Communications Environment

The first section of this book describes the *external environment* in which firms operate. Environmental factors, which include competitors' actions, can both aid and interfere with marketing communications. Therefore, it is imperative that an advertiser's position, personality, and message be clear, consistent, and accurate so that consumers feel they know the firm based on the advertising, and so that the firm's products will confirm this image. In a marketing and brand-conscious society, a store in a sense becomes a kind of branded product.

EXHIBIT 1-9 An Information-Processing Model for Communications
Source: Used with permission. Keith Crozier, "Towards a Praxiology of Advertising," *International Journal of Advertising*, 2 (April-June, 1983), figure 1, p. 225.

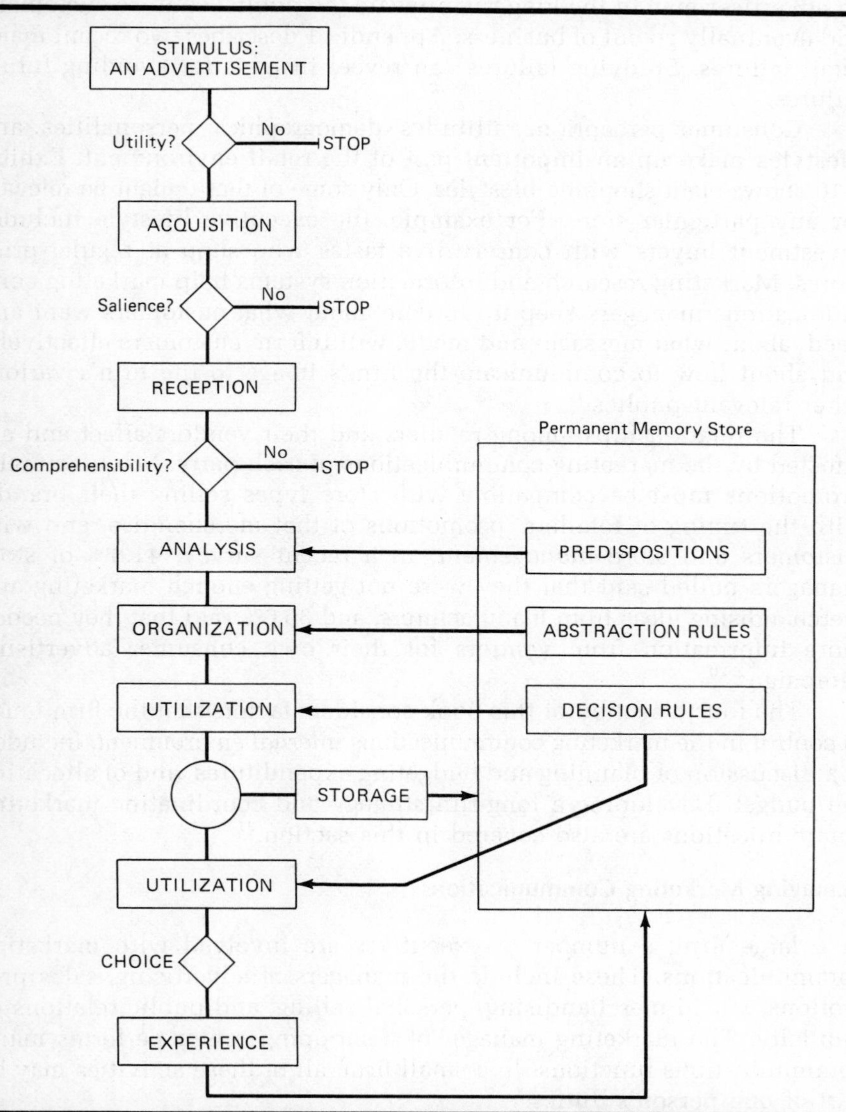

Because a change in the environment may require a change in image to allow a firm to continue to meet company goals, management must be aware of environmental trends.[18] By ignoring environmental trends, an advertiser may in the long run alienate the public, confuse customers, and eventually go out of business. Appendix 1 describes two recent major retail failures. Studying failures can reveal insights for avoiding future failures.

Consumer perceptions, attitudes, demographics, personalities, and lifestyles make up an important part of the retail environment. Exhibit 1-10 shows eight shopping lifestyles. Only some of these might be relevant for any particular store. For example, the executive lifestyle includes investment buyers with conservative tastes who shop at regular-price stores. Marketing research and information systems help marketing communications managers keep up to date about what customers want and need, about what messages and media will inform customers effectively, and about how to communicate the firm's image to the firm's various other relevant publics.[19]

The relationships among retailers and their vendors affect and are affected by the marketing communications of each party. Manufacturers' promotions must be compatible with *store types* selling their brands, with the *timing* of retailers' promotions of that merchandise, and with *customers* and *store management*. In a recent survey, 41.6% of store managers polled said that they were not getting enough marketing and merchandising ideas from manufacturers, and 36.6% said that they needed more information from vendors for their own consumer advertising campaigns.[20]

The fourth section of this book considers factors that the firm tends to control in the marketing communications *internal environment*. Included is a discussion of planning and budgeting expenditures, and of allocating the budget. Developing a long-run strategy and coordinating marketing communications are also covered in this section.[21]

Managing Marketing Communications

In a large firm, a number of executives are involved with marketing communications. These include the managers of advertising, sales promotions, visual merchandising, personal selling, and public relations or publicity. The marketing manager of a shopping center performs many communications functions. In a small firm, all of these activities may be part of one person's duties.

Regardless of firm size, a marketing communications manager does not necessarily do all of the work alone. Other employees, outside agencies, and media representatives can help. However, the manager should (1) *define what needs to be done*; (2) *understand what can be done* and by whom, given personnel and financial resources, current technology, and

EXHIBIT 1-10 Eight Shopping Lifestyles

Source: Adapted from R. Quarles, "Shopping Centers Use Fashion Lifestyle Research to Make Marketing Decisions," *Marketing News*, 16 (January 22, 1982), section 1, p. 18. Used with permission of *Marketing News*.

	INVESTMENT BUYER	UTILITY BUYER
REGULAR PRICE NOVELTY TASTE	Clothes Horse	Daddy's Dollars
REGULAR PRICE CONSERVATIVE TASTE	Executive	Reluctant
BARGAIN SHOPPER NOVELTY TASTE	Savvy Shopper	Trendy Saver
BARGAIN BUYER CONSERVATIVE TASTE	Sensible	Make-do

computer-based information systems; (3) *decide priorities* for what to do, taking some calculated risks to try new ideas; and (4) *evaluate what was done* and learn from experience. Information in this book should help management determine what the company's communications problems are, choose an appropriate marketing and communications mix, and evaluate whether their goals have been reached within cost and other resource constraints.

SUMMARY

Marketers communicate with their target markets using some or all of these methods—advertising, sales promotion, visual merchandising, personal selling, and publicity. Various types of vendors and retailers use different mixes of these marketing communications tools depending on their environment and targets. From large national and regional firms to firms in cities and towns, retailers and manufacturers must learn about their potential customers in order to send them effective messages.

Early firms and managers were so close to their customers that they knew what customers wanted and could personally tell customers what they had for sale. As the distance between marketer and customer increased, it was necessary to develop effective methods of finding out what large numbers of customers wanted and of telling them about merchandise through mass communication. Most retailers no longer manufacture all of their own merchandise, so producers must now work with vendors to coordinate communications to customers.

The communications model describes the process of communication from the encoding of the message through the sending of the message, decoding, and feedback. An information-system approach to understanding communication assumes that consumers are more active than does the stimulus-response model. Consumers often actually seek out and interact with marketing communications, because for some consumers the communications are entertainment.

In addition to keeping up to date with what consumers want and need, both manufacturers and retailers must also watch for changes in the external environment, including actions of competitors. The internal environment is also relevant. Coordination of marketing communications with other parts of the marketing mix and the business's other activities should be a factor in allocating budgets.

QUESTIONS

1. Explain the difference between advertising and publicity. Give examples of this difference (a) for a shopping center marketing manager, and (b) for a large national manufacturer.
2. Explain how effective sales promotion for a large discount department store might differ from that of a small specialty apparel store. How would promotions differ for a large consumer durable manufacturer and a large consumer non-durables manufacturer?
3. Explain what visual merchandising is. Explain how it differs from personal selling in a small independent book store.
4. A small, local independent retailer and a large national retailer like J.C. Penney might emphasize different marketing communications tools. Suggest which tools each might prefer and explain why.

5. Explain how "noise" in the communications model might interfere with marketing communications.
6. Explain why you agree or disagree with the statement that communications is a stimulus-response situation in which consumers respond to marketing communications stimuli.
7. What kinds of manufacturers should understand retail marketing communications, and why do they need this understanding?
8. What four major responsibilities should a marketing manager be able to handle in working with marketing communications?

NOTES

1. Brooks Brothers ad in New York Public Library picture collection.

2. "AMA Board Approves New Marketing Definition," *Marketing News*, 19 (March 1, 1985), p. 1. Also, Phillip Kotler, *Marketing Management*, 5th ed. (Englewood Cliffs, NJ: Prentice-Hall, 1984), p. 4, and other marketing texts.

3. "Mervyn's Deceptively Simple Approach," *Retail Week* (July 15, 1981), p. 38.

See Kotler, *Marketing Management*, note 2. Kotler's addition is the societal marketing concept in which the consumer's and the society's well-being are enhanced.

4. "Clothing Makers Go Straight to the Consumer," *Business Week*, (April 29, 1985), pp. 114–115.

5. See the following books for information about other parts of the marketing mix: J. Evans and B. Berman, *Marketing* (New York: Macmillan, 1982); J.B. Mason and M. Mayer, *Modern Retailing* (Plano, TX: Business Publications, Inc., 1984); C.D. Schewe and R.M. Smith, *Marketing Concepts and Applications*, 2nd ed. (New York: McGraw-Hill, 1983); Kotler, *Marketing Management*. See also Chapter 5 of this book for vendor information.

6. J. Engel, M. Warshaw, and T. Kinnear, *Promotional Strategy*, 4th ed. (Homewood, IL: Irwin, 1979), p. 12; B. Rosenbloom, *Retail Marketing* (New York: Random House, 1981), p. 289; R. Stanley, *Promotion*, 2nd ed. (Englewood Cliffs, NJ: Prentice-Hall, 1982), p. 5.

See also Chapter 11 of this book.

7. *Promotion Marketing Association Glossary*, a booklet of the Promotion Marketing Association of America, 322 8th Ave., Suite 1201, New York, NY 10001.

See Evans and Berman, *Marketing*, p. 414; Rosenbloom, *Retail Marketing*, p. 312; and Ray, *Advertising*, p. 11.

8. See references in notes 5 and 6, and Part II of this book, Chapters 6–10.

9. See Rosenbloom, *Retail Marketing*, p. 233; references in notes 5 and 6; and Chapter 12 of this book.

10. See references in notes 5 and 6, and Chapter 13 of this book.

11. See Rosenbloom, *Retail Marketing*, p. 312; references in notes 5 and 6; and Chapter 14 of this book.

12. *Survey of Buying Power*, (New York: *Sales and Marketing Management*, July 25, 1983), p. A-48. These Census definitions also appear in other sources.

13. Ibid. See also *Predicast F&S Index-United States* (New York: Funk & Scott, 1983), pp. 412–413.

14. I. Barmash, "How They Plan," *Stores* (September 1983), pp. 7–15; J. Sharp, "Making It All Work for You," *Advertising Age*, 52 (July 6, 1981), p. S8.

15. See Kotler, *Marketing Management*, pp. 604–605.

16. See Evans and Berman, *Marketing*, and other references in note 5; also, H. Assael, *Consumer Behavior and Marketing Action* (Boston: Kent, 1984), pp. 202–203.

17. K. Crosier, "Toward a Praxiology of Advertising," *International Journal of Advertising*, 2 (April-June 1983), pp. 215–232, has a more complete discussion of this topic.

18. See Chapter 2 of this book.

19. See Chapters 3 and 4 of this book.

20. "Trade Ads, Promotions Flunk Test of Retailer Relevance," *Marketing News* (December 23, 1983), p. 1.

21. See Chapters 15–16 of this book.

APPENDIX 1

COMMUNICATIONS LESSONS FROM RETAIL FAILURES

Management can learn much by carefully analyzing the causes of store failures. Let us examine the failures of two well-known retailers. Failures of Grant's and Korvette involved hundreds of millions of dollars.

W.T. Grant's

Grant's failure was the biggest loss in retail history. This company was founded in 1906 as an old-line "dry goods" store chain. Later, Grant's added apparel lines and staple soft goods. All merchandise was moderately priced. Until about 1963, the company made good profits. It had an image of a soft goods and apparel retailer with good values at reasonable prices. In 1963, Grant's embarked on a rapid expansion program. From 1963 to 1973, the company opened 612 new stores and expanded 91 other stores. In 1973, Grant's had 1188 stores throughout the United States, and employed about 82,500 people.

Grant's suffered from poor communications internally and externally at this time. In addition, the company decided to change its merchandising direction from emphasis on soft goods and apparel to appliances, hard lines, and major items such as television sets, refrigerators, washing machines, and radios. Most of these items were sold under Grant's private label, which was virtually unknown. At the same time, Grant's sought to trade up in the soft goods and apparel lines, thus completely confusing existing customers. Making all these changes at once, without doing sufficient marketing research or building expectations sufficiently via marketing communications, resulted in a loss of $177 million in 1974!

To help turn the business around, Grant's offered liberal credit terms, believing that credit would help sell its more expensive items. Grant's accepted poor credit risks, and soon its customers owed over $600 million, much of it past due. Grant's had to borrow still more money even though it was already in debt and paying huge interest on its previous loans. There was a chain reaction. It was difficult to keep inventories at proper levels. Often, customers walked out because they could not find what they wanted. Given these circumstances, it was inevitable that Grant's would fail. Rescue attempts proved futile. When Grant's finally closed its doors, the liabilities were over one billion dollars, making it the largest retail failure in history.

What can be learned from Grant's failure? First, too-rapid expansion puts a strain on any company and can lead to a poor cash-flow position and a shortage of operating funds. Also, when interest rates are rising, it is the wrong time to borrow money on a large scale for expansion. Third, radical changes in marketing and/or merchandising policies cannot be undertaken without careful research, accompanied by marketing communications to set expectations. A pilot test might have been tried at a few of the stores before any major moves were made. Such tests would have shown that the changes drove old customers away without attracting new ones. Lastly, adequate inventory controls must be operating to guard against over- and understocking. Had Grant's acted differently in these four key operational areas, it might still be in business today.

Grant's greatest failure was probably one of marketing communications. As policymakers tried to change Grant's from one type of operation to another, they confused their own personnel and also their regular customers by failing to explain what they were trying to accomplish. Marketing, advertising, and public relations tools were not used properly to help make the transition understandable and acceptable.

Such major changes in policies and image must be carefully planned, slowly put into place, and communicated on a step-by-step basis. At each step the company must make certain that they are taking their customers along with them and maintaining their patronage and good will. Grant's failed completely in this area. When management finally realized this, rescue efforts were too little and too late.

E.J. Korvette

A second big retail failure was that of E.J. Korvette, one of the largest of the discount chains. This type of store entered the retail field late, after World War II, and began to flourish in the 1950s and 1960s. In the beginning, discount houses were divided into two main groups: (1) those specializing in the sale of hard goods and appliances, and (2) those emphasizing the sale of soft goods and apparel. Korvette began as the former.

Discount stores differ from regular retail stores in the following characteristics: merchandise priced below traditional margins; limited service; self-selection; open long hours and on Sundays; and less reliance on statistical control systems. After World War II and the Korean War, Eugene Ferkauf realized there was a tremendous pent-up demand for major appliances—refrigerators, television sets, washing machines, and dishwashers, as well as for smaller electrical appliances, such as toasters, clocks, radios, and blenders. Korvette also offered watches, electric shavers, luggage, and other consumer goods at bargain prices.

Ferkauf began by opening a small store on the second floor in an office building on a side street in New York's midtown. Marketing communications was in the form of business cards passed out to customers to give to their friends, and given out in offices with hundreds of workers. The cards stated that brand-name merchandise in the categories mentioned above was available at prices from 20% to 40% off listed prices. Customers began flocking to Korvette to save sizable amounts of money. If on a visit to Korvette, a shopper didn't see what was wanted—for example, a particular model television set or refrigerator—Korvette's personnel would send the shopper to the nearest department store for the item's model number, then return to Korvette and buy it off price. Consumers could also select items from the manufacturer's catalog. The larger items were "drop shipped" to the customer directly from the manufacturer at the promised savings.

By the 1970s, hard lines—refrigerators, ranges, washing machines, TV sets, radios, etc.—were no longer difficult to obtain. In order to compete with discount houses, department stores reduced their prices. Responding to these trends, Korvette moved into the fashion and soft-goods business with which it had no experience. It positioned itself halfway between mass merchandise stores like Sears and J.C. Penney and bargain department stores like K mart. Bargain-hunting customers who had bought General Electric refrigerators and Zenith televisions at Korvette had an image of the store as an appliance dealer, not a soft-goods fashion outlet. Such customers were not interested in shopping at Korvette for fashion merchandise made in Taiwan or South Korea, some of it cheap and shoddy. Changing customers' image of Korvette would have required an extensive marketing communications effort focusing on image. But instead the advertising plan stressed savings via four-day sales, fewer products in ads, and end-of-week newspaper advertisements. The theme was "Korvette's gives you discounts plus".[1] The merchandise advertised was neither good fashion nor great value.

[1] See sources in note 5 for Chapter 1; also, "Korvette's," *Advertising Age*, 51 (November 3, 1980), p. S-8; "New Marketing Strategy Positions Korvette's as 'Promotional' Chain," *Marketing News*, (March 21, 1980).

Korvette's profits were dropping, hard-line sales were falling off and apparel sales were not successful. By 1979, Korvette's profits had turned to losses. From then on, it was downhill all the way. A large French corporation wishing to enter the American market bought Korvette in late 1979. Agache/Willott closed some of the least profitable stores, put more capital into the remaining ones, and tried to turn the operation around. But Korvette failed in 1981 after three years of increasing losses.

What went wrong? First, once the image of selling certain merchandise is established, a change requires an extensive and coordinated marketing and marketing communications effort. After experience with the initial Korvette, the public expected to buy brand-name soft goods at bargain prices there. Without a clearly communicated retail image, customers tend not to buy "blind items" and badly made non-brand-name merchandise even if the merchandise is a so-called "bargain."

Second, in order to compete in fashion soft goods, Korvette advertised, relocated on expensive real estate, and fixed up the inside of the stores to imitate department stores. No longer was this a "no frills" operation. By selling bargain shoddy merchandise in an expensive high-class location, the "Other Korvettes" confused its customers and lost its profits. While marketing communications alone cannot solve all a firm's problems, an understanding of communications sheds light on what radical changes in business practices can do to store image. Marketing communications can help and be a key factor in communicating transitions to a store's various publics.

2
ENVIRONMENT AND POSITIONING

INTRODUCTION

The two major components of the marketing communications environment are: (1) the more-controllable environment created by the firm itself, and (2) the less-controllable environment of the community, competitors, the nation, and the world. This external environment is called "less-controllable" instead of "non-controllable" because some firms can adapt effectively so that the external circumstances work to their advantage. The environment created by the firm itself includes the basic nature of the firm which results from prior management decisions, and, for retailers, store atmosphere. The less-controllable environment includes historic changes and technological developments; physical and community changes; legal and geographic constraints; and consumer activities.[1]

Marketers assume positions to show where they stand with respect to their environments, their communities, and their competitors. They use marketing communications to help actual and potential customers learn about these positions. When environmental changes render a current position obsolete, a business must consider how to change to a new position that will be consistent with its current environment and current goals.

Because intensive communication is now so much a part of our current society, words themselves can change perception of the environment. For example, to which of these signs or advertising headlines do you believe consumers would be more likely to respond: "Sporting Goods" or "Health, Fitness and Sports"? "China and Glassware" or "Dining Decor"? Would a vacation-minded person be more likely to visit "Smith's Woods" or "Enchanted Forest"?

Manufacturers, through their consumer advertising and retailers with their signs and other visual merchandising, can change shoppers' perceptions of both products and stores. Through their total communications efforts, both retailers and manufacturers can deliberately take a "position" in the market with respect to competition. "Positioning" is explained later in this chapter. Although the producers of consumer products and the stores that sell them have less control over the external environment than over their internal environments, the part that they *can* control is often of immense importance. Therefore, good marketing communications is the essence of successful business.

THE HISTORICAL AND TECHNOLOGICAL ENVIRONMENT

Communications History

Because history often repeats itself, managers can learn from past successes and mistakes to deal with similar situations in the present. When a colleague suggests a "hot new communications strategy," the manager with information about its results in similar past situations can evaluate its present potential. A "hot new strategy" repeated several times in similar circumstances is no longer new and tends not to be successful. A historical perspective helps managers choose wisely between alternative strategies.

Before widespread use of print and other mass communications media, communication was relatively local. Wall signs announced gladiator combats to the Romans, and town criers announced merchants' wares. Pictorial signs informed the illiterate about store merchandise in these local environments and served as translation for those who did not understand the language of the area. Sales promotion efforts consisted of fairs, travelling entertainments, and free samples of wine and other wares.

After the Industrial Revolution, improvements in printing and literacy facilitated newspaper advertising. At the same time, increased business competition was requiring innovations in communications. As early as the 1880s, Schuster's Department Store in Milwaukee issued trading stamps. By 1900, advertising agencies were helping marketers buy media space, write copy, and design packages. Magazines like *Ladies Home Journal* and *Cosmopolitan* made it possible to communicate with special market segments. To regulate this communications explosion, businesses formed the Association of National Advertisers in 1910 and the American Association of Advertising Agencies in 1917.[2]

Radio sold time to advertisers beginning in 1922 and television became popular in 1949. Changes in transportation, communication, and lifestyles made broadcast media more effective than previously for communicating retail and manufacturers' messages. Heavy teen use of radios, narrow and deep segmentation of some magazines, and national targets of mass merchandisers and specialty chains made retail advertising effective in these newer media. However, newspapers have remained a major medium for retailers.[3]

Technological Developments

New developments in technology continue to influence media selection and usage. Technology (how to send the message) and usage (what message to send) for videotex ads are currently being developed. Videotex advertising is usually created by a computer. It is delivered by computer or television screen, and the consumer usually responds by computer or phone. Exhibit 2-1 has videotex ads and some of the jargon associated with this new technology. Videotex is discussed at length in Chapter 8. At present, owners of personal computers can call up a variety of videotex services for shopping and banking.

There are even electronic "shopping centers." CompuServe in Columbus, Ohio, is a videotex shopping service that allows customers to shop at 80 firms 24 hours a day via personal computers. Subscribers can ask questions, provide feedback and information, and place credit card orders through their computers. The average CompuServe subscriber is a male college graduate aged 35 with a $40,000 annual income. Advertising space is available for small ads at the bottom of CompuServe catalog pages. The merchandise is organized into 11 categories, and an electronic bulletin board, updated weekly, informs subscribers about new merchandise, services, and merchants. Similar videotex services in California, Florida, and Illinois allow subscribers to purchase tickets, read news, receive electronic mail, pay bills, and help children with homework. Gateway, in Orange County, CA, takes advertising and shares information from the videotex operations with newspaper publishers. Sears, Waldenbooks, American Express, Bloomingdale's, Kinney Shoes, Montgomery Ward, a number of banks, and several other businesses are involved with these videotex operations.[4]

EXHIBIT 2-1 **Computer Ads: Videotex, Graphics, and Jargon**

Source: "Videotex Advertising," AT&T Consumer Information Services (December, 1983). Used with permission of AT&T Information Systems. M. Kalis, "Talking the Language," *Advertising Age*, 54 (December 19, 1983), p. M-26. Reprinted with permission of *Advertising Age*. Copyright 1983 by Crain Communications, Inc.

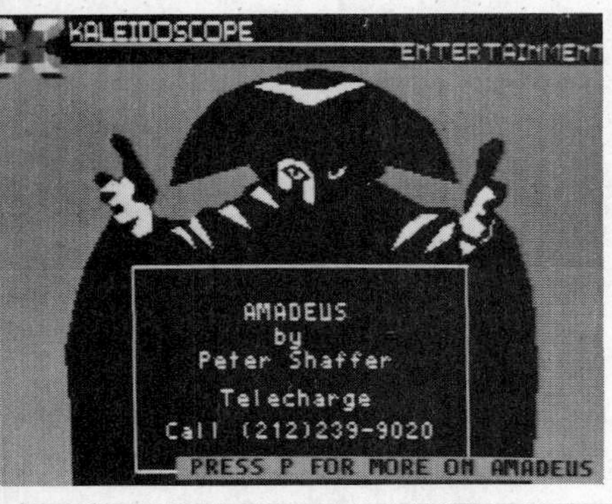

Computer graphics: This is specifically using the computer to create the actual designs.

Computer-like (or pseudo-computer): Using conventional animation to give the appearance or "look" it was done by a computer. Can often be done cheaper than using a computer.

Computer simulation: Making an environment in the computer that is like something either real or imagined. Also can mean using the computer for effects that could be done with conventional animation and models.

Digital animation: Another term for computer animation. Also means using the computer to create the in-between steps needed to animate from one position to the next, rather than drawing them by hand.

Digitizing: Feeding a design into the computer by transmitting points laid over the drawing. For instance, a square would be digitized with four points.

Television sets now come in such small sizes that they can be worn on the wrist. This mobility of television sets means that people who attend live sporting events with a wrist TV can watch the actual event then see the instant replay on their wrists—plus the commercials.[5] The environment in which active athletes can use biomechanical computer techniques to improve their performances inspired the "catazine" ad in Exhibit 2-2. A catazine—combination magazine and catalog—is a new media vehicle in the environment.

TV cassettes allow stores to put fashion shows, demonstrations, and even advertisements on television screens throughout a store. Laser beams

EXHIBIT 2-2 **Catazine Advertisement with Apparel for Biomechanics Environment**
Source: Jordan Marsh, *JM Magazine*, 3 (April, 1984), p. 22. A "catazine" or "magalog" is a combination retail catalog and magazine. Size of original, 8½ × 11". Used with permission of Jordan Marsh, Boston, MA.

allow advertising in 3-D forms even in the sky. Fiber optics outdoor billboards can create any colors, change them in sequence, and create the illusion of motion.[6] Computer-generated graphics can be used to design art for advertisements.

Scanners collect more and more data which can be analyzed by sophisticated and user-friendly computers to evaluate the effectiveness of communications in reaching company goals. A new scanning system links television viewing and lifestyles to purchasing.[7] New computer software agencies and research consultants have developed to help marketers simulate communications campaigns and evaluate effectiveness before embarking on the actual campaign. By keeping informed about past and new developments, the communications executive can select from the growing arsenal of communications weapons the mix most appropriate for achieving company goals.

As technological change results in a variety of communications media, and in directing media vehicles toward specific market segments, consumers will have a wider choice among media vehicles. (A *media vehicle* is a specific carrier of advertising messages, for example, a radio station.) By the year 2000, this wider choice may include a cable television channel for almost every splinter group—consumer, sports, hobbyist; "zap-proof" commercials built into "free" lending library cassettes; the transmission of smells, feels and tastes into the home; interactive radio and television; 3-D ad inserts and optical chips in newspapers and magazines; advertiser-sponsored video magazines sent free to subscribers; and advertiser-sponsored home cinema.[8]

Effects of Historical Changes in the Environment

Over the years, communications and media marketing institutions have grown and changed. The Hudson Bay Company established the first general store in North America in 1670. Because customers of general stores had few alternatives, communication was relatively unimportant. One went to the store once a year, and either bought what was there or did without. By the 1860s, improvements in transportation and communication made possible larger stores, such as department stores. In the 1930s, the first supermarket, King Kullen, opened in Jamaica, NY, and the first discount store, Masters, opened in New York City. The first regional shopping center, Northgate, opened in Seattle, Washington, in 1950. A variety of regional and national chains opened in the 1960s: fast-food restaurants, home-improvement centers, furniture warehouse showrooms, and catalog showrooms. Also, department stores developed branches for the shopping centers.[9]

Developments in print and broadcast media facilitated advertising to the wider markets served by the chains in shopping centers. Geographic dispersion of retail outlets made national or regional television cost-effective. National product manufacturers cooperated with retail tenants to create traffic in shopping centers. For example, sporting goods manufacturers helped support athletic-based promotional events.[10]

Non-store retailing expanded in the 1980s as working women had more money and less time, and as the high cost of fuel for cars discouraged extra driving. Catalog shopping and direct marketing substituted for some in-store shopping. To accommodate this new lifestyle, the Abraham & Straus department store in Brooklyn, NY, and the Sears Roebuck mass merchandiser put some catalogs on television. Other department stores broadened the distribution area of their catalogs, even advertised their catalogs in magazines, as if the catalogs themselves were store merchandise. Exhibit 2-3 has such an advertisement for a catalog.

EXHIBIT 2-3 **Catalog Advertised in Magazine**

Source: Appeared in *The New York Times Magazine* (July 29, 1984), p. 49. Size of original, 5½ × 5¾″. Used with permission of Bloomingdale's, New York, NY.

bloomingdale's
BY MAIL LTD

No one has ever been quite as at home with home furnishings as we. Now, the best in the house can be yours. For only $4 *(which goes toward your first purchase)* we'll send you the first in a series of home furnishings catalogues. Others will follow.

Send your check for $4 and this coupon to:

Bloomingdale's By Mail Ltd.
115 Brand Rd., Dept. 098
Salem, VA 24156

NAME__________
ADDRESS__________
CITY__________
STATE__________ZIP__________

098

MORE-CONTROLLABLE ENVIRONMENTAL FACTORS

The basic components of a firm's nature include type of business, size, location, method of operation, product line, and goals. These factors determine what kind of marketing communications will be effective. However, they are not necessarily under the control of those who manage marketing communications, unless the communications managers are in top management. Store atmosphere is likely to be controlled by retail marketing communicators, subject to guidance from top management.

For example, a store can be conventional, off-price, promotional, factory outlet, or some other type of outlet. To attract customers, a conventional store advertises about merchandise newly arrived and characteristics of existing merchandise. An off-price store uses lower prices as its major attraction. A promotional store offers sales and special events to attract customers. A factory outlet store is usually located near a factory and sells merchandise at near-wholesale prices; however, a new development is a factory outlet shopping center of stores that may not be physically near their factories.

In terms of volume, supermarkets and large department stores have large dollar sales. The major share of all food products is sold in supermarkets. In recent years supermarkets are also capturing a larger share of the drug, toiletry, and home products market. Once in a supermarket, it is easier for the consumer to purchase many household products other than food or cleaning items, including kitchen gadgets, cooking ware, towels, books, hosiery, cosmetics, glassware, dishes, and housewares.

In recent years, supermarkets have often been the ones to introduce the latest concepts in marketing. Checkout counter scanning devices, automatic itemizing, computing prices of purchases, the amount of change given to customers, inventory control, total sales by category and item, and other desired statistics are all coordinated by new sophisticated computers. Computers help count and tabulate coupons, compute discounts, and reimburse customers. Efficiency in supermarkets is essential, as the markup on most supermarket items is considerably lower than the apparel and other items carried in department and specialty stores. Many successful malls and shopping centers have a leading supermarket and/or a leading department store as anchors.

Store locations include urban, downtown, suburban, and regional; also, *in* or *not in* a shopping center. Method of operation can be full service, semi-service, or self-service. Product lines can be wide or narrow, shallow or deep. *Wide/narrow* refers to the variety of products stocked. *Shallow/deep* refers to the amount of a given product stocked. *Narrow/deep* means a small variety with much stock. Firm and employee goals range from having the largest market share or sales growth in the area, to getting rich and/or being promoted to a high management position, to fulfilling a dream of owning a small business.

LESS-CONTROLLABLE ENVIRONMENTAL CHANGE IN THE COMMUNITY

Managers should consider their firms "local" even when they work for chains that operate in widely separated communities. Most retail customers, except tourists, are relatively local. Therefore, retail managers must understand their local communities.

Physical Changes

Appendix 2 contains information about a small independent store with units in two very different local environments, one on the east side and one on the west side of Fifth Avenue in New York City. One environment is changing as a result of redevelopment. The other is more stable. An environmental consequence of redevelopment is construction interfering with shopping routes. Retailers who face construction interference must resort to creative communications techniques to encourage their customers to brave the obstacles.

Likewise, store remodelling changes familiar routes and areas within a store, and road construction can make it quite difficult for shoppers to get to some stores by car. Special promotions and communications are needed to retain customers in these cases.

Another such obstacle is delayed construction of a nearby business which is expected to draw traffic to the area of a store. For example, the opening of a large civic center was delayed for several months. Many small independent retailers had opened stores near the center, counting on it to generate traffic for them. Generating traffic was beyond the communications resources of these small independent retailers. The lack of traffic caused by the delayed opening of the civic center forced some of these small businesses to close.

Redevelopment changes can ease the communications situation by upgrading the environment. A recent redevelopment change involved a famous site, Herald Square in New York City, and nearby stores, Macy's and Gimbels. Herald Center, located near a large commuter railroad station, has room for 140 stores and restaurants. This complex inspired area redevelopment including office buildings, cooperative housing, and a convention center. By attracting a better residential and office population, this redevelopment planned to help attract more affluent consumers to the existing stores as well as to the stores in the new shopping center.[11]

Community Changes

Community history, folklore, customs, institutions, heroes and myths affect customers' perceptions, attitudes and shopping preferences. One recent change in community environment is the growth of the Hispanic population. Marketers whose environments contain a large and growing Hispanic segment need information about communicating to Hispanics.

The more a firm learns about and adapts to its community environment, the more profitable it will be. A successful business today must be a friend to the community, a service organization, and an integral part of society so that it becomes essential to that society. The businesses in an area or community may work together through an informal association or a division of a larger business to create and maintain a favorable environment. This environment might include such factors as good transportation, parking facilities, traffic regulations, store hours, uniform seasonal openings and closings, cleanliness and attractiveness of old landscaping. For Procter & Gamble, the environment included a 1981 rumor that its 135-year-old "Man in the Moon" logo was linked with devil worship and the Church of Satan. P&G attempted to dispel this rumor using a toll-free phone number.[12]

Nothing is permanent in the environment; the only permanent component is change. The demise of many former leading businesses that did not understand their changing environments attests to environment's importance. In addition to Grant's and Korvette, many famous local stores have disappeared: Arnold Constable, New York (140 years old); Best & Co., New York (125 years old); Halle Bros., Cleveland (87 years old); Goldblatts (40 years old) and the Davis Company, Chicago (65 years old); S. Klein, New York (70 years old); and many more. Buildings in some communities have different tenants each year, as businesses move in with hope and move out in debt.

Marketing Communications in the Regulatory Environment

Government regulators watch advertising to decide whether advertising makes false claims, interferes with product development, fosters monopoly, or raises prices. Media and competing advertisers watch advertising to make sure they are treated fairly by other media and advertisers, and by government. Regulation of advertising is covered extensively in marketing and advertising texts and in current periodicals.[13] A few examples are mentioned here to indicate the complexity of the regulatory environment.

One target of government regulation is *bait and switch advertising*—falsely offering to sell one product or service in order to gain prospective customers for some other, usually more expensive product. This is an unfair practice. Evidence of bait advertising includes refusing to show the advertised product; disparaging the product; failing to have enough of the product on sale; and refusing to take orders for delivery in a reasonable time. Proof of illegal bait and switch advertising includes lack of sales at the advertised price, or a large advertising expenditure on products which have minimal sales.[14]

The membership of the Federal Trade Commission (FTC), a government regulatory agency created in 1914, changes over time, depending on who is appointed to serve on the FTC. The effort of the FTC towards regulation of advertising depends on the interest of the members and of their constituency in this subject. The FTC has recently investigated the 1971 regulation that supermarkets must have advertised items in stock and conspicuously available for sale, and has asked for input from consumers on this matter. The last FTC complaint under this regulation was in 1978; the FTC has since questioned whether the costs of inventory and record-keeping outweigh potential savings to shoppers which might occur if this regulation were abolished.[15]

Federal courts also make judgments about communications. An Ohio federal court refused to stop a Cleveland florists' association from using the Anheuser-Busch beer marketer's slogan, "This Bud's for You." The reason was that there was no attempt by the florists to expand into beer marketing and that there was no evidence of confusion.[16]

An example of self-regulation is the creative code of the American Association of Advertising Agencies. Briefly, this code states that advertisers must not knowingly make false or misleading visual or verbal statements, unfairly disparage competitors' products or services, or use poor taste. Violations will be referred to the Association's directors. The updated 1984 code of the American Advertising Federation requires (1) truth, including facts which, if omitted, would mislead the public; (2) substantiation prior to making claims; (3) refraining from misleading comparisons with competitors; (4) no bait and switch advertising; (5) explicit, sufficient information about guarantees and warranties available for examination before purchase; (6) no misleading price claims; (7) testimonials of honest and competent witnesses; and (8) taste and decency.[17]

Non-government agencies also monitor advertising and influence what advertisers do. Consumers Union has consistently fought to bar commercial use of its findings and ratings.[18] Consumers Union sued Remington Products and two department stores to stop marketers from exploiting the product ratings published in *Consumer Reports*. Competitors' and others' complaints about advertising are published regularly in *Advertising Age*. Usually, these are requests for substantiation; *Advertising Age* also reports whether the offending ads have been substantiated or withdrawn. The Children's Advertising Review Unit of the Better Business Bureau offers guidelines for advertising to children. These guidelines include making clear the size of the product and whether batteries or assembly are needed; not showing children or adults doing something unsafe; not suggesting that owning the product may make the child superior to friends or more popular; and other guidelines shown in Exhibit 2-4.

Current regulatory advertising issues include whether ads deceive

EXHIBIT 2-4 Guidelines for Advertising to Children

Source: Children's Advertising Review Unit, National Advertising Division, Council of Better Business Bureaus, Inc., New York. Size of original, 8½ × 9″.

As A Parent — Or A Concerned Non parent

Your watchful eyes and attention to children's advertising are important. Here are some things to look for:

If the answer to any of the following questions is NO, the advertising may be questionable.

- Is the size of the product made clear?
- Does the ad clearly indicate what is included in the original purchase?
- Are separate purchase requirements clearly indicated?
- If batteries are needed, is this clearly stated?
- If assembly is required, does the ad clearly say so in language that a child will understand?
- Are other essential disclosures clearly voiced or worded, legible, prominent and in language understandable by the child audience?
- In ads featuring premiums, is the premium offer clearly secondary?
- If fantasy elements are used, are they clearly "just pretend?"

If the answer to any of the following questions is YES, the ad may be questionable.

- Are children shown using a product in a way that the average child couldn't?
- Does the ad show more than the number of toys that might reasonably be expected for a child to own?
- Is the child or adult shown doing something unsafe?
- Is the child or adult shown using a product not intended for children?
- Is a child-directed advertising appeal being used for vitamins or medication?
- Does the ad suggest that a child will be superior to friends or more popular if the child owns a given product?
- Does the ad employ any demeaning or derogatory social stereotypes?
- Does the ad suggest that an adult who buys a product for a child is better or more caring than one who does not?
- Does the ad reflect unfavorably on parental judgment and other generally recognized sources of child guidance?
- Does the ad show bad manners or use offensive language?
- Is a food product not shown within the framework of a balanced diet?
- Does the ad imply that one food provides all the nutrients contained in a well-balanced food plan?
- Does the ad suggest overconsumption of a particular food product?
- Does the ad urge children to ask parents or others to buy the product?
- Does the ad use words as "only" or "just" to describe price?
- Do program hosts or characters appear in commercials within their own program?
- In print publications, are the title characters of the publications used in ads within their own publications?
- Is there anything misleading in the ad about the product's benefits?

Where To Write

If you have a complaint about a particular advertisement, or would like a copy of the guidelines, please write to the Children's Advertising Review Unit, National Advertising Division, Council of Better Business Bureaus, Inc., 845 Third Avenue, New York, N.Y. 10022. Keep in mind that the Children's Unit concerns itself only with national or broadly regional **advertising** directed to children, and not **programming.**

(discussed above); whether ads have *subliminal messages;* and whether *clutter* should be regulated. Subliminal messages, which might involve suggestive graphics, are those which are perceived subconsciously. Wilson Bryan Key has written *Subliminal Seduction* and other books about subliminal advertising. Advertisers have repeatedly denied that they have supervised subliminal ads or had any knowledge of their firms or competitors' using subliminal ads. However, some computer software allegedly contains subliminal messages.[19]

Clutter occurs when there are so many ads that the viewer or reader either misses some ad messages, or confuses ads, messages, and sponsors. Broadcast clutter is no longer prohibited. In 1982, a federal court ruled that because of antitrust implications the National Association of Broadcasters could no longer limit the volume, frequency, or format of commercials within a given time period. Clutter also appears in newspapers and magazines. The difference between print and broadcast clutter is that the reader has a chance to reread a print ad, but does not necessarily hear a repeat of a broadcast ad. A new aspect of clutter is the *split-30 commercial*, which means that two 15-second ads will be put into one 30-second commercial. The split-30 may become widespread as network television audiences grow smaller, and as advertisers turn to other types of media to reach their target markets.[20]

In addition to external regulation of advertising, consumers regulate what they will accept from ads. Seeing is not necessarily believing. In a recent nationwide survey, the average credibility rating of advertising seen, read, or heard was slightly above "somewhat unbelievable."[21]

Also, critics of marketing communications publish their criticisms, and these criticisms might influence advertisers and consumers. Critics claim that such communications encourage people to buy things that they do not need, and that communications exploit genuine sentiments to make such holidays as Christmas, Hanukah, and Independence Day nothing but commercial events. As a result, they argue, billions of dollars of unwanted and unneeded goods are sold. The communicators respond that in a large geographic market where producers and consumers do not live near each other, there must be some method of communicating what is available for sale. Marketing communications serve this *information* function. Also, *psychological* needs exist as well as physical ones. Marketing communications help some products serve the former, and sometimes the latter as well. Further, the communications system makes possible the dissemination of information about new products. These products can be produced and sold only because communications vehicles tell consumers about the products and where to buy them.[22]

Marketing Communications and Geographic Markets

Markets are usually either cities and suburbs, or combinations of cities with specific demographic and other characteristics. These characteristics can change over time. Each of the 100 leading markets in the United States is described annually in *Advertising Age*. For example, New Haven-Meriden, CT, the 85th largest market, had a population of 500,474 in 1980 and an estimated 1982 income of $8,028 million. With the help of

Yale University, New Haven is having a "facelift," and corporations are accepting invitations to relocate there. Its theater district is attracting New York plays while its renovated downtown attracts professionals.

Tucson, AZ, which at 78th place, has about the same rank and population as the New Haven market, and also has relocating companies, differs from New Haven in other characteristics. Its largest employer is the government, with an Army base, an Air Force base, and a state university. It has several copper mines, a large percentage of retired households, and a tourism business markedly affected by the value of the Mexican peso.[23]

Descriptions of changes in markets help marketing communications managers keep track of where their communications targets are located. Marketers who put northeastern corporate executives and professionals in their target markets need to know about their new residences in New Haven, as well as where they lived previously. Marketers interested in military and mining target markets in Tucson need to know about national military policy and international developments involving Mexico.

Marketing Communications and Market Share

Because of the slowdown in population growth and the growing competitiveness in all commercial areas, *market share* is of increasing importance. In the years ahead, the competition for the consumer's dollar will be fierce. Not only will similar products be competing, but stores will fight to get the consumer to spend money in a particular store for a particular product category. If consumers spend their discretionary income on an expensive vacation or travel, they will have less to spend on apparel, gourmet foods, and other consumer items. Every day consumers will be voting with dollars in an election that retailers and manufacturers cannot afford to lose.

Hence, in the future it is expected that there will be an all-out war to maintain and if possible increase market share. This will place heavy responsibility on all forms of marketing communications, as well as on costs of production and distribution. Pricing will be under close scrutiny. Tight inventory control will be mandatory. Funds for communication must be expertly targeted to obtain maximum results for the investing firm.

CONSUMERS IN THE ENVIRONMENT

Consumer Decisions

Consumers in their local environments make shopping decisions about locations, about businesses within a shopping location, and about shopping areas within a store. The term *shopping location* refers to a retail business or group of businesses within one area, for example, a shopping center. Stores within and among shopping locations compete for consumer dollars by using communication tools. Consumer decision models for choosing among manufacturers' brands can be adapted for choosing among stores, as shown in this section.

Consumers need more information for complex decisions than for simple decisions that are based on habit or low involvement. *Low-involvement* stores are stores about which consumers care little, or about which they have no attitudes,[24] for example, a convenience store, which is selected mainly for convenient hours and/or location. A low-involvement store for one person may be a high-involvement store for another. Consumers tend to receive passively any marketing communications information about low-involvement stores, and do not evaluate these stores until after shopping there.

Although consumers who purchase by *habit* seek some information about stores, they seek out retail alternatives only to a limited extent. A loyal consumer chooses by habit to minimize the shopping time and the risk involved in searching through several alternatives.

A *high-involvement* store is chosen through complex decision-making. "Shopping" for the right store, like shopping for goods, requires evaluating alternatives. Consumers who choose among various stores learn about stores' attributes from the stores' merchandise and marketing communications, as well as from their own friends and shopping experience.

Sometimes stores' desirable features *compensate* for undesirable features. In the *compensatory model*, consumers evaluate each alternative according to criteria related to their needs. These criteria include merchandise quality, service, atmosphere, and other factors. High evaluations of a store on some attributes can compensate for low evaluations on others. For example, a superior store-brand shirt may compensate for a store's inconvenient location.

In the *non-compensatory model*, consumers evaluate retailers on one attribute at a time, eliminating all unsatisfactory alternatives. Under this model, a customer might avoid all retailers with inadequate parking regardless of their excellent merchandise, services, or marketing communications, because these other attributes do not compensate for unsatisfactory parking. Parking may be viewed as unsatisfactory because of icy conditions, theft and mugging, or for some other reason important to consumers.

Even after a customer has chosen a store, purchasing merchandise there is not inevitable. Changes in price, arrival of new information, or unavailability of a favorite brand may interfere. The experience of buying from a store may influence repeat visits and purchases either positively or negatively.[25]

Shopping Plans and Preferences

Only some consumers make decisions about stores or merchandise in advance. Impulse purchasers tend to postpone decisions until after they enter the shopping area.

Likewise, only some consumers like to shop. Researchers do not agree on whether a consumer who likes shopping spends more time shopping than one who does not. Budget constraints can force consumers who dislike shopping to spend more time at it than do affluent consumers who like shopping but have no spending limit. Or consumers may enjoy shopping for some types of merchandise but not others. There is some evidence that consumers do not shop around for convenience goods regardless of their attitudes toward shopping.[26]

Some consumers shop for diversion, physical exercise, information, social experiences, or self-gratification, not necessarily to buy merchandise. Many consumers make impulse purchases while visiting shopping locations for reasons other than planned shopping. Consumers who enjoy shopping tend to make more impulse purchases than those who do not enjoy shopping.[27]

There are several types of impulse purchasing. Consumers may buy (1) for variety or novelty, (2) because a display reminds them that they need the product, (3) because a display suggests a new product, or (4) because special conditions are met. For example, a consumer who has planned to buy merchandise when it is on sale waits to find the sale before making the purchase.[28]

Marketing Communications Strategies for Decision-Making Types

Ash's and Dale's are hypothetical low-involvement retailers. Ash's marketing communications task is to get consumers to shop at Ash's instead of at Dale's. Knowing that consumers do not evaluate low-involvement stores until shopping there, Ash's uses displays, coupons, and special promotional events to get customers into the store. Ash's would benefit from shifting consumers to high-involvement or habit decision-making in order to convert them into loyal customers. This store might want to use coupon booklets with weekly, dated coupons for a five- or six-week period to influence its customers' shopping habits.

Hypothetical high-involvement marketer Birch can use advertising to inform consumers of distinctive differences between Birch and competitors. Birch's actual or perceived differences must be sufficient to change consumers' behavior. If Birch offers little physical difference, it can use image advertising to reassure customers that it has the appropriate merchandise to meet their needs. While the customer is in Birch's store, or buying Birch-brand merchandise, the merchandise, store atmosphere, and store personnel should be consistent with the consumer expectations created by the images promoted in store or brand advertising.

Store and brand advertisements can be used as a source of information for shopping planners. In-store promotions and displays help attract impulse purchasers. Displays and special sale promotion events are important visual stimuli for such customers. Salespersons can influence impulse purchasing by suggesting new merchandise, uses, and related accessories.

POSITIONING—IN THE ENVIRONMENT

Positioning

Positioning, a concept which originated in about 1969, grew out of Rosser Reeves' 1950s "unique selling proposition" for a product and David Ogilvie's 1960s "long-term investment in the image of a brand." While the product and image continue to be important, both retailers and manufacturers of products must gain a *position* in the consumer's mind. In order to do this, the seller must be able to describe its target customer. Exhibit 2-5 contains J.C. Penney's description of its target customer, positioning objective, and positioning creed. The target is current Penney customers and consumers who have easy access to Penney's but who do not believe that the company meets their expectation for fashionable merchandise. Penney's positioning objective is to have recognizable values in consistently good-quality fashionable and functional merchandise. Its positioning creed includes up-to-date store atmosphere, good quality, timely merchandise, and prices 10% to 20% below comparable merchandise in department and specialty stores.

The position focuses on consumers' *perceptions* of the place that the product or store occupies in a specific market, locating the product or store *relative to competing brands or stores* in consumers' minds. For example, by claiming to be "the savings place," K mart takes the position that it is the kind of store in which consumers can save money. This position is very appropriate for K mart's new venture into selling financial services, which are associated with monetary savings. In another example, by continually changing displays, events, and even departments, Bloomingdale's stores support their position as avant-garde leaders of fashion. The chart in Exhibit 2-6 suggests a method of choosing goals to position stores against competitors with respect to merchandise, service, convenience, and other dimensions.[29]

There are various types of positioning. Competitive "head-on" positioning is *attacking* the industry leader. This can be done by using advertising to compare the merchandise, values, and services of one firm with that of another. An attack can be dangerous when the non-leader makes comparisons with the leader, and consumers think that the leader

EXHIBIT 2-5 J.C. Penney's Target Consumers, Positioning Objective, Excerpts from Creed

Source: "J.C. Penney Stores Positioning Statement" (January, 1982). Courtesy J.C. Penney Co., Inc.

Target Consumers

Primarily, consumers who currently shop at Penney's. Secondarily, consumers who have convenient access to Penney stores, but do not shop at Penney's because they do not believe their expectations for fashionable merchandise will be satisfied.

Within the primary target, we recognize that many Penney shoppers buy a disproportionately small amount of their fashionable merchandise at Penney's, compared to what they purchase at Department and Specialty Stores. This segment represents a key target group.

Positioning Objective

To be perceived by target consumers as having appealing selections of consistently good quality, fashionable merchandise, with recognizable value reflected by a price advantage in the majority of items, while continuing to be perceived as a retailer offering good quality, functional merchandise.

We define fashionable merchandise as any item where such characteristics as style, appearance, and timeliness are considered important by the target consumer.

Positioning Creed (Excerpts)

We want consumers to have an enjoyable experience—so that they "feel good"—shopping at the Penney store. We want to instill confidence in consumers that in all of our actions we are competent, fair and of the highest integrity. . . .

We will be sensitive to meeting our target consumer expectations for shopping assistance and in support services, such as credit, product services, and catalog desks. All of our associates will conduct themselves in a friendly, knowledgeable way, and present an appearance that supports the character of the store and merchandise.

We want target consumers to feel that Penney's offers a selection of merchandise by providing a variety of styles, colors, fabrics, and name identifications, along with the needed depth in appropriate items. The main thrust in most lines will be the Penney name and Penney private labels. Manufacturers' brands will be offered to enhance the consumers' perception of quality, selection, and timeliness, or when they are the only practical choice in the market. We will attempt to provide consistency and longevity in the Penney name identifications we use in order to help consumers make repeat purchases. . . .

Everything we do gives a signal to consumers as to who we are, what we believe in, and what we want to be. All elements must be coordinated to communicate our positioning effectively. Store elements—sales associates, services, fixtures, signs—need to be in harmony; so must the character of each department and the merchandise assortments, one to another; so must pricing and advertising support the total effort.

***EXHIBIT 2-6* Positioning Method and Chart**

Source: "How to Position for Success," New York: Newspaper Advertising Bureau. Modified, with permission, by L. Rubin. Size of original, 8 × 11″.

POSITION A STORE

	Positioning Dimensions	Store Now
1.	Merchandise Diversity	
2.	Store Size/Customer Range	
3.	Fashion Distinctiveness	
4.	Price Competitiveness	
5.	Convenience	
6.	Service Quality	
7.	Innovativeness	
8.	Lifestyle Awareness	
9.	Dependability	
10.	Community Identification	

The above chart lists ten ways retailers are perceived by customers. Use the columns for a store and its four most important competitors. Here's how to develop a positioning table:

1. Rate Yourself

Assign 0-10 points to each dimension. The number you give each dimension represents your effectiveness now, that is, how you think customers see the store. For example, assigning 8 points to fashion distinctiveness means you feel the store is currently perceived as a fashion leader. Assigning a 3 to price competitiveness means that prices do not presently play a significant role in distinguishing the store.

EXHIBIT 2-6 (continued)

A MARKET

e Goal	Competitors			

2. Rate competition
In the same way, assign points to express the effectiveness of each dimension for the four most significant competitors.

3. Establish goals
Compare store position profile in each dimension with competition. Are you satisfied with the way you compare or would you like to strengthen store positioning in one or more dimensions? The "goal" column should indicate which dimensions need strengthening during a specified period.

is doing the advertising. In that situation, the non-leader is spending its money to promote the leader. Taking a position *relative* to the leader is another option. This kind of positioning uses the leader's familiar position as a reference point for communicating a competitive position. Avis Rent-a-Car successfully positioned itself relative to the leader, Hertz, with the slogan "We're Number 2—We Try Harder".[30]

Repositioning

Repositioning is an option when a current position is no longer effective in a current competitive environment, and when additional customers are needed to generate sufficient sales. Boston's Jordan Marsh department store's former conservative image failed to attract young, single career persons. Jordan Marsh moved to a new position, trying to attract this new group without turning away its original customers. This is known as *lifestyle* positioning. Sears repositioned itself as "The Store of the Future" and is remodelling stores to look more like fashionable merchandisers, less like utilitarian retailers of durable goods. Montgomery Ward is repositioning itself with the slogan "The Seven Worlds of Wards."[31]

J.C. Penney commercials state, "There's a change in Penney's because there's a change in you." By hiring Halston to design a fashion line, J.C. Penney has changed from a middle-of-the-road apparel position to a fashion-conscious position. The repositioning included phasing out hard lines like large appliances (now only 25% of Penney's stock) and stressing soft lines like fashion merchandise (75% of Penney's stock). Penney eliminated appliances, paint and hardware, lawn and garden, and fabrics, which now are carried in specialty outlets and home improvement centers, and not necessarily in regional shopping centers. Penney's brand mix of 85% private label and 15% national brands remained the same after the repositioning. However, private labels have been upgraded to be highly competitive with national brands in terms of fashionability, quality, and timeliness.

Penney's repositioning effort aimed at dominance in the marketplace. For Penney, this meant becoming the leading resource of the key merchandise lines found in regional shopping centers. Penney pursued dominance in five ways. Three of these involved marketing communications: presentation, staffing, and communications to the customer. The other two were adding designer lines and eliminating the hard lines. Communications included weekly preprints in local newspapers or by mail to two-thirds of the metropolitan households in America, bi-weekly preprints to reach almost half of all households in America, national television advertising, and several catalogs. Only the designer lines were featured in a recent television campaign, an indication of the attempted change in image.[32]

Store and Product Positioning

Retail positioning strategy is both similar to and different from manufacturers' positioning strategy. Both must communicate a corporate position consistent with their various brands and roles in their markets. However, the retailer sells merchandise from numerous manufacturers and has little control over the individual manufacturers' positions except to choose whether to carry the manufacturers' merchandise. The retailer must take into account the consistency of the manufacturers' positions when deciding on a merchandise mix. This merchandise mix and communications about the various manufacturers' brands must be consistent with the retailer's position. Store-brand merchandise (85% at J.C. Penney) does not have any manufacturers' identification, aiming instead to build a strong retail image.

Some manufacturers offer cooperative funds to help pay for retail advertising of their brands. Sometimes they furnish prepared ads, illustrations, manufacturers' logos for the stores' own advertisements and signs, and point-of-purchase display materials. Retailers should evaluate all of these communications aids with respect to their consistency with the retailer's own position. If their use supports the retailer's position, then they are helpful to both retailer and manufacturer. But if their use is inconsistent with the retailers' image, they will help only the manufacturer, with the retailer incurring little benefit from its advertising costs.[33] As mentioned earlier, in modern concepts of marketing, the store itself can often become "the product."

SUMMARY

From early times, firms have created marketing communications appropriate for their operations and environments. These communications are dictated by the nature of each business and its environment. Even when part of a national chain, businesses are often constrained by local situations. Firms must fit into communities with unique customs, institutions, and lifestyles, all of which tend to change over time. Communications are also constrained by government regulation and by the pressure of relevant others: competitors, advertising associations, and consumers.

Information about their particular environment helps firms keep track of customers, competitors, and relevant businesses moving in and out of an area, as well as competitors' activities in the marketplace. Consumer decision-making methods, shopping plans, and preferences are part of the environment. Marketers can use information about the environment in planning how to deploy all appropriate communication tools: advertising, visual merchandising, personal selling, special promotions, and publicity.

Marketing communications positioning must create a clear image in the minds of the target consumers. Position is the image of what the marketer stands for; the firm through its communication projects its personality. As times change, repositioning is sometimes necessary to create an image more appropriate for the environment. Marketing communications must therefore be consistent with position.

QUESTIONS

1. Explain how the basic nature of a business affects its marketing communications choices.
2. Explain why communications managers need to have some knowledge of how past marketing communications have succeeded or failed in their environments.
3. Which of the new forms of communication made possible by modern technology do you think will be the most widely adopted? Explain, and give examples.
4. Why should marketing communications managers understand the community environment? In your opinion, what aspect of the community environment has the most critical impact on whether a particular marketing communication will succeed?
5. Which is preferable, self-regulation or government regulation of advertising activities? Explain.
6. Think of a low-involvement and a high-involvement store that you have visited recently. Did customers go to these stores because of marketing communications? If so, why, and how did the communications differ for these stores? If a customer did not receive marketing communications about these stores, but visited them anyway, explain why retail marketing communications would still help the stores.
7. Explain similarities and differences in marketing communications for (1) people who like to shop, (2) people who dislike shopping, (3) people who tend to buy on impulse.
8. Explain positioning. Explain how and why J.C. Penney's position differs from K mart's position.
9. You own and manage a small independent store in a shopping center where J.C. Penney is an anchor store. Your store sells merchandise that is similar to merchandise in one department of J.C. Penney. State your position. How is it like or different from the position of J.C. Penney? Explain. Explain why you would or would not recommend a head-on position.

NOTES

1. "Shopping Centers Will Be America's Towns of Tomorrow," *Marketing News* (November 28, 1980), pp. 1, 10; store atmosphere is discussed in Chapter 12.

2. For more extensive history, see marketing and retailing texts cited in notes 2, 5 and 6 of Chapter 1, as well as O. Kleppner, T. Russell, and G. Verrill, *Otto Kleppner's Advertising Procedure*, 8th ed., Englewood Cliffs, NJ: Prentice-Hall, 1983.

3. See Chapters 7 and 9.

4. R. Crain, "Videotex: 2-Way Ticket Nowhere," *Advertising Age*, 55 (May 10, 1984), p. M-10 and letters to editor in subsequent issues; "Compuserve Unveils 'The Electronic Mall'," *Marketing News*, 18 (November 9, 1984), p. 3; "Times-Mirror Opens up Gateway," *Marketing News*, 18 (November 9, 1984), p. 5.

5. B. Hulin-Salkin, "Growing Market Seen for Shrinking Products," *Advertising Age*, 55 (June 7, 1984), pp. 26, 28.

6. J. Snyder, "Fiber Optics Boards Launched," *Advertising Age*, 55 (February 13, 1984), p. 12.

7. S. Yuspeh, "Syndicated Values/Lifestyles Segmentation Schemes: Use Them as Descriptive Tools, Not to Select Targets," *Marketing News*, 18 (May 25, 1984), pp. 1, 12.

8. "Ads in Year 2000: Agency Executives Forecast Their Appearance and Delivery," *Marketing News*, 18 (December 21, 1984), pp. 1, 10.

9. J. Evans and B. Berman, *Marketing*, New York: Macmillan, 1982 (inside front cover).

10. V. Ruthig, "Malls Act as a Center for Marketer Promos," *Advertising Age*, 55 (May 4, 1981), p. S-13.

11. P. Sloan, "Retailers from Uptown New York Are Remembering Herald Square," *Advertising Age*, 55 (June 4, 1984), p. 54E.

12. L. Freeman, "After Devil of a Fight, P&G Gives Up," *Advertising Age*, 56 (April 29, 1985), 3, 100.

13. See note 2.

14. Commerce Clearing House, *CCH Trade Regulation Reporter*, 2, (3-20-72) p. 12,601, No. 12-22, (Chicago: Commerce Clearing House, 1972).

15. "FTC Reconsidering Grocery Ad Sale Rule," *The Morning Union*, (Springfield, MA) 121 (December 27, 1984), p. 9.

16. W. Borchard, "Federal Judges Display Sense of Humor," *Advertising Age*, 56 (February 11, 1985), p. 44.

17. "AAF Approves Ad Code Revisions," *Advertising Age*, 55 (August 17, 1984), p. 20; R. Scheidker, *What Every Account Representative Should Know about the Law and Advertising*, New York: American Association of Advertising Agencies, 1982, pp. 22–23.

18. G. Jervey, " 'CR' Suit Nicks Remington's Ad for Shaver," *Advertising Age*, 55 (December 24, 1984), p. 2.

19. J. Haberstroh, "Ad Professor Deliver Subliminal Education," *Advertising Age*, 56 (March 4, 1985), p. 52; "Can't Ignore Subliminal Ad Charges," *Advertising Age*, 55 (September 17, 1984), pp. 1–42; and letters to the editor in subsequent issues, October 8 & 22, p. 22 and November 5, p. 24; T.E. Moore, "Subliminal Advertising: What You See Is What You Get," *Journal of Marketing*, 46 (Spring, 1982), pp. 38–47. D. Rainer, "Not Seeing Is Believing," *Advertising Age*, 55 (January 16, 1984), p. 20, a letter in response to "Subliminal Chip Shots," *Advertising Age*, 54 (December 5, 1983), p. 16. This topic is covered in most advertising texts. See also: Sidney Weinstein, "Beware Subliminal Laws," *Advertising Age*, 55 (June

25, 1984), pp. 20–22. "Subliminal Ad Tactics: Experts Still Laughing," *Marketing News*, 19 (March 15, 1985), pp. 6–7.

20. "Clutter: Who Decides?" *Advertising Age*, 54 (December 5, 1983), p. 16. This topic is frequently in the news. See also, "Ads in the Year 2000," in note 8; and Chapter 6.

21. "Ad Quality Good; Believability Low," *Advertising Age*, 55 (May 31, 1984), pp. 3, 54.

22. M. Albion and P. Farris, *The Advertising Controversy*, Boston: Auburn House, 1981.

23. "New Haven-Meriden, Conn," and "Tucson, Ariz," *Advertising Age*, 55 (December 5, 1983), pp. M-14, M-56.

24. Adapted for stores from H. Assael, *Consumer Behavior and Marketing Action*, 2nd ed., Boston: Kent, 1984, Chapters 2–4.

25. J. Stearns, L. Unger, and J. Lesser, "Intervening Variables Between Satisfaction/Dissatisfaction and Retail Patronage Intention," *AMA 1982 Educators' Conference Proceedings*, B. Walker and others, eds., Chicago: American Marketing Association, 1982, pp. 179–182. For current articles about satisfaction, see *Journal of Marketing* and *Journal of Retailing*.

26. E. Hirschman and M. Mills, "Sources Shoppers Use to Pick Stores," *Journal of Advertising Research*, 20 (February, 1980), pp. 47–51.

27. D. Bellenger and P. Korgaonkar, "Profiling the Recreational Shopper," *Journal of Retailing*, 56 (Fall, 1980), pp. 77–92; L. Berry, "The Time-Buying Consumer," *Journal of Retailing*, 55 (Winter, 1979), pp. 58–69; P. Hendrix and C. Martin, "Evaluating Classification of Shoppers: Temporal and Enjoyment Dimensions of Patronage," *Retail Patronage Theory Workshop Proceedings*, W. Darden and R. Lusch, eds., Norman, OK: U. of Oklahoma, 1981, pp. 192–196.

28. Assael, *Consumer Behavior*, p. 560; H. Stern, "The Significance of Impulse Buying Today," *Journal of Marketing*, 26 (April, 1962), pp. 59–62.

29. J. Trout and A. Ries, "The Positioning Era," *Advertising Age*, 43 (May 1 and May 8, 1972); R. Markin, *Marketing Strategy*, 2nd ed., New York: Wiley, 1982, pp. 116–117. J. Snyder, "K mart Says, 'Come on Down,'" *Advertising Age*, 56 (February 11, 1985), p. 84.

30. Ibid.

31. "Marsh Brings Back Couple," *Advertising Age*, 53 (May 17, 1982), p. 49E; R. Reed, "Wood Prepares for Selling the 'New Sears'," *Advertising Age*, 54 (May 9, 1983), pp. 1, 88; R. Reed, "Ward's Sets Test of Specialty Plan," *Advertising Age*, 55 (January 30, 1984), p. 6; "Sears Committed to Expansion Despite Cutthroat Retail Market," *The Morning Union*, (Springfield, MA), 121 (December 26, 1984), p. 35.

32. David F. Miller, President of J.C. Penney Stores and Catalog, "J.C. Penney 1984: Pursuing Dominance in the Marketplace" (address to a Merrill-Lynch Field Trip), January 25, 1984; "Penney's Pitch: Change for the Better," *Advertising Age*, 55 (September 17, 1984), pp. 6, 90; Robert B. Gill, Vice Chairman of the Board of J.C. Penney, "Serving Today's Consumers, J.C. Penney's Strategic Plans" (address to the Morgan-Stanley Retail Forum), November 15, 1983; P. Sloan, "Penney's Saying 'Ciao' to Staid Image," *Advertising Age*, 55 (April 9, 1984), pp. 4, 69.

33. See the section on cooperative advertising in Chapter 14.

APPENDIX 2

SMALL RETAILER IN TWO ENVIRONMENTS

oberta Lingerie Couture: Telling Its West Side Story

NEW YORK—As business lit-
rally builds around her intimate
pparel boutique on the Upper West
ide, Roberta Liford is slowly build-
ıg business.

Like her cross-town store, the
reamy, wedge-shaped shop at 410
olumbus Ave. is dubbed Roberta
ingerie Couture, Inc.—Roberta for
ıort.

But unlike the Madison Avenue
ocation, the West Side store has been
oth blessed and cursed by its ad-
ress: It is on a block across from
ıe popular American Museum of
atural History, but it's a block that
under construction.

"That hasn't helped," Liford
ıid with a sigh one recent afternoon,
aring through her display window
the scaffolding that lines the street.
Fortunately, the huge crane that was
ut there for weeks just left."

Unfortunately, the construction
f storefronts and a 35-story con-
ominium is expected to continue
ırough the summer and into fall.
ut Liford is trying to make the best
f it. Ever since the scaffolding went
p she's had a rack of swimsuits,
veats and tops outside her door un-
er a sign that reads, "Construction
ıle; drastic reductions."

The lure, she admits, is
something I would never do on
Iadison Avenue," where the East
ide clientele isn't exactly shopping
r bargains.

"The Madison Avenue cus-
mer comes into the shop with a
efinite purpose, and that is to buy something," she said. "They set a definite time to shop and there's no nonsense."

"That type of customer is starting to come in here from Central Park West and Riverside Drive," she noted. "But mostly we've been getting the weekend customers who come strolling in with yogurt or cookies or ice cream. They do a lot more impulse buying."

. . .

Liford has also noticed some other contrasts between East and West. Most notably, she said, Columbus Avenue customers are younger and less affluent, with tastes to match. "They love a lot of cotton, terry cloth and daywear," she said.

A higher percentage of her customers there—as much as 25 percent—are also men. "They buy mostly silk pajamas, sexy panties and bras, and teddys," Liford said.

Popular among all buyers are camisoles, cotton sweatpants, "interesting" socks and big, bulky terrycloth robes. But one more thing appears to have captured an audience.

"Shoulder pad T-shirts," Liford said. "Since 'Dynasty,' everybody wants to look like Linda Evans, so that sells well"—at $34 each.

. . .

For now, the challenge of running similar shops in different parts of the city is enough for Liford. She opted to go into business for herself in 1977 and claims she's somewhat surprised by the sudden proliferation of shops like hers.

Source: By Kevin Haynes, excerpts from *Women's Wear Daily* (May 31, 1984), p. 19.

3
CONSUMER PERCEPTIONS, ATTITUDES, DEMO/PSYCHOGRAPHICS

INTRODUCTION

People don't buy *products*. They buy solutions to problems.[1] Understanding what motivates consumers to buy is essential for planning how to communicate to consumers. This chapter includes information about perception, attitudes, demographics, and psychographics (lifestyle and personality) to help marketers understand how to communicate about image, products, and services. While these topics are explained generally in consumer behavior chapters and texts,[2] this chapter presents them from a marketing communications perspective and suggests relevant strategies.

PERCEPTION

Perception is the way in which individuals gather, process, and interpret information from their environments.[3] Individuals tend to perceive selectively and in their own manner. When exposed to marketing communications, they often see and hear only what they want to. They tend to turn pages of a newspaper or magazine without "seeing" certain advertisements unless there is something to attract their attention. They selectively tune out television and radio commercials unless they have some reason for paying attention.

Balance and Dissonance

Even when an advertisement attracts attention, selective perception can interfere with its message. A message consistent with prior beliefs tends to communicate completely and clearly, but one that is not consistent upsets the balance between beliefs and message. A person can restore balance by changing opinion about a brand or store, or source of information, or both.[4] Displays in Macy's "Cellar of Specialty Shops" send a message (creative) different from that sent by displays in the former "Bargain Basement" (dull). Customers can change opinions of Macy's to restore the balance upset by this change in displays and merchandise.

Cognitive dissonance, a kind of mental discomfort, also tends to arise when a perceived piece of information is contrary to prior beliefs. A person tries to reduce this dissonance by distorting or denying the information.[5] This dissonance occurs when well-known firms attempt to change their images. Pepperidge Farm, a Campbell Soup Company, had a quality image for bread and cookies. Low-quality products like Deli's, Star Wars Cookies, and apple juice failed because consumers bought Pepperidge Farm products for high quality and the low quality Deli's, etc., caused dissonance.

Sears' original attempt to change from its conservative, middle-America image to an upscale fashion image in a short time failed because it created cognitive dissonance: at that time, mass marketers did not have a fashion image. Somewhat later, after the historical impact of the Sears change, Penney was more successful in changing from middle-class merchandise to middle-class-plus-designer merchandise (Halston). Similarly, K mart, Montgomery Ward, and again Sears are adding higher-margin fashion merchandise at a time when the Penney experience has made this kind of change more acceptable and less dissonant. In the interim, Sears' expansion into financial services (Dean-Witter) and real estate (Coldwell-Baker), and its change to a more modern logo have helped change its original image to a more updated fashionable one, further reducing the dissonance which had originally been associated with the Sears fashion image.[6]

Organizing Perceptions

People organize perceptions by putting them into categories or adding them to the existing information in memory. Remembering an advertisement from a previous exposure, they tend to pay relatively less attention to a repeat of that advertisement once their exposure to the message has reached a certain threshold. Some people cease to notice frequently-

EXHIBIT 3-1 Threshold, Optimum Frequency, and Decreasing Impact of Marketing Communications over Number of Exposures

Source: Reprinted with permission from *Strategic Advertising Campaigns* by Don E. Schultz, Dennis G. Martin, William P. Brown, published by Crain Books, a division of Crain Communications Inc. Copyright 1984 by Don E. Schultz, Dennis G. Martin, William P. Brown.

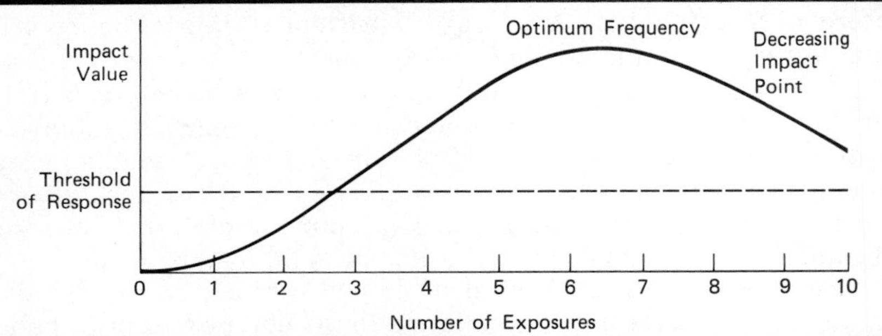

repeated advertisements sooner than others. Exhibit 3-1 shows the optimum frequency and decreasing impact point for exposures to messages about brand-name goods. At least three exposures per month or during a purchase cycle are needed to reach the threshold of response. After six or seven exposures, succeeding exposures become less valuable. Then, the curve falls towards the threshold level again, and may fall below the threshold in certain situations.

Consumers generalize from past experience. For example, they recognize distinctive print typefaces and art styles without having to read the store or brand name. If they like the store or brand and need the advertised merchandise, they tend to pay attention to the ad; if not, they tend to ignore it. For example, a customer sees a sale ad for suits in one store, and generalizes from past experience that other stores also have suit sales, or that other merchandise is on sale at the store which advertised the suit sale.

Individuals tend to complete patterns by filling in missing parts. An incomplete message attracts attention when completing it brings satisfaction to a person. The Lord and Taylor department store chain, whose main store is in New York City, repeats a short phrase in print advertisements each year. A recent phrase is "American Refinement." This and former phrases like "The Classic Look" enable customers to complete the message with their own specific interpretations of the Lord and Taylor image.

Image

Perception and image Image represents consumer perceptions about a firm as a whole, a *gestalt*. Firms, like people, have distinctive personalities and images, such as a low-price image, a good-service image, or a prestige image. Research implies that low-image apparel retailers benefit from association with high-image brands, but low-image manufacturers do not benefit from association with high-image retailers. Promotions, publicity, advertising, helpful employees, and store atmosphere communicate images. Customers enjoy shopping in stores and for brands that reinforce their self-images. If firms have similar images with respect to major characteristics, a relatively minor incident such as a pleasant or unpleasant encounter with one salesperson tends to have a greater effect on customers comparing these firms than if firms have different images.[7]

Exhibit 3-2 contains a semantic differential scale which collects information about perceptions. By observing where customers place hypothetical Art's Store on this scale versus where they place other stores rated similarly, one can learn about customer perceptions of Art's Store relative to a competitors'. This type of scale, with other adjectives, has been used for brands. Because customers do not necessarily agree with the marketer about what a store's or brand's image is, this feedback is very important. Cognitive dissonance can arise when customers perceive that a store or brand is not the way its ads lead them to believe. Exhibit 3-2 can be modified to collect information about brands.

EXHIBIT 3-2 A Sample Semantic Differential Scale for Retailers*

Source: Selected from Robert Kelly and Ronald Stephenson, "The Semantic Differential: An Information Source for Designing Retail Patronage Appeals," *Journal of Marketing,* 31 (October, 1967), p. 45. Reprinted with permission from *Journal of Marketing.*

Please check the category that you think best describes Art's store.

	Very		Neither		Very	
Wide merchandise selection	___	___	___	___	___	Limited merchandise selection
Unattractive decor	___	___	___	___	___	Attractive decor
Helpful employees	___	___	___	___	___	Employees not helpful
Difficult to find	___	___	___	___	___	Easy to find
Believable advertising	___	___	___	___	___	Misleading advertising
Well-known to friends	___	___	___	___	___	Not known to friends
Prices relatively low	___	___	___	___	___	Prices relatively high

* *This scale can be used for brands by substituting bi-polar adjectives relevant for evaluating a particular brand. Examples: sweet–sour; updated–conservative; long lasting–perishable; easy to clean–difficult to clean.*

Models of image development In the *internally-based* model of image development, image is based on the founder's original ideals and on the business traditions developed over time. As the environment changes, this image may lose relevance. In the *trade-based* model, managers stress attributes in relation to those of competitors and of similar non-competing firms elsewhere. Emphasizing similarity does not differentiate a firm from its peers, but does take advantage of clear images already communicated by others. Changing from either of these models to the *market-based* model allows a firm to use customers' responses as important input into communications plans.[8] The Stew Leonard store is an example of an internally-based model. Stew Leonard's is a dairy-produce retail store selling only a small number of items compared to the standard supermarket. Leonard's is an example of a retailer doing everything right from a marketing standpoint. The customer is *always* right. There are always numerous bargains and special values. All displays are mass displays indicating that the store has confidence in the merchandise it is offering. (Leonard's earns over $85 million in a one-store operation!) After the customers enter the store, they must follow a wide curving aisle that takes them through the entire store. Thus, every customer is exposed to all merchandise being offered. The store has a wall of celebrity customers' pictures, together with those of regular customers who have carried Leonard's shopping bags all over. Alongside the parking lot is a small zoo to interest the children who accompany their parents.

Internally-based and trade-based strategies are often associated with failure unless these strategies remain appropriate as the environment changes. As explained earlier in this chapter, Sears' original internally-based image did not change until other changes in the environment made this change acceptable to the public. The "Other Korvette," an updated branch of Korvette, tried a trade-based strategy to be a fashion department store like its neighbors. However, it could not supplant the old Korvette discount image and went out of business.[9] J.C. Penney is a good example of a change from an internally-based model to a market-based model. Penney phased out appliances, which tend to be sold in discount stores; and phased in moderately-priced designer fashions in addition to its regular lines at a time when these were popular but not generally affordable elsewhere.

Weber's Law and Image-Change Thresholds

Below a certain threshold, individuals do not notice a difference in stimuli. Weber's Law states that the stronger the initial image or stimulus, the greater the impact required for the change to be recognized.[10] Therefore, relatively small changes in brand characteristics, packaging, display, and advertising style can be made over a period of time without changing the basic image. On the other hand, changing a long-time image requires relatively large and noticeable changes in packaging, display and advertising style for both manufacturers and retailers.

For example, Jordan Marsh, a conservative Boston department store, made a noticeable change in its catalog presentation. In March 1981, it produced an updated catalog, targeted at ages 22–35, and accompanied by newspaper and television backup.[11] This controversial catalog told of the adventures of a young Boston couple, Jack and Jill. It was perceived as inconsistent with the demographic and social environment of that time and generated substantial publicity. Protesters marched on Jordan Marsh, attracting the attention of both regular customers and the new, young, upscale target who then came in to buy the updated merchandise.

Marketing Communications Strategy Related to Perception

Increasing awareness Increasing the size of a print advertisement or using an announcer whose voice fits the message in a broadcast advertisement increases the likelihood of a message being perceived.[12] Awareness of advertisements also can be increased by offering coupons that customers might cut out and carry with them, and by using displays which reinforce the visuals of advertised messages. On the other hand, changing colors and logos on packaging, and on store bags and boxes may help change brand and/or store image in some cases because this is a change that the consumer takes home.[13]

A moderate amount of ambiguity can be used to increase awareness by letting customers complete an advertised message to suit themselves. This indefinite quality also allows one ad to attract different segments of the target market. Ambiguous mixed messages can be part of the background audio or visual as well as of the basic concept.

Reducing dissonance or misunderstanding Reassurance that the firm sells quality merchandise reduces potential dissatisfaction and dissonance arising from a purchase. Thus, customers feel that they "did the right thing by making the purchase." The reassurance that the retailer both sells quality merchandise and accepts merchandise returns also reduces the perceived risk of purchasing merchandise, especially if the merchandise is expensive.[14] In addition to providing a positive image for a store, this reassurance builds a positive image for *store brands* which helps them compete with heavily-promoted manufacturers' brands, further building store loyalty. The "Penney Fox" emblem is an example of store brand competition with the "Izod Alligator" manufacturer's insignia.

Projecting a consistent image Because individuals tend to organize visual perceptions into images, the quality and other images projected in advertisements must be consistent throughout the marketer's brands or stores. The various personalities of different parts of a brand or store and its marketing communications should be well enough integrated for the consumer to form a *gestalt*—a unified image of the marketer. Before the original Bonwit Teller fashion store for women closed in New York City, its departments had a variety of images, mixed messages that confused potential customers. The new Bonwit Teller in New York City, located in the elegant Trump Tower, presents a distinctive and unified personality for a more consistent image.

Weber's Law implies that changes in packaging, and atmosphere and other marketing communications contribute to a change in image once they exceed the perceptual threshold. Therefore, unless management wants to change image, these changes should occur below the awareness level of the target market so that consumers do not perceive a difference when none is intended.

ATTITUDES

Attitudes are "learned predispositions to respond to an object or class of objects in a consistently favorable or unfavorable way."[15] Knowledge about attitudes helps to identify market segments and to evaluate communication and marketing strategies.

Marketers can benefit from understanding theories of attitudes and behavior. When customers are only slightly disappointed, assimilation/contrast theories suggest that their attitudes will adjust to their expectations; that is, that customers will forget their disappointment and remember their expectations. On the other hand, a negative change in attitude is likely when a customer is very disappointed.

For example, a retailer who has always carried the Prestige shirt brand may decide to switch to a comparable brand. A disappointed customer who wants only the Prestige *brand* may dislike the retailer who no longer sells Prestige shirts. Other customers who want Prestige *quality* may accept the same quality in a comparable brand, and continue to like that retailer. Their disappointment is not great enough to affect their attitudes.

Attitudes develop over time. They are influenced by family, peers, personality, information, and experience. They are related to beliefs about a store's image, the products and brands it carries, and its benefits and attributes, or inherent characteristics. Examples of *benefits* are: good values, pleasant salespeople, and a liberal return policy. Examples of store *attributes* are: carrying certain brands and accepting national credit cards. Customers tend to shop at stores that have preferred and desirable benefits and attributes.

Functions of Attitudes

Attitudes have several functions.[16] First, they help customers satisfy their needs by helping them to choose among alternative stores and brands. Customers go to areas and stores and buy products that they like because past experience, word of mouth, or advertising communicate that these will meet their needs.

Next, attitudes express a self-concept of identity and a value system. People who like natural foods tend to buy natural foods at natural foods stores. People who like classic styles tend to like brands and stores with a classic image.

Finally, attitudes serve an ego-defensive function by helping the consumer avoid anxiety-producing situations. Customers who like to have the Ivy League look in order to feel confident about themselves tend to like brands and stores with an Ivy League image.

Measuring Attitudes, Intent, Need Components

An *overall evaluation* of a firm can be obtained either by rating the firm on a scale from "like very much" to "do not like at all," or by ranking a group of firms in order of preference. Both of these alternatives are shown in Exhibit 3-3. However, an overall evaluation can be misleading.

EXHIBIT 3-3 **Two Methods of Measuring Overall Attitude Evaluation of Retailers or Brands**

Source: Adapted from Henry Assael, *Consumer Behavior and Marketing Action,* 2nd ed. (Boston: Kent Publishing Company, 1984), pp. 180–181. © 1984 by Wadsworth Inc. Reprinted by permission of Kent Publishing Company, a division of Wadsworth Inc. See also the monadic preference scales in Kevin J. Clancy and Robert Garson, "Why Some Scales Predict Better," *Journal of Advertising Research,* 10 (1970), p. 34.

1. Rate the following by checking the category that best applies.

In general, I like A very much.	___ ___ ___ ___ ___	In general, I do not like A at all.
In general, I do not like B at all.	___ ___ ___ ___ ___	In general, I like B very much.
In general, I like C very much.	___ ___ ___ ___ ___	In general, I do not like C at all.

2. Please assign a number of 1 to the store (or brand) you prefer most, a number of 2 to your second choice, and so on.

A _____

B _____

C _____

Many firms sell merchandise from several categories. A person can like a manufacturer or retailer for one category and not for another. Therefore, some specific category should be used as a reference point in measuring overall evaluation, such as the "stereo category" or the "canned cat food category."

A consumer may like a store but not shop there because of location, pricing, or other constraints. For example, not all consumers who like an elegant, expensive New York jewelry store like Tiffany's can afford to buy expensive jewelry or silver there. Similarly, customers who like expensive car brands may not be able to afford to buy them. Therefore, *intent*, the subject of Exhibit 3-4, may be more relevant for sales than favorable *attitude* because intent is closer to action than attitude is. "Definitely will" is the category of interest to new stores or brands. Brand studies have shown a close relationship between percentage of respondents expressing intent to buy and subsequent consumer trial of a product.[17]

Marketing communicators need to know: how consumers evaluate certain store or brand attributes, how much satisfaction consumers get from these attributes, and how consumers rate the ideal store or brand on these attributes. This information, plus some ranking of the relative importance of these components, shows what kind of store or product the respondents want and need. Exhibit 3-5 has questions about what respondents value and consider important. By comparison, answers to questions in Exhibit 3-2 provides information about the attributes that the respondents think firms provide. An alternative method of analyzing the consumer-firm interface is in Appendix 3-C, where the *management* perception of the relationship is explored. Consumer perceptions can differ from management perceptions.

EXHIBIT 3-4 **Intent to Shop at Store A or Buy Brand A**

Source: Adapted from Henry Assael, *Consumer Behavior and Marketing Action*, 2nd ed. (Boston: Kent Publishing Company, 1984), pp. 180–181. © 1984 by Wadsworth Inc. Reprinted by permission of Kent Publishing Company, a division of Wadsworth Inc. More than one brand or retailer can be included.

What is the likelihood that you will shop at Store A (or Buy Brand A) next time you shop for a business suit?

Definitely will _____

Probably will _____

Might or might not _____

Probably will not _____

Definitely will not _____

EXHIBIT 3-5 **Measures of What Customers Value and Consider Important**

Source: Adapted from Henry Assael, *Consumer Behavior and Marketing Action*, 2nd ed. (Boston: Kent Publishing Company, 1984), pp. 180–181. © 1984 by Wadsworth Inc. Reprinted by permission of Kent Publishing Company, a division of Wadsworth Inc. Many stores or brands and 10 to 20 attributes can be included. Beliefs importance (Fishbein) has been modified to ask for intent, not importance.

```
                         VALUE OR NEED COMPONENTS

1.  Indicate your evaluation of the following for Art's Store.*

                      Wide Selection of Merchandise
    Good     __A__  _B,I_  _____  _____  __C__  _____  _____  Poor

                            Helpful Employees
    Poor     _____  _____  _____  __A__  _____  __B__  _C,I_  Good

2.  Indicate the degree of satisfaction you get from the
    following at Art's Store.

                      Wide Selection of Merchandise
    Very satisfied ___ ___ ___ ___ ___ ___ ___ Not very satisfied

                            Helpful Employees
    Not very satisfied ___ ___ ___ ___ ___ ___ ___ Very satisfied

3.  Think about your ideal store for shopping for a business
    suit, and rate it on the characteristics listed below.

Wide merchandise selection  __ __ __ __ __ __ __ Limited Selection

Employees not helpful       __ __ __ __ __ __ __ Helpful employees

                          BELIEFS IMPORTANCE **

Rate each of the following characteristics based on how important
you think they are in determining your selection of a store in
which to buy a business suit.

               Right width of merchandise assortment
Very important  ___ ___ ___ ___ ___ ___ ___  Not important at all

               Right level of helpfulness of employees
Not important   ___ ___ ___ ___ ___ ___ ___  Very important
```

* *After results of a survey are compiled, the averages for each store can be posted on the questionnaire as shown in 1. Then, average evaluations for stores A, B, C, and I (ideal) can be compared.*

** *In longer lists, the order of the bipolar terms, i.e., good/poor, can vary at random to avoid a halo effect.*

Marketing Communications Strategy Related to Attitudes

An example of *adaptive strategy* is to send special mailings to credit customers who have shown a positive attitude by buying and charging certain merchandise categories. Such a strategy would notify customers who charged shoes about shoe promotions, and notify customers who charged housewares about housewares and home furnishings promotions. This strategy might include sending discount coupons to customers who have bought moderately priced or sale merchandise.

A strategy designed to *induce change* tries to modify consumer priorities and attitudes, in order to attract new customer segments. There are four change strategies: change consumer beliefs, change the relative importance of those beliefs, change the store or brand's image, and change consumer behavior or intended behavior. These strategies use informatin from Exhibits 3-2 through 3-5 above. For example, Boston's Jordan Marsh department store used its controversial Jack and Jill catalog to change potential customers' beliefs that Jordan's was a conservative store.[18]

Another strategy is to *change the overall attitude evaluation* measured in Exhibit 3-3 by changing the *perceived mood* of the shopping experience. Changes in store atmosphere, decor, personal service, and store image can be used to change customers' overall attitude evaluation. In a recent survey, about one-third of the respondents (42% of the men and 28% of the women) said they considered shopping for food, clothing, housewares, furniture, and other items an unpleasant experience. Further, about two-thirds considered salespeople only "somewhat knowledgeable."[19] These findings, based on personal in-home interviews from a national probability sample, indicate that stores have plenty of room for changing attitudes.

Changing *intent*, as measured in Exhibit 3-4, is another possible strategy. Inducements to buy a brand or to visit a store, such as special sales, special purchases, coupons, or special events can be used on a temporary basis to change intent. Once customers have been induced to visit the store, the merchandise, atmosphere, personnel, and events influence their intent to return to the store another time. Brand trial also can influence intent to buy the brand again if the trial creates a positive attitude.

Lastly, information from Exhibit 3-5 helps determine whether market segments would be receptive to changing their perceptions about a store's ability to meet their needs. For example, if a wide selection of merchandise is important, and the store has or plans to have wide merchandise selection, then advertising, personal selling, and display can be coordinated to communicate information about a wide selection of merchandise. Need components for brand attributes, like flavor or durability, could be evaluated in a similar way.

DEMOGRAPHICS

Demographic Data

Demographic data (age, race, sex, education, occupation, income, region, national origin) provide objective, measurable information about actual and potential customers. The United States Census counts the entire population every ten years and takes sample counts in other years. Given trends in birth and death rates, immigration, and emigration, the government can project the data into the future. For example, children born in the Baby Boom at the end of World War II are 20–29 years old in the 1980s and will be 30–39 years old in the 1990s, as shown in Exhibit 3-6.

Even though estimates of future demographics are available today, local environmental changes can invalidate the projections. Current changes in the environment include such factors as more women working, more college graduates, smaller families, non-traditional living arrangements, the aging World War II Baby Boom, the boom in children of baby-boom parents, and the larger percentage of senior citizens. The "baby boomers" earned about half of the U.S. personal income, had almost half of the civilian jobs, purchased about 70% of the homes and stereo equipment in 1984, and buy many premium products.[20] Also new is the redistribution

EXHIBIT 3-6 **United States Population Profiles by Age Groups, Including Baby Boom, 1980 and 1990**

Source: B. G. Yovovoch, "Baby Boomers Battle Mid-Level Bulge," *Advertising Age*, 53 (January 4, 1982), p. S-16. Reprinted with permission from the January 1982 issue of *Advertising Age*. Copyright 1982 by Crain Communications, Inc.

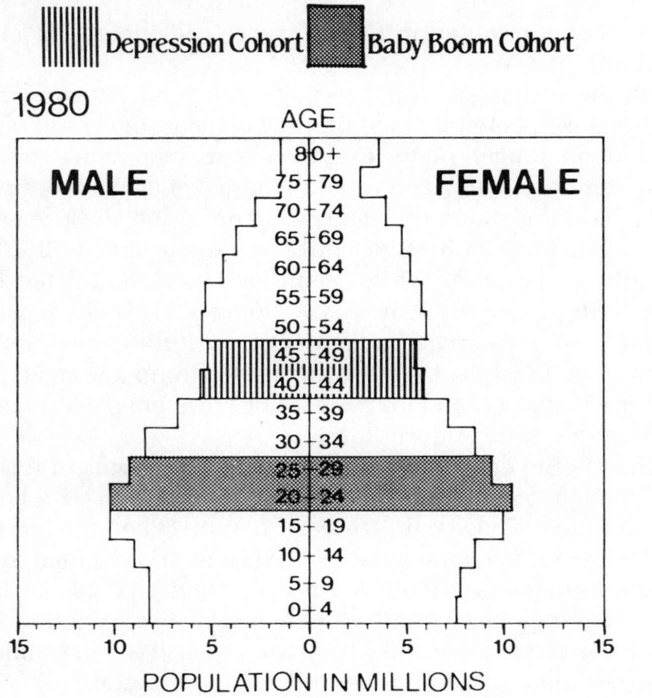

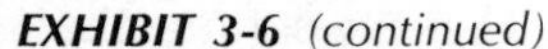

EXHIBIT 3-6 (continued)

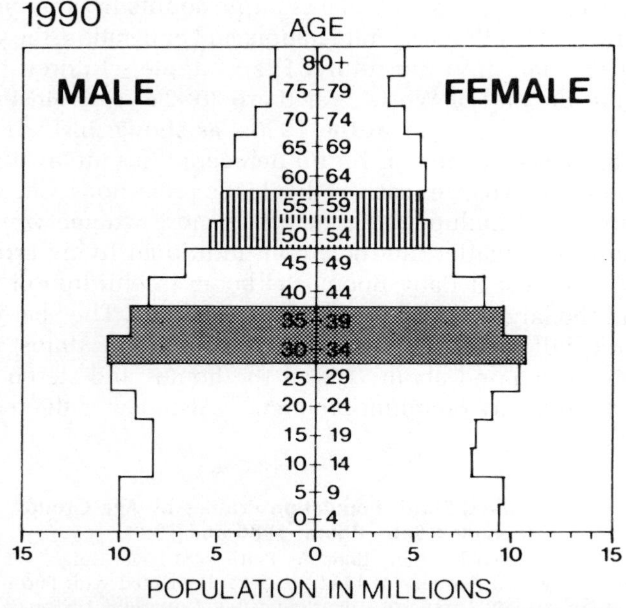

of United States population by age, race, and income from North and East to South and West.

With these changes in the demographic environment come changes in definitions. For example, as of the 1980 Census, the "head of household" designation no longer refers exclusively to men when the household contains women as well. The respondent designates the household head, who may be either male or female depending on the preference of the respondent. Changes in lifestyles influence the counts in the "household" and "family" categories. While "families" (persons related by blood or marriage living together) still exist, "households," (all persons, related or unrelated, who occupy a housing unit, excluding group quarters) are a more common lifestyle than in the past. Group quarters includes an "institutions" category, and "other": 10 or more unrelated persons sharing a unit, includes college dormitories.[21]

Demographic data show whether or not segments of the population are large enough to constitute a target market, and indicate where segments can be combined. These data are most helpful when the target has identifiable demographic characteristics, that is, men or women; homeowners or apartment-dwellers; urban or rural residents; people of high or low mobility, age, income, or educational levels. For example, adolescents and middle-aged consumers may be more responsive than senior consumers to subjective advertising claims and vague superlatives.[22] Exhibit 3-7

EXHIBIT 3-7 **Descriptions of Selected Demographic Groups**
Source: Reprinted with permission from Donnelly Marketing Information Services, Stamford, CT.

CLUSTERPLUS℠

BG/ED CLUSTER DESCRIPTIONS

Cluster Code	Demographic Characteristics
S 01	Highest SESI, Highest Income, Prime Real Estate Areas, Highly Educated, Professionally Employed, Low Mobility, Homeowners, Children in Private Schools
S 02	Very High Income, New Homes and Condominiums, Prime Real Estate Areas, Highly Mobile, Well Educated, Professionally Employed, Homeowners, Families with Children
S 03	High Income, High Home Values, New Homes, Highly Mobile, Younger, Well Educated, Professionally Employed, Homeowners, Married Couples, High Incidence of Children, Larger Families
S 19	High Incidence of Children, Larger Families, Above Average Income, Average Education, Younger, Married Couples, Homeowners, Homes Built in 60's and 70's, Primarily Rural Areas
S 20	Areas with High Proportion of Group Quarters Population, Sub-divisions Available Including College Dormitories, Homes for the Aged, Mental Hospitals and Prisons
S 28	Below Average Income, Less Educated, Younger, Mobile, High Incidence of Children, Mobile Homes, Primarily Rural Areas
S 29	Older, Low Mobility, High Proportion of Foreign Languages, Average Income, Below Average Education, Old Homes and Apartments, Urban Areas, Northeast Region
S 30	Low Income, Poorly Educated, Higher Vacancy Rates, Families with One Worker, Farms, Rural Areas
S 46	Poorly Educated, Very Low Income, Hispanic, Families with Children, Apartment Dwellers, Unskilled, High Unemployment
S 47	Lowest SESI, Urban Blacks, Very Low Income, Less Educated, Unskilled, Very High Unemployment, High Incidence of Female Householders with Children, Old Housing

Donnelley
Marketing Information Services
(203) 965-5454

Simmons
Market Research Bureau, Inc.
(212) 867-1414

gives the demographic characteristics of some demographic groups. These groups, sometimes called clusters, range from high-income, well-educated professionals in prime real estate areas to low-income, unskilled workers in rural areas.

Sources of Demographic Data

Demographic data are available from government agencies, in various publications and from media that sell advertising time and space.[23] Exhibit 3-8 describes some of the data available from the 1980 Census of Population. Census data are available in various forms—tape, print, microfilm; and from various sources—libraries, extension services, and private data services. The Census provides demographic data for states, standard metropolitan statistical areas (SMSAs), counties, cities, towns, and blocks.

Sales and Marketing Management publishes annual demographic data in its *Buying Power Data Service,* and in its July issue. Five-year projections are in its October issue. The July issue contains tables by counties and cities for median age; percentage of population by age groups—18–24, 25–34, 35–49, and 50 and over; number of households; total and median effective buying income (EBI, or disposable income) in thousands—$10–19.9, $20–34.9, $35–49.9, and $50 and over; and a buying power index (BPI). The *Data Service* contains finer breakdowns of age and income data, as well as three buying power indices. Books, other periodicals, and research firms also provide demographic data, which often come from a Census source.

Demographic data provided by research firms includes population densities of executive and managerial employees in an SMSA; computer displays of population, household size, ethnic background, sex, age, and other demographics; and computer-generated site maps. Demographic data are available by ZIP code with forecasts of the future and comparisons with the past. A computer data base offers demographics with economic, attitudinal and quality of life factors.[24]

Marketing Communications Strategy Related to Demographics

When both husband and wife work, the household has less time for shopping and for perceiving marketing communications. This means that communications art and copy, and in-store atmosphere must be efficiently targeted at those who do the household buying, regardless of age and sex. In some households with two working parents, teenagers do the grocery shopping. With the new variety of household lifestyles, manufacturers and retailers need to know whether different messages and media vehicles are needed by various target segments, such as singles without children, parents, and unrelated adults living together.[25]

EXHIBIT 3-8 **Description of Selected Data Sources for 1980 Census of Population Available from the Government**

Source: "Census Publications: An Update," in *Printout* (Summer 1983), p. 1. Data are available from the Government Printing Office, Supt. of Documents, Washington, D.C. 20402. *Printout* is a publication of The Center for Massachusetts Data at the University of Massachusetts at Amherst, MA.

Massachusetts

Number of Inhabitants: Massachusetts *(PC80-1A23). Basic population totals, shown over time; totals and percent change from previous census are shown from the first census in 1790. Contains maps, charts and graphs. Data are presented for the state, SMSA's, counties, cities and towns, as well as for the component parts of SMSA's: central city and area outside central city. 52 pages. Issued December 1981. $4.25. 003-024-02712-7.*

General Population Characteristics *(PC80-1B23). Complete count population characteristics, such as age, race, Spanish origin, sex, marital status and household composition. Data are fairly extensively cross-tabulated by race and Spanish origin. Includes maps for counties and urbanized areas. Data are presented for the state, SMSA's, counties, cities and towns, and Census Designated Places (CDP's) of 1,000 or more. Totals are also available for the categories of urban and rural areas, central cities, and urban fringe. 335 pages. Issued June 1982. $9.00. 003-024-02769-1.*

General Housing Characteristics *(HC80-1A23). Complete count housing characteristics such as total number of units, persons per unit, tenure (renter or owner occupied), value or contract rent and plumbing facilities. Detailed cross-tabulations by race and Spanish origin. Includes maps for counties and urbanized areas. Data are presented for the state, SMSA's, counties, and cities, towns, and CDP's of 1,000 or more. Totals also presented for the categories of urban and rural areas, central cities, and urban fringe. 294 pages. Issued July 1982. $8.50. 003-024-03053-5.*

Advance Estimates of Social, Economic and Housing Characteristics *(PHC80-S2-23). Sample data. Population characteristics include age, race and Spanish origin, sex, household composition, marital status and presence of children, language spoken, veteran status, education, labor force status (including limited occupation and industry information), poverty status and income. Housing characteristics include tenure, year moved into unit, year built, number of bathrooms and bedrooms, kitchen facilities, source of water, central heating and air conditioning, telephone, vehicles available, and water and home heating fuels used. Selected characteristics cross-tabulated by race and Spanish origin. Data are presented for the state, counties, and cities and towns of 25,000 or more. Contains information on sample size at the city and town level. 126 pages. Issued December 1982. $6.00. 003-024-04897-3.*

The change in age distribution over the decades means that marketers with a market targeted by age have a different-sized customer pool each decade. Also, there is a new group of consumers who reach target age each year and need information about stores or brands. Firms with age-group targets that are numerically small in some decades need to reevaluate whether they can stay in business with this small group, or whether they should direct communications towards additional segments to generate sufficient sales.

Mobility is of interest to marketers because population in a targeted region can change over time in its mix of race, occupation, and income. By understanding the changes in residence in a target area, marketers can choose their communications targets. Possibilities include the same target population in the same location; the same target population which has now moved to a different location; and a new demographic target which now lives in the original target location.

PSYCHOGRAPHICS

Psychographics are those psychological characteristics of consumers which can be quantified, including lifestyle and personality.[26] Lifestyle can change with age and social class. Personality tends to be more permanent than lifestyle.

Lifestyle

Lifestyle is a distinctive mode of living which can be identified in part by *activities, interests,* and *opinions*. Examples of *activities* are work, sports, hobbies, cultural interests, and shopping. *Interests* include family, recreation, food, media, and fashion. *Opinions* of self, society, and the future are examples of opinion variables. Exhibit 3-9 has some sample lifestyle categories matched with sample statements from activity-interest-opinion (AIO) questionnaires. The "Credit User" lifestyle is associated with the activity of buying many things with a credit card. "Yuppies", young urban professionals, and "Yumpies", Young Upwardly Mobile Professionals, have money and are willing to spend it on designer clothes, pasta makers, and electronic pagers. They are neat perfectionists and like to believe they are independent, although they too follow patterns, such

EXHIBIT 3-9 Lifestyle Categories and Associated Statements

Source: Selected from William D. Wells and Douglas J. Tigert, "Activities, Interests and Opinions," *Journal of Advertising Research* 11 (August 1971), 35. Reprinted from the *Journal of Advertising Research*. © Copyright 1971 by the Advertising Research Foundation.

CATEGORY:	*STATEMENT*
Credit User	"I buy many things with a credit card or a charge card."
Fashion-Conscious	"When I must choose between the two, I usually dress for fashion, not for comfort."
Price-Conscious	"I usually watch the advertisements for notices of sales."
Self-designated Opinion Leader	"My friends or neighbors often come to me for advice."
Sports Spectator	"I usually read the sports page in the daily paper."

as jogging while listening to Sony Walkmans.[27] Lastovicka has suggested a need for improving the validation of lifestyle traits.

Marketing research can provide profiles of lifestyle traits. Exhibit 3-10 and Appendices 3-A and 3-B describe work styles and fashion concerns of professional, clerical, and other working women. Appendix 3-A shows that professionals have a strict dress code and invest in clothes for a fashion image, whereas assembly workers prefer practical clothing for their jobs, expressing themselves in their non-work apparel. Exhibit 3-10 shows that women in some occupational groups—back-office clericals, assembly-line workers, and production-oriented service workers—have dual wardrobe requirements desiring both advanced fashion and functional wardrobes. On the other hand, professionals tend to have either classic or functional wardrobes. Appendix 3-B describes the buying habits of "formal" professionals, like accountants, lawyers, and administrators. Various groups of working women purchase different types of apparel in different types of stores for different reasons and with different frequency.

After 20 years of research, the Values and Lifestyles Program (VALS) developed by Stanford Research Institute has identified nine consumer types that will influence marketing strategies in the 1980s and 1990s.

EXHIBIT 3-10 Fashion Preferences of Major Women's Occupational Segments
Source: Working Women, 1980–1985, An Emerging Market (Celanese Fibers Marketing Company, January, 1980), p. 35.

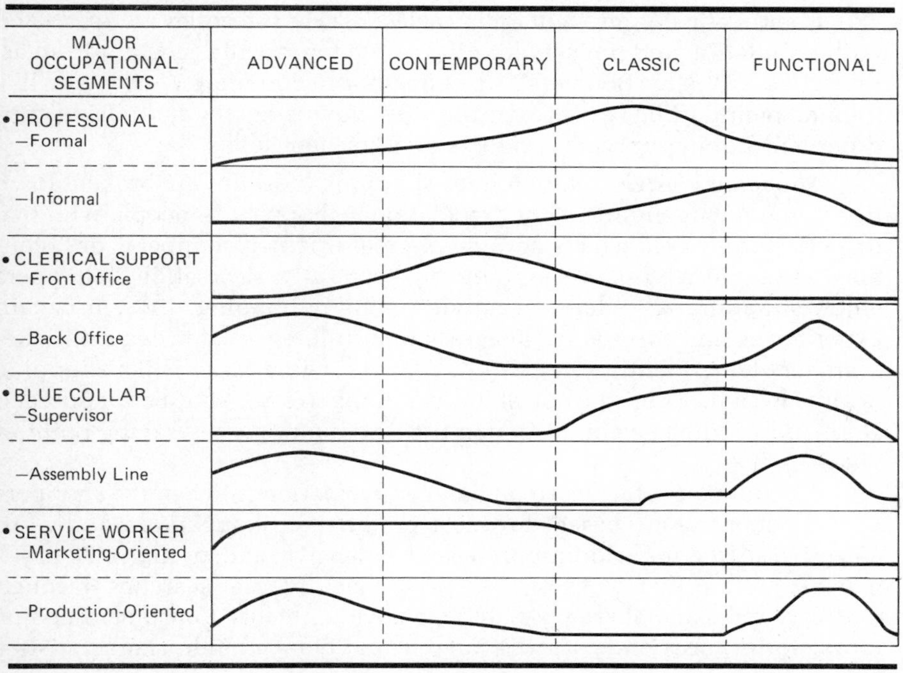

MAJOR OCCUPATIONAL SEGMENTS	ADVANCED	CONTEMPORARY	CLASSIC	FUNCTIONAL
• PROFESSIONAL —Formal				
—Informal				
• CLERICAL SUPPORT —Front Office				
—Back Office				
• BLUE COLLAR —Supervisor				
—Assembly Line				
• SERVICE WORKER —Marketing-Oriented				
—Production-Oriented				

These types include Need-driven, Belongers, Achievers, Inner-directed, and Outer-directed. Other evaluation scales include such types as Maker, Preserver, Taker, Changer, Seeker, Escaper; and Experimental, Following, Pleasure-seeking, Self-denying, Practical, and Ostentatious. While schemes like these have been criticized as too remote, rigid, and unreliable for selecting consumer targets, demographic data alone may be insufficient for characterizing consumer behavior. Two people with the same demographics can behave very differently in the marketplace because of their different lifestyles. For example, the "Emulators" and "Experimentals" have similar demographics but different lifestyles; on the other hand, the old and young "Achievers" have different demographics and similar lifestyles.[28]

Three lifestyle examples, "Achievers," "Working Women," and "Sunday Shoppers," follow. "Achievers" do not always marry; however, they do tend to buy homes. These households often lack spouses and children, and their members want convenience products and services. Achievers buy quality goods, but not status symbols. They treat their leisure as an extension of their jobs.

"Working women" prefer contemporary to traditional commercials, and like money management seminars and personal shopping services. There are three types of "Sunday shoppers": serious, family, and recreational. Recreational shoppers tend to like displays and special exhibits.[29]

Other lifestyle categories available from research suppliers include: "Pools and Patios," and "Sun Belt Singles." These categories are associated with population and household information for specific geographic areas. Lifestyles of "Baby Boomers"—persons born soon after World War II—include maintaining two-income families, buying homes and raising children, and buying upscale products and gourmet foods.[30]

Shopping lifestyles Sometimes shopping lifestyles are broken down into "enjoyment shoppers" or "recreational shoppers"—people who like to go to stores to see what's new—and "goal-oriented shoppers" or "planners"—people who plan shopping trips carefully. Recreational shoppers enjoy shopping as a leisure activity. While shopping, they also gain experiences and form store images which influence later decisions. Researchers have identified types of shoppers who either dislike shopping or are neutral. They do not enjoy shopping. These shoppers approach store and product selection from a time-saving or money-saving point of view.[31]

Shopping is often based on habit and experience, when the shoppers need frequently-purchased, low-cost product(s). Shoppers do engage in an active search for seldom-purchased, expensive, and/or high-risk products. There are two types of active searches: internal searches, through memory, and external searches, through advertisements, *Consumer Reports*, news stories, or friends. Time available and demographic characteristics help determine the relationship between internal and external searches.[32]

For example, Shaw Ping, a hypothetical college student, needs a stereo to facilitate studying for exams next week. Shaw has not bought a stereo before, and does not own one. Because a stereo represents a relatively large investment for a student, Shaw reads *Consumer Reports*, scans newspapers and catalogs for stereo ads, and talks with stereo owners, like Con Sumer. Shaw learns that Con bought an MSC-brand stereo from a likeable salesperson at hypothetical Shore's Store, and that Con likes the stereo very much. Noticing this week's Over's Store advertisement for a sale of MSC stereos, Shaw goes to hypothetical Over's Store and buys a stereo like Con's.

Timing is important. Sometimes a person will decide to buy some merchandise during a shopping trip but will not be ready to make a purchase at the time of this decision. Budget constraints or a psychological need to postpone satisfaction can delay implementation of the buying decision. The actual purchase can occur as a result of information gathered on previous shopping trips, print or broadcast advertisements, or word-of-mouth information.

While shoppers who do not like shopping might want to spend the least possible time buying what they need, saving money might be more important for them than saving time, especially when buying expensive merchandise like consumer durables. On the other hand, some shoppers might enjoy shopping but have time constraints. Whether the shopper has done any planning, the shopper's sex, and other variables may be more significant predictors of shopping time than shopping enjoyment.[33]

Impulse purchasing is associated with shopping enjoyment. This type of purchasing is unplanned; the shopper makes the purchase decision after entering a store and seeing the merchandise or related stimuli. Impulse purchasers tend to be younger than 35 or older than 65. Choosing stores in a shopping center on impulse is similar to choosing merchandise on impulse because display communications from stores along the shopping route can influence shoppers. Attractive visual displays play an important role in this regard.[34]

Lifestyle information is available from research projects like the Stanford Values and Lifestyles Program, and is published in current books and periodicals. Retail personnel can learn about the lifestyles of customers in their stores by observing what customers wear, what they say while shopping, and what they buy.

How marketing communications strategies relate to lifestyles The lifestyle categories in Exhibit 3-9 can guide communications strategies. For example, copy in sale advertisements can be directed at price-conscious consumers, while advertisements for sports merchandise and services can be placed in the newspapers' sports pages. Marketers can direct communications about new merchandise and retail services to the self-designated opinion leaders whose friends ask them for advice. Retailers can put ad inserts in billings to their credit card customers, selecting ads for merchandise types these customers have charged. Different messages can be sent in different media vehicles to professional and blue-collar workers described in Exhibit 3-10.

Marketing communications strategy for VALS groups might include high-contrast colors, such as orange and yellow, and attention-grabbing sight and sound in ads for the *need-driven* group; a conservative environment for *belongers;* an exciting environment for the *achievers;* and natural colors and textures for the *inner-directed.*[35] These components can be included in advertising, displays, packaging, and special promotions. Information from VALS and other marketing research about psychographics can be referred to when choosing advertising media and messages for specific market segments.

Catalog shopping, discussed in Chapters 5 and 8, is becoming popular with customers who prefer to spend their time on work and recreation and who therefore need time-efficient shopping. In-store displays and promotional events can be designed to educate and attract segments who consider shopping a recreational activity. Newspaper advertising can be designed to inform planners about current merchandise and prices. Lifestyle information is also useful for selecting timing for advertising and promotions, and for designing repositioning communications.

Personality

Personality theories Many theories of personality are of interest to marketing communications managers, including trait theory, psychoanalytic theory, social theory, and self-concept theory. *Trait theory* asserts that personality is a set of traits. Psychological instruments take inventories of traits which are analyzed and grouped into a small number of underlying dimensions. Some of the personality variables on the Edwards Personal Preference Scale, a psychological test for traits, include exhibition (want others to notice you), affiliation (participate in groups), and change (frequently do new and different things).[36]

Psychoanalytic theory explores the unconscious aspect of personality. Depth interviews and projective techniques, like interpreting ink-blots and ambiguous pictures, are used to learn about motives that are repressed or difficult to express. *Social theory,* on the other hand, emphasizes conscious motives and social variables. Cohen's compliance-aggressiveness-detachment (CAD) scale was constructed to measure how compliant or aggressive target customers are or think they are, for marketing applications. Finally, *self-concept theory* deals with individuals' ideal and realistic concepts of who they are.[37]

How marketing communications strategy relates to personality Psychologists' studies of personality include helpful clues to store–customer–product interactions. Recently, marketers have adapted information about personality from psychologists to use in marketing strategy. Consumers have multiple-personalities; their feelings and actions depend on where they are. If any generalization is possible, today's consumers are in the "sensation" generation of participators who want to touch and feel, not just to watch.[38] Information about traits from tests like Edwards' can be used to identify market segments known to have certain traits, to direct advertising copy to these segments, and to choose advertising and store displays for these segments. Words and phrases such as "be noticed," "new," "inspires confidence," and "sophisticated," can be used where appropriate in copy and on in-store signs.

Social theory offers many helpful insights for writing advertising copy and directing marketing communications to specific personality segments. Also important for advertising copy is knowledge of the discrepancy between consumers' real and ideal self-concepts, and of whether consumers purchase according to actual or ideal self-image. Along these lines, recent communications have stressed the "I'm worth it," message. A clearly communicated image helps consumers select retailers and brands to fit their real or ideal self-images.[39]

SUMMARY

Individuals perceive reality in different ways. They see and hear advertising and displays selectively. Because individuals tend to organize stimuli into images, a marketer must project a consistent image. To be successful, marketing communications must break through the perceptive screens of the target customers to deliver the firm's message clearly. Successful businesses use marketing communications to create a unique image that other firms cannot steal or copy.

Whether or not consumers choose to buy products and services from a certain firm is determined in part by how they perceive that firm and the extent to which they have favorable attitudes about it. Attitudes develop over time, are related to shopping behavior, and can be influenced by effective marketing communications. An example of an adaptive communications strategy might be to send special mailings about sales of particular merchandise to customers whose purchases have indicated a favorable attitude toward that merchandise.

Target customers are distinguished by age, sex, race, income, education, occupation, and other demographic factors. These characteristics help marketers determine what media vehicles consumers will select and what messages will interest them. Demographic data that reveal who is moving in and out of the geographic target market show where and to whom to send marketing communications and what to communicate.

People have different lifestyles that are characterized by particular activities, interests, and opinions. Shopping lifestyles range from "shopping-for-pleasure" to "shopping-in-least-possible-time." Displays and special promotions provide entertainment for pleasure-seeking shoppers. Marketing communications can appeal to time-savers by providing advance advertising information that will shorten shopping trips or facilitate mail or phone orders. Understanding personality helps marketers communicate store or brand images in terms such as "helps you be noticed" and "inspires confidence." These communications help consumers find stores and product brands to fit their real or ideal self-images.

QUESTIONS

1. Why do marketers need to know about consumer behavior in order to plan marketing communications?
2. How should a marketer use information about perception, cognitive dissonance, and gestalt in planning advertisements?
3. Discuss the relationship between the perceptual threshold and changes in store or brand images. Give examples.
4. What is an attitude? What does a marketing communications manager need to know about attitudes in planning marketing communications strategy? Give examples.
5. How can a marketing communications manager use the information about customers obtained in the charts in Exhibits 3-2 through 3-5?
6. How do current demographic trends influence marketing communications strategies? Give examples.
7. What is lifestyle? How can lifestyle be determined? Give examples of some shopping lifestyles and suggest appropriate marketing communications examples for these lifestyles.
8. Suggest an advertising message consistent with one of the personality theories mentioned in this chapter.

NOTES

1. Theodore Levitt, *The Marketing Imagination* (New York: Macmillan, 1983), cited in "Customer 'Problem' is Key to Marketing Success," *Advertising Age,* 55 (March 12, 1984), p. M-21.

2. Topics in this chapter are covered in greater detail in consumer behavior texts such as the following:

Henry Assael, *Consumer Behavior and Marketing Action,* 2nd ed. (Boston: Kent, 1984); Del I. Hawkins, Roger J. Best, and Kenneth A. Coney, *Consumer Behavior, Implications for Marketing Strategy,* 2nd ed. (Plano, TX: Business Publications Inc., 1983); James F. Engel and Roger D. Blackwell, *Consumer Behavior,* 4th ed. (New York: Dryden, 1982); David Loudon and Albert J. Della Bitta, *Consumer Behavior Concepts and Applications,* 2nd ed. (New York, McGraw-Hill, 1984); Douglas W. Mellott, Jr., *Fundamentals of Consumer Behavior,* (Tulsa, OK: Pennwell Books, 1983); Leon Schiffman and Leslie Kanuk, *Consumer Behavior,* 2nd ed. (Englewood Cliffs, NJ: Prentice-Hall, 1983).

3. Assael, *Consumer Behavior and Marketing Action,* p. 37; Loudon and Della Bitta, *Consumer Behavior Concepts and Applications,* p. 416.

4. Fritz Heider, *The Psychology of Interpersonal Relations* (New York: John Wiley, 1958).

5. Leon Festinger, *A Theory of Cognitive Dissonance* (New York: Harper & Row, Pub. 1957).

N. Giges, "Pepperidge Farm's Fallow Ground," *Advertising Age,* 56 (February 21, 1985), pp. 2–3.

6. "Sears' About Face," *Business Week* (January 8, 1979), p. 80. See also foonotes 31 and 32 in Chapter 2.

7. James M. Kenerdine and Jack J. Katsulis, "The Relationship Between Changes in Perceptions of Store Attributes and Changes in Consumer Behavior," in Robert F. Lusch and William R. Darden, eds., *Retail Patronage Theory 1981 Workshop Proceedings* (Norman, OK: University of Oklahoma, 1981), pp. 93–99; Robert A. Peterson and Roger A. Kerin, "Image Measurement and Patronage Behavior: Fact and Artifact," in the same volume, pp. 221–228; Jacob Jacoby and David Mazursky, "Linking Brand and Retailer Images—Do the Potential Risks Outweigh the Potential Benefits?" *Journal of Retailing,* 60 (Summer 1984), pp. 105–122; Pierre Martineau, "The Personality of the Retail Store," *Harvard Business Review,* 36 (January-February 1958), pp. 47–55; Kent Monroe and Joseph Guiltinan, "A Path Analytic Exploration of Retail Patronage Influences," *Journal of Consumer Research,* 2 (June 1975), pp. 19–28.

8. Bert Rosenbloom, "Congruence of Consumer Store Choice Evaluative Criteria and Store Image Dimensions," in Lusch and Darden, *Retail Patronage Theory,* pp. 82–85; Leonard J. Berry, "The Components of Department Store Image: A Theoretical and Empirical Analysis," *Journal of Retailing,* 45 (Spring 1969), pp. 3–20.

Berry's is mentioned in the book, *A Passion for Excellence* by T. Peters and N. Austin (New York: Random House, 1985).

9. See Appendix 1.

10. Assael, *Consumer Behavior,* pp. 131–134; Stuart H. Britt, "How Weber's Law Can Be Applied to Marketing," *Business Horizons,* 13 (February 1975), pp. 21–29.

11. Alan Radding, "Jordan Marsh Back to Basics," *Advertising Age,* 52 (April 6, 1981), p. 38E.

12. R. Barton, *Advertising Media* (New York: McGraw-Hill, 1964), p. 109; A. John Prusmack, "Consumer Perceptions—Can They Be Measured?" *Advertising Age,* 49 (September 18, 1978), p. 84.

13. See Chapters 6 and 11.

14. Ted Roselius, "Consumer Rankings of Risk Reducing Methods," *Journal of Marketing,* 35 (January 1979), p. 56.

15. Gordon W. Allport, "Attitudes," in C. A. Murchinson, ed., *A Handbook of Social Psychology* (Worcester, MA: Clark University Press, 1935), pp. 798–844.

16. Daniel Katz, "The Functional Approach to the Study of Attitudes," *Public Opinion Quarterly,* 24 (Summer 1960), pp. 163–204.

17. Martin Fishbein, "Attitudes and the Prediction of Behavior," in Martin Fishbein, ed., *Readings in Attitude Theory and Measurement* (New York: John Wiley, 1967), pp. 477–492; Assael, *Consumer Behavior,* Chapter 7.

18. "Marsh Brings Back Couple," *Advertising Age,* 53 (May 17, 1982), p. 47E.

19. "Update on America, A Study of America's Attitudes," presented at the ARF Conference by R.H. Bruskin Associates, (New Brunswick, NJ: March, 1984).

20. "The Year 2000: A Demographic Profile of Consumer Market," *Marketing News,* 18 (May 25, 1984), Section 1, pp. 8, 10; B. G. Yovovich, "Getting a Reading on the Baby Boom," *Advertising Age,* 55 (October 18, 1984), pp. 11, 12.

21. D. Bogue, *The Population of the United States,* NY: Macmillan, 1985, pp. 440, 443.

22. Targets and segments are discussed in detail in marketing texts cited in Note 2. See also David J. Lill and Donald A. Mitchie, "Puffery, Retail Image and Patronage: The Cases of Senior and Adolescent Markets," in Lusch and Darden, *Retail Patronage Theory,* pp. 44–49.

23. Chapter 9 has more information about demographics and media.

24. Before using continuous data for a long time period, it is necessary to find out, usually via footnotes, whether the data definitions have changed enough during this time period to make data for one period not comparable with data for another period. For example, one definition is used until 1972, and another definition is used for 1972 and later.

"Data Base Offers Consumer Profiles from 'Nine Nations,' " *Marketing News,* 18 (May 25, 1984), Section 1, p. 13;

"DEMO + GRAF Area Comparison 1980, Beverly Hills, CA: Santa Monica Bl. & Wilshire 2.0 Mile Ring," (Urban Decision Systems Inc., August 8, 1983); "Executive and Managerial Employees, Bloomington, IN SMSA by Tracts," (Donnelley Marketing Information Services, 1983); Lori Kesler, "Behind the Wheel of a Quiet Revolution," *Advertising Age,* 53 (July 26, 1982), p. M-13; "New Sourcebook Features Up-to-Date ZIP Demographics," Ibid., p. 11. This book is *The 1984 Sourcebook of Demographic and Buying Power for Every ZIP Code in the USA,* (Arlington, VA: C.A.C.I., 1984). "SITE.MAP," (New York: C.A.C.I., 1983).

Most of this information came from handouts at the National Retail Merchants Association annual meeting, vendors booths.

25. See Assael, *Consumer Behavior,* pp. 231–233; P. Francese, "One-Parent Families Joining a Crowd," *Advertising Age,* 55 (August 2, 1984), p. 36.

26. William D. Wells, "Psychographics: A Critical Review," *Journal of Marketing Research,* 12 (May, 1975), pp. 196–213.

27. William D. Wells and Douglas J. Tigert, "Activities, Interests and Opinions," *Journal of Advertising Research,* 11 (August 1971), pp. 27–35; " 'Yuppies Willing to Pay: Study," *Advertising Age,* 55 (June 25, 1984), p. 14. A statistical technique called "factor analysis" can be used on a computer to translate many statements into a few independent categories. Each category contains a group of related statements.

John L. Lastovicka, "On the Validation of Lifestyle Traits: A Review and Illustration," Journal of Marketing Research, 19 (February 1982), pp. 126-38.

28. Paul Nebenzahl, "Will The Values/Lifestyles Program Developed by Stanford Research (SRI) Encourage Retailers to Take the Marketing Approach?" *Hear, There and Everywhere,* No. 148 (February 1981), pp. 1–4; Douglas Tigert and T.C. Bourgeois, "Retail Fashion Segmentation: A Lifestyle Application," (presented at Canadian Association of Administrative Sciences meeting in Edmondton Alberta), June 2–3, 1975; Jonathan Gutman and Michael K. Mills, "Fashion Lifestyle ınd Store Patronage: A Different Approach," in Lusch and Darden, *Retail Patronage Theory,* pp. 155–160.

Brooke H. Warrick, "SRI's Response to Yuspeh: Demographics Aren't :nough," *Marketing News,* 18 (May 24, 1984), Section 2, p. 1.

29. Norma G. Barnes, "Sunday Shoppers Divided into Three Distinct Cat- :gories," *Marketing News,* 16 (October 1, 1982), p. 9; Rena Bartos, "What Women .ike and Don't Like in Ads," *Advertising Age,* 53 (March 8, 1982), p. M-3; Jody ßeckman, "Retailers Alter State to Suit Busy Women," *Advertising Age,* 53 (July :6, 1982), pp. M-26, M-28; M. Machlowitz, "Reaching Achievers," *Advertising \ge,* 55 (January 16, 1984), p. 18.

30. "Baby Boomers Push for Power," *Business Week,* (July 2, 1984), pp. ;2–58; "Prizm Neighborhood Lifestyle Clusters: Area Composition," (Los Angeles: :laritas Corporation, Urban Decision Systems, September 6, 1983).

31. Elizabeth C. Hirschman and Michael K. Mills, "Sources Shoppers Use o Pick Stores," *Journal of Advertising Research,* 20 (February, 1980), pp. 47–51; Villiam L. Moore and Donald R. Lehman, "Individual Differences in Search ßehavior for a Non-Durable," *Journal of Consumer Research,* 7 (December, 1980).

32. Joseph W. Newman and Richard Staelin, "Prepurchase Information ieeking for New Cars and Major Household Appliances," *Journal of Marketing Research,* 9 (August, 1972), pp. 249–257.

33. Jon C. Udell, "Prepurchase Behavior of Buyers of Small Electrical \ppliances," *Journal of Marketing,* 30 (October 1966), pp. 46–49; Danny Bellenger ınd Pradeep K. Korgaonkar, "Profiling the Recreational Shopper," *Journal of Retailing,* 56 (Fall 1980), pp. 77–92; Leonard L. Berry, "The Time-Buying Consumer," *ournal of Retailing,* 55 (Winter, 1979), pp. 58–69.

34. Claude R. Martin, Jr., and Phillip E. Hendrix, "Evaluating Classifications of Shoppers: Temporal and Enjoyment Dimensions of Patronage," in Lusch and)arden, *Retail Patronage Behavior,* pp. 192–196; Danny Bellenger, Dan H. Rob- :rtson, and Elizabeth C. Hirshman, "Impulse Buying Varies by Product," *Journal of Advertising Research,* 18 (December 1978), pp. 15–18; Edward M. Tauber, 'Why Do People Shop," *Journal of Marketing,* 36, (October 1972), pp. 46–59.

Impulse purchasing is discussed further in Chapter 12.

35. Barnes, "Sunday Shoppers"; Bartos, "What Women Like"; Beckman, 'Retailers Alter State"; Machlowitz, "Reaching Achievers."

36. Excerpted from Allen L. Edwards, *Edwards Personal Preference Schedule Manual* (New York: Psychological Corporation, 1957). See also Assael, *Consumer Behavior,* p. 269. The same type of computer program for factor analysis used or the lifestyle AIO questionnaires can be used here.

37. Joel B. Cohen, "An Interpersonal Orientation to the Study of Consumer ßehavior," *Journal of Marketing Research,* 4 (August 1967), pp. 270–278; Edward .. Grubb and Harrison L. Grathwohl, "Consumer Self-Concept, Symbolism and Market Behavior: A Theoretical Approach," *Journal of Marketing,* 31 (October 969), pp. 22–27.

38. "Marketers' Target is Multiperson: Light," *Advertising Age,* 53 (May ;, 1982), p. 39.

39. Leon Schiffman, J. Dash, and William Dillon, "The Contribution of Store-Image Characteristics to Store-Type Choice," *Journal of Retailing,* 53 (Summer 977), pp. 3–14; Danny Bellenger, E. Steinberg, and W. Stanton, "The Congruence of Store Image and Self Image," *Journal of Retailing,* 35 (Spring 1976), pp. 17– 32.

APPENDIX 3-A

DRESS CODES AND FASHION IMAGES FOR SELECTED WOMEN'S OCCUPATIONS

I. *Formal Professional* This group includes accountants, lawyers, sales managers, executives and administrators who work in a highly structured and formal environment. They can be characterized by a strict dress code and overriding concern with representing a professional image. Members of this group wish to convey occupational status at work and in nonwork activities and can be considered an investment dresser. *Their major fashion concern is professional image.*

II. *Informal Professional* This group includes teachers, artists, engineers, decorators, librarians, social service workers, computer science technicians, advertising and medical personnel. They are concerned with self expression and conveying individuality. Members of this group are less influenced by the need to play a role or to conform either on or off the job. They demonstrate a preference for functional styling in their apparel. *Their major fashion concern is self expression and individuality.*

III. *Front Office Clerical* The women in this subsegment are secretaries, receptionists, typists, bookkeepers who are highly visible to their employers and employer's clients. They are strongly influenced by the environment and a need to conform to a dress code which requires that they be physically attractive. Members of this group wish to communicate an image. *Their major fashion concern is physical attractiveness.*

. . .

VI. *Assembly Line Worker* This group includes manual laborers, sewers, packers, handlers and porters. They are not subject to a dress code but tend to counter their low work status by establishing their individuality in nonwork activities. Members of this group prefer practical clothing on the job. *Their major fashion concern is self expression in non work apparel.*

Source: *Working Women, 1980–1985, An Emerging Market* (Celanese Fibers Marketing Company, January 1980), pp. 13–15.

APPENDIX 3-B

WHY, HOW, WHERE, AND WHAT FORMAL PROFESSIONAL WOMEN BUY

1. Why Purchase Apparel?
   a. Occupational status
   b. Conformity to dress code
   c. Physical attractiveness

2. How They Purchase?
   a. Frequently—once a week they shop and buy
   b. Limited number of stores, due to time constraints
   c. Loyal customer to stores who meet their needs

3. Where They Purchase?
   a. Department stores (better)
   b. Specialty stores (better)
4. What They Purchase?
   a. Classic, with a touch of contemporary
   b. Quality
   c. Care not most important
   d. Versatile

Source: *Working Women 1980–1985, An Emerging Market* (Celanese Fibers Marketing Company, January 1980), pp. 20, 23.

APPENDIX 3-C

MARKETER IDENTITY PROFILE

Management should fill out this profile to compare the firm with major competitors, A, B, C, and more if necessary. Questions 1–3 refer to characteristics of the firm. Questions 4–9 refer to marketing communications. This management view of the situation should be compared with a customer view, using a similar questionnaire in a survey of actual and potential customers. See Chapter 4 for information about surveys.

IDENTITY FACTORS; RATE FIRMS ON A SCALE OF 1–6 WHERE 1 = TERRIBLE, 2 = POOR, 3 = FAIR, 4 = GOOD, 5 = VERY GOOD, 6 = EXCELLENT.	*RATINGS*			
	YOUR FIRM	*COMPETITORS* A	B	C
1. Appropriateness of *location* for target: part of town, neighboring firms, access and exterior, surroundings	____	____	____	____
2. Merchandise *assortment,* uniqueness for firm, and rightness for target customers	____	____	____	____
3. Adequacy of *services* associated with effectively selling the product(s)	____	____	____	____
4. Match of firm's *image* with demographics, lifestyle, and image objectives of actual and potential customers in target market	____	____	____	____
5. *Interior* design and maintenance appropriateness for times and merchandise	____	____	____	____
6. *Salespersons'* effectiveness in resolving customer uncertainty and selling product(s)	____	____	____	____
7. Special *promotions'* effectiveness in attracting customers to buy product(s)	____	____	____	____
8. *Advertising* effectiveness overall:	____	____	____	____
a. Reach with respect to appropriate target (actual and prospective) customers	____	____	____	____
b. Balance in emphasis with respect to different types of products	____	____	____	____
c. Frequency in markets of primary, secondary, and tertiary customers	____	____	____	____
d. Coverage in available media	____	____	____	____
9. Newsworthiness	____	____	____	____

Source: Adapted by P. Anderson from suggestions provided by the Newspaper Advertising Bureau.

4

MARKETING RESEARCH AND INFORMATION SYSTEMS

INTRODUCTION

In marketing, what you don't know *can* hurt you. The former "production" and "selling" general business approaches required little or no consumer input. The newer "marketing" approach uses information about consumer wants, needs, and behavior obtained from marketing research and information systems to direct the manufacturing and sale of products. Today, a marketing operation without these tools is like a ship without a rudder; it cannot move where it should be going. Information lowers decision-making risks by reducing uncertainty and increasing knowledge. Through research, marketers can find out not only who and where customers are but also what they want, need, and do. Research reveals how to inform customers about stores and brands more effectively so that customers' purchases will enable firms to meet sales goals.[1] Information systems collect, store, and retrieve the information considered necessary for effective communications.

This chapter on marketing research and information systems will help marketing communications managers distinguish between acceptable and sloppy research. Decisions based on fuzzy thinking or bad information can badly harm a business. Marketing managers can monitor the quality of research only if they can tell good research from bad.[2] Then they can insist on quality, making inferences from high-quality research to guide their marketing communications decisions.

PROBLEM DEFINITION AND RESEARCH DESIGN

Marketing research consists of identifying specific problems, collecting and analyzing relevant information, and drawing conclusions and strategy implications from the results of the analysis. Such research is "the *systematic* gathering, recording and analysing of data about problems relating to the marketing of goods and services."[3] *Systematic* methods must be defined in advance to obtain specific answers to specific questions: who, what, when, where, why, and how. To get useful answers to these questions, managers need to know (1) how to define the problem, (2) how to get needed data at an affordable price, and (3) how the analysis of that data can shed light on solving the problem.

Evaluation skills are necessary for marketing managers because some sloppy researchers use whatever data collection and analysis methods are conveniently available, whether or not these are accurate and relevant. Sloppy researchers generate erroneous, but neatly printed, computer printouts. Their method is called GIGO, "garbage in, garbage out." GIGO means that when research input is incorrect, research output is at best worthless, at worst misleading.

Defining the Research Problem

The most important step in doing research is *defining the problem.* The real problem may not necessarily be the apparent problem. A careful definition of the research problem can save time and money, preventing poor decisions based on answering the wrong question. As Peter Drucker, a famous business consultant, pointed out, it is better to do the right things than to do (the wrong) things right. Because of the popularity of its competitor's product, PepsiCola, the Coca-Cola Company embarked on a massive blind taste test research project. It tested the *taste* of its regular Coca-Cola, as well as PepsiCola, and a new formula Coca-Cola. Initially Coke did not identify the beverages, and thus omitted *brand name* and *image* from the testing. As a result of this research, it was announced that henceforth the company would sell the new formula Coke, and it would replace the old Coke. However, after announcing this important change in a much publicized press conference and distributing the new product nationwide, thousands of consumers who liked the old Coke better made such a clamor that the company decided that the old Coke would still be produced and called Classic Coke. This is an example of research that did not consider all the market factors. Only the taste factor was considered, and that test was clouded by the fact that there now existed diet cokes, lemon cokes, and other variations. Actually other aspects of this marketing problem should have been evaluated at the same time. Consumer attitudes about cola beverages, consumer psychology about the branded colas, and open testing of various cola drinks should have been carried out. These other factors, when researched, would have brought out the fact that there were many thousands of "old-Coke" consumers who would resist change. The Coca-Cola Company would have avoided the embarassment of a decision reversal that gave their competitors a big boost. On the other hand, Coca-Cola has achieved a large amount of publicity and a product-line extension.[4]

Operational definitions and research questions Once the real question or problem is identified, it must be stated in *operational* terms. These serve as guides for data collection and analysis. An example of an operational question is: "How many households with disposable income of $15,000 to $40,000, children aged 12–17, located within a four-mile radius of Fact City, saw the Fast Music Hour on Channel 3 on March 31, and recalled the advertisement inviting them to Fact Store's spring sale of stereos?" A question like: "Did people see our TV ad last night?" provides inadequate information for doing research.

Research questions related to marketing communications concern the benefits that target consumers want, the target's response to various media, and potential customers' perceptions of the marketer's image. By separating targets into primary, secondary, and tertiary areas of importance, researchers can determine to what extent marketing communications and media reach differ for these different areas. Sometimes different research methods can result in drawing different geographic boundaries for a market area. In one study, the geographic boundaries differed depending on whether the map was drawn based on number of visits or sales dollars.[5] Marketing research explores how consumers choose among stores and brands, and how they are influenced inside a store by promotions, sales-persons, and displays.[6]

Some research questions generate more than one research project. Trying to learn too much from one research project can generate "noise" and confusion. A series of separate, simpler projects may be more affordable and more understandable.

Problem definitions that miss the problem In the following real situations, retailers tried to find out why advertisements did not bring people into their stores. In each case, advertising was not the problem. The problem was that customers had trouble finding the store. The stated question was, "What is wrong with my advertising?" The question should have been, "Why are my sales lower than would be expected, given my advertising?"

One small store, one of several stores located in a former factory, ad *no sign*. Nor was there a map of store locations in this former factory. Therefore, customers who responded to this store's advertising had trouble inding the store. The store needed to have a sign, and a map in its ads, efore evaluating whether the ads were effective.

Another store was in a strip shopping center that was perpendicular o a highway instead of parallel to it. This store's only sign was over the oof of the walkway. Thus customers standing in front of the store *could ot see the sign*. Nor did the store's door and window display identify he store. The shopping center was adjacent to the eastbound lane of the ighway, but it was visible only from the westbound lane. Customers ad difficulty finding both the shopping center and the store. This store eeded both a sign on the door, and location directions for store and hopping center in its advertising.

A third store in another strip shopping center had an attractive sign on the roof. However, the store name on the sign was in *illegible script*. The script did not contrast enough with the background of the sign to be visible from the road or from the parking lot. The store logo on all he store's printed materials was in block letters, and used a different olor scheme than did the sign. Unifying logo, print type, and color cheme on all signs and printed materials would have helped customers ind the store after they read an ad and looked for the store. Similarly, hanging a logo, print type, or color of packaging without informing ustomers can cause customers to pass by brand-name items on supermarket helves when they are looking for the old packaging.

Research Design

Once the problem is identified, an appropriate research design must be elected. *Research design* is the specification of methods and procedures o obtain relevant information objectively and economically. Research designs can be *exploratory, descriptive,* or *causal.*

Exploratory *Exploratory* studies should be flexible. They can be used to identify and formulate problems to the point where management knows enough either to make a decision or state hypotheses for further testing.[7] Typically, observation, interviews, studies of similar situations, nd secondary data (described in the next section) are used in exploratory esearch. Putting a discount coupon in an advertisement and counting the returned coupons is an example of an exploratory study.

Descriptive *Descriptive* research has a research question and a preplanned, structured design. It can include both primary and secondary data. Descriptive research looks for the extent to which variables are ssociated with each other. For example, what is the relationship, if any, between an ad on the Sunday before Mother's Day in one local paper and sales of the advertised item during the following week?

Causal *Causal* research answers questions about what causes what. *Natural* causal experiments, as in comparing retraining salespeople with not retraining them, require little intervention. In *controlled* causal experiments, the researcher keeps some variables constant while varying others. For example, a chain with similar stores in similar markets uses radio ads for some stores, newspaper ads for others, and no ads for a *control group*. Sales are compared before, during, and after the period of the experiment to find if there is a *significant difference*[8] in sales "caused by" radio, newspaper, or no advertising.

DATA AND COLLECTION OPTIONS

Secondary Data

Definition and nature *Secondary data* are data that have already been collected for some purpose other than the research being planned. Some data may have been collected by the firm itself as part of ongoing record-keeping, for its information system, or for earlier research projects. Other data may have been collected by other organizations, such as government agencies, trade associations, research firms, or media.

Secondary data are sometimes sufficient for making a decision. Even when not sufficient, they may help management determine what *primary data* to collect for a specific project. Since secondary data already exist, they can be less expensive to obtain than primary data. However, because they were collected for some other purpose, secondary data are not necessarily in the appropriate form for current research, and they may not be sufficiently useful for solving the problem.

Researchers need to determine the extent to which secondary data are appropriate for the new research. Using inappropriate data leads to misleading results and wrong decisions. Researchers should consider whether the time period of the study, the demographic base of the respondents, and the variable definitions in the secondary data fit current research requirements. Data may require adjustments, varying in cost. Footnotes in Census and other published data may make a great difference in interpretation and subsequent use of the data, especially when definitions and series change substantially from year to year.

Sources of secondary data The government publishes data about persons and businesses. Private firms and trade associations also provide data.[9] Appendix 4-A has an executive summary of a current research article about the effects of changes in parking costs and suburban competition on the attractiveness of a shopping area. Exhibit 4-1, prepared for *Sales and Marketing Management*, shows population, effective buying income, and retail sales for newspaper and television markets.[10] Exhibit 4-2 shows excerpts from a conversation with a computer in which the user selects desired information from a list, in a search for information about the demographics and sales potential in a given geographic area.

Shopping center trade periodicals have secondary data and articles about data sources for information on how many customers are in a trade area, where they live, and what they are likely to buy. "Customers in a trade area" includes people who live, work, pass through, and visit the area. The suggested core area for a store is that area in which live a high percentage (60 to 80%) of the customers living closest to the location. This area is usually defined by street boundaries rather than by concentric circles. Research firms can take demographic information from Census tracts and blocks and update it from the last Census count to get a profile of the customers in the core area. Then they can merge this information with clusters of lifestyle groups of "best customers". The National Decision Systems data base has three types of reports for shopping centers: one lists consumer expenditure potential by store type within one, two, and three-mile radii of a site; another lists all centers over 100,000 square feet in the radii of one, two, and three miles of a center; and the third lists current and projected demographics for the same areas. A researcher can use the data base to look for areas with certain characteristics specified by a client; most reports are in the mail within 24 hours of the request.[11]

Many research studies are private and confidential. However, some general research results are published. These may provide helpful information for planning research. The essence of research results can be reported without divulging firm names and numbers. For example, research implies that specialty stores should stress sales expertise and product variety, and that department stores should stress their convenient locations.[12]

The National Retail Merchants Association and the *Journal of Retailing* publish research about retailers.[13] The American Marketing Association (AMA) publishes both a bimonthly newsletter, *Marketing News*, and two quarterly journals, *Journal of Marketing* and *Journal of Marketing Research*. The AMA Information Center in Chicago directs marketing professionals, educators, and students to secondary sources of desired information. Members of AMA may borrow books from the Center. Non-members pay a small fee to request information by phone.[14]

Other periodicals like the *Journal of Advertising Research, Journal of Consumer Research, Journal of Personal Selling and Sales Management,* and *Journal of Consumer Marketing* publish marketing research of interest to advertisers. Trade publications like *Advertising Age, Chain Store Age Executive, National Mall Monitor, Stores,* and newspapers like *Women's Wear Daily* and *Daily News Record* report news about specific manu-

EXHIBIT 4-1 **Media Market Information for Newspapers and TV Markets**

Source: *Sales and Marketing Management* (October 31, 1983), p. 118, 167.

a. Newspaper

	ESTIMATES 1982									
	POPULATION 12/31/82		EFFECTIVE BUYING INCOME	RETAIL SALES BY STORE GROUP						
STATE *NEWSPAPER MARKET (Home County) . . .* *Dominant Counties (50% or more penetration)* *Effective Counties (20%–49% penetration)*	*Total Pop. (Thous.)*	*Total House-holds (Thous.)*	*Total EBI ($000)*	*Total Retail Sales ($000)*	*Food ($000)*	*General Merchan-dise ($000)*	*Furnit./Furnish./Appl. ($000)*	*Auto-motive ($000)*	*Drug ($000)*	*% Hslds. Cov. Total Area*
LOUISIANA										
ALEXANDRIA (Rapides) . . . Over 50%: Rapides; 20–49%: Avoyelles, Grant.	199.5	68.3	1,423,118	725,271	194,270	113,756	26,134	136,775	28,167	47.5
BATON ROUGE (East Baton Rouge) . . . Over 50%: East Baton Rouge, West Baton Route; 20–49%: Ascension, East Feliciana, Iberville, Livingston, Pointe Coupee, West Feliciana.	618.1	206.7	5,597,698	2,646,722	705,040	473,535	105,016	462,262	84,872	48.0
LAFAYETTE (Lafayette) . . . 20–49%: Lafayette.	162.3	57.2	1,749,641	1,011,731	212,906	148,074	52,276	188,405	22,659	43.0
LAKE CHARLES (CALCASIEU) . . . OVER 50%: Calcasieu; 20–49%: Beauregard, Cameron, Jefferson Davis.	247.8	85.4	2,185,247	1,158,498	354,079	110,815	45,966	228,451	35,252	46.2
MONROE (Ouachita) . . . 20–49%: Caldwell, Franklin, Ouachita, Richland, Tensas, Union, West Carroll.	245.4	85.4	1,680,330	960,456	246,961	139,957	37,858	201,615	29,996	37.6
NEW ORLEANS (Orleans) . . . Over 50%: Jefferson, Orleans, St. Bernard; 20–49%: Plaquemines, St. Charles, St. John the Baptist, St. Tammany.	1,331.2	481.1	12,024,913	6,030,256	1,777,180	711,181	276,714	889,962	185,517	51.7
SHREVEPORT (Caddo) . . . Over 50%: Bossier, Caddo; 20–49%: Bienville, Claiborne, De Soto, Red River, Webster.	457.8	165.6	3,932,763	1,918,068	454,873	267,900	84,072	396,455	43,577	57.4

b. Television

	ESTIMATES 1982												
	POPULATION—12/31/82										EFFECTIVE BUYING INCOME	RETAIL SALES	
					Population by Age Group (Thousands)								
STATE ARBITRON TV MARKET (AD)	Total Pop. (Thous.)	Total House-holds (Thous.)	Black Pop. (Thous.)	Spanish-Origin Pop. (Thous.)	2–11 Years	12–17 Years	18–24 Years	25–34 Years	35–49 Years	50 & Over	Total EBI ($000)	Total Retail Sales ($000)	Buying Power Index
KANSAS													
TOPEKA	359.2	133.8	19.9	11.3	48.1	29.4	61.3	61.3	54.1	93.0	3,320,329	1,531,851	.1493
WICHITA-HUTCHINSON	1,086.9	418.7	40.7	33.7	152.4	96.4	137.3	175.9	176.2	311.8	10,579,683	5,345,837	.4825

EXHIBIT 4-2 Demographics and Other Information from Research Firm's Computer

Source: Compuserve, 5000 Arlington Centre Boulevard, PO Box 20212, Columbus, Ohio 43220, an H&R Block Company.

```
Request Recorded,
One Moment, Please
Thank you for Waiting

GEOGRAPHIC AREA
1 Zip Code
2 County
6 Demonstration Reports

Key digit or H for help !6

          Demographic and Sales Potential Demonstration Reports

 1 1980 Summary                21 Apparel Store
 2 1980 Demographic Profile    22 Drug Store
 3 Demographic Forecast        23 Grocery Store
 4 1980 Income Profile         24 Department Store
 5 Income Forecast             25 Restaurant
 6 1980 Housing Profile
 7 1980 Education Profile
 8 1980 Employment Profile     26 Shopping Center
 9 1980 Energy Profile         27 Footwear Store
10 1980 Hispanic Profile       28 Hair Salon
11 1970 Demographic Profile    29 Dry Cleaners
12 1970–1980 Comparison        30 Optical Center

Key digit(s) separated by commas (ie. 2,8,10) or H for Help
!1,21,3,4,5*
 -

                    1980 SUMMARY REPORT (excerpt)

ANYCOUNTY, U.S.A.          AREA REFERENCE:          INCLUSION/EXCLUSION

****************************************************************************
```

	1970 CENSUS	1980 CENSUS	1970–1980 CHANGE
POPULATION	553370	524472	−28898
HOUSEHOLDS	174219	189850	15631
FAMILIES	142181	140335	−1846
AVG HH SIZE	3.1	2.7	−0.4
AVG FAM SIZE	3.6	3.3	−0.3

DATE 9/10/84

* *Note: The user types the "6" and "1, 21, 3, 4, 5" in the lines beginning with the words "Key digit." "6" gets "Demonstration Reports," and the following "1" gets "1980 Summary Report."*

facturers and retailers from a newspaper or magazine point of view. Current information about possible target markets, environment, and life-styles is also available in publications like *The New York Times, The Wall Street Journal,* and *Business Week,* and in the broadcast media.

Other information sources include current books on market research (usually advertised in the current periodicals mentioned above), seminars and exhibits at the annual meeting of the National Retail Merchants Association, and relevant business seminars.[15] Current texts on marketing, retailing, advertising or promotion, and consumer behavior cite and summarize research data as well.

Primary Data

Nature of primary data *Primary Data* are collected specifically for a particular research project. If an experiment, extensive survey, or interviewing project is involved, primary data are usually more expensive to collect than secondary data. However, collecting primary data can sometimes be less expensive than making secondary data fit the special needs of a research project. Primary data can be collected through (1) personal interviews and focus groups, (2) mail and telephone surveys, (3) observation by people or machines, (4) experiments, and (5) simulation studies.[16]

Each data collection method has its own strengths and weaknesses and is more appropriate for some situations and less so for others. Budget and time constraints might force a choice between reaching relatively few people with in-depth personal interviews, or surveying a large number in less detail via mail or telephone. The focus of this section is on understanding and evaluating different methods of data collection, with collection techniques themselves treated only briefly. Appendix 4-B and this chapter's footnotes list additional references with more information on collection methods.

Interviews and focus groups Personal interviews and focus groups are used to interview people in depth. Personal interviews, which are one-on-one, can be more expensive in terms of interviewer time. But unstructured in-depth interviews are useful for finding out what motivates consumers to behave in certain ways, and also for exploring what kinds of questions might be needed in a wider, briefer survey. *Unstructured* means that there is not a formal questionnaire such as exists in *structured* interviews. Unstructured interviews with, say, persons who can examine new products during the actual interview can reveal which aspects of the product are most attractive to consumers, and so should be emphasized in marketing communications.

Structured survey interviews can be done using a questionnaire. Once done mostly in homes, survey interviewing is now often done in shopping centers, where interviewers can safely find respondents and where respondents can feel safer than when admitting a stranger into their homes. Interviewers using prepared questionnaires need to learn how to approach potential respondents, ask questions, and record answers.[17] Their work is similar to phone interviewing, but there is a visual component too, and the interviewers are harder to supervise when not concentrated in one room. Checks are needed to insure that all recorded interviews are genuine.

Focus groups, like personal interviews, provide opportunities for face-to-face interaction, with the chance to observe body language. A focus group may contain from six to fifteen persons. Under the guidance of a trained interviewer, the group discusses some topic, such as an advertising campaign or a sales promotion that may still be in the exploratory stages. Clients can observe and take notes behind a one-way mirror without disturbing the focus group. A variety of focus groups can be used to get information about different segments of the target market, such as teens, working women, or urban dwellers. Highly trained interviewers are needed for focus groups and unstructured in-depth personal interviews.

Questionnaires The questionnaire is a crucially important part of mail and phone surveys, as well as of door-to-door and shopping center interviews. Either the introduction section of the questionnaire, or the cover letter for mail surveys, must interest the respondent in answering the questionnaire. The questions must continue to hold the respondents' interest and motivate them to answer all questions accurately. Vague questions are hard to answer and so discourage responses; for example, "What do you like?" Multiple-choice questions remind the respondent about possible answers, as well as organize the information for coding. For example, "What kind of breakfast-cereal TV commercial will make you want to buy this product? (a) musical, (b) dramatic, (c) celebrity, (d) attack-the-competitor, (e) other (please specify) ____."

Creating questionnaires is an art as well as a science. Questionnaires must cover all information needed while omitting unnecessary questions that only add length. Long questionnaires with unclear questions inspire respondents to file them in the waste paper basket. As in advertising copy, brevity and clarity are essential.

Pretesting is necessary to insure that respondents will understand what the questions want to find out, and will provide relevant answers.[18] Questions should not be biased or slanted to elicit desired answers. Pretesting the questionnaire on friends, co-workers, or sample respondents helps eliminate ambiguities. Comparing a list of needed information with the list of questions can reveal which questions are unnecessary and whether additional questions are needed. Another method of finding out what questions to omit or add is to plan tables showing what the research results will look like in the final report.

Mail and phone surveys Mail and phone surveys obtain information from relatively large numbers of customers. Mail surveys are less expensive than phone surveys because they do not involve hiring, training, and monitoring persons to make phone calls. Respondents can answer mailed questions at their leisure, while they must answer phoned questions at the time of a phone call. Sometimes mail is used to solicit respondents for phone surveys; sometimes the phone is used to ask for cooperation in mail surveys and to remind respondents to return mailed questionnaires. The mail response rate tends to be relatively low compared with phone survey and interview responses. Sending a followup letter including various incentives, such as a discount coupon or free sample, can increase the response rate. The relevance of a mailing list to the survey has a large effect on the response rate. A list of persons interested in the subject—that is, customers who are heavy users of a product category—tends to get a higher response rate than a general list.

The respondent cannot ask questions in a mail survey. While it is physically possible for respondents to ask questions in a phone survey, interviewers may not have been given the information they need to be able to answer. Phone numbers can be selected from customer records or by random digit dialing. Making several callbacks to reach respondents may increase the phone survey response rate. Many persons consider an unsolicited phone call to be an interruption of their privacy and cooperate reluctantly, especially if the interview takes longer than the agreed-upon time.

ELEMENTARY STATISTICAL ANALYSIS

Marketing executives who make wrong decisions because they do not understand simple data analysis lose credibility. Therefore, this section provides some very basic information about simple data analysis techniques. More sophisticated techniques are beyond the scope of this book, but Appendix 4-B lists reference sources for data analysis techniques, as well as for data collection techniques.

Marketing research reports do not always use statistical techniques appropriately. A recent presentation at a retailers' national meeting implied that there were differences in means (averages), but did not use tests to find out if these differences were statistically significant. When someone from the audience asked about these tests, none of the five panelists seemed to know what they were. Thus, the credibility of the presenting firm was damaged.

Significant Differences Among Groups

Means or averages *Standard deviations* are indications of error. Much research is based on taking *samples* and making inferences about the *population* from which the samples were taken. A population is the entire group that the researcher wants to study; for example, all married women in New York in full-time employment. For a variety of reasons beyond the scope of this section (see Appendix 4-B), sample means (i.e., averages) will be different from the population means, due to errors. The standard deviation indicates whether an error is large or small relative to the sample mean. If we know the standard deviations of two sample means that we want to compare, we can tell whether these means are significantly different from each other by doing a test which uses the standard deviations.

For example, a sample of 300 coupons was taken from 1000 coupons submitted in response to the same shirt advertisement in two newspapers in the Los Angeles area which claimed to reach the same demographic markets. The research question was which paper's ad had more influence on shirt sales involving coupons. Mean dollar sales of the shirt per customer were computed from a sample of redeemed coupons for each newspaper to learn about the effectiveness of this promotion. Mean shirt sales per customer were \$56 for one paper and \$47 for the other. A significance test, using standard deviations, was used to find out whether the average sales per customer for those who redeemed coupons was in fact significantly different between the two newspapers. The coupons in one paper were redeemed for significantly higher average shirt sales per customer than the coupons in the other. Perhaps, other things being equal, the money spent for space in the other newspaper could be used more effectively elsewhere when using coupons in ads for that type of shirt. A related question to answer is whether the paper associated with the *smaller* coupon sales actually stimulated greater sales; perhaps many customers forgot to turn in coupons. Tests of significance and more sophisticated analyses introduced below can be done on microcomputers and other computers.[19]

Cross tables Other simple statistical tests can be used to determine whether groups in a sample belong to the same population market segments or to different ones. For example, Exhibit 4-3 has a cross table of radio-program listening habits of two groups, 100 persons aged 12–19 and 100 persons aged 20 and over. Thirty teens and sixty adults listened to program type A once a week or less. Seventy teens and forty adults listened to this program type more than once a week. A *chi square statistic,* which can be computed by a computer program, can indicate whether these groups have statistically significant differences in listening habits for radio program type A. A significant difference might indicate that teens

EXHIBIT 4-3 **Crosstable of Radio Program Listening Habits by Age Group**

Source: Hypothetical crosstable designed by P. Anderson for illustration purposes.

	Number of Persons Listening to Radio Program Type A Each Week:	
	Once or Less	More than Once
Age 12 - 19	30	70
Age 20 and Over	60	40

and adults are really different populations with respect to listening habits for radio program type A. A manager could use this information to help decide whether to air commercials for both teens and adults on this type of radio program.

Preferences

From rank-order decisions made by respondents, researchers can infer respondents' preferences for different brands or stores. Exhibit 4-4 shows a perceptual map that might result from computer processing of such rank-order decisions made by a group of consumers according to quality and price criteria. In Exhibit 4-4, Store or Brand A, which is in the upper

EXHIBIT 4-4 **Perceptual Map of Quality and Price for Store or Brand A, Competitors, Ideal Point**

Source: Hypothetical crosstable designed by P. Anderson for illustration purposes.

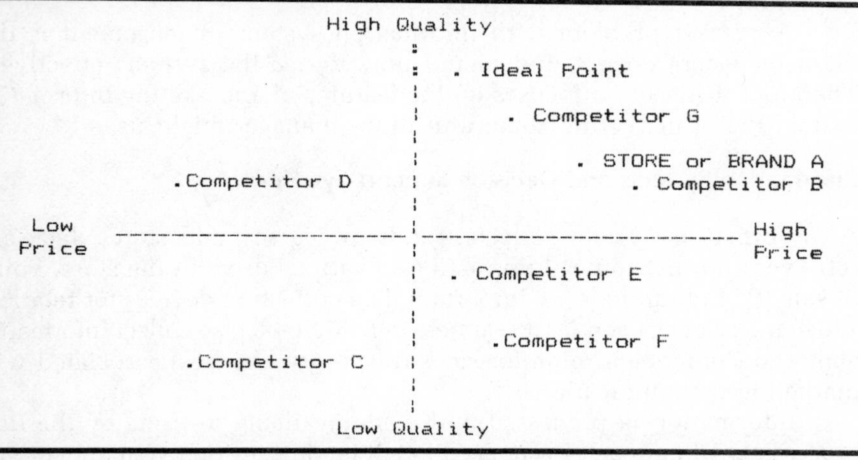

right quadrant, is perceived to have relatively high quality and price. Store or Brand C, which is in the lower left quadrant, is perceived to have relatively low quality and price. The ideal store or brand, in the upper right quadrant near the vertical axis, has a higher quality and lower price than competitors G, A, or B.

Knowing how customers perceive a store or brand relative to competitors helps managers direct marketing communications either to build on some positive characteristics indicated in the customer rankings, or to change position on the perceptual map. The usefulness of this information depends on (1) the extent to which all important competitors are included, and (2) the extent to which the persons doing the rank-ordering resemble the target customers.[20]

USING INFORMATION SYSTEMS TO AID MARKETING COMMUNICATIONS DECISIONS

Information systems help marketers mine overlooked "acres of diamonds." Since most firms get 75% of volume from 25% of their customers, the greatest sales potential might come from the 75% of customers who contribute only 25% of the sales. The information system helps firms see which customer types have the greatest sales potential, *however defined* by management, helping managers plan communications which can emphasize the products of interest to these customers, making advertising more productive.[21]

In order to obtain an effective information system, management needs to know (1) *what* information is needed in the total system, (2) *who* needs which parts of this information *when*, (3) *how* to obtain this information, and (4) *where* to deliver it most effectively within the budget limitations.

A current problem with information systems management is that often managers do not understand how to use the systems effectively. Therefore this section focuses on the features of a marketing information system that a marketing communications manager might use.

Information Systems and Decision Support Systems

An information system collects, sends, processes, and stores data; and retrieves and distributes information to various users in the store. Point-of-sale (POS) terminals are important data collection devices for retailers. Video interviewers and laser scanners in Exhibit 4-5 also collect information about consumers and monitor sales (inventory changes) associated with marketing communications.[22]

Information is processed and made available to users by the *data processing* (DP) system. Users need to tell the information system managers

EXHIBIT 4-5 **Video Interviewers and Laser Scanners for Collecting Data**
Source: Video: *Marketing News* (November 25, 1983), Section 2, p. 26; Laser: W&H Systems, Carlstadt, NJ 07072, from National Retail Merchants Association 1984 Annual Meeting.

MARKETING TECHNOLOGY BRIEFS

The VIDEO-INTERVIEWER, a technology for in-store interviewing of consumers, is being used by the Heritage Food Warehouses chain in Montreal. The device—which consists of a videoscreen, microcomputer, and numeric keyboard—questions shoppers about their likes and dislikes, preferences, needs, and level of satisfaction. It is programmed to amuse consumers with humorous remarks and reactions to their answers, and will even wish "happy birthday" when the occasion arises.

For CSA, hand held laser scanners are being teamed with WHizscan® to provide the required input to the CSA computers. As loads arrive from manufacturers, computer-generated labels are affixed. These carry two codes; WHizscan for High Speed Sortation, and BarCode, for the hand held laser. The label is in two parts—one gummed, the other not. As a case is loaded outbound, part is torn off and sent to the office in a batch for optical scanning. When the case arrives at the member's break bulk center, the label on the case is scanned with the hand held laser. With these three scans, connected to computers, CSA and its members are able to both sort merchandise and to maintain an audit trail through this physical distribution operation.

what information they want, when they want it, and in what form they prefer it. These managers have other customers besides marketing communicators, and must plan the system to service their entire clientele.

The purpose of an *information system* (IS) is to facilitate decision-making by providing pertinent support information in a systematic way. A *decision support system* (DSS) also provides information that can be retrieved to facilitate decision making.[23] Note that IS and DSS *support decisions;* they *do not make decisions.* Managers make decisions based on information and decision support systems and other relevant factors.

DSS is sometimes called "ad hoc-ery." DSS works on urgent, immediate, specific problems related to a particular situation. By involving users in problem solving, DSS can be flexible. Data processing (DP), on the other hand, is called the "bureaucracy" because it works on ongoing, necessary, routine problems instead of special exceptions.[24] In planning computer capacity to handle DP and DSS, managers of the computer facilities must consider not only timeliness, accuracy and reliability, but also cost-effectiveness.

It is possible that other divisions of the firm will share the IS with marketing communications. This increases the number of transactions and the maintenance time, which may delay getting information from the system. The fact that computers can work very fast does not necessarily mean that requested information will always be delivered immediately.

Quick service is less of a problem when there are many decentralized computers. Then the problem is to arrange the data into a data base so that several computers can use it. *Distributed data processing* means that the firm has several computers in a network instead of one central computing facility. Data base management involves organizing the data base so that its various users—sales, finance, accounting, etc.—can get the information that they need in a cost-effective manner.[25] The most frequently used data should be accessed most efficiently.

The IS and DSS have not only the data, but also the computer instructions for processing data through various models which facilitate decision-making. Some of the models are trial and error models (*heuristic models*). Others produce "what if" scenarios (*simulation models*). Still others look for the best solution (*optimization models*). Models forecast the future by extending information from the past, assuming that the future is an extension of the past. For example, regression analysis can be used to show the extent of the historical association of advertising and sales.

Specialized computer programs are available commercially. For example, BRANDAID predicts sales-advertising relationships. A manager considering cutting the advertising budget in half could use BRANDAID to predict what would happen to sales if the future is expected to be like the time period during which the data were collected.[26]

User-Friendliness of Systems

Now that many computer information models are available, the current problem is to make IS and DSS "user-friendly." "User-friendly" systems require relatively little computer programming expertise from users. They are often *interactive* models, with the computer asking what information the user wants, providing it, and asking another question. An interactive conversation with the computer involves many small management decisions. The questions take one small step at a time to help the manager think systematically. An actual conversation would take smaller, more specific steps than the example in Exhibit 4-6. Because the computer can provide alternative scenarios based on changing information from the manager, the manager can explore different possible strategies. With a simulation model like the one in Exhibit 4-6, the manager can see the effect of alternative back-to-school plans and budgets on projected sales of children's shoes for the back-to-school season.

Making or Buying Necessary Information

The managers of the IS must decide between creating the data base and programs themselves or buying them elsewhere. It is advisable to buy

EXHIBIT 4-6 Example of a Manager/Computer Conversation

Source: Hypothetical conversation designed by P. Anderson for illustration purposes.

Computer (C): What do you want to do?
Manager (M): Choose advertising media.
C: Merchandise classification?
M: Children's shoes.
C: Season?
M: Back to school.
C: Budget?
M: 105% of last year's back-to-school advertising budget.
C: Costs? (Enter only changed costs.)
M: Newspaper = $1200; catalog = $5000; Radio = $1000.
C: Based on average annual productivity of advertising/sales in last 5 years "back-to-school" shoes, use: 10% radio, 35% catalog, 55% newspaper. Breakdown within media?
M: Yes.
C: Which media?
M: Newspapers.
C: Add or delete any newspaper?
M: No.
C: Use 50% newspaper budget for each of the two papers. Do you wish another plan?
M: Yes.
C: What changes?
M: Raise ad budget to 108% of back-to-school last year.
C: New plan follows . . .
Do you wish another plan?
M: No. Bye.

data that are expensive to collect, infrequently used programs, and information for which the firm loses no competitive advantage. Demographic and psychographic data bases that help the marketer understand target customers are usually accessible on a phone-in basis. For a fee, the firm's computers can phone the current data base for up-to-date information. The data base contains secondary data which are collected by others but are likely to be expensive for a firm to collect itself. Libraries and trade associations have information about current sources for such data. On the other hand, the retailer might want to customize some extensively used programs, and to collect private data that only the firm's managers should see.

When using bought data, the following attributes must be considered.

1. Coverage (how far back in time; what items? how relevant?)
2. Timing (how recent? how often—daily, weekly, etc.?)
3. Accuracy (how many estimated errors?)

4. Cost (how much?)
5. Compatibility with the firm's programs and data (which?)
6. Possible use by competitors (which and when?)

Recent advances in color computer graphics might be added to the information system, if useful. Maps of trading areas, of areas covered by various media, and of productivity categories provide visual aids to facilitate advertising decisions.[27]

A potential problem arises when employees who have their own personal computers try to interact with the central information data base. There must be some protection for data that the firm wishes to keep from being erased or misfiled by users who are not IS personnel.

Evaluating an Information System

An information system is effective if it accomplishes its predetermined objectives. However, marketing, finance, and other areas may have conflicting objectives. The overall objective for the system is to provide information quickly and accurately, with better tables and graphics than in the past, and better user training guidance and control. The IS should facilitate user decision-making and encourage positive attitudes of users towards the IS.[28]

Problems arise in developing an information system. For example, managers and consultants may agree that the system will be on-line, but computer programmers may not be able to get the system to operate that way, so switch to a method that they *can* implement. The method that the programmers like may be so inconvenient for the client that no one uses the system at all.[29]

However, basic problems affecting marketing communications are not generally caused by information systems. When customers complain about late delivery of orders that they placed in response to advertisements, this could be a problem with IS but could also be caused by salespersons not processing orders promptly; order clerks making errors; inventory not having adequate stock; the shipping department being poorly managed; or the credit department delaying approval of credit.

IS should help managers make better decisions. Initially, managers tend to ask for more information than they need. Management users should be involved in developing a new system so that they can provide feedback to improve the system. This user involvement can lead to dissatisfaction, but might motivate users to help improve the system rather than trying to remove it.[30]

The human element must remain dominant, for it is human input that must direct computers and information systems. A system can store, analyze, present, and project information; it can provide alternatives and project scenarios. But ultimately the user must analyse the information in the setting of the current environment and the user's previous experience.

The user must make the decisions, implement them, and live with their consequences, good or bad. For maximum effectiveness, humans and computers should each do what they can do best.

USING CONSULTANTS, AGENCIES, AND MEDIA RESEARCH

A marketing communications manager who does not have in-house expertise can hire a consultant, a research firm, or can use the research facilities of media, advertising agencies, university faculty, or graduate marketing and advertising students. Graduate students will often work on companies' research problems for experience and course credit.

Alternative outside researchers should be evaluated with respect to quality and bias versus relative cost. Quality can be determined by reviewing the researcher's record and by talking with former and present clients. Bias can be estimated by analyzing the goals of the research facility. A newspaper, for example, is interested in selling newspaper advertising space. It therefore tends to provide research information that puts its circulation and readership in a favorable light in order to sell advertising space.[31]

Evaluating Research of Others

The questions in Exhibit 4-7 provide a step-by-step approach for evaluating a research report. They ask what the research question is; whether the data and analysis techniques are appropriate for answering the research question; and whether the conclusion follows from the data and analysis used. They ask how the shortcomings of the research will affect the results and the marketing implications of the results.

Sometimes rough research is sufficient; other times the nature of the research problem is such that a small error can lead to a substantial change in marketing implications. Using the questions in Exhibit 4-7, it is possible to find errors in many reports. However, the important question is not whether or not errors exist, but whether they affect the research results sufficiently to change the implications for marketing strategy.

For example, a firm wants to reach 250,000 customers in an advertising campaign. Results say that 275,000 will be reached. There is an error in the research: in fact, the campaign will reach only 250,000 customers. This error will not change advertising strategy based on a goal of 250,000. However, if the actual number reached is only 25,000, the research error would have been quite serious, as it would have hidden the need for a change in strategy.

In another example, a decision is needed for whether to use radio spots or to spend an equivalent amount on newspaper advertising. Errors cause research results to indicate that the spots are three times more

EXHIBIT 4-7 **Questions to Ask When Evaluating Research**
Source: Compiled by P. Anderson.

When evaluating a research report, answer the following questions:

1. State the *research question* in your own words and explain why it is necessary, given the past research mentioned in the report. What is this research trying to learn?
2. Explain whether or not the *operational definitions of the variables,* and the *measurement techniques* and *sampling methods* resulted in collecting data appropriate for answering the research question. An operational definition is one that defines a variable specifically enough to collect data to represent that variable.
3. Explain why the *data analysis* methods were or were not appropriate for answering the research question.
4. Briefly state the authors' *conclusion* and explain the extent to which the collected data and use of statistical analysis techniques justify this conclusion.
5. On a scale of 1–7 where 7 is excellent, 4 is acceptable, and 1 is useless, *rate* this report on its quantitative and qualitative aspects. Estimate what might happen if this report deserves a rating from 1 to 3 and you take the action suggested by the report. Then, *pretend that this report is excellent* and explain the marketing implications of the research results.
6. If you have decided against using the recommendations of this report because you have rated it 1 to 3, can some of this research be salvaged? Can data be analysed by a more appropriate method, should the sample be larger, etc.? Explain how you will improve any items in questions 1 through 4 above, and how your changes will affect the results. Support your answer to this question with information from other relevant sources.

effective than newspaper ads. Correct results are that newspaper ads are in fact ten times more effective than the spots. These erroneous results might lead to choosing a less effective media strategy.

Marketing Research Firms and Services

Exhibit 4-8 shows some of the leading United States-owned research firms, their gross research revenues, their rank by revenue, and the areas they research. This is not a complete list and the firms and their services may change over time, but it shows what kind of research help may be available.

The types of research services provided by the firms in Exhibit 4-8 are indicated by code letters to the right of the firm name. Firms coded "S" provide information from *common data pools* like audits, mail panels, and audience share. Arbitron Ratings Company, a wholly-owned subsidiary of Control Data Corporation, is in this group. Arbitron provides local market measures of television, cable television, and radio audiences collected from mail diaries and electronic meters. The company's

EXHIBIT 4-8 **Some Leading U.S.-Owned Research Companies**

Source: Adapted from table entitled: "How They Rank," in J. Homomichl, "Top Research Companies' Revenues Rise 13.7%," *Advertising Age* (May 23, 1985), p. 17. Reprinted with permission from the May 1985 issue of *Advertising Age*. Copyright 1985 by Crain Communications, Inc. See also similar tables in *Advertising Age* (May 17, 1984), p. M-17 and (May 24, 1982), p. M-7; and J. Pope, *Practical Marketing Research* (NY: AMACOM, 1981), p. 249.

TYPE	*RANK*	*RESEARCH COMPANY*	*RESEARCH REVENUES*
B S	1	A.C. Nielsen	$491.0
B S	3	SAMI	118.4
S	4	Arbitron Ratings Co.	105.8
C T	5	Burke Marketing Services	66.0
M C	7	Market Facts	35.9
PST	10	NPD Group	29.2
C	12	WESTAT, Inc.	24.5
C T	13	Elrick & Lavidge	23.3
C T	15	YSW Group	17.0
C	16	Chilton Research Services	16.5
T	17	ASI Market Research	16.4
C S	18	Louis Harris & Associates	15.3
C	19	Opinion Research Corporation	14.5
C	20	Erhart-Babic Group	13.2
C	23	Data Development Corporation	10.5
C	28	Custom Research	8.6
S	33	Starch INRA Hooper	7.5

Note: 1984 rank is for gross research revenues in millions for research activities only; for some companies, total revenues, which include nonresearch activities, are higher. Type codes: B = report market share data for grocery, drug, and discount stores; C = do custom research projects; S = provide information from common data pools; M = maintain mail panels; P = maintain purchase diary panels; T = use same standardized techniques to provide studies for different clients, but work on proprietary data.

Other research firms and ranks are: 2, IMS International; 6, M/A/R/C; B, Information Resources; 9, NFO Research; 11, Maritz Market Research; 14, Walker Research; 21, Winona, Inc.; 22, Simmons; 24, Decisions Center; 25, Harte-Hanks; 26, McCullum/Spielman; 27, Admar; 29, National Analysts; 30, Decision/Making/Information; 31, Management Decision Systems; 32, Gallup Organization; 34, Mediamark; 35, Market Opinion Research.

"Arbitrends" delivers ratings to radio and television stations via microcomputers, while "Target AID" merges ratings and lifestyle information.[32]

Arbitron has been testing a remote-control keypad, or "people meter." Viewers punch in a code to indicate that they are watching, and punch out every time they leave the set. The meter also records all channel selections. Respondents are instructed to remove the wand attached to the people meter and to wave it over the universal product code of the products they buy. Because of the expense of installing this equipment, respondents are told to use the people meter daily. The diary panel, which recorded viewing only one week per month, will probably be phased out after the completion of the people meter testing.[33]

Firms coded "T" in Exhibit 4-8 use standardized techniques to do studies for different clients, but work with data private to the client (*proprietary data*). "T" firms conduct such studies as advertising recall, response to commercials or parts of commercials, and simulated sales tests to find out what consumers might buy. Burke, a research conglomerate partly owned by Arbitron, is in this group. Burke has an AdTel unit which specializes in advertising testing; a joint venture with Time Inc.'s SAMI that counts numbers of products that leave warehouses as opposed to the counts sold from retail stores; Universal Product Code (UPC) scanner-equipped store panels; and consumer purchase panels for promotion testing. Burke has services for pretesting and posttesting television commercials; and other services. Burke also worked with Arbitron on the people-meter pilot study in Denver.[34]

Most research is custom designed; firms with code "C" do custom research projects. Elrick and Lavidge, wholly-owned subsidiary of Equifax, is in this group. Elrick and Lavidge does computer-assisted personal surveys, telephone and focus group interviewing, and operates eighteen mall interviewing centers. This firm has shoppers pose as customers to rate salespersons on promptness of service, suggestion selling, attitude and courtesy of employees, and other sales attributes.[35]

Research firms can also be categorized by type of data provided. The A.C. Nielsen Company is in the code "B" group that reports custom and syndicated market share data for grocery, drug, and discount stores. Nielsen has a television meter sample of households. This has increased in order to include cable stations with a minimum of ten million households, and may increase further as cable stations increase. Nielsen can detect which programs are recorded on videocassette recorders, even while another program is being watched. Advertisers want Nielsen to report playbacks of recorded programs, and to measure whether the remote control channel-switching devices avoid the commercials. Nielsen meters measure viewing every minute; advertisers prefer their measuring every five seconds to tally viewing of 30- and 60-second commercials.[36]

Nielsen, bought by Dun & Bradstreet in 1984, reports weekly brand sales and prices from more than one hundred retail grocery outlets equipped with UPC scanners. To compete more aggressively, Nielsen will track an individual's purchases through use of a card similar to a credit card, following the lead of Behaviorscan. Panelists sometimes get prizes for using their cards. While Burke and Information Resources Inc. allow advertisers to *substitute* test commercials for regular commercials on cable television, Nielsen's ERIM Testsight allows marketers to send *different* commercials to test and control groups and then to compare purchase behavior for the two groups in several grocery and drug stores in test areas. Microprocessors on the respondents' television sets admit either the test or the regular commercial, as specified by the control center. Because the panelists' homes have special antennae on their residences, dummy antennae are put on other homes to ward off guerilla actions of competitors.[37]

NPD/HTI, privately held, has a diary panel for packaged goods, a mail panel, more than twenty-five local market panels, a division to measure out-of-home eating habits, and purchase panels for nonpackage goods. Market Facts, a public company, has a consumer mail panel, six shopping mall interviewing facilities, several telephone interviewing centers, and extensive focus group and television evaluation facilities.[38]

Research is available from many firms not in Exhibit 4-8. For example, a recent similated network originated by The Pretesting Company in Fair Lawn, NJ, which works at shopping mall locations, allows advertisers to insert test commercials into videotapes of actual network television programs. Respondents at the shopping center locations are asked to evaluate the programs. Before and after seeing the programs, they fill out product choices on a questionnaire in order to compete for a $25 prize. Another firm, Customer Keypad in Turtle Creek, PA, markets a microcomputer software package to allow salespersons to enter a customer phone number or other code on a keypad near the cash register at time of purchase. The computer enters the transaction into the customer file, which can then be used to update mailing lists and to target communications campaigns.[39]

On Being a Good Research Client

"The best research client is a well-informed client . . . the more informed the better."[40] A well-informed client tends to take the following steps to work effectively with the research supplier. First, the client compares research needs with the capabilities of the suppliers, and seeks proposals from at least three suppliers if suppliers have not been used before. A client should visit researchers' places of business, meet the people who will work on the research, and make clear what research is needed.[41]

Once the supplier has been chosen, the client should provide all the necessary background for the research. Withholding "secret" information can mislead the researchers. The client should explain timing, cost, and implementation constraints so that the research will be consistent with schedules, budgets and company politics. It is acceptable for the client to challenge the supplier to provide alternatives and suggestions, and to save money. The supplier can also help to define the research problem, and should be asked to explain any confusing jargon. The research agreement should be put in writing, and all parties should sign it. A considerate client will avoid last-minute changes, and will leave the researcher alone unless there are specific suggestions about performance.[42]

Lastly, the client should tell the researcher what happens after the firm has acted on the research results. A smart client will be loyal to a researcher who does good work. Researchers that are familiar with a firm's business can spare a firm from lengthy and costly explanations that would be required to begin a relationship with a new firm.[43]

SUMMARY

Marketing communications managers need to know how marketing research and information systems can help them learn about the effectiveness of their marketing communications, and about their customers. Although these managers may never actually conduct research, they do make decisions based on research and information services. They therefore need to know how to select, work with, and evaluate consultants, agencies, and published research.

Research and decision support systems work on specific, immediate problems, whereas information systems provide ongoing information for routine decisions. To use an information system, marketing managers need to know what information is available, and how to communicate with the information system and its managers. The human element is an essential factor in this process.

Accurate problem definition enables researchers to look for answers to the right questions. Data can be collected from secondary sources, personal interviews and focus groups, mail and phone surveys, and experiments. Managers need to know enough about data analysis to evaluate research results.

QUESTIONS

1. What is the difference between marketing research and a marketing information system?
2. Why should a marketing communications manager understand (a) marketing research, and (b) marketing information systems?
3. (a) Discuss the advantages and disadvantages of using primary and secondary data in research for marketing communications. (b) Suggest good sources of secondary data that will be useful in marketing communications research for a specific store or product type that you suggest.
4. Compare and contrast interviews, mail surveys, and phone surveys for gathering information to evaluate marketing communications for a product or service of: (a) a small local store, (b) a chain of specialty stores in shopping centers, (c) a large national mass merchandiser like Sears or J.C. Penney, (d) a large department store chain, and (e) a discount store chain.
5. Explain why defining the research problem is of major importance in marketing research.
6. What is the most important factor to look for in a marketing consultant's report on research about some aspect of your marketing communications? Explain why this is the most important factor.
7. What is the most important information to give a consultant who has been hired (a) to research marketing communications and (b) to design an information system? Explain.
8. How can point-of-sale cash registers linked to computers, and other computer technology help in (a) research and (b) an information system related to marketing communications?

9. Choose a store or brand that interests you. Select from Exhibit 4-8 the types of research suppliers that would be most helpful to you in planning marketing communications for the store or brand you selected. Explain.

NOTES

1. H. Zeltner, "Research Must Meet Greater Demands than Ever," *Advertising Age,* 54 (August 15, 1983), pp. M4–M5, M46–M47.

2. See J. Wind, "Research and Management," *Journal of Marketing,* 45 (Spring 1981), pp. 8–10.

3. R. Alexander, *Marketing Definitions: A Glossary of Marketing Terms* (Chicago: American Marketing Association, 1960), pp. 16–17; see also H. Boyd, R. Westfall, and S. Stasch, *Marketing Research,* 5th ed., Homewood, IL: Richard D. Irwin, 1981).

4. P. Drucker, *Managing in Turbulent Times* (New York: Harper & Row, Pub., 1980); see also, D. Tull and D. Hawkins, *Marketing Research,* 3rd ed. (New York: Macmillan, 1984), pp. 27–30; J. Homomichl, "Missing Ingredients in 'New Coke's' Research," *Advertising Age,* 56 (July 22, 1985) pp. 1, 58.

5. Edward Blair, "Sampling Issues in Trade Area Maps Drawn from Shopper Surveys," *Journal of Marketing,* 47 (Winter 1983), pp. 98–106; D. Huff and R. Rust, "Measuring the Congruence of Market Areas," *Journal of Marketing,* 48 (Winter 1984), pp. 68–74.

6. See B. Rosenbloom, *Retail Marketing* (New York: Random House, 1981) pp. 78, 159; J. D'Antoni, Jr., and H. Shenson, "Impulse Buying Revisited: A Behavioral Typology," *Journal of Retailing,* 49 (Spring 1973), pp. 63–76; and notes to Chapter 3.

7. See J. Evans and B. Berman, *Marketing* (New York: Macmillan, 1982), pp. 59–64.

8. These are statistical terms; see statistics texts in Appendix 4-B, especially Berenson, *Intermediate Statistical Methods,* and Wonnacott, *Introductory Statistics.*

9. See Chapter 3. See also "Retail Trade Statistics," *Factfinder for the Nation,* issued monthly by the U.S. Bureau of the Census, and the annual July and October issues of *Sales and Marketing Management.*

10. Secondary data are also in Exhibits in Chapters 3 and 8, and in current texts like Evans and Berman, *Marketing.*

11. C. Curtner, "New Database Pinpoints U.S. Centers," and J. Paris and L. Crabtree, "New Tools for Trade Area Analysis," *National Mall Monitor* (Sept./Oct., 1984), 90–99.

12. See Rosenbloom, *Retail Marketing,* pp. 88, 132; I. Fenwick, "Advertising Experiments by Retailers," *Journal of Advertising Research* (August 1978), pp. 35–36; S. Keiser and J. Krum, "Consumer Perceptions of Retail Advertising with Overstated Price Savings," *Journal of Retailing,* 52 (Fall 1976), pp. 27–36; A. Oxenfeldt, "Developing a Favorable Price-Quality Image," *Journal of Retailing,* 51 (Winter 1974–5), pp. 8–14; D. Pathak, W. Crissy, and R. Sweitzer, "Customer Image versus the Retailer's Anticipated Image," *Journal of Retailing,* 51 (Winter 1974–5), pp. 21–28; B. Rosenbloom, "Improving Personal Selling in Small Retail Stores," *Small Marketers Aids,* No. 159 (Washington, DC: U.S. Small Business Administration, November 1976), pp. 1–5; L. Schiffman, J. Dash, and W. Dillon, "The Contributions of Store-Image Characteristics to Store-Type Choice," *Journal of Retailing,* 53 (Summer 1977), pp. 12–14.

13. *Journal of Retailing,* issued quarterly by the Institute of Retail Management of New York University, 202 Tisch Hall, Washington Square, NY 10003.

14. American Marketing Association, Suite 200, 250 Wacker Drive, Chicago, IL 60606; "AMA's Information Center Expansion Serves Reference Needs of Marketers," *Marketing News,* 19 (February 15, 1985), pp. 8–9; I. Broh, "Measure Success of Promotions with In-Store Surveys," *Marketing News* (May 13, 1983), p. 17; R. Schmitz, "Research Tool Developed to Pretest Effectiveness of Brand-Featuring Strategies in Retail Print Ads," *Marketing News* (September 16, 1983), p. 2.

15. National Retail Merchants Association, 100 W. 31st St., New York, NY 10001; NRMA runs microcomputer seminars for independent retailers and publishes the *Directory of Retail Software* (R6983) and related handbooks.

The Advertising Research Foundation, 3 East 54th St., New York, NY 10022, has an annual advertising research conference.

16. See current issues of *Marketing News;* and also C. Chase and K. Barasch, *Marketing Problem Solver* (Radnor, PA: Chilton, 1977); P. Green and D. Tull, *Research for Marketing Decisions,* 4th ed. (Englewood Cliffs, NJ: Prentice-Hall, 1978), p. 94; F. Kerlinger, *Foundations of Behavioral Research,* 2nd ed. (New York: Holt, Rinehart, & Winston, 1973), Chapters 17–21; J. Pope, *Practical Marketing Research* (New York: AMACOM, 1981), and G. Lilien and P. Kotler, *Marketing Decision Making* (New York: Harper & Row, 1983).

17. See Appendix 4-B, especially Breen, *Do It Yourself Marketing Research;* Chase, *Marketing Problem Solver;* Leedy, *Practical Research;* Pope, *Practical Marketing Research;* and Sudman and Bradburn, *Asking Questions.* Exhibits 3-1 through 3-4 in Chapter 3 illustrate some question types.

18. See current issues of *Marketing News;* also Chase, *Marketing Problem Solver;* Green, *Research for Marketing Decisions;* Kerlinger, *Behavioral Research;* and Pope, *Practical Marketing Research.*

19. "Software for Marketing and Marketing Research," *Marketing News* (March 16, 1984), Section 2, p. 10.

20. See Appendix 4-B, especially Aaker, *Multivariate Analysis;* Luck, Wales, Taylor, and Rubin, *Marketing Research;* Hair, ed., *Multivariate Data Analysis;* and Yaremko, *Reference Handbook.*

Questionnaires for image and ideal points are in Exhibit 3-5.

21. "Information System Helps Retailers to Mine Overlooked 'Acres of Diamonds,' " *Marketing News* (May 11, 1984), p. 4. This article reports a speech by Marvin Rothenberg.

22. "New Possibilities for POS," "Gold Circle Sets Up to Scan," "Strawbridge & Clothier: 100% Data Capture at POS," and "Allied's POS System Speaks for Itself," *Chain Store Age Executive,* 60 (January 1984), pp. 57–73.

23. P. Keen, speech at annual meeting of the Northeast Region American Institute for Decision Sciences, Philadelphia, 1983; see also P. Keen and M. Scott Morton, *Decision Support Systems, An Organizational Perspective* (Reading, MA: Addison-Wesley, 1978).

24. N. Ahituv and S. Neumann, *Principles of Information Systems* (Dubuque, IA: Brown, 1982), p. 5; and R. Sprague and E. Carlson, *Building Effective DSS* (Englewood Cliffs, NJ: Prentice-Hall), 1982.

25. J. Buchanan and R. Linowes, "Understanding Distributed Data Processing," *Harvard Business Review,* 58 (July-August, 1980), pp. 143–153; Buchanan and Linowes, "Making Distributed Data Processing Work," *Harvard Business Review,* 58 (Sept./Oct., 1980), pp. 143–154; S. March and G. Scudder, "On the Selection of Efficient Record Segmentations and Backup Strategies for Large

Shared Databases," *Working Paper Series MISRC-WP-82-19* (Minneapolis: University of Minnesota, 1982); R. Nolan, "Computer Data Bases: The Future is Now," *Harvard Business Review,* 51 (September 1973), pp. 98–114.

26. Keen, *Decision Support Systems;* L. Lodish, "A Marketing Decision Support System for Retailers," *Marketing Science,* 1 (Winter 1982), pp. 31–56.

27. H. Takeuchi and A. Schmidt, "New Promise of Computer Graphics," *Harvard Business Review,* 58 (Jan./Feb., 1980), pp. 122–131.

28. S. Hamilton, "Evaluation of Information System Effectiveness: A Comparison of Evaluation Approaches and Evaluator Viewpoints," *Working Paper Series MISRC WP-81-03* (Minneapolis: University of Minnesota, 1980).

29. G. DeSanctis and J. Courtney, "Toward Friendly-User MIS Implementation," *Working Paper Series MISRC-WP-83-04* (Minneapolis: University of Minnesota, 1982).

30. G. Dickson and J. Wetherbe, "Increasing the Productivity of MIS Personnel: The Motivation Issue," *Working Paper Series MISRC-WP-81-08* (Minneapolis: University of Minnesota, 1981).

31. See Chapter 10.

32. See. J. Homomichl, "Nation's Top 35 Market Research Companies," *Advertising Age* (May 17, 1982), p. M-17; *Advertising Age* (May 24, 1982), p. M-7; and T. Barker, "Nielsen Reacting to Foes' Pressure," *Advertising Age,* 55 (February 20, 1984), p. 6.

33. "Arbitron and Burke Announce Test of 'ScanAmerica Meter,' " *Marketing News,* 18 (November 9, 1984), p. 1; S.B. Smith, "Who's Watching TV? It's Getting Hard to Tell," *New York Times* (January 6, 1985), pp. H1, H23.

34. See Appendix 4-B, especially Pope, *Practical Marketing Research.* See also Homomichl, "Top Research Companies' Revenues Rise," p. M-17; *Advertising Age* (May 23, 1985), p. M-7; Barker, "Nielsen Reacting," p. 6; "Arbitron and Burke," p. 1; and S.B. Smith, "Who's Watching TV?" pp. H1, H23.

35. See Homomichl, "Nation's Top 35 Market Research Companies," p. M-17; *Advertising Age* (May 24, 1982), p. M-7; Barker, "Nielsen Reacting," p. 6; and L.G. Gulledge, "Evaluation Services Pay Off in Bigger Bottom Lines," *Marketing News,* 18 (October 12, 1984), p. 30.

36. See Homomichl, "Nation's Top 35 Market Research Companies," p. M-17; *Advertising Age* (May 24, 1982), p. M-7; Barker, "Nielsen Reacting," p. 6; "Arbitron and Burke," p. 1; and K. Higgins, "Nielsen Introduces ERIM Commercial Testing Service," *Marketing News,* 18 (October 12, 1984), pp. 1, 45.

37. Ibid.

38. See Homomichl, "Nation's Top 35 Market Research Companies," p. M-17; *Advertising Age* (May 24, 1982), p. M-7; Barker, "Nielsen Reacting," p. 6; "Arbitron and Burke," p. 1.

39. "A Microcomputer Software Package," *Marketing News,* 18 (November 9, 1984), p. 2; B. Whalen, " 'Simulated Network' Debuts," *Marketing News,* 18 (November 9, 1984), pp. 1, 47.

40. J. Pope, "Tips for Research Clients," *Advertising Age,* 51 (November 24, 1980), p. 42; and Pope, *Practical Marketing Research.* The information in the "On Being a Good Research Client" section comes from these two sources.

41. M. Katz, "Selecting the Right Research Firm: Step-by-Step Guidelines," *Marketing News* (January 6, 1984), p. 41.

42. Pope, "Tips for Research Clients," p. 42; and Pope, *Practical Marketing Research.*

43. Ibid.

APPENDIX 4-A

EXECUTIVE SUMMARY FOR A CURRENT RESEARCH ARTICLE

The article presents a retail center demand modeling and forecasting approach which is an application of techniques pioneered for predicting metropolitan travel patterns. The technique can be used to forecast future market shares for different shopping centers on the basis of expected changes in population characteristics, the store characteristics of existing and planned new shopping areas and the nature of auto and transit access characteristics to those areas. Initial model calibration requires a small scale survey of current shopping trips in the area, together with easily accessible information on characteristics of shopping districts and the transportation system. It efficiently utilizes information on each individual trip concerning the characteristics of the chosen shopping alternative and the characteristics of the alternatives that were not chosen. Forecasting under various future scenarios can then be accomplished by calculator or microcomputer-based methods.

Use of this approach for managerial decision-making depends on the specification of alternative future scenarios. Effects of new centers, expansions of existing centers or shifts in their retail mix, changes in transportation cost and service, and growth or relocation of population in the market area can all be forecast. Opportunities for given shopping locations can be identified and their vulnerabilities assessed.

One of the most important potential uses of this "disaggregate model" approach stems from its potential for evaluating effects in terms of the age and income distribution of the potential market. Changes in competitive shopping areas, in transportation characteristics, or even just in the size and location of neighboring populations can imply differential changes in demand depending upon the age and income of affected shoppers. Among the examples explored in the study, reduced parking charges in the Central Business District would attract low-income shoppers disproportionately, and increased gasoline prices would mainly discourage downtown shopping by upper-income households.

Defining a practical, moderate-cost approach for forecasting shopping area market attraction necessarily requires tradeoffs and compromises in specification from what a research analysis model would be. For example, although use of psychological scaling and perceptual image information can yield insight regarding behavioral decision-making, it can be less

Source: Excerpt from Glen E. Weisbrod, Robert J. Parcells, and Clifford Kern, "A Disaggregate Model for Predicting Shopping Center Market Attraction," *Journal of Retailing* 60 (Spring 1984), pp. 80–81.

easily amenable to forecasting alternative scenarios. The relative power of objective measures compared to perceptual data will continue to be topics for future research. At the same time, it is important to differentiate the objectives of research analysis and the requirements of applied market estimation techniques for management decision-making and to improve incrementally the information available for managerial decisions.

APPENDIX 4-B

REFERENCES FOR MARKETING RESEARCH

Aaker, David A., *Multivariate Analysis in Marketing,* 2nd ed.. Palo Alto: The Scientific Press, 1981. Regression, discriminant, conjoint, factor, cluster analysis; experiments.

Andrews, F. et al., *A Guide for Selecting Statistical Techniques,* 2nd ed. University of Michigan, 1981.

Berenson, Levine & Goldstein, *Intermediate Statistical Methods.* Englewood Cliffs, NJ: Prentice-Hall, 1983. Computer packages.

Breen, G. and A. Blankenship, *Do It Yourself Marketing Research,* 2nd ed. New York: McGraw-Hill, 1982. Questionnaires.

Chase, C. and K. Barasch, *Marketing Problem Solver.* Radnor, PA: Chilton, 1977. Samples, interviewing.

Conover, W. *Practical Nonparametric Statistics,* 2nd ed. New York: John Wiley, 1980.

R. Ferber, ed., *Readings in the Analysis of Survey Data.* Chicago: American Marketing Association, 1980.

Hair, J., ed. *Multivariate Data Analysis with Readings.* Tulsa: Pennwell, 1979.

Jain, A., C. Pinson, and B. Ratchford, eds. *Marketing Research.* New York: John Wiley, 1982. Recent articles about data collection and analysis.

Kerlinger, F., *Foundations of Behavioral Research,* 2nd ed., Ch. 17–21. New York: Holt, Rinehart & Winston. 1973. Experiments.

Leedy, P., *Practical Research,* 2nd ed. New York: Macmillan, 1980.

Lilien, G., and P. Kotler, *Marketing Decision Making.* New York: Harper & Row, 1983.

Luck, D., H. Wales, D. Taylor, and R. Rubin, *Marketing Research,* 6th ed. Englewood Cliffs, NJ: Prentice-Hall, 1982.

Pope, J. L. *Practical Marketing Research.* New York: AMACOM, 1981.

Prince, M. *Consumer Research for Management Decisions.* New York: John Wiley, 1982.

Sudman, S., and N. Bradburn, *Asking Questions*. San Francisco: Jossey-Bass, 1982.

Wonnacott, T. H. and R. J. Wonnacott, *Introductory Statistics for Business and Economics,* 2nd ed. New York: John Wiley, 1977.

Yaremko, R. et al., *Reference Handbook of Research & Statistical Methods in Psychology*. New York: Harper & Row, 1982.

5
SELLING AND COMMUNICATING TO AND THROUGH RETAILERS

INTRODUCTION

'he total marketing efforts of both the manufacturer and the retailer ome into sharp focus at the retail cash register. It is there that the onsumer determines whether the merchandise and the prices are right. t is truly the payoff for all concerned. Successful marketing ultimately epends on sales to the final consumer. Manufacturers, sales agents, vholesalers, and others who sell merchandise to retailers are called *vendors* n this chapter. Vendors and retailers are in the same boat: both must nderstand retail marketing communications in order to sell their merhandise to retail customers. To be effective, communications from all ources must be consistent and not contradictory. Henry Dreyfuss, industrial esigner and believer in the human factor, at one time suggested that ie attributes of a successful product are value, convenience, easy mainenance, attractiveness, and sales appeal. These attributes should guide endors and retailers in formulating communication strategies.

Manufacturers' aid to retailers can include cooperative funds to help ay for advertising manufacturers' brands, and art and copy materials or use in retailers' advertisements. Manufacturers' ads can list retailers vho sell the advertised merchandise. Manufacturers can also provide

EXHIBIT 5-1 Excerpts from a Booklet for Copywriters Provided by a Supplier

Source: *Pocket Guide to Copywriters* (New York: The Wool Bureau), p. 14.

Carpeting and Rugs

You're going to live with your carpeting a long, long time. Choose carefully. Choose wool. For wool is a natural fiber. A small fact but it makes a large difference. Wool bounces back when you step on it and is naturally fire-resistant and static-resistant. Wool resists soil which makes it easier to clean than other fibers. Most important of all, wool carpeting wears longer and keeps its beautiful color and sheen. Year after year after year.

Wool carpeting. You'll love it for itself. You'll keep loving it for the way it acts. Time will slide by, but your wool carpeting will keep its natural beauty, its natural resistance to soil and fire and static. And what can match wool's natural affinity for color? Or the joyous years of wear it will give you? Or the pride you'll feel in owning wool?

Almost everybody had a grandmother who said "you get what you pay for". Think about that, and you'll choose a wool rug. You can buy lesser fibers at lesser prices, of course. But you won't get the long and lovely wear only wool can give you. The way it springs back to hide footsteps and furniture marks. The way it resists soil and fire and static. The way it glows with rich colors. Buy a wool rug and we predict: someday when you're a grandparent, you'll point to your rug proudly and say "you get what you pay for".

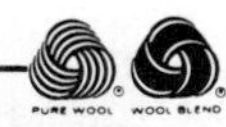

point-of-purchase display materials, seminars for store personnel, and informative product literature in booklets, folders, signs, television cassettes, and tags. Manufacturers' suppliers can also provide information for retailers. Exhibit 5-1 shows excerpts from a booklet provided for advertising copywriters by the Wool Bureau.

DISTRIBUTION FROM THE MANUFACTURER TO THE RETAILER

Depending on their size, manufacturers selling products to and through retailers have several distribution options. They can (1) sell directly to retailers, (2) use agents, (3) use wholesalers.[1] Agents and wholesalers can often provide promotional assistance, salespersons, and research in addition to distribution services. A given amount of resources can be used effectively or ineffectively, depending on the amount of duplication or coordination of marketing communications among various distribution channel members.

Selling Directly to Retailers

Marketers who sell effectively use every possible relevant communications tool. Manufacturers who sell direct to retailers have several communications options: their own salesforce, catalogs for retailers, showrooms in merchandise marts in major cities, trade shows, and contact with retail buying offices. Using salespersons to call on all retail customers is usually cost-effective when there are a few large customers or customer groups that purchase large amounts of merchandise. Manufacturers' catalogs can be sent directly to smaller, geographically dispersed retailers.

Merchandise marts, trade shows, and buying offices allow manufacturers to deal directly with many retail customers without travelling to all retail sites. Merchandise marts in major cities like Atlanta, Chicago, Dallas, and Los Angeles, have space available for continuous displays of manufacturers' merchandise. Trade shows, which are held from time to time, but not continuously, also have merchandise displays. Retail buyers benefit from shopping at regional merchandise marts and trade shows because they can comparison-shop for merchandise and marketing communication ideas from several manufacturers in a relatively short time. They can also save money, as they do not have to travel to New York City or to manufacturers' home offices.

Trade shows are especially useful for those manufacturers located a great distance from their customers. For example, at a recent annual meeting of the National Retail Merchants Association in New York City, the Hong Kong Trade Development Council staged a series of events around an extensive exhibition of their products: clothing, furniture, sports equipment, toys, computers, and housewares. The exhibit area was in the convention hotel, and all retail conferees received invitations. The admissions "fee" was a business card or business name and address.[2]

Another option that saves time for manufacturers and retailers is to work with a buying office. Buying offices represent client stores. They buy merchandise from manufacturers on behalf of their member stores, and also provide information to the stores about merchandise availability and current trends. Retailers pay a fee or commission for this service. Manufacturers can save sales-force time by working directly with these buying offices whenever possible.

These direct contacts, however made, are very important to both retailers and manufacturers because they facilitate the exchange of information. The manufacturer needs to know what customers are like, how the retailer plans to advertise and promote the merchandise, and what communications help the retailer will accept. In order to cooperate with the manufacturer, the retailer needs to know how the manufacturer plans to advertise, price, and promote the merchandise, and what retail communications support is available.

Enthusiastic vendors sell to retailers, hoping that the enthusiasm is then passed on to the consumers. This is a circular situation, requiring a constant updating for retailers and manufacturers to be informed about each others' plans for marketing communications. An indication of a lack of communication between retailer and manufacturer is manufacturers' ongoing complaint that retailers often fail to make use of manufacturers' cooperative advertising funds. Manufacturers can help retailers understand how to use these funds only if the manufacturers fully understand retail marketing communications.[3]

Selling Indirectly Through Agents

To substitute for or augment a direct sales force, manufacturers can pay independent agents and distributors to represent them. *Selling agents* sell the entire output of one manufacturer. *Manufacturers' agents* serve a number of different non-competing manufacturers. While they sell for manufacturers they do not take title to merchandise. These agents carry non-competing merchandise lines in order to avoid conflict of interest. However, they tend to specialize in related lines that might all be purchased by their target groups of retail buyers. For example, an agent might specialize in children's apparel, carrying one manufacturer's line of infant wear, and another's line of clothes for toddlers.

Selling Indirectly to Wholesalers

Wholesalers differ from agents because they buy and take title to merchandise. They also tend to specialize by merchandise type. For example, there are food wholesalers, dry goods wholesalers, and so on. A wholesaler will buy large quantities from manufacturers and sell small quantities to retailers. Thus, retailers can buy a smaller amount than the manufacturer considers an efficient order size. For example, a major firm that sells directly to retailers may require a minimum order of one gross (144 pieces). This may cause a problem for a small store that requires only six pieces; however, a wholesaler can buy the gross and sell only six pieces to the small retailer. Retailers can make contact with just one wholesaler and buy small quantities of a number of different manufacturers' lines or items.

A *rack jobber* is a type of wholesaler who stocks store racks with merchandise several times a week in a busy store, or at least once a week in stores with less traffic. Jobbers get a commission for stocking racks. Rack displays take up little floor space and produce high sales volume when constantly stocked. L'eggs hosiery racks are stocked in supermarket

XHIBIT 5-2 L'eggs Logo on Truck and L'eggs Packaging
ource: *The First Sixty Years*, Dancer Fitzgerald Sample.

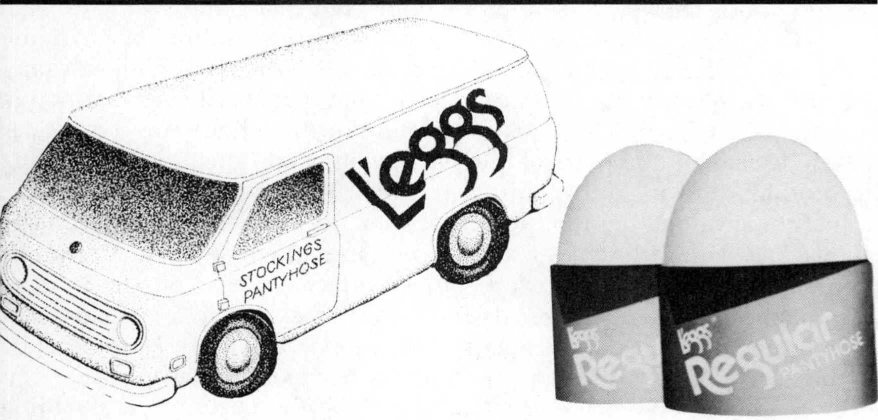

nd drug stores by rack jobbers. The L'eggs logo on a truck and on an gg-like package is shown in Exhibit 5-2. L'eggs ads and packaging elp *presell* the merchandise that is displayed on self-service racks in ores. Appendix 5-A describes L'eggs' selling, advertising, and display echniques.

Even when a manufacturer sells indirectly to retailers, there is still need to coordinate information about marketing communications plans. Ianufacturers need to work with retailers to insure that both manufacturer nd retail communications project a consistent image, protecting consumers om any mental discomfort created by conflicting messages. Manufacturers nust inform retailers about the merchandise itself and about available narketing communications aids, either indirectly through agents and holesalers, or directly through their own sales force in person, by mail, r by phone. In order to develop effective aids, manufacturers must nderstand retailers, their customers, and their communications needs. gents and wholesalers can tell manufacturers about the market situation nd the customers at the stores they serve.

THE INTERACTION BETWEEN THE VENDOR AND THE RETAILER

ypes of Retailers and Product Brands

ew if any products can be sold in all types of retail stores. Store and rand image are such that if a product is sold in one type of store, it nay not be accepted by another type. For example, certain products sold in drug or variety stores are not sold in some department stores that want to project a different image. Manufacturers can change image by changing both marketing communications and retail outlets.

Some manufacturers choose to create a variety of brands, each one aimed at a different type of retail store. In this case, packaging can play a key role, especially if the product is an item that is not very distinctive without its package. The package communication helps the consumer make a decision at the point of purchase by attracting attention, identifying the product, and instantly telling its story. The package must not only protect the product, but remind the customer of the desired brand image. The package can differentiate a relatively undistinctive product into different brands for different store types and customers, not to deceive customers, but to emphasize distinctions. For example, a special scent in perfumes or a special durable feature in a product like batteries may not be discernable until the product has been used. The package can point out distinctive product attributes while the customer is deciding which brand to buy.

Once the manufacturer has defined the target customers, the next step is to determine the types of stores in which these customers will buy the manufacturer's merchandise. For example, toiletry products such as soap or cologne are sold in department stores, drug stores, variety stores, and even supermarkets, but each of these store types carries different brands. The best sales results will come from the best match of brand image with store image. Without a match, either the store has a better image than the brand, or the brand has a better image than the store. Marketers should investigate to what extent this image mismatch affects a particular brand and store.

In another example, a hosiery manufacturer makes a "status" brand for the better department and specialty stores, another line for discount department and variety stores, and a third line for drug and chain stores. This same firm may also manufacture private brands for major chains or mail order houses. This manufacturer would distribute by matching different brand images to different images of retailers that serve different customer types.

Exhibit 5-3 shows two pages of a department store catalog displaying seven brands of merchandise from several "neo-classic" manufacturers for the "modern male" who is "comfortable with tradition, yet eager for the new." These manufacturers tend to sell the same brand to some specialty stores with prestige images, but not to discount, drug, or grocery stores. Manufacturers can evaluate their sales by store type to determine the role of each store type in their distribution strategy.

Some years ago, retailers with sufficient market power were able to require manufacturers to sell exclusively to their stores. For example, Sears carried Easco tools. When Sears reduced inventories, Easco had to

Catalog Information about Merchandise Characteristics, Seven Brands

Source: Jordan Marsh, "Modern Moves" Catalog, August 1983. Size of originals, 8½ × 11″.

find additional customers to make up for the lost Sears business. It can be dangerous for manufacturers to sell a major part of their output to one retailer because loss of business from that retailer can harm the manufacturer. However, a manufacturer can have an exclusive retailer for some brands in each of several non-competing geographic areas, while still selling other brands elsewhere. The less exclusive the brands, the more work retailers must do to differentiate their stores from competing stores.[4]

Most products require traffic to generate volume sales. If a combination of drug and variety stores has the required traffic, the manufacturer could sell through these types of stores. Some products require demonstrations and sales explanations. Appropriate stores for these products are department or specialty stores that have salespeople. Brands that can be presold by national advertising are appropriate for supermarkets and other self-service stores.

Communicating to and Through Retailers

In addition to informing, reminding, and persuading customers about products, vendors' marketing communications can generate customer *expectations* of what types of stores carry their merchandise. This can be done by advertising which lists stores that carry the brand. The image ad in Exhibit 5-4 lists store names and cities for a manufacturer's brand.

Other vendor communications include coupon sales promotions, point-of-purchase displays, and store signs. Often manufacturers will provide outside signs which feature the store's name as well as name of the manufacturer's brand. For example, a store sign provided by Puch Bikes tells customers that the store carries that brand. Of course, the store will want this sign to communicate the store name equally well.

In a constantly changing environment, marketing communications are needed to keep the customer up-to-date about which store types carry which brands. This is especially necessary when some store types invade the traditional territory of other stores. For example, supermarkets now carry health and beauty aids and drug stores carry candy, cosmetics, and greeting cards. The L'eggs story in Appendix 5-A is an example of the invasion of grocery and other stores by a product formerly sold only in department stores.

The Revlon story in Appendix 5-B is an example of a double invasion supported by various tools in the marketing communications mix. Originally, Revlon products were personally sold by manicurists in beauty shops. They were later sold by manufacturers' ads and point-of-purchase displays in drug stores. Finally, they were sold by salespeople working in department stores. Publicity generated by a Revlon-sponsored television show, and by national print advertising in prestige media added value

EXHIBIT 5-4 Manufacturer's Magazine Ad Listing Store Names and Cities

Source: "*The World of Gianni Versace*," *Vogue*, 1984. Size of original, 8½ × 11".

to the Revlon product image. Exhibit 5-5 shows one side of a two-page color advertisement which appeared in several issues of prestigious national magazines to create consumer demand for Revlon nail polish and lipstick. The other side of the ad continues the eight color stripes, with the name of the color printed on each stripe. Between the fourth and fifth stripes are lips and three fingers with polished nails. Sometimes the name of a retailer is printed in the lower right corner of this ad.

EXHIBIT 5-5 **Revlon Magazine Ad about Colors of Lipstick and Nail Polish**

Source: *Vogue* (June 1984), pp. 10–11; (August 1984), pp. 18–19. Size of original, 8½ × 11″.

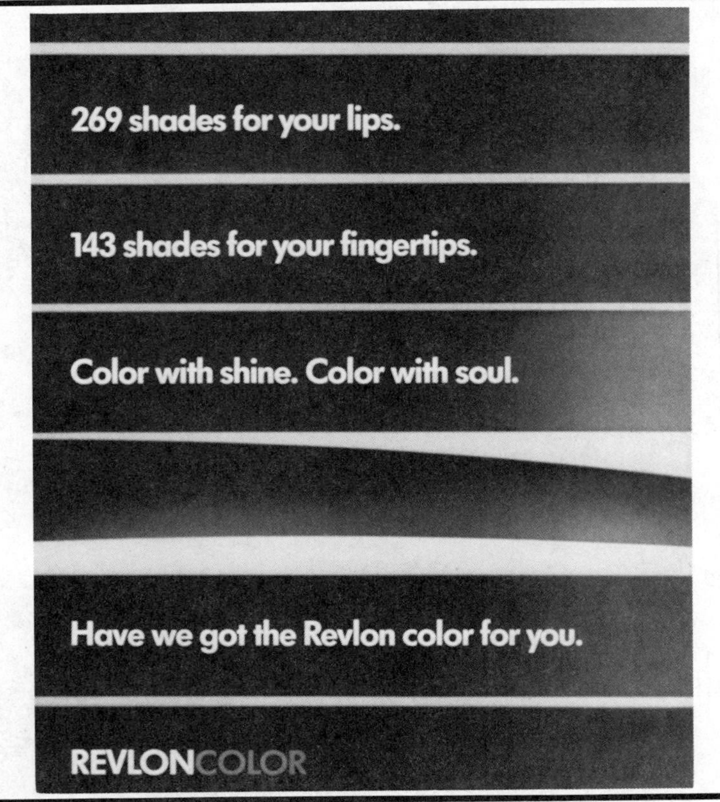

For moderately priced impulse merchandise, available in many types of stores, manufacturers tend to provide coupons in their national advertising, as well as funds for retail advertising. In this case it is important for a manufacturer to realize that retailers advertise the manufacturer's brand only to get sales in their own stores. Retailers must use the manufacturer's cooperative funds cautiously to avoid spending money on an ad that might send customers to competitors who also sell the advertised brand. On the other hand, a recent retail coupon strategy has been to accept coupons from competing brands or retailers, thus benefiting from competitors' coupon efforts.

Sometimes, related merchandise from more than one manufacturer can be used in an advertisement. In Exhibit 5-4, the left side of a manufacturer's two-page magazine ad, an apparel manufacturer, Versace, featured a prestigious car, the Ford Continental Mark II. Ford had asked

Versace for design assistance (see ad copy). The copy listed some of the stores which carry the Versace fashion apparel. In Exhibit 5-6, a retail advertiser listed vendors. This is the reverse of the Exhibit 5-4 ad in which the manufacturer listed retailers.

VENDORS AND RETAIL CATALOGS

This section explains the vendor-retailer interactions involved in selling merchandise to consumers via store catalogs. The example here is for a large catalog; however, the general idea can be adapted as a guideline

EXHIBIT 5-6 **Retail Magazine Image Ad Listing Vendors**
Source: *Vogue* (September 1982), p. 161. Size of original, 8½ × 11″.

for smaller stores and their catalogs. The issues involved in selling merchandise through catalogs are mostly ones of timing and planning ahead. Providing catalog merchandise for sale in stores tends to allow less flexibility than providing non-catalog merchandise, as the merchandise included in the catalog must be available throughout the period covered by the catalog. The catalog is expected to describe and depict the item accurately, and to adhere to expected sizing conventions.

Also, while newspaper advertising tends to send an immediate message to come to a store, catalog advertising is less urgent. The catalog sends a message to buy merchandise this month or this season. Often it is not even necessary to come to the store to buy catalog merchandise; mail and phone orders are usually accepted.

Large chains and mail-order firms purchase catalog merchandise from three to five thousand different vendors. For all lines of merchandise, large retailers might buy from eight to ten thousand manufacturers. How does a manufacturer become one of that number? If already in, how does a manufacturer acquire still more business, particularly the catalog business of Penney, Sears, Spiegels, or Ward?

Planning a Consumer Catalog

Exhibit 5-7 presents a time plan for a Fall General Catalog which has from 1,500 to 2,000 pages of four-color and one-color rotogravure printing. Millions of these fall mail order catalogs should be in customers' hands by mid-June. The logistics of getting to that point involves buyers and their suppliers at several crucial steps along the way.

Retailers hold a general strategy meeting in late August to discuss corporate plans for the season (See the Aug./Sept. column in Exhibit 5-7). Then each buyer analyzes his or her general and catalog performance at about the mid-point of the previous fall season. This analysis takes into consideration actual versus planned sales rates for each item by size and color. Seasonal sales trends and expected environmental conditions are factored into both figures.

Competitors, particularly those stores and manufacturers offering merchandise of similar quality, image, and price, are evaluated as well. Can the latest European and New York designer fashions be interpreted for the mass retail market? What are the trends? Manufacturers can give retailers information about the market, about manufacturers' advertising and promotion plans, and about what's happening with other retail accounts . . . no names, just numbers. Buyers also have sales input from their retail sources. Computer printouts, or hand tallies for non-computerized stores, provide more facts.

After merchandise is chosen for each catalog page, picture-page layouts are roughed out with the help of the Catalog Sales Manager and presented to the Merchandise Manager. They are included in a departmental

Source: Adapted from information furnished by A.E. Huettel, Merchandise Development Manager, Montgomery Ward.

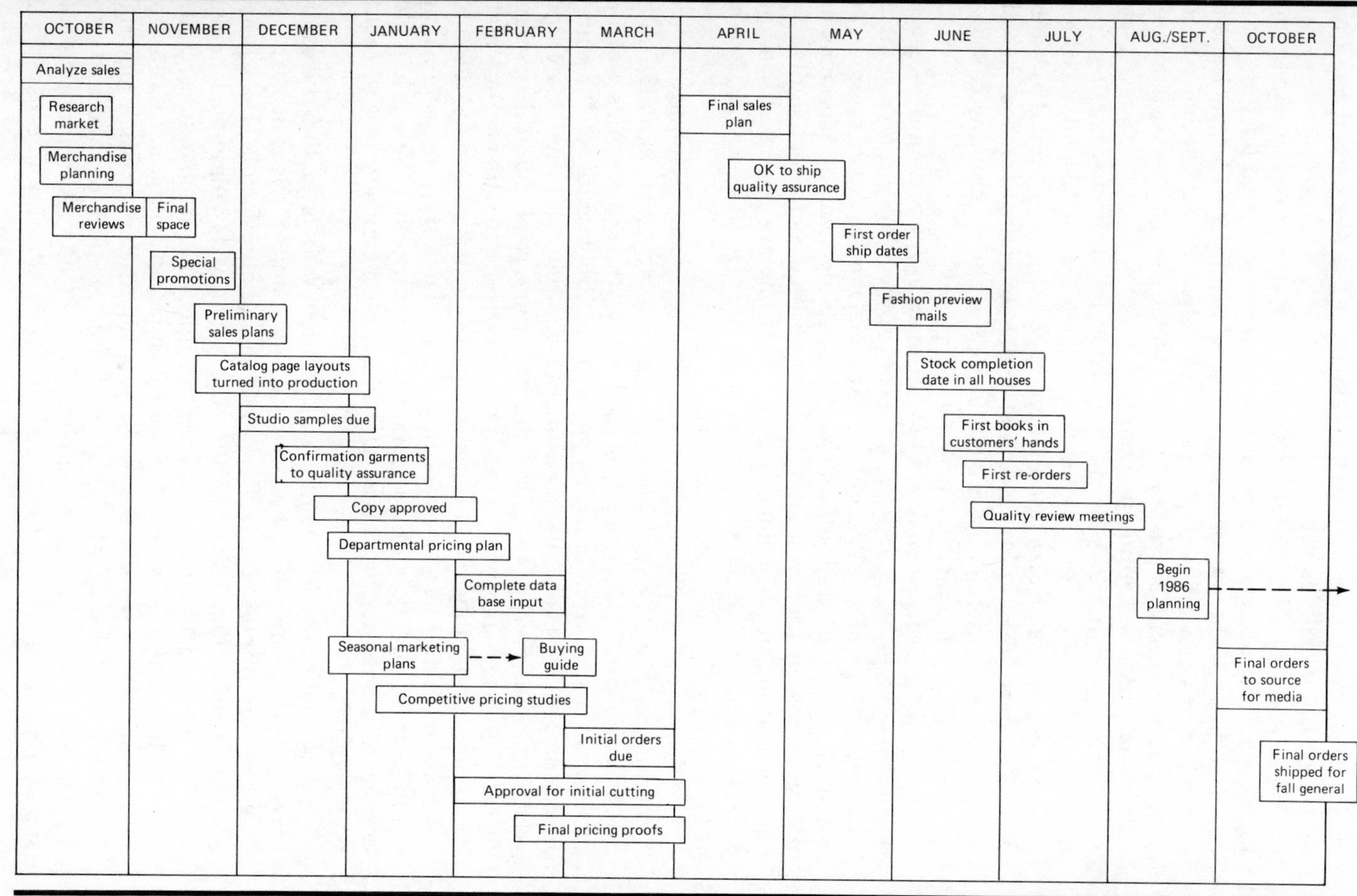

preliminary marketing plan for the catalog, and in the overall retail marketing communications plan.

The plans of all of the departments in a given division are brought together so that all concerned can evaluate the interrelationship of merchandise lines in the catalog concept. Someone must decide which themes or promotions can relate different merchandise categories, and whether catalog space should be reallocated to take advantage of manufacturers' marketing communications programs?

Finally, the initial stage is completed by allocating catalog space based on the retailer's general merchandise plan, departmental allocations, and manufacturers' programs and themes. For example, Exhibit 5-8 shows a catalog page for a cooking theme, which includes cookbooks, woks, and accessories. Merchandise includes one manufacturer's wok set and cookbook plus a store-brand wok set.

Once buyers have finalized the fall plans—by about mid-November according to Exhibit 5-7—they can begin to develop prototypes for the selected merchandise. The buyers examine merchandise samples and evaluate results of quality tests before specifying size and workmanship requirements for each vendor. Catalog pages and merchandise plans are turned in from mid-November through mid-January. Merchandise specifications must be decided upon as the catalog's art and copy become firm.

From these specifications, manufacturers submit samples for confirmation and photography. These samples should arrive about December 15 through January 15, depending on the department schedules. Retailers can accept some variation between a studio photograph of the sample merchandise and the actual confirmation sample, but only if they know what those differences are. The confirmation sample should be manufactured in the same way as the merchandise that will fill the catalog order, and preferably in the same shop. The confirmation sample must perform in quality tests, pass sizing and workmanship inspections, and conform to catalog copy. If the catalog copy states that the fabric is 60% cotton/40% polyester, that's exactly what the manufacturer and retailer must deliver.

The retailer needs the following information in order to write catalog copy: Does the product have any unique features? Does it carry any guarantees or implied warranties? Is the material washable? Does it have a special finish that resists stains? If a garment is guaranteed to wear longer or keep customers warmer than competitive merchandise, retailers want to test that quality and mention it in catalog copy. Exhibit 5-3 has information from several manufacturers about merchandise materials: hand knit Irish wool, heathered wool flannel, supple leather; and about how to use and combine the merchandise. The ad suggests that tie color should pick up a color in the tweed jacket. The illustrations also suggest

EXHIBIT 5-8 **Catalog Page with One Vendor's Wares and Store Brand**

Source: Home Economics Catalog, Jordan Marsh Store. Size of original, 8½ × 8½″.

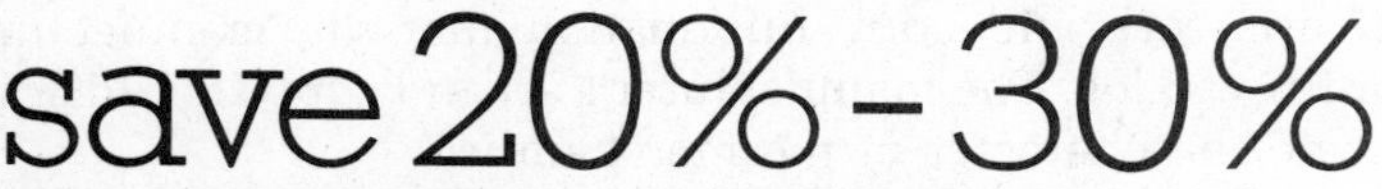

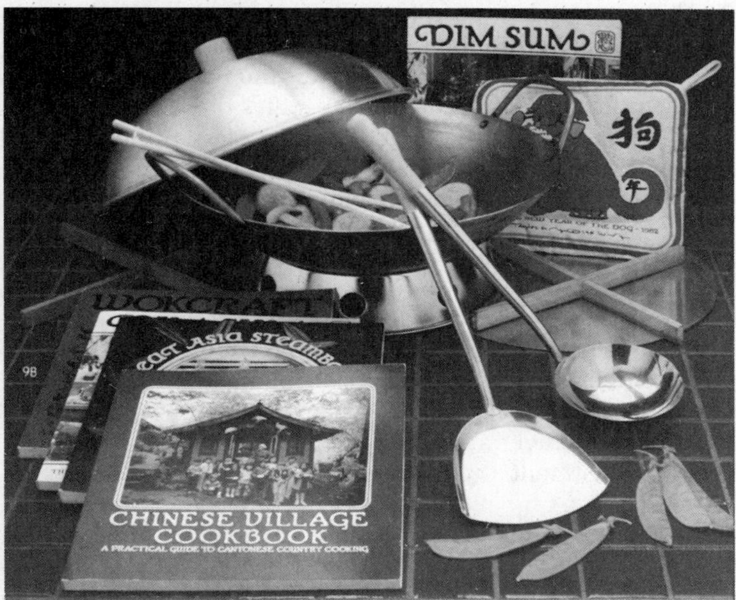

sale 40.00
9A. TAYLOR & NG WOK SET WITH DIM SUM STEAM SET and pot holder. 8 pc. set includes: 14″ wok, cover, ring, cooking chopsticks, steam rack, cookbook, stainless steel spatula and ladle. Dim Sum Steam Set includes: cookbook, 11″ steam rack, aluminum disc and instructions. (Dim Sums are bite-sized morsels of stuffed meat or dumplings to be steamed, baked or fried and served with a variety of dips!) Plus, a Chinese New Year potholder. If purchased separately 58.00

sale 3.95
9B. SAVE 20% ON COOKBOOKS from Taylor & NG. Select from Chinese Village, Wokcraft, Great Asia Steambook and Dim Sum. Reg. 4.95

sale 20.00
9D. SAVE 20% ON OUR OWN STAINLESS STEEL WOK SET. 4 pc. set includes: 14½″ stainless steel wok with copper plated bottom, ring, cover and steamer. Reg. 25.00
Gourmet Cooking D6707

combinations. This information helps both the manufacturer and retailer sell more goods.

Within about 30 days, an efficient retailer should be back to a manufacturer with the corrections needed to help the sample conform to catalog sizing and workmanship standards. During this period, the retail buyer is reviewing artwork, proofing copy, and doing a comparative study of competition to help develop a final pricing plan. This plan is then compared with the sales and markup goals established for the catalog or store operation, and modified where necessary due to competition. The retailer and the manufacturer must also negotiate the content and quality of art work and copy information that the manufacturer will supply for the catalog. The manufacturer's art and copy should accurately communicate the character of the merchandise.

In early February, all pertinent data for the Fall General Catalog is fed into the catalog data base for the use of buyers. Each catalog entry has its own number and includes all the information needed to generate mechanized orders for merchandise. After the retailer approves the manufacturer's confirmation samples and specifies the labeling, tagging, packaging, and marking, the manufacturer can start production. This can happen as early as February or as late as the first week in April, depending upon (1) the buyer's or store's schedule (early or late catalog or merchandising forms), and (2) special arrangements that may have been worked out with the buyer, such as producing a part of the order early to take advantage of lower production costs during a slack period.

About mid-February, the buyer checks the final copy and pricing proofs to evaluate whether or not prices are right for the period of June through December. Once again, all the elements that went into proposing each catalog page or merchandising plan are reviewed. Now the catalog proofs go to the engraver and printer. Manufacturers who tell the retailer about price adjustments at this point will probably receive no future business.

It is crucial that manufacturers meet the initial order shipping date (early May through early June) on time since all catalog orders are in a total schedule of shipments that are timed to arrive over a period of several weeks. Shipping cartons and carton markings must conform to retailers' requirements so that the merchandise will go through the receiving process faster, and manufacturers will be paid faster.

Evaluating and Acting on Catalog Results

Because buyers are rated on how well their merchandise performs in the catalog or merchandise plan, vendors who cause delivery problems will probably not get future orders. Insufficient merchandise means lost business and lower page productivity for the retailer and lost space in future catalogs for the vendor.

If the buyer buys the correct merchandise and prices it correctly; if the manufacturer meets specifications and delivers merchandise on time; and finally, if customers respond with orders as planned, *reorders* should begin coming to the vendor about late June. A manufacturer continues to get orders from a Fall Catalog through October for November delivery. Sometimes, the retailer estimates wrong and demand exceeds supply. When a retailer needs more merchandise to sell in a store, vendors can provide merchandise which is similar to but not identical with previous stock. But catalog reorders are less flexible because merchandise in a catalog should match its copy and illustration. If not, the retailer will have to cope with customers whose expectations based on the catalog are not met by the merchandise.

For example, a delivered game does not look like the game shown in the catalog. Even if the delivered game is better than the game shown in the catalog, the retailer, not the manufacturer, has to assure customers that the substitute merchandise is acceptable. If the substitute is not acceptable, the retailer has to accept the returned merchandise and send it back to the manufacturer. This situation tends to discourage retailers from dealing with vendors who cannot supply enough suitable merchandise to meet catalog requirements.

In negotiating with the catalog buyer, the vendor has to cover estimated costs for a shipping period that spans over six months. It takes long-range planning for the manufacturers and all of their suppliers to provide catalog merchandise over this extended period without inconveniencing the retail buyer. Vendors must tell buyers about potential manufacturing problems that might affect delivery during the life of each catalog, so that the buyers can prepare for any difficulties ahead of time.

To get a first order from catalog and mass merchandisers, a manufacturer must be known as a trusted retail resource on whom buyers can depend for reliable delivery and quality. A manufacturer with a good product should not stop trying for catalog business after one rejection, since numerous catalogs are developed every year. A manufacturer can expect that a Spring Catalog will be planned approximately six months after the Fall Catalog. The time-line diagram in Exhibit 5-7 makes it easier to visualize the overall timing for selling to large catalog operations and chains.

CONDUCTING RESEARCH ABOUT RETAILERS

Preliminary Questions

Vendors can use research to learn whether a retail market is large enough for a particular product, and to find out which stores are suitable. In the example of men's hosiery, Census data show that there are over 100 million adult males in the United States, each of whom wears hosiery of some type. A few big retailers—Sears, K mart, Penney, and Woolworth—probably sell from 25% to 30% of all men's hosiery. Twenty giant retail organizations, such as Macy's, May Co., Federated Stores, A.M.C., Allied Stores and Associated Dry Goods, account for another 15% to 20%. Retail giants take the lion's share of all sales in the other merchandise categories as well.

Merely by looking at a Sears Roebuck Catalog, a J.C. Penney catalog and shopping a K mart store, a typical manufacturer can get a prett good idea of where the mass market is. After selecting a market segmen the manufacturer needs to analyse the major competitors and their retai customers as well as the retailers' customers. The next step is to compar competing product offerings for quality and for related services, such a delivery timing.

Input From Retailers

Store buyers and managers of a manufacturer's best retail customer generally have a good understanding of why their store does well with this manufacturer's product. Because good vendor resources are importan to them, retailers tend to go out of their way to help good suppliers do more and better business. Vendors can tell one store about the successfu communications effort of other non-competing stores. Also, retail buyers can explain to their vendors why their store's customers are not buying the vendor's products.

While verbal reports of successful retailers can be invaluable feedback to manufacturers, the most important input comes from sales figures When a retailer does well with a product, the manufacturer-retailer com bination is "doing something right," with the store-product combination the marketing communications, or both. If the members of the retailer manufacturer combination find out what they are doing right, they car repeat it while the situation stays the same, and make modifications to fit changing situations.

In addition to evaluating verbal input and sales figures, retailers and vendors can experiment to find out what communications techniques work best. For example, Exhibit 5-9 shows a coupon section of a catalog that tests various sale offerings for manufacturers' brands of a wide variety of merchandise. Some savings are in percentages, and some are in dolla amounts. This mix of percentage and dollar savings arrangements may be the natural result of store-vendor negotiations. However, it provides a basis for finding out whether the percentage or the dollar savings generate more sales on comparable merchandise. Another aspect of this catalog page is the timing required for reduced-price promotions, a retail phenomenon that vendors should understand. This catalog page is designed to increase sales and traffic on one normally slow day in retailing, Tuesday.

The type of store in which a product is sold often helps determine the packaging requirements. In a store where salespeople wait on customers, the merchandise may have to be displayed on hangers or shelves, but not on a package. Such merchandise would be placed in a store bag or box after the customer purchased it. On the other hand, preselling through advertising, reinforced by point-of-purchase display, helps packages attract customers' attention in self-service stores. In some cases, manufacturers

EXHIBIT 5-9 **Sale Catalog Coupons with Percentage and Dollar Discounts on Various Brands**

Source: Steiger's 86th Anniversary Sale Catalog. Size of original coupon, 2⅝ × 2¼″.

Great Savings on Newest Spring Fashions!

These coupons are valid on Tuesday, April 20th. One coupon per item.

test products in their own stores. For example, Hallmark, a "social expression" business, is testing products in its three new store types: a store with trendy greeting cards and products for teens and young adults, a store with select cards and products for classics consumers, and a partyware store.[5]

Another major factor in package design is stores' methods of displaying the product. Will it lie flat, stand up, be hung up, or be hung on hooks? Some stores use display fixtures provided by the vendors. Store management can provide feedback about displays or cooperate in experiments to find out such things as whether products sell well in multiples (several of the same items banded together or placed in a single package). Store management can also help to test package copy, art, color, shape, and size.

Product Quality and Marketing Communications

A number of leading manufacturers of consumer products have installed manufacturing quality control methods. They have also used product-testing laboratories to put their merchandise through rigid tests of strength, durability, and other quality standards. This reduces the testing work that retailers must do. A number of manufacturers issue guarantees or warranties, building consumer confidence and projecting a quality image, particularly when there is brand identity. Advertising copy can include warranty information.

When selling merchandise through retailers, manufacturers should know what makes products most acceptable to customers, and what advertising, promotion, personal selling, and display are most effective. Retailers should understand clearly to what extent the manufacturer stands behind the product so that the store in turn can guarantee satisfaction to the consumer. When the product is an honest value, priced properly, placed in the right stores, and has its advantages brought to appropriate consumers' attention through the good teamwork of manufacturers and retailers, it should be successful.

SUMMARY

Good vendor brands and resources help build the image of a store, while good retail images help build consumer sales. Vendors are able to provide effective support for marketing communications only when they understand retail marketing. Successful selling is a result of vendors producing and the retailers providing good products at prices consumers are willing to pay, and of both parties effectively communicating product information to consumers. A good product that satisfies consumers usually results in repeat sales and increased consumer confidence in store, brand, and vendor.

Because modern consumers are better informed than those of the past, vendors should provide accurate product information directly to consumers as well as through retailers. Information can be provided via advertising, displays, tags, packages, and labels. Catalog selling additionally requires accurate product descriptions, as well as advance planning and prompt merchandise delivery by vendors.

Both vendors and retailers benefit by integrating their research into consumer preferences, and into the effectiveness of marketing communications on consumers. Consumers benefit when improved marketing communications facilitate their learning what products benefits exist, where to buy products, and how to use and take care of them. Satisfied customers are those whose product and service expectations have been met.

QUESTIONS

1. Why is it important for manufacturers who sell through retailers to understand retail marketing communications?
2. What types of stores and retail marketing communications should manufacturers seek for (a) mass-merchandise apparel, (b) exclusive fashion apparel, (c) housewares, (d) computers, (e) presold, packaged small items like cosmetics and hosiery?
3. Manufacturers sell their merchandise to a number of stores in order to increase sales, market shares, profits and meet other goals; while stores want to have a number of vendors who will help them reach similar retail goals. These goal similarities and differences may result in a potential conflict. Explain how the conflict would affect marketing communications, and how it might be resolved.
4. What potential retailer-vendor conflicts might arise when vendors who do not have the information in this chapter try to sell through retailers' catalogs?
5. Why is vendors' delivery timing so important to retailers?
6. Why is consistency between (a) merchandise samples provided to retailers by vendors, and (b) the delivered order of merchandise, especially important for retail *catalog* marketing? Is this difference as important for merchandise *advertised in newspapers,* as for *unadvertised* merchandise? Explain.
7. Why and how can vendors and retailers cooperate to do research about retail marketing communications? Under what conditions would you recommend that manufacturers have their own stores?
8. Compare and contrast the use of distribution channels and related retail marketing communications by Revlon and L'eggs, as described in Appendices 5-A and 5-B.

NOTES

1. Sources for this chapter include V. Buell, *Marketing Management* (New York: McGraw-Hill, 1984); J. Evans and B. Berman, *Marketing,* 2nd ed. (New York: Macmillan, 1985); P. Kotler, *Marketing Management,* 5th ed. (Englewood Cliffs, NJ: Prentice-Hall, 1984); M. Mandell and L. Rosenberg, *Marketing,* 2nd ed. (Englewood Cliffs, NJ: Prentice-Hall, 1981); J.B. Mason and M. Mayer, *Modern Retailing,* 3rd ed. (Plano, TX: Business Publications Incorporated, 1984). See also

L. Cheskin, *Why People Buy* (Boston: Severight, 1959); L. Cheskin, *Business Without Gambling* (Chicago, Quadrangle, 1963); H. dePaola and C. Mueller, *Marketing Today's Fashions* (Englewood Cliffs, NJ: Prentice-Hall, 1979); E. Grey, *Levis* (Boston: Houghton Mifflin, 1978); D. Rachman, *Retail Strategy and Structure*, 2d ed. (Englewood Cliffs, NJ: Prentice-Hall, 1975); L. Rubin, *World of Fashion* (New York: Harper & Row, Pub., 1977); J. Weitz, *Man in Charge* (New York: Macmillan, 1974); G. West, *Sears Roebuck, USA* (New York: Stein and Day, 1977); See also Direct Marketing Association and *Catalog Page*.

2. J. Bergman, "Creating a Better Image," *Stores* (January 1984), pp. 29–37.

3. See Chapter 15 for more information on cooperative advertising.

4. "EASCO: Using Profits from Aluminum to Repair its Tool Business," *Business Week* (July 2, 1984), p. 90; Ruth Stroud, "Tattered Levi Seeks Diversity," *Advertising Age*, 55 (June 25, 1984), pp. 3, 114.

5. "At 75, Hallmark Cards Diversifying Products," *The Morning Union* (Springfield, MA), 121 (January 2, 1985), p. 27.

APPENDIX 5-A

L'EGGS: SELLING, ADVERTISING, AND DISPLAY

At one time, women's hosiery was sold mostly in department and specialty stores. Hanes, a major hosiery firm, decided that by using a different type of packaging, designed for mass-market products, it could sell large quantities of women's hosiery through mass-market retailers. Hanes decided to use rack jobbers to distribute the new packages to drug stores, grocery stores, and supermarkets.

Selling hose through mass market retailers required different marketing communications than selling in department stores. Department stores had salespeople to answer questions about hosiery, which was packaged in flat envelopes, and displayed on leg mannequins. In mass-market, self-service stores, products were presold by manufacturer's advertising. The packaging task was to avoid damage to merchandise and to sell merchandise from self-service store displays.

Hanes designed packaging to communicate an image of hosiery as an appropriate product for a grocery store. L'Eggs hosiery was packaged in egg-like hard plastic containers and displayed in special racks. The egg package suggested a grocery item—eggs. This innovative package itself attracted otherwise indifferent hosiery buyers because it was easy to find, protected the merchandise, and could later be used in craft projects.

At least twenty-seven packages are required for a display of L'Eggs: three sizes times three lengths times at least three colors. To have six of each size, length, and color, the store must stock at least 162 pairs of hose! The racks must be filled constantly to attract buyers. Using rack jobbers to stock the displays, L'eggs built up a huge volume in drug stores and supermarkets, taking away some business from variety and department stores. By 1983, more than 40% of hosiery was sold in food stores or drug stores. To provide more variety and fashion for consumers, L'eggs added colors in 1981, sheer colors in August 1983, and new colors in the fall of 1984.[1]

APPENDIX 5-B

REVLON: SELLING, ADVERTISING, DISPLAY, PUBLICITY

Distribution of Revlon nail polish, cosmetics, and toiletries changed marketing channels and communications twice. Charles Revson's first product was Revlon nail polish. Woolworth, Kresge, and major department stores then carried Cutex, the leading brand of nail polish at that time. Because those stores would not add another brand from a new, unknown manufacturer, Revson distributed his nail polish in beauty shops where manicurists used large quantities of nail polish. Revlon nail polish seemed superior to existing nail polishes in durability on the consumer's nails, as well as in quality and variety of color. Soon hundreds of beauty shop manicurists were using Revlon.[2] The predominant marketing communications tool was then personal selling.

To sell his nail polish in larger volume, Revson changed colors each season, creating obsolescence and tying in with the newest apparel colors. Revson used national print advertising to inform customers about the new colors. After he had built a good demand for Revlon nail polish through manufacturer's advertising, he convinced druggists that they could take some of the nail polish business away from department and variety stores. Sales of Revlon nail polish in drug stores were profitable and achieved considerable volume.

With thousands of drug stores selling his product, Revson added matching lipstick to his nail polish line. This created still larger volume and customer acceptance for the drug store as a place to buy these items. Revlon began a huge advertising campaign with colorful double spreads in fashion magazines and Sunday newspaper supplements. These spreads were made into counter cards and window displays for the drug stores. Revson had added another communication tool to help the retailer, point-of-purchase display materials. Soon Revlon nail polish and lipsticks were the top sellers in their field.

[1] "L'eggs Joins the Color Crowd," *Sales & Marketing Management* (August 13, 1984), p. 24.

[2] A. Tobias, *Fire and Ice* (New York: Morrow, 1976).

When department-store and variety-store buyers asked Revlon to sell them his hugely successful products, he refused at first. Later, he developed new and expensive beauty products and brands especially for department store customers: Ultima II, a treatment line, plus colognes and perfumes—"Charlie," "Chaz," and other expensive products. These products were sold by Revlon-paid salespersons at leased or shared-cost cosmetics counters in department stores.

The Revlon-sponsored TV show "The $64,000 Question" was a top-rated show on television in the 1960s. Millions of viewers watched each week as contestants were tested for their knowledge of a particular subject. On several occasions, Charles Revson himself appeared on the program to discuss Revlon products. One of the winners in this program, Dr. Joyce Brothers, went on to a prominent career as a columnist, consultant, and popular psychologist. The publicity generated by this television show and its guests and contestants added value to the product image.

In 1985, Revlon introduced Scoundrel Musk, a scent targeted at ages 13–24. This benefited from the brand name of the four-year-old Scoundrel scent, targeted at ages 25–49. Communications included a national TV ad featuring Joan Collins (a star in the well-known "Dynasty" TV program); displays featuring a jewelry offer, a gift set of Musk cologne, and a Joan Collins book; and free Scoundrel-Musk-scented bookmarks.[3]

Manufacturer-aided retail marketing communications for Revlon began with personal selling. Next, national advertising created sufficient demand to move into new channels twice. Point-of-purchase display materials helped out both types of channels, and a Revlon-sponsored television show generated publicity and a consequent huge demand for Revlon products. Today, Revlon products are extensively advertised, well known and sold in large quantities throughout the United States, and in many other countries as well.

[3] R. West, "Revlon Moves for Piece of Musk Market," *Womens Wear Daily*, 49 (February 8, 1985), p. 11.

PART TWO

Advertising

The best advertising brings a fine, useful, or valuable product or service to the attention of the public.—L. Rubin

6
THE ADVERTISING DEPARTMENT

INTRODUCTION

Advertising is a major marketing communications tool. Marketing communications managers need to understand how to organize a creative team that will produce effective advertising. Advertising management includes art, copy, production, and scheduling. Although this chapter focuses on the in-house advertising department, those who manage advertising without a special department, and those who use outside agencies can also benefit from reading this chapter. Because of the large volume of retail advertising, we use as example a retail operation. However, often manufacturers also have internal advertising departments.

THE ADVERTISING TASK

Reasons for Internal Control of Advertising

Most large and some medium-size retailers and manufacturers have their own advertising departments. The huge volume of day-to-day retail advertising, the large variety of merchandise to advertise, and the close advertising deadlines make it almost imperative for buyers, merchandise managers, and other store personnel to be involved in advertising decisions. At times, even an hour can be crucial when changes are necessary. Also copywriters, artists and, or photographers should have close contact with the merchandise itself so that they can get samples to describe, sketch or photograph in time for use in an advertisement. And of course, each store knows its customers best, and so can educate its advertising department about its particular target audiences. A store's own staff members can better maintain continuity of approach and build an identity, as they develop and record experience over time. Even though copywriters, artists or photographers may change from time to time, those who take their places can learn the store's desired image, style, and approach to advertising.

An advertising agency usually works for a number of non-competing clients and does not necessarily specialize in retailing. Thus, agency personnel are not as motivated or as flexible as the store's own employees to make necessary last-minute changes. Stores often need to change an ad at the last minute, due to such problems as non-arrival of merchandise, severe weather, or "upstaging" by a competitor. An internal staff can learn quickly of these last-minute changes and act on them immediately because the store is their only "client".

Large retailers with adequate internal resources will probably save money by preparing their own advertising. Assuming the same personnel at the same salaries worked for an outside agency, the agency would charge the store for agency overhead and profit as well. Most newspapers give stores special low retail advertising rates based on a sliding scale with the cost per line or per inch going down as the amount of space purchased increases.

Advertising Management in Smaller Firms and Shopping Centers

When small firms do not have advertising departments, their personnel or free-lancers can do the work of an advertising department. Managers can hire outside advertising agencies, artists, photographers and any other help they need. Media representatives and manufacturers provide help with art and copy. Help can also be obtained through the Chamber of Commerce, independent consultants, and college marketing and advertising students and professors.

Shopping center marketing managers plan advertising and promotions that include tenant stores. Managers of small specialty chain stores located in shopping centers get help from central chain management, which often sends art and copy to its stores, or does the advertising itself.

ELEMENTS OF PRODUCTION

Leaving the question of budgets to Chapter 15, this chapter will focus on the preparation of the advertising itself. The preparation of advertising is basically the same whether or not there is an internal advertising department. The main difference between a small operation and a larger one is the number of people involved. Both operations must accomplish the same tasks, but on different scales and levels of complexity. For example, a large retail operation will have a number of copywriters specializing in different areas: women's fashion, children's clothes, men's fashion, accessories, home furnishings, housewares, toys, books, and so on. In a small retail operation, one person may write copy for the entire store, or the local newspaper or radio station may perform this service.

Managers of the various marketing communications functions report to top management, or to a marketing vice president or manager. Separate managers may be assigned to public relations, visual merchandising (sometimes called visual presentation or display), special events (also called sales promotion), media advertising, and direct response advertising (including catalogs). Exhibit 6-1 shows the possible organization of an advertising department.

As the chart in Exhibit 6-1 indicates, there are three major categories: print, direct response, and broadcast. (Specific details for specific media

EXHIBIT 6-1 **General Organization of an Advertising Department in a Medium-to-Large Store**

Source: L. Rubin and National Retail Merchants Association.

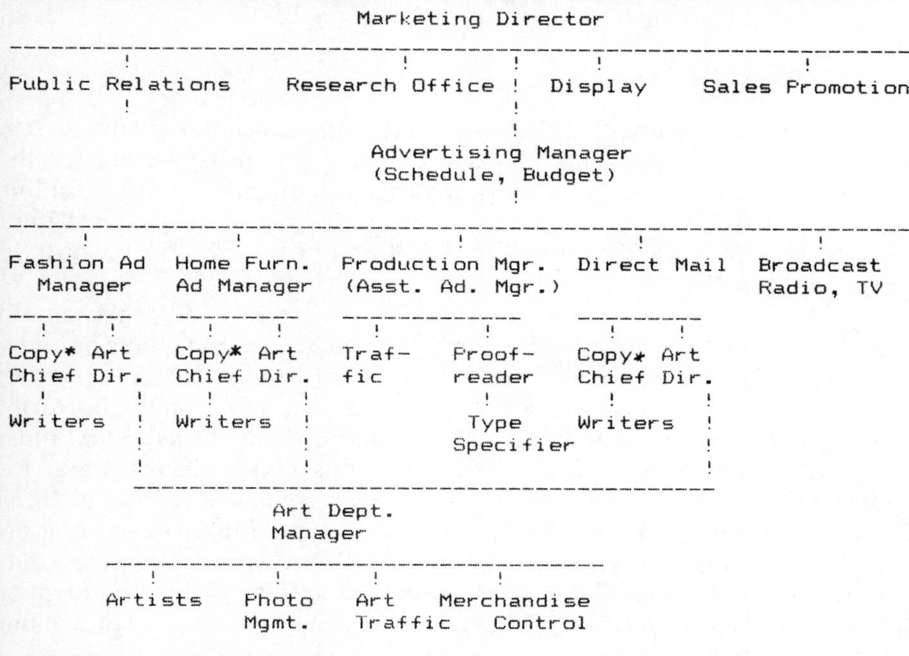

* *Sometimes copywriters work in several areas.*

are covered in Chapters 7, 8, and 9.) Advertising is divided into three major functional groups: copy, art, and production. The chart for the advertising department in Exhibit 6-1 shows the services associated with these functional groups. Numerous variations can be made on this structure according to the needs of the firm.

Generally, each functional group handles all media. However, in a large operation, specialists for each medium help the functional groups. For example, the copy department writes for newspapers, magazines, direct response advertising, radio, and television, but, say, a newspaper specialist is available to give advice when copywriters are preparing copy for newspapers.

Layout, art, photography, and copy, the principal creative ingredients of print advertising, offer many possibilities for individuality and distinctiveness. It is essential, from a marketing viewpoint, that a business express its character and personality through these advertising ingredients. Therefore, it is essential that top management constantly confer with the advertising managers about the firm's current position and the image that management wants to project, and that they discuss how best to project this image through marketing communications. Top management should also provide feedback to advertising managers about research results concerning sales response to advertisements and what customers think about the firm's position, image, and advertising. Top management and advertising managers need to discuss the implications of these research results for future advertising.

Copy Management

Copy, the advertising text, has been called the backbone of advertising. In the long run, copy may be one of the determining factors for the success or failure of a firm's marketing communications. Both the headline and the body copy communicate company image, no matter what their overt content. The "headline" is the "title" of the ad. Other words in the ad are called "body copy."

The copywriter deals in printed and spoken words that should represent creative, effective concepts.[1] On some occasions there are only a few words in a printed or broadcast advertisement; for example: "Tools for Mom," or "A duo of textures . . ." in Exhibit 6-2. Usually, however, advertising requires detailed copy and descriptions. Copywriters must be skilled at writing copy for various kinds of merchandise and for different media. In most cases, copywriters specialize in one of three areas: fashions, hard lines (housewares, home furnishings), or accessories. By specializing, individual copywriters become familiar with the terminology and special vocabulary used for specific categories of merchandise. The newspaper ad in Exhibit 6-3 has specialized copy about a "double-scoop top."

EXHIBIT 6-2 Two Small Ads with Minimal Copy

Source: Shoe Bin ad in local newspapers of Amherst, Massachusetts (Fall 1984); Grand Lake Hardware ad in *The Christian Science Monitor* (May 9, 1984), p. 18. Sizes of originals, 1¾ × 6″, 4 by 5″, respectively.

One of the roles of a good advertising manager is to coordinate the efforts of various copywriters, so that while each writer is a specialist, at the same time the business seems to speak in a unified voice. The manager must also strive for good team-work between the layout artist and the copywriter, so that the ad is well coordinated in terms of copy and art or photography, or oral or visual elements in the case of radio and television.

Many good copy chiefs take as a model the mail order catalogs of the leading retail firms. This type of copy is often considered the best basic copy written, because it must leave no possible question unanswered in the consumer's mind. Customers who buy by mail must know every fact about the item under consideration, particularly the details that cannot be seen by looking at the picture accompanying the copy. It may not be necessary to mention two pockets when they can be clearly seen in an illustration, but it is essential to describe the fabric, its feel and

EXHIBIT 6-3
Specialized Copy
Source: Tacoma News Tribune (October 28, 1983). Size of original, 6 columns full.

fiber content and performance, as none of these can be projected by a work and photographs. The catalog copy in Exhibit 6-4 includes the siz ranges, colors, pockets, and materials of suits, and descriptions of sever accessories.

A good copywriter must be able to write good headlines and lead to attract the attention of readers or viewers. (See "CLASS ACT" i Exhibit 6-3.) Some top copy experts believe that the headline determine the success or failure of a print advertisement. Clyde Bedell, a gre copywriter during 1940–60, made some experiments in this area. He too

***EXHIBIT 6-4* Catalog Copy**

Source: Brooks Brothers Spring 1984 Catalog, p. 2. Size of original, 8½ × 11″.

particular ad, changed only the headline, ran it on different occasions, nd carefully checked the responses. He found that one headline con-istently drew more business than the other for identical merchandise dvertised in identical space in the same medium.[2] Additional copy esearch supports the idea of the importance of the headline. No wonder nany of the best copywriters spend most of their time on the headline. xhibit 6-2 shows one ad in which the headline, "Tools for Mom," is ne only copy except for store identification, and another ad in which ne short body copy, "A duo of textures . . .," also serves as the headline.

Because stores do not have different copywriters for different media nd their copywriters are often specialists in merchandise categories, retail copywriters can usually adapt their skills to radio and television copy. Radio copy often requires a certain amount of repetition because the listener cannot refer back to printed information when the message is completed. Television copy does not need explanations of how products work, because the merchandise can be shown in actual use.

Art Management—Layout and Visuals

Art directors express concepts graphically, first in rough *layouts* or *storyboards* and then in specifying illustrations, photography and typography, and supervising finished ads.[3]

A key function of the Art Department is creating the *layout*. The layout—or storyboard in the case of television—is the blueprint for an advertisement. It tells the illustrator, photographer, or camera operator the amount of space devoted to the illustration, photograph, or visual concept, and the approach that should be taken in the execution of the visual elements. It also tells the copywriter for print media the amount of space to be devoted to the headline and the copy text.

Some layouts and storyboards are "comprehensive." They show in great detail exactly how the artwork or photography is to be executed. However, often "rough" layouts are sufficient, giving the general idea of the approach to be used. Layouts are sometimes made with scissors and paste by cutting up old ads or visuals and reassembling them in a new manner.

It is important that layouts and visuals for a particular store be consistent with one another and with the store image. This maintains the store identity. A good test for whether a store or brand is maintaining its identity in its advertising is to cover the nameplate or logo in an ad and see if the sponsor can be identified immediately by the remainder of the ad. The *stack* ad—a series of small related ads arranged in a column—in Exhibit 6-5 has a distinctive style of art and layout that has been repeated in many ads over a period of years.

The completed layout is passed on to the artist, photographer, copywriter or television producer involved. Often duplicates are made so the art, copy, and television production departments can proceed independently without waiting for each other.

Generally, the best print layouts or television concepts are *simple*. When advertising is too complex, it discourages the reader from reading the ad or the television viewer from watching. It must always be assumed that the reader or viewer is a busy person and perhaps disinterested. Everything in the presentation must be done with the idea of making the ad pleasant, easy, and perhaps entertaining to the consumer.

The art department is responsible for the actual illustration and photography in an ad. In the case of television, illustrations, slides, and

EXHIBIT 6-5 Stack Ads for Outside Borders of Newspaper Pages

Source: B. Altman & Co.

live action may be used in various combinations. Some advertisers use both art and photography: art for fashion, and photography for hard lines and housewares. Others may use all art or all photography to give the presentation a certain internal consistency. However, the most important aspect of the visual presentation is that it consistently reinforces store or brand image. Many advertisers take great pains to select certain artists and use a unique art approach for fashion merchandise. Once this approach is determined, the artists involved are directed to keep the art along certain lines and to use certain techniques to project this distinct image.

The late, great Dorothy Shaver, President of Lord & Taylor for many years, set the pace in this respect. For over forty years, that store has helped build its identity by maintaining a consistent art and layout style. An example is shown in Exhibit 6-6.

There are many types of art and photography approaches to depicting merchandise in retail advertising. Artists can use wash techniques, line drawings, combination line and wash, charcoal, "scratchboard," and various combinations of all these techniques. Wash techniques are black and white with all shades of gray, like watercolor paintings but without the color. Line art is black and white only. However, when fine black lines are placed close to one another, the eye may see the area as gray. Scratchboard is rough-surfaced paper which gives special effects to both line and wash techniques. Photographers can use square halftones, silhouetted photographs, combination square and silhouette, especially cropped photos, "soft background" shots, out-of-focus techniques, special lighting effects, montages, and combinations of different techniques.

Good art directors generally want a consistent approach to both art and photography, so that like layout, the art and photography themselves express the unified look for a store or brand. Such unity is possible even if a number of artists or photographers are involved in an ad, since the art director can instruct everyone to follow a particular approach.

An important factor that must be worked out is the ratio of copy space to space for illustration. Some retail advertising directors believe that copy should be brief and that the illustration should carry the main impact of the presentation. Other managers believe that copy is very important and should be given almost equal space. Such questions have no "right" answers but depend on the advertising philosophy. Both approaches have been taken successfully by leading retailers. Fashion in particular is often a very sensitive matter, and the possibilities for handling it are numerous.

Many entirely different, but successful, approaches can be taken in advertising. The ad in Exhibit 6-3 has a modern look; those in Exhibits 6-2, 6-5, and 6-6 are all more classic, but each has a different treatment. The ad copy is relatively short in Exhibits 6-2 and 6-7, longer in Exhibits 6-3, 6-4, 6-5, and 6-6.

EXHIBIT 6-6 Distinctive Art, Copy, Layout Style in Newspaper Ad

Source: Lord & Taylor. Size of original, 2 full newspaper pages.

Lord & Taylor

American refinement

Head-to-toe dressing
—total Lord & Taylor fashion dedicated to
the American woman's way of life.
Devoid of artifice, nothing extraneous.

All the essentials are here
—the perfect dress, suit, coat or sportswear
—and the carefully edited Lord & Taylor nuances
to make you look and feel
beautifully put together—always.

Lord & Taylor

American refinement

Lord & Taylor head-to-toe dressing.
Bred-in-the-bone good looks.
Good manners. Assurance.
After all, isn't this what fashion is all about?

Our Gloria Sachs cashmere sweater takes a tattersall skirt, bravura beret and big, striped shawl.

Come meet Gloria Sachs here tomorrow from 12 to 2
and see informal modeling of her beautiful new fall collection
typified by these sumptuous textures mixed with her refined sense of wit.
Long cashmere pullover in charcoal grey with intarsia argyles, S, M, L, 500.00
Tattersall checked dirndl skirt of cashmere-wool, heathery grey with white
and charcoal, 4 to 12, 330.00 Striped cashmere-wool shawl to match, 130.00
Third Floor, Lord & Taylor, Fifth Avenue at 39th Street—(212) 391-1199
Open daily 10 to 6 Thursday 10 to 8 The sweater, skirt and shawl also
at Westchester and Stamford. Shop Sundays 12 to 5 in our Westchester and Stamford stores.

***EXHIBIT* 6-6** (continued)

EXHIBIT 6-7 Ads with Minimal Copy and Varying Type Styles

Source: These ads are from *The Christian Science Monitor,* 1984. Dau (May 8, p. 36), size of original, 3½ × 2⅝″; Andersen's in CA (January 25, p. 18), size of original, 3½ × 4″; Oscar's (May 7, p. 17), size of original, 1¾ × 3″.

Art Management—Typography

Typography is the setting and arranging of copy in particular typefaces, styles, and sizes using metal or photographic composition.[4] Although typography is often taken for granted in the creation of advertising, the choice of type-faces for headlines, subheads, and copy can greatly affect the total appearance of the retail ad. It is wise to spend time to evaluate carefully the typefaces being used, to decide whether they contribute to the image that the store is trying to achieve. If possible, a store's type should be of a somewhat different style from that of other stores, particularly from those with whom it is in direct competition. The type selected should be clear, easy to read, and distinctive. Compare the variety of type among the small ads in Exhibit 6-7 with that in Exhibits 6-2 through 6-6. Type ranges from almost an electronic print in Exhibit 6-3 through some script print in Exhibits 6-5 and 6-6 for the store names. The headline type in Exhibits 6-5 and 6-6 are similar, except that one is entirely upper case and the other is mostly lower case.

Once decided upon, the typography should remain constant to help build the identity of the advertiser. It should be changed only when a store changes its image. The linear logo on the sign outside the New York Bloomingdale's store goes with the store's former conservative image. The rounded logo used in advertisements goes with the new, updated image. This logo is shown in Exhibit 2-3. Similarly, Sears' new logo was created at a time when Sears was in the process of changing from a conservative image to a new, updated image.

Production Management

Art and copy personnel create communications about merchandise, image, and information such as the advertiser's toll-free telephone number, store location, and hours of business. Advertising production management concerns the mechanics of getting the advertising into print. It includes specifying ("specing") and setting the type, correcting the proofs, sizing and scaling the art and photography, assembling all of the ad's elements, inserting the logos, setting borders and rules, creating the boxes around the ads, and integrating all the elements into a coherent whole.

The major elements of any advertisement include: creative work, production, and printing. Creative work includes layout, art, photography, and copywriting. Production includes reproducing the illustrations and copy on the printed page. Printing concerns paper and printing costs, including delivery.

The *specing* of type is a skilled occupation. *Specing* is short for "specifying the size and face of the type to be used in each ad." This must be done carefully, so that the type fits properly into the space alloted for it and is the best size and weight possible under the circumstances. Specing is not as simple as it may seem, for a single typeface may offer the choices of styles in Roman or italic; weights of regular, medium, bold or extra bold; and sizes from 6-point to 72-point. Because a firm usually uses several faces in its advertising, the possible combinations of type styles, weights, and sizes can be extensive. See the type styles in Exhibits 6-2 through 6-7 as an illustration of the extent of type variety.[5]

Today, most newspapers are printed by the *offset method*, which vorks from a printed image, rather than from the metal plates (*cuts*) or natrixes (*mats*) that are part of the *photoengraving process*. The original orinted image of typographic and pictoral elements pasted up in exact oosition is called a *mechanical*. The picture taken from this image is ultimately reproduced through the offset printing process.[6]

The old method of typesetting was done with "hot type" set in netal by a Merganthaler linotype machine. Headlines and special type vere set by hand by a typesetter. Today most type is set by the photo process, in which type is photographed after being properly sized on the ohoto-typesetting machine. Appendix 6 explains the three major methods of printing: letterpress, offset, and gravure.

The important point for those managing copywriting, art, or pho-ography is to remember that almost any effect can be created through production techniques. The original photograph or artist's drawing can e *blown up* (made larger) or *reduced* to fit the layout as required. Pho-ographs and wash drawings are called *halftones* because they must be roken down into tiny dots before they can be reproduced. *Line copy*, vhich is black and white only, does not have to be broken down into lots through the screening process. When line copy and halftone copy re used together, they are called *combination artwork*.

All personnel in the advertising department should be familiar with he terminology used in advertising production, and should know what an and cannot be done with the various elements involved. A copywriter vho has overwritten for the space allotted for copy will have to edit the opy to fit it into the allotted space. The writer might think the copy ould be set in smaller type to fit the space, and so should know that it ooks bad for a firm's advertising copy to be set in too many different izes of type.

Skilled production people and typographers can help the look of he type within an ad by *justifying* and *letter-spacing*. *Justifying* is inserting larger or smaller amount of space than normal between words so that vords come out even at the end of a line. *Letter-spacing* is adding extra pace between each letter of a line of copy to make it fit the space more venly or to match another line above or below it.

These and hundreds of other production techniques are used by xperienced advertising personnel to achieve the best possible appearance or ads. The entire graphic process requires a great deal of expertise. Marketing and advertising personnel usually enlist the aid of printers, ypographers, and plate-makers to give advice, quote prices, and cooperate enerally in the entire process. Large sums of money are often involved n advertising, so it is important for those involved to be knowledgeable n these areas.

It is likewise important to have good communication between the reative and the production people in the advertising department. Through such team work, many problems can be solved and the ads themselves improved. With changes in technology, many previously unknown and unattainable effects are now available. These technological advances are publicized in trade journals, at trade shows, and by word of mouth. Effective managers should also find out about new technological innovations used by competitors.

The production manager needs to work with the art and copy managers to solve problems concerning layout, typography, and wording.[7] The art department can help solve a problem by redoing the art work when more room is needed for copy. Or the copywriter might edit the copy to allow for a larger or more impressive sketch. Still another possibility is changing the size of the copy or the headline for a better fit.

MANAGING THE SCHEDULE

A normal advertising flow pattern should be established to meet the deadlines that are a constant pressure in producing advertising for the media. These pressures can build to a frantic point if there is not sufficient lead time worked out and allowances made for schedule changes and emergencies.

Here is how an advertising schedule might be worked out: Let us say that the newspaper deadline is three working days, and the radio and television deadline two working days prior to date of appearance. This means that the ad for Wednesday's paper must be in the hands of the newspaper by Monday noon and in the hands of the radio or television station two days prior to broadcast. Sunday ads must be in the newspaper's hands by noon on Wednesday. Time must also be allowed to proofread and approve the newspaper's printing. To save time on proofing, some of the larger stores are doing their own production in-house with typesetting and preparation of Velox prints so proofing time is reduced and there is a better chance of meeting deadlines. A typical newspaper schedule is in Exhibit 6-8. Microcomputer programs are available to help plan schedules.[8]

The National Retail Merchants Association (NRMA) monthly planning schedule can also serve as a planner's guide; one page is shown in Exhibit 6-9. This calendar has space to note last year's and this year's sales and weather each day. It also notes the number of selling days in the month and the number of Mondays, Tuesdays, etc. this year, last year, and next year. If a month has partial weeks, the days of the preceding and following months are filled in to make complete weeks.

To facilitate advertising requests, some firms provide printed request-for-advertising forms and requests for proof approval to their own personnel. These standardized forms help the advertising manager learn which de-

EXHIBIT 6-8 Typical Newspaper Schedule
Source: L. Rubin and Newspaper Advertising Bureau.

12 working days before ad appears: Buying office must have request for ad and specific information.

11 working days before: Start layout, and have copywriter and artist or photographer schedule ad.

10 working days before: Layout approved; copywriter and artist get layout and start work.

9 working days before ad: First copy draft due.

8 working days before: Art completed; buyer returns corrected first copy to ad department.

7 working days before ad: Newspaper gets copy, art, and layout for proofs.

6 working days before ad: Newspaper may need two days to show proofs.

5 working days before ad appears: Buyer makes final corrections and changes in proof; merchandise manager and ad manager approve.

4 working days prior to ad appearance: Newspaper final "running proof"; can make only emergency changes.

3 working days before ad: Final OK and release due at newspaper by noon.

Day before ad appears: Buyers and merchandise managers get running proofs, which are also posted for salespeople.

Day the ad appears: Get newspaper "tearsheets," and save them in advertising scrapbook with date of ad and, eventually, sales data. Send copies to accounting department for cost of advertising posted to budget and paying newspaper.

partments want what advertising. The forms encourage personnel to operate in a simple, systematic, routine manner, and provide a uniform set of records for evaluating the advertising procedure. They also provide a record to guide advertising plans for the future, reminding managers what did and did not work under certain conditions.

Formats will vary in each firm, but here are some items that may be included on a form. First, for sketching merchandise, artists need to know whether to sketch from the front, back or side and, if a person is in the sketch, how old the person should be. Also, artists need to know whether this sketch is to be the featured item in a group, whether it should be sketched exactly as is, and what additional special instructions should be observed. In stores, the buyer usually provides this information.

The copywriter needs to know the important selling features worthy of headline emphasis, as well as other features worth mentioning in the copy. The copywriter also needs to know whether material, fiber content, washability, sizes, colors, or brands, must be mentioned. Related information useful to the copywriter includes comparative prices—"regularly $5.00," "originally $15.00," "sold X days ago for $Y"; mail and phone

EXHIBIT 6-9 **Calendar for Scheduling Advertising**

Source: Marketing-Sales Promotion-Advertising Planbook (New York: National Retail Merchants Association, 1984), pp. 42–43.

NO. OF SELLING DAYS		
1984	1985	1986
26*	26*	26*

*New Year's Day **Not** Included

*Sundays **Not** Included

DAYS OF MONTH COMPARISON							
YEAR	M	T	W	TH	F	S	SU
1984	5	5	4	4	4	4	4 *
1985	4	4 *	5	5	4	4	4
1986	4	4	4 *	5	5	4	4

*New Year's Day **Not** Included

JANUARY 1984						
S	M	T	W	T	F	S
1	2	3	4	5	6	7
8	9	10	11	12	13	14
15	16	17	18	19	20	21
22	23	24	25	26	27	28
29	30	31				

JANUARY 1985

JANUARY 1986						
S	M	T	W	T	F	S
			1	2	3	4
5	6	7	8	9	10	11
12	13	14	15	16	17	18
19	20	21	22	23	24	25
26	27	28	29	30	31	

MONDAY	TUESDAY	WEDNESDAY
Sales l.y. $.....t.y. $......... Weather l.y. ......t.y. **31**	Sales l.y. $.....t.y. $......... Weather l.y. ......t.y. .... **1** New Year's Day	Sales l.y. $.....t.y. $........ Weather l.y. ......t.y. **2**
Sales l.y. $.....t.y. $......... Weather l.y. ......t.y. **7**	Sales l.y. $.....t.y. $......... Weather l.y. ......t.y. **8**	Sales l.y. $.....t.y. $....... Weather l.y. ......t.y. **9**
Sales l.y. $.....t.y. $........ Weather l.y. ......t.y. **14**	Sales l.y. $.....t.y. $........ Weather l.y. ......t.y. **15**	Sales l.y. $.....t.y. $...... Weather l.y. ......t.y. **16**
Sales l.y. $.....t.y. $....... Weather l.y. ......t.y. **21**	Sales l.y. $.....t.y. $........ Weather l.y. ......t.y. **22**	Sales l.y. $.....t.y. $........ Weather l.y. ......t.y. **23**

order information; delivery charges; and store locations where merchandise is available. The copywriter should know the name of the newspaper in which the ad will appear, the name of the event or sale, the number of lines allowed, what art, photos, or coupons will be in the ad, the vendor's copy, and fiber requirements. If there is a manufacturer's warranty, information about the warranty must be in the ad. It is helpful to let the copywriter know who is the target audience for this ad, what copy style (narrative or other) is needed, and what behavior the advertiser expects of the readers.[9]

Signs and posters related to ads should probably be ordered at least five working days in advance. The number of signs and posters for each store, the dimensions, the headline used in the ad, and the three most important but not obvious selling points must be specified when ordering. Also, if a comparative price is used, is it the regular, original, special purchase price, or the price for "imperfect" or irregular merchandise? Is the sign for a promotional event, mailer, daily advertising, or special need?

All persons writing copy or designing signs should know the firm's definitions for prices and other terms. Definitions include *regularly* (last previous price for the most recent 18 days, and following the sale); *originally* (implies a permanent markdown because the "original" price is the first price in current selling season); *comparable* (items of like grade and quality are currently available in this trading area); *usually* (most recent price or customary price in trading area); *formerly* (sold substantial amounts at the former price; must also specify any intermediate markdowns). In headlines, *sale* means that a price has been reduced at least 10% for items priced at $100 or less and at least 5% for items priced over $100. *Clearance* means at least the same price reductions on a broad assortment of odds and ends or broken sizes, with plans to sell out all the stock. *Special purchase* means that goods are probably not available at this price in the trading area.

All persons working on the ad and related signs and posters should know the deadlines for submitting the ad. The buyers need to know when the ad will run so that an adequate amount of the advertised merchandise will be available. The selling supervisors need to know dates in order to inform salespersons.

WORKING WITH AN ADVERTISING AGENCY

Although all firms do not necessarily work with advertising agencies as discussed earlier, it may be financially advisable for a firm to use an agency for some special function that cannot be done internally. Because an advertising agency usually works with a number of clients, it may have a broader perspective than an in-house department. By working with several clients, the agency acquires experience in performing some functions that any single client might require only rarely.

Both the client and the advertising agency must agree on precisely who is responsible for which activities and expenses. There is often confusion about who should pay for rough art, and about how research such as copy testing should be charged—at cost, marked up, or absorbed. There is also potential disagreement about conflict of interest, especially when stores expand into new lines and territories, or when newly combined agencies inherit new accounts from the merger.[10]

Agency services usually include creative execution and production, creative strategy, media planning and placement, marketing strategy, research, public relations, direct mail, and copy testing. Agencies need sufficient input from clients to do their work, clearcut decisions, access to top management, effective approval procedures, and reasonable demands. To work productively with an agency, a client should be loyal and cooperative; require short, clear, written strategy that defines the suggested advertising direction; build campaigns, not ads; and be willing to experiment and take risks.[11] Because larger agencies have many account executives and creative personnel, it is advisable to interview persons who will work with an account to see if their work is compatible with the company's desired image and position.

Information about local agencies is readily available by observing their ads in print and broadcast media. Current telephone directories, periodicals, and books also publish information about agencies, their clients, and creative material.[12]

It is in the best interest of businesses to use the time of agency representatives effectively because this minimizes the number of hours that the agency charges to the client. Therefore, the client should observe the following procedures. First, set and keep appointments with agency representatives. Agency personnel should not be kept waiting because this takes their time from doing advertising. Clients should meet agency representatives in a situation which has no distractions, to make most effective use of the meeting time. Agency representatives are most effective when they understand a firm's business and products and know what the firm wants its advertising to accomplish. It is usually helpful to give the representatives a tour of the premises, and to provide them with samples of the products or other materials that will be illustrated.

Agency representatives should always be treated courteously. Good treatment will induce a positive attitude towards a firm, which in turn helps the agency create a positive, inviting ad for their client.

If a firm's managers do not know exactly what they want, they should listen to suggestions of the agency representatives and give them some creative freedom. The client is paying for the agency's creative

EXHIBIT 6-10 Newspaper Ads in Small Towns Produced with Agency Help
Source: *New Haven (CT) Advocate* (May 30, 1984), p. 25, designed by The Little Apple Agency, Clinton, CT.; (July 25, 1984), p. 9. Sizes of originals, 2¾ × 4¾″, 4¾ × 5″.

time, and should make use of the agency's creativity. Taking a calculated risk on something new might work better than past advertising. If it does not, then the next ad can be different.[13]

Several small firms can use agency representatives' time effectively by cooperating with each other to give a joint order to the agency. This tends to result in a better rate and coordinated advertising with a bigger overall clout. Another way for small firms to afford agency ads is to order a good-quality general-approach ad layout, and then pay for a variety of merchandise illustrations that can be introduced into this general format.

Two ads for small stores in a small town are in Exhibit 6-10. These are simple ads for stores that offer a variety of merchandise. The Jabberwocky store sells sportswear, jewelry, accessories, and gifts, and features jewelry in its illustration. This ad was prepared by representatives of a small agency in a small town.[14] The Zimmerman and Fink store, which has a wide variety of merchandise, features hammocks, beach chairs, and picnicware in its copy. The whimsical illustration is very much in character with the store's ambiance. Both ads appeared in a free, weekly, shopper-type newspaper.

SUMMARY

The combined efforts of art, copy, and production workers, when successful, enable marketers to create interesting, cost-effective advertising that attracts customers. Over the years, many medium-sized and large firms have found that it is more efficient to have their own advertising departments instead of employing an outside agency. The urgency of retail advertising deadlines requires close and constant contact between merchandise buyers and advertising personnel. In smaller firms where each manager performs several functions, there may be no formal advertising department. Their advertising can be handled by store personnel, media, or agencies. Shopping center marketing managers and the central management of retail chain stores may also help with advertising functions.

All print advertising, whether handled by the firm or by others, is structured in a similar manner. Print advertising involves three major areas: copy, art and production. Merchandise art and copy specialists operate in several media, with specialists available for advice in every media. Photographers, layout specialists, mechanical artists, type specifiers, proofreaders, and coordinators work on advertising production.

The advertising manager must organize these people into a team to produce effective advertising on schedule to reach clearly defined store goals. The advertising itself must be consistent and technically well-produced so that it enhances the reputation of the firm. It must also be consistent with other marketing efforts.

QUESTIONS

1. Why is it important for some retailers to produce their own advertising?
2. What help is available for small businesses for creating and producing advertising?
3. What are the major functional groups in creating advertising, and why must they work together?
4. How is catalog copy like and unlike copy for newspaper advertisements?
5. Exhibits 6-2 through 6-7 contain ads for large and small stores. Choose a type style from one ad. Would it be appropriate for any of the other ads? Explain.
6. Choose an art style from one of the ads in Exhibits 6-2 through 6-7 and explain whether or not it would be appropriate for some other ad in Exhibits 6-2 through 6-7.
7. The ads in Exhibit 6-7 appeared in a national newspaper. They are ads for several stores located throughout the United States. Explain why they have so little copy, and why the particular copy they have is or is not appropriate.
8. Given the newspaper schedule in Exhibit 6-8, explain what you think might happen if, on the day before the ad is to appear in the newspaper, (a) the merchandise in the ad has not arrived in the store, or (b) merchandise ordered for the ad arrives, but does not look like the illustration in the ad because of some mixup beyond the buyer's control. What might happen to the ad? If you were the store president, what would you do to avoid problems (a) and (b)? If you were the marketing vice president of the vendor, what would you do?
9. Explain the conditions which might persuade an advertiser to work with an advertising agency. What advice would you give a client for working successfully with an advertising agency?

NOTES

1. Carl K. Hixon and John Noble, *What Every Young Account Executive Should Know About the Creative Function* (New York: American Association of Advertising Agencies, 1979), p. 4.

2. For a general overview and historical background, see William H. Backus, *Advertising Graphics* (New York: Macmillan, 1970); John Caples, *Tested Advertising Methods* (New York: Harper & Row, Pub., 1932); Judy Young Ocko, *Your Sale Advertising Can Be Better* (New York: National Retail Merchants Association, 1981); Ocko, *Retail Advertising Copy, the How, the What, and the Why,* rev. ed. (New York: National Retail Merchants Association, 1977); Rosser Reeves, *Realities in Advertising* (New York: Knopf, 1961); M.L. Rosenblum, *Revise! How to Design Effective Store Advertising* (New York: National Retail Merchants Association, 1974); Rosenblum and Ocko, *How to Be a Retail Advertising Pro* (New York: National Retail Merchants Association, 1977); *Women's Ad Review,* published by Retail Reporting, 101 Fifth Avenue, New York, NY 10003.

3. Hixon and Noble, *The Creative Function,* pp. 4, 10.

4. Walter E. Conway, Jr., and Klaus F. Schmidt, *What Every Young Account Executive Should Know About Print Production* (New York: American Association of Advertising Agencies, 1978), p. 20.

5. Conway and Schmidt, *Print Production,* p. 5.

6. Ibid., p. 20.

7. Chapter 7 will explain more about layout changes in the IFSOS section.

8. Suggested by a Prentice-Hall referee; see also Conway and Schmidt, *Print Production,* pp. 13–20.

Microcomputer software for scheduling using IBM personal computers was advertised in *Business Week* (September 17, 1984), p. k.

9. Bert Holtje, *How to Be Your Own Advertising Agency* (New York: McGraw-Hill, 1981).

10. Herb Zeltner, "Client Agency Conflicts," *Advertising Age,* 55 (March 5, 1984), pp. M64–M68; Zeltner, "Sounding Board: Clients, Admen Split on Compensation," *Advertising Age,* 52 (May 18, 1981), pp. 63–76.

11. Joseph D. Brown, "Satisfaction: Easy to Promise, Hard to Deliver," *Advertising Age,* 54 (April 4, 1983), pp. M48, M50; William E. Whitney, Jr., "15 Ways to Use Your Ad Agency More Productively," *Marketing News* (March 18, 1983), pp. 10–11.

12. See *Advertising Age,* annual issue featuring advertising agencies; also, *The Agency Book,* 540 Madison Ave., New York, NY 10022, published by the publishers of *Business Week.*

13. The preceding three paragraphs are based on an interview with Earl and Rachael Killeen of the Little Apple Studio, Clinton, CT, on July 24, 1984.

14. Jabberwocky ad designed by the Little Apple Studio, Clinton, CT, Earl and Rachael Killeen, owners.

APPENDIX 6

PRINTING WITH LETTERPRESS, OFFSET, GRAVURE, COLOR

There are three major methods of printing: letterpress, offset lithography, and gravure or rotogravure. Each method can include color. Marketing and advertising managers must evaluate in detail each task involving printing with respect to the comparative pricing of all elements and the desired quality of the advertising.

Letterpress

Letterpress printing can still be accomplished in the old-fashioned flatbed manner as well as on rotary presses. The old flatbed method was used by Gutenberg and Benjamin Franklin. The flatbed method involves setting metal type and woodblock or other illustrations in a flat frame form. The raised surface is inked, a sheet of paper is placed over the surface, and a roller impresses the raised ink images and type on the paper. Today, most letterpress printing is done on rotary presses. A curved metal plate is placed around the roller which is automatically inked as it revolves.

Offset Lithography

In offset lithography, the image, configuration type, and illustration to be printed are rendered on a thin, flat, zinc or aluminum sheet which is treated to retain ink in desired areas and to repel ink in other areas. Offset printing is also sometimes described as planographic printing by indirect image transfer from photomechanical plates, and is sometimes called *photo offset*. When paper mats are used instead of metal, the process is called *multilith* or mimeograph.

Gravure or Rotogravure

Gravure or rotogravure printing is a total reproduction process using photomechanically etched plates or cylinders. Intaglio printing means that an image is incised below the surface of such plates. Gravure is best used for large production runs such as mail-order catalogs and Sunday newspaper supplements because its initial cost of preparation is high. The lower setup costs of letterpress and offset lend themselves to shorter runs.

Color

Color can be achieved in letterpress, offset, or gravure at varying additional costs. Multicolor ads are more costly than two-color ads. The four-color process achieves the entire spectrum of colors using only four colors as input: black and the primary colors of red, yellow, and blue. For example, green is made from tiny yellow and blue dots. More yellow dots than blue dots makes yellow-green.

Color separations are achieved by photographing full-color artwork through filters which separate the primary colors. Printing plates are made from the photo films and inked in the four process colors. Some four-color proofs do not have the depth and brilliance of transparencies on film because they are on paper and are not backlighted.[1]

[1] Conway and Schmidt, *Print Production*, pp. 6, 20. See color plates in Kenneth E. Runyon, *Advertising*, 2nd ed. (Columbus: Chas. E. Merrill, 1984), pp. 390–391.

7
ADVERTISING IN NEWSPAPERS, MAGAZINES, AND OUTDOORS

INTRODUCTION

Newspaper advertising is a very important medium for both retailers and manufacturers. When available, manufacturers' cooperative funds can help retailers advertise brand-name products. In some cases, retailers and newspapers have a symbiotic relationship, depending on each other for their existence. Advertisements create interest in and large revenues for newspapers, magazines, and outdoor media. These media create traffic for stores, and sales of the advertisers' products.

We discussed the structure of the advertising department, the duties of its personnel, and the mechanics of print advertising in Chapter 6. Newspaper, magazine, and outdoor advertising are essentially print advertising with several characteristics in common. Because of the importance of print advertising, we will now focus on some of the greatest print advertisers' discoveries, and on the best ways to use this medium.

Manufacturers of brand-name merchandise have used magazines and outdoor advertising for some time. Although less important to retailers than is newspaper advertising, magazine and outdoor advertising are now being used more often by retailers than in the past. Direct-response print advertising, including catalogs, will be covered in Chapter 8.

ATTRIBUTES OF GOOD PRINT ADVERTISING

Most advertising that has produced good results has had the following attributes:

1. Consistent presentation of company image
2. Interesting and informative headline (the *title*) and body copy (the remaining print in the ad)
3. Attractive art and/or photography
4. Easy-to-read layout

When all of these elements are excellent, and the products presented are of good quality, desirable, and competitively priced, advertising usually helps meet company goals.

While most advertising sells a specific merchandise or service, often the cumulative total effect of these ads is to promote an institutional message—a total image of the firm and its various products or services. Print ads can build an image of prestige, good value, great bargains, the most up-to-date fashions, or some other special identity.[1]

Some years ago, Ohrbach's in New York City ran a series of institutional ads promoting the store rather than the merchandise it sold. Although these ads had attention-getting photographs, it was the headlines that created the greatest impact. An example: "I Found Out about Joan," is shown in Exhibit 7-1. The body copy supports the "catty" headline and illustration. It presumes that everyone likes a bargain but some won't admit it.

Once an advertiser develops consistently exciting art, copy, and themes in advertising week after week, customers become familiar with that firm's personality. When art and copy are so distinctive that one can identify the firm merely by glancing at an ad before reading it, the firm has become a good communicator. Customers can find the firm's ad and get its message with minimum time and effort.

Illustrating this consistent art and copy is the ad in Exhibit 7-2, a full-page Altman's merchandise ad in *The New York Times*. The slanted headline communicates that the merchandise, of which one example is shown, has elegant simplicity. The headline repeats the slant of the main zipper in the illustration. The newspaper medium is ideal for the timely message in the body copy: "See the whole, just-unpacked collection tomorrow."

This message is a joint effort of the advertising department—copywriters, artists, production—and those involved in merchandising decisions. Their decisions result in the words, headlines, body copy, and art that will best motivate customers to buy the merchandise. The copy must be in keeping with the image of the advertiser for which it is written. A dignified firm should have dignified copy. Copy of any sort can have humor, but it should still represent the character of the advertiser.

***EXHIBIT 7-1* Institutional Ad with Creative Headline**
Source: L. Rubin, *The World of Fashion* (New York: Harper & Row, Pub., 1976).

Five Important Guidelines for Advertising Copy[2]

Advertising copy should perform the following five functions: involve readers' self-interest; use a new or news approach; be straightforward; be positive; and suggest the easiest way to get what is advertised. Because excellent copy should be based on facts and research, there is room for imagination only after the headline and body copy have given all essential

EXHIBIT 7-2 Newspaper Merchandise Ad with Sketched Illustration

Source: B. Altman's, N.Y. Appeared in *The New York Times* (February 5, 1984), p. 11. Size of original, entire newspaper page.

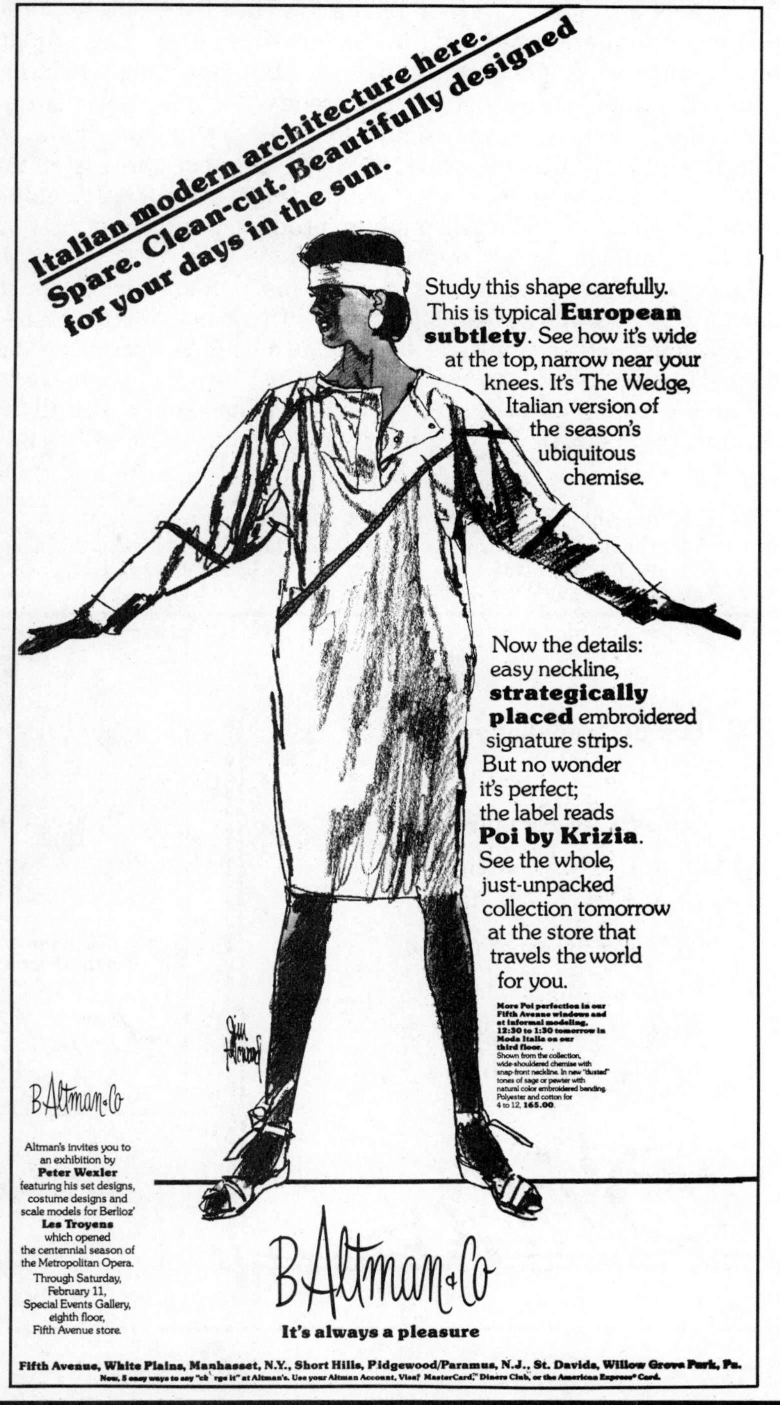

information. From the marketing viewpoint, the ability to use imagination to "romance" a product, service, or the firm itself is quite important, as this sets the *climate* for the entire advertising effort. The climate can become a major marketing force on its own. If, for example, Bloomingdales can convince the public that it is a "trendy, fashion-right" store, then its day-to-day trendy, fashion-right advertising will have more weight and impact. In the following ads, the copy enhances and is enchanced by appropriate illustrations. These examples enlarge on the five guidelines. They represent a variety of firms and products, and their use may be varied for a number of different businesses.

First, an ad should always involve the *readers' self-interest*. The ads in Exhibit 7-3 speak to this. The ad in Exhibit 7-3a asks *questions* about consumer satisfaction with the merchandise: "Is everybody happy?" (with size, color, etc.). If not, the retailer invites customers to make returns or exchanges before a deadline date. No art is needed in this ad. The ad communicates concern for customer welfare and a reminder about the

EXHIBIT 7-3 **Ads that Involve Readers' Self-Interest**

Source: a. Albert Steiger Inc., Springfield, MA, and *The Morning Union*, Springfield, MA (December 26, 1979), p. 6. Size of original, $4\frac{1}{2} \times 4\frac{1}{2}''$. b. *The Christian Science Monitor* (December 11, 1981), p. B9. Size of original, $1\frac{3}{4} \times 3\frac{1}{8}''$.

Is everybody happy?

If the choice wasn't wise,
Or if you goofed on the size,
Or the color was too bright,
We'll be glad to make it right.
Bring back the boo-boos...
please, before JANUARY 5th...
for an exchange or return.

a.

You'll be warm and cozy in new winter boots.

250 Main Street

b.

store's return and exchange services. The very small ad in Exhibit 7-3b makes a *personal appeal*: "You'll be warm and cosy in new winter boots." The kitten in the boot illustrates "warm and cosy."

Unusual headlines attract attention. "Is everybody happy?" in Exhibit 7-3 reminded people to return merchandise. The copy in Exhibit 7-3 communicates *immediacy* by suggesting a deadline for merchandise returns.

Second, an ad should use *new or news approach* whenever possible. The ad in Exhibit 7-4 offers *newness*, an important aspect of most products. People want to look good; hence "The New Good Looks . . . " has a strong appeal. The modernistic illustration further emphasizes "new."

EXHIBIT 7-4 **The New/News Approach to Headlines**

Source: Henri Bendel, Bob Hiemstra, photographer. Appeared in *The New York Times* (February 5, 1984), p. 2. Size of original, 4¼ × 7″.

Announcing a dramatic new product also attracts attention. The headline in Exhibit 7-5 is a designer's name, with the body copy announcing the "sophisticated, elegant, dramatic" product. The model's arm, another diagonal (see also Exhibit 7-2) points to the headline. Diagonals are active and dynamic, compared to the more static horizontals. The large vertical columns in the ad communicate the elegance and splendor mentioned in the copy.

EXHIBIT 7-5 **Vendor Name in Headline; Photography in Illustration; Body Copy Explains Product**

Source: Saks Fifth Avenue. Appeared in *Vogue* (February, 1984), p. 24. Size of original, 8½ × 11".

Bill Blass

The sophistication, the elegance—the splendour!—is pure Bill Blass. His inspiration...the very drama of the seas! For there, he has stolen the design-intricacy of coral for sequined black and white beading swirling from shoulder to waist. And too, captured its graceful curves and arcs for the sweep of a great fishtail hem. As photographed amidst the brilliant luxuries of New York's Parker Meridien, truly this is a gown born of nature and the natural genius of Blass. In black silk crepe. In American Designers Collections.

Saks Fifth Avenue

Third, an ad should use a *straightforward* approach, as in Exhibit 7-6. The copy in that ad explains what is on sale and the sizes, colors, and prices. The art also makes suggestions. Customers like to know what an ad is getting at without having to spend time and effort trying to figure it out. The new store ad is *informative* and gives customers specific information about special sale merchandise.

A *price appeal* is an old and basic straightforward approach which should be used for sales and off-price advertising. "Sale" is the first word in the headline of a blanket ad in Exhibit 7-7. Because current *sale* and *free offer* newspaper ads and inserts from discount stores, mass merchandisers, and supermarkets are readily available, they are not included as exhibits.

Testimonials, also straightforward ads, tend to be used by manufacturers. When using a celebrity in a testimonial, it is important to make

EXHIBIT 7-6 **The Straightforward Approach**
Source: The Door Store. Appeared in *The New York Times* (February 16, 1984), p. 26. Size of original, 4½ × 5¼″.

EXHIBIT 7-7 Headline and Art from Creative Sale Ad
Source: Bloomingdale's, N.Y. Size of original, entire newspaper page.

sure that the advertiser is remembered from the ad and not only the celebrity.[3] Actress Lauren Bacall has done effective ads for the Fortunoff's store.

Fourth, *be positive.* A positive approach includes a money-back *guarantee* to show that the retailer has confidence in the merchandise. Avoid neutral or negative copy. Many experts are against the negative approach even though it may be attention-getting. It gets the wrong kind of attention.

Last, suggest the best, *quickest* and *easiest* way for the reader to get what is advertised. New stores or shopping centers might advertise quick and easy transportation routes for mass transit or car, and also advertise quick and easy parking. Sometimes, the easiest way to get what is advertised is by mail or phone order. These are covered in Chapter 8.

Headlines

A headline serves as the "title" in a print ad in Exhibit 7-8. Examples of good headlines are reviewed here. An example of a creative headline in a merchandise ad is: "6 Pak of Light Bear," in Exhibit 7-9. This stuffed-toy-bear ad won a NoRMA award for Brandeis of Omaha, NE, in the $50-100 million category.[4]

Several different approaches for *headlines* are illustrated in the exhibits in this chapter:

1. *Descriptive:* naming the product, "Toys by Roy" (7-11a)
2. *Informative:* "6 Pak of Light Bear" (7-9)
3. *Audience selective:* "Italian Modern Architecture Here" (7-2)
4. *Interest arousing:* "Most of Our Customers Have Top Jobs" (7-11b)
5. *Label or brand:* Bill Blass, designer (7-5)
6. *Command:* "Count Sheep" (7-7)
7. *Slogan:* "Von's Is Going to $ave You" (7-10)
8. *Direct promise:* "You'll Be Warm . . . " (7-3b)

These approaches are not mutually exclusive. They can be combined, particularly if a subcaption is used. The most important aspect of writing both headline and body copy is to keep clearly in mind the consumer target for a particular ad.

Skillful copywriters are also aware that the language used largely defines the target audience. Notice how the following variations on the same theme affect the basic concept:

> *"Hey Cats—Catch this disco dress!"*
> *"With this dress, you can dance all night."*
> *"A Great Dress that can also go Dancing."*
> *"If dancing is your thing; this is your dress!"*

Over the years some of the greatest copywriters have suggested basic approaches that they believe helped sell millions of products. Rosser Reeves suggested the Unique Selling Proposition (USP) to differentiate a product from similar competing products. The USP involves researching a product or service to discover *the most powerful benefit* from all the

EXHIBIT 7-8 A Timely Ad That Makes Suggestions.

Source: Used with permission of Eugene Bachand, owner, Floor Trends, Amherst, MA. This ad ran in the September 11, 1985, *Amherst* (MA) *Bulletin*, p. 5. Size of original, $3\frac{1}{2} \times 8\frac{1}{2}$''.

EXHIBIT 7-9 Merchandise Ad with Creative Headline

Source: Newspaper Advertising Bureau. The Brandeis store is in Omaha, NE.

possible benefits that might be advertised. Giving logical reasons to buy a product is the most powerful and successful basic idea in copywriting.[5]

Body Copy

Headlines, and some body copy that substitutes for headlines, do the work of attracting attention and arousing interest in store or merchandise. The rest of the body copy or *text* has the task of telling the story and providing details about the product or service in a manner that satisfies the reader and answers all the reader's questions. Let us examine some

EXHIBIT 7-10 Example of Slogan in Headline

Source: This ad has been used in several 1984 issues of *The Christian Science Monitor* newspaper. Von's is a California supermarket chain. Size of original, 5¼ × 2¾″.

of the major approaches to body copy, some of which follow up the themes in our discussion of headlines.

Some of the best *factual copy* is found in major mail-order catalogs. This copy must describe accurately and in detail the merchandise pictured. An example is shown in Exhibit 7-12. There must be no questions left unanswered about construction, colors, sizes, and functions of merchandise. Some copywriters keep handy a Sears catalog or similar books for reference. Direct-response advertisers know which ads sell and which don't, because customer orders provide this feedback.[6]

A story about how a product is created, or *romance* as it is sometimes called, can attract buyers. The ad in Exhibit 7-5 has romantic copy. This story idea is a type of news story.

An *imaginative approach* to copy was shown in Exhibit 7-2. Following a headline which compares a dress to modern architecture, the copy continues to make this analogy. Sometimes, suggesting a role the customer could play with the merchandise helps sell better than merely describing the product. For example, copy in a toy ad stated "Be a French Foreign Legionnaire," instead of "sturdy black plastic gun".[7]

Reason-why copy contains facts and evidence for why the consumer should buy the product and the benefits to be gained. The copy in Exhibit 7-12 states that customers buying the book pack will be able to carry several items and also will be visible while walking in the dark. This is straightforward copy.

Superlatives should be used only where justified. This may seem to contradict the positive approach suggested above, but is really part of

EXHIBIT 7-11 Two Different Approaches to Headlines in Newspaper Ads

Source: a. *The Christian Science Monitor* (January 17, 1984), size of original, 1¾ × 3⅛", p. 11; b. Ibid. (June 7, 1984), size of original, 1¾ × 7⅝", p. 26. Note: a. also appeared in June 19, 1984, p. 10; and in January 3, 1984, p. 36, and July 3, 1984, p. 28, for Wichita, KA. In the last case, the copy was next to the art, instead of below the art. Toys by Roy is located in Amarillo, TX. The Andover Shop is in San Marino, CA.

a.

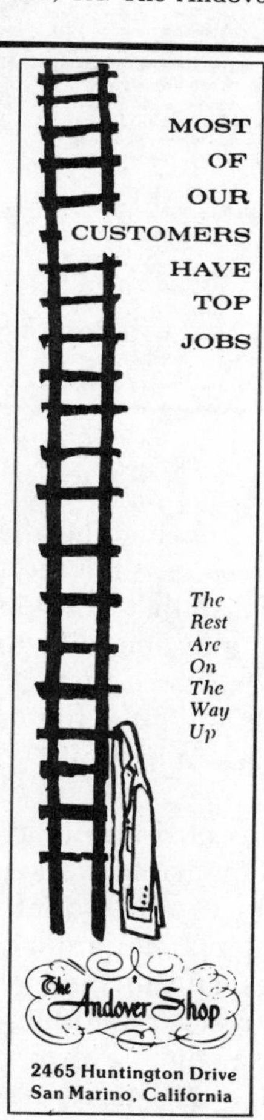

b.

EXHIBIT 7-12 **Bookpack Descriptions from a Direct-Mail Ad**
Source: L.L. Bean Catalog, Christmas 1984; 3M®. Size of original, 4 × 8".

Bean's Book Packs

Day packs designed to carry books and other campus gear as well as camera gear and clothes. Manufactured from tough 8 oz. coated nylon pack cloth. Adjustable padded shoulder straps. Self-repairing nylon coil zippers.

Easily holds ring binder and several oversized books. External zippered pockets that hold smaller items such as pens, calculator, note pad. 3M® reflective strip provides extra margin of safety while walking or cycling on dark nights. Carry handle on top.

Book Pack. Sized for adults and has two handy storage pouches inside; the smaller has a zippered closure for pens or pencils, the larger holds folders and papers. Waist strap with ¾" Fastex® side-release buckle. Measures 16" high x 11" wide x 5" deep. Wt. 13 oz.

Five colors: Plum. Navy. Gray. Royal Blue. Teal.

5127K Bean's Book Pack, ppd.

L. L. Bean, Inc. Freeport, Me. 04033

this approach. When making the product the hero, it is not necessary that a product be *better* than the competitors'; but it should be perceived as positively *good,* so that a customer who is uncertain about a competitive product will buy the one with the "good" image.[8]

Humorous and clever copy is difficult to write; only expert copywriters should attempt it. Included in this type of copy is the "insider" approach for the knowing, as in Exhibit 7-1. See also the humorous copy in Exhibit 7-9.

A new and controversial kind of copy is the *advertorial.* Advertorials appear in a newspaper or magazine advertising section that is organized around a theme. An advertorial is shown in Exhibit 7-13. Advertorials look like news items, but are labeled "advertising." Their acceptability, sales for retailers, and income for media vehicles depend on whether or not consumers treat advertorials as credible.[9]

Regardless of the cleverness of the art and copy in a single advertisement, the advertiser loses in the long run unless the ads are generally consistent over time. While creative personnel may not consider consistency glamorous, consistent advertising builds the long-term values of a good image and repeat purchasing. The right set of words can create unique and memorable feelings and also communicate rational reasons for making a purchase. *Consistency* extends beyond the advertising copy and must include packaging, displays, media, product, and company image.[10] All of these elements must be mutually consistent.

EXHIBIT 7-13 **An Advertorial for a Shopping Center**

Source: *The Christian Science Monitor* (July 16, 1984), p. 22.

Mall offers a trip back through time

Memory Lanes Antique Mall in Harbor City, Calif., is much more than antiques. It is a nostalgic and memorable experience for the whole family. Since its opening in 1978, Memory Lanes Antique Mall has been growing in reputation as a favorite shopping center for thousands of visitors.

Because of the more than 154 different dealers, merchandise is constantly being replenished as it sells. The variety also changes as new dealers move into the mall and others bring in bargains they have discovered at auctions, sales, and on buying trips out of state.

Advertiser **profile**

For this reason, each trip to the mall is a whole new experience, and many customers return often to keep up with the kaleidoscope of merchandise. Memory Lanes Antique Mall lends itself to leisurely, yet convenient, shopping. This Harbor City shopping center is billed as the largest mall of its type.

Memory Lanes is stocked with collectibles from nearly all eras. The merchandise of 154 dealers is attractively displayed in small shops separated by "streets" with names that evoke a time when life was slower and quieter. You may stroll down Sunset Strip on Route 66 to find Hollywood memorabilia dating from 1932, or you can land on Boardwalk and Park Place to find Carnival, Depression, and hand-blown glassware. You may even wind up on Easy Street.

Along the lanes, dealers display everything from museum-quality antiques to small items suitable for any décor. In addition, there are many fine pieces of antique furniture and accessories.

Strollers, as well as an enclosed play area, are available for the little folks. There is also a section in which older children may play games or read. There's even a snack area and television lounge. The mall provides wheelchairs which, along with the entrance ramp, make the center a convenient outing for those in need of help in getting around.

If it's the unique you seek, visit Memory Lanes Antique Mall, located at 24251 Frampton Avenue in Harbor City, one-half mile west of the Harbor Freeway.

Regular store hours are from 10 a.m. to 6 p.m. Monday through Saturday, and noon to 8 p.m. on Sunday.

(Please see related ad on this page.)

Advertisement

NEWSPAPER ADVERTISING

Characteristics of Newspaper Advertising

Newspaper advertising plays a key role in marketing communications for most retailers and, indirectly, for the manufacturers who sell their products through stores. Supermarket ads feature manufacturers' brands of grocery products and related items. Department stores give much advertising space and attention to apparel. Approximately 90% to 95% of all stores that advertise spend from 60% to 85% of their advertising budget on newspaper advertising.[11] Most newspaper advertising consists of daily black-and-white ads which attract traffic to stores and inform customers about the special daily offerings in various merchandise categories. The advertised merchandise must present a representative picture of the marketer's wares.

Stores, unlike manufacturers, need to include location, business hours and phone numbers so that customers will know where and when to buy the advertised merchandise. Recently, manufacturers have included a toll-free telephone number to get feedback from concerned customers. The daily presence of a firm's ad in a familiar location in the newspaper reassures customers that the firm exists. If the ad is missing, customers who expect to see it tend to wonder what happened—did the firm go out of business?

"IFSOS"—Improving Newspaper Advertising

Good advertising creative people are constantly updating and improving advertising methods. Some tried and true techniques may have become a little too familiar to consumers who expect change. In recent years a number of attempts have been made to help retailers improve newspaper advertising. Unlike magazine and outdoor advertising, newspaper advertising sometimes includes many items of merchandise in a single ad. Creative organization puts the various elements of an ad together to form the best possible total picture.

The Newspaper Advertising Bureau (NAB) has created the IFSOS method to improve retailers' newspaper advertising. IFSOS is an acronym for a five-point checklist: identify, focus, simplify, organize, and sell. The purpose of IFSOS is to move more traffic into stores, to move more merchandise out, and to increase customer loyalty. The IFSOS method suggests improvements that give daily ads a fresh, contemporary look, provide a change of pace, and motivate both store personnel and customers. Of course, increased product sales benefit the manufacturers as well.

Identify means to bring the store's identity to the attention of the store's target customer. *Focus* means to choose an ad's dominant element to make readers focus on the ad. *Simplify* means to define the purpose or each ad; then omit everything that is not essential. *Organize* means o make retail multiple-item advertising a "pre-shopping service" to help usy customers make the best use of their time. *Sell* is the object of all dvertising, but "sale" messages are more urgent than others. A sale nessage implies a price reduction which is usually limited to a specific ime period.

Top retail advertising professionals from the U.S. and Canada formed ive task forces, each concentrating on one element of the IFSOS formula. Their task was to demonstrate how to use the five points to improve tore advertising. They worked with a series of ads for "Baxter's," a ypothetical retail conglomerate with all kinds of stores under its umbrella. The experts had free rein to update and improve some actual newspaper ds with one stipulation: they had to include in their remake every item of merchandise shown in the original.

Identify Advertising must communicate a firm's identity to its cus-omers. The ad in Exhibit 7-14a has disconnected items of merchandise out no advertiser identity. The revised ad in Exhibit 7-14b puts the nerchandise together on a person who resembles Baxter's target customer.

Focus Focus uses a dominant, visually striking element to force eaders to take notice. The "before" ad in Exhibit 7-15a gives equal weight o all its elements, and the background of the photographs obscures the nerchandise. It is not clear what the word "profiles" means because not ll of the merchandise is in profile.

The "after" version in Exhibit 7-15b focuses on one important item, shoe. The background is white space which sets off the shoe. The rofile of the shoe ties in with the word "profiles" in the headline. Art nd copy for the other merchandise are in a column on the left side of he ad. This stack of merchandise points to the store name, "Baxter's." The ad in Exhibit 7-15b has the same amount of merchandise as the ad n Exhibit 7-15a, but the ad in Exhibit 7-15b is easier to read because of ts focus.

Simplify One of the best ways to demonstrate why it is important o do something is to show the effects of *not* doing it. The ad in Exhibit 7-16a is very busy. Simplifying the ad, as in Exhibit 7-16b, can make it nore effective. The less readers are distracted by extraneous copy, the nore they can concentrate on the message of the ad. The purposes of his ad are to announce and create interest in a sale, to give time and lace, to list special offers, and to show many items of merchandise. The d in Exhibit 7-16a misses that goal by forcing readers to wade through nnecessary artwork, multiple typefaces, and confusing layout.

The ad in Exhibit 7-16b eliminates unnecessary artwork and copy. Now readers can see the news of the sale because it is nearer to the enter of the page and set off by white space. Brief copy which lists the

EXHIBIT 7-14 IFSOS Method for Evaluating and Improving Ads: I = Identify.
Source: Newspaper Advertising Bureau.

a. Before

b. After

types of merchandise on sale is located above the sale notice, "20% to 50% off." A large merchandise grouping puts together curtain, lampshade and bedspread. Below are other curtain types and slipcovers. Each block of the layout leads the eye into the next and ultimately to the store name. The store name was hidden in the top left margin of Exhibit 7-16a.

Organize Multiple-item advertising should be as easy to go through and as clearly defined as the aisles and departments in a store. This especially holds true when advertising essential items that customers must shop for but would prefer to buy as quickly as possible. In the ad for Baxter's 100-year anniversary sale in Exhibit 7-17a, related items are not together. This ad forces readers to hunt for related items. Many of them will turn the page rather than make the effort.

EXHIBIT 7-15 **IFSOS: F = Focus**

Source: Newspaper Advertising Bureau.

Before

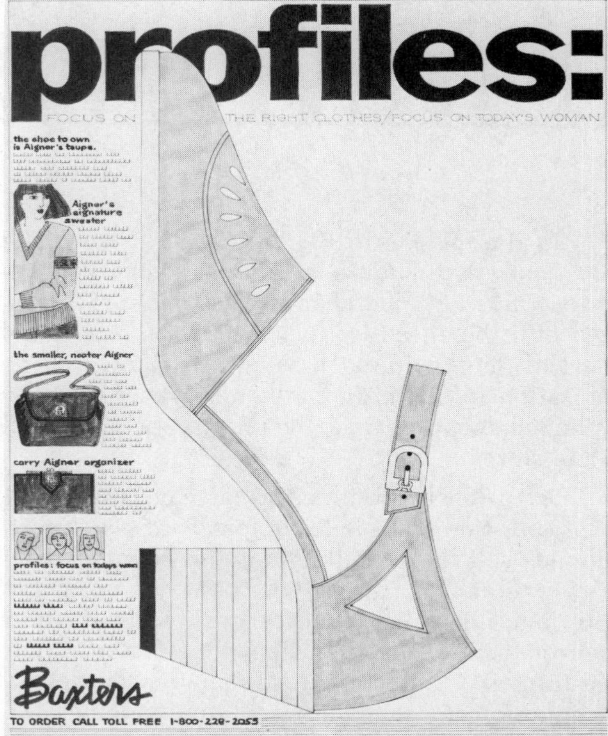

b. After

EXHIBIT 7-16 **IFSOS: S = Simplify**

Source: Newspaper Advertising Bureau.

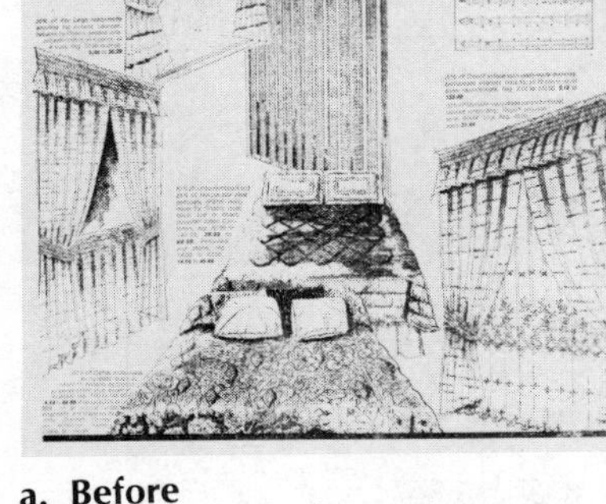

a. Before

b. After

In the remake in Exhibit 7-17b, the bold headline announces the sale. The art illustrations serve as subheads under which is copy that corresponds with merchandise categories. Shoppers can check off items, then pull the ad out of the paper for a shopping list. They can buy the checked items without having to backtrack for forgotten items. The organization in the ad helps the advertiser and customers make the most of limited shopping time, the prospect of which will help entice customers to the store.

Sell Sell is the fifth and last checkpoint of IFSOS. All advertising must sell. Some ads sell company image. Others sell product benefits. Sale ads sell the benefits of buying now to save money.

Exhibit 7-18a has a "before" version of the sale ad. It points out how much customers can save on each illustrated item. This restricts interest to the illustrated item. The "after" version in Exhibit 7-18b is less limited. This general treatment tends to generate more traffic because it communicates that additional items are on sale. The sale is not limited

EXHIBIT 7-17 IFSOS: O = Organize
Source: Newspaper Advertising Bureau.

. Before

b. After

o the illustrated items. Also, the ad presents some ambiguity about articular items on sale, which allows customers to read into the ad what hose items might be. The headline states the range of savings: "15% to 0%."

Ogilvy and IFSOS

FSOS is a coined word that reminds advertisers about the five key elements in an effective print ad. Ogilvy's hints for good advertising, isted here, complement IFSOS. Ogilvy points out that headlines below in illustration, as in Exhibits 7-1 and 7-11a, are read by 10% more people han headlines placed above. Likewise, more people read captions under llustrations than read body copy. Copy in all capital letters is difficult o read. Short lines of copy as in Exhibits 7-3b and 7-11b increase readership. Ogilvy suggests that two-page ads should be used only for a long product hat needs to be shown horizontally. Otherwise, the same money could buy twice as many ads, doubling a store's frequency of advertising.[12]

EXHIBIT 7-18 **IFSOS: S = Sell**
Source: Newspaper Advertising Bureau.

a. Before

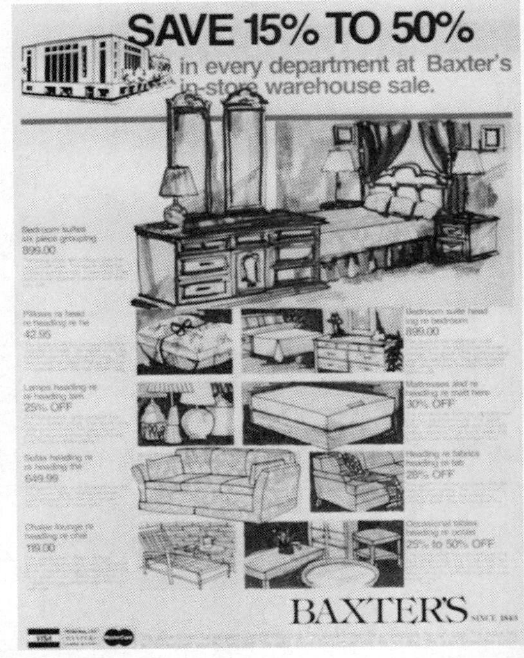

b. After

MAGAZINE AND OUTDOOR ADVERTISING

Magazines expand the advertiser's reach to a wider geographic area than do newspapers, while outdoor media concentrate on a relatively more local area than do newspapers (for example, billboards along a highway). In both cases, the exposure to advertising lasts longer than does the exposure in a daily newspaper. The special characteristics of magazines and outdoor print must be evaluated against an advertiser's needs when planning advertising for these areas.

Magazine Advertising

If a firm is national or regional, a relatively large part of its advertising budget can be spent on magazine advertising; otherwise, magazine advertising tends to cover a wastefully large area for a firm's purposes. National magazine advertising can be used to build an image, making the advertiser into a national institution.

Magazines are major print media for brand-name merchandise that is sold to and through stores. By building a national brand name and identity, manufacturers presell brands like Arrow and Manhattan shirts, Estee Lauder and Revlon cosmetics, and Crest and Colgate toothpaste to millions of consumers. This gives retailers a strong incentive to carry the advertised brands.

The development of local city magazines and local sections of other magazines makes magazine advertising more feasible for local advertisers.[13] The Sunday Magazine sections of many newspapers are good local magazines, usually including color as well as black-and-white advertising. Like newspapers and regular magazines, they are full of advertising in the big retail seasons like Christmas, and have relatively few ads in the slow seasons.

A magazine advertisment generally concentrates on one or two items of well-known, national brand-name merchandise as shown in Exhibit 7-5. Occasionally, suppliers to manufacturers, like the Wool Bureau or Cotton, Inc., sponsor national advertising through retail stores, promoting the brand-name fibers of leading manufacturers.[14] Most retail magazine ads feature apparel, accessories, and cosmetics and appear in Sunday Magazine sections of newspapers, large city magazines (*New York, The New Yorker, Chicago, Los Angeles*), national fashion magazines (*Vogue, Harper's Bazaar, Mademoiselle, Glamour, Seventeen*), or male-oriented magazines like *Gentlemen's Quarterly* and *Esquire*.

Manufacturers advertising on regional pages of magazines can list local stores in their various regions. For example, eastern stores will be listed in the eastern edition, and southern stores in the southern edition. These listings are called *credits;* they credit the store with carrying the merchandise pictured. This is a double selling tool: it helps the vendor sell merchandise to the stores, and helps the stores sell merchandise to the consumers who read the ad. Often, magazine advertisements are in color and are cooperatively financed with costs shared by the manufacturers, retailers, fiber, textile or car firms, and sometimes other firms.[15] The magazine ad in Exhibit 7-19 lists participating stores in the inside column of the left-hand page with the illustration on the right-hand page.

All the rules of good advertising and copywriting that apply to newspaper advertising also apply to magazine advertising. Magazine ads have a longer "life" than news ads because magazines are passed on to others, and left in waiting rooms of doctors, dentists, and other professionals. Therefore, their content should be less time-bound, such as image advertising rather than reduced-price advertising. The paper in magazines is of a quality designed to last longer than newsprint. This makes possible better art and color reproduction, which help to build image. Because magazine pages tend to be smaller than newspaper pages, there are fewer ads, and fewer items per ad, on a magazine page. Ads in exhibits 5-4, 5-5, 5-6, 7-5, and 7-19 are magazine ads.

EXHIBIT 7-19 Vendor Ad Mentioning Stores
Source: Vogue (October 1983), pp. 136–137. Size: 8½ × 11″.

Outdoor Advertising

Outdoor advertisers include hotels, resorts, cities, utilities, lotteries, zoos media vehicles, manufacturers, restaurants, banks, retail consumer services grocery stores, and some department stores. Because outdoor advertising is local, it tends to be a reasonable option for augmenting newspaper advertising. Outdoor advertising has a time duration more like a magazine than like a newspaper, because a billboard is rented for a longer period than a day or week. A sidewalk sign, bus shelter or subway station; a bus, train or subway car; a store's truck or suppliers' trucks also can carry ads or a distinctive logo for a longer period than a day or a week For a short period, advertisers can hire a small airplane to skywrite or to fly ads on a trailing canvas over targets at beaches or other crowded outdoor areas.

In large cities, billboards may be huge, lighted signs on the tops or sides of buildings. A store building and its windows might be lighted or floodlighted, thus making the store itself into an outdoor advertising medium. Its roof might include a large electrical or spotlighted sign advertising it or its wares. Times Square in New York City and similar squares elsewhere are known for their huge, colorful, flashing, blinking, or smoking signs which are newsworthy enough to be shown on television news programs.

A new technological development, fiber optics, allows advertisers to create changing colors in a billboard ad and to be more energy-efficient. Fiber optics ads cost more to produce and install than painted outdoor advertising.[16]

Where not prohibited by law, and when space can be rented, advertisers can use billboards located along roads and highways. Here, the challenge is to attract attention of high-speed traffic safely. The long, traditionally rectangular shape of billboards, the speed of cars and trucks in passing billboards, and the sign's distance from the reader dictate very simple art and minimal copy for billboards, as well as for ads on trucks. Exhibit 7-20 shows two examples of art and copy appropriate for billboards.

The Institute of Outdoor Advertising, in New York, reports large spending increases in outdoor advertising sales to beer and wine makers, car and gas dealers, hotels and restaurants, communications companies and radio stations, computers, banks, and footwear. Cooperatively funded advertising, which accounts for 12% of all outdoor revenues, is also growing. Fashion advertising, which sells image, and retail advertising that sells fashion are a good match for cooperative outdoor advertising near retail outlets. Helzberg Diamond Shops erected an outdoor video board in a midtown area of Kansas City where the traffic pattern was slow. Two-thirds of the board was painted for daytime; one third was white, on which a 30-second film featuring jewelry was shown from dusk until midnight. This film generated much media publicity and created an original image for Helzberg.[17]

Telephone booths offer a different shape for outdoor advertising. They tend to be tall and narrow instead of short and wide. They are even more local than roadside billboards, and can be targeted very specifically at pedestrians and commuters near the merchandise's point of sale. Burlington used telephone booth ads successfully to advertise apparel in the garment district of New York City.

Commuters spend about 30 minutes on a mass transit ride, making them a regular audience for transit ads. The Shelter Advertising Association in Minneapolis, a two-year-old trade group, reports that there are about 3500 shelters nationwide, most concentrated into 25 cities. Advertisers

EXHIBIT 7-20 Retail Billboards

Source: a. B. Flood, "Bottom Line is Creativity," *Advertising Age*, 52 (July 13, 1981), p. S19; b. A. Sobczynski, "A Lot More than just Twinkling Lights," *Advertising Age*, 54 (August 8, 1983), p. M22. Reprinted with permission from the July 1981 and August 1983 issues of *Advertising Age*. Copyright 1981 and 1983 by Crain Communications, Inc.

Wife preserver.

a.

"Harmony and a clever twist."

b.

in bus shelters include firms doing business in publishing and media, travel and entertainment, alcohol, tobacco, health and personal care products, and real estate, as well as restaurants and fast food stores, and financial institutions.[18]

In smaller markets, the outdoor companies offer customized, complete advertising services to local advertisers, such as banks, car dealers, retailers and restaurant owners. The relatively low cost of outdoor advertising makes it an appealing medium to local advertisers who have fewer media choices than do advertisers in large cities. Information about funds available for cooperative advertising can make outdoor advertising appealing to small local advertisers.[19]

Advertisers large enough to own trucks can benefit from technological advancements in using the free advertising space on their own vehicles. Screen-printed vinyl decals are less expensive than fiberglass signs, and take less time to apply to the trucks. In addition to advertising the company colors and logo, trucks can carry advertising messages and the firm's toll-free telephone number.[20]

Other outdoor advertising media include sidewalk signs outside a mall store telling of new merchandise or events; sandwich boards; and utdoor banners.

CLUTTER IN PRINT ADVERTISING

:lutter in newspapers, magazines, and billboards is related to the number f ads on a page, the number of pages in an issue, or the number of illboards or trucks in a given location. There is no legal restriction to dvertising in newspapers and magazines, but some legal restraints to utdoor billboard clutter have arisen in response to needs for highway afety. Environmental groups have also complained.

A magazine problem related to clutter is the position of the ad within ne magazine. Starch, a firm that measures magazine ad readership, claims nat position has no effect on readership, but not all advertisers agree. Aany are concerned about their ad's position with respect to the articles nd editorials that attract target customers, and their position relative to ompeting ads. By paying a higher rate, advertisers can request a particular osition, for example, "page 3." Then, customers can always know where o look for a firm's ad in each issue of the magazine. A new position in nagazine advertising is the bottom halves of two facing pages.[21]

While page clutter can also be a problem in newspaper advertising, newspaper tends to have fewer pages than a magazine. Also, large dvertisers, like Sears, Penney, and K mart, tend to use newspaper inserts vhich collect all of their ads into a "circular." That way a reader can hoose whether or not to read the Sears circular, for example. While this elps the clutter within the newspaper itself, there can still be clutter mong a large number of advertising inserts. Then the challenge is to et the customer to read a particular insert by giving the insert a special istinctive appearance.

Some newspaper pages contain a number of advertisements. Indi-idual advertisements on such pages must stand out from the clutter on page. This can be done by using contrasting white space or black areas, epending on the background of surrounding ads, and by using contrasting rt and graphics. If the ad is "run of paper (ROP)," the advertiser tends ot to know what competing ads will be on the page; then, the challenge s to stand out whatever the clutter! ROP means that the newspaper ecides where to place the ad. Examples of distinctive small newspaper ds are shown in Exhibits 7-3, 7-4, 7-6, 7-9, 7-10, and 7-11. Another ocation for part-page ads in newspapers is the outside borders of news ages, as in Exhibit 6-5.[22]

Outdoor billboards also contend with clutter of other billboards, nd of trees and buildings. The advertisement and the billboard must tand out from this clutter. Further, as in page locations of newspapers and magazines, the billboard must be located in a place where passersby will be thinking about buying products, possibly even travelling in the direction of stores.

SUMMARY

Print advertising is one of the most important marketing communications tools. It informs target customers about brands and stores that might satisfy their wants and needs. It conveys the characteristics of the advertiser's firm and products. It communicates an image that the customer might attain as a result of buying, giving, or using the advertised merchandise. Effective print advertising consistently communicates an advertiser's image and personality, through informative headlines and body copy, attractive illustrations, and easy-to-read layout. Copy should follow four guidelines: involve the reader's self-interest; use a new or news approach; be straightforward and positive; and suggest the easiest way to get what is advertised.

An important difference in product advertising as opposed to store advertising is that the manufacturer aims to build brand image and sell products from all stores that carry these products, while a retailer aims to get customers into a particular store on a day-to-day basis. In the past, manufacturers were more likely than retailers to advertise in magazines and outdoor media because these are more long-term, while retailers used newspaper ads for day-to-day advertising messages about changes in merchandise. Changes in technology, and growth of local magazines or magazine sections of newspapers enable retailers to use magazines and outdoor media more than they did in the past.

Print advertising can be improved by designing each ad to identify, focus, simplify, organize and sell. A newspaper page can hold more information and ads than can a smaller magazine page. The much larger outdoor media vehicles have simpler art and less copy than newspapers or magazines because they must attract people who are moving.

Print ads must appear in the right place to attract target customers. They must stand out from the clutter on a page, from the clutter of ad pages in a newspaper or magazine, or from the background clutter of outdoor advertising. Color, which reproduces differently in newsprint, magazines, and outdoor materials, can be used creatively to help ads stand out from clutter, and to deliver their messages. Color is discussed in Appendix 7 from the point of view of advertising management, and from the production point of view in the appendix to Chapter 6.

QUESTIONS

1. What are the major differences in newspaper, magazine, and outdoor media art and copy?

2. Why have retailers allocated a large part of their total advertising budget to newspaper advertising?
3. Select from the exhibits in this chapter or Chapter 6 an ad that illustrates at least two of the five important guidelines for retail advertising copy: arouse reader self-interest, use a new or news approach, be straightforward, be positive, and suggest an easy way to obtain the product. Explain how the ad illustrates these guidelines. Do not use the ads cited in the text as examples.
4. From an exhibit in this chapter, select an ad that has body copy. Explain why you think this body copy is effective or not effective. Include in your explanation the relationship of the copy to the illustration, if any.
5. Explain why you would or would not recommend the use of advertorials.
6. Use IFSOS to redo an ad from an exhibit in this chapter. Explain why you have made your revisions.
7. Pretend that Chapter 7 is a magazine and that the Exhibits are ads in this magazine; or pretend that Chapter 7 is a newspaper, and the smaller ads are on one page of this newspaper. Choose one ad that attracts your attention most. Explain why this ad stands out from the clutter in this "newspaper" or "magazine."
8. Describe the ideal location for a billboard for one of the ads in Exhibit 7-15. Explain why you have chosen this location.
9. From the exhibits in this chapter or Chapter 6, select an ad that you think would be more effective in color than in black-and-white. Explain why you think color would make this ad more effective. Ads in Exhibits 5-4, 5-5, 5-8, 6-4, 7-5 and 7-12 were in color.
10. Choose one of the outdoor media described in this chapter. Select a newspaper or magazine ad from this chapter and explain how it could or could not be changed into an outdoor ad for the outdoor medium you have chosen.

NOTES

1. Ed Zoti, "Reading Between the Lines of Corporate Ads," *Advertising Age*, 55 (January 24, 1983), pp. M9-M16, and other articles in this "Corporate Image" section.

2. Newspaper Advertising Bureau, 485 Lexington Avenue, New York, NY 10017.

See also current advertising texts from Crain, Dryden, Fairchild, NRMA, Prentice-Hall, Random House, and other publishers. Also, *Marketing Communications*, 8 (September, 1983), pp. 52–53, has a list of merchandising magazine support services for relevant magazines. Services include help with market research, in-store promotions, public relations, and designing ad campaigns.

3. D. Ogilvy, *Ogilvy on Advertising* (New York: Crown Publisher, Inc., 1983), p. 108.

4. Picture obtained from Newspaper Advertising Bureau. See article entitled "Best of Class," STORES, (January, 1984), p. 86. "NoRMA" is the nickname for National Retail Merchants Association.

See also the Bloomingdale's sale ad with the sheep, in Chapter 6.

5. "Ad Pioneer Reeves, 73, Dies; Proponent of Hard Sell, USP," *Advertising Age*, 55 (January 30, 1984), pp. 4, 85; Rosser Reeves, *Reality in Advertising* (New York: Knopf, 1961).

6. Ogilvy, *Ogilvy on Advertising,* p. 23. See the wok ad in Exhibit 5- and Exhibit 7-12 for factual copy.

7. Mike Cafferata, "Good Copy is Alive and Well," *Advertising Age,* 5 (May 3, 1984), p. M-10.

8. Ogilvy, *Ogilvy on Advertising.*

9. Stuart J. Elliott, "Advertorials, Straddling a Fine Line in Print," *Advertisin Age,* 55 (April 30, 1984), pp. 3, 36–37.

10. This information is from a speech by Robert E. Jacoby, chairma president, and chief executive officer of Ted Bates Worldwide, Inc., New Yor reported in "Advertisers Achieve Consistency, Longevity with Right Words, *Marketing News,* 18 (December 21, 1984), p. 3.

11. The Newspaper Advertising Bureau provided these statistics and als the information about IFSOS in the next section.

12. Ogilvy, *Ogilvy on Advertising,* pp. 19, 89, 91, 97. The IFSOS sectio is from the Newspaper Advertising Bureau.

13. See magazine ads in other chapters.

14. J. Neher, "Magalogs Latest Vehicle for Advertisers," *Advertising Age* 51 (November 3, 1980), p. 10; "Stores Try Publishing Their Own Magazines, *Business Week* (July 27, 1981), p. 34; Pat Sloan, "Wool Bureau Boosts Spending, *Advertising Age,* 55 (February 27, 1984), p. 37; and see Barney's ad in Chapte 5, Exhibit 5-6.

15. See cooperative advertising section in Chapter 15.

16. "Out-of-Home" Section 2 of *Advertising Age,* 52 (July 13, 1981), pp S1–S20; A. Sobczynski, "A Lot More than just Twinkling Lights," *Advertisin Age,* 54 (August 8, 1983), pp. M22–M23.

17. K. Hoffman, "Outdoor Boards Get Down to Business," *Advertisin Age,* 55 (December 20, 1984), pp. 16, 18; P. Thomas, "Boards' Future Look Larger than Life," *Advertising Age,* 55 (December 20, 1984), p. 11; L. Weisberg "Fashion Industry Finds Outdoor a Perfect Fit," *Advertising Age,* 55 (Decembe 20, 1984), p. 12.

18. B. Gloede, "Bus Shelter Ads Covering the Cities," *Advertising Age* 55 (December 20, 1984), pp. 25, 26; "Mass Transit Making Strides," *Advertisin Age,* 55 (December 20, 1984), p. 22; and L. Weisberg, "Fashion Industry," p. 12

19. L. Freeman, "Small Markets Have Big Potential," *Advertising Age,* 5 (December 20, 1984), pp. 26, 27.

20. "Trucks Keep Messages on the Move," *Advertising Age,* 55 (Decembe 20, 1984), pp. 20, 21.

21. S. Emmrich, "Magazines Pressed on Positioning of Ads," *Advertisin Age,* 52 (September 28, 1981), pp. 1, 92; Starch INRA Hooper, Inc., 566 Bostor Post Road, Mamaroneck, NY 10543.

The L'eggs ad in the February 1984 issue of *Vogue* is on the bottom half of two pages.

22. See the Altman's stack ad in Chapter 6, Exhibit 6-5, and other smal ads in other chapters.

APPENDIX 7

COLOR IN PRINT ADVERTISING

All the rules for headline writing, copy writing, layout, and production apply to color advertising. However, one need not use copy to describe colors and details which are obvious when shown in color. According to recent research, the eye follows a color line so that if one of the colors used in an ad is run in a tint block under an article on the facing page, the reader will be drawn from the article to the ad.[1]

The major concern in producing color advertisements, whether for newspaper, magazine, or billboard, is the quality and realism of the color art or photography to be used. With respect to color photography, a great deal of effort must be made to get photographs that will reproduce well. The lighting must be just right to assure that the end result will reproduce effectively. Also the processing must be done skillfully to assure proper reproduction on paper. These steps must be properly checked and color corrections made where necessary. Otherwise, color reproduction in the ad tends to mislead customers about the color of the actual merchandise.

When color art is used, the finished work is called *representational* art, meaning that it represents the merchandise but is not as exact as a photograph. This art is processed in a method similar to that of reproducing color photographs on paper. Newsprint can never quite achieve the same variety of art reproduction as process color achieves on the glossy stock used in magazines, but color advertising in newspapers is improving with new technological developments.

Ads in Sunday Magazine sections of newspapers are generally done by the rotogravure processes and come much closer to the fine reproduction that can be obtained by magazines.[2] Advertisers who use color advertising only rarely are advised to employ an advertising agency for color work.

When color advertisements in magazines are produced by the vendors with retailers' names merely listed in the ad, the retailer has fewer responsibilities for color. The retailer has only to make sure that the color and art accurately represent the merchandise and are consistent with store image—and that the store name is emphasized enough for the reader to find and read it.[3]

[1] "New Woman Scores Well with Synergism," *Magazine Age*, 4 (December, 1983), pp. 59–60.

[2] Gravure printing is economical only in quantity. Newspapers have sufficient quantity printing to justify gravure. The printing surface of the plate is below the non-printing part, and the ink is held in the wells thus made. For more information about types of printing, see Richard E. Stanley, *Promotion*, 2nd ed., (Englewood Cliffs, NJ: Prentice-Hall, 1982), pp. 194–202.

[3] See section on cooperative advertising in Chapter 15. For more on color, see Appendix 6.

8
DIRECT-RESPONSE ADVERTISING: MAIL AND OTHER

INTRODUCTION

Direct marketing is an interactive system of marketing which uses one or more advertising media to effect a measurable response and/or transaction at any location.[1] *Direct marketers* use *direct-response advertising* to contact their customers, especially those for whom face-to-face contact is too expensive. Direct-response advertising can involve mail and other media such as telephone, broadcasting, computers, and mail-order forms in newspapers and magazines singly or in combination. Direct-response advertising can be used by manufacturers, retailers, service businesses, and other distribution channels. Consumers can either buy directly from these advertisers, or go to a store to buy the advertised merchandise or similar merchandise.

DIRECT MARKETING AND DIRECT-RESPONSE ADVERTISING

Direct marketing is an *interactive* system of marketing which involves (1) building and maintaining a *data base* of customer and prospect names,

(2) using a vehicle, often a computer, to store purchase information, and (3) having a method of measuring the results of the advertising in terms of advertising costs versus sales. A data base includes names, addresses and other relevant information, i.e., credit status, past mailings and past purchases. An *information system* integrates the firm's customer information with the advertising and purchase information.[2] Information on past lists of customer prospects can be compared with current information about the prospects and with information about customers. One reason for comparing information is to remove duplicate entries. This avoids the embarrassment and nuisance of duplicate mailings.

Exhibit 8-1 shows how direct marketing and other marketing communications interact. Note that marketing research connects direct marketing with direct-response advertising media, which include direct mail, telephone, interactive television forms, network and cable television, radio, newspapers, magazines, outdoor car cards, matchbooks, bill inserts, and package inserts. Measurable responses and transactions include mail, phone, and personal visits.

In recent years, the development of new electronic technology has made data collection and retrieval, and hence direct marketing, more and more efficient in terms of targeting audiences. As a result, the total investment in direct-response advertising by mail and phone has been increasing measurably, increasing home ordering.[3] For many marketers, direct-response advertising is an important aspect of their total media mix of print and broadcast advertising and personal selling. For example, Sears' mail-order catalog produces billions of dollars in sales. Some specialty stores claim that one-third to one-half of their business is accounted for by mail and telephone orders.

Although the local newspaper has been generally the most important advertising medium for most retailers, direct-response mail advertising can be rated as the second most important, with radio and television advertising as third and fourth, respectively. Catalog marketers advertise their catalogs in magazines. Sometimes, retail stores grow out of successful mail-order businesses, and sometimes adding a mail-order division can provide a department store chain with at least as great a return on investment as opening a branch store.

DIRECT-RESPONSE MAIL ADVERTISING

Characteristics

Likely prospects for direct mail are people on mailing lists who have already purchased from previous mailings, and charge-account customers whose credit is established. Customers can be classified as renters or home owners, married or single, with or without children, males or

EXHIBIT 8-1 A Direct Marketing Flow Chart

Source: Direct Marketing Magazine, 224 Seventh St, Garden City, New York 11530, USA, reprinted from July 1984, vol. 47.

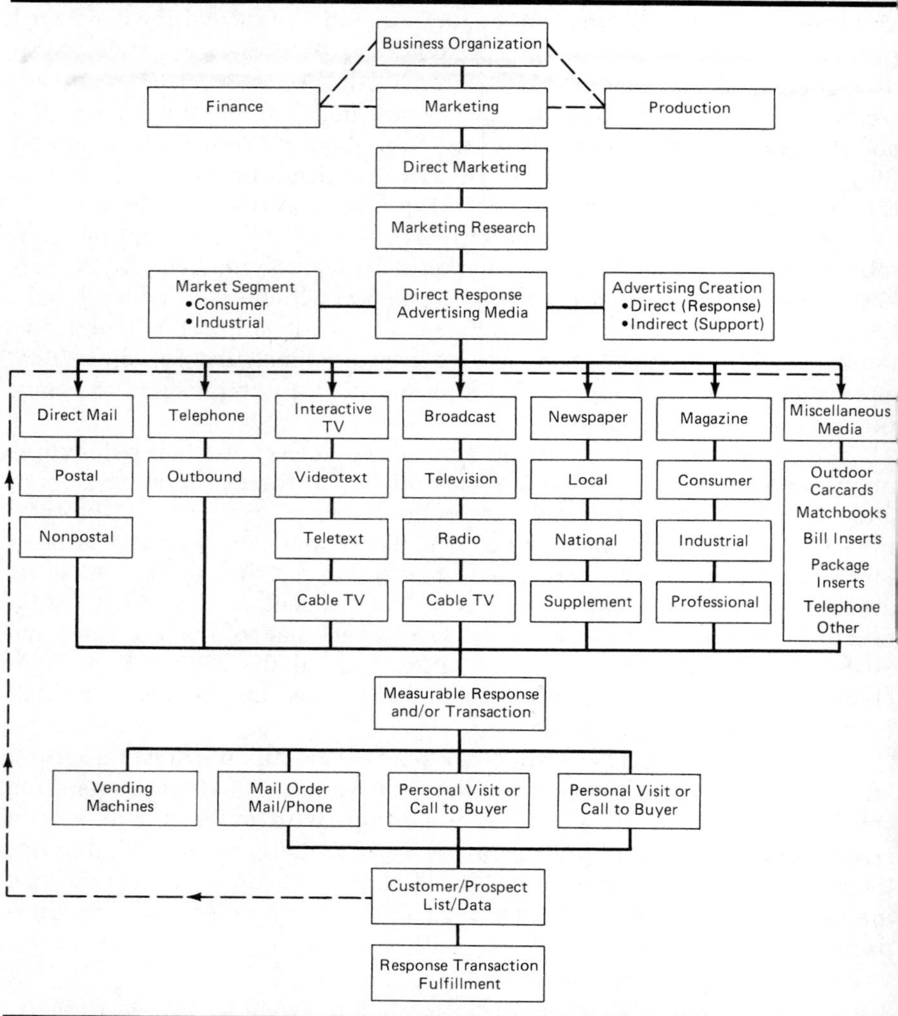

females, owning or not owning an automobile, etc. Coding customers in this way ensures that only those segments with an interest in specific merchandise categories are included in a mailing.

In general, retail mail order customers are likely to be educated, higher-income females aged 35–44. They will take the risk of buying merchandise without actually seeing it. People who live in the vicinity of a retail store and fit the description of the store's target consumers are likely prospective walk-in customers. However, those who fit the target description but live further away in the region or even elsewhere in the nation can become direct-mail customers. By sending direct-response mailings only to customers who fit the target description and meet certain other criteria, the retailer can control costs to improve return on advertising investment. The other criteria include recency, frequency, and dollar amount of purchases, what products were purchased, demographics, and merchandise return habits. Retailers might want to know whether a direct mailing generates a mail order, phone order, or a trip to a store. However, the salespersons may fail to collect this information, and the customers might not remember which communication inspired the purchase.[4] Response can vary from less than 0.5% to 6% or 7%. The lower responses are for random mailings. The higher percentages result from mailings to known audiences—charge customers, those who have responded to particular types of merchandise or product categories, regular mail-order customers, or selected target groups.

Direct mail has a "half-life," the point at which about half of the responses will arrive. This means that an advertiser can predict response within a few days for first-class mailings or a few weeks for third class. By sending all mailings on the same day and recording responses daily, the advertiser can find the half-life—when the response has peaked.[5] The mailing list can later be revised to exclude non-respondents and poor credit risks.

When a direct-mail piece arrives in a customer's mail, it often must compete for the customer's attention with all other clutter in that mail delivery. Whether the customer reads the piece or throws it away depends on its appearance, the mailer's image, loyalty, and other factors in the customer's environment at that time. Whether mail clutter is more or less than the clutter in print and broadcast advertising depends on many factors, including media vehicles and time of year. Exhibit 8-2 contains some ideas on how to help direct-mail advertising stand out from mail clutter. Clutter should not be a problem when the firm mails to customer types who, experience has shown, buy the merchandise.

Advantages and Disadvantages of Direct Mail

The main advantages of direct-response mail advertising are that it is *selective* and based on *market segmentation*, and that sales can be *measured* via coded responses. Early direct mail segmentation was by merchandise, with separate farm equipment and clothing catalogs from Sears and Montgomery Ward. In the 1970s, retailers segmented by lifestyle, selling the same sweater as a classic in a Brooks Brothers catalog and as contemporary in a Bloomingdale's catalog. In the 1980s, Spiegel tried to get the attention of the segment of working women with household incomes of $40,000 who wanted to shop at a "sexy convenience store in print." Spiegel and

EXHIBIT 8-2 10 IDEAS FOR PROFITABLE DIRECT MAIL

Source: Adapted from information provided by Direct Marketing Association. See also E. Mayer, Jr. "The Seven Cardinal Rules for Direct Mail Success" (New York: Direct Marketing Association, 1985).

1. *Build and Maintain your Mailing List*
   Nothing is more important than this. Your internal or customer lists are one of your *most valuable marketing resources.* Large firms can afford to buy additional or outside mailing lists with the help of expert brokers. Small or local firms can contact local and county government for local and Census data.
2. *Target your Mailings*
   Direct mail can be *selective.* Customers who bought most recently, most frequently, and spent the most money are the best targets. Where possible, match merchandise offerings with potential audience.
3. *Present your Best Offerings*
   The potential customer usually knows values. Use your best offerings and make your offer difficult to resist.
4. *Sell Benefits, not Features*
   The most profitable direct mail sells benefits rather than features. Tell your customers *why* they should buy the items presented. A great value is the best benefit. Promise your most important benefit in the headline or first paragraph.
5. *Write Believable Copy that Will Get a Response*
   Don't exaggerate. Good, plain, simple copy that accurately describes the merchandise is best. Tell readers exactly what they will get. Use proofs and endorsements to back up your statement. Ask for action.
6. *The Me-To-You Approach is Best*
   Direct mail is a *personal* medium. Take advantage of this relationship by relating to the *individual.*
7. *Where Possible, Use Personalization*
   What better way of telling a person he or she is important than by directing the mail to a person rather than "occupant."
8. *Design Direct Mail to be Opened and Read*
   Make certain the outside of the mailing is appealing either by its simplicity or its teasing copy. If your firm is well known, make certain to have your name on the outside.
9. *Develop the "Right" Mailings*
   Your mailing package should be clear, easy to read and understand, and well-implemented for response—a toll-free phone number, a postage-paid envelope or card.
10. *Test, Test, Test*
    Try out various techniques and approaches as well as products and prices. Find out what frequency of mailings, combinations of factors, products, offers, copy, lists, timing seem to work best. Where possible, try small-scale mailings before using entire lists.

---

others advertised their catalogs in fashion magazines. Each Spiegel advertisement comes with a tear-out, already addressed mail order form/envelope, and toll-free telephone number, for ordering the catalog.

The development of computers facilitated this segmentation to the point where a Catalogia store chain offered a computer service to help customers locate the right catalog for the merchandise they wanted.[6] Use of information from direct mail response is of use to find out where to open up stores.

The big advantage of direct mail is that there is *little or no wasted circulation*. In newspaper, radio, or television advertising, the advertiser pays to reach thousands of people who are not potential customers and never will be. For example, a newspaper ad by a children's specialty store will be delivered to thousands of people with no interest in this category.

Because of the many forms that direct-mail advertising may take, it is flexible in format and timing. It can be easily adapted to a specific audience, time of year, or category of merchandise. It can be used in split-run testing such that some prospects get one mailing and other prospects get a different one.

Direct mail is personal and private. Other firms do not necessarily know the reach and frequency of your firm's direct mailings. A mail piece may be more informative than a salesperson, and it can communicate in many languages. In addition, direct mail can be used to test copy approaches, pricing, and advertising cost per item and per order.[7]

Direct mail also has some disadvantages. The individual cost of a particular mailing may be high in comparison to other media. However, the type of mailing piece in large part determines its cost, and the marketer controls this factor. Also, vendor help is available to help retailers with direct-response advertising of brand-name products.

Mailing lists can have wasted circulation if not kept up to date as people move away, die, or get married. If desirable, advertisers can arrange to have undelivered mailings returned so that the list can be corrected. The claim that all advertising sent through the mail is "junk mail" is only true of mailings which have no relevance for the recipient. Store mailings generally go to customers who are usually interested in what a store with whom they trade has to offer.

Guidelines for Ethical Business Practices

These guidelines are offered by the Direct Marketing Association: Offers should be clear, honest, and complete. When an offer illustrates goods which are not included or cost extra, this should be clear. Claims regarding time and quantity limitations should be legitimate. Photographs and artwork should accurately portray the merchandise. When "free," "half-price" or "two-for-one" offers are made, the original price should not be increased or the product quantity or quality decreased. List owners who sell, exchange, or rent lists should inform individuals on the list and delete names on request. Phone soliciters should not tape conversations without consent.[8]

TYPES OF DIRECT-RESPONSE MAILINGS

Direct mail has a number of forms, according to the type of merchandise presented. These are the most important direct mail forms:

1. Catalogs and Booklets
2. Letters and Postal Cards
3. Statement Enclosures/Stuffers
4. Folder, Brochures, Broadsides
5. Loose-Leaf Mailers
6. Newspaper Tabloids and Supplements

Catalogs and Booklets

There is no exact definition of when direct-mail booklets leave off and catalogs begin. However, a catalog is usually defined as a rather large multi-page book of eight or more pages that provides the recipient with all the information necessary to purchase one or more of the items described often with illustrations and descriptions. The name comes from the Greek *katalogos*, "a list or register of items arranged in some kind of alphabetical or numerical order, or by classification with descriptions of each item." There are business-to-business catalogs, full-line consumer catalogs and specialty catalogs. Business-to-business catalogs can supplement salespeople for smaller customer-firms and for routine purchases of standardized items.[9] Full-line consumer catalogs such as Sears' have thousands of items in numerous merchandise classifications. Sears has partially replaced its unwieldy and expensive main catalog with separate catalogs: farm implements, automotive, paint and related items, and other catalogs for special targets. Bloomingdales and L.L. Bean mail specialty catalogs. The steps in preparing a large catalog are described in Chapter 5.

A *booklet* is a little book with a self or paper cover, with fewer pages and a more limited merchandise assortment than a catalog, perhaps several hundred or so items. A booklet cover is shown in Exhibit 8-3. This seasonal booklet, or small catalog, has an attractive painting on the cover to entice recipients to keep and use the catalog during the season depicted on the cover.

The rise of the two-earner household has increased incomes and decreased time available for shopping. This is one of many factors that have resulted in more shopping from catalogs, including the diminished quality of sales training, the smaller number of salespersons available to customers, the proliferation of bank credit cards, and the toll-free 800 phone number.[10]

Today's catalogs and booklets are used to build consumer awareness of the marketer in addition to selling merchandise. They usually are well organized to facilitate purchasing, with postage-paid self-addressed envelopes, order forms, and complete instructions for the use of the forms.

EXHIBIT 8-3 **Watercolor Fishing Scene on L.L. Bean Spring 1984 Catalog**
Source: L.L. Bean Catalog, Spring 1984. Size of original, 7⅝ × 8¾″.

The self-addressed envelope can also communicate much information, such as a toll-free telephone number; shopping hours and locations of branch stores, if any; information about how to pay for delivery, sales tax and C.O.D.; and even advertisements for services such as a bridal registry or gift certificates. L.L. Bean and Sears catalogs have detailed instructions for selecting sizes and taking measurements for clothing and footwear. Exhibit 8-4 contains a sample of these instructions.

Catalogs or booklets for merchandise purchased mostly by mail tend to have more information about a given item than do circulars inserted in Sunday newspapers for merchandise purchased mostly in stores. Exhibit

***EXHIBIT 8-4* Catalog Instruction for Selecting Sizes**

Source: L.L. Bean Catalog, Christmas 1984.

SIZE GUIDELINES

Chest

Measure just under the arms and across shoulder blades holding tape firm and level. Women measure at the fullest point of the bust and across shoulder blades holding tape firm and level.

Gloves and Mitts

Measurement in inches around the knuckles with hand flat. (Exclude thumb.) Number of inches equals glove size.

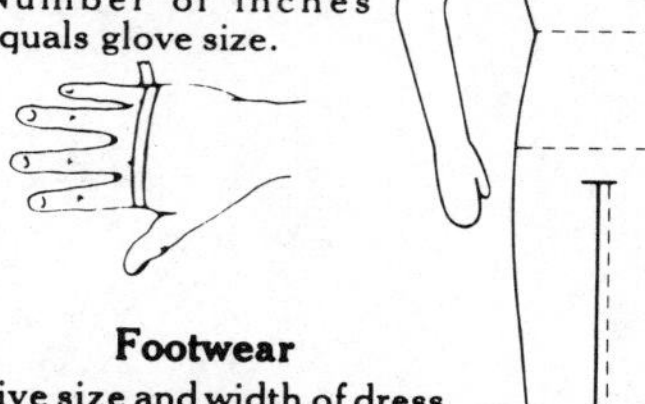

Footwear

Give size and width of dress shoe and/or enclose outline of bare foot. Hold pencil straight up when tracing foot. Also advise type of stockings you plan to wear (light, heavy, etc.)

Hat and Caps

Measurement in inches around the largest part of the head with tape above brow ridges. Convert to hat size using the chart below.

Shirts

Measurement in inches of a shirt collar that fits you well. Lay collar flat. Measure from center of collar button to far end of button hole.

Belts

Measurement in inches around the outside of the waistband of trousers that fit you well.

Inseam

Measure pants from the crotch seam to the bottom of the pants along inside pant leg seam.

Trousers, Slacks, Skirts

Measurement in inches over shirt around your waist, where you normally wear trousers or slacks. Hold tape firmly but not tight.

Hat Sizes: Unless otherwise stated the following conversions apply:

Head Measurement:	20½	20¾	21⅛	21½	21⅞	22¼	22⅝	23	23½
Hat Size:	6½	6⅝	6¾	6⅞	7	7⅛	7¼	7⅜	7½

Women's Shirts and Jackets:

Size:	Sm.	Med.	Lg.	XLg.
	6-8	10-12	14-16	18-20

Women's Skirts and Slacks (Actual Body Measurements)

Waist:	25	26	27	28	30	31	33	35
Size:	6	8	10	12	14	16	18	20

Stockings:

Shoe Size:	4-5½	6-8	8½-10	10½-11	11½-12½	13-14
Sock Size:	9(S)	10(M)	11(M)	12(L)	13(L)	14(XL)

100% Guarantee

All of our products are guaranteed to give 100% satisfaction in every way. Return anything purchased from us at any time if it proves otherwise. We will replace it, refund your purchase price or credit your credit card, as you wish. We do not want you to have anything from L.L. Bean that is not completely satisfactory.

7-12 has backpack descriptions from L.L. Bean. The Bean description includes weight, size in inches, and description of the number and types of books that will fit in the pack. A person shopping in a store would be able to see and touch the bookpack. Therefore, a store circular would require less description than the Bean's mail-order piece.

Generally, catalogs have at least a season's life. They are considered a basic reference until the stated expiration date, after which a new catalog is sent out. Formerly, retailers mailed two catalogs per year; recently, they have mailed a variety of specialized catalogs for various sales—white sales, china and crystal, back-to-school, Christmas, and others. There are so many catalogs that a direct-marketing management consulting company has developed a historical data base of 500 mail-order catalogs, including 35 business-to-business catalogs. The data base is indexed by 90 variables including merchandise, vendors, prices, and delivery terms. Firms wanting to begin catalogs, add more catalogs, or sell to catalog marketers can order reports from this data base.[11]

A new development is a *catazine* or *magalog* which has feature articles as magazines do, but promotes merchandise like advertisements do. Some store catalogs now carry manufacturers' ads. This is consistent with using direct-response advertising to build consumer awareness while at the same time selling merchandise. Another new development is to send catalogs into homes via television or home computers. Electronic in-store catalogs with video screens and computers for taking direct orders allow customers in stores to order items not in the store inventory. If this electronic catalog generates sufficient sales, it might be expanded into in-home electronic shopping.[12]

Creatively designed catalogs employ attractive art and graphics to lure customers. Occasionally they use unusual merchandise to attract publicity, and feature an adaptation of the airlines frequent-flier plans. Attractive art is shown in Exhibit 8-3 and in Exhibit 8-5, "Steiger's brass candlesticks and other treasures." A Jordan Marsh catalog has featured residents and llamas in Peru, with scenes of Peru on pages that also offered store merchandise. Neiman Marcus has offered ostrich pairs, camels, Chinese junks, and other extravagant merchandise to add to its luxury image and attract attention. Sakowitz has offered a flying recreational vehicle, a home ice rink, and a year of ghost-written weekly love letters. Filene's has offered a $10,000 gift certificate and a $10,000 charity donation on behalf of the person who accurately counted the number of times cats and other symbols appeared in their cat-a-log. A recent Filene's Christmas catalog offered the chance to participate in a drawing for a $10,000 gift certificate to customers who checked through the pages for clues to decode a secret message. Burdine's has used a 3-D catalog with enclosed viewing glasses for a back-to-school mailing. The Sharper Image catalog has offered $50 to $300 gift certificates for 750 to 2500 points accumulated in a one-

EXHIBIT 8-5 Photography and Layout for Inside Catalog Page
Source: Albert Steiger, Inc., Springfield, MA. Catalog, Christmas 1983. Size of original, 8½ × 11″.

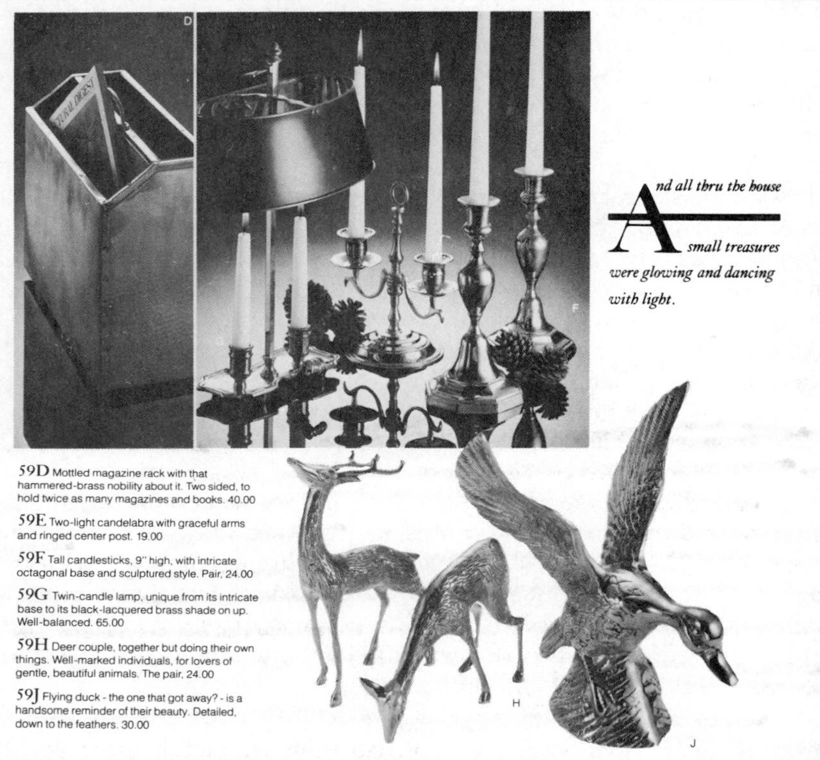

year period. As frequent fliers have accumulated points for air tickets, sharper customers get one point for each dollar spent (less refunds) toward merchandise purchases.[13]

Catalog mailing costs can be reduced by using bulk mailing privileges, and by pre-sorting and following certain postal regulations. The United States Postal Service has a variety of booklets explaining bulk mailing. Because postal regulations change periodically, the best current information source is the post office. Catalogs and other bulk-rate mailings often bear the following instruction below the mailing label: "Postmaster: If addressee has moved, please deliver to current resident." If not mailed, catalogs can be inserted in newspapers or handed out at stores.

Letters and Postal Cards

The letter was the first form of direct-mail advertising. It was probably used first by manufacturers and merchants to write to potential customers telling them about the new items available for sale.

The letter is still the most personal form of direct mail. Recently, manufacturers have been using letters to market products directly to other businesses and to consumers. Letters are usually used by retailers to invite customers to stores for special events or sales. Such letters are often sent to charge customers or other special groups to notify them of special sales events prior to a general public sale. The letter package consists of (1) the outer envelope, (2) the letter, and (3) a reply device for the customer to send back.

Well-written letters can be a powerful communications instrument. They may be long, but they must not be dull. Letters to customers can be used not only to solicit sales, but also to announce changes in company policies, credit terms, etc. Thanks to developments in computer technology, the body of a letter can now be automatically typed and personalized to look as if it were especially prepared for the addressee. Even certain parts of the body of the letter may be customized. Mass-produced letters can be made to look handwritten by simulating handwriting even though printed.

Because the customer must be persuaded to open the envelope and read the letter, the size and shape of the outer envelope, and the wording on the envelope must arouse interest of approximately 10% of the prospects who will actually read the letter. The offer can begin on the envelope. Loyal customers may be persuaded to read letters when they notice the logo of a favorite firm on the envelope. The J.C. Penney envelope in Exhibit 8-6 has the store logo, a national brand name, and a free trial offer on the envelope.

The purpose of the letter is to communicate the offer. It also must get attention so that it is read; therefore, it must start with an exciting sentence. The letter in Exhibit 8-6 begins: "This may be the most exciting . . . " The letter communicates product, price, payment, commitment, and guarantee. Also, it can do positioning, and test leads and response methods. Sometimes a brochure about the product is enclosed. The order card enclosed with the letter makes ordering easy by requiring only a checked payment choice, a phone number, and a signature.

Letters have been very effective when used as specific invitations—to meet a celebrity or to attend a fashion show or special event. Letters should be used sparingly. If used too often by the same firm, they begin to lose their effectiveness. However, when used from time to time and supplemented by other direct-mail pieces, they stand out by their contrast and infrequency.

Postal cards can be used for the same purposes as letters but are less costly in terms of postage, preparation, and printing costs. One common use by department and specialty stores is to advise particular customers that certain special merchandise has arrived or is in stock, or that there is an advance sale for charge customers prior to a public sale. Another use is to tell a specific customer that a special order has arrived.

EXHIBIT 8-6 Left End of Envelope, Letter, Reply Card in a Direct-Mail Advertisement

Source: J. C. Penney. Used with permission.

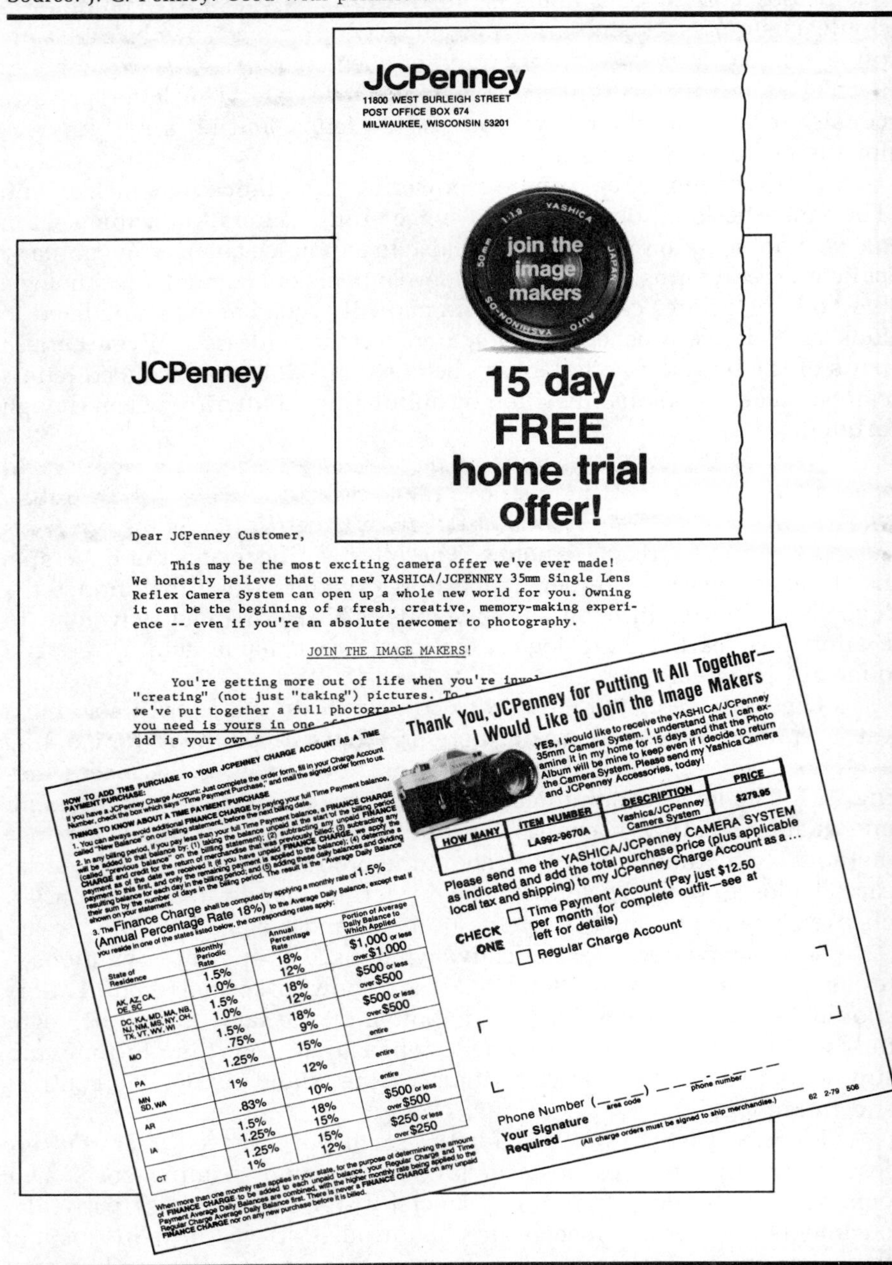

Dear JCPenney Customer,

This may be the most exciting camera offer we've ever made! We honestly believe that our new YASHICA/JCPENNEY 35mm Single Lens Reflex Camera System can open up a whole new world for you. Owning it can be the beginning of a fresh, creative, memory-making experience -- even if you're an absolute newcomer to photography.

JOIN THE IMAGE MAKERS!

You're getting more out of life when you're invol... "creating" (not just "taking") pictures. To ... we've put together a full photograp... you need is yours in one ... add is your own ...

HOW TO ADD THIS PURCHASE TO YOUR JCPENNEY CHARGE ACCOUNT AS A TIME PAYMENT PURCHASE:
If you have a JCPenney Charge Account: Just complete the order form, fill in your Charge Account Number, check the box which says "Time Payment Purchase," and mail the signed order form to us.

THINGS TO KNOW ABOUT A TIME PAYMENT PURCHASE

1. You can always avoid additional **FINANCE CHARGE** by paying your full Time Payment balance, called "New Balance" on our billing statement, before the next billing date.

2. In any billing period, if you pay less than your full Time Payment balance, a **FINANCE CHARGE** will be added to that balance by: (1) taking the balance unpaid at the start of the billing period (called "previous balance" on the billing statement); (2) subtracting any unpaid **FINANCE CHARGE** and credit for the return of merchandise that was previously billed; (3) subtracting any payment as of the date we received it (if you have unpaid **FINANCE CHARGE**, we apply the payment to this first, and only the remaining payment is applied to the balance); (4) determine a resulting balance for each day in the billing period; and (5) adding these daily balances and dividing their sum by the number of days in the billing period. The result is the "Average Daily Balance" shown on your statement.

3. The Finance Charge shall be computed by applying a monthly rate of 1.5% (Annual Percentage Rate 18%) to the Average Daily Balance, except that if you reside in one of the states listed below, the corresponding rates apply:

State of Residence	Monthly Periodic Rate	Annual Percentage Rate	Portion of Average Daily Balance to Which Applied
AK, AZ, CA, DE, SC	1.5% 1.0%	18% 12%	$1,000 or less over $1,000
DC, KA, MD, MA, NB, NJ, NM, MS, NY, OH, TX, VT, WV, WI	1.5% 1.0%	18% 12%	$500 or less over $500
MO	1.5% .75%	18% 9%	$500 or less over $500
PA	1.25%	15%	entire
MN SD, WA	1%	12%	entire
AR	.83%	10%	entire
IA	1.5% 1.25%	18% 15%	$500 or less over $500
CT	1.25% 1%	15% 12%	$250 or less over $250

When more than one monthly rate applies in your state, for the purpose of determining the amount of **FINANCE CHARGE** to be added to each unpaid balance, your Regular Charge and Time Payment Average Daily Balances are combined, with the higher monthly rate being applied to the Regular Charge Average Daily Balance first. There is never a **FINANCE CHARGE** on any unpaid **FINANCE CHARGE** nor on any new purchase before it is billed.

Thank You, JCPenney for Putting It All Together—I Would Like to Join the Image Makers

YES, I would like to receive the YASHICA/JCPenney 35mm Camera System. I understand that I can examine it in my home for 15 days and that the Photo Album will be mine to keep even if I decide to return the Camera System. Please send my Yashica Camera and JCPenney Accessories, today!

HOW MANY	ITEM NUMBER	DESCRIPTION	PRICE
	LA992-9670A	Yashica/JCPenney Camera System	$279.95

Please send me the YASHICA/JCPenney CAMERA SYSTEM as indicated and add the total purchase price (plus applicable local tax and shipping) to my JCPenney Charge Account as a ...

CHECK ONE

☐ Time Payment Account (Pay just $12.50 per month for complete outfit—see at left for details)

☐ Regular Charge Account

Phone Number (area code) — phone number

Your Signature Required ____ (All charge orders must be signed to ship merchandise.)

62 2-79 508

Postal cards come in regular sizes, double, or jumbo sizes. The double postal card, of which one card has the sender's return address, is often used when a reply is desired.

Exhibit 8-7 shows a post card announcement of a one-day sale and wine party, and a newsletter from the same store. This store, Webs, sells supplies to weavers and knitters. The newsletter informs customers about craft events in the area, and about new merchandise, courses, workshops, and discounts for quantity purchasing.

EXHIBIT 8-7 **Postcard and Newsletter from Small Specialty Store**
Source: Webs, Amherst, MA 01002. The store has moved from 109 Main St. to larger quarters in Amherst. Size of postcard original, 4¼ × 5½"; size of newsletter, 5½ × 8½". Used with permission.

Webs

box 349 · 109 main st. · amherst, ma 01004 (413) 253-2580
1225 sumner ave. springfield, ma 01118 (413) 782-0748

March 1, 1983 **Newsletter** Vol. III No. 1

Our anniversary sale has come and gone for another year and we met and continue to welcome hundreds of weavers, spinners and knitters to our shops. We thank you all for your confidence and patronage. We will continue to keep your needs foremost as we search out new yarns and products and reflect your interests and expectations back to our suppliers and manufacturers.

Statement Enclosures

For stores that have regular charge accounts or mailings to customers, the enclosure may be the most often used direct-mail piece. It was discovered many years ago that an invoice or statement in an envelope was considerably underweight in terms of ounces allowed for first-class mail. Retailers, often with manufacturers' cooperation, took advantage of this situation, and began enclosing little folders or statement enclosures featuring various types of merchandise. Single-sheet enclosures usually have a picture of the merchandise on the front and an order blank on the reverse side.

Such enclosures are inexpensive to mail as they get a "free ride." Many manufacturers are willing to provide enclosures imprinted with the store logo and featuring the manufacturer's merchandise, all without charge to the retailer. The manufacturers also benefit from this extensive advertising, even if only a small percentage of the millions of enclosures sent out are converted to orders.

Single-sheet enclosures offer flexibility in targeting specific merchandise selections to the appropriate market segment. When stores have a coded mailing list, these single-sheet enclosures can be adapted to mailings. For example, if all red-tabbed nameplates mean families with children, these can be mailed an enclosure with children's merchandise, while people without red-tabbed plates receive only adult merchandise. As an alternative to the colored tabs, microcomputer programs will sort mailing lists into desired segments and print address labels. Many stores use split mailings in order to give mailing exposure to several departments. For example, the total mailing is divided into four parts; each of four departments advertises in one-fourth of the total mailing.

Because charge customers tend to buy more than random customers, the return on statement enclosures tends to be higher than direct-mail efforts that use purchased mailing lists. The charge customer merely has to check the "charge" box on the order form to initiate payment for the merchandise. Often a postage-paid return envelope is provided to make purchasing convenient. Ease and convenience are the major reasons for mail-order success.

Folders, Brochures, Broadsides

Generally, brochures and broadsides are classified as *self-mailers*. The reason for this nomenclature is that a space for the customer's name and address is provided on the mailing piece itself; no envelope is required. Such pieces should be considered bulk mailing. They carry a permit number, a permanent number bought by a firm for a one-time fee with additional yearly renewal fees.

Generally, a *folder* is a simple, medium-sized sheet folded in half or quarters for mailing. A *brochure* is an elaborate, image-building booklet that usually has pages in multiples of four, and is bound into a cover. A *broadside* is usually a large sheet of paper folded down to comfortable size for ease in handling. All have the same purpose: to create a good presentation of merchandise when a complete catalog is not needed, and to be relatively economical. Economy is achieved by the absence of an envelope, and pre-sorting by zip code to achieve the lowest possible bulk mailing rate. A folder is shown in Exhibit 8-8. This folder has the store address, the customer's name and address, and the bulk-rate permit number on the outside, and the sale announcement with illustrations, store phone numbers, and addresses on the inside. The word *Confidential* is printed on the outside to encourage recipients to open the folder.

Coupon booklets also can be mailed without an envelope and by bulk mail. These booklets can be either mailed to charge customers or delivered to "occupants" in a target area. These booklets usually require shoppers to come to the store to redeem coupons for special savings. In one example, one coupon in the booklet offers $5 off the price of any fabric handbag, and another offers 20% off the price of selected women's fashion boots. Using manufacturers cooperative funds, coupons can offer savings on manufacturers' brands, such as Jello, Ivory, Campbell's soup, Coke. As does a direct-mail envelope, coupon booklets can also carry advertisements of store services. For instance, the coupon book mentioned above advertised a special lunch price on Friday and Saturday, and free parking in the parking garage on Sunday afternoon. Coupons usually have a time limit, to encourage consumers to respond quickly. Coupons from this booklet were honored during the second weekend in December.

Loose-Leaf Mailers

In recent years, loose-leaf mailers have become popular with stores and customers because of their flexibility and ease of use. The individual sheets are identical to the enclosures used in billing statements. The merchandise is featured on one side, with the order blank on the reverse side. While a statement may only be able to accommodate a few of these single sheets, direct-mail advertising specialists have created a cover-pocket slightly larger than the individual sheets. As many as twenty or thirty of the individual sheets can be mailed in this loose-leaf mailer cover-pocket. This pocket is enclosed in an envelope to prevent the individual sheets from being lost in the mail.

Newspaper Tabloids and Supplements

A *tabloid* is defined as a half-standard size newspaper. Many cities have tabloid-size daily newspapers, particularly in large cities where people

EXHIBIT 8-8 A Folder (Inside Contents at Top, Address Space at Bottom)
Source: Alan Bilzerian, 32 Newbury St., Boston. The store has moved to larger quarters. Size of original, 8½ × 11″. Used with permission.

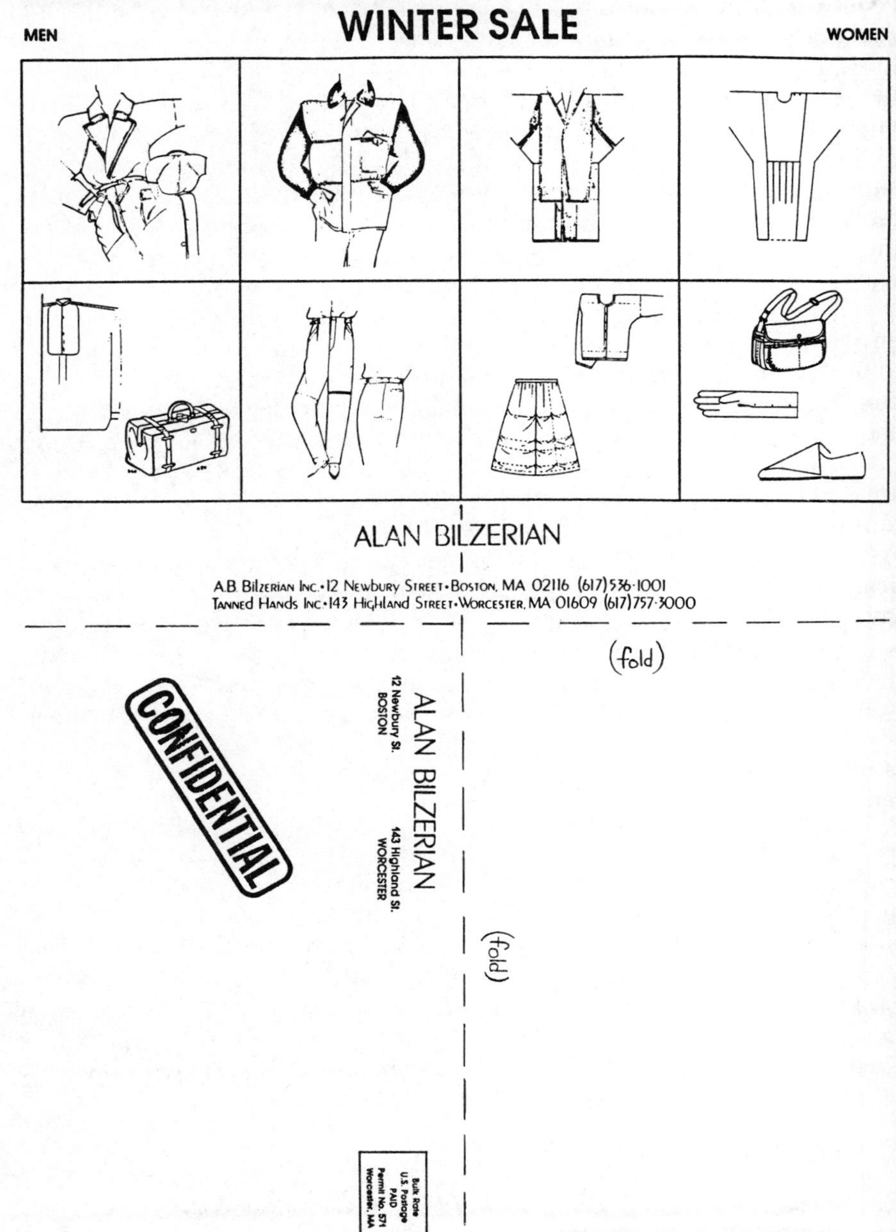

commute to work in crowded buses, subway cars, or trains. The smaller size of a tabloid makes it easier to handle under such conditions. In other cases, the standard-size paper is used. With current newspaper technology, tabloids can have color as well as black-and-white illustrations. A *supplement* is a tabloid contained in a newspaper. Because of its "newsy" appearance and approach, a newspaper supplement tends to be especially effective for sale-type presentations, bargains and off-price merchandise.

Marketers who like to feature price find tabloids and newspaper supplements effective. Food stores and mass-merchandising chains use tabloids and supplements weekly. Tabloids and supplements are not included here as exhibits because current examples are available every week in local newspapers, at stores, or from home mailings.

Some advertisers have found it effective to send tabloids to customers on a regular basis. Tabloids can be mailed, delivered by circulation agencies to all residents in a shopping area, or inserted as supplements in newspapers. Regular delivery of tabloids or supplements reminds consumers about the advertiser and about what merchandise and specials are available.

Marriage mail is defined as two or more advertising pieces which are not in an envelope but which are wrapped around each other. Large retailers like J.C. Penney and K mart use marriage mail.[14] The mailings are not distributed through newspapers, but by advertising-distribution firms that fine-tune the markets by ZIP codes. When several firms are involved, the cost of marriage mail can be divided among sponsors.

Although marriage mail has a large distribution, there is no guarantee that every recipient will read it. Therefore, it is important for marketers to find out whether their target reads ads in paid newspapers, free newspapers, marriage mail, all of these, or none of these. One way to find out is to put coded coupons in these media vehicles, and compare coupon redemption rates.

MANAGING DIRECT MAIL

Planning and Preparation of Mailing Pieces

In most cases, retail advertising personnel who work on regular print advertising also work on direct-mail pieces, and the layout artists in the art department make up a dummy of the proposed piece. A *dummy* is a work-up of what the finished piece will look like, with space allocated to various departments and products. The copywriters, artists, and photographers will use this layout as a guide in their work.

Often the local newspaper produces tabloid advertising pieces because these are printed on newsprint paper. Catalogs, booklets, enclosures, and other direct-mail pieces may be printed in color, and so may require different printing facilities.

Some retailers and manufacturers who use direct mail extensively assign personnel full-time to direct mail. Major mail-order firms like Sears have thousands of people involved in direct mail working from six months to a year before the publication of major direct-mail pieces.

Each direct-mail operation is structured to fit a firm's particular needs. Manufacturers generally use an advertising agency to prepare catalogs and direct marketing pieces. Also, small stores often employ advertising agencies. Avon has an electronic publishing system linked to a data base of product descriptions and prices.[15] Some stores use existing advertising personnel and maintain a low budget, using mostly manufacturer-supplied pieces as well as modest pieces of their own. Major department stores often produce several major catalogs a year, as well as other somewhat elaborate mailing pieces for special fashions, housewares, home furnishings, cosmetics and beauty products, domestic products, and children's back-to-school apparel and accessories.

Some stores share catalogs. For example, Jordan Marsh in Massachusetts and Joske's in Texas have used the same Christmas catalogs. These stores belong to the same parent corporation, Allied Stores, and operate in separate, non-competing geographic markets. Using the same catalog is economical in terms of catalog production and merchandise buying, but is effective only if there are similar customer wants in the two markets.

Mailing Lists

One of the keys to successful direct-mail operations is the selection and maintenance of appropriate, productive mailing lists. At one time, only firms with their own mailing lists could use direct mail. Firms can maintain charge accounts or other up-to-date proven lists of their own customers and prospects that bring a fairly high percentage of return on the direct-response advertising investment.

Now, with Census tracts, ZIP codes, computers, and firms that specialize in mailing lists, relatively large marketers can buy or rent lists for various demographic and psychographic market segments. The Direct Marketing Association has current information about mailing lists.[16] Lists rent or sell for a variety of prices, depending on the source. Sources include magazines and catalog retailers. ZIP codes identify areas of wealth and unemployment, and also areas of houses, apartments, or condominiums. Firms too small to afford to buy or rent lists can develop their own lists from responses to ads in print and broadcast media.

Catalog marketers benefit from supplying lists to non-competing firms. A customer who buys Christmas foods, fruits, candies from one firm's catalog may be interested in apparel from catalogs of other firms having the same demographic and psychographic target market. Direct marketers benefit from encouraging customers to request that their names e deleted from mailing lists. This saves the cost of printing and postage r non-productive mailings.

One important factor for all mailing lists is how up-to-date they re. The return to the marketer on rented or purchased lists depends oth on the percentage of actual and potential target customers on the sts, and on the accuracy of the lists themselves. To be accurate, lists eed to be updated frequently to delete those moving out or dying, and add those moving in. An old mailing list may have a high percentage f *nixes*, mailing pieces that cannot be delivered for various reasons: ddressee deceased, moved with no forwarding address, addressee unnown, no such person at address given, etc.

A mailing of ten percent or more non-deliverable items is costly to e mailer because postage and printing have been paid to no purpose. owever, there is a trade-off between the cost of mailing non-deliverable ems and the cost of having pieces returned in order to correct old lists. o have undelivered mail returned to the sender requires using the firstass postage rate. If thousands of returns are involved, depending on e postal rate structure, old lists may be no bargain even if purchased low cost.

A simple method for retailers who do not have charge accounts is have customers fill out address cards when they make purchases. These istomers are familiar with the store and so are good candidates for mail der solicitation. A new computer package marketed by Customer Keypad eates files listed by customer phone numbers. The file for each customer rovides information about items purchased, purchase frequency and ollar volume. Non-retailing direct marketers can update mailing lists om the mail-order addresses. Postcards offering a small discount to istomers who make purchases with these cards by a certain date can iild customer loyalty and keep the mailing list up to date. One creative arketer sends postcards to gift recipients to ask if the gift arrived safely d if the recipient would like to be on a mailing list for catalogs.[17]

/here Direct Mail Works Best

etail direct mailings work best in the following areas:

1. To replace or augment advertising in nearby suburban local newspapers and nearby metropolitan papers that are too expensive for such fringe circulation.
2. To notify special customer segments about special sales for them prior to public announcement.
3. To invite existing customers to special events.
4. To reach specifically targeted groups of people, condo owners, families with children, those making recent purchases, or purchasing large dollar amounts.
5. To promote single categories of merchandise, such as housewares, computers, records, or toys.

6. To spend a small amount of advertising dollars in order to move limited quantity of merchandise.
7. To reach new potential customers in housing being built in the vicinit of the store.
8. To collect data for marketing research through questionnaires solicitin customer opinions about the merchandise, services, and operation.
9. To inform customers about credit, charge accounts, returns, an complaints.

Note: Response can vary from 0.5% to 5% or 6%; with a lower retur from a random mailing, a higher one from a mailing to charge or regula customers.

OTHER DIRECT-RESPONSE ADVERTISING

Direct-response advertising can be done by telephone, broadcasting, vid eotex, and mail-order information in newspapers and magazine adve tisements. These media can be combined. For example, prospects ca be notified by mail to expect a phone call, or can be asked to respon by postpaid mail coupon if they want a phone call about a particula product or service and to indicate what hours they can be reached b phone.

Telephone

In this paragraph, customers are defined as buyers who are willing t consider a repeat purchase. There are two types of telephone advertisin (1) telephoning the customer (outbound), and (2) advertising a toll-fre number for the customer to call (inbound). Telephoning the custome may be cost-effective compared to paying salespersons to interact wit customers in person. Generally, only department and specialty store some mass merchandisers and large firms telephone customers. For ma keters with customer data bases showing who has purchased what, callin customers offers a high rate of return compared with cost; but this typ of soliciting is usually best left to firms that have sufficient personnel t make the calls, sufficient inventory to fill the orders, and sufficient resource to pack and send out the merchandise in a reasonable time.

Firms that benefit most from telephoning customers have an infor mation file for each customer with such details as customer characteristic and previous phone-order history. This information tells the markete what the customer is likely to buy. The caller's approach might be a follows:

"Hello, Mr. Jones. This is Lee Doe from Hill's. We have a specia this week on oak chairs. Since we only have a limited number, we ar alling a few of our best customers about the special. How many oak hairs would you like us to send you today?"

Another successful method is to encourage individual retail salespeople to call customers, if these salespeople have established a following nd are aware of particular customers' needs. The approach may be done n the following manner:

"Hello, Ms. Johnson. This is Jay Wilson at the Day Store. We have ıst received the new shipment of X Computers. You have told us that X is your favorite brand. To give you first choice, I am calling you to let ou know before we advertise in the paper. When would you like to ome in to see the X Computer?"

Some retailers do thousands of dollars worth of business through uch solicitations. Salespeople may do telephone marketing in addition o face-to-face selling or instead of it. Telephoning is often done to sell elatively expensive merchandise to customers who have a known record f purchasing a particular type of product, such as a designer's line.

Motivation to do phone selling as well as face-to-face selling needs o be built into a salesperson's expectations during training. Telephone elling can be used to tell regular customers about special products, sales nd promotions, or direct-mail advertising. For credibility, phone calls an be preceded by direct mail.[18] Phone orders must be coordinated with nail orders and retail sales in the store so that there is enough merchandise o fill all orders. If phone orders are not filled promptly, not only is the ustomer disappointed by the delay, but also the merchandise inventory nay be depleted until there is no merchandise to send. Prompt processing f phone and mail orders builds good will and avoids having disappointed ustomers spread the word that your store cannot manage to fill orders.

Computerized telemarketing is becoming feasible for the larger marketers. It requires a data base, data communications equipment, multiple hoice questions, automatic redial, and other new technology. It also equires computer programs that meet the specific needs of each firm nd are compatible with other software in the firm's information system. AT&T claims that response to a toll-free number in a mailing is 20% greater than to a mailed reply card, and that sales from those who inquire y telephone are likely to be as much as four times greater than from hose who inquire by mail. However, telephone robots who do telemarketing an be annoying and are being constrained by government restrictions. To ward off government regulation, the Direct Marketing Association rovides a toll-free number for people to remove their names from telephone ists dispensed by that association.[19] Marketers whose lists are not available o that association should realize that telephoning those who do not want hone solicitation is non-productive. Appendix 8 has information about elemarketing successes and mistakes, and about how to recruit effective elemarketers.

Broadcast Media, Including Cable Television[20]

The advantage of radio for direct-response advertising is that station and programs are aimed at specific market segments. Radio viewers ten to be station loyal. The disadvantage is that the audience cannot se what is being advertised and may not remember how they can phone o write to get it. Television viewers tend to be program loyal. Televisio has the advantage of visual aids and demonstrations, but also has th same memory problems as radio. Advertisers should (1) realistically de scribe merchandise, (2) clearly explain order terms and (3) advise customer to print name and address legibly, use checks or credit cards and expec delivery in X days.

An effective use of broadcast is to augment other direct-respons media; for example: "Watch for this newspaper ad," or "Wait for thi mailing or phone call." This type of advertising is best placed on program whose audience is less involved with the programming—early and lat fringe and daytime shows, where 90- and 120-second commercials ar available. Because broadcast time is perishable, unsold time may b available at a reduced price. Successful broadcast ads can be repeate and unsuccessful ads deleted. Side benefits of broadcast advertising ar awareness, image communications and reinforcement of buyer satisfaction.

Several firms have tested cable television catalogs. Because the tele vision catalog situation is new and subject to rapid change, the bes source of information is in current periodicals. For example, "Request," a one-way cable television service, has a home shopping service availabl through Comp U Card, a national computerized shopping service. "Re quest's" programming includes news, weather, sports, and soap operas

Videotex

Videotex, introduced in the "Technological Developments" section o Chapter 2, is a two-way information service that operates via computer and phone lines.[21] The advertiser communicates information via televisio screens and the customer responds either on a computer linked via a modem to a telephone line, or by telephone. Subscribers can order ai tickets, make restaurant reservations, check for prices, order machin tools, etc. Some videotex services are available on television sets, an some on home computers. Some subscribers pay for special equipmen to access some videotex, and some pay a monthly fee. The price of th equipment and the size of the fee influence purchase decisions. Videote can operate as a joint venture of marketers and media, for example, IBM Sears and CBS. Dayton-Hudson and J.C. Penney are also experimentin with videotex.

One problem with videotex is the shortage of viewers, which reduce the amount of advertising, thus further cutting down on the number o iewers, and so on. Also, copy and art professionals need to be comfortable sing computer graphics, and consumers need to be comfortable with wning and operating computers connected to phone lines. Because of apid changes in this area, marketers should keep up with current in- rmation by reading current periodicals.

The advantage of videotex is that it can use computer technology r storing information in a data base, organizing files, and retrieving ata. In video catalogs, *prices* can be changed in the data base and new *erchandise* added to the data base as soon as the information is available. here is not as long a production wait to enter the data base as to change print catalog, because computer graphics software packages are available create illustrations and various print sizes and styles. With ability to easure response, direct marketers can use videotex to test ideas quickly nd to find out which idea is most effective. Users can enter criteria, cluding price, into the computer and products/services that meet the riteria can be shown on the screen. Travel agents who use this method an show video tapes of vacation resorts which meet customer criteria. lso, videotex can be used to present advertising layouts and storyboards clients in their own offices, and to enable viewers to order print atalogs. There should be a small charge for the catalogs to discourage eople who do not intend to buy the catalog merchandise.

Once the idea of advertising by computer becomes familiar, the lderly and other convenience-minded groups can become a big market, rovided that they can acquire and operate the equipment. The hard nes, such as television sets, stereos, toaster ovens, and computer wares, ight be the first big sellers because their consumers tend to know what rands they want. As computer graphics improve so that it is possible get a good picture of merchandise, and as experience with the type f merchandise suitable for videotex accumulates, merchandise currently n mail-order catalogs can be marketed in videotex. Eventually, ordering irectly by computer will be widespread. Videotex can be used for news, veather, banking, shopping, games, electronic mail and other uses.

SUMMARY

Direct marketers use direct-response advertising to attract customers. esponse to such advertising can be measured. Direct marketing can be onducted by mail and other print media, telephone, broadcast media, nd computers. Appropriate updated customer lists help to prevent wasted fforts. Reaching existing and potential customers beyond the reach of ther print and broadcast media can be cost-effective with direct-response dvertising. Computer data bases and information systems enable marketers o adjust their advertising efforts to measured responses.

A wide variety of mailing formats allows marketers to adapt mailing to budgets of all sizes. These mailing formats include catalogs, booklets, letters, postal cards, statement enclosures or "stuffers", folders, brochures, broadsides, loose-leaf mailers, and newspaper tabloids and supplements. Managing direct mail can require substantial staff or help from outside agencies for printing and mailing, and for maintaining mailing lists. The results can be well worth it: for example, L'eggs sells $40 million of imperfect hose by mail.[22]

New developments in technology have facilitated the growth of direct-response telephone, broadcast, and videotex advertising by both manufacturers and retailers. In addition, newspaper, magazine, radio and television advertisements can serve as direct-response advertisements by including a mail coupon, mail-order directions, or a toll-free telephone number.

QUESTIONS

1. Direct-response advertising aims to be personal, because it is sent directly into the home. What ethical issues arise from the personal nature of direct-response advertising, and how should a marketer handle these? In answering this question, consider your past experiences, if any, with ethical issues and direct-response advertising.
2. You have a small independent toy store in a medium-size town or medium-size shopping center. You have decided to try direct-response mail advertising, and to experiment with two types. Which two types of direct mail will you try and why?
3. You are the direct-response marketing manager of a large, national retail chain of department stores. You already use direct-mail catalogs. Which other direct-response advertising methods should you use and why?
4. You are responsible for direct-response advertising for a national chain of small retail specialty stores in shopping centers. Your chain has stores for women's clothing, men's clothing, shoes, and convenience items. What type of direct-response advertising, if any, should you do for each of these store types? Explain.
5. Answer question 4 for a manufacturer of the same types of merchandise. How would your direct-response effort affect your sales and marketing effort to retailers?
6. What kind of firm would most benefit from telemarketing? Explain. Recommend a telemarketing campaign for a specific product type, or for fund-raising of your college.
7. What kind of firm would most benefit from television direct marketing? From videotex? Explain. Recommend a direct-response campaign for a specific merchandise classification using television or videotex. Discuss prices for a) equipment and b) monthly service fee with respect to attracting the desired number of customers for videotex.
8. Suggest a direct-response media mix for the following firms in the current year: (a) small store downtown, (b) small specialty chain stores in shopping center, (c) large city department store, (d) chain of discount department stores, (e) national mass merchandiser, (f) manufacturer

In each case, suggest who should be the target of this direct-response communication, and how you will find out names, addresses, and locations of this target. Also, explain what kinds of merchandise would benefit most from direct-response advertising.

NOTES

1. Direct Marketing Association, Inc. (DMA), 6 E. 43rd St., New York, NY 10017 and their publications. The authors appreciate the input of various speakers at the DMA Educational Foundation Institute for Professors, May 20–23, 1985, in New York City.

"Direct Marketing Sales Far Outpace Estimates," *Marketing News,* 18 (November 23, 1984), pp. 1, 8; J. Kobs, *Profitable Direct Marketing* (Chicago: Crain, 1979); E. Nash, *Direct Marketing* (New York: McGraw-Hill, 1982); B. Stone, *Successful Direct Marketing Methods* (Chicago: Crain, 1979); The Association of Direct Marketing Agencies, 342 Madison Ave., Suite 1818, New York, NY 10017.

See also Chapter 2 of this book.

2. Association of Direct Marketing Agencies. Chapter 4 explains information systems. See also P. Edwards, "Resurgence Seen for Direct-Response Ads," *Advertising Age,* 55 (December 6, 1984), pp. 6–7; E. Fitch, "Agencies Teach Clients Some New Steps," *Advertising Age,* 55 (October 11, 1984), pp. 11, 16.

3. Stewart Alter and Gay Jervey, "Agencies Catch Direct-Marketing Fever," *Advertising Age,* 55 (July 23, 1984), pp. 45–46; "Direct Marketing Statistics on Hold," *Advertising Age,* 56 (April 1, 1985), p. 68; Jules Silbert, "Should a Retailer Establish a Separate Catalog Business," *Retail Control,* 52 (January 1984), pp. 45–52; A. Sobczynski, "Which Comes First: The Catalog or the Store?" *Advertising Age,* 54 (January 17, 1983), p. M-50.

4. DMA FACT BOOK, (New York: Direct Marketing Association, 1984), and Ken Schenker, "Databases, What Are They?" at the DMA Institute for Professors, NY, May 21, 1985.

5. E. Burnett, "How to Calculate the 'Half-Life' of Direct Mailings," *Marketing News* (June 27, 1980), p. 4.

6. Eileen Norris, "Spiegel Takes Corporate Climbers to the Summit," *Advertising Age,* 55 (April 2, 1984), p. M-18; J. Paganetti, "Sales Sprout from the Seeds of Segmentation," *Advertising Age,* 55 (January 17, 1983), p. M-9; see also other articles in this and the November 28, 1983, issue; also, Jim Powell, "The Lucrative Trade of Crafting Junk Mail," *The New York Times* (June 20, 1982), p. F7.

7. D. Daly and R. Franklin, *What Every Young Account Representative Should Know About Direct Mail Advertising* (New York, American Association of Advertising Agencies, 1977); Henry L. Hoke, "The Concept of Direct Marketing," DMA Institute for Professors, NY, May 20, 1985; Wendy Kimbrell and Lewis Lazare, "Sears Book Gets Breezy Look," *Advertising Age,* 55 (July 9, 1984), p. 24; S. Marcus, "The Creative Will Best Survive," *Advertising Age,* 50 (July 30, 1979), p. 119; "Penney Sends More Spanish Catalog Guides," *Advertising Age,* 50 (August 6, 1979), p. 34.

8. *Ethical Business Practices* (New York: Direct Marketing Association, 1984). Write DMA "Mail Preference Service," 6 E 43rd St., New York, NY 10017 to delete your name from mailing lists.

9. William Dean, "Catalogs," at the DMA Institute for Professors, NY, May 21, 1985.

10. Ruth Drizen, "Retail Advertising: The Media Connection," *Californi Apparel News* (March 7, 1980), p. 79; B. Stone, "Consumer Trends Pace Shoppin by Catalog," *Advertising Age,* 50 (March 26, 1979), p. 61.

11. "CatalogScan to Offer Mail-Order Database," *Advertising Age,* 5 (September 27, 1984), p. 6.

12. P. Sloan, "Bloomie's Book Adds Ads; Will Editorials Come Next?" *Advertising Age,* 56 (July 29, 1985), pp. 3, 63. P. Sloan and R. Reed, "Fate o Catalogs Rides on Santa's Sleigh," *Advertising Age,* 54 (November 28, 1983), p. 98; D. Snyder, "Donnelley Plugs into Retail Venture," *Advertising Age,* 55 (December 24, 1984), p. 38; Patricia Strand, "Spiegel Stretching Direct Response," *Advertising Age,* 55 (May 21, 1984), p. 38.

See also section on videotex in Chapter 2.

13. "Burdines Adds Dimension to Catalog Sales," *Advertising Age,* 54 (August 22, 1983), p. 42; *JM Magazine* (Boston: Jordan Marsh, 1980 issues); "N-M, Sakowitz Battle for the Ultimate Catalog," *Advertising Age,* 51 (November 3, 1980), p. 46; *The Sharper Image* (San Francisco: Sharper, 1983); A. Radding, "Filene's Asks Its Customers to 'Cat-alog' Holiday Symbols," *Advertising Age,* 54 (November 14, 1983), p. 89E; Radding, "Filene's Catalog Makes Game of Holiday Shopping," *Advertising Age,* 55 (November 26, 1984), p. 60E; W. Robinson, "Wishbooks: Those Big Books of Dreams, Updated," *Advertising Age,* 50 (January 15, 1979), p. 52; S. Stiansen, "Sakowitz Selling Romance via Mail," *Advertising Age,* 55 (October 25, 1984), p. 7. Norris, "Spiegel Takes Corporate Climbers," p. M-18; Paganetti, "Sales Sprout," p. M-9; Powell, "Lucrative Trade," p. F7. See also *Advertising Age,* 53 (November 28, 1983).

14. "Marriage Mail: A Letter-Perfect Match," *Advertising Age,* 54 (May 30, 1983), p. M-15.

15. S. Shamoon, "It's Avon Calling . . . With Computers," *Management Technology* (May 1984), pp. 56–58.

16. Direct Mail Marketing Association; "Direct Marketing Sales," *Marketing News,* 18 (November 23, 1984), pp. 1, 8; J. Kobs, *Profitable Direct Marketing*; E. Nash, *Direct Marketing*; B. Stone, *Successful Direct Marketing Methods*; Association of Direct Marketing Agencies.

See also Chapter 2 of this book.

17. Atkins Fruit Bowl, Amherst, MA, sends followup postcards to gift recipients. Also see "System Builds Store Lists," *Advertising Age,* 55 (September 6, 1984), p. 9.

18. A. Jordan, *How to Increase Sales via the Telephone* (New York: National Retail Merchants Association, 1983).

19. "Nebraskans Hope to Silence Telephone Robots and 'Junk Calls,' " *The Christian Science Monitor* (February 27, 1984), p. 5; "Staying User-Friendly Pays Off," *Advertising Age,* 55 (April 16, 1984), p. M-40; Bob Stone, "Dial 800-SUCCESS," *Advertising Age,* 55 (January 30, 1984), p. M-32; G. Walther, "Taking the Plunge: How to Computerize Your Telemarketing Department in Four Easy Steps," *Telemarketing,* 2 (December, 1983), pp. 12–17. *Telemarketing* is published by Technology Marketing Corporation, Norwalk, CT 06581.

20. "At Sears, 'Thumbs Up' to the Video Catalog," *Business Week* (May 11, 1981), pp. 33–34; "Group W Schedules Trial for Teletext," *Advertising Age,* 55 (July 12, 1984), p. 33; H. Hoke, "How New Technologies will Change Direct Marketing," DMA Institute for Professors, New York City, May 23, 1985; B. Stone, "A Message to Media Reps from a Direct Marketer," *Advertising Age,* 51 (November 10, 1980), p. 60; "Sears' Wish Book Enters New Video Era," *Advertising Age,* 52

(May 4, 1981), p. 10; P. Sloan, "Stores Boost Direct Mail, Eye Cable," *Advertising Age*, 52 (May 26, 1981), p. 4; N. Weiss, "N.Y. Retailer Offers In-Home Video Catalog," *Women's Wear Daily* (December 28, 1981), p. 14.

See also material on videotex in Chapter 2.

21. Scott Armstrong, " 'Teleshopping' Inches Forward," *The Christian Science Monitor* (January 3, 1984), p. 27; Tom Mach, "High Tech Opportunities Getting Closer to Home," *Advertising Age*, 55 (April 16, 1984), pp. M60–M61; James R. Brown, Robert F. Lusch and Darrel D. Muehling, "Differential Effects of In-Home Shopping Methods," *Journal of Retailing*, 59 (Winter, 1983), pp. 29–52; "Three Big Backers Give Videotex a Shot at Success," *Business Week* (February 27, 1984), pp. 36–37; Joel E. Urbany and W. Wayne Talarzyk, "Videotex: Implications for Retailing," *Journal of Retailing*, 59 (Fall 1983), pp. 76–92; *Videotex Applications Briefs for Advertising and Direct Marketing*, AT&T Customer Information Services, 1983; Hoke, "How New Technologies."

See also Chapter 2.

22. "Advertisers Should Take Plunge Now into New Ad Media," *Marketing News*, 18 (November 23, 1984), p. 4.

APPENDIX 8

TELEMARKETING

With changing technology and changing consumer acceptance, telemarketing is a rapidly growing and changing field. This appendix summarizes recent information about telemarketing, and explains briefly how to recruit and train telemarketers. More information is available in current periodicals.

As a direct marketer, a telemarketer should appreciate the importance of a data base in keeping track of productive phone numbers and purging non-productive ones. Controlled-dialog call guides can be used to increase productivity, and alternative guides tried to compare effectiveness. Telemarketing should be coordinated with other marketing efforts in direct mail, catalogs, print, and broadcast media. Because phone representatives are subject to burnout, this job works best on a part-time basis—after five hours a day, burnout leads to low productivity and high turnover. Acoustical partitions and other efforts to decrease the noise level in the phone room will also increase productivity. Because this is a growing field, some phone representatives should be trained for the higher-level positions of trainers and supervisors.[1]

Prospective phone representatives should be interviewed on the phone. Applicants can display their communication skills by explaining their present jobs in detail. A telemarketer should look for aggressive, goal-oriented, decisive, strong-willed, and persistent people. Different products or purposes require different emphases on these qualities. But

[1] R. Bencin, "The Biggest and Most Repetitive Mistakes Telemarketers Make," Telemarketing, (November, 1984), pp. 21–23.

in most cases, a phone representative must at least be able to tell when the customer has been sold on a product, or when the customer will not buy under any circumstances.[2]

Telemarketers who understand their target markets should know who will welcome calls about a particular product or service and what are the best times to call. This information can be obtained from mailed response cards to ads or direct mailings. In a phone call, the salesperson should explain the advertiser's name and purpose, be prepared to substantiate claims, explain costs and terms, ship prepaid orders within 30 days, honor order cancellations within three days of the order, and avoid making unsolicited phone calls to unlisted numbers.[3]

Practice enables a phone representative to speak from a call guide so well that it does not sound like reading. Speech should be louder than in person-to-person conversation, but should adjust to the needs of the client. Salespeople should be enthusiastic and should learn how to overcome objections. They should keep track of every call and its success or failure.[4] A telemarketer should tape and evaluate at least one phone call from each salesperson each week.

[2] M. Larson, "How to Recruit and Select Quality Telemarketers," *Telemarketing* (November, 1984), pp. 38–39.

[3] "Guidelines for Telemarketing," New York: DMA 1985; M. Pierce, "The Future of Direct Marketing" and G. Gautman, "Telemarketing," DMA Institute for Professors, New York City, May 22–23, 1985.

[4] S. Billue, "20 Shortcuts to Success in Telemarketing," *Telemarketing* (November, 1984), pp. 30–33.

9
BROADCAST ADVERTISING: RADIO AND TELEVISION

INTRODUCTION

The twentieth century brought about major innovations in communication. Previously, newspapers changed the lives of most people by making communication faster than in pre-newspaper times. Later, radio and television—the broadcast media—made newspaper communication seem relatively slow. Both radio and television usually capitalize on their timeliness compared with print media. As a result, the broadcast media have an immediacy when used for commercial messages as well as for news and other programs. This chapter explains how marketing communications managers can use radio, cable TV, and regular television effectively.

RADIO

The senior broadcast medium, radio has been a major source of communication and a commercial success since the 1920s. When television arrived after World War II, many thought radio would become a less important medium. However, the number of radio sets in use grew from 100 million in 1956 to 478.7 million in 1983. About 99% of all homes have more than one radio (an average of 5.5 radios per household), and 95% of all automobiles have radios.[1]

Characteristics of the Radio Medium

With improvements in technology, radios have become lightweight and portable. Of the portable tape players, 75% have radios. This enables radio owners to listen privately, even in public places, while sitting, exercising, and travelling. Radios are often carried to the beach, on picnics, and on vacations. Also, in many factories, workplaces, and retail stores, radio music and news reports are played over public address systems all day. Of adults in multi-paycheck households, 84% listen to the radio at work.[2]

In 1950, there were approximately 580 FM radio stations and 2100 AM radio stations in the United States. In 1983, there were six times as many FM stations (3527) and over twice as many AM stations (4773). The Radio Bureau of Advertising, a trade association of radio stations in the United States and some other countries, estimates that radio reaches 81% of Americans age 12 and over each day and 96% of that population in a week.[3] Exhibit 9-1 compares radio with other media as a news source, morning and midday, for some age, education and occupation segments.

Radio can perform four important tasks: audience segmentation, creating a mood, instant communication, and reaching a mobile consumer. Radio advertising is relatively inexpensive and flexible. It offers a great creative visual freedom because listeners create their own pictures in their minds.[4] Radio is often local, giving local news, entertainment, weather reports, and advertising local businesses. Radio is a background medium. A unique and important aspect of radio is that people can engage in other activities while listening.

In the 1920s and 1930s, network radio soap operas were major late-morning programs for homemakers, following the morning news programs. A small number of networks tried to appeal to a huge cross-section of the population. Today, radio programming is different. With many more radio stations, more local stations aim at segmented audiences with different demographic, psychographic, and language characteristics. A typical area may have eight or ten radio stations, each with its special audience and programming. Adult contemporary music is the format of 22.5% of the AM stations and 18% of the FM stations, followed by country music (18.7%) and nostalgia (15.0%) on AM; and rock (19.1%), country (16.4%), easy listening (13.4%), and album-oriented rock (12.9%) on FM. Other radio programming includes continuous news, talk shows, or other specialties. A Spanish programming format is on 3.1% of the AM and 0.6% of the FM stations, and Black-oriented or rhythm-and-blues programming is on 5.3% of the AM and 4.2% of the FM stations.[5]

Audiences are segmented by time of day, days of the week, and type of program. Exhibit 9-2 shows the programming and advertising

EXHIBIT 9-1 Radio Compared with Other Media as News Source

Source: *Radio Facts* (New York: Radio Advertising Bureau, 1984), p. 17.

First News Source: Morning and Midday

Morning (6 A-10 A)	Radio	Tv	News-papers	Other	None
Persons 12 +	56%	21%	16%	1%	7%
Teens 12-17	56	23	13	—	7
Adults 18 +	56	20	16	1	7
Adults 18-34	62	19	12	1	6
Adults 25-54	57	18	18	1	6
College Grads	56	15	23	—	4
Prof./Mgr. Males	56	16	24	1	2
Working Women	66	20	10	1	4

Midday (10 A-3 P)	Radio	Tv	News-papers	Other	None
Persons 12 +	38%	23%	13%	2%	25%
Teens 12-17	24	22	22	2	30
Adults 18 +	40	23	12	2	24
Adults 18-34	50	20	12	2	17
Adults 25-54	41	18	13	2	27
College Grads	43	9	16	1	32
Prof./Mgr. Males	41	5	16	4	34
Working Women	40	18	13	2	27

plan for a news, weather, and "beautiful music" station targeted at adults age 18 and over. This station advertises itself in transit ads, on billboards, and television spots.

The matching of radio audiences with a firm's target market can be complicated because audience and target may have a different geographic spread. Retailers must compare their own reach with target areas for some local stations that may reach only a very limited area. However, some stations with strong signals may reach most of a retailer's target market. Exhibit 9-3 shows the geographic reach of a radio station with a range from northern New Jersey to southeast New York, including most of Connecticut and some of Rhode Island.

Radio Advertising

In Exhibit 9-4, Jeffrey Martin, Sears, Cotter (True Value Hardware), AT&T, and General Motors are the top five network radio advertisers; Anheuser-

EXHIBIT 9-2 News, Weather, and Music Station—Programming/Advertising Plan

Source: WSRS FM 96, Worcester, MA.

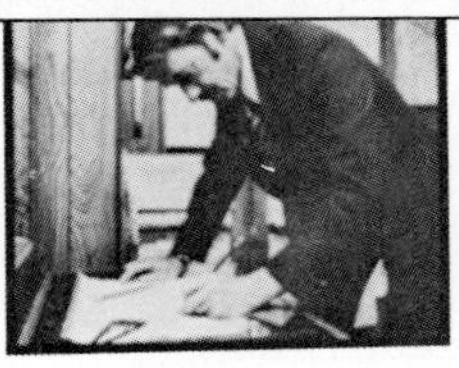

Listeners depend on **WSRS** for constant updates of news and weather information.

WSRS has **18** news casts every day combined with complete weather summaries featuring meteorologists Art Douglas and Dave Watts.

The **WSRS** listener is well informed and yet WSRS presents more pure music than any other radio station in the area. That's because **WSRS** gives the listener just the news and weather. No nonsense. Just news, weather and music which is the proven modern radio programming technique to put the advertisers message in the foreground.

The advertising plan for **WSRS** calls for year round use of almost every available medium . . .

- Big, colorful outdoor painted bulletins to promote our unparalleled format.
- Transit card advertising to spread the word about **WSRS.**
- Spot Television ads to inform our listeners about special programming.

We also use listener contests that are advertised with newspapers, car bumper stickers and retail window banners. Not to mention our on-air promotion for practically everything we're doing. It all adds up to make **WSRS** one of the most actively promoted radio stations in New England.

A Knight Quality Group Station

Busch, General Motors, AT&T, Coors, and Miller are the top five spot radio advertisers. Such marketers can use radio effectively for the large geographic areas they cover. Advertisers in the 12th and 24th ranks—American Home Products and Bayer in network, and Southland (7-11 Stores) and Zayre in spot radio—are also large firms.[6] These firms advertise nationally, but local retailers can advertise on local stations, choosing their audiences effectively. For example, teen apparel can be advertised on teen music stations, and men's products on news and sports stations.

Many types of marketers advertise on local radio. Exhibit 9-4 shows that auto dealers, department stores, and banks are the largest local radio advertisers, followed by clothing stores, restaurants, supermarkets, and other retailers. The wide usage of radio is a testimony to its effectiveness

EXHIBIT 9-3 Geographic Reach of Radio Station
Source: WCBS Radio.

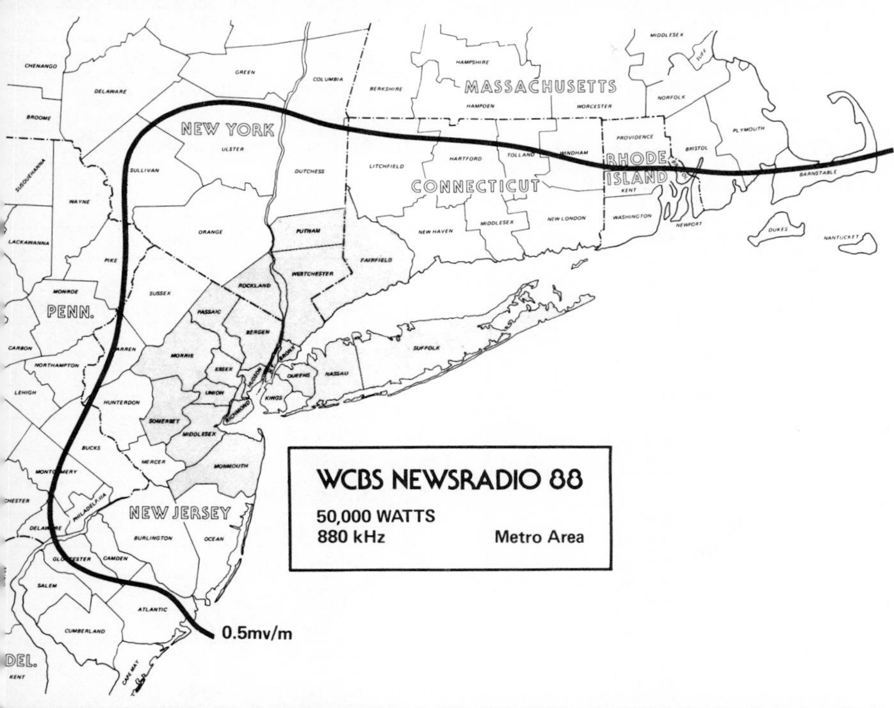

as a local advertising medium. Bigger firms use radio to back up large-scale sales promotions, while smaller firms use it for sales or special offerings.

Some stores have a live radio program on which people talk from he store itself or members of the store staff tell listeners about the store's merchandise or values. Some retailers gain good will by offering tips on dressing which tie in with their own apparel departments, or recipes hat tie in with their housewares department. Some offer early morning news and women's items for the women working inside the home and he career woman on her way to the office. Other advertisers may find hat spot advertisements aired throughout the day reach a wide audience, bringing customers into the store in response to the specific offers made.

Radio Commercials

Unlike newspapers and magazines, which are available for reference and n which the art and copy can be read in any order, broadcast messages

***EXHIBIT 9-4* Types of Advertisers on Network, Spot, and Local Radio**

Source: *Radio Facts* (New York: Radio Advertising Bureau, 1984) pp. 26, 27, 29.

Top 25 Network Radio Advertisers, 1983	*Top 25 Spot Radio Advertisers, 1983*
1. Jeffrey Martin, Inc.	1. Anheuser-Busch, Inc.
2. Sears, Roebuck & Co.	2. General Motors Corp.
3. Cotter & Co. (True Value Hardware)	3. American Telephone & Telegraph
4. American Telephone & Telegraph Co.	4. Coors, Adolph Brewing Co.
5. General Motors Corp.	5. Miller Brewing Co.
6. Dow Jones & Co.	6. Chrysler Corp.
7. Warner-Lambert Co.	7. Delta Air Lines Inc.
8. Campbell Soup Co.	8. United Airlines
9. Ford Motor Co.	9. Van Munching & Co. (Heineken
10. Anheuser-Busch, Inc.	10. PepsiCo, Inc.
11. Nabisco Brands, Inc.	11. Ford Motor Co.
12. American Home Products Corp.	12. Southland Corp. (7-11 Stores)
13. U.S. Government	13. American Honda Motors
14. RCA Corp.	14. Martlet Importers (Molson)
15. Dart & Kraft, Inc.	15. Nissan Motors (Datsun)
16. American Express Co.	16. Stroh Brewing
17. Hartz Mountain Industries, Inc.	17. Pillsbury Co.
18. Wm. Wrigley Jr. Co.	18. Eastern Air Lines, Inc.
19. Chrysler Corp.	19. Greyhound Corp.
20. Schering-Plough Corp.	20. Ralston Purina Co.
21. Purex Industries, Inc.	21. American Airlines, Inc.
22. Gillette Co.	22. Coca-Cola Co.
23. State Farm Insurance Co.	23. Bank of America
24. A.G. Bayer	24. Zayre Stores
25. Honda Motor Co. Ltd.	25. General Mills, Inc.

Local Radio Advertisers Include A Wide Range of Businesses

1. Auto Dealers	13. Theaters
2. Dept. Stores	14. Lumber Dealers
3. Banks	15. TBA Stores
4. Clothing Stores	16. Drug Stores
5. Restaurants	17. Shoe Stores
6. Supermarkets	18. Entertainment
7. Furniture Stores	19. Agricultural
8. Bottlers	20. Stereo/Record Stores
9. Appliance Stores	21. Other Financial
10. Savings & Loans	22. Religion
11. Shopping Centers	23. Real Estate
12. Jewelers	24. All Others

re received in the order sent. Unless listeners record a program, they annot rerun it later in order to listen to the commercials again. However, he ear takes in information 22% faster than the eye, and auditory stimuli re retained four or five times as long as visual ones. The "Pepsi-Cola its the Spot" commercial, originating in 1950, is still remembered today. herefore, radio commercials have a good chance of being remembered;[7] ut they need to be aired more than once to build awareness of the dvertiser's name, location, image, and message.

Radio spots are generally created in three lengths: 15-second, 30-econd and one minute. The 15-second spots are sometimes referred to s *station breaks*. Commercials can be scheduled for specific times. For lower cost, they will be scheduled at the *best time slots available* BTA), and if better times become available, spots will be moved into hem. This lower-cost scheduling is also called *run of schedule* (ROS).[8]

Radio spots run the gamut from very elaborate productions with ound effects, several voices, original music, and scoring, to very simple ne-voice statements. Nationally advertised brands tend to have more xpensive and complicated spots.

For small, local firms, simple and straightforward announcements an be as productive as elaborate spots. Most radio advertisers have found hat it is the offer made on radio that gets the response, rather than the nusic, singing, or sound effects. A consistently-used musical theme or ound effect does alert interested listeners to pay attention to a particular ponsor's commercial.

Important words for radio commercials are: *sale, save,* and *now.* he typical 15-second commercial shown in Exhibit 9-5 offers savings t a sale in a big-city store. It is simple and inexpensive to make, requiring nly the voice of an announcer. Such copy can be written by a person n the store's advertising department or advertising agency, or by someone t the radio station. If used often, the commercial can be recorded.

Although the immediacy of radio makes it an ideal medium for sale ommercials, it can also be used for information commercials. A 30-econd information commercial is shown in Exhibit 9-6. It has sound ffects (SFX) in the form of a musical theme that is aired with every

XHIBIT 9-5 **Script for a 15-Second Radio Commercial—City Store Sale**
ource: Leonard Rubin and Radio Advertising Bureau.

---

t's **here** and it's **hot**! The **summer sale** at **Bach's store**! For a summer f **hot days** and **simmering nights**, the best answer is **'specially selected lothes**—selected for **coolness, comfort, softness** and **class.** The *savings* izzle—if a **sale** can be **hot,** this is a heat wave. Don't miss the **summer ale** at **Bach's**!.

EXHIBIT 9-6 Script for a 30-Second Radio Commercial—Small Town Shopping Center

Source: WTTT Radio Station, Amherst, MA.

You'll find visiting the **Carriage Shops** uptown in Amherst a pleasant change of pace. **Ample parking** in their **tree-lined** lot . . . lovely wooden **benches** set among mini-flower beds . . . interesting **window displays** . . . and the many lovely **shops** lining the walkway. In one small area of town there are products and services available to fill almost any want or need. **The Mercantile** . . . **La Mia Pizza** . . . **Once More with Feeling** . . . and **Adventura Travel**. . . . A sample of the shops you'll find when you stop in at the **Carriage Shops** . . . on **East Pleasant Street** in DOWNTOWN AMHERST.

commercial from this downtown strip shopping center. The 30-second commercial describes the shopping center's environment—lovely wooden benches set among flower beds, with ample parking—and names four of the shops. The names mentioned depend on which shops in the shopping center have paid for that particular ad.

This small-town commercial has a much slower pace than the city commercial in Exhibit 9-5. The one-minute version of this spot repeats the convenient-parking message and describes in detail the merchandise and services of two other shops. For example, the ad might say that The Creative Needle is taking reservations for knitting and other classes, and has a sale of selected materials and craft books. In addition to sharing the cost of these shopping center ads, the shops in this center can buy additional radio time relatively inexpensively because the shopping center has already purchased large blocks of radio time for commercials.

Aids for Radio Advertisers

The Radio Advertising Bureau (RAB) has available printed aids for advertisers, and scripts in print and on tape. The RAB also offers a guide for planning annual advertising campaigns and for making sales comparisons with the previous year's sales. Relevant library materials are available through local RAB member stations. These include (1) clippings from 100 trade papers and magazines about industry trends, (2) research about advertising, costs, and audiences, and (3) commercials categorized by merchandise and business types.[9] Since 1949, Arbitron has been mailing quarterly reports to radio station subscribers to report on the number of listeners by program, age, sex, and other characteristics. A 1984 attempt to make this service monthly and available by computer was not well received.[10]

Through cooperative funds provided by manufacturers for retailers to buy radio time, the retailer helps customers find out about manufacturers'

›roducts, with the purpose of increasing both retailers' and manufacturers' ales. This augments the retail advertising budget and helps the retailer—ınless listeners decide to buy the advertised merchandise from a competitor. ˜he Radio Advertising Bureau works to promote cooperatively funded adio advertising by publishing a booklet of sources of such funds. The Vational Retail Merchants Association and advertising representatives of adio stations help retailers understand this funding system.[11]

Cooperative funds are usually based on a percentage of the amount ›f merchandise bought by the retailer from a particular manufacturer. ˜he manufacturer may earmark certain percentages of these funds for 'arious media. The problem for radio and other broadcast advertisers ıas been to prove that these funds were spent as directed. Print advertising :an be verified by sending the manufacturer a copy (tearsheet) of the ›rint ad. The radio station can send a notarized affidavit signed by the tation manager to the manufacturer or the Advertising Checking Bureau, n auditing company. The Radio Advertising Bureau has developed an electronic tearsheet" which combines an affidavit with the script of the adio commercial and the station's invoice for the ad.[12]

Radio, because it can be targeted at specific audiences, is one of he most selective of all media. Local businesses find that it produces esults on a cost-effective basis.

TELEVISION

'elevision has become a home entertainment and news center for millions f households. Of the approximately 85 million households in the United tates, about 98% have television sets.[13] Viewers can watch sports, the-trical, and public events. The prediction that television might make ıovie theaters obsolete has not been realized; but television has changed ıe nature of the motion picture industry. Some movie theaters now how advertisements before projecting the movies, while many motion ictures are made especially for television viewing.

The impact of television on our society is tremendous. Television ıfluences children who insist that their parents buy the food and toys ıey see advertised there. Adults are influenced by the apparel and lifestyles f the television personalities on television soap operas and other programs.

Possibly one of the most misjudged areas of commercial television ; its impact as a retail advertising medium. Early prognosticators in the 960s and 1970s predicted that millions of shoppers would respond to ɘlevision ads by placing phone and mail orders. This has not happened; owever, many people have taken time to incorporate some new technology ıto their habits and lifestyles. Experience with electronic games and ⁄ith *infomercials* (two-minute or longer commercials) is paving the way ɔr interactive television purchasing. Thus, while television has changed institutions and how they do business, it has not yet replaced stores or become a major factor in retail sales. Its growing impact on direct marketing was discussed in Chapter 8.

Television Advertising

Television commercials are credited with selling billions of dollars worth of merchandise every week. This has been done mostly through manufacturer's advertising on network television to presell brand-name products and create a brand image. Supermarkets and drug stores that sell brand-name packaged goods have benefited more from network TV brand advertising than have department and specialty stores. TV advertising volume was $18,800 million in 1984, of which 44% was network; 30%, spot; and 26%, local.[14] Local tie-ins with network television programs and with cable have created new opportunities for local advertisers.

Many national TV commercials and their music have been extremely popular. Some of the phrases have become widely used cliches such as Avis's "We try harder." J. C. Penney's Halston apparel has been modeled on television. Sears' Winnie-the-Pooh television specials for children have advertised Sears' clothing line of that brand name.

By 1980, a number of department stores had expanded their use of television, notably, Macy's, San Francisco; Foley's, Houston; Gimbels, New York; Broadway, Los Angeles; Elder-Beerman, Dayton; Gottschalk's, Fresno; and Marshall Fields, Chicago. Eastover Shopping Center near Washington, DC featured stores, merchandise and prices on television, and Rouse's Perimeter Mall in Atlanta promoted Christmas sales. In 1983, Bloomingdale's incorporated television into its media mix in promoting home furnishings, swimwear and its France promotion. As of 1984, Burdines in Florida, Sanger Harris in Dallas, Younker's in Des Moines, and Carson Pirie Scott in Chicago, among others, have used television advertising. K mart was a sponsor for the 1984 Olympics, targeting fashion and home electronics ads at viewers aged 18–44. Sears was also an Olympics sponsor.[15]

It is much easier for large firms with national markets to use national television than it is for small local firms. The larger firms can amortize the costs of producing and broadcasting an expensive commercial over substantial sales. The top network and spot TV advertisers include manufacturers of food and food products, automotive products, toiletries and toilet goods, beer and wine, proprietary medicines, and confectionary and soft drinks.

Local firms can use less expensive alternatives like cable and local tie-ins. Top local TV advertisers include restaurants and drive-ins, auto dealers, food stores and supermarkets, banks and savings and loans, and furniture stores. The top 25 network, spot and local categories are shown in Exhibit 9-7.

EXHIBIT 9-7 **Types of Advertisers on Network, Spot, and Local Television**
Source: Television Bureau of Advertising, from data supplied by Broadcast Advertisers Reports.

Top 25 Network Advertisers, 1984

1. Food & Food Products
2. Toiletries & Toilet Goods
3. Automotive Products
4. Proprietary Medicines
5. Beer & Wine
6. Soaps, Cleaners, & Polishers
7. Confectionary & Soft Drinks
8. Office Equipment, Computers, & Copiers
9. Household Equipment & Supplies
10. Restaurants & Drive-Ins
11. Consumers Services
12. Apparel, Footwear, & Accessories
13. Pet Foods & Supplies
14. Home Electronics Equipment
15. Department Stores
16. Jewelry, Optical Goods, & Cameras
17. Movies
18. Sporting Goods & Toys
19. Insurance
20. Publishing & Media
21. Travel, Hotels, & Resorts Outside U.S.
22. Building Materials, Equipment, & Fixtures
23. Freight & Industrial Development
24. Investment Brokers
25. Gasoline, Lubricants, & Other Fuels

Top 25 Spot TV Advertisers, 1984

1. Food & Food Products
2. Automotive Products
3. Confectionary & Soft Drinks
4. Toiletries & Toilet Goods
5. Beer & Wine
6. Soaps, Cleaners, & Polishers
7. Consumers Services
8. Household Equipment & Supplies
9. Travel, Hotels, & Resorts
10. Proprietary Medicines
11. Home Electronics Equipment
12. Publishing & Media
13. Apparel, Footwear, & Accessories
14. Sporting Goods & Toys
15. Gasoline, Lubricants, & Other Fuels
16. Office Equipment, Computers, & Copiers
17. Insurance
18. Pet Foods & Supplies
19. Building Material Equipment & Fixtures
20. Jewelry, Optical Goods, & Cameras
21. Freight & Industrial Development
22. Horticulture
23. Household Furnishings
24. Agriculture & Farming
25. Smoking Materials

Top 25 Local TV Advertisers, January–June 1984

1. Restaurants & Drive-Ins
2. Auto Dealers
3. Food Stores & Supermarkets
4. Banks, Savings & Loans
5. Furniture Stores
6. Radio Stations & Cable TV
7. Department Stores
8. Amusements & Entertainment
9. Leisure Time Activities & Services
10. Movies
11. Home Improvement Contractors
12. Discount Department Stores
13. Appliance Stores
14. Hotels & Resorts, U.S.
15. Auto Repair & Service Stations
16. Medical & Dental Services
17. Drug Stores
18. Builders & Real Estate Agents
19. Clothing Stores
20. Local Education Services
21. Auto Supply & Accessory Stores
22. Health Clubs & Reducing Salons
23. Carpet & Floor Covering Stores
24. Shore Stores
25. Investment Brokers

The Television Advertising Bureau (TvB) is eager to help firms use television for advertising. TvB will develop a presentation for a firm based on its size and position in the market place, offering such helpful information as mass media trends for the target market, television commercials for similar firms, comparative reach and frequency analyses in the media schedule, budget suggestions for different months, and sources of cooperative funds.

The TvB also provides television case histories for various types of stores that have advertised on television, such as furniture, jewelry, drug, discount, department, carpet, appliance, and shoe stores, as well as shopping centers. A sample case history is that of Plaza Pharmacy in Atlanta, which has been running the same television commercial for 20 years. This is a 30-second spot that states: "Everyone in Atlanta knows that the Plaza Pharmacy is open 24 hours a day." Kirkwood Plaza Shopping Center in North Dakota is another case history. Kirkwood uses television 20 to 25 weeks a year to publicize events, airing ads the week before the event. Kirkwood increased television usage to compete against a new shopping center coming into the area.

Reach and Program Strategy

In television's early days, retailers selected mostly daytime spots to reach women, many of whom then worked inside the home and were a major audience for soap operas. Now that many women work outside the home during the day, some retailers advertise in the evenings, and television evening programming also includes "soaps". Because of the large audiences for soap operas, space on these programs is often purchased by nationally advertised brands of products that women are perceived as likely to buy. Thus, local firms have difficulty buying time on evening soaps. However, local television stations usually have time available for local firms. Before buying that time, managers should do their demographic homework to find out how many of their target customers watch that station in that time period.

The dollar amount of local television expenditures by retailers is growing. The increase has been most marked for apparel specialty stores, least so for department, discount, and bargain stores, although bargain stores have also increased local television spending.[16] A good portion of this increased dollar amount is, of course, influenced by inflation.

Advertisers have used television commercials successfully for two major approaches: to boost a firm in a general manner, and to sell specific merchandise. The former method calls for the firm to present its image as a "fashion firm," a "firm famous for values," or a "firm known for both fashion and value." Brand-name products can be advertised coperatively by retailers and manufacturers. A type of general television pot used widely by retailers promotes a major departmental sale or a tore-wide sale.

Large chain and mail-order firms have often used television comercials to promote their own private brand names. Local brands do not ave the wide appeal of nationally recognized names nor of the private rand names of major retailers who have spent millions of dollars building rese name identities. However, a local advertiser can build customer yalty by positioning itself as a friendly local firm that knows its customers.

Until recently, the Federal Communications Commission (FCC) pecified the maximum amount of time that could be used for commercials a given time period, and required that some commercial time be vailable for public service commercials. Because of recent deregulation, re FCC no longer puts a limit on the amount of commercial time per our. Therefore, there is a potential problem of clutter for television ommercials if the time used for commercials increases markedly. Unlike ewspapers and magazines, which can expand the number of printed ages, or radio and cable, which can expand the number of stations, rere is a limited amount of time available on network television. In rder to avoid the clutter arising from expanded time for commercials n network TV, some advertisers might switch to cable TV.

Another new development is the *split 30* commercial, which allows dvertisers to put two unrelated products in a 30-second commercial. ome argue that the 15-second spot commercial will become more widepread and that ads will become correspondingly more informative because rey will not have time to be emotional. It has been also suggested that onsumers suffering from ad overload will prefer shorter broadcast ads. thers suggest that advertisers may resort to longer, one-to-seven-minute fomercials in order to stand out from the clutter.[17]

In an initial test related to split-30s, 30 viewers watched a halfour comedy show with three commercial breaks. The first break had rree 30-second commercials; the second, two 30s and four 15s; and the rird, ten 15s. Viewers remembered only four of the ads, and these ads aried in length. It would be important for an individual advertiser to nd out why specific ads were remembered.[18]

Technological improvements are adding quality and new capabilities television sets. Soon, new sets will be stereo-capable. They will be ble to display images from computers, videocassette recordings, and ideotex data bases simultaneously. A monaural subaudio channel will e available for bilingual broadcasts so that, for example, Hispanic audiences an receive audio in Spanish. All of these changes will expand the range f people who watch television, and will certainly affect which programs eople select.[19] Advertisers must be aware of these changes and their amifications for television advertising.

CABLE TELEVISION

Cable television is relatively new compared with radio and broadcas television. Cable television is a form of communications whereby broadcas TV signals, satellite signals, original programming, and other signals ar distributed by means of a coaxial cable or optical fiber. One requiremen of working with the new cable technology is learning the vocabulary Exhibit 9-8 provides a glossary of new words. Especially important word for retail advertisers are *huts, puts,* and *crawl space.* Huts are "home using television"—the number of homes in which people are watchin broadcast or cable television at any one time. Puts are "people usin television"—the number of people watching at a particular time. Craw space is space on the television screen, usually at the bottom, for alpha numeric characters, moving from right to left under the picture.[20]

The oldest of today's leading cable networks began in Decembe 1976. The Cable TV Advertising Bureau, formed in 1980, is patterne after the Radio Advertising Bureau and Television Bureau of Advertising In 1983, total cable advertising revenues were estimated at $300 million up from $58 million in 1980, but below industry estimates of the amoun needed to cover costs and make a profit. The *Electronic Media Repor for the Retailing Industry,* published monthly by the American Medi Council and Retail Advertising Conference, has advised retailers tha television is a secondary advertising medium for retailers, and that cabl television is not a high priority, with the exception of MTV for youn viewers. The Broadway in California, Rich's in Alabama, Georgia an South Carolina, and Foley's in Houston have advertised on MTV. Becaus cable is so new, advertisers should watch constantly for changes whic may make cable television a more viable medium for advertising. Vid eocassette recorders represent one change that will affect cable an broadcast television advertisers. At least ten million Americans, abou 12% of all households, already own videocassette recorders.[21]

One of the problems of advertising on cable arises from the newnes of this medium; services which measure the effectiveness of cable ad vertising are still in their infancy. Another uncertainty is the implicatio of the Cable Communications Policy Act of 1984, which deregulates cabl service rates after two years. Advertisers need to know who is watchin what and when. Services that answer this question for radio and televisio already exist. Whether or not cable advertising costs should be measure in the same way as the costs of regular broadcast advertising is no being studied. Broadcast television involves a certain amount of wast by reaching many persons who are not in the store's target market. Becaus its audience is narrower, cable tends to have less wasted circulation People meters and electronic diaries are being investigated as means o learning more about cable listeners.[22]

EXHIBIT 9-8 Glossary of New Words Associated with Cable TV

Source: *Advertising Age*, 54 (June 13, 1983), p. M-10. Reprinted with permission from the June 1983 issue of *Advertising Age*. Copyright 1983 by Crain Communications, Inc.

Community antenna television (catv). *This is what they used to call cable tv. What will they call it next?*

Crawl space. *Homeowners, it's not what you think. It is actually space on a tv screen (usually the bottom) used for alpha-numeric characters. And the text is called, you guessed it, a crawl.*

Direct broadcast satellite (dbs). *From all reports, this satellite service is one to watch. The signals are delivered directly to a viewer's home, or to be technical, a viewer's own personal earth station in the form of a dish. And it's all done without the benefit of an intervening cable system.*

Downlink. *Programming that's transmitted from a satellite transmission system has to eventually come to earth. So no programming gets home without this.*

Earth station. *Moving right along, there are structures, called "dishes," and they receive and/or transmit electromagnetic signals from the birds.*

Footprint. *The geographic area (whether wide or narrow) in which a satellite signal can be received.*

Head-end. *The brains of the cable system. It's the site of the receiving antenna and the signal processing equipment needed to make all (cable) systems go.*

Homes passed. *Don't look now, but you may be living in one of the total number of homes that have the potential for becoming part of a cable system.*

Homes using television (hut). *Huts at one time rarely had tv. But now a new age has dawned, and Huts designate the total available video audience at a given time, as reflected by the number or percentage of tv homes watching broadcast or cable programs.*

Interconnect. *Centel's Videopath is a good example of this. It's several cable systems in a given area that join to sell advertising—and it makes for easier billing.*

Low power tv (lptv). *Not a reference to daytime programming, but rather to tv stations licensed to operate at low power without observing current standards of minimum geographical separation established for full power tv stations on the same channel.*

Multiple system operator (mso). *A company that owns and operates more than one cable tv system throughout the country. (The big operators.)*

Multipoint distribution system (mds). *A pay service devised for the transmission of programming (largely movies with some specials and sports) via microwave for generally short distances. Subscribers have converter boxes and special antennae (especially if they're very receptive).*

Pay cable. *If the basic fare is not enough, cable subscribers can pay an additional charge and get even more programming (especially movies, sports and specials). HBO and Showtime, for example, are extra.*

Pay per view. *(Known in some circles as ppp—pay per peek.) Pay tv for which subscribers pay for each program viewed rather than per month. So did you all catch Linda Ronstadt in "Pirates of Penzance"?*

Persons using television (put). *Instead of tossing a 16-lb. metal ball around, the puts are home being included in the total number or percentage of people watching broadcast or cable tv at a particular time.*

Satellite-fed master antenna television (smatv). *A mouthful. Also a minicable system for buildings connected to a private satellite antenna. It provides multichannel video to large apartment buildings and condo complexes.*

Will cable pull its advertising dollars away from radio or local television? Both radio and local TV appeal to the local audience; both are less expensive than national television, and both have a variety of formats that appeal to specific loyal segments. Cable has rock music, news networks, and health programming. There is even a Campus Network to provide entertainment directed at college students. A cable movie channel advertises on radio, broadcast television, and in print.[23]

At present, radio programming is free, while cable requires a monthly payment for programming. Radios are more mobile than television sets, and demand only listening: one can drive and walk while listening to radio, but not while watching television. The differences between radio, cable, and network television should direct advertisers to make wise choices. Radio and cable are more personal than network television because radio is narrowly targeted, and the cable audience has to subscribe to the cable service. The psychographics and demographics of some local radio or cable audiences may be more appropriate for some advertisers than for others. Firms can obtain information about radio and cable listeners from media vehicles, and decide which have audiences best suited to their advertising needs and target markets.

At first, cable companies expected only their subscribers to generate revenues. As audiences have increased, local advertising has also become an effective, efficient revenue source. Because cable advertising is less expensive than network television, longer commercials are affordable. These are called *infomercials.* Infomercials inform customers about products and stores. The success of infomercials on cable has inspired ABC television to run test infomercial series in New York and Chicago. Marshalls, the Melville Corporation's discount clothing chain, has run 60-second commercials on ABC following a series of infomercials on fashion and news.[24] The infomercial thus provides two kinds of opportunities for advertisers. They can use infomercials to inform customers about a firm and its products, and then follow up with commercials on stations that aired related infomercials.

Several cable options are available in addition to commercials and infomercials. These include *cable shop, cable coupon, video mail order,* and *Qube.* For cable shop, viewers phone to request specific infomercials of from two to seven minutes, and then place orders by telephone. Short video programs will also soon be available on this service, with infomercials and programs listed in local cable guides. Cable coupon networks allow advertisers to include coupons in the monthly cable bill. Video mail order divides a 24-hour catalog service into one-hour segments by merchandise category. Infomercials will be included. Users will interact via a toll-free number.[25]

Qube is interactive television that allows customers to shop from home and register their opinions. Gold Circle, Federated's discount retail chain which sells apparel, records, and stereos, sponsored a video jukebox on Qube and was mentioned in all Qube promotional materials, including the program guide. Gold Circle also had three 30-second commercials and four or five verbal and logo slide mentions, although it did not use the direct-response selling capability of Qube. Finally, Gold Circle provided prizes for quiz segments on the program.[26]

Many manufacturers are using these cable services. As customers become more familiar with these facilities, more retailers will also use them. Customers will then be able to use cable services to shop for various merchandise categories at home, rather than going to many stores.

MAKING TELEVISION COMMERCIALS

Making television spots is a demanding task, requiring technical skill similar to that involved in filming of full-length motion pictures. The television spot is a "movie in miniature," telling a story on film in order to sell merchandise, an institution, or both in 60 seconds or less.

A television spot can cost as much as $50,000 to $1 million because it may be produced in London, Paris, Hong Kong, Africa, the Andes, the Arctic or other faraway places. While it is true that some local people can be hired to help make the spot on location, it may be necessary to send as many as six or more support people from the United States. Transportation of so many people and their equipment, and putting them up in hotels or rented homes for the time period allotted for production can cost thousands of dollars before the shooting has even begun.

If extras are needed for crowd scenes, or musical groups for background, thousands of dollars can likewise be spent on personnel before any shooting has been started. Even if the music is dubbed in later, the cost of the musicians is still high, especially if original music is to be written. Writers and production people's salaries must be added to the other costs.

Production time must be booked before the client approves scripts. One of the differences between retail ads and manufacturers' ads is the urgency. Thus retail ads must often be produced in-house to save time. An ad for a manufacturers' brand can be repeated over time, but a retail ad for a one-day event must be changed after the event has taken place. Therefore a retail commercial often takes less than half a day to produce, because it is not cost-effective to take more time for a short-lived ad. Money is often saved by using the same cast and production staff to produce more than one retail commercial per day. The shooting of four to six simple, related retail commercials may be done in the morning and early afternoon, with reviewing and editing completed in the late afternoon.[27]

After the commercial is filmed, the film needs to be cut, edited, and fitted with the sound track. The commercial must then be submitted to relevant managers for approval. If not approved, it must be re-shot or re-edited, requiring more expense. Because large retail clients hire advertising agencies to produce and air 50 to 175 television commercials in a year, agencies should have enough experience to get the commercials right the first time, especially since shooting scripts are usually approved in advance. After the commercial is aired, accounting must be arranged to pay residual fees to the talent acting in the commercials.[28]

All television spots do not have to cost thousands of dollars. Spots have been done on very modest budgets with the help of local stations and the advertiser's own personnel. Advances in the time-compression technique allow radio and television broadcasters to speed up the sound track. For example, a 34-second commercial can be speeded up to take 30 seconds.[29] This allows an advertiser to deliver a 34-second message but pay for a 30-second spot.

A local camera operator can be hired for a half day or an entire day to shoot on nearby locations, in a store, or in the local television studio. An advertiser's own models or those hired especially for the shooting can be used. Perhaps other employees can also be used as background or for other help with the commercial, building employee morale and increasing favorable word-of-mouth communications about the advertiser. Employees who are in the film tend to want family and friends to watch the commercials.

Still shots and computer graphics can be integrated with motion pictures. Scripts can be written by writers in a firm's advertising department; perhaps the advertising manager or an assistant can act as director-producer. Recently, a shopping center created a commercial using color slides of various stores in the shopping center, and a crawl space for a moving line of print.[30] The words in the crawl space were changed regularly to go with current shopping center events.

Advertisers can make television spots with the help of agencies, local television stations, or their own personnel. For cost-effectiveness, the ad's concept should be essentially simple and straightforward, and require a reasonable time to accomplish. Appendix 9 contains a checklist for making a simple retail television commercial. This might be made with cooperation of manufacturers whose merchandise is featured. Briefly, the checklist includes selecting interesting products and an appropriate background location, writing a flexible script to allow input from the director, shooting extra footage which can be edited later into commercials of various lengths, using a voice-over commentary and canned music, allowing room for the advertiser's logo at the beginning and the end, and working with the local television station to book slots economically.

A typical 10-second television spot commercial might have one model in action, another as foreground, and music from the public domain.

The copy might consist of two short sentences that include the advertiser's name and location. The visual would include the advertiser's logo.

A McDonald's television commercial described in Exhibit 9-9 offered collectors some glassware decorated with five familiar Peanuts cartoon characters. Glassware could be purchased after buying a medium or large soft drink during a five-week period. The target included children and Peanuts fans. Exhibit 9-10 shows a "photoboard" for an institutional commercial targeted at an ethnic group. The Zayre commercial explains, in Spanish, that a mother may return an electric mixer bought by her daughter. Knowledge that a retailer will accept returns reduces the perceived risk of buying merchandise from that retailer.

New Technology

Advances in technology facilitate the shooting and editing of television commercials. A major technological advance is videotape, which is less expensive than film and can be reviewed immediately. While film is slower to develop, it has higher quality and so is better for repeated airings, such as for institutional image advertising. If an advertiser wants to change commercials frequently, videotape is adequate.

Light pens can be used by experienced editors to assemble commercials quickly. The pens can make scenes roll forward and back, fast and slow. Computers can be used to design unique pictures and backgrounds. Software designed for producing animated movies on home computers could be used by smaller stores.[31] Drawing can be done with the computer's arrow keys and joystick. Illustration quality is improving steadily as computer graphics improve. Designing a computer-made commercial still requires artistic talent and creative ideas, but production is certainly simple and less costly then using film and live models.

EXHIBIT 9-9 **Television Commercial Tie-In with Comic Strip**

Source: R. Ebert and G. Siskel, "At The Commercials," *Advertising Age*, 54 (October 13, 1983), p. M-46. Reprinted with permission from the October 1983 issue of *Advertising Age*. Copyright 1983 by Crain Communications, Inc.

Linus: *Where's my blanket?*

Charlie Brown: *Good Grief! The struggle for security is no picnic.*

Voiceover: *Linus and the gang are camping out at McDonald's. On 16 oz. glasses specially designed by Charles Schulz. This week get the Linus glass for just 49 cents when you buy a medium or large soft drink, like Coca-Cola. Collect all five. One each week.*

Linus: *Witness, the blanket is quicker than the eye . . .* quod erat demonstrandum.

Lucy: *Can't he just say ta-daaa!?*

Singers: *Linus, McDonald's and you.*

EXHIBIT 9-10 Photoboard for Commercial Targeted at Hispanic Audience, Zayre's "Hispanic/Friendly Service"

Source: Zayre Corporation, Framingham, MA.

ZAYRE

"HISPANIC/FRIENDLY SERVICE"

COMMERCIAL NO.: ZAYR 3322

LENGTH: 30 SECONDS

(MUSICA DEBAJO)
HIJA: Mama, al fin compre la Batidora que querias.

(MUSIC UNDER)
DAUGHTER: Mama, at last I bought the mixer you wanted

MADRE: Ah...yo tambien.

MOTHER: Ah... me too.

(RIENDO)

(LAUGHTER)

LOCUTOR: En Zayre, le aceptamos su devolucion

ANNCR: At ZAYRE we accept your returns

con una sonrisa.

with a smile.

HIJA: Las dos compramos lo mismo.

DAUGHTER: We both bought the same.

DEPENDIENTE: Les gustaria otra cosa? CANTAN: VENGA Y AHORRE

CLERK: Would you like something else? SINGERS: COME AND SAVE

EN ZAYRE

AT ZAYRE

SERVIRLE ES UN PLACER. MADRE: Esto es perfecto!

SERVING YOU IS A PLEASURE.. MOTHER: This is perfect!

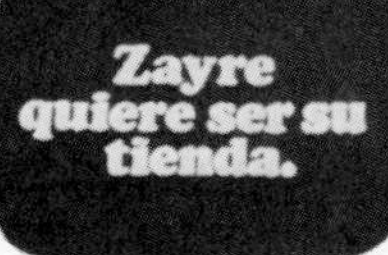

CANTAN: ZAYRE QUEIRE SER SU TIENDA

SINGERS: ZAYRE WANTS TO BE YOUR STORE.

Z-A-Y-R-E

ZAYRE

ZAYRE QUIERE SER SU TIENDA. HIJA: Hemos hecho de Zayre nuestra tienda. CANTAN: ZAYRE QUEIRE SER SU TIENDA ...

ZAYRE WANTS TO BE YOUR STORE. DAUGHTER: We have made ZAYRE our store. SINGERS: ZAYRE WANTS TO BE YOUR STORE...

A technological development which may be more acceptable to viewers than to advertisers is a *zapper*. This patented device memorizes the audio and video signals of a commercial and removes or replaces it when the viewer presses the control box. The zapper also can be used to edit commercials out of videotaped programs.[32]

Evaluating Television Commercials

It is important to evaluate the extent to which a commercial helps the advertiser reach the goals set for it. Criteria for evaluating television commercials are as follows: First, target customers should become *aware* of the message, and *understand* the message. Then, the commercial should arouse *interest* and *liking* for the firms or merchandise advertised. Third, the commercial should get the target customer to *buy merchandise* from the advertiser in the near future. Slogans, jingles and benefit statements generate awareness. High production quality, a relaxing tone, a focus on the product's personal usefulness, interest in the product, retention of the message, and motivation to buy.[33]

Creative art and copy persons should be involved in evaluating commercials so that they will understand the marketing communications issues involved. In addition to evaluating a commercial's art and copy, its content should also be evaluated. Evaluators disagree over whether the same commercial performs differently with TV programs of different types.[34]

One research firm claims that it is possible to determine accurately how people really feel about commercials by giving them small wireless computers on which they can press buttons to indicate reactions. Because the computers are synchronized with what appears on the television screen, every second of the commercial can be analyzed. Viewers can be shown the points at which their feelings changed and discuss the reasons with the researchers. CBS pretests programs in this manner.[35]

AN ADVERTISER'S OWN TELEVISION PROGRAM

Some advertisers have developed their own television programs. This is a much greater commitment than is airing spots. Having a program involves booking time on television for a half-hour or an hour and filling that time with programming and commercials.

Such a program might be a typical morning show with a local personality or an employee acting as the anchor person. Viewers could be given tips on nutrition, books, fashion, latest local news, perhaps cooking if the advertiser sells housewares. Buffum's has a 30-minute cable television show that offers beauty and fashion tips.[36] Demonstrations of beauty aids and cosmetics make interesting visual programs. Leading manufacturers of toiletries and cosmetics are glad to have their repre sentatives perform demonstrations on television as well as in stores.

From time to time, fashion shows might be televised, or celebritie who are visiting the city could appear. Many leading figures from th fashion world make personal appearances in various cities to promot their lines and merchandise. They are glad to appear on television show as well as in stores. Visiting authors would also be glad to appear t promote their books.

Special audience television shows might be popular, such as a po music show aimed at high school or college students late in the afternoon with the students themselves providing the entertainment or selectin the show's music and visual material that would be presented. The progran might include dancing, a display of apparel and other products aimed at the young audience, and perhaps some student athletic stars in interviews.

An advertiser might also sponsor special shows for particular holiday featuring such events as a Thanksgiving Day Parade, Christmas with Santa Claus, or a New Year's Eve show of local dancing and music. There could also be Easter Egg hunts on television and perhaps a Fourth of July fireworks show sponsored by the advertiser and televised as well. There could also be a cooperative show in which a manufacturer and retaile jointly present merchandise on local television in the form of a fashion show or demonstration. In this case, the manufacturer could pay for a large percentage of the TV time costs if the manufacturer's merchandise were featured exclusively.

Another special television show that an advertiser might produce is the broadcasting of games played by a popular local athletic team. This is a good opportunity to present brand-name merchandise for men. A firm might sponsor and televise games of a local or nearby college or high school team that has wide local support.

WORKING WITH AN ADVERTISING AGENCY

Many firms produce newspaper advertising in-house but hire an agency to produce television commercials.[37] When an advertising agency is employed to produce television spots, the agency should understand the client's goals and budget constraints. The cost of air time is set by media, but production budgets must be negotiated between client and agency. Client and agency must also decide who is responsible for designing, producing, and airing the commercials.

When employing an advertising agency, a client must make sure that the agency clearly understands what marketing communications objective is to be addressed by this advertising effort. A superb campaign focused in the wrong direction wastes money. Therefore, all information needed to clarify the objective should be provided quickly and completely.

Clients do not benefit when agency personnel have to grope around in the dark for essential information, or make erroneous assumptions.

Whenever possible, suitable models and personnel from the client should be used for the filming. The client's advertising department should only provide scripts if it can do so adequately and appropriately. In most cases, the client's writers will know more about the products and their uses than will the agency people, but the agency people have had more experience writing scripts for television.

Locations for filming commercials might be obtained in museums, libraries, and other public organizations that want exposure from the commercial. Credits in the ad naming the public buildings tend to increase awareness of these institutions and thus help them solicit funds. Customers who have beautiful private grounds or homes may let the advertiser use them for the prestige of being able to say, "Watch that television commercial; that's our home." Usually, there is much additional film footage after a shooting. This footage can be saved for possible use in other commercials.

The agency's contribution can be the skillful use of the camera, technical support, and the many creative touches that go into creating commercials. Another important agency contribution is coordinating all the elements: models and timing, location, and support people—camera operator, director, sound person, prop person, script person, and others.

SUMMARY

Radio's advantages as an advertising medium are (1) it can be directed at specific, segmented audiences, (2) it is an instant, relatively local communication adaptable to last-minute changes, and (3) it can reach a mobile consumer. For example, a new shipment of rock records can be advertised on an area rock station to which people listen on earphones while biking or jogging. Firms can advertise location, hours, image, mood, general sales, and specific merchandise on radio, and refer listeners to newspapers and other advertisements for details.

Large advertisers can afford to use network and spot television effectively, but network television has been used only in a limited way by most local firms. However, local television has been widely used for short institutional ads by local firms and shopping centers. Smaller and regional firms can benefit from improvements in local and cable television. Production costs vary with complexity of ads. Commercials should create awareness, interest, and understanding for a firm and product(s), encouraging customers to like the sponsors and buy the products.

New technological developments make it necessary for marketers to watch carefully what is happening to television and other broadcast media vehicles, and what competitors are doing with broadcast advertising. Shorter, split-30 commercials, longer multi-minute informercials, television sets with stereo, bilingual broadcasting, interactive television, videocassettes, and computer graphics are changing the television scene. But creating commercials that overcome broadcast ad clutter can be a worthwhile challenge.

QUESTIONS

1. How might an advertising message differ for the various media: radio, television, newspapers? Choose a radio or television commercial described in this chapter and adapt it for a different broadcast media vehicle.
2. Compare a radio commercial described in this chapter with a television commercial as to message and target.
3. For the radio commercials shown in this chapter's exhibits, compare messages and targets. Explain why radio is or is not more appropriate than newspapers for these commercials.
4. How would you evaluate a television commercial? Apply your criteria to a television commercial in this chapter.
5. In the next five years, will broadcast media become more important than print media for retailers? for manufacturers? Explain. If this will be true for some types of retailers or manufacturers and not for others, explain which types will use relatively more broadcast than print media in the next five years. Which broadcast media will be most important for these types? Explain.
6. You are a small, independent retailer with one record store in a downtown area. Explain why you will or will not include cable television in your advertising plan.
7. Which of the present and future technological developments affecting broadcast advertising will be most important for broadcast advertisers five to ten years from now?
8. Under what conditions would you employ an advertising agency to help your firm with broadcast advertising? Specify type of advertiser when you answer this question.
9. Under what conditions would you have your own television program? Specify type of advertiser when you answer this question.

NOTES

1. *Radio Facts* (New York: Radio Advertising Bureau, 485 Lexington Ave., NY 10007, 1984), pp. 4, 5, 7.

2. *Radio Facts,* pp. 6, 9.

3. *Radio Facts,* pp. 12, 17, 34, 35.

4. Miles David, "How to Work Effectively with your Local Radio Stations," in *How to Profit from Radio Advertising* (New York: National Retail Merchants Association, 1975), p. 60.

5. *Radio Facts,* p. 32.

6. *Radio Facts,* pp. 26, 27.

7. A. Ries and J. Trout, "The Eye vs. the Ear," *Advertising Age,* 54 (March 14, 1983), pp. M-27, M-28.

8. "Glossary of Radio Language," in *How to Profit From Radio Advertising,* pp. 76, 82.

9. Miles David, "How to Work Effectively," pp. 59–65.

10. S. Williams, "New Arbitron Service Receives Rough Rating," *Advertising Age,* 55 (September 13, 1984), p. 24.

11. Sonja Larsen, "The Facts about Radio Co-op," in *How to Profit from Radio Advertising,* pp. 23–35.

12. C. Canape, "Co-op Ads: An Overlooked Bargain," *Advertising Age,* 53 (September 13, 1982), p. M-14; Diane Mermigas and Steven Colford, "Don't Burn Those Logs, Ad Units Tell TV Stations," *Advertising Age,* 55 (July 2, 1984), pp. 1, 42. "Coop" is discussed more fully in Chapter 15.

13. Television Bureau of Advertising.

14. Television Bureau of Advertising.

15. "Department Stores Ready Fall Campaigns," *Advertising Age,* 55 (August 2, 1984), p. 38; Margaret Opsata, "Center TV Advertising Moves into 'Hard Sell' Gear," *Shopping Center World,* 10 (November 1981), pp. 32–34; Pat Sloan, "Bloomingdale's Future in Expanding Its Mystique," *Advertising Age,* 54 (October 3, 1983), pp. 3, 58–59; Jesse Snyder, "K-mart Buys Fit Long-Term Plan . . . as Company Eyes More TV Ads," *Advertising Age,* 55 (August 6, 1984), p. 52.

15. *Our Business is Helping Your Business Grow Bigger, More Competitive, More Profitable,* undated brochure of the Television Bureau of Advertising, 485 Lexington Avenue, New York, NY 10017, received January 1984; and other Television Bureau of Advertising materials.

16. Good sources of information about retail television advertising include: H. Abrahams, *Making TV Pay Off* (New York: Fairchild, 1975); Michael M. Klepper, *Getting Your Message Out: How to Get, Use and Survive Radio and Television Air Time* (Englewood Cliffs, NJ: Prentice-Hall, 1984); J. Rowen, ed., *Profitable Retail Television Advertising* (New York: National Retail Merchants Association, 1977); Roy S. Singleton, *Telecommunications in the Information Age: a Nontechnical Primer on the New Technologies* (Cambridge, MA: Ballinger, 1984).

See also Television Bureau of Advertising.

17. Maurine Christopher, "ARF Warned on TV Clutter by Nielsen," *Advertising Age,* 55 (March 2, 1984), pp. 4, 61; Diane Mermigas, "New-Format TV Ads Expected," *Advertising Age,* 55 (July 9, 1984), p. 61.

18. V. Gay, "JWT & ABC Ask: To Split, or Not to Split," *Advertising Age,* 55 (November 29, 1984), pp. 1, 54.

19. Arlene Zeichner, "TV Sets Wising Up with Innovations," *Advertising Age,* 55 (June 7, 1984), pp. 33–34.

20. "Of Head Ends and Footprints," *Advertising Age,* 54 (June 13, 1983), p. M-10.

21. "Cable Ad Bureau Gets Broad $upport," *Advertising Age,* 51 (August 11, 1980), p. 3; "Cable Report Sees Basic Services Moving to Pay," *Advertising Age,* 55 (January 23, 1984), p. 55; J. Cleaver, "The Medium is Potent, if the Message is Clear," *Advertising Age,* 54 (June 13, 1983), pp. M-28, M-32; "Department Stores Ready Fall Campaigns," *Advertising Age,* p. 38; Jack Myers, "Networks Stake Survival on Ad Revenues," *Advertising Age,* 55 (May 31, 1984), pp. 32, 36; Susan Spillman, "Cable Sees Growing Threat from VCRS," *Advertising Age,* 55 (May 7, 1984), p. 60.

22. M. Kingman, "The Cost of Learning About Cable," *Advertising Age,* 53 (September 6, 1982), p. M-28; B. Hulin-Salkin, "How the Electronic Media Measure Up," *Advertising Age,* 54 (October 31, 1983), pp. M-36–M-41; D. Veraska,

"Cable Marketing Still a Murky Art," *Advertising Age,* 55 (December 6, 1984) pp. 1, 12.

23. C. Allen, "Locally, the Fight Heats Up," *Advertising Age,* 53 (Septembe 13, 1982), p. M-16; S. Spillman, "Movie Channel Tunes in Ads," *Advertising Age* 55 (December 6, 1984), p. 3; "People Meters" are explained in Chapter 4; Spillman "TV Network Tries to Extend Campus Reach," *Advertising Age,* 55 (August 6 1984), p. 46.

24. "ABC Infomercials Rerun in New York," *Advertising Age,* 55 (Januar 9, 1984), p. 40E; S. Donavon, "Local Ads Hit the Spot for Operators," *Advertisin Age,* 55 (December 6, 1984), p. 13.

25. "Cable, Marketing's Newest Dish," *Advertising Age,* 53 (April 26, 1982) p. 21; "Cableshop Plans National Launch in January 1985," *Marketing News,* 1 (November 9, 1984), p. 23; "Long Spots Long Shots that Pay," *Advertising Age* 55 (May 31, 1984), p. 36.

26. "Qube in Sponsored Programming Again," *Advertising Age,* 52 (Apri 13, 1981), p. 69.

27. P. Schulman and B. Reid, *What Every Young Account Representative Should Know About Television Commercial Production* (New York: America Association for Advertising Agencies, 200 Park Avenue, 10017, 1979).

28. Schulman and Reid, *What Every Young Account Representative Shoul Know.*

29. M. Schlinger, L. Alwitt, K. McCarthy, and L. Green, "Effects of Tim Compression on Attitudes and Information Processing," *Journal of Marketing* 47 (Winter 1983), pp. 79–85.

30. Marketing Director Ruth Brandt, Holyoke Mall, Ingleside, MA, 1980

31. H. White, "Five Ways to Get the Most Out of Production Dollars," *Advertising Age,* 51 (October 20, 1980), p. 66; White, Chapter 15, *How to Produce an Effective TV Commercial* (Chicago: Crain, 1981); D. Salisbury, "A Compute Program for Budding Walt Disneys," *The Christian Science Monitor* (January 14 1984), p. 17.

32. "Marketing Technology Briefs," *Marketing News,* 18 (November 9 1984), p. 23.

33. J. Myers, "Effective Retail Television Advertising," *Promotion Exchange* (April 1980), p. 3.

34. J. Myers, "Effective Retail Television Advertisers," page 1; J. Honomichl "TV Copy Testing Flap: What to Do About It," *Advertising Age,* 52 (January 19 1981), pp. 59–62; Sonia Yuspeh and David Leach, "A Recall Debate," *Advertising Age,* 52 (July 13, 1981), pp. 47–48.

See also Chapter 16 of this book.

35. "New Technology 'TRACES' Reaction to TV Ads," *Marketing News* (May 25, 1984), Section 1, p. 3.

36. "Department Stores Ready Fall Campaigns," *Advertising Age,* p. 38.

37. Ibid.

APPENDIX 9

SUGGESTIONS FOR MAKING A SIMPLE TV SPOT COMMERCIAL

1. Select appropriate merchandise for the forthcoming season that is visually colorful and interesting and perhaps has a story.
2. Use store models if possible, or hire models on a daily basis rather than an hourly basis. Spots usually take many hours to shoot; once on location it is wise to make several at the same time.
3. Select an interesting location suitable for the merchandise to be shown, and one that might give atmosphere to the spot. If this is not possible, it may be appropriate to add a few props to a studio shooting or shoot in some interior that already has furniture, such as a store's own home furnishing section or a home that is made available for this purpose.
4. Shooting can be done on 16mm color film or videotape, whichever is the easiest and most economical.
5. Write a simple *shooting script* with plenty of flexibility so director and producer have plenty of leeway.
6. Always shoot much more footage than will actually be used, redoing the scene several times for long, medium and close-up shots. Later the editor can select footage which gives the best effects.
7. Use a voice-over commentator rather than live sound. Use canned music softly under commentary, louder when there is no voice.
8. Time various versions to make 10-second, 30-second, and one-minute spots from the same material, with appropriate commentary changes.
9. Combine all elements, visual, voice, and music, for the best total effect and proper lengths, allowing room for the store's identification logo at the beginning, the end, or both.
10. Work with the local television station to find the best time for spots to be aired, and to decide how frequently they should be broadcast. Usually there are savings in booking a number of time slots over a week or a month.

10
COMPARING AND SELECTING ADVERTISING MEDIA

INTRODUCTION

The late Marshall McLuhan, Director of the Center for Culture and Technology of the University of Toronto, was the author of the famous phrase, "The medium is the message." He argued that the medium shapes the scale and form of known associations and actions. Each media vehicle has its own image which sends a message about those who advertise in it. McLuhan facetiously asked if the following lines that Shakepeare's Romeo spoke to Juliet could describe television:[1]

> But, soft! What light through yonder window breaks? . . .
> She speaks, yet she says nothing . . .

He should have added the remainder of that thought: "what of that? Her eye discourses." On television, sometimes the action and visuals in commercials speak louder than the words.

Media vehicles are the instruments through which advertising is communicated. Each has its own image, advantages, and disadvantages. Marketing communications can involve a major investment in media time and space. We have discussed the production and evaluation of newspaper, magazine, radio, television, direct mail, and other advertising separately in previous chapters. This chapter describes the characteristics of the various media vehicles in relation to one another and to communications objectives. It gives examples of how the various media vehicles can be used, combined, and coordinated for effective advertising.

While media planning plays a key role for all advertisers, it is especially vital to retailers because merchandise advertising must be maintained and changed on a day-to-day basis. Manufacturers' brand and retailers' image advertising both build name recognition and long-term identity; such ads can be planned months in advance and run for a period of time. Not only effective messages but also effective media placements are needed to get the most "bang for the buck," and to reach a firm's goals for image, profits, market share, sales, and growth.

THE SELECTION PROCESS

Knowledge of just who and where the targeted customers are becomes an important factor in media decisions. Previous experience and marketing research determine the targets. Then the matching process begins. Effectiveness is measured by comparing dollar sales, traffic, and number of specific items sold with the cost of the marketing communications involved.[2] There is not an exact cause and effect relationship because other variables, like weather, competitive advertising, and other marketing communications by the firm also influence sales.

Selecting Media Categories

The first step in making a selection is to evaluate the major media in relation to each other: newspaper, radio, television, direct mail, and perhaps magazine, transit advertising, and billboards as well. The type of each business will influence media selection. Manufacturers and stores with national distribution can use network television and magazines. Local firms tend to use newspaper and radio advertising.[3]

These decisions are part of other marketing decisions which include expenditures for sales promotion, display, publicity, and related matters. The marketing manager coordinates both the allocation and the timing of each aspect of promotion. In some cases, a firm's own labeled shopping bags and boxes are included in media allocations. In other cases, these items are charged to sales promotion or operating expenses. In either case, packaging is an important medium for manufacturers.

Each media vehicle tries to make the best case for itself in order to sell more advertising time or space to more advertisers. In Exhibit 10-1, a radio news station describes its power, coverage, format, staff, and features in a print advertising piece prepared for potential advertisers.

EXHIBIT 10-1 **Radio Station Description of Image, Programming, Audience**
Source: WCBS Radio.

WCBS NEWSRADIO 88

A CBS Owned Station Represented by CBS Radio Spot Sales • 51 W 52nd Street, New York, New York 10019

STATION PROFILE

POWER: 50,000 watts, 880 kHz

COVERAGE: Metro Area: 20 counties (N.Y., N.J., CT.)
0.5 mv/m area: 42 counties in 6 states
Nighttime Skywave Contour: Florida to Great Lakes

FORMAT: All news — 24 hours a day, seven days a week. Summaries, headlines, on-scene reports, analysis, backgrounders and enterprise/investigative series. Wide range of information features. CBS News on the hour.

STAFF: Twelve anchors. Dual anchor team weekdays:
AM Drive - Jim Donnelly and Robert Vaughn
Midday - Rita Sands and Harvey Hauptman
PM Drive - Ben Farnsworth and Tom Franklin

Eight general assignment reporters, one chief investigative reporter, five suburban stringers. Largest staff of reporters in New York radio. Three sports reporters. Seventeen feature broadcasters.

World and national coverage: CBS News, RSNS, AP, UPI, Reuters and special sports and feature wires.

FEATURES: Helicopter Traffic: 13 reports in AM Drive, 13 in PM Drive. Pilots: Neil Busch, Lou Timolat and Tom Salat.

Sports: At :15 and :45 during AM Drive, PM Drive, nighttime and weekends. Ed Ingles reports mornings. Bill Schweizer from 4PM to 11PM and Barry Landers on the weekends.

Weather: Complete forecasts by Craig Allen 26 times each weekday. Weekend reports by Steve Sambol.

Business: Hourly reports in AM Drive and from 3PM to 11PM, weekdays. Ken Prewitt is the reporter.

Other features include reports on medicine (Mel Granick), entertainment (Jeffrey Lyons), law (Neil Chayet), consumer news (Elaine Rose), food and dining (Anthony Dias Blue), money management (Marshall Loeb), business and industry (William S. Rukeyser), books (Don Swaim).

6/84

Selecting Media within a Category

The next step in the selection process is to evaluate each medium separately to determine which media vehicles will produce the best results for the money expended within a category—for example, which radio stations should be used, or which newspapers. Then, each of the different media vehicles must be compared on a cost-effective basis with the others. Finally, the selection of individual media is made on the basis of reaching the most potential customers for the least cost. At this point the list of media vehicles should be specific. The newspapers, radio stations, television stations, direct-mail programs, and other media are named, and the proportions of the advertising budgeted for each are assigned.

The essential factors in a firm's evaluation of individual media vehicles include the relevant geographic market and the advertiser's and brand's particular characteristics. The *retail trading area* is the geographic region containing a retailer's actual and potential customers. This must be compared with the *geographic reach* of the various media. For example, if an appropriate newspaper reaches only a certain portion of the total targeted area, then a mailing piece, hand-distributed circular, or a broadcast medium may be needed to achieve total coverage. In addition to the primary trading area, retailers usually designate *secondary* and *tertiary areas* from which they also draw customers, but to a lesser and lesser degree. The actual and potential customers of a firm are also defined by demographic and lifestyle research. The marketer then determines how best to reach the demographic and lifestyle targets in a trading area.

The retailer needs to define specifically the exact size and shape of the trading area, depending on transportation routes, the number and types of competitors in the vicinity of a store, and the shopping habits of target customers. Census data are available for small geographic units called *blocks, block groups,* and *tracts* to help marketers understand particular geographic areas.

The central business district (CBD) is the downtown area of a central city in a Standard Metropolitan Statistical Area (SMSA), or of other cities of 50,000 or more people. It is in an area of high land valuation with a high concentration of retail businesses. Within the boundaries of the central city are various barriers like rivers and highways which affect travel from one part of the city to another. An area of interest to retailers is a shopping center, also called a *major retail center* (MRC) by the Census. This is a concentration of at least 25 retail stores in a Standard Metropolitan Statistical Area but outside the central business district. At least one of the stores must be a general merchandise store with a minimum of 100,000 square feet of total under-roof floor space.[4]

It may be difficult for the uninitiated to use Census data. It is probably most efficient to get help from Census data services at universities or to use Census information that has been processed by commercial firms, rather than trying to use Census data without help.

Defining a trading area has been the subject of recent research. For example, survey data obtained by interviewing customers can be misleading. In one experiment, researchers used four different types of criteria: (1) number of visits to a shopping center, (2) sales dollars, (3) location of interview in shopping center, and (4) time of interview in shopping center—and they drew four different trading area maps for the same shopping center![5] Coordinating the geographic trading area of a store, however defined, with the areas covered by media vehicles, is an art as well as a science, and requires an understanding of the environment beyond mere numbers.

Selecting Location or Time in a Media Vehicle

In addition to the selection of a list of media vehicles, retailers try to select specific pages and page locations for print media, and specific time slots and programs for broadcast media. For example, the managers of a men's store might select the sporting and financial pages in a newspaper and drive time on radio. Sunday papers are targeted at the entire family with comics for children and articles about households, food, news, recreation, and sports for adults. Retailers with these targets advertise in Sunday papers because consumers have more time on weekends for reading the paper.

Media programming, advertising content, and costs of time and space change as lifestyles and demographics change. The increase in the number of employed women has caused broadcast programmers to move some types of soap operas from daytime to evening. Prime time can change its meaning as consumers change their listening habits.

MEDIA BACKGROUND

Jargon and Strategy

A basic tool for comparing media is *cost per thousand*, (CPM). This means the cost per thousand households or individuals reached, depending on the survey definition. CPM is based on a ratio of (1) the cost of advertising time or space to (2) the estimated number of households or individuals reached by a particular media vehicle. Those reached have not necessarily paid attention to the ads or remembered them; nor are all of those persons interested in a particular firm or product/service. CPM is only a rough yardstick for comparing various media vehicles.

CPM can be supplemented by demographic and psychographic data A higher CPM for a media vehicle which reaches a firm's target audience is more cost-effective in terms of potential purchasers than a media vehicle with a lower CPM. For instance, marketers who wish to reach an affluent audience might use a particular radio station or local magazine hat reaches most of their target customers at a very high cost per thousand f there is a very high profit in reaching that group. The higher cost per housand is cost-effective if the media vehicle reaches a high percentage of actual and prospective customers, for then the advertiser's message is eaching a high percentage of the right people. On the other hand, a nedia vehicle with a low cost per thousand which reaches a very low percentage of the right people can be effectively very costly—or it may be so inexpensive that reaching only a low percentage of the target is till cost-effective. The effective CPM is the CPM-of-people-reached adjusted by the percentage of the right people reached.

Reach, for a media vehicle, is the total unduplicated audience exposed o that media vehicle in a specified time period. Reach for an advertiser s the number of the media vehicle's target customers exposed to that irm's advertisements in a specified time period. If 70% of 100,000 listeners eard a commercial last week, reach is 70,000.

There are two factors to consider when evaluating reach: where and who. *Where* refers to the media vehicle's geographic reach compared with an advertiser's trading area. *Who* asks, "What percentage of persons eached by the media vehicle have demographics and psychographics ike those in the advertiser's target market? Most newspapers, magazines, nd radio, and television stations have collected demographic and psychographic data about their audiences, and provide this information to prospective advertisers. *Effective reach* is the number of the advertiser's arget customers within the media vehicle's reach. *Wasted reach*, also alled *wasted circulation*, is the number of households or individuals not in the advertiser's target market, but in the media vehicle's reach.[6]

Two examples of wasted reach follow: A large store in a shopping enter on one side of a big city uses city media vehicles that reach both he entire city and the area on the opposite side of the city which has ts own shopping center. This retailer pays for reaching those who are not expected to be customers. Another retailer is located in a suburb of large city. Most inhabitants of this suburb read the city newspapers nd listen to the city broadcast media. This suburban retailer cannot fford to pay the high price of the city media to reach only a small egment of its own audience.

Some media vehicles have special rates and programs for advertisers ocated in outlying areas. Some newspapers have special sections which irculate only in particular areas with news, features, and ads targeted t those areas. Broadcast media tend to have special rates for advertisers who cannot afford to pay for reaching thousands of people who are not ikely to be customers.

On the other hand, some retailers get multiple value from an advertising investment because they have several stores within the area of media reach and all of their stores benefit from the same advertising ffort. This is one reason for a retailer's locating branches in clusters thoughout the country, instead of having only single stores, geographically dispersed.

Frequency is the number of times an advertising message reaches the same person or household within a given time period. For example, of ten million target customers, five million target customers saw three ads, and five million saw nine ads last week. The average frequency would equal six, the total exposures to the message divided by reach ([5 million × 3] + [5 million × 9]) ÷ 10 million persons or households. A certain number of ads are needed to get consumers to notice a store or brand. After noticing an ad, consumers must remember the ad's message when planning a shopping trip or when at the point of purchase. The consumer can always refer back to a newspaper advertisement for any detail. But a broadcast message must be coordinated with reminders in other media or repeated often enough for consumers to remember—but not so much that consumers get tired of it and cease to notice.[7]

Continuity is related to frequency; it is the regularity with which a retailer's advertising appears in the media over a period of time.[8] Regularity reassures customers that the advertiser is there, ready to serve them, and has not gone out of business. The less a store or brand is known, the more frequency and continuity are required to build awareness. One-shot advertisements for relatively unknown stores or brands are generally ineffective.

Once target customers are aware of a firm, then it can maintain its presence in the market with continuous advertising in the appropriate media. Continuity is reinforced by placing ads in the same page, time slot, or program type so that customers know where to find the ads when they want information about a store or brand. Requesting a particular place is more expensive than having the media management choose the location for ads, and this may influence how often the advertiser can choose the location. Likewise, it costs more to request that an ad run before a certain date. The less expensive alternative, called *run of press* (ROP) or *run of schedule* (ROS), means that media representatives determine the placement of the ads. However, when timing is essential, as in announcing a retail sale on a particular day, it is false economy to take a chance that the ad will be run on time. In that case, paying more to be sure of chosen placement is advisable.

An exception to continuous advertising would be several short, intensive advertising campaigns to maximize reach and frequency at certain times of year. Because retailers are usually in business during all months of the year, they need continuous advertising. But cooperative funds may come from different manufacturers at different times of the year depending on the seasonality of the merchandise; for example, lawnmowers in spring and snowblowers in winter.

A popular current practice is to use a message in one medium to reinforce a message in another. For example, announcing a special event in all local media, or using radio to mention key items in a mailed catalog or newspaper insert. This practice can overcome some of the reach problems of a particular media vehicle.

Gross rating points (GRP) are computed for each market by multiplying the percentage of the population reached times frequency: GRP = (audience reached by ad/total audience) × frequency. For example, if 70,000 people in an audience of 100,000 were reached six times (average frequency) last week, GRP = 70 × 6 = 420. Different sources disagree as to whether *reach* should be expressed as 70%, or as 70,000. If reach is expressed as 70%, then GRP = reach times frequency. If reach is expressed as 70,000, then GRP = reach/total audience times frequency. Definition of *total audience* differs for different media. For TV, it is households having TV sets; for radio or magazines, it is a particular target group—number of teens, males, etc.; for outdoor media, the total is the number of people passing the sign in one day.[9]

If an advertiser's goal is 840 GRP and only 420 GRP are being attained, the average frequency could be doubled, the reach could be changed by choosing other media vehicles, or some combination of changing both reach and frequency might be tried. Increasing frequency would depend on whether the advertiser could afford to buy more time slots for ads and on whether these slots were available. It might be necessary to reallocate media selection plans if the current plan does not meet the firm's goals. This GRP calculation is only quantitative and does not measure the non-quantitative aspects of the ad's effectiveness.

Media Markets

Most media vehicles have a demographic and psychographic profile of their audiences, and comparisons with those of competitors. Media vehicles also provide information about how to use a particular medium most effectively.[10] Marketing and advertising consulting firms analyse markets and help select media for a fee. Telephone directories and libraries have current names and addresses of these firms and agencies. Microcomputer and mainframe computer programs for media selection and placement are also available. The Newspaper Advertising Bureau, Radio Advertising Bureau and Television Bureau of Advertising have retail specialists to help retailers match local media with retail trading areas.

Information provided by newspapers about their markets can be confirmed in other sources like the *Sales & Marketing Management* Survey of Newspaper Markets and the *Editor and Publisher* annual *Market Guide*. *Sales & Marketing Management* provides information for cities with at least one daily newspaper having a minimum paid circulation of 25,000. Information is available for the *home* county of the newspaper, the *dominant* county where household newspaper penetration is 50% or more, and *effective* counties, where coverage ranges from 20% to 49%. Information comes from the data bank of the Audit Bureau of Circulation. Total net retail sales, excluding refunds, return allowances, taxes, and credit carrying charges, are available for food stores, general merchandise establishments including department stores, furniture and appliance stores, automotive and tire stores, and drug stores engaged primarily in retail trade. These sales are an approximation because shoppers travel to and from adjacent areas. Circulation totals are expressed as a percentage of all households covered, using the Census definition of *household*—groups of up to nine individuals living together, whether families or unrelated individuals.[11]

Editor and Publisher provides surveys of over 1600 daily U.S. and Canadian newspaper markets, including location, transportation, population, households, industries, retail areas, and distance of shopping centers from downtown. A sample of this information is shown in Exhibit 10-2. *Editor and Publisher* also provides market guide maps which show cities and county seats with daily newspapers. A sample is shown in Exhibit 10-3.

EXHIBIT 10-2 **Media Market Information**

Source: *Market Guide* (New York: Editor & Publisher, 1982), p. II-165.

ALPENA, MI

1 - LOCATION: Alpena County, E&P Map D-3, County Seat. Located 234 mi. N of Detroit, on Thunder Bay, Lake Huron. On U.S. Hwy. 23 and State Hwy. M-32.

2 - TRANSPORTATION: Detroit and Mackinac R.R.
Motor Freight Carrier-1.
Intercity Bus Lines-Great Lakes; Greyhound.
Airlines-Simmons.

3 - POPULATION:
Corp. City 80 Cen. 12,214; Loc. Est. 11,663
CZ-ABC: (70) 22,806; (82) 24,500
RTZ-ABC: (70) 27,087; (82) 32,700
County 80 Cen. 32,315; Loc. Est. 32,354
City & RTZ-ABC: (70) 49,893; (82) 57,200
Demographic Information available from Newspaper. See paragraph 14.

4 - HOUSEHOLDS:
City 80 Cen. 4,574; Loc. Est. 3,820
County 80 Cen. 11,151; Loc. Est. 11,509
CZ-ABC: (70) 6,574; (82) 8,300
RTZ-ABC: (70) 8,132; (82) 11,600
City & RTZ-ABC: (70) 14,706; (82) 19,900

5 - BANKS:	**NUMBER**	**EST. DEP.**
Savings	2	$205,600,000
Savings & Loan	2	$48,700,000

6 - PASSENGER AUTOS: County 16,206

7 - ELECTRIC METERS: Residence 5,400

8 - GAS METERS: Residence 5,650

9 - PRINCIPAL INDUSTRIES: Industry, Number of Wage Earners (Av. Wkly. Wage)-Cement 1,000 ($280); Machines 650 ($220); Auto Trim 130 ($160); Paper 200 ($220); Hardboard 550 ($240); Foundry 125 ($210).

10 - CLIMATE: Min. & Max. Avg. Temp.-Spring 41-59; Summer 54-72; Fall 30-43; Winter 15-30.

11 - TAP WATER: Alkaline, soft; fluoridated.

12 - RETAILING:

Nearby Shopping Centers

Name (No. of stores)	Miles from Downtown	Principal Stores
Alpena Shopping Center(15)	NA	Lakeshore Shoprite, Kresge, Cunningham
Giantway Plaza	2	Giantway, Midway
Ripley Square	1	A&P, Fisher Big Wheel, TG&Y, Mont. Ward.
Thunder Bay(14)	1	Kroger, Revco, Sears
Alpena Mall(3)	1	K mart, J.C. Penney

Principal Shopping Days-Mon., Fri., Sat.; stores open 6 nights & Sunday afternoon.

13 - RETAIL OUTLETS: Department Stores-J.C. Penney; Vaughn; Kotwicki's.
Discount Stores -Big Wheel; Giantway K mart.
Variety Stores-McLellan's; Kresge's; T.G.&Y.; Disco; Western Auto; Gambles.
Chain Drug Stores -Spen's Walgreen; Cunningham's; Revco Drug.
Chain Supermarkets-A&P; Midway 2; Hamady; Perch's IGA; Lakeshore Spartan.
Other Chain Stores-Kinney Shoes; Three Sisters; Sherwin-Williams; Singer; Montgomery Ward (catalog); Sears (catalog); Gately's; Gittleman's; Western Auto; Radio Shack; Holiday Inn; Erb Lumber; Wickes Lumber.

14 - NEWSPAPERS: NEWS (e) 12,599; Mar. 31, 1982 ABC.
Local Contact for Advertising and Merchandising Data: Edward Robin, Adv. Mgr., NEWS, 130 Park Place, Alpena, MI 49707; Tel. (517) 354-3111.
National Representative: None.

EXHIBIT 10-3 Map of Daily Newspapers
Source: *Market Guide* (New York: Editor & Publisher, 1982), p. II-155.

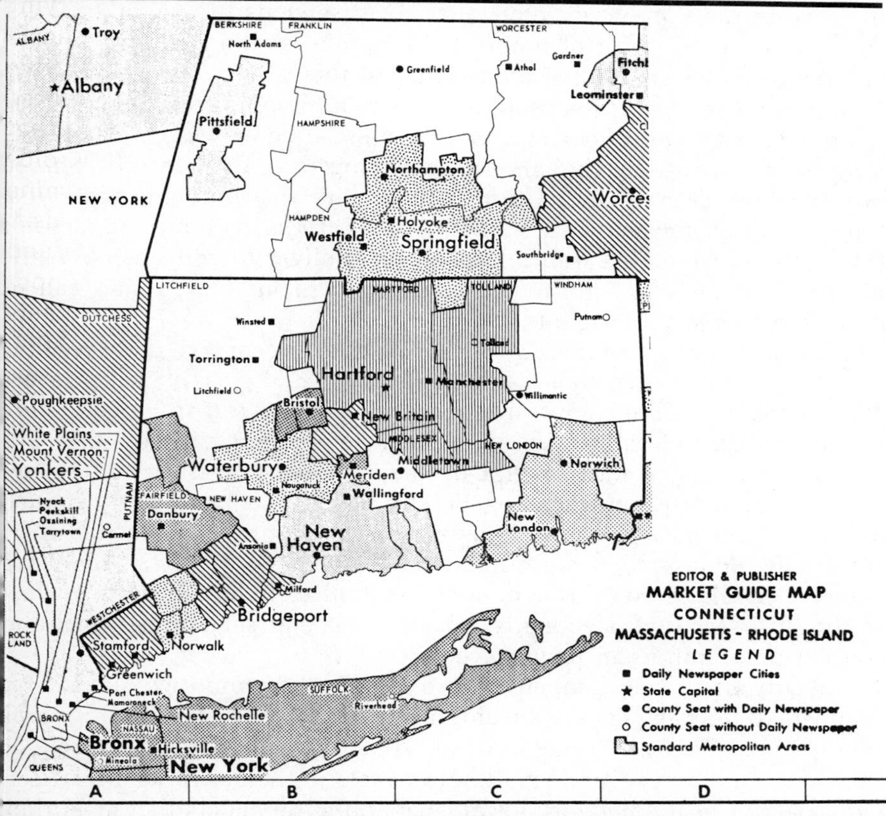

Media Characteristics and Information Sources

Advertising Age provides articles about media, and summaries of media research for radio, magazines, newspapers, and network and local television. This summary lists the media covered, audience definition, methodology, data supplied, subscriber universe, and other information, including evaluations of the research services provided by advertising agencies. *Advertising Age* also reports numbers of advertising pages for U.S., Canadian, and foreign consumer publications by merchandise category each month, with the year-to-date totals.[12]

Recent articles have reported some interesting information about media. Media people in ad agencies can now advise clients about cable TV as well as print and broadcast media. Recent Scarborough and Simmons studies make inter-media comparisons possible both nationally and on a market-by-market basis. Of 510 men and women, 45.8% reported that they had read one out of four issues of some non-existent magazines. An increase in the number of retail sale advertisements in regular sections and also in the number of preprinted separate retail advertising inserts has reduced the amount of advertising in the Sunday newspaper sup- plements, possibly because supplements require more lead time than do the regular ad pages of newspapers. Retailers are now using 20% of their newspaper advertising dollars on producing their own inserts. Shared mail and direct-mail pieces to consumers are also reducing somewhat the amount of newspaper advertising. *Shared mail* is grouping tabloids from different retailers into one packet to deliver to consumers. While most newspapers go only to those who buy them, shared mail can be delivered to every household.[13]

With the growth of free circulars or newspapers comes a new diversity *Free community newspapers* are usually delivered weekly. They devote 30% of their space to news, mostly local, and the rest to grocery store advertising and classified ads. *Suburban newspapers* can be either free or paid. They have local, regional, and national advertisers and news ratios of about 40%. *Shoppers* generally have just advertising, "canned features," and no local news; they are distributed by local carrier or by U.S. mail. *Pennysavers* are similar to shoppers or circulars, but have readers' classified ads throughout the tabloid to induce readers to look at the ads. Retailers frequently advertise special sale promotions and coupon redemptions in pennysavers.[14]

With all of the competition from larger communities and shared mail, small newspapers are developing networks with other nearby small newspapers. This allows advertisers to submit and pay for a single ad that will appear in several small newspapers in the network. Advertisers can select from the network newspapers only the papers that meet their needs. This minimizes waste circulation.[15]

Many towns and cities have colleges located nearby. These colleges often have student-run weekly newspapers that can be effective advertising media vehicles for local firms that consider college students to be in their target market. The college papers are for students, a relatively well defined age and lifestyle group. Some large colleges and universities have newspapers with larger circulations than many small-town newspapers.

Other print media include the various printed materials available to college students, and the electronic print media available in shopping centers. Examples of print media vehicles for college students include *The Directory of Classes,* published three times a year to inform students of class schedules and including advertisements, and *The Wallpaper Journal,* a semi-weekly poster-sized information sheet with articles of interest to students, also including ads. *Colormedia* is a computerized message board that displays news, weather, sports, local notices, and ads.

ı colored moving print and illustrations. Located in shopping centers, ıis board allows advertisers to change ad messages several times a day.[16]

Sources of information about print media also provide information bout broadcast media. *Sales & Marketing Management's* survey of TV ıarkets uses Arbitron's Areas of Dominant Influence (ADIs). For each .DI, the magazine gives population, broken down to show Black and panish-origin population, population by age group, retail net sales, and uying power index.[17] Exhibit 10-4 shows a map provided by *Newspaper*

***KHIBIT 10-4* Media Map for Newspapers, Radio and Television**

ource: Map © Rand McNally & Co. Used by permission. *Newspaper Rates and Data* Vilmette, IL: Standard Rate & Data Services Inc., Oct. 12, 1983), vol. 65, #10, p. 74.

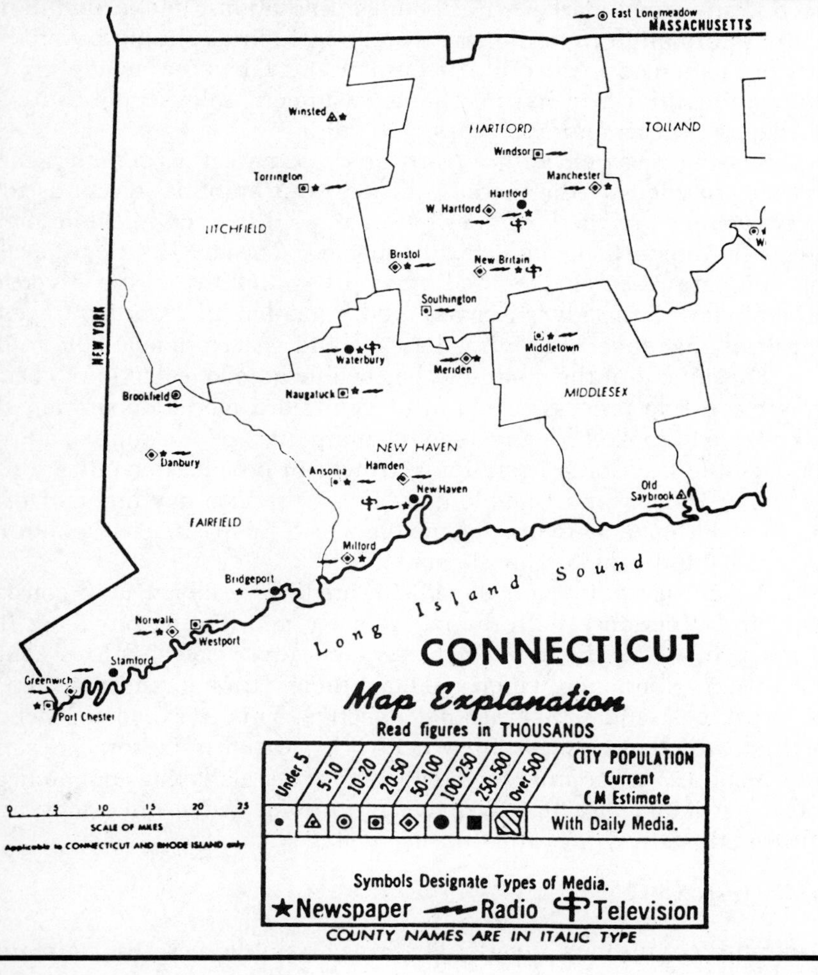

Rates and Data which shows the locations of newspaper, radio, and television stations. This source lists retail sales by store type for ADIs, as well as giving ADI rankings. It also lists names, closing times, and rates for newspapers and magazines. Arbitron provides a map which is color coded for cable penetration levels by ADI.

ACQUIRING INFORMATION FOR PLACING ADS IN MEDIA

Media Research

To information provided by the media, advertisers can add their own information about actual and potential customers, so as to match media reach to the target market within budget limitations. In addition to using media information to minimize wasted reach, firms should have current lists of customers for use in direct-mail and telephone marketing communications. If a firm has no charge customers, salespeople can collect customers' names and addresses.

Sharing research with advertisers is a marketing communications service provided by the media. This research information tends to put media vehicles in the best possible light, as it is done in the interest of the media vehicle that conducted the research. The advertiser must evaluate and compare research provided by media vehicles from the advertiser's point of view. If the advertiser wants additional help, advertising agencies and firms that specialize in media time and space are available to help.

The advent of the computer has enabled media selection to become a more creative process. Large firms can afford media departments and task forces to look at long-run media alternatives. For example, a Procter and Gamble task force is studying growth in broadcast syndication and cable TV. Procter and Gamble continues to reduce daytime and prime-time spending in network television while increasing its spending in magazines and Sunday supplements.[18]

Advantages of frequent advertising are that the advertiser is constantly acquiring experience with the media used, and that no one ad is likely to make or break the firm. However, the advertiser should be able to learn from experience which media vehicles, timing, and placement of ads work best and which are not effective. This is called the *heuristic* method, which means learning what works by trial and error. One caution here: a success arises from the combination of a marketing communication and a particular situation. What is successful at one time may not be successful again if the situation has changed.

Media Tests

Even with continuous advertising, firms do not necessarily maintain the same level of advertising every month. There are slow seasons and busy easons. Many retailers do about 25% of their annual business in November nd December, and so do more advertising at that time. Experience has hown that best results come from "striking while the iron is hot." A ecent test by the Newspaper Advertising Bureau explored whether some hristmas-season advertising allocations should be moved to off-season. he idea was that people bought in the Christmas season anyway, but eeded encouragement to buy in a slow season. Thus total sales would e improved without increasing the annual advertising budget. However, esults showed that the newspaper advertising obtained better results in eak seasons than in slow seasons.[19]

Often, media tests can be made on a limited scale before large funds re invested. Examples include (1) placing a small ad in a newspaper nd checking the results, (2) using various appeals: "sale at good savings," bring in coupon for dollars off," "one-day sale or three-hour sale," and 3) combining two alternative media with two alternative appeals in an xperiment. By counting unit sales and coupons redeemed under special ffers, advertisers can measure customer response, approximating the esults of more sophisticated tests and acquiring an understanding of heir firms' special circumstances.[20]

Sophisticated computer simulations are available through consultants. niversity professors and graduate students can help advertisers with nedia research. Trying various advertising messages, techniques, and lacements in the same medium over a period of time has also been ffective in learning what gets the best response. When good overall esults are obtained, the advertiser is probably doing something right. owever, while *everyone* usually does well during good times, effective dvertising also does relatively well even in poor times.

It is easier to compare similar media vehicles than to compare ifferent ones. For example, the same coupon ad in two different newsapers can be evaluated by counting the number of coupons redeemed om each paper. It is more difficult to compare radio or television ads gainst each other or against newspaper ads. Broadcast listeners can be sked to mention the ad and the station to get a discount when making purchase; however, some might find this embarrassing. To avoid emarrassment, listeners can be asked to design a discount coupon and ubmit it at purchase time, with the best coupon winning a prize.[21]

To evaluate cost-effectiveness among media, a retailer should select taple items and invest, say, $200 in advertising these items for one week. llow a second week for "slow response time," then invest another $200 advertise the identical items in another medium. Allow two more veeks for response; then compare the results. If the advertiser owns two r more stores in different but comparable areas, media vehicles in these ifferent areas can be compared in the same time period. For example, dvertise in newspapers in Texas and on radio in Ohio. *Noise* in the orm of word-of-mouth communication between newspaper readers and broadcast listeners can distort the results of these experiments when the comparable areas have customers who know each other. That is, someone in the area covered by the ad can phone a friend in the no-ad area to communicate the ad information. The advertiser must evaluate the extent to which this noise will interfere with the experiment.

Direct Contact with Customers

Direct marketing and direct-response advertising were discussed in Chapter 8. Direct-mail tests of advertising usually involve coded coupons, with a different code for each media vehicle in which the advertisement is placed. Coupons can also include questionnnaires, with rewards for returning coupons with filled-out questionnaires. Coded customer lists updated regularly from customer purchases, and returned questionnaires reduce wasted circulation. Demographics of the lists need updating because families change their age compositions over the year. If a mailing information card shows no school-age children in a certain family, no back-to-school advertising will be sent to them—but the family may have school-age children later. Children grow up and leave the family residence to form new households. Immigration, emigration, mortality, and lifestyle shifts can change the number of adults in a household.

Media that have direct contact with customers are many and varied. A few are mentioned here. Cash register tapes can be used to create customer loyalty by offering a reward for saving a specified dollar amount in tapes. Coupons advertising other branches or brands can be printed on the back sides of cash register tapes. Sales receipts, stationery, and envelopes can have advertising. Advertisements may be placed on plastic covers made for telephone books. Exhibit 10-5 shows ads in a calendar.

MEDIA—THE BIG PICTURE

Media Allocations by Large National Firms

Looking at media allocations of large, successful firms may provide clues about media priorities. Exhibit 10-6 shows media spending as percentages of advertising spending for large national advertisers. There are five retailers among the 100 largest national advertisers: Sears, K mart, McDonald's, J.C. Penney, and Wendy's. In Exhibit 10-6, Sears, the largest retail advertiser and the second largest national advertiser, is shown to have spent a smaller percentage of sales on advertising than did Wendy's, the 97th largest national advertiser. Wendy's spent a smaller percentage of sales on advertising, than did its larger competitor, McDonald's. The great success of Wendy's "Where's the beef?" commercial showed that advertising effectiveness is not necessarily proportional to money invested. Sears spent the largest measured percentage of its media budget on network

EXHIBIT 10-5 Coupon Ads in Calendar for Students

Source: Reprinted by permission of Harvard Cooperative Society, 1400 Massachusetts Ave., Cambridge, MA 02138.

television and magazines. Penney and McDonald's spent their largest percentages on spot and network television.

Some large stores that have clusters of branches in various sections of the nation, advertise in national magazines. Their objective is to achieve a national image and to attract mail orders and tourists. Manufacturers who distribute brand-name products nationally also advertise in national media.

EXHIBIT 10-6 **Media Spending as Percentage of 1983 Total (Measured and Unmeasured Estimates) Advertising Spending for Some of the 100 Largest National Advertisers**

Source: Percentages are computed from data for each firm in *Advertising Age*, 55 (September 14, 1984). Reprinted with permission from the September 1984 issue of *Advertising Age*. Copyright 1984 by Crain Communications, Inc. Note the large amounts of advertising expenditures that are *unmeasured*.

ADVERTISER	1983 NATIONAL RANK	1983 SALES, $ MILLION	ADVERTISING, PERCENT SALES	MEDIA SPENDING AS PERCENT OF AD SPENDING							
				NEWSPAPER	MAGAZINE	TV		RADIO		OUTDOOR	UNMEA
						SPOT	NET	SPOT	NET		
Procter & Gamble	1	12,946	6.0	1.3	5.2	29.6	47.3	0.4	0.3	0.0	15.9
Sears	2	35,883	2.0	0.0	4.6	4.0	19.8	0.7	1.3	0.0	69.4
K mart	9	18,600	2.1	0.0	2.8	2.5	6.0	1.2	0.0	0.0	87.5
Genl Foods	10	8,600	4.5	0.1	8.5	1.9	44.0	0.1	0.1	0.0	26.2
McDonalds	16	8,687	3.6	0.0	0.1	34.1	26.0	0.6	0.0	1.2	37.9
Johnson & Johnson	17	3,610	8.1	0.7	7.7	3.0	44.4	0.0	0.7	0.0	43.0
J.C. Penney	19	12,078	2.4	0.0	6.5	6.2	10.9	0.0	0.0	0.0	76.0
Anheuser-Busch Cos	20	6,658	4.3	1.4	3.4	20.3	40.0	14.1	2.4	1.4	16.6
Campbell's Soup	52	3,292	3.8	4.0	9.5	16.7	50.0	3.2	5.6	0.0	10.3
Revlon	53	2,379	5.2	0.6	12.9	12.9	37.9	0.6	0.8	0.0	33.9
Hershey Foods	89	1,700	4.0	0.4	10.3	23.5	42.6	0.9	0.6	0.0	20.6
Wendy's Internat.	90	1,923	3.3	0.0	0.6	48.4	28.1	1.4	0.0	1.6	18.8

Exhibit 10-6 gives newspaper advertising budgets for all national dvertisers except the retailers. However, the tabloids that Sears, Penney, nd K mart produce for delivery in newspapers might be in the unmeasured ategory, which is a very high percentage of the advertising spending hown in that exhibit. Unmeasured expenditures include point-of-purchase dvertising, coupons, direct mail, premiums, and other forms of national ales promotion. Many large retailers would be included in the top 100 dvertisers if criteria other than *national* and *measured* spending were sed. *Local* advertising, used by many retailers, is likewise not shown n Exhibit 10-6.

In 1983 Sears was the seventh largest magazine advertiser, the second argest network radio advertiser, and the tenth largest network television dvertiser. McDonald's was the third largest spot television advertiser, nd the 14th largest outdoor advertiser. Zayre Corp, not in the top 100 ational advertisers, was the 25th largest spot radio advertiser. Advertising as a very low percentage of sales for these retailers compared with ales percentages spent on advertising by the other firms in the top 100 ational advertisers. Cosmetics, gum, soft drinks, soap, and drug advertisers ad the higher percentages, up to 10% of sales and more.[22]

In addition to the annual issue of "100 Leading National Advertisers" ublished by *Advertising Age,* there are periodicals which offer current nformation on media advertising. Each annual issue of the Leading National dvertisers' (LNA) *LNA Ad Dollar Summary*[23] lists the advertising dollars pent by the top 1000 companies in six major media: magazines, national ewspaper supplements, network and spot television, network radio, and utdoor. Media advertisements in current trade periodicals offer information n target demographics and psychographics. For example the magazine *bony* advertises that it has almost nine million readers, including 63% f upper-income Black females in the United States, and 50% of all Black orporation presidents, executives, managers, and entrepreneurs.[24]

ompanies That Own Media Vehicles

n addition to publishing annual information on the 100 largest advertisers, *dvertising Age* reports on the 100 largest media companies. These companies are ranked by revenue and their activities are described. For xample, Time Inc., the 3rd largest media company in 1984, owns *Fortune, ife,* and *Sports Illustrated* magazines; cable/video, including Home Box)ffice (HBO); also, Book-of-the-Month Club, Selling-Areas-Marketing, Inc. SAMI), Little, Brown & Company; and Time-Life books. The New York 'imes Company, the 12th largest media company in 1984, owns television roperties in Alabama, Arkansas, and Tennessee, the WQXR radio station n New York, cable TV in southern New Jersey, five magazines (*Cruising Vorld, Family Circle, Golf Digest,* and *Tennis*), and newspapers in eleven states. McGraw-Hill, the 14th largest media company, owns many magazines, newsletters, newswires and services, television companies, boo companies, and financial and information services. The four largest medi companies in 1982 thru 1984 were American Broadcasting Company CBS, Inc., Time Inc., and RCA, the owner of NBC.[25]

Circulation Audits and Broadcast Ratings

The Audit Bureau of Circulation aims to give objective circulation dat so that print advertisers will have accurate facts. The Audit Bureau protect print advertisers from false circulation claims of print media. A non profit organization, the Audit Bureau is funded by newspaper and magazin publishers, advertising agencies, and advertisers. Full-time auditors evaluat circulation claims, using data that members provide. Bulk newspape sales, bought by hotels and others to give to guests, are not included i audited circulation figures because small and medium newspapers oppos this. Advertisers, especially Sears, want ZIP codes included in the Audi Bureau reports to reveal more about demographics.[26]

Similarly, Arbitron and others provide "circulation" estimates fo television broadcasting. The *rating* is the estimated percent of all televisio households or persons tuned to a specific station. The *gross impression* is the average number of persons that view at a time a commercial run multiplied by the number of times the commercial is run. Arbitron als computes the average time spent viewing per household—number o quarter hours times average audience divided by *cume* households. *Cum* is the same as circulation and reach, as previously described. *Viewin* is defined as watching television at least once for five minutes durin the average week for the reported time period. Arbitron also reports th area of dominant influence (ADI), "an exclusive geographic area consistin of all counties in which the home-market commercial stations and satellit stations reported in combination with them received a preponderance o viewing hours." For example, Denver is the 19th ranked ADI, with almos one million households covering 1.12% of the United States. Arbitro reports demographics; for example, Denver has 422,800 women aged 18-34, ADI rank 16.[27]

Media Selection Examples for Six Stores

Appendix 10 contains media selection examples of six hypothetical stores in two competitive situations. In the first competitive situation, a departmen store and a specialty store are located in a typical city outside a large metropolitan area. In the second competitive situation, there are two department stores and two specialty stores in the same trading area. While ıese examples are more complicated than needed by a small firm, they rovide ideas for variations in media selection based on variations in ıe situation.

SUMMARY

Media selection decisions are a very important component in adertising effectiveness. Media selection decisions affect whether or not firm gets the optimum value for each advertising dollar and also whether r not the firm reaches its advertising goals. In a competitive environment, ood or poor media decisions can make the difference between business uccess and failure. Because of constant changes in media, customers, nd the environment, a firm's entire media program should be reviewed t least quarterly to evaluate whether the existing allocation can be nproved.

In addition to choosing among media types, advertisers choose media ehicles within a type, and time and space locations within a media ehicle. Media, periodicals, agencies, and research publications provide ıformation about reach, advertising costs, and usage of various media ehicles, and about consumers' response to advertising. This information elps advertisers minimize wasted reach.

Magazines and national television, which tend to have wider reach, re used by firms with national markets or clusters of markets throughout ıe nation. Local radio, newspapers, cable television, and direct mail can e used by firms with smaller trading areas. When the reach of a media ehicle does not coincide with the advertiser's trading area, a mix of ehicles can be used. Appendix 10 includes examples of media allocation.

QUESTIONS

1. Which media vehicles are most often used by retailers, and why? Which are more often used by manufacturers? Explain. See Exhibits 9-4 and 9-7 for information on broadcast advertisers.
2. For which types and sizes of manufacturers and retailers is national television an effective advertising medium? Explain.
3. You are the manager of a small local jewelry, toy, or sheet-towel-table linens store. Your trading area consists of your small town and small surrounding towns, with one regional shopping center 20 minutes from town by car. There are several colleges and universities in and near your town. Describe your target market and suggest a media mix for your store for the season September through December. Describe the media mix for manufacturers who sell the merchandise listed in this question to stores.
4. Answer question 3 for a large national store chain with a store located in the regional shopping center described in 3. See Appendix 10 for helpful information.

5. You have a small store in the regional shopping center described in question 3. Explain what resources are available to you for evaluating your advertising media.
6. What is the difference between evaluation processes for selecting media types and those for selecting media within types? For example, (a) which evaluation process would you use to decide whether or not to use radio? (b) If you decide to use radio, what evaluation process would you use to decide on stations, time slots, and a program type (news, talk show, or music; what type of music?)? In answering this question, use a store example, i.e. college book store, card-print-poster store, restaurant, deli. Also, use a manufacturer example, i.e., book, card, meat.
7. Your store is in a shopping center near a large city, or is in a suburb of a large city. Explain why and to what extent you will advertise in the media of that large city if many of your customers work in that city.
8. If you are concerned about the credibility of a salesperson from a local print media vehicle, where can you find out whether the information provided by this salesperson is accurate? Answer this question for a salesperson of a local radio station.
9. Explain the timing of your advertising for (a) a small local candy store, (b) a medium-sized jeans store in a regional shopping center, (c) a large mass merchandiser, (d) a branded product.

NOTES

1. Marshall McLuhan, *Understanding Media, The Extension of Man* (New York: McGraw-Hill, 1964); William Shakespeare, *Romeo and Juliet,* Act II, Scene II.

2. See Chapter 15.

3. See Chapter 9, Exhibits 9-4 and 9-7, for national, spot, and local radio and television advertisers.

4. U.S. Bureau of the Census, *Census 80 Projects for Students* (Washington DC: U.S. Government Printing Office, 1981), p. 25; and associated product primers as on "Census Tracts," (PHC80-2), issued August 1984.

5. Edward Blair, "Sampling Issues in Trade Area Maps Drawn from Shopper Surveys," *Journal of Marketing,* 47 (Winter 1983), pp. 98–106; Avijit Ghosh and C. Samuel Craig, "Formulating Retail Location Strategy in a Changing Environment," *Journal of Marketing,* 47 (Summer 1983), pp. 56–68; E.T. Grether, "Regional-Spatial Analysis in Marketing," *Journal of Marketing,* 47 (Fall 1983), pp. 36–43; David L. Huff and Roland T. Rust, "Measuring the Congruence of Market Areas," *Journal of Marketing,* 48 (Winter 1984), pp. 68–74; See the entire issue of *Journal of Retailing,* 60 (Spring 1984).

See also Exhibit 3-8 in Chapter 3.

6. Richard E. Stanley, *Promotion,* 2nd ed. (Englewood Cliffs, NJ: Prentice-Hall, 1982), p. 233; D. Aaker and J. Myers, *Advertising Management,* 2nd ed. (Englewood Cliffs, NJ: Prentice-Hall, 1982), p. 431; C. Bouvee and W. Arens, *Contemporary Advertising* (Homewood, IL: Irwin, 1982), p. 467; W. Dommermuth, Promotion (Belmont, CA: Wadsworth, 1984), p. 522.

7. Ibid. See also Exhibit 3-1 in Chapter 3, about thresholds.

8. Ibid.

9. Ibid.

10. See also these references: Harvey R. Cook, *Selecting Advertising Media: A Guide for Small Business* (Washington DC: U.S. Small Business Administration, 1977); M. Davis, *The Effective Use of Advertising Media* (London: Business Books, 1981); S. Jain, *Marketing Planning and Strategy* (Cincinnati: Southwestern, 1981), pp. 378–383; G. Lilien and P. Kotler, *Marketing Decision Making* (New York: Harper & Row Pub., 1983), pp. 511–524; M. Mandell, *Advertising* (Englewood Cliffs, NJ: Prentice-Hall 1980); A. McGann and J. Russell, *Advertising Media* (Homewood, IL: Irwin, 1981); "Media Outlook, 1984", *Advertising Age,* 54 (November 7, 1983), pp. M9–M50; J.R. Pierce, *Symbols, Signals and Noise* (New York: Harper & Row Pub., 1961); David J. Riesman, *The Lonely Crowd* (New Haven: Yale University Press, 1950); Jay R. Schoenfeld and William J. Donnelly, *What Every Account Representative Should Know About Media* (New York: American Association of Advertising Agencies, 1981); Jack Z. Sissors, *Advertising Media Planning* (Chicago: Crain, 1976); C. Sutton, *Advertising Your Way to Success* (Englewood Cliffs, NJ: Prentice-Hall, 1981); H. Taha, *Operations Research,* 3rd ed. (New York: Macmillan, 1982), Chapters 7 and 8.

11. *Sales and Marketing Management,* (October 31, 1983), pp. 92, and 118, corresponding issue in subsequent years; *1983 Market Guide,* (New York: Editor & Publisher, 1982), and corresponding information in subsequent years.

12. "Media Outlook" *Advertising Age,* 53 (November 8, 1982), special section beginning on p. M-9, and corresponding information in subsequent years; for example, the entire June 27, 1985, issue; "Ad Linage," *Advertising Age,* 55 (February 20, 1984), p. 57. This section is updated regularly.

13. "A Bad Pitch," *Advertising Age,* 55 (July 9, 1984), p. 29. This responds to several articles in the June 14, 1984, issue. It is an ad by Advo-System, a Direct Media company.

See also James Dunaway, "Two Studies Could Boost Newspaper Advertising," *Advertising Age,* 55 (January 30, 1984), p. M-30, M-31; Nancy Millman, "A Day in the Life of a Media Wizard," *Advertising Age,* 53 (November 8, 1982), p. M-40; Stuart Emmrich, "Future Cloudy for Sunday Supplements," *Advertising Age,* 54 (March 18, 1983), pp. 3, 61–62; Clark Schiller, "Remembered, but Never Read," *Advertising Age,* 52 (October 26, 1981), pp. S14–S15; Anna Sobczynski, "Retailers' Preprints Saturating the Land," *Advertising Age,* 55 (June 14, 1984), pp. 34, 36, 38.

14. Thea B. Few, "Definitions," *Advertising Age,* 52 (July 20, 1981), p. S-2.

15. M. Breslauer, "Boston Hears Big BAND Sound," *Advertising Age,* 55 (August 16, 1984), p. 25; Anna Sobczynski, "Networks Present a United Front," *Advertising Age,* 55 (June 14, 1984), pp. 39–40.

16. Colormedia, Inc., Pembroke, MA 02359; Stuart J. Elliott, "Youth Voice Spurs 13-30 Move," *Advertising Age,* 55 (January 9, 1984), p. 55; " 'Wallpaper Journal' Hits Campuses," *Advertising Age,* 51 (November 10, 1980), p. 22.

17. *Sales & Marketing Management* (October 31, 1983), p. 167.

18. See Mark Albion and Paul Farris, *The Advertising Controversy,* (Boston: Auburn House, 1981), Chapter 6. Get current addresses of agencies and media firms from phone book or reference librarian; V. Gay, "P&G Cuts New Media Pie," *Advertising Age,* 55 (December 3, 1984) pp. 1, 92; A. Sobczynski, "Media Carrot May Need Gilding," *Advertising Age,* 55 (November 29, 1984), pp. 30–32.

19. Suggested by the Newspaper Advertising Bureau.

20. See Chapter 4.

21. Suggested by Andrew Barylski, Sales Manager radio stations WESC AM and WQUR-FM in Worcester County, MA, on May 9, 1984.

22. *Advertising Age,* 54 (September 8, 1983), pp. 78, 140, 114, 98, 148, 126 166.

23. Published in Norwalk, Connecticut.

24. "Straight Talk about Black Media," advertisement in *Advertising Age* 54 (September 8, 1983), p. 125.

25. *Advertising Age,* 54 (June 27, 1983), pp. M4, M46–48, M59–60; and 5 (June 28, 1984), pp. 12, 13, 52, 68; and 56 (June 27, 1985), pp. 1, 42, 48, 57. Thes are the issues of the "100 Leading Media Companies."

26. Robert Reed, "Audit Bureau Makes the Numbers Count," *Advertising Age,* 55 (January 9, 1984), pp. M4–M5.

27. *Arbitron Ratings—Television* (Control Data: Arbitron Ratings Company 1983), inside front cover, and pp. 1, 37.

APPENDIX 10

MEDIA SELECTION EXAMPLES

Media selection examples are given here for six hypothetical stores in two typical environments. These examples can be used as prototypes for similar firms, or to generate ideas for other advertisers.

Typical City: Department and Specialty Stores

A department store, Anderson's, and a specialty store, Rubin's, are located in a typical city of about 800,000 persons. The city is outside a large metropolitan area. This city has the following media:

1 Daily and Sunday newspaper
Daily Circulation 165,000
Sunday Circulation 225,000

Radio station # 1 programmed to reach higher-income families; evening audience estimated at 35,000, daytime audience 20,000

Radio Station # 2 programmed to reach medium-income families; evening audience 46,000, daytime audience 16,000

Radio station # 3 programmed to reach mostly young people ages 14 to 30 with popular music; estimated daytime audience 8,000, evening audience 12,000

Radio station # 4 programmed to reach young rock music fans; estimated daytime audience 9,000, evening audience 11,000

Radio station # 6 all-news station aimed at adults and those driving automobiles. Estimated evening audience only 6,000 but a very large daytime audience of 30,000 where the station is turned on in the morning and left on all day.

TV station # 1—National network, daytime audience 15,000, evening audience 90,000

TV station # 2—National network, daytime audience 115,000, big soap opera, popular programs; evening audience 65,000

TV station # 3—National network, daytime audience 45,000, evening audience 55,000.

TV station # 4—Local station general programming, daytime audience 12,000, evening audience 28,000

TV station # 5—Local station, runs many movies during day and evening; daytime audience 18,000, evening audience 60,000

Bus cards in public transportation—220,000 riders daily

Anderson's has one downtown location with an annual sales volume of $12.5 million. The marketing communications budget, which includes advertising, sales promotion, and publicity, is $625,000, or 5% of net sales. About half of this, or 2.5% of net sales, is allocated for advertising. Anderson's media allocation is shown below. It is difficult to compare this allocation with those of the large mass merchandisers in Exhibit 10-6 because advertising costs have two components: time/space costs and production costs. Exhibit 10-6 probably includes expenditures for media time and space. The list below covers Anderson's entire advertising allowance, which includes production costs as well. Anderson's one department store spends a relatively large proportion of its budget on newspapers and direct mail, and relatively less on broadcast. Anderson's has its own mailing list of 44,000. In contrast, national stores like Sears buy network television time and magazine space because of the larger geographic market of these retailers and the corresponding wider reach of magazines and network television.

Media Allocation Plan for Anderson's Department Store

		Budget	Percent
Newspaper Daily and Sunday		$145,000	46%
Radio Station # 1		10,000	3
Radio Station # 2		6,000	2
Radio Station # 3		2,400	1
TV Station # 1	Daytime	5,200	2
	Evening	8,000	3
TV Station # 2	Daytime	5,200	2
	Evening	8,000	3
Bus. cards		9,000	3
Direct Mail		110,000	35
Misc.		3,200	1
		$312,000	100%

By selecting this media mix, Anderson's expects to reach a large percentage of the people in the city who could be expected to shop in this store. The demographics indicated by the radio stations listed above are a good match for Anderson's customers. Its mailing list is made up of current and recent charge customers who receive mailings at least once a month. Each monthly mailing consists of different statements and enclosures.

Anderson's media allocations are made according to the criteria recommended above, and summarized here.

1. The target customers in the *Trading Area* must be reached by one medium or another. This includes the primary, secondary, and tertiary areas. Overlapping of media helps to reinforce the message.
2. The *merchandise* used in the advertising has been evaluated and judged appropriate for the targeted audiences.
3. Advertising in each media vehicle is evaluated in terms of its *intrinsic value* and *against costs of other media* vehicles and other marketing communications efforts.
4. This particular media mix is the most *cost-effective* that can be made at this time under the given circumstances. Next month there might be some adjustments based on seasonal or other factors.

Let us take another example. In the same city, there is a women's specialty store, Rubin's, with an annual sales volume of $4.5 million. Rubin's, located in the northern section shopping center, budgets 3% of sales for advertising. Any media vehicle selected by Rubin's can only be partially effective as it would reach many east, west, and south section people who are not likely to be customers. What can Rubin's do? Through experience, stores such as Rubin's find that their own mailing list is by far the best medium, as it reaches only their own customers with no wasted circulation. Rubin's also gives out occasional handbills in various locations near the store such as bus stops and entrances to the shopping center.

Media Allocation Plan for Rubin's Specialty Store

	Budget	***Percent***
Direct Mail	$121,500	90%
Mass Circulars by Hand, Posters	13,500	10
	$135,000	100%

Compared with the next example, media selection for Anderson's and Rubin's has been relatively simple since the relevant media have been relatively limited.

Large City: Downtown and Shopping-Center Stores

Now, let us take a larger city with a population of 1,750,000, several suburbs and two outlying shopping centers, one north, the other south. Let us concern ourselves with four stores:

Madison's Department Store, locally owned with a downtown store and a branch store in the north shopping center.
Leonard's Department Store, a national chain with one store each in the north and south shopping centers.
Carol's, a Women's Specialty Store, in the south shopping center.
Russell's, a Men's Specialty Store, with stores in both the north and south shopping centers.

This city has the following media:

Media Available in Large City with Suburbs

Morning newspaper—circulation 365,000
Morning newspaper's Sunday edition—circulation 565,000
Evening newspaper—circulation 265,000

TV Station # 1, National Network	*Daytime Audience*	*85,000*
	Evening Audience	*254,000*
TV Station # 2, National Network	*Daytime Audience*	*165,000*
	Evening Audience	*190,000*
TV Station # 3, National Network	*Daytime Audience*	*60,000*
	Evening Audience	*150,000*

Radio Station # 1 Classical music audience, 25 and older
Radio Station # 2 All-news, older audience
Radio Station # 3 News, heavy on sports; heavy men's audience
Radio Station # 4 Popular music, 22 to 60 age group
Radio Station # 5 Country music station, 20 to 45 age group
Radio Station # 7 Rock music, 15 to 30 age group
Radio Station # 8 Disc jockey, current popular music, 18 to 40 age group
Radio Station # 9 Hard rock, 15 to 30 age group

Let us evaluate the media decisions of the four stores listed above. Madison's Department Store has annual sales of $22 million, and can economically consider all media because its trading area matches the reach of media coverage. Hence its media decisions can be made on the basis of which media vehicles best match its customer demographics. Madison's has merchandise for all age groups, but aims at mainly the middle and upper-middle-income families in the area, so sends it advertising to this audience. Based on these considerations, suggested media percentages for Madison's are shown in the table below:

Media Allocation Plans for Four Stores in Same Area

a. Madison's Department Store: sales = $22 million; ad budget = 2%

Morning and Sunday newspapers	55%
Evening newspaper	27
National network TV station #1: evening	3
daytime	3
Local TV station: daytime	1
Radio station #1, #2, #4 (1% each)	3
Radio station #3, #5 (.5% each)	1
Direct mail	6
Miscellaneous	1
	100%

b. Leonard's Department Store: sales = $26 million; ad budget = 2%

Morning and Sunday newspapers	50%
Evening newspaper	25
National TV network #1 daytime—allocated by national	3
evening—allocated by national	3
National TV network #2 daytime—allocated by national	3
evening—allocated by national	1
National TV network #3 daytime—allocated by national	1
evening—allocated by national	1
Circulars, hand distributed	7
National magazine, share of nat'l magazine budget	3
Miscellaneous	3
	100%

c. Carol's Specialty Store: sales = $5.5 million; ad budget = 2.5%

Morning and Sunday newspapers, society page	48%
Local TV station, fashion news	7
Radio stations #1, #2 (4% each)	8
Direct mail and telephone	36
Miscellaneous	1
	100%

d. Russell's Specialty Store: sales = $6.6 milion; ad budget = 2%

Newspaper, daily, Sunday, men's, sports	30%
Newspaper, evening, financial pages	20
TV station #2, national network local time	5
Radio station #1 (classical) #4 (popular)	10
Radio station #6 (all news)	4
Direct mail and telephone	26
Miscellaneous	5
	100%

At one time, Leonard's had a downtown store, but gave it up and built a store in the south shopping center. Leonard's management made that decision in response to declining traffic downtown and growing building developments for high-priced residential sections south of the urban center. Leonard's two stores are direct competitors of Madison's, the locally owned department store which still has a downtown store. These stores use a high percentage of newspaper advertising. Leonard's two stores have a total volume of $26 million and a total advertising budget of approximately $520,000, including allocations from the Chicago headquarters of its organization. These stores are charged for their share of national network television sports and national magazine advertising, and must include these costs in their advertising budget. Leonard's media plan is also shown in the table above.

The women's specialty store, Carol's, has one location in the south shopping center with a volume of $5.5 million, of which 2.5% is allocated for advertising. Carol's caters to the upper-middle and higher-income women of the city who live in the south suburban area. Advertising in the general media is ineffective for Carol's because it has considerable wasted circulation. Therefore Carol's advertising pattern must be entirely different from those of the local and national department stores, Madison's and Leonard's who also want to sell to the upper-middle income women in this area.

The breakdown of Carol's media allocations in the table above reveals an emphasis on direct mail. Carol's uses a lower percentage of its allocation for newspaper advertising compared to the department stores. The evening newspaper was entirely omitted from Carol's media list. Because of the extensive wasted circulation of advertising in the regular media, Carol's prefers to reach known customers with continuous mailings. Carol's store depends on shopping center advertising and promotions to draw traffic into the shopping center.

Finally, let us examine the media pattern for the men's specialty store, Russell's, which has two stores, one in each shopping center. Russell's has an annual volume of $6.6 million; its advertising budget is 2% of sales, as shown in the table above. Because Russell's stores cater to the more affluent, its media mix is heavily weighted to reach that audience. A good part of Russell's business consists of suits worn by businessmen and the more prosperous adult men; hence the emphasis on the financial and sports pages in print media, and on the radio stations, including the all-news station, that have a more adult audience.

Media decisions in all of the above cases were made by comparing rate cards for comparable media and evaluating cost versus effectiveness of various choices—direct mail, newspapers, radio, and television. For example, radio allocations were based on evaluating eight different radio stations which had different audiences. It is not enough to compare medi cost per thousand persons reached. In choosing media, it is essential t look at the overall picture: alternative uses of the money, productio costs of the commercial, the actual and potential relevant environment and demographics and psychographics of the target market.

PART THREE

Sales Promotion, Publicity, Visual Merchandising, and Personal Selling

When you blow your own horn, make certain that the notes ring clear and true.—L. Rubin

11 SALES PROMOTION

INTRODUCTION

Definitions

Sales promotion includes an element of show biz. Here comes the parade! Seat the children for a magic show! Hear our musical treat! Meet the celebrities! Come to our party! Watch our demonstration! Compete in our contest! These and other sales promotions can be sponsored by individual firms and groups of firms.

"Win a free trip!" "Buy two for the price of one!" "Try this free for 30 days!" Sales promotion includes games and contests; reduced-price events such as sales; inducements to try a product such as offering coupons or free samples; merchandise demonstrations; personal appearances; events; foreign-country and theme promotions; exhibits and entertainments such as parades, musicals, fashion shows, seminars, store openings, and anniversaries. Sales promotion is sometimes defined as a catch-all—marketing communications that are *not* advertising, personal selling, visual merchandising, or publicity. "Sales promotion," in some cases also has been used as a synonym for *marketing communications*, which in this book means the overall effort that goes into creating sales advertising, public relations, publicity, sales promotion, visual merchandising and personal selling.[1]

Of all the marketing communications tools, sales promotion is the one most likely to be accompanied by the others. Advertising and publicity about special events help potential customers plan product purchases and store visits. While attending these events, customers can be influenced to buy merchandise by on-site product displays and personal selling.

Promotion can play a key role in some cases and a supporting role in others. For example, a sales promotion is *advertised*, generates *press releases*, attracts *publicity* as a newsworthy event, often inspires related *displays*, and usually involves *sales personnel*.

Sales promotion has also been described as making the most out of the traffic created by advertising. The term *promotion* or *sales promotion* has been used to describe *special events*—fashion shows, parades, and personal appearances related to introduction of new merchandise. Manufacturers' and retailers' *coupon* and *free sample* sales promotions also introduce new merchandise. Retail sales promotion includes special *sales* of merchandise—anniversary sales and storewide or departmental sales such as white sales, which move large quantities of new and dated merchandise.

Manufacturers have a slightly different definition of sales promotion "the direct inducement or incentive to the sales force, the distributor or the consumer, with the primary objective of creating an immediate sale," including "displays, shows and exhibitions, demonstrations, and various nonrecurrent selling efforts not in the ordinary routine," as well as consumer education and sales literature.[2] Manufacturers translate "not in the ordinary routine" as "relatively temporary" events that do not adhere to a predictable schedule. Non-routine timing is used for brand promotions because manufacturers want consumers to buy their brands at the regular price as well, and not to wait for coupons or other special incentives to buy.

For manufacturers of mass-market merchandise brands, sales promotion includes sales force efforts to get good *shelf space* for their brands in supermarkets. These efforts involve both *discounts*—inducements to stores to carry the brands—and *coupons*—inducements to consumers to buy the brands. Point-of-purchase display materials are often included in manufacturers' sales promotions.

Purpose and Functions

The purpose of sales promotion is to dramatize the selling of merchandise and to get actual and prospective customers to buy merchandise. It is not enough just to bring people near or into stores; the point is to get *more* customers to buy *more* merchandise. Sales promotion also builds store and brand *image* as the various efforts communicate store and brand personality and generate publicity.

Unlike manufacturers' brand promotions which are scheduled to be temporary and unpredictable, retail sales promotions are a continuing phenomenon, but the featured products change. To encourage customers to visit their stores regularly, retailers constantly work with various vendors to insure that there is always a sales promotion event of some sort going on. Particular merchandise categories and manufacturers' brands are promoted to attract various segments of the store's target market. Retailers also add their own sales promotions to their vendors' promotions. For example, food retailers tend to have occasional double or triple-coupon days for manufacturers' nationally advertised brands. For example, if a customer has a 25-cent-off coupon for brand-A coffee, the store will give 75¢ off for that coupon on a triple-coupon day. The manufacturer decides the 25¢ coupon; the retailer decides the 75¢-off for the coupon.

The sales promotions which occur at retail locations tend to attract people to participate in events or to be entertained. Creating traffic and sales is the goal of the events. Sales promotion also communicates store and brand image and develops customer habits of store and brand loyalty. As shoppers make fewer and faster trips to save time and energy, marketers must increase their sales per customer visit. Sales promotion events have the potential for increasing customer time in stores and increasing the number of visits to stores and shopping centers.

Different retail sales promotions are planned for different seasons and merchandise categories. Exhibit 11-1 shows suggestions for retail promotions for one month, November, and also lists November events and dates that might inspire other promotions. Some promotions suitable for November include early gift items, pre-Christmas sales, Election Day sales, Thanksgiving Day Sales, and glove, coat, and toy promotions. Exhibit 11-2 describes spring and early summer events planned by one town's Chamber of Commerce. These include an Easter Egg hunt with prizes provided by merchants, sidewalk sales run on the days of the community fair, and contests and raffles related to a Teddy Bear Rally and Crafts Fair.

Sales Promotion Management and Strategy

In a large firm, the sale promotion manager or director reports to the vice president of marketing as do the other marketing communications managers. Often, the retail personnel director reports to both the marketing director and the vice president for operations. In a shopping center, the marketing manager does the promotions, and reports to the shopping center manager. In a small firm, the owner, manager, or some other designated person plans the promotions, or someone from the Chamber of Commerce organizes community promotions as shown in Exhibit 11-2. For the rest of this

EXHIBIT 11-1 One Month from Calendar of Suggested Promotion Events

Source: Marketing-Sales Promotion-Advertising Planbook (New York: National Retail Merchants Association, 1984), p. 49.

NOVEMBER

Flower of the month—Chrysanthemum *Birthstone of the month—Topaz*

China, Glassware, Silverware, Linens
Christmas Layaways
Dryers
Early Gift Items Presentation
Election Day Sales
Electric Blankets
Evening Wear
Fashion Accessories
Furniture, Home Furnishings, Bedding
Fur Sales
Girls', Infants Wear
Gloves
Gourmet Foods
Intimate Apparel
Lamps, Shades
Men's Clothing, Furnishings, Hats
Pre-Christmas Sales
Radios, TV's
Rugs, Carpets, Linoleum
Stationery
Thanksgiving Day Sales
Toys, Games
Traffic Appliances
Veterans Day Sales
Wines & Liquors Sales
Women's Misses' Coats
Woolen Fabrics

November	1	World's Fair in Paris, 1889 National Author's Day
November	2	James K. Polk born 1795 Warren G. Harding born 1865
November	3	Roger Williams Day
November	6	Volunteers of America, incorporated, 1896 Election Day
November	7	Marie Curie, discoverer of radioactivity, born 1867
November	11	Veteran's Day Remembrance Day in Canada
November	12	Elizabeth Cady Stanton Day
November	16	Sadie Hawkins Day Oklahoma entered Union, 1907
November	17	Congress convened in Washington for first time, 1800
November	19	James A. Garfield born 1831 Lincoln's Gettysburg Address, 1863
November	21	No. Carolina joined Union, 1789
November	22	Lyndon B. Johnson became 36th Pres. of U.S. upon assassination of Pres. John F. Kennedy in Dallas, Tex., 1963. Reelected Nov. 1964. Thanksgiving Day
November	23	Franklin Pierce born 1804
November	24	Zachary Taylor born 1784 Latin America Day
November	30	Winston Churchill, born 1874 St. Andrew

section the term *sales promotion manager* refers to whoever manages sales promotions, whatever the actual title of that position.

The sales promotion manager plans and supervises special events exhibits, and educational programs such as investment classes and cooking instruction. If paid parking facilities are available, the manager might promote sales with free parking, or reduce parking fees for customers who show proof of purchasing from the cooperating stores. A retailer's liaison with leased departments, like cosmetics and shoes, and with outside services is often supervised by the sales promotion manager Outside services include appraisals, babysitting, beauty salon, sewing and cooking classes, medical services, parking, and restaurants.

Many of these services are quite important to customers. Special services can make a firm unique and different. If the retailer, downtown,

EXHIBIT 11-2 Excerpts of Events Announced to Members in Chamber of Commerce Newsletters

Source: Chamber of Commerce, Amherst, MA.

AMHERST CHAMBER OF COMMERCE NEWSLETTER

Easter Update: *We had a huge turnout on the Common for the egg hunt. Our thanks to Price Chopper for the donation of the eggs (need more next year), Louis' Foods and the downtown merchants who supplied prizes for the children.*

May Sidewalk Sales and Community Fair: *May 19, 20, 21. . . . Our food booth at the fair this year will once again be selling those scrumptious sausages on a roll (Chick's famous recipe). Directors will be asked to sign up for a shift at the booth during the weekend. (We hope to also sell our Chamber Center of Distinction stationery and T-shirts).*

Merchants will have super bargains displayed on the sidewalks beginning on Thursday. Promotional ads will be on radio (WTTT & WHMP) and in the papers. Our thanks to WTTT for their cooperation.

. . .

July Event: *The July Sidewalk Sales are scheduled for 14, 15 and 16. Events and happenings being planned for the Teddy Bear Rally and Crafts Fair on the 16th are beginning to solidify. Some of the activities are: coloring contest, beekeepers exhibit, "Winnie the Pooh" readings, Teddy Bear Hospital, theater presentation and a competition for various bear categories. Raffle ticket sales for a fine quality Steiff Teddy Bear are currently in progress (to benefit Hampshire County Retarded Citizens) and we will have Teddy Bear T-shirts available early in June at the Chamber office. If you don't have a Teddy Bear button, you're not with it!!!!!*

or shopping center does not have all of them, management often encourages individual entrepreneurs to provide these services to attract more customers. In recent years, Sears has gone into the real estate and stock brokerage businesses.[3] Diversification is a growing trend.

As are other marketing communications, sales promotion is aimed at existing and potential target customers to help achieve marketing goals. Both manfacturers and retailers must stay competitive. If young fashion customers are the desired audience, a junior fashion show or rock show can be promoted. If housewares sales needs to be stimulated, a cooking demonstration or series of housewares demonstrations can be arranged to attract customers. In modern times, men as well as women maintain homes, cook, and are interested in fashion, so many promotions can be targeted at both sexes. When an entire store wishes to boost its sales and increase its traffic, store-wide events can be scheduled and coordinated with other marketing communications efforts.

Firms that are too small or too inexperienced to put on their own special events can hire special events consultants or marketing consultants. Consultants may only help develop a concept or strategy, or they may help with implementation as well. Some consultants provide newsletters with suggestions for timely events each season. Consultants may work with manufacturers on projects such as designs for in-store retail promotions. Many ideas for events involve specific products because the purpose of sales promotion is to sell merchandise.[4]

RETAILERS' AND MANUFACTURERS' PROMOTIONS

Merchandise demonstrations, samples and coupons, personal appearances, and brand-name or famous-name events are cooperative efforts which involve both manufacturers and retailers. In recent years, marketers in both fields have shifted substantial funds from media advertising to sales promotion efforts.[5]

Merchandise Demonstrations

Many products are best shown through demonstrations. Employees of stores or manufacturers can demonstrate the products. Occasionally, some items can be demonstrated by the customers themselves. Items such as the following can benefit from a demonstration:

Beauty, hair products, makeup
Toiletry preparations
Kitchen utensils, gadgets
Housewares, blenders, mixers
Food and cooking techniques
Toys and games
Sporting and exercise equipment
Home entertainment
Recorders and cassettes
Computers
Videotapes
Hobbies and tools

While demonstrations are almost a necessity to sell expensive, unfamiliar, or somewhat complex items such as food processors, video games, and computers, demonstrations of all types add color and show-biz interest to stores. Retailers have organized cooking lessons on a regular basis in their housewares and kitchen departments. Celebrities promoting their cookbooks will show how to prepare certain recipes. "Show barkers" provided by vendors will demonstrate kitchen gadgets.

There are also various "sporting week" promotions where professionals in such sports as tennis, badminton, ski, golf, or table tennis demonstrate tips for improved games. These can be tied in with local sports contests sponsored by retailers or manufacturers. Home decorating seminars can be scheduled for a week to include such topics as "defining the decorating problem," "mixing furniture periods," "arranging artificial flowers for centerpiece or accent piece," "decorating with sheets," and "tabletop decor." Lecturers can be provided by the store and by cooperating vendors.[6]

Toiletry and cosmetic firms, by agreement with large retailers, often place permanent demonstrators at their particular counters in the cosmetics department. Demonstrators show customers how to improve their appearance by using specific brand-name products. Small stores can get allowances from the firms to compensate for the demonstrators provided to large stores.

Samples, Coupons, Gifts

Samples, coupons, and gifts are among the easiest to implement of all sales promotion techniques. People usually like getting something free. Often, manufacturers will create small sample-size packages of their product for retailers to give customers to take home and try. Either vendor representatives or store personnel can give out samples of a product. For example, if the product is a food item, small portions can be placed on a tray and offered to customers as they pass by. If the product is a fragrance, demonstrators can spray some on the hands of interested customers so they can smell the fragrance on their own skin. Stocked for sale immediately behind or near the demonstrator should be packages of the product, so customers can be encouraged to buy the item after trying the sample.

One retailer invited entire towns to a large-scale sampling. To celebrate the opening of a new branch in Hadley, MA, the Bread and Circus Natural Food Supermarket put up a huge circus tent and invited people in the target market area to lunch. Invitation folders were sent by mail. Each folder contained a map and information about the store's commitment to selling high-quality natural foods. Billboards en route to the store repeated the natural foods message. In the tent, which was in the parking lot in front of the store, many manufacturers had booths to offer sample of food sold by the store. Also included with the invitation were thre $2-off coupons for making purchases of $10 or more at the store in eac of the next three weeks. This event attracted a large crowd.[7]

In addition to passing out merchandise samples, marketers sometime give small gifts like pens, pencils, matchbooks, pads, key chains, an calendars on which the firm's name, address, and telephone number ar printed. As long as the small items last, they remind customers of th marketer's name and phone number. Talbot's, which has a catalog operatio and a chain of women's apparel stores in the Northeast, has given ou flowering plants with each apparel purchase to promote spring and summe merchandise.[8]

Another promotional method is to place coupons in print adver tisements or to mention discounts on broadcast advertisements. By pre senting print coupons at the store, or reporting that they heard the broadcas customers then get free samples or discounts. Many variations or com binations of these sampling techniques have been used successfully b stores and manufacturers to promote new items.

Coupons are generally offered at two levels: (1) by the manufacture of a product, and (2) by a store or a group of stores. Manufacturers coupons tend to be placed in national magazines, Sunday supplement tabloids, or direct mailings. Manufacturers' coupons are often used t get customers to try new products, particularly packaged grocery product Formerly, only retailers redeemed most manufacturers' coupons. Now some coupons can be mailed directly to a central address for rebate Manufacturers' coupons can have expiration dates several months in th future.[9]

A new coupon-dispensing machine in supermarkets can be activate by shoppers' specially encoded cards. Information from this dispensin machine, about which coupons are dispensed and where, enters a dat base that might provide, for a fee, information of use to retailers an manufacturers.[10]

Retailers tend to run store and vendor coupons in local papers enclose coupons in retail catalogs, send letters and appreciation coupon to charge customers, give out coupons in the store or deliver coupo books to special customer groups like students. National retail chain often put coupons in national magazines.

Store coupons can be used to get customers to visit a new store o a new branch of a store, as in the case of Bread and Circus just described Store coupons can also be used to get new customers to try an existin store, and to build store loyalty or *habit shopping*. One shopping cente near a state university used a full-page newspaper ad to announce th mailing of coupon booklets sent to college students. The ad also mentione ten weeks of entertainment events which began at the beginning of th pring semester. This ad appeared in a free newspaper which was available ɔ students.[11]

Other important functions of retail coupons are to build traffic, and ɔ clear out merchandise by reducing the price of a merchandise category; ɔr example, "Save 25% on any regular price picture frame in stock—n April 19 only," or "save $10 on any swimsuit—July 17–19 only."[12] ;xhibit 11-3 shows coupons from a five day coupon-sale catalog. This ;imbels catalog had sixteen pages of back-to-back coupons, perforated ɔr easy separation. A potential problem with back-to-back coupons is ı record-keeping. Someone must mark the turned-in coupons to indicate vhich side customers have redeemed.

Store coupons are also used to encourage customers to come to tores during slow times. These include (1) the period between the Back-ɔ-School promotions and the Christmas shopping season—about mid)ctober; (2) the period following Christmas, the January sales, and the esort season and before Easter and Passover—sometime in March; and 3) the period after Easter and before the summer sales promotions—in ıne. Other good coupon times are Tuesdays or any other slow days of ıe week, or in slow hours of the day, such as the early morning just fter the store opens. A coupon might be valid only until noon on the rst Tuesday morning in February. Retail coupons tend to expire sooner han manufacturers' coupons. Some retail coupons may be good for only ours or days; others may last as long as two weeks.

ersonal Appearances

)ccasionally a personal appearance by a celebrity has drawn such crowds ıat it ties up the area around a store for blocks. This has occurred several mes in recent years when some very well-known rock music stars appeared ɔ autograph their records. In some cases the police had to be called to estore order. However, most personal appearances draw reasonable crowds ıat are easily controlled. Authors of current books, stage stars who have ecorded numbers from their hit shows, sports stars who appear for articular sporting goods firms, and celebrity chefs who demonstrate their ecipes often make personal appearances at sales promotions.

Sometimes a personal appearance is tied in with another sales pro-ıotion event, such as a famous designer appearing at a fashion show of is or her clothes, or a famous TV or film star endorsing a particular osmetic or toiletry item as part of a demonstration. Personal appearances ave even been made by costumed comic-book characters like Spiderman nd the Hulk. Exhibit 11-4 shows some publicity generated by these ersonal appearances, special displays, and advertisements for the Sanger Iarris department store in Dallas, Texas.

EXHIBIT 11-3 Coupons from a Five-Day Coupon-Sale Catalog

Source: Gimbel's Coupon Sale (May 3–7, 1984), p. 5.

INTIMATE APPAREL
Short gowns at big savings
Save $5
With coupon only
Without coupon $16-$17
Waltz-length gowns in your choice of pretty pastels or prints. Lots of assorted trims and styles. (D384)

INTIMATE APPAREL
Polyester/cotton tailored pajamas
Save $5
With coupon only
Without coupon $17-$18
Man-tailored pajamas in a huge variety of solid colors and prints. Machine washable. Sizes 32 to 40. (D384)

INTIMATE APPAREL
Summer shifts and sundresses
Save $5
With coupon only
Without coupon $16-$18
Cotton/polyester fashion look styles. Assorted new prints in pretty colors and trims. S,M,L. (D402)

FASHION ACCESSORIES
Cubic Zirconia earrings, pendants
Save 40%
With coupon only
Without coupon $27-$40
Dancraft 14K-gold filled earrings and pendants in solitaire, pear or marquise shapes. (D046)

FASHION ACCESSORIES
Fabric, vinyl, straw bags $21 to $39
Save $6
With coupon only
Without coupon $21-$39
Choose from camera bags, double handles, satchels, shoulder bags, hobos and more. (D130, 131)

FASHION ACCESSORIES
Baronet small leather goods
Save 40%
With coupon only
Without coupon $18-$29
Selection of french purses, mini clutches, credit card cases, indexers, organizers and more on sale. (D132)

EXHIBIT 11-4 Spiderman Visits a Store and Generates Publicity

Source: Advertising Age, 52 (October 19, 1981), pp. S35, S38. Reprinted with permission from the October 19, 1981 issue of *Advertising Age*. Copyright 1981 by Crain Communications, Inc.

A meeting was arranged with op execs of Sanger Harris and the *Times Herald*. Marvel laid it on hick, passing out comics books and superhero paraphernalia. "It was not your typical executive uncheon," Mr. Wolf recalls.

Sanger Harris brass ate it up. Ms. Allen dreamed of a fat Christmas bonus.

Then a snag developed—or so it seemed. Sanger Harris wanted to go co-op on all the display space. "I said, 'oh, boy,'" Ms. Allen says. "I thought it was dead."

Not to worry. Sanger Harris made the rounds of its suppliers, and they loved the idea. "We were looking to sell 16 pages plus cover," Ms. Allen says. "We not only sold that, we oversold. We went to 36 pages overnight, with other people waiting to get in."

The result was "Pipeline to Peril," a specially drawn comics book distributed July 26 featuring Spider-Man and the Incredible Hulk struggling against wickedness in Dallas, with a Sanger Harris store displayed prominently on the cover. Inside, alongside the usual Marvel superheroics, were 18 pages of back-to-school fashion advertising, featuring such well known marketers as Izod, Gloria Vanderbilt for Murjani and Brittania. . . .

But that wasn't the end of it. Sanger Harris made the comics book the kickoff for a five-week-long back-to-school promotion centering around Marvel's superheroes. "Spider-Man" and "Hulk" point-of-purchase displays were installed in key departments. Copies of the comics book and Marvel balloons were distributed free.

Sanger Harris scheduled live appearances by Spider-Man, the Hulk and Spider-Woman (or reasonable facsimiles thereof, anyway). The characters were also on hand for back-to-school fashion shows. Children got a chance to sneak-preview Spider-Man tv cartoons scheduled for airing this fall, and were given free access to Marvel pinball machines.

Young shoppers could participate in superhero sweepstakes contests, with Marvel merchandise and a birthday party visit from Spider-Man as prizes. They could also select from a full lineup of regular Marvel comics on display in children's department.

■ The *Times Herald*, for its part, promoted the special comics book with full-page house ads *and radio spots*, and printed up color display cards for its dealers and coin boxes. Sanger Harris bought still more newspaper and radio advertising, and put together a special mailing to 20,000 key customers.

The verdict? "One of the best marketing and sales promotion ideas that I have seen in a long time," Mr. Wolf says. "It was great

EXHIBIT 11-4 (continued)

publicity and great public relations for us," says Cecil Snodgrass, Sanger Harris vp for publicity. "The grownups enjoyed it just as much as the kids."

Neither the newspaper nor the retailer will release figures, but Sanger Harris says its sales exceeded projections, and the Times Herald enjoyed a noticeable jump in circulation. Both organizations report enthusiastic comments from customers. Marvel comics fanatics offered to buy all the extra copies of the comics book, as well as Sanger Harris' store displays. And souvenir-hunting children made off with all the coin box display cards.

Brand-Name or Famous Name Events

This type of promotion features a famous brand or designer name. Leading designers like Bill Blass, Pierre Cardin, Hubert Givenchy, Calvin Klein, Mary Quant, Yves St. Laurent, Diane Von Furstenberg, Yamamoto and others have appeared in stores to promote the merchandise bearing their names. Since many of these designers have franchised their names to several different categories of merchandise, many items are included in the promotion. For example, Pierre Cardin designs women's dresses, gloves, scarves, umbrellas, sun glasses, jewelry, perfume, cologne, shoes, hosiery, lingerie, and more. Some designers have luggage, sheets, towels, toiletries, and belts as well.

SPECIAL STORE PROMOTIONS

Some sales promotions involve several departments or even the entire store. These promotions include foreign country and U.S. city promotions, color and theme promotions, exhibits and contests, anniversary and other sales, and rewards for quantity purchases.

Foreign Country and U.S. City Promotions

Stores may want to base promotions on merchandise from a foreign country. Appendix 11 has information about a Japan-related promotion, which was quite extensive. Newspaper and magazine ads explained the purpose of the promotion, a directory included cultural events throughout the store, an advertising supplement to *The New York Times* included a letter from the Japanese ambassador, and special shopping bags were designed to go with the promotion.

In recent years the Orient has attracted a good deal of attention with China, Japan, and India promotions. For these storewide promotions, number of buyers purchase merchandise from the particular nation eing featured. Not only apparel, but also home furnishings, food, and ther items are featured in advertising and in the store. Windows and nteriors are decorated with the flags, artifacts, and colors of the nation eing featured, in addition to the promoted merchandise. Usually the romotion is opened with a leading personality from the nation being onored at an opening or a preview.[13]

The media often send photographers and reporters to report—and pread—the news of such promotions. The publicity shown in Exhibit 1-5 included a description of Japanese drum players and dance ritual n Wanamaker's Japan promotion in Philadelphia. Such promotions make nteresting, colorful additions to the stores' reputation.

A related promotion can be done for a U.S. city. In a manner similar o Bloomingdale's and Wanamaker's Japan promotions, Lord & Taylor's taged a New Orleans promotion with parties and events, New Orleans

XHIBIT 11-5 **Japanese Promotion at Wanamaker's**

ource: "Japan '83—Wanamaker's Storewide Tribute," *Body Fashions Intimate Apparel* 'ebruary, 1984), pp. 6B, 19.

Centuries of Japanese tradi- ons and innovations were lauded n nine floors of the Wanamaker uilding during the spectacular wo-week celebration, making a isit to the store an international, hopping and cultural experience.

Discoveries from the classic hrine rising three stories in the rand Court to the super-futuristic ony home entertainment center lled each department. Japan's nost influential fashion designers ppeared, including the famed **Ianae Mori.** Art exhibits, foods repared by visiting chefs, Olym- ic class athletes and a variety of raftspeople were all part of the ffair. In particular, the highly tylized furniture designer, **George Jakashima** displayed his collec- ion.

In the auditorium were the ashion shows, Samurai Kendo demonstrations, concerts, the Taiko Drum Corps, Minyo dancers, Japanese gymnastic Olympic hopefuls and two full-scale English productions of Puccini's Madame Butterfly by the Curtis Institute of Music. A nearby stop at the Sanyo Shop pointed up classic and avante garde styling, wool fabrics and meticulous tailoring in suits, separates and raincoats.

Playful moods extended in children's activities on the same floor with puppet shows, origami demonstrations and a calligrapher.

In line with pen and ink was the book store's collection of Japanese books. Martha Stewart, author of *Entertaining*, also made an appearance to introduce her new book, *Quick Cook*, for Japanese appetites. For the fifth course, Tempura of deep-fried vegetables was served in the cafe.

products, Cajun art, Louisiana country antiques, Creole gumbo, back-country basketmaking, and other related merchandise.[14] This promotion was supported by advertising, and also generated publicity.

Color and Theme Promotions

Each season, certain colors or groups of colors seem to dominate the fashion picture. With this in mind, retailers have often done fashion color promotions or even occasional store-wide color promotions. "Citrus Colors" have been featured including Orange, Lemon, and Lime, with tie-ins to Sunkist fruit growers. Coffee promotions have been worked out with tie-ins to Columbian or Brazilian coffee growers. The coffee color is highlighted with bags of coffee beans and perhaps free coffee given out in the store during the promotion. Other color promotions might include "Stained Glass" colors, "Scotch Plaids," and "Earth Colors."

A theme promotion might be something like "The Age of Elegance" or "America Goes Western." Such themes can be presented successfully to tie in with the latest moods or fads, like roller skating, disco, or Western, taking advantage of media publicity about the fads themselves.

Exhibits and Contests

Stores have sometimes assembled impressive exhibits as sales promotion efforts. Art exhibits of various kinds are among the most common. A Gucci newspaper advertisement invited readers to an exhibit of modern paintings, tapestries, Roman marbles, and sculptures at the store.[15] Stores that sell drawings and paintings can use one-person shows to attract traffic to their art departments. Retailers who do not have art departments can use exhibits to create traffic for the store in general.

Contests can attract a wide variety of people, from the grade schoolers in the advertising contests, shown in Exhibit 11-6, to adult artists. Exhibit 11-6 contains a newspaper ad inviting children to participate in an ad contest, a child's ad that was printed in the newspaper, and the certificate that was sent to each child who participated. This contest can interest children in reading ads in order to compare them with their own work.

Contests can be associated with shows of individuals' submitted art, of employees' art, or of art furnished by various local clubs. Many friends and relatives of those represented in an exhibit come to the store, so an exhibit of several hundred pieces can attract hundreds if not thousands of people. Prizes can be awarded by media or stores; for example, a $100 gift certificate for the first prize. Posters by older students can be community service-oriented, and the winning poster can be offered to the city for duplicating and posting.

During an anniversary sale, prizes can be offered for the best pictures of "fifty years ago," or whatever else would be appropriate for the an-

XHIBIT 11-6 Newspaper Advertising Contest for Children
ource: Amherst Morning Record, Amherst, MA.

niversary. Often the police and fire department archives contain many interesting photos and memorabilia that make interesting exhibits. Local libraries also tend to have a lot of material. Because of most stores' central location and easy access, good exhibits are usually popular and well attended. Often, they can be set up inexpensively with the cooperation of local club members.

Rewards for Quantity Purchases

From time to time, retailers issue trading stamps. The purpose of stamps is to build customers' loyalty. Stamps are issued based on the amount of the customer's purchases. They are ultimately redeemed by the stamp company that issued them to the store, or by the store itself. Customers redeem stamps at the store, at a redemption center, or from a catalog. Each item is priced by the number of trading stamps required to obtain it.

There seem to be cycles for promotional tools as a particular tool becomes boring when its novelty wears off. The use of trading stamps likewise runs in cycles. If all stores are offering them, there is no advantage in trading with one particular store. Trading stamps peaked in 1969, were replaced by price cutting in the 1970s, and later by double coupons and cash prize games. Stamps began to be popular again in the mid-1980s.[16]

Sales

In-store sales, shopping center sales, and sidewalk sales connected with local community activities are so familiar that most readers have probably experienced them. Occasions for these sales can be found in the National Retail Merchants Association monthly sales promotion calendar of which one month was shown in Exhibit 11-1. Sales can offer special purchases or price reductions in order to clear out merchandise. In the past, summer white sales of sheets, towels, and related merchandise have been typical. Recently, when the federal tax refund was later than usual and sales at the regular price did not reach expectations, the summer sales were in September. Marketers must be aware of state and national legislation which specifies how long merchandise must be sold at the regular price before it can be sold at a reduced price. Competition for reduced-price promotions comes from discount and off-price stores. In addition to meeting this competition with price reductions, retailers have options of promoting their private labels, their services, and their images to their target customers.[17]

SPECIAL ENTERTAINMENT EVENTS

More and more marketers are realizing the importance of making shopping an interesting and exciting experience. Retailers, often in cooperation ith manufacturers, are making greater effort towards entertainment as ›mpetition increases. Special entertainment events include parades, pares, and presentations of musical groups such as bands, rock groups, ıd folksingers. Solo appearances of stars, marionette shows, and fashion ıows are also popular. Special events (1) are usually leisure pursuits,) involve participation of consumers as an audience, (3) have a definite ›ening and closing, and (4) generate publicity spontaneously.[18]

arades and Parties

nly a few major stores in the nation put on big parades; for example, acy's in New York City, J.L. Hudson in Detroit, Wanamaker's in Phillelphia. These are usually Thanksgiving Day Parades to initiate the ›liday buying season. The parades receive wide publicity and are carried ı network television. Often, various organizations participate and unerwrite part of the costs: a record company whose popular recording ar appears, movie stars who are plugging their most recent release, and ›pyrighted cartoon figures like Walt Disney's Mickey Mouse. A parade :ene is shown in Exhibit 11-7. Huge inflatable figures, like the one in is exhibit, make a parade a newsworthy event and attract attention of ewspaper and television photographers.

A few other stores have smaller parades in cooperation with other cal institutions. In smaller towns, stores participate in parades on special :casions like the Fourth of July with many local organizations such as

:HIBIT 11-7 Inflatable Figure in Macy's Parade
urce: Macy's, New York, NY.

realtors, advertising agencies, school bands, athletic organizations, scouts, and various clubs. Police and fire departments and local manufacturers may also contribute floats. These parades can be announced by posters in store windows and fliers in cooperating stores, banks, and realty offices. They generate publicity in local media also.

Parties, including benefit parties for charity, are special promotions that generate publicity and project store image. A recent benefit party at Jordan Marsh in Boston had movie and television stars as guests, musical events including music for dancing throughout the store, and refreshments. Parties are often held in connection with the foreign country and U.S. city promotions mentioned earlier.[19]

Musical and Other Entertainment

Small bands and musical groups can easily be set up in shopping centers, in the stores themselves, or downtown. Such musical groups can be selected for their appeal to certain segments of the stores' target markets. Rock groups can be used to promote jeans and young people's merchandise. Folk singers can be used to attract a wider audience of both old and young. Church choirs can be invited to sing carols during the Christmas holiday season. Smaller groups of singers can sing carols in individual store entrances to entertain shoppers who are waiting for a store to open. Symphony orchestras and opera companies have performed in shopping centers.[20] Exhibit 11-8 shows an ad for Woodward & Lothrop's sing-a-longs for children near Washington, DC. In addition to the musical component, gifts in the form of a muppet poster and other prizes were included in this promotion.

Other entertainments for children include magic shows, and puppet, muppet, or marionette shows given in the toy departments, or in central areas of shopping centers. Many stores also plan small giveaways for children during the holiday season, such as balloons or snack food. Gifts are also handed out by Santa Claus or his helpers. Some stores supervise kiddie entertainment and play areas, on a permanent basis or during the Christmas shopping season, to allow parents to leave their children long enough to shop in the store.

Entertainments for children during school vacation periods have wide appeal. These entertainments give parents and children a reason for wanting to go to stores at times when going merely for shopping may not be as palatable as going elsewhere for entertainment. At the other extreme of the age continuum are entertainments for older customers. Famous Barr stores of the May Company parent firm have had Christmas and Easter breakfasts, gift certificates, early store opening hours, dancing classes, and other courses for adults age 60 and older. The number of older persons is increasing as persons live longer and as the baby boom generation grows older. It is a challenge to direct promotions towards

EXHIBIT 11-8 Store Muppet Show and Sing-a-long

Source: The Washington Post (August 12, 1981), p. 12. Size of original, 2⅞ × 9″.

Bring the kids
to a tune-filled
Muppet™ sing-a-long

Friday, Aug. 14
11 a.m. at Fair Oaks Mall
2 p.m. at Montgomery Mall
Children's World

Join Judy Knotts as she and her Muppet™ friends sing-a-long with you and your children. Every child will receive a Muppet™ poster and become eligible for prizes from the Billy the Kid™ and Calamity Jane Muppet™ collections.

Employees of Woodward & Lothrop, their families, agents and representatives are not eligible.

lder persons to create interest and sales, while not projecting a negative ttitude towards senior citizens.[21]

A popular summer entertainment is fireworks on the Fourth of July. Iacy's fireworks are held on the rivers surrounding Manhattan. Newspaper ds and handouts announce the time and place of the fireworks, describe ie fireworks display, explain plans for including the handicapped, and ell when the fireworks can be seen on television. They also give directions for getting to the place by car, bus, and subway, and thank the variou governmental agencies and media for helping with the event. There i no merchandise in this institutional advertising for the fireworks. Howeve the advertising lists store hours for all area Macy's stores which are ope on the holiday.[22]

On a smaller scale, a small town has run one-day Teddy Bear Rally during a slow time in retailing, a Saturday in midsummer. This participator entertainment included a bear contest with prizes for many categorie donated by local merchants, educational displays about honey, a "bea repair" hospital, musical entertainment including the Teddy Bear song and a theater production of "Goldilocks and the Three Bears." The purpos of this rally, sponsored by the Chamber of Commerce, was to generat shopping traffic in the center of a town that is near suburban shoppin centers. Booth rentals and the sale of teddy-bear decorated t-shirts an balloons raised money for a charitable organization. The infant-size t-shir was a best-seller because it also fit the bears. Store windows were decorate with bears. Over 50,000 toy bears and from 15,000 to 20,000 person attended the rally. Hot weather was no problem; the bears wore sunglasse and hats to keep cool. Retailers, especially restaurants, reported goo business from this event.[23]

Fashion Shows and Seminars

A popular special event frequently used by individual stores, shoppin centers, and store groups is the fashion show. This can be a dramati and colorful event, accompanied by sound effects, music, and even slide or motion pictures. The reason for frequent fashion shows is that fashio is constantly changing and in the news, hence a fashion show is a logica focal point for apparel and accessories retailers. This kind of event i like a financial investment which generates a stream of revenue ove time.[24] Monthly fashion show themes might include wardrobes for va cations, going back to school and college, and winter sports. Timing wil depend on when manufacturers have new products to introduce.

Individual retailers and shopping centers put on fashion show during the year, especially in spring and fall, which are the major season for style changes. A show sponsored by a group of stores must be rep resentative of all of the participating stores. For public relations, som stores or groups of stores cooperate with local civic groups to put o fashion shows to raise money for a charity. Exhibit 11-9 shows a progran for a fashion show with five sponsoring apparel retailers plus two floris sponsors that provided flowers. The purpose of this show was to rais money for a college scholarship fund.

Most stores announce their shows through publicity in the new columns as well as mentioning them in their own advertising. They plac

EXHIBIT 11-9 Fashion Show Program That Lists Retail Sponsors

Source: The program was designed by Louise Currin for University Women, Amherst, MA.

osters and show cards around the store and shopping center, and often ıail invitations to actual and prospective customers.[25]

Some retailers plan small daily or weekly shows with models parading ırough their selling floors, lunch rooms or restaurants. Either the models arry cards which describe the garments shown, or cards are displayed n the restaurant tables. Other retailers send models to restaurants outside ıe store. These models carry cards printed with descriptive information ıcluding price, and discuss the fashions with the customers. Some stores' ıshion shows in specific apparel departments to highlight their merhandise are known as *informal modeling*. Still other retailers have as ıany as 30 to 35 shows per year, including some especially for men, 'omen, or children. Videotapes of vendors' fashion shows, or of store ıerchandise representing several vendors, can be run continuously in arious departments. Manufacturers and groups of manufacturers often resent fashion shows at meetings of retailers.[26]

In another method of promoting apparel, Casual Corner, a women's apparel store chain in the Northeast, provides store representatives to give a fashion seminar at meetings of local clubs and civic organizations to help fund-raising efforts. This seminar informs potential customers about the store's wardrobe-investment-advice-service and other services. It also provides an opportunity for the retailer to hand out cards on which attendees can request an individual appointment, an invitation to a store wardrobe seminar, or a presentation at the meeting of another local civic organization.[27]

Store Openings and Anniversaries

Store openings and anniversaries tend to involve several special promotional events: ribbon cutting, concerts, exhibits, parades, personal appearances, coupons, and samples. Anniversaries present annual opportunities for creating excitement. These events can be announced in an invitation like the one for a store opening in Exhibit 11-10, or in newspaper advertisements. Newsworthy openings and anniversaries usually generate publicity in the media.

SUMMARY

Retail sales promotion is the show-biz tool of marketing communications. It includes special events, appearances, demonstrations, entertainments, exhibits, contests, seminars, sales, offering coupons and free samples, and fashion shows. It has been defined as "marketing communications other than advertising, personal selling, visual merchandising, and publicity." It usually works best in coordination with one or more of these other marketing communications tools. Manufacturers define sales promotion as "the direct inducement or incentive to the sales force, the distributor, or the consumer, with the primary objective of creating an immediate sale" and including such activities as "displays, shows and exhibitions, demonstrations and various nonrecurrent selling efforts not in the ordinary routine," as well as consumer education and sales literature.

The purpose of sales promotion is to generate sales. It tends to project image and attract publicity as well. Promotions can be used to generate traffic in stores and to sell products during slow seasons, months, days, and hours. Promotions are also a key competitive tool during important retail seasons like Christmas.

In addition to involving other tools in the marketing communications mix, promotions can involve manufacturers, retailers, local institutions, governments, and even other countries. Therefore, cooperation and coordination are necessary to insure that all of these components work

XHIBIT 11-10 Invitation to a Store-Opening Party

ource: Used with permission of Alan Bilzerian. The store in the Exhibit has moved to 4 Newbury St. The invitation and illustration were each on 7 × 9″ cards.

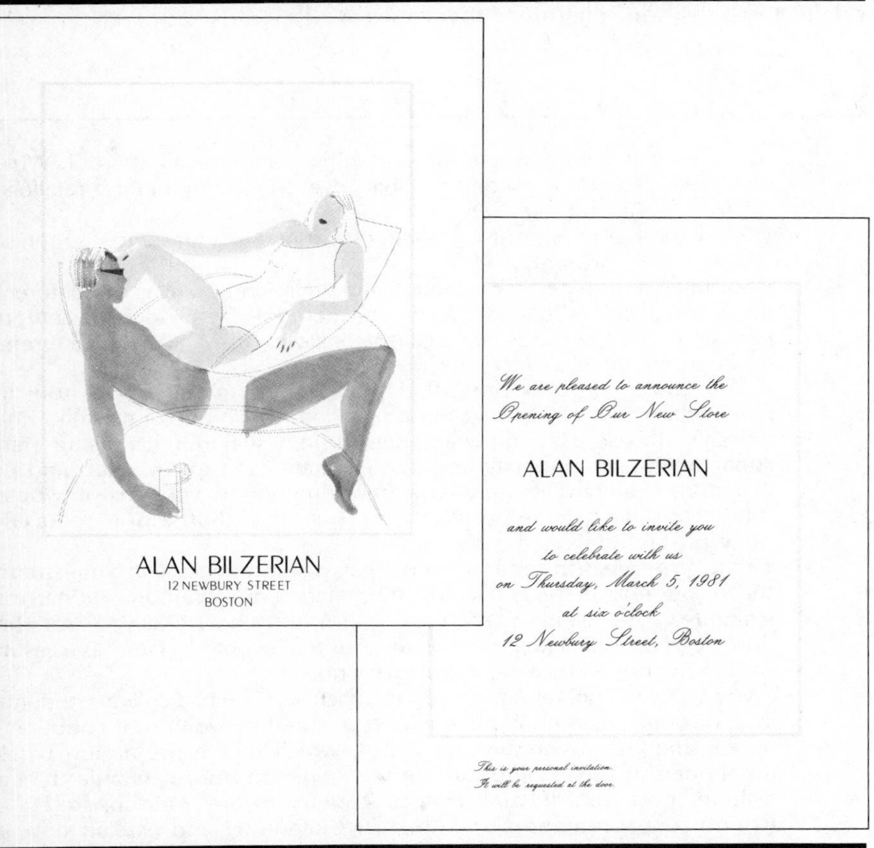

ogether to communicate store or brand image, in order to get customers nto the store to buy merchandise. Poor coordination of marketing comnunications tools can waste a firm's resources, confuse customers, and ail to reach communications goals.

Special events arranged cooperatively by retailers and manufacturers nclude product demonstrations, offering free samples and coupons, and ersonal appearances and brand-name events that reinforce advertising. hese events result in increased sales appeal for manufacturers' merhandise and greater traffic for the store.

Special promotions and entertainment events also call attention to tores and the brands. These include foreign country or U.S. city pronotions, theme promotions, exhibits and contests, rewards for quantity purchases, and sales. Parades, musical and other entertainment, fashion shows and seminars, store openings and anniversaries are entertainment promotions that build good will and traffic. They should build present and future sales, and customer loyalty as well.

QUESTIONS

1. Advertising is a very important marketing communications tool. What does sales promotion accomplish that advertising cannot (a) for retailers, (b) for manufacturers?
2. Why is it often important for retailers and manufacturers to cooperate in retail sales promotions?
3. How are various types of promotion and their timing similar and different for (a) small stores in small towns, (b) medium-sized shopping centers near small cities, (c) large city department stores, (d) small manufacturers, (e) large manufacturers?
4. If you could use only one other marketing communications tool in conjunction with a planned sales promotion, which one of the following tools would you use, and why: advertising, visual merchandising, personal selling, or publicity and public relations? Explain what kind of promotion you have in mind. Explain whether or not your answer would differ for a Christmas promotion versus an end-of-season reduced-price promotion.
5. Think of a sales promotion event that you attended. Did you attend the promotion in response to other marketing communications, for example, advertising? If so, why; if not, why not? Did you buy the promoted products (a) immediately after that event, (b) later, as a result of that event? If so, why; if not, why not?
6. If you were an apparel retailer or manufacturer who had college students in your target market, explain why you would or would not cooperate in a fashion show promotion. If not, which of the promotion types mentioned in this chapter are, in your opinion, more suitable than a fashion show for attracting college students to buy your apparel?
7. Choose one promotion described in Chapter 11 and explain how it will attract the attention of a target market made up of Baby Boomers, people born soon after World War II. Also, using this target market, explain whether or not you think Baby Boomers will respond actively or passively to this promotion. That is, do they need considerable effort of other marketing communications tools to attract their attention to promotions, or are they so actively looking for excitement, entertainment, and purchases that they do not need extensive advertising to get them to seek out promotions? Next, answer this question for a college-student target market.

NOTES

1. O. Kleppner, *Advertising Procedure,* 8th ed. (Englewood Cliffs, NJ: Prentice-Hall, 1983); L. Spalding, "Push for Productivity," *Stores* (January 1981), pp. 56–59; R. Stanley, *Promotion, Advertising, Publicity, Personal Selling, Sales Promotion,* 2nd. ed. (Englewood Cliffs, N.J: Prentice-Hall, 1982), p. 302.

See also the point-of-purchase section in Chapter 12.

2. D. Schultz and W. Robinson, *Sales Promotion Management* (Chicago: Crain, 1982); R. Strang, *The Promotional Planning Process* (Holt, Rinehart & Winston, 1980); E. Mahany, *Mahany on Sales Promotion* (Chicago: Crain, 1982); D. Schultz and W. Robinson, *Sales Promotion Essentials* (Chicago: Crain, 1982).

See also: S. Britt, *Consumer Behavior and Behavior Sciences* (New York: John Wiley, 1966), pp. 425–443; G. Donahue, "Testing and Evaluating Promotion," *Marketing Communication* (October 1979), pp. 76–78; E. Hamburger, *Fashion Business, Its All Yours* (San Francisco: Harper & Row, Pub., 1976), pp. 91–92; M. Harriman, *And the Price Is Right* (New York: William Collins Publishers, Inc., 1958), pp. 241–269; J. Jarnow and B. Judelle, *Inside the Fashion Business* (New York: John Wiley, 1974), pp. 388–397; L. Rubin, *The World of Fashion* (San Francisco: Harper & Row, Pub., 1976), pp. 193–218; D. Schwartz, *Marketing Today,* (New York: Harcourt Brace Jovanovich, 1977), pp. 1–24, 261–264, 325–329; G. Weil, *Sears Roebuck USA* (Briarcliff Manor, NY: Stein & Day, 1977), pp. 119–130; L. Wendt and H. Kogan, *Give the Lady What She Wants* (Skokie, IL: Rand McNally, 1952), pp. 351–364; A. Winters and S. Goodman, *Fashion Advertising and Promotion,* 5th ed. (New York: Fairchild, 1978).

3. I. Barmash, "Shaping a Sears Financial Empire," *The New York Times* (February 12, 1984), pp. 1, 6; A. Bates and J. Didion, "Special Services Can Personalize Retail Environment," *Marketing News* 19 (April 12, 1985), p. 13.

4. P. Phillips, "On Stage," *Stores* 62 (March 1980), p. 49.

5. D. Schultz, "Why Marketers Like the Sales Promotion Gambit," *Advertising Age,* 54 (November 7, 1983), pp. M52, M54.

6. Steigers ad in *Sunday Republican,* Springfield, MA (March 9, 1980), Section 1, p. A12.

7. Mail folder from Bread and Circus natural foods supermarket, Hadley, MA branch opening. The original store was started by Tony and Susan Harnett in Brookline, MA in 1975.

8. Talbot's ad in *The New York Times* (March 11, 1984), p. 48.

See also Schultz and Robinson, *Sales Promotion Management;* Strang, *Promotional Planning;* E. Mahany, *Mahany on Sales Promotion;* Schultz and Robinson, *Sales Promotion Essentials;* Britt, *Consumer Behavior,* pp. 425–443; Donahue, "Testing and Evaluating Promotion," pp. 76–78; Hamburger, *Fashion Business,* pp. 91–92; Harriman, *Price is Right,* pp. 241–269; Jarnow and Judelle, *Inside Fashion,* pp. 388–397; Rubin, *World of Fashion,* pp. 193–218; Schwartz, *Marketing Today,* pp. 1–24, 261–264, 325–329; Weil, *Sears,* pp. 119–130; Wendt and Kogan, *Give the Lady,* pp. 351–364; Winters and Goodman, *Fashion Advertising.*

9. L. Haugh, "Pass the Coupon, Please," *Advertising Age,* 54 (December 12, 1983), p. M30.

10. "A Coupon Machine at the Supermarket," *Business Week* (March 5, 1984), p. 68; "In-Store Pioneers Clip Coupon Competition" *Advertising Age,* 56 (January 24, 1985), p. 6.

11. *Valley Advocate* (Springfield, MA) 12, February 2, 1979, p. 22A.

12. Steiger's 88th Anniversary Sale Catalog, Springfield, MA (April 8, 1984).

13. G. Mahany, "Fall Promotions Set Big 'Sails,' " *Advertising Age,* 51 (November 3, 1980), p. 64; Edwin McDowell, "How Bloomingdale's is Selling China," *The New York Times* (September 7, 1980), Section 3, p. 1; P. Sloan, "China Chic Blooms in N.Y.," *Advertising Age,* 51 (September 22, 1980), p. 104; M. Stevens, *"Like No Other Store In the World,"* Chapter 4.

14. Lord & Taylor ad in *The New York Times* (April 8, 1984), p. 19. There were similar ads on pp. 7 and 18.

15. Gucci ad in *The New York Times* (March 21, 1982), p. 9.

16. Betsy Gilbert, "Retailers Stamp Out Loyalty Problems," *Advertising Age,* 55 (May 10, 1984), p. M-34.

17. Kathryn Eickhoff, Executive Vice President, Townsend-Greenspan Co. Inc., New York, at "Forces Reshaping our Future" session of the National Retail Merchants Association (NRMA) meetings in New York City, January 14, 1985; Samuel Feinberg, "From Where I Sit," *Women's Wear Daily* (February 24, 1984), p. 12; "Sales Promotion/Marketing Idea Exchange" session of NRMA on January 13, 1985; see Eickhoff, "Forces Reshaping our Future."

18. L. Ukman, "All the World's a Stage for Blooming Events Era," *Advertising Age,* 54 (April 18, 1983), pp. M29–M31, including "What Makes an Event Special," on p. M-31.

19. Donald M. O'Brien, Senior Vice President of Marketing, Jordan Marsh Company, Boston, visual presentation at "Using Events and Public Relations to Enhance Store Dominance" session of 1985 NRMA.

20. Kathy Riley, "Promotion at the Chestnut Hill Mall," *Marketing East,* 2 (February, 1981), p. 4.

21. Laurent Belsie, "Dance Class at the Local Department Store? Seniors Give it a Whirl," *The Christian Science Monitor* (April 18, 1984), p. 5; Eickhoff, "Forces Reshaping our Future."

See NRMA idea exchange reference in note 17.

22. Macy's ad in *The New York Times* (July 3, 1984), p. A5.

23. "Bears' Day Out," *The Daily Hampshire Gazette,* Northampton, MA (August 6, 1984), pp. 1, 9; "Bring on the Marmalade, Bear Fans," *The Daily Hampshire Gazette* (May 29, 1984), p. 11; "Teddies Take the Common," *Amherst Bulletin* (August 8, 1984), p. 2.

24. A. Estes, "How Retailers Promote, Entertain," *Advertising Age,* 52 (April 6, 1981), pp. 47–48.

25. See Alan Bilzerian invitation in Exhibit 1-3, Chapter 1.

26. NRMA fashion show on January 15, 1985, sponsored by the Polyester Fashion Council, featured apparel from Mary McFadden, Bill Blass, Bill Haire, Fernando Sanchez and Pietro Dimitri.

27. Folder from Casual Corner about Appointment Consultations and Wardrobe/Investment Seminars, No. 630-51, received during presentation in Amherst, MA, Spring 1984.

APPENDIX 11

JAPAN PROMOTION AT BLOOMINGDALE'S

This appendix contains three examples of print communications related to the Japan promotion. The first, which appeared in newspapers and magazines, sets the tone and thanks cooperating firms. The second describes some of the many products, events, and dates in the New York store; special books about Japan, pearls, computerized skin analyzer, etc. The third is a letter from the Japanese Ambassador that emphasizes the importance of international cooperation. This letter appeared in a Bloomingdale's booklet.

VITALITY. CREATIVITY. INDIVIDUALITY. FROM A CHILD'S FIRST BRUSHSTROKE TO THE 21ST CENTURY OF DESIGN, ONE THING IS CLEAR: A UNIQUE RESPECT FOR THE PAST. AN INSATIABLE CURIOSITY FOR THE FUTURE. AN INNOVATIVE, INTERNATIONAL QUALITY OF LIFE FOR TODAY.

THE KEY TO JAPANESE DESIGN: "TO ARTISTICALLY MATERIALIZE ONE'S WILL". THE KEY TO OUR PRESENTATION IS ONE AND THE SAME. COME SEE IT ALL IN EVERY BLOOMINGDALE'S, BEGINNING SEPTEMBER 12.

We thank our colleagues for their special support in our exhibits and programs:

Pan American World Airways	**The American Express®Card**	**Kirin Beer**
American Honda Motor Co.	Sanyo Fashion House	Sanrio Inc.
Mitsubishi Electric/Diamond Vision	I.S. Cosmetics	Toshiba American
Sotheby Parke Bernet	Albuquerque Museum	Sony

bloomingdale's

Source: Bloomingdale's. Appeared in various publications, such as *The New York Times Magazine*, Fall 1984. Full-page ads.

- 1 -

JAPAN AT BLOOMINGDALE'S

An event as expansive as the Japanese influence sweeping the world. Now, at Bloomingdale's.

In fashion. Home design. Cuisine and cosmetics. Eelctronics and ceramics. Bloomingdale's and Japan on the cutting edge of design. A dynamic panorama of contemporary style, going on from September 13 to November 4 in New York and selected branches.

SHOPS AND SPECIAL MERCHANDISE

Metro Level	Tomorrow's World. Video magic and sound spectacular. Visit the future in the Electronics Center.
	Books. Tokyo Access, the latest in travel guide books, features everything you want to know and more on Tokyo. Explore our large selection of special literature on Japan.
Lower Level	Au Kimono. Exclusive styles for private hours from international designers. Intimate Apparel.
	Kiddo. Boys designs for your favorite mischief-maker and Dick and Jane - 50's looks for little people. Both in The Next Generation.
The Arcade	Mikimoto. For nearly a century the name has been synonymous with exquisite pearls.
	Accessories. Oversized scarves, embossed rubber "schoolbags" like buffalo and snake, computer-graphic socks, velvetized pearls...the list goes on. Also on 4.
B'way	Shiseido. The Shiseido computerized skin analyzer is a magic wand guided by your personal advisor, who will relay information on the best use of color for your immediate future. Meet Masu Ohtake. Internationally known Shiseido make-up artist. Consult him in The Beauty Spot, September 13th to 24th.
	Intelligent Skincare. Exclusively in Bloomingdale's. Introducing the I.S. beauty computer to B'way and the world. It magnifies your skin to thoroughly analyze every pore. A printout gives the program to follow for flawless skin at any age. In The Beauty Spot, September 25th to October 1st.
	I.S. Computer Charts. The I.S. computer graph charts your skin, eyes and hair while a printout states which make-up colors are scientifically correct for you alone. Visit the new I.S. counter.

Source: Bloomingdale's handout, Fall 1984. Directory of exhibits and demonstrations included some exhibits mentioned in newspaper ads. Whole-page newspaper ads were used for related apparel.

A MESSAGE FROM JAPAN

EMBASSY OF JAPAN
WASHINGTON, D. C.

Message from
His Excellency Yoshio Okawara,
Ambassador of Japan
at the Opening of "Salute to Japan,"
Bloomingdale's Exhibition of Japanese Culture and Products

It is a great pleasure for me to send you greetings on the occasion of this "Salute to Japan." This exhibition will provide an opportunity for the American people to broaden their understanding of Japan and its people through exposure to Japanese art, fashion and technology. It will also serve to illustrate how the heritage from the past combines with the future in forming a harmonious modern society.

Last November in Japan, Prime Minister Nakasone and President Reagan jointly affirmed the importance of increasing cultural exchange between our two nations. This embodies the interest and enthusiasm in culture of other shores held by our peoples. Therefore, an opportunity to experience another culture through an event such as this exhibition is very important. It is my belief that through mutual understanding and the appreciation of the similarities as well as the differences between our cultures, we are able to enrich each other and improve the quality of our lives. Certainly an exhibition of this magnitude will make valuable contributions toward this goal.

I would like to extend my most sincere wishes for the success of "Salute to Japan," and also would like to congratulate all the people involved who have worked hard to put this exhibition together.

Yoshio Okawara
Ambassador of Japan

JAPAN

An opportunity to experience another culture.

17

Source: Bloomingdale's booklet.

12
VISUAL MERCHANDISING

INTRODUCTION

It is said, "There's no business like show business"; that is why successful marketers do not underestimate the pizazz factor. While advertising, special promotions, and publicity help bring customers into stores, dramatic in-store displays help sell the merchandise by creating atmosphere. Manufacturers help create dramatic displays by providing colorful packaging, signs and attention-attracting point-of-purchase (POP) display materials. Visual merchandising is the coordination of all display components to create atmosphere both inside and immediately outside the store and manufacturers' showrooms. Like personal selling and some promotion events, visual merchandising is located at the selling site.

Displays are arrangements of merchandise, backgrounds, props, and signs which are usually temporary and moveable, as opposed to store *design,* which includes large-scale fixtures and architectural elements.[1] Exterior display includes windows, signs, and landscaping. Interior display includes merchandise or images of merchandise on signs, counters, shelves, walls, ceilings, and in rooms.

The function of exterior display is to get persons passing by to enter then or later. The function of interior display is to create an attractive environment, attract attention to specific merchandise, and provide information about how to cook, use, or wear the merchandise. The purpose of all visual merchandising is to communicate image, develop store and

EXHIBIT 12-1 Publicity about a Store with Unusual Displays

Source: *The Christian Science Monitor* (January 15, 1981), p. 17. © The Christian Science Publishing Society. All rights reserved. See also, "A New Twist: Supermarkets with all the Frills," *Business Week* (August 17, 1981), p. 122.

Chandeliers and cabbage: elegant shopping at Byerly's

By Phyllis Hanes
Food editor of
The Christian Science Monitor

People in Minneapolis can go to the supermarket expecting to buy a porcelain sculpture for $15,000 or to choose a pot of mustard from 47 varieties – if they shop at a place called Byerly's.

They will also shop in comfort at this unique market, with carpeting covering the extra-wide aisles and chandeliers with soft lighting. They can also use the services of a post office, bank, pharmacy, or florist shop or even take a cooking lesson.

Well-dressed customers roam around, choosing exotic foods if they like, such as ground buffalo meat, killer-bee honey, live lobsters and live fish, frog's legs and Spanish octopus, cactus leaves and taro root.

• • •

A French pastry chef works in a glass booth creating masterpieces of dough and pastry. A home economist is available for advice. All bakery products, chilies, soups, and many other foods are cooked fresh on the premises.

• • •

Byerly's not only sells food but tells how t prepare it. Each store has a college-educated home economist to give out recipes and advice. A store will even plan a dinner party for customers who want to entertain at home.

The store also offers a schedule of ethnic, dietary, and basic cooking classes in a beautifully organized cooking-school kitchen.

• • •

One wonders how the store can make a profit with such lavish services. One answer is that there's no advertising, except for special holidays or a new-store opening.

Another reason is that Byerly's entices the customer to buy high-margin items that other supermarkets don't offer. The stores' customers spend about $19 on an average trip. The average, nationwide, is just $12.

brand loyalty, sell merchandise, and attract attention of both customer and the press.[2] Exhibit 12-1 shows a sketch and excerpts from an articl about effective visual merchandising in an unusual supermarket whicl does not advertise. This supermarket, Byerly's in Minneapolis, has car peting, chandeliers, soft lighting, and displays of live lobsters, cactu leaves, and French pastry as it is being made.

VISUAL MERCHANDISING AS A MARKETING COMMUNICATOR

Functions of Visual Merchandising

With its theater-like dramatic lighting, props, staging and sometimes music, display *reminds, informs,* and *persuades.*[3] It *reminds* by reinforcing messages sent by other marketing communications such as advertising and special promotions. For example, interior display reminds customers about merchandise that has been advertised.

Display can *inform* customers about unadvertised special sales and newly arrived merchandise, and demonstrate how merchandise can be used or worn, as shown in Exhibit 12-2. In addition, displays inform

EXHIBIT 12-2 **Display Showing How Merchandise Can Be Used or Worn**

Source: Advertisement by Poly Form U.S.A. Inc., in *Visual Merchandising and Store Design* (December 1983), p. 35.

customers about how merchandise can be combined or coordinated with other merchandise, where the merchandise is, what it costs, and perhaps how to take care of it. Display *persuades* by including other merchandise or props that make the featured merchandise look especially attractive and desirable to the target customers.

It is estimated that over 25% of all fashion merchandise is sold primarily through displays. In-store display is a main source of product information for bathroom accessories, serving and buffet products, and other housewares.[4] Display substitutes for some personal selling of merchandise whether or not the merchandise has been presold. When displays sell some of the merchandise, salespersons have more time to sell other merchandise for which personal selling is especially effective. When poorly trained salespersons do not know where to find, or how to demonstrate merchandise, display can help customers find it and learn about it. Displays in Exhibit 12-3 show consumers what merchandise is available for sale.

Visual merchandising can add a psychological value which differentiates merchandise available in one store from the same merchandise available from a competitor in the same trading area. The overall image of price, quality, and service that displays create should clearly distinguish a store from its competitors. Customers in or passing by a store should know which store they are in, even without seeing a sign.[5]

Display creates an on-site message about store image which should reinforce the image communicated by advertising and other marketing

***EXHIBIT 12-3* Displays Showing Merchandise in Macy's Cellar**
Source: Macy's, New York, NY.

communications.[6] Visual merchandising should communicate a clear overall image when a store has several merchandise categories and departments. Design and allocation of store windows and other display space should be part of a coordinated marketing plan for the store. Customers who are confused about a store's character tend to buy merchandise in another store which has a clearer image.

The Store as Theater[7]

Colorful, dramatic visual merchandising is enjoyable entertainment. Like a play in a theater, visual merchandising in a store has stage lighting, settings, props, and costumed actors. The store is unlike most theaters in that the customers join the actors—employees—on the stage—selling floor—and interact with them and the props—merchandise, mannequins, display fixtures, and displays. For example, the customers could be seen interacting with the merchandise in Exhibit 12-3.

The short-run purpose of visual merchandising is to sell merchandise. The long run purpose is to project an image of the store as a center for ideas and entertainment, a place that customers will want to visit repeatedly for more enjoyment—and more purchases.[8] The entertainment aspect is also important for shopping center marketing managers who use visual merchandising in common areas to attract attention to the shopping center and its tenant stores.

The more a person enjoys shopping in a store or shopping center, the more likely the person will return. Enjoyment includes a time element. Customers who have little time to shop will enjoy being able to find the merchandise they want in the limited time they have available for shopping. Effective visual merchandising can make it easier for customers to find what they want. Making the store or shopping center an enjoyable place to spend shopping or leisure time is especially important in a competitive environment.

Customers are exposed to print and broadcast advertisements for similar merchandise sold in several competing stores or shopping centers. For example, flowers are advertised by two competitors on facing pages of the Sunday paper. When customers can visit several stores or shopping centers in the same shopping trip, and when several stores are the same perceived distance from customers' homes, visual merchandising helps differentiate stores and brands by adding an image or psychological component. Recently a newspaper article featured a distinctive series of interior window displays in Bergdorf's, a New York specialty apparel store. These displays had a large amount of white space, communicating an image of expensive merchandise.[9] Such an image might attract customers trying to choose among several similar stores.

EXTERIOR AND INTERIOR DISPLAYS

Store Exteriors and Shopping Centers

Store exteriors communicate some *image,* from *value-conscious* to *avant-garde.* An exterior includes facades, night lighting, windows, signs, a logo, and landscaping. Unattractive buildings with little potential for exterior improvement may have to rely on advertising, sales promotion, and interior displays.

The first on-site impression of a store or shopping center comes from the exterior. Because landscaping and parking facilities also communicate image,[10] their appearance should be consistent with the advertised image. Exteriors should send clear, inviting image signals to target patrons passing by in cars, buses, or on foot. Exterior signs should give exit directions to cars on turnpikes.

The interior walkway of a shopping center also sends messages to customers about image. For this reason marketing directors of shopping centers monitor store signs and displays along the interior walkway so that these are consistent with the shopping center's image.[11] A torn sign or dirty display at the entrance to a store detracts from the overall image of the center. Rules must be enforced so that one store does not outdo other stores and set off a competitive situation that would also detract from the consistency of the shopping center image.

Retail managers should evaluate what image their store facades are communicating. In the absence of store windows, the store signs, interior displays, and store personnel near store entrances serve as a facade. A facade that sends no message fails to differentiate a store from its competitors. Display cues help customers find the store. The impact of store advertising is reduced when no external cue tells customers that this is the store with the enticing advertising.

Window Display

Effective window displays use props and color to dramatize merchandise in an exciting manner. Just as creative advertising personnel fit illustrations and copy into newspaper pages or into broadcast time slots, creative display personnel adapt displays to window sizes and shapes. A window has about three seconds to attract a person who is walking by the store, and possibly less time to attract those passing by in cars and buses.[12] Even to passers-by who do not stop, the window can communicate a number of different messages, such as *value, exclusiveness, attractiveness, clutter,* or *clearance sale.* Clear, exciting, and rapid communication encourages passers-by to remember the firm and merchandise and return at a later date.

As the art and copy support the message of a print advertisement, merchandise and props support the message sent by the window display. Theme windows (holiday, foreign) augment the messages sent by interior display and other advertising and promotional events. While the merchandise displayed in the window need not be what most customers actually buy, it should appeal to the target customer's aspirations or desired image. A window display of merchandise that is more expensive, prestigious, and striking than merchandise that customers actually use differentiates their perception of the store's merchandise from their perception of the same merchandise sold by competitors. Creating a store identification for merchandise, brand-name or not, supports this differentiation. Exhibit 12-4 shows an example of a prestigious window display.

To attract attention, a store window needs lighting that focuses on the merchandise but does not change its color or texture. Research indicates that most windows should have price signs. These should be small and

EXHIBIT 12-4 **A Prestigious Window Display**
Source: D.G. Williams

de-emphasized in a prestige store, and larger and more visible in a promotional store. Signs help sell merchandise when they are consistent with the window image and, for large stores, when they give the department name and floor location.[13] Television, also used for in-store displays, can be used in windows to arouse interest as well.

Simple exteriors and neat, clean windows that communicate a clear image of the store are more likely to attract customers than are dusty, dirty, cluttered exteriors and windows. The latter communicate that the store is not careful with details and does not care about merchandise and customers.

Window displays must be changed frequently, weekly in high-traffic areas, less often in areas of less traffic. One exception to this principle is the special holiday window that serves as a tourist attraction in the Christmas shopping season. Perceptual screening—the blocking out of unnecessary sensory data[14]—makes customers cease to notice a window display they have seen many times before.

Special attention-grabbing windows tend to attract not only passers-by but also the press, resulting in publicity for the store. Pictures of outstanding windows that have been published in newspapers attract attention of potential customers, reminding them to visit the store. An innovative robot window display in a New York clothing store, Charivari, attracted attention of the press and was featured in a news article with a photograph.[15] In that case, the window did not have a back wall, so the interior displays become part of the window display as well.

Visual merchandising managers should use window displays to tie in with popular events in local museums or visits of celebrities to the store's city. These windows also tend to attract newspaper publicity. A favorable newspaper article adds status to the store. Christmas windows, which also tend to attract newspaper publicity remind people to come to the store during the Christmas shopping season. If customers have to stand in line to see the windows, they realize that the display is valued by many others.

A small store in a larger city used *space* to attract attention to windows in the same way that Bergdorf's display mentioned earlier or a prestigious newspaper ad uses *white space.* This small store's target market was affluent men and women who like high-fashion apparel. Nearby competitors had larger windows with more merchandise in them. In contrast, this store's simple window displays with strategically placed empty space stood out from the surrounding store windows.

Interior-Exterior Displays

Some display ideas can be used both for windows and for interior display. Larger stores like Bergdorf Goodman, for example, divide interior space into little shops which have windows inside the store.[16] Macy's Cellar has a series of little shops with interior window displays facing the walkway. These shop windows are inside Macy's Cellar, but serve as exterior displays for the shops. Some of these shop windows are shown in Exhibit 12-5.

Stores in shopping centers can use ceiling displays to enable people passing by to see merchandise inside the store. Customers inside the store also see high-rise merchandise and signs hanging from ceilings above counters and floor fixtures. Ceiling displays have two advantages. First, they are relatively hard to reach, and so minimize temptation to shoplift. Second, they direct customers to specific merchandise, whether these customers are inside or outside the store. For example, a large railroad train suspended from the ceiling can identify the toy section, or a sign with large letters can locate the housewares department.[17]

Interior Displays

Wall displays and displays on raised platforms or above counters can be better used to guide customers than less visible low fixtures. K mart uses a variety of wall and floor fixtures with merchandise arranged so that customers can see a variety with little effort. Department signs are displayed near ceilings so that merchandise displays will not obscure the signs. New displays were part of K mart's change in image to the "store of the '90s." This new, upscale image of brand names and higher-quality merchandise was supported by a $40 million television and print

EXHIBIT 12-5 **Interior Shops Window Displays in Macy's Cellar**
Source: Nate Silverstein, photographer.

campaign. The new merchandise mix featured sporting goods, leisure products, and electronics, and de-emphasized floor coverings and automotive products. Brand-name items had better displays than unbranded merchandise. Tiled main traffic aisles helped steer customers through the displays.[18]

In a recent speech, several key points about strategic display planning were made by Joseph Weishar, President of New Vision Studios in New York City.[19] Weishar explained that the point of visual merchandising is to get customers through the merchandise on the floor to the wall displays. K mart's tiled main traffic aisles, for example, smoothly lead customers through the merchandise areas. Weishar also pointed out that merchandise should appear to be within arm's reach. Again, K mart's merchandise, displayed on floor stands and walls, seems to be within arm's reach of a customer standing between two floor fixtures or between the floor fixtures and a wall. Light intensity also influences mood, Weishar said, so there should be good lighting in fitting rooms, by mirrors, and near cash registers. Light should illuminate merchandise, not empty spaces. K mart's lighting on ceiling tracks is a good example of effective lighting.

Because most customers turn right when they enter a space, and because they prefer to try on items upon entry, managers should put merchandise to try on where customers enter, with impulse items at locations that customers will pass upon leaving a space. Thus many stores put racks of impulse items near checkout registers. The shades of black and white tend to fade away from displays and so should be put in the center, surrounded by more striking colors. The key color in a color-assortment display should be put in the place that customers see first, recommended Weishar.

Weishar's suggestion for wall display was to put the largest assortment below a striking display, and when that sells, to move the striking display to another assortment. For example, display a row of men's shirts with ties along a wall, near the ceiling. One of the shirts has a bow tie. Below each shirt-and-tie display are shelves of shirts in stock. The shirts below the bow tie will sell fastest. When that stock is depleted, move the bow tie to another display shirt. Weishar also suggested that if there are small items to display on walls—for example, hammers and screwdrivers—turn them into a display design.[20]

Model Room displays show how various pieces of furniture and accessories look when placed together, and save customers the time and trouble of trying to imagine how separate pieces would look together in a room. They also sell by suggestion, reminding customers about accessories that go with furniture. More than one customer has bought an entire room display! Model rooms have been furnished by and for celebrities to attract attention. One clever display featured a room complete with a life-sized photograph and a biographic sketch of a role-model figure for customers.[21]

Logos and Signs

Symbols and logos are important because they are shorthand for quic identification. The store or brand logo can be a name, sign, or symb which, together with the store or brand color scheme helps build a uniq identity that differentiates one establishment or product from all other Customers should be able to identify the color and shape of a log recognizing a store or brand without even having to read the logo. Th logo can differ from the complete corporate name, which tends to l longer than the logo. The logo should be flexible enough to look appropria on packaging, in print and television advertising, and on various siz of signs and other printed materials.

A logo's design is an important marketing communications devic A clearly defined, easily recalled logo helps customers find a store o brand easily. To insure that the logo is compatible with overall marketin strategy, the design should be approved by top management. Exhibit 1 6 shows several logos. The competitors Macy's and Bloomingdale's hav

EXHIBIT 12-6 **Store Logos**
Source: Newspaper ads and circulars for the below stores.

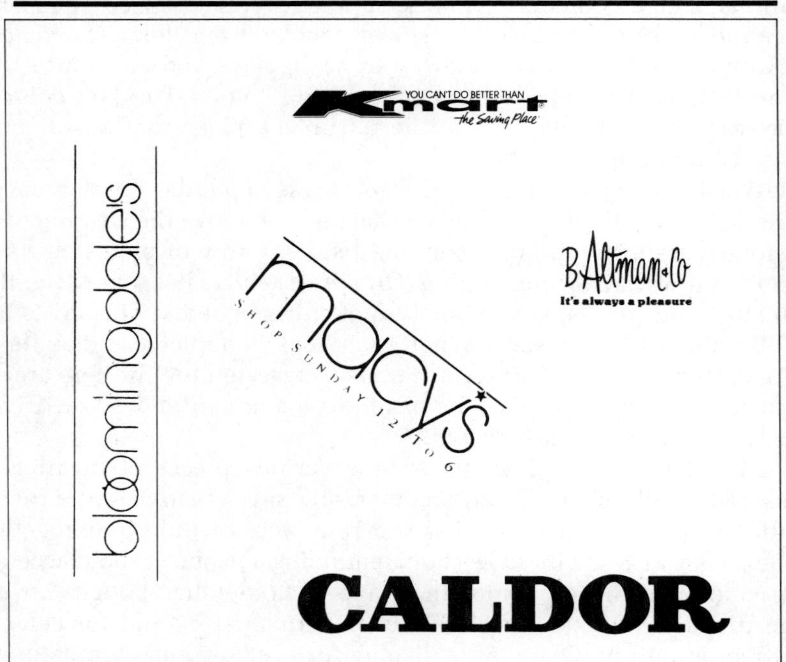

unded logos; Caldor has a bold logo; Altman's has a script logo. The mart and Altman's logos are accompanied by brief position statements. acy's logo is underlined by its store hours.

The logo and the type style used for other words in advertising ›py, on signs, and on packaging helps communicate store or brand image the public. A change in logo communicates a change in image whether not the marketer intends it. Filene's department store in Boston changed om a logo in script to a block-letter logo to announce a more modern ore. Another Federated Department Store, Bloomingdale's, changed from straight-letter logo (which is still on the external sign of the New York ity store) to the rounded logo shown in Exhibit 12-6. Because the logo ıange does tend to be perceived as an indication of actual changes in ore or brand, logo revisions should be reviewed carefully with regard the perceptual threshold.[22] Marketers wishing to communicate change ould make noticeable changes in logos; those wishing to change the go but not the image would make these changes below the perceptual ıreshold. Complications arise because different people have different ›rceptual thresholds.

ıckaging

a sense, packaging is both external and internal display. Bags, boxes ıd other containers can be seen inside and outside stores and on public utes to and from stores, as well as in media publicity pictures of crowd enes or general sidewalk scenes. Often, clever salespeople will offer rge store bags to customers who are carrying competitors' bags. This ›t only gives customers pleasant feelings about being helped and cared r, but also sends the store logo throughout the store and along the ıstomers' routes, at the expense of the competitor's logo.

At one time, customers' purchases were either wrapped or unwrapped; ere were no bags. Shopping bags descended from bandboxes which estigious stores used to contain delivered merchandise in the 19th ›ntury. These bandboxes were used to hold the hats and detachable ›llars that gentlemen fastened to their shirtbands. Shopping bags in the ›30s were somewhat plain compared with the colorful paper and plastic ıgs of today. By the 1960s bags were so artistic that the Cooper-Hewitt useum exhibited 150 of them as "Portable Graphic Art."[23]

As just described, the shopping bag can extend the store display ea beyond the store premises, reminding people about the store as long the bag is used and reused. An attractive, reusable shopping bag or ›x can induce customers to buy generally available items in a particular ore just to get the store bag or box. As with many symbols of today, e logos of leading stores and brands become status symbols. People are proud to wear the logos and carry the packages associated with fine reputations. They tend to carry packages of status stores with the name side exposed. They tend to carry packages of no-name stores with the name side hidden.[24]

DISPLAY AIDS AND FIXTURES

Visual Electronics

Because electronic display aids are developing and changing rapidly, it is necessary to consult current periodicals for new developments. Some examples are given here. The newest developments involve computers and television.

Computers and television have been used (1) to tell customers where merchandise is located, (2) to analyse customers' cosmetic and wardrobe requirements and to offer suggestions, and (3) to provide information about merchandise and its use and care. Electronic directories in shopping centers indicate the routes to stores that sell the desired merchandise. These directories also include information about gift suggestions, and daily sales and promotions. A hard-copy printer provides coupons to consumers interested in free samples or discounts. Print advertising space is available on the directory kiosk for stores or manufacturers. With electronic aids, televised fashion shows, interviews with designers, and merchandise demonstrations can run continuously or when activated by a customer. Computers at cosmetic counters can analyse customers' needs, provide printed shopping lists, and store consumer information collected in this manner. In a promotion of *Gentlemen's Quarterly* magazine and a cognac marketer, touch-sensitive computers in clothing stores asked questions about each male customer's lifestyle and personality and printed out accessories suggestions for two fashion basics named by the customer.[25] Retailers and manufacturers can use these data about lifestyles and personalities to understand target customers.

Various electronic display aids allow one-way or interactive video presentations. In one shopping center, a mime is available to help customers notice and use an electronic aid.[26] Until this technology is more widespread people are needed to help customers learn how to use the machines. The VideoSpond videotex terminal is able to talk, ask questions, listen and respond to customers. Customers can stop and replay videos. The device keeps track of the number of times each program is played. Manufacturers and retailers can be represented on this device.[27] The video aid described in Exhibit 12-7 has a gift guide service which asks questions about the recipient and then suggests gift ideas and stores.

Other electronic displays include Christmas-gift and bridal-gift computers which collect customers' gift preferences, print gift lists for the

XHIBIT 12-7 **Electronic Display Aids**

ource: "Mall Uses Touch-Screen Video," *Marketing News* (November 25, 1983), p. 22, ection 1.

MALL USES TOUCH-SCREEN VIDEO SYSTEM AS MERCHANDISING, SALES-PROMOTION TOOL

VHEN SHOPPERS at Ingram Park ʎall in San Antonio, Texas, want nformation, they let their fingers lo the walking—on the touch-ensitive screens of a videotex-like ystem.

Two video terminals are set ıp at a centrally located booth in-ide the mall, and five remote ter-ninals are located at various mall-ntry points. Using the interactive touch screens," shoppers access wide range of consumer-related nformation stored in a central data ase.

For example, the system features a gift-guide service that will narrow down product selections based on a person's preferences and demographic characteristics.

The system displays a series of questions (Is the gift for a man or woman? Age? What are his/her interests or hobbies? How much do you want to spend?) which the shopper answers by pressing certain areas on the screen. After going through this process of elimination, the computer suggests personalized gift ideas and indicates stores in the mall where they can be purchased.

ustomers' friends, suggest specific gifts, and point out the locations of his merchandise. Still other aids are closed-circuit television monitors vhich narrowcast brand and store commercials to customers waiting in heckout lines in supermarkets. These commercials can also appear on ome television.[28]

Ion-Electronic Selling Aids, Including Signs

Ion-electronic display aids include tags, signs, and accessories. Display ıanagers can order them from vendors through catalogs and conventions. ʌn alternative to buying display aids is making them. Parts and equipment an also be ordered from vendors through catalogs and conventions. Sign-ıaking equipment enables retailers to make colorful and attractive signs uickly. Technological changes have resulted in the modern sign-printing quipment displayed by vendors at trade shows. Specialized computers an be programmed to make signs from directions typed into the computer eyboard. The appendix has information about signs and print styles.

The newest developments in display aids are also available at trade hows. Signs can take the form of banners and streamers for indoor and utdoor use, tickets and tags can be self-sticking or tied on, and free-tanding box and tent-signs, mobiles, and card toppers for display stands are also available. Display props include trees, snowflakes, icebergs, an bears for winter, and palm trees, citrus fruits, and related items appropriat for other seasons. Display aids and props contribute to store atmospher and should be consistent with store image created by other marketin communications.

Fixtures

Today, decor is taken seriously, and the surroundings of the merchandis helps create a mood. Store fixtures are part of the store environment When possible, fixtures should help customers evaluate the merchandise.[2] Fixtures that display merchandise so that customers can see it withou effort communicate that the store knows its business. Crowded displa racks hide some merchandise from view; customers must move othe merchandise to see it. This slows down shopping, tires customers an communicates poor management.

Display fixtures should have a capacity related to store inventor and stock turnover policies. Large-capacity fixtures can be used either i stock turnover is low or if fixtures can be restocked quickly. Otherwise fixtures with a smaller capacity should be used so that they will loo full and well-stocked when customers are in the store. A small amoun of empty space in fixtures will suggest to customers that some merchandis has been purchased. Neat stocks of merchandise in fixtures will encourag customers to fold and put back merchandise.[30]

Robots can help stock display fixtures by determining how muc merchandise is needed and by moving needed merchandise to fixtures.[3] They cannot recognize damaged stock and arrange displays. Seibu, supermarket in Japan, uses robots to reduce the number of employees and to allow remaining employees the time to be with customers.

Display Deterrents to Shoplifting

As fewer salespeople are available to help customers, display fixture that discourage shoplifting become more important. Management mus balance crime prevention against customers' inconvenience. When coat are chained to fixtures and hangers, shoplifters have trouble stealin them, but customers have trouble trying them on in front of mirrors, an trying to imagine what they would look like if not on a leash.

Technological advances offer two general alternatives. First, th merchandise can be locked onto display fixtures, or tagged with device that emit signals when customers leave the store with merchandise the have not purchased. The other alternative is a store surveillance syster with mirrors, television, and detectives. The first method serves as display which tells customers that the store is taking action to discourag shoplifting. Signs that tell customers that "if the bell rings, our personne will assist you," and prominently placed security guards in bright uniforms, also communicate to customers that the store is concerned about theft. The choice between these two alternatives depends on store image, customer type, the environment surrounding the store, the extent of crime-prevention training, the availability of salespeople and security personnel, the crime prevention budget, and the type of merchandise.[32]

Exhibit 12-8 shows lockable display fixtures. Jewelry and purses can be locked onto racks. Apparel can be locked onto hangers with chains or can be locked onto racks. Small items, like video disks, handbags, and computer software, can be locked into cases. Various non-fixture

EXHIBIT 12-8 Lockable Display Fixtures

Source: National Retail Merchants Association Meeting, Securax, Inc., Fort Worth, TX.

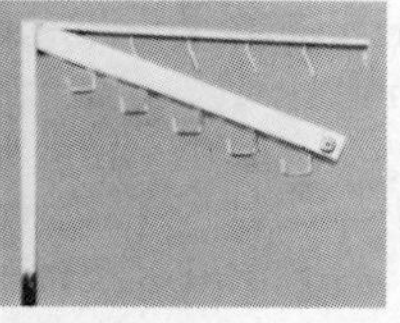

Securax™ anti-theft fixtures are available for use with all types of merchandise, including handbags. Our contemporary handbag unit utilizes a typical J-hook.

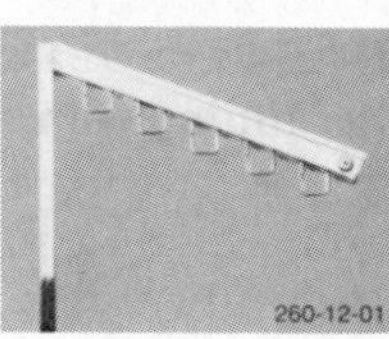

When the unit is unlocked, any handbag may be individually removed. When the J-hook is closed, all handbags are completely secured, yet they may be handled by customers.

devices also display merchandise while simultaneously deterring shoplifters. A small, lockable package holds a single cassette or eight-track tape. The package is removed when the cassette or tape is purchased. A tag that will adhere to any flat, non-metallic surface can be removed by machine at the checkout counter. A clear plastic jacket can be used to hold a store name or fashion tag, which sets off signals as the customer leaves the store or other sensitive area. Another device allows pairs of socks or gloves or other small merchandise to be hung on display fixtures, while keeping pairs together as well. Information about the latest versions of these devices is available from vendors at trade shows. The devices can be seen at work in up-to-date stores.[33]

MANAGING VISUAL MERCHANDISING

While large stores tend to have a somewhat formal distribution of visual merchandising tasks among various employees and managers, smaller stores tend to assign the work to only one or two people. In the larger stores, a visual merchandising manager coordinates displays within a division or store. Helpful advice is available from the Small Business Administration, seminars run by the local Chamber of Commerce, and university faculty and students. Many manufacturers provide display materials to stores of all sizes.[34]

The Visual Merchandising Task

Using the jargon of the communications model, the visual merchandising manager *sends a message* from the store to the customers through the use of merchandise and props at various store sites. The manager also collects feedback about how effectively the visual merchandising helps reach management goals. This feedback comes from (1) monitoring the effect of specific displays on sales of specific merchandise, (2) observing customer response to displays in own and competitors' stores, and (3) asking customers and employees what kind of shopping environment they enjoy. For example, a Neiman-Marcus buyer noticed that some competing stores displayed gift merchandise as it would be used in the home. The buyer informed display personnel about this as well as telling them about display information received from manufacturers.[35]

Experiments with visual displays are one way of determining the relative influence on sales of display and other communications tools. Field experiments have been done to determine the sales effect of signs in stores.[36] After experimenting with different presentations and different merchandise in displays, managers should observe passers-by from time to time, noting how many stop, look, and buy. This information can be used to compare different displays for effectiveness, allowing for changes in environment, weather, seasons, and holidays.

Visual merchandising managers must make both long-run and short-un plans. For the long run, they get plans from the merchandise managers nd from other marketing communications managers, set their annual udget and get it approved by top management. Then, they develop easonal, monthly, and weekly schedules for interior and exterior displays.[37] isplays in the schedule must be consistent with other marketing com-unications themes and copy, and with store image and budget. When veeds are advertised, tweeds should be displayed. When weekly grocery pecials are advertised, they should have special displays. Bookstores isplay books on the best-seller list.

Short-run scheduling for a specific display includes preparation me for acquiring or refurbishing fixtures, props, and decor within budgeted llowances. Storage of display props and fixtures is an important part f planning because reuse of existing fixtures releases funds for additional rops needed later. Both monetary and non-monetary costs and benefits f attic and warehouse storage must be evaluated when deciding whether) keep props for reuse.

Installation of displays must make efficient use of personnel and ther resources without inconveniencing customers or making the shopping xperience dangerous. Tools left on the floor of customer routes, and nproperly anchored displays are dangerous.

'isual Merchandising Personnel

. *visual merchandise manager* or *display director* coordinates displays vithin a division or store. The *display manager* title is sometimes given) art professionals whose interests include designing and creating displays or artistic expression. Professional display personnel tend to have art aining, using principles of emphasis, harmony, balance, and rhythm, nd also combining color, lighting, and composition to create an effect. uch staff either work full-time for one large store or part-time for several mall stores. Whereas art professionals create displays, marketing profes-ionals manage visual merchandising to achieve store sales, profits, and ther goals.

Other display professionals are associated with the stores' suppliers. hese might be food wholesalers or manufacturers' agents whose respon-bilities include delivering and shelving merchandise. They and their mployers are concerned with getting the most advantageous space for isplaying their products.

Still other display professionals are logistics consulting firms that elp retailers, manufacturers, brokers, wholesalers, and baking companies lan shelf displays of products in stores. These consultants use micro-omputer programs to evaluate product sales by shelf space location, nd to plot shelf allocations among brands and products to maximize rofitability of the shelf space. A sample allocation for fabric softener in a supermarket is shown in Exhibit 12-9. Because the retailer wants to maximize retail profit while the manufacturers and brokers want to maximize their profits, there may be a need to negotiate these allocations. Negotations would include a discussion of whether the sales results are caused by experience with a product itself, by advertising of retailer or manufacturer, or by the location of the product in the store.[38]

***EXHIBIT 12-9* Shelf-Space Allocation Planned by Computer**

Source: Logistics Data Systems, 11325 Seven Locks Road, Potomac, MD 20854.

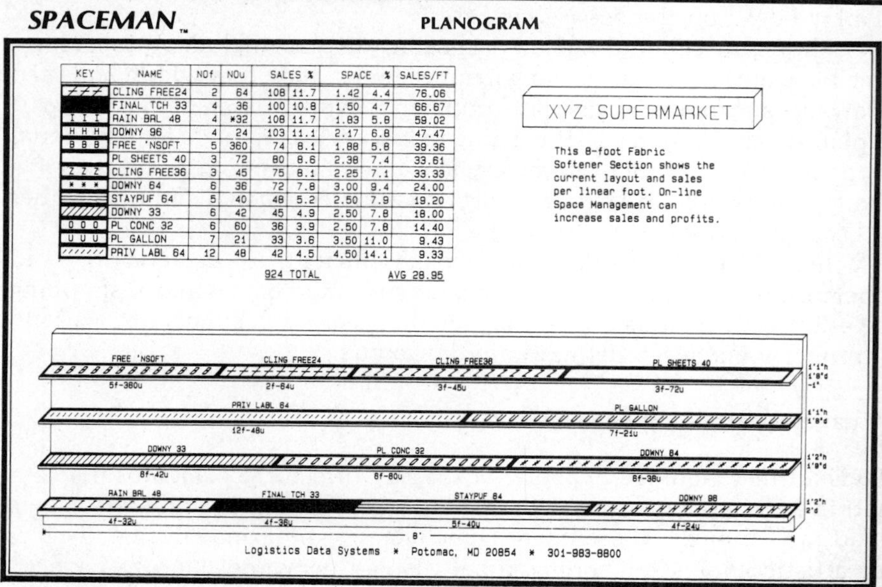

KEY	NAME	NOf	NOu	SALES	%	SPACE	%	SALES/FT
	CLING FREE24	2	64	108	11.7	1.42	4.4	76.06
	FINAL TCH 33	4	36	100	10.8	1.50	4.7	66.67
I I I	RAIN BRL 48	4	*32	108	11.7	1.83	5.8	59.02
H H H	DOWNY 96	4	24	103	11.1	2.17	6.8	47.47
B B B	FREE 'NSOFT	5	360	74	8.1	1.88	5.8	39.36
	PL SHEETS 40	3	72	80	8.6	2.38	7.4	33.61
Z Z Z	CLING FREE36	3	45	75	8.1	2.25	7.1	33.33
* * *	DOWNY 64	6	36	72	7.8	3.00	9.4	24.00
	STAYPUF 64	5	40	48	5.2	2.50	7.9	19.20
	DOWNY 33	6	42	45	4.9	2.50	7.8	18.00
O O O	PL CONC 32	6	60	36	3.9	2.50	7.8	14.40
U U U	PL GALLON	7	21	33	3.6	3.50	11.0	9.43
	PRIV LABL 64	12	48	42	4.5	4.50	14.1	9.33
				924 TOTAL				AVG 28.95

MENU ORIENTATION

I. Products	Defines product color, code, and description for planogram as well as height, width and depth and minimum stocking requirements.
II. Performance	Enters data for sales, profit, market share and movement.
III. Space	Allocates space for each product on the shelves; distributes products based on performance; generates vertical distributions; meets minimum stocking requirements.
IV. Draw	Produces the planogram on the graphics plotter.
V. System	Saves and retrieves planograms on floppy diskettes.
VI. Restart	Clears the screen to start another planogram.
VII. Stop	Ends the ***SPACEMAN*** session.

EXHIBIT 12-10 News of Winning Display

Source: "Sweet Dreams Win Prize for Shoe Bin," *The Amherst News* (December 31, 1981), p. 1.

The Shoe Bin, 187 North Pleasant St., is the winner of the annual Amherst Chamber of Commerce Window Display contest. The theme of the display is a little girl's bedroom, delightfully arranged with handmade bedspread and ruffle, dressing table and stool with padded cusion, and even "Poochy" lying on a rug next to the bed. The little girl is dreaming of beautiful shoes arranged on clouds with little elves precariously hanging on the edges. The Shoe Bin received an engraved plaque to be hung in the store for this year.

Honorable mention went to Town and Country Realtors, 79 South Pleasant St., for their entry.

"The store windows of the Amherst shops were particularly attractive this year and the judges had a difficult decision," said Ann Campney of the Chamber ofCommerce. Judging was based on, originality, creativity, overall design, and appropriateness for the business involved, she explained.

Artistic display professionals are most often found in large cities. tores in shopping centers and small downtowns are not always within 'avelling range of these professionals. Specialty chains either employ isplay professionals to travel from shopping center to center to set up isplays, or to provide detailed instructions to store managers, or both.[39] wners of small downtown stores often take a personal interest in doing isplays, or they teach a salesperson to do them. High school or college :udents who work in the store while studying art or retailing can also o the displays. A news article about a display contest sponsored by the .mherst Chamber of Commerce stated that the winning display was reated by a part-time store employee who was a university student ıajoring in design, as shown in Exhibit 12-10.[40]

Students in marketing courses might work on displays as a class roject. Before accepting student help, managers should spend time acuainting students with store philosophy and image, and should work 'ith them on planning. Unguided students may misunderstand the store nage and create displays that conflict with it.

In earlier years, the display director reported to the promotion director nd received directions from top management second-hand, through the ıterpretation by the promotion director. Recently, some display directors ave become vice presidents of display or visual presentation. As such, ıey are directly responsible to the president or to a senior vice president of marketing.[41] This change enables the visual merchandising manager to be in on the store's marketing plans at an early stage and to have an effect on the decision process. Thus the manager gets an insight into store needs and available resources, as well as longer lead time for planning ahead.

Coordination with the Marketing Mix

The high cost of energy illustrates the need for coordinating visual merchandising with overall store marketing management. A decision to reduce overall lighting in the store so as to reduce energy consumption can involve several store managers. While lighting is important for effective display, relative lighting is more important than absolute lighting level. Sloan's Supermarket, a chain of 43 stores in New York, changed to a different type of light fixture to save energy, but the dim lights reduced sales. Another change produced a negligible dimming of lights, used about 20% less energy than the original lighting, and increased sales. A manufacturer, Pillowtex, replaced overhead lighting with tiny spotlights in a showroom at the Dallas World Trade Center and attributed about one-third of its $3.13 million annual showroom sales to the lighting change.[42] These examples show that it is possible to reduce energy costs and increase sales with a creative combination of general lighting and display lighting.

When general lighting is reduced, the relatively brighter lighting in the display areas attracts more attention. In this reduced lighting, visual merchandising managers might work with store designers to use (1) colored lighting, (2) lighter colors in decor and fixtures, and (3) more mirrors and light-reflecting surfaces to attract attention to displays.[43] However, store management must provide adequate light near mirrors and in fitting rooms where customers try on apparel. Customers who try on store apparel in the store can be considered to be displays. If customers cannot see how they look because of poor lighting, they may shop elsewhere where the lighting is adequate. If they do buy the merchandise, they may return it after finding out what it looks like in adequate lighting at home.

Displays must be backed up by adequate merchandise in stock. Displays must also contain directions for finding the merchandise. Signs in store windows and near the merchandise area are needed for this purpose. Salespeople need to be told where the merchandise is and what has been the message of advertising and other marketing communications.

Customers who want merchandise that they see on display but have trouble finding, tend to generalize from this experience: "The store does not have what it says it has; no one in the store knows where anything is; the store is badly managed." Negative generalizations like these conflict with positive messages being sent by other marketing communications.

A new display that helps customers, retailers, and vendors manage .me is a superclock. This large clock, suspended from the ceiling, takes p the right-hand third of a two by seven-foot aluminum board. The rest f the board is available for brand or store advertising. Advertisers are uaranteed that the board will never be blocked by other signs. Sales of ampbell's Le Menu frozen entrees increased 25% during a 12-week eriod of advertising on a superclock in the Boston area.[44]

isplay Principles and Errors

ood displays sell merchandise, image, and excitement; bad displays nterfere with marketing communication efforts. Visual merchandising nanagers who have more of a marketing background than an art background till need to be able to evaluate whether a display will be effective. The elative proportions of the merchandise, and of the merchandise to the isplay area should be consistent with the key message of the display. 'he focal point of the display can be heightened through color, texture, ontrast, or size. The various parts of the display should harmonize with ne another. Props, fixtures, lighting, signs, and merchandise should be ompatible with each other and with the store image. The display in xhibit 12-11 has one model and several artistic props—a table, a branch rrangement and a scroll—to make a focused arrangement.

Color is important in both inside and outside displays. Color can e used to set a mood or theme. For example, yellow can be used to ommunicate cheerfulness. Color also can be used to help a display stand ut from its background. For example, a red display will stand out from green or neutral background. Artistic arrangement of fruits, vegetables, nd salad bar with attention to color makes produce look better in one tore than the same produce elsewhere that is not well displayed. The rofusion of flowers in a crisp green and yellow color scheme adds to ne attractive appearance of the Bread and Circus natural foods supermarket nside and out. Some of the flowers are for sale.[45]

A good display sells merchandise. The merchandise, a very important art of the display, should look fresh and clean, not soiled, faded, wrinkled r wilted. Small items scattered about with no apparent pattern, props nat are out of proportion, and too much merchandise for the space make isplays look confusing and crowded. Displays in narrow travel routes nterfere with the traffic pattern and tend to invite accidents. Too little nerchandise, and merchandise which is in the wrong proportion for the isplay space, make the display look empty.

Consumers tend to ignore displays that feature merchandise few eople want. Dirty windows, fixtures, or signs; uncollected display tools; nproper props or accessories; and displays that can be seen from several ides but which look good on only one side are details that produce a

EXHIBIT 12-11 Model with Artistic Props in Focused Display

Source: Saks Fifth Ave., New York, NY.

negative effect for store image and sales. Construction mechanics, suc as pins and nails, should be hidden, or they communicate sloppiness These errors diminish the selling power of display.[46]

SUMMARY

Visual merchandising, which includes display, communicates in formation and image. In addition, display shows customers the type o merchandise available and where to find it. Displays sell by suggestio as they show customers how merchandise items can be used, worn, an combined, and how rooms might be furnished. Visual merchandisin helps a store to be a theater, an exciting, entertaining place to shop, place in which to spend recreational time and money. To integrate visua merchandising into the total marketing mix, the manager should interac with top management to coordinate strategy for projecting image and promoting merchandise.

The purpose of windows and other exterior displays is to communicate image and attract target customers. The purpose of interior display, point-of-purchase displays, and packaging is to create a pleasing environment for the target customers, to provide information about merchandise, and to sell merchandise. Visual merchandising and packaging help other marketing communication tools differentiate stores and brands from their competitors and add a psychological value to products.

Logos on store exteriors, packaging, interiors, and such printed materials as signs are part of visual merchandising. Customers carry store logos away from the store on packaging and printed materials. Electronic and non-electronic display aids and fixtures help allocate shelf space, project image, enable customers to find products, and discourage shoplifting.

QUESTIONS

1. How does the role of display differ from the role of advertising in the marketing communications mix?
2. Explain how and why the purpose of exterior display is like and different from the purpose of interior display.
3. Think of a store that you visited recently, and explain how it was like a theater, and how it could have been more like a theater to sell merchandise.
4. Beach's store sells the Prestige brand widget, and so do Beach's three competitors in the same shopping center. Explain how to use display to add a psychological difference to the Prestige brand widget sold in Beach's store.
5. Why is it so important to have the same total image communicated by displays, logo, packaging, and all printed materials associated with a business?
6. How do store windows attract the attention of passers-by? Is it enough to attract attention, or does display have a further task?
7. Displays should encourage customers to want merchandise, but the customers are expected to pay for this merchandise. What can visual merchandising managers do to deter shoplifting?
8. The visual merchandising manager has both long and short-run planning responsibilities, and needs access to top management in order to work effectively. Discuss and explain.
9. A visual merchandising manager with a marketing background evaluates displays from a marketing viewpoint, and considers display principles in evaluating whether a particular display is effective. What principles of display should be used in this evaluation and why? What errors should be watched for?
10. You are assigned to put a point-of-purchase display into a store for your brand-name products. Suggest a product and explain what you will consider and discuss with the retailer concerning where to locate this display.

NOTES

1. K. Mills and J. Paul, *Applied Visual Merchandising* (Englewood Cliffs, NJ: Prentice-Hall, 1982); *Visual Merchandising* (New York: National Retail Merchants Association, 1980); Barbara D'Arcy's definition, in Pat Sloan, "Bloomies Expands Deco Decor," *Advertising Age,* 51 (March 3, 1980), p. 42E.

2. W. Davidson, "To Understand Retailing in the 1980s, Analyze Firms' Response to Trends," *Marketing News,* 8 (March 7, 1980), pp. 1, 12–13; R. Marquardt, "Merchandise Displays are Most Effective When Marketing, Artistic Factors Combine," *Marketing News* (August 19, 1983), p. 3; John A. Murphy, "The Changing Role of Visual Merchandising," *Promotion Exchange* (January, 1980), pp. 7–8. The visual merchandising section was added in 1980 because of the growing importance of visual merchandising. This periodical has since merged into *Ad Pro*.

3. See H. Assael, *Consumer Behavior and Marketing Action* (Boston: Kent, 1984).

4. James M. Reynolds, "The Fourth Media," *Promotion Exchange* (July, 1980), pp. 5–6, 8; "Study Tracks Housewares Buying, Information Sources," *Marketing News* (October 14, 1983), p. 16.

5. "Tips on Effective Use of Store Design," *Stores* (February 1981), p. 37. This summarizes a speech by Joseph Hoppe, Foley's Divisional Manager of Visual Merchandising, at the National Retail Merchants Association (NRMA) Convention in New York, January 1981.

See also "Establishing a Unique Image," *Stores* (February 1981), p. 37. This summarizes a speech by Bernard Newberg, Margo's Executive Vice President, at NRMA.

6. "Building Brand Character," *Stores* (February 1981), p. 36. This summarizes a speech by Shirley Young, Executive Vice President of Grey Advertising, at NRMA.

7. J. Kornbluth, "The Department Store as Theater," *The New York Times Magazine* (April 29, 1979), pp. 30–32, 65–74; and Mark Stevens, *Like No Other Store in the World.*

8. This is the *show biz* mentioned in Chapters 1 and 11.

9. "Bergdorf's, A New Kind of Specialty," *Women's Wear Daily* (January 30, 1984), pp. 6, 7.

10. See "Remodelling Gives New Look to Discounters," *Chain Store Age Executive* (August 1978), 90–92.

11. Suggestions from Ruth Brand and Carolyn Kennedy, Marketing Directors of Holyoke, MA, and Worcester, MA, Center super-regional shopping centers respectively, 1980, 1981.

12. Kenneth Mills and Judith Paul, *Create Effective Displays* (Englewood Cliffs, NJ: Prentice-Hall, 1974).

13. Brand and Kennedy.

14. See Chapter 3.

15. John Duka, "A Charivari in Midtown," *The New York Times* (June 17, 1984), p. 44.

16. J. Greenberg, "Promoting the Executive Work Shirt," *Men's Wear* (September 7, 1979), p. 54.

17. Marjorie Axelrad, "Macy's New York: 'Growing up on 5'." *Men's Wear,* 178 (September 22, 1978), pp. 118–119.

18. "K mart: The No. 2 Retailer Starts to Make an Upscale Move—at Last," *usiness Week* (June 4, 1984), pp. 50–51; J. Snyder, "K mart Moves to Sell 'Store f the '90s' Idea," *Advertising Age,* 55 (March 12, 1984), pp. 52–53.

19. Speech by Joseph Weishar, President of New Vision Studios, New 'ork, at the National Retail Merchants Association meeting, session entitled, Visual Merchandising: Your No. 1 In-Store Marketing Tool" (January 13, 1985).

20. Ibid.

21. "The Chinese Library," *The Lord & Taylor Rose* (November 1977), p. 2; 'People Rooms' Personalize Impersonal Furniture Stores," *Marketing News* ugust 22, 1980), p. 1.

22. See Chapter 3.

23. "The Shopping Bag, Portable Status," *The New York Times* (December , 1978), p. C2.

24. Attributed to the late Dorothy Shaver, former president of Lord & aylor department store in New York City.

25. Computer Helps Shoppers Pick Fashion Accessories," *Marketing News,* 8 (November 9, 1984), p. 40; "High-Tech Mall Directory Debuts," *Marketing Iews,* 18 (November 9, 1984), p. 18; "High-Tech POP Display is Here to Stay: urvey," *Marketing News,* 18 (November 9, 1984), p. 40.

See also Howard P. Abrahams, "Television: A New Merchandising Fron-er," *Promotion Exchange* (January 1980), pp. 5–7; Paul Kamezura, "Retailers sk Audio-Visual To Show Way to Higher Sales," *Advertising Age,* 51 (June 23, 980), p. S20; "POP-AV Displays Boost Retail Sales," *Marketing News,* 15 (November 7, 1981), Section 2, p. 18; "Revlon Develops a Computer Touch," *Advertising ge,* 51 (August 4, 1980), p. 76.

26. "Videotex, Computer Technologies," *Marketing News* (December 9, 983), p. 2.

27. "Yes, You Can Talk to Your Customers," *Marketing Communications* December 1983), p. 64.

28. "Touch-Sensitive Computer Brings Data to Fingertips," *Marketing News,* 3 (November 16, 1979), p. 14; "Two Supermarkets Test New Video Ad System," *larketing News,* 14 (June 30, 1980), p. 1.

29. "A&S's Meyer Proposes Changes," *Stores* (February 1981), p. 33. This ummarizes a speech by Lasker Meyer at NRMA, January 1981.

30. Weishar, NRMA, January 13, 1985.

31. Geoffrey Murray, "High-Tech Bean Stockers Invade Japanese," *The hristian Science Monitor* (April 5, 1984), p. 9.

32. See current articles about retail crime in *Stores, Chain Store Age xecutive,* and related periodicals.

33. The annual meeting of the National Retail Merchants Association in lew York City in January has exhibits of display aids, signs and fixtures.

34. G. Valenti, *Interior Display: A Way to Increase Sales* (Washington, DC: J.S. Government Printing Office, May 1974 reprint), SBA Small Marketers Aids, Jo. 111; and other SBA materials.

See also "Popai Honors Displays," *Advertising Age,* 55 (February 27, 984), p. 56. *Popai* is the Point-of-Purchase Advertising Institute, sponsored by nanufacturers like Schwinn, Kimberly Clark, Max Factor, Rexall, and Procter and Gamble.

35. J. Crabtree, "How I Almost Became a Retail Display Pro," *Menswear,* 77 (March 10, 1978), pp. 130–134; "Taking a Swank Tack to Giftware," *Retail Veek,* (May 1, 1981), pp. 37–39.

36. G. McKinnon, J. Kelley and E. Robinson, "Sales Effects of Point-of-Purchase In-Store Signing," *Journal of Retailing,* 57 (Summer 1981), pp. 49–63; J. Wilkinson, C. Paksoy and J. Mason, "A Demand Analysis of Newspaper Advertising and Changes in Space Allocation," Journal of Retailing, 57 (Summer 1981), pp. 30–48.

37. See "Display Checklist," *Promotion Exchange* (January 1980), p. 8.

See also E. Brill, "Not Just Window-Dressing," Worcester *Magazine* (November 11, 1981), pp. 65, 67; M. Saijbel, "Contemporary Store Windows Use Fewer Props, Garments," *California Apparel News,* 35 (June 22, 1979).

38. Jan S. Aaron, "Microcomputer-prepared Shelf Designs Boost Sales Results, *Banking Industry* (March 1984); "Software Program Aids Whlslr, Retailer in Allocating Space for Maximum Profit," *Supermarket News* (June 25, 1984), p. 35.

See also Laurie Freeman "Battle for Shelf Space," *Advertising Age,* 56 (February 28, 1985), p. 16.

39. See M. Liebeskind, "Merchandise Presentation and Display in the Specialty Store Chain," *Promotion Exchange,* (March 1980), pp. 1–3.

40. *The Amherst News* (December 31, 1981), p. 1.

41. "New Status for Visual Merchandise Executives," *Stores* (June 1979), pp. 38–39.

42. Mark Harris, "Evaluate Lighting Systems as a Marketing Device, not Overhead," *Marketing News,* 18 (October 26, 1984), pp. 1, 10.

43. "Bullock's Interior Design: Lighting a la Chameleon," *Chain Store Age Executive,* 58 (May 1982), pp. 68–70; D. Crabtree, "Energy and Display," *Stores,* (June 1979), pp. 36, 39; "Revamping the Lamping," *Shopping Center World,* 10 (November 1981), p. 28.

44. "Shoppers Find Time for Superclock," *Marketing News,* 18 (November 9, 1984), p. 43.

45. J. O'Connell, "Big Natural Foods Supermarket Grew from Owner's Beliefs and Experiences," *The Morning Union* (Springfield, MA, May 23, 1984), p. 25.

46. See Mills and Paul, *Applied Visual Merchandising* and *Create Effective Displays.*

APPENDIX 12

SIGNS AND PRINT TYPES FOR SIGNS

With the improvement in computer graphics technology, it is possible to reduce printing costs and increase the quality of signs, and also to increase uniformity of signs among stores. No longer is it necessary to wait for an artist to design the signs, or for a print shop to print them. Computers can produce a large quantity of signs quickly, printing them with a dot-matrix printer, on thick paper with colored stripes or in one color only. The ability to produce signs quickly has allowed Milgrams, a food store chain in Kansas City, MO, to pass on vendor discounts to consumers as soon as these temporary price reductions become available.

Computer hardware and software for producing signs is available from a variety of vendors, many of whom take booths at trade shows. Some computers will print bar codes, labels, and business signs as well as in-store signs. Signs and other information can be stored on computer disks for recall at a future date.[1]

Various non-computer signmaking machines are also available to print signs automatically or manually from a variety of types, once the type is set into the machine. Standard typefaces, display faces, and exclusive script faces are available in different sizes. Samples of type are shown in the following examples:

TYPE FACES FOR SIGNS

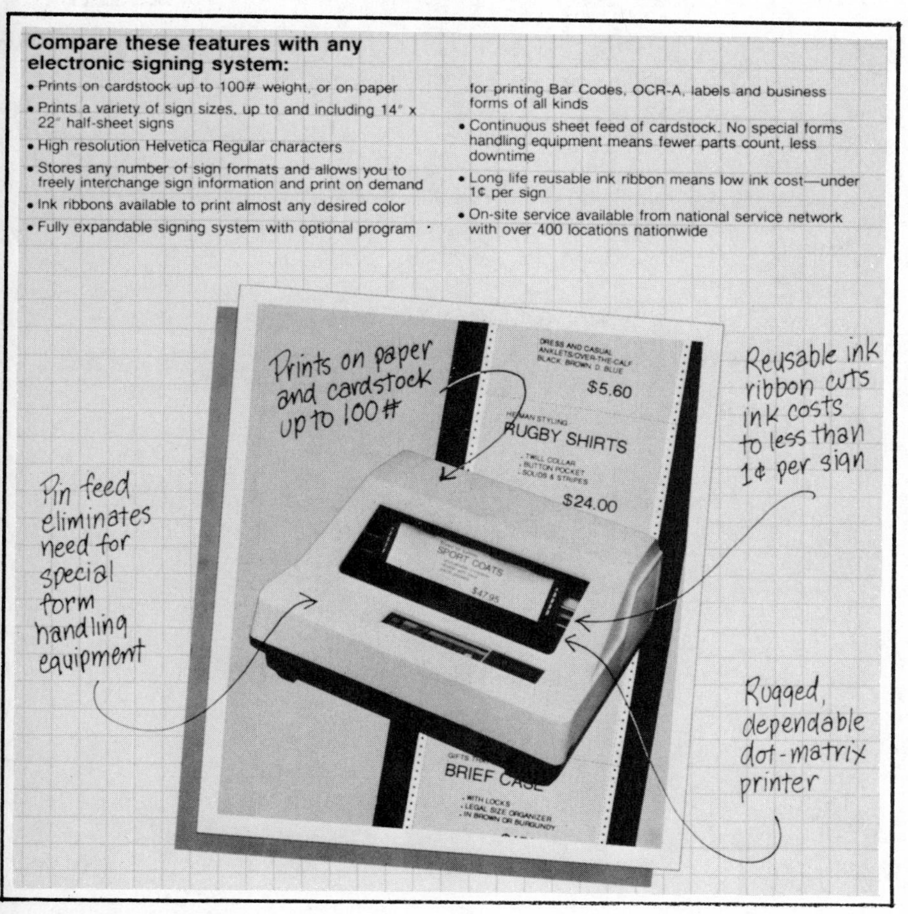

[1] "Perk up Promotions with Computer-Printed Signage," *Marketing News*, 18 (November 9, 1984), p. 46; and *Sign Up with the Showcard Machine*, Showcard, 1985, IL.

Futura LIGHT
Futura MEDIUM
Futura MEDIUM CONDENSED
Futura SEMI-BOLD
Futura BOLD
Futura BOLD CONDENSED
Radiant BOLD
Cooper BLACK
Century NOVA

SALE sale 1234
FT sem 72
AB ab 12
AB ab 1

Brush
Coronet Bold
DOM CASUAL
Lydian BOLD
Showscript
BALLOON
CLARELAN
PUEBLO BOLD
HELVETICA MEDIU

Source: Showcard Machine Company, 320 West Ohio Street, Chicago, IL 60610.

13
PERSONAL SELLING

INTRODUCTION

A firm's personality in a sense is created by its communications and its employees. The firm reflects the creativity, conscientiousness, and loyalty of all employees from top management to the service workers who clean the premises. Personnel, and particularly the selling force, constitute a major factor in the success of every business operation, especially when personal selling makes up a large part of the marketing communications mix.

A salesperson has an advantage over impersonal communicators because the salesperson receives customer feedback at the point of sale. Learning the customer's wants, needs, and reactions to products, salespeople can answer questions, overcome objections, perhaps even close a sale while inspiring the customer to buy more, then and in the future.[1] Positive interactions between salespersons and customers are crucial; salespeople often "are the firm" as far as customers are concerned. This chapter discusses selection, training, motivating, and scheduling of sales personnel to work towards increasing sales, developing the firm's image, and other goals.

While inadequately trained salespeople who ignore or antagonize customers harm sales and image, customers' experiences with *any* employee influence their attitudes toward a firm. Encounters with managers, telephone operators, cashiers, and stockpersons can negate or reinforce the total impression that customers should receive from marketing communications. At a time when customers can buy the same brand-name merchandise in several stores, maintaining effective sales force quality is one of the biggest problems in retailing.[2] Exhibit 13-1 shows excerpts from a newspaper article about the positive effect of supermarket checkout cashiers on customer attitudes.

EXHIBIT 13-1 **The Positive Effect of Checkout Cashiers on Customer Attitudes**
Source: "Supermarket Cashiers," *Daily Hampshire Gazette* (May 22, 1984), p. 25.

SUPERMARKET CASHIERS

Biggest Responsibility

"Being a cashier is the biggest responsibility in the whole store because we are the last person the customer sees before walking out the door. We have to make sure the customer leaves here happy," explains Harriet Golash, a cashier at Bread and Circus supermarket in Hadley. Meeting and interacting with people is precisely why the Northampton resident finds her job "a lot of fun." Having worked as a cashier for other supermarkets and as a bartender for eight years before starting at Bread and Circus six months ago, Mrs. Golash enjoys working with people, especially the "sober public."

Similarly, Theresa "Tess" Kinlock, a cashier at Big Y Supermarket in Northampton, "loves every minute" of her job, especially the people. "It's always such a pleasure to see them and to follow up on each other's interests," says Mrs. Kinlock.

Friendly Greetings

As she walks down the aisle on her break, she greets an elderly woman clad in grey. "Hi! How are you doing?" inquires Mrs. Kinlock, gently touching the woman's arm.

"People come here, sometimes just to talk, and they know someone will listen to them, even for just a moment."

Mrs. Kinlock, a grandmother from Easthampton, has been working part-time for Big Y for four years and knows many of the regulars. "They come in every day, oh maybe to pick up bread and milk, but mostly to talk and joke," she says. One regular, "an elderly, but very spry lady," invited some of the cashiers for brunch. For the most part, however, Mrs. Kinlock, like many cashiers, limits her socializing with customers to the check-out line.

"We know more about some people than their friends know about them," says Shirley Lauder, cashier for Louis' Foods in Am-

***EXHIBIT 13-1* (continued)**

herst. Mrs. Lauder, of Amherst, also has a circle of "friends" she sees only at the cash register. Many elderly residents from the neighboring apartments shop at Louis' daily for provisions.

Awkward Moments

Whether it's an awkward moment in the check-out line or simply a bad mood brought into the store, the cashiers must face up to the inevitable not-so-friendly customer. Mrs. Lauder says she tries to ignore them because "you never say the right thing, and I certainly won't argue with them." Of grumbly customers, Mrs. Kinlock raises her eyebrows with a smile and says, "I say 'hi' or 'good morning' and then I shut up."

Fan Clubs

Each cashier has her own fan club, those who will stand only in her line no matter how long. "I always try to help out the older people, pregnant women, or people having a bad day," says Mrs. Kinlock. She often encourages them to sit down on a nearby bench while she rings up the order. Similarly, Mrs. Lauder helps the older women get money, especially coins, out of their wallets. And Mrs. Golash, known by her co-workers as "Mama Harriet," particularly enjoys seeing the new mothers with their babies and "watching them grow week to week."

THE IMPORTANCE OF PERSONNEL

Personnel and Image

Marketers spend large amounts of money building and communicating an image.[3] The marketing communications budget usually does not include salaries of retail salespeople and other employees, who are generally under the category *operations*. Integrating retail employees into the marketing communications mix requires top management commitment and coordination because marketing managers and operations managers tend to have different priorities. For example, marketing likes to maximize sales whereas operations likes to minimize costs. Top management needs to restructure the incentive system for marketing and operations managers to encourage retail personnel to communicate image effectively.

Several recent studies suggest that selling assistance is one of the most important components of a service store's image, and that rapport between salespeople and customers has a profound effect on sales and the role of personal service differs in various cultures, e.g., United States versus Japan.[4] Exhibit 13-2 has two illustrations of store service. In the first, a small appliance store uses personal service to differentiate itself

***EXHIBIT 13-2* Two Illustrations of Store Service**

Source: a: *Christian Science Monitor* (February 13, 1984), p. B7. Reprinted by permission from the *Christian Science Monitor,* © 1984 by The Christian Science Publishing Society. All rights reserved. b: Appeared in *The New York Times* (March 18, 1984), p. 9.

a.

Owners says service is key to store's success

Seattle

Sure, Bill and Bob Almvig can't really say their business is famous. After all, they aren't "jeweler to royalty" or "furrier to the stars."

But, says Bill Almvig, their appliance store has sold washing machines, televisions, and freezers to people like Seattle Mayor Charles Royer and Washington Gov. John Spellman. And to a lot of other customers who return again and again to Almvig's in the university area of Seattle.

The family-owned business is over 50 years old and has been in its present location for more than a quarter century. The key to this longevity has always been service, says Bill Almvig.

Advertiser **profile**

"We get terrific referral business because we can offer a little more personal service than the discount stores," he says. "A woman with a broken washing machine can't wait for days while a discount outlet or a big department store gets around to delivering a machine — if it will deliver at all. If she comes in here, we'll come out and install her new machine the next day.

"It's true we can't always compete on price. But we feel there'll always be room for businesses that can offer personal service. That's how we stay alive."

As new products are introduced, says Bob, they search for a selection of quality brands — foreign and American — to offer their customers. Among brand names they carry are Sony, Amana, GE, and Maytag.

One of the hot items today is video cassette recorders. "Young families are buying the video camera with the recorder," says Bill Almvig. "On a $15 tape, they can record six hours of their family's history — in full color and sound."

b.

"It's wonderful! My own Personal Fashion Advisor at Lord & Taylor"

She's Gail Kittenplan —and she'll help you with every important fashion decision from giving your wardrobe a fresh spring outlook to selecting gifts and solving other shopping dilemmas. For an appointment call (212) 391-3519 Third Floor, Lord & Taylor, Fifth Avenue at 39th Street

from discount stores that also sell appliances. Personal service and knowledge of customers can make small stores competitive with the larger stores that sell similar merchandise. In the second illustration, a large department store offers the personal service of a fashion advisor who helps select wardrobe and gifts, and solves shopping dilemmas. Exhibit 13-3 describes the personal service of a specialty store. This store encourages one-to-one salesperson-customer continuing relationships in which the salesperson keeps a purchase history of customers, so as to offer informed advice concerning personal purchases and gift selection. Personal service saves time for customers, many of whom are willing to pay for this service.

Sales personnel communicate store image through their appearance, body language, and verbal exchanges with customers. For example, a

EXHIBIT 13-3 The Personal Service of a Specialty Store

Source: M. Turner, "Miss Jackson's: Building on Tradition," *Women's Wear Daily* (June 7, 1984), vol. 149 p. 19.

TULSA, Okla.—Big city retailers, such as Sakowitz from Houston, and Sanger-Harris from Dallas, are bulldozing their way into Tulsa, but Miss Jackson's—indisputably this oil city's preeminent high fashion specialty store—isn't going to topple off its time-honored pedestal without a fight.

Instead, it's accepting the challenge, and responding by enlarging its 24,000-square-foot store another 12,000 square feet. Additionally, it is expanding its higher-price designer and weekend wear categories, concentrating on upper price points in both dresses and sportswear, and focusing its efforts on the fitting rooms, where William F. Fisher, Jr., chairman and chief executive officer, believes about 70 percent of the store's $11 million volume is generated.

The key to selling in any fine specialty store is personalized service. Fisher and his 40 sales associates know Miss Jackson's 77-year history was built on it, and, now, its survival depends on it. . . .

The younger Fisher, a native Tulsan, had 10 years of Sears, Roebuck & Co. training under his belt, and had been general manager of Miss Jackson's before his family took it over. His greatest challenge, he says, was overcoming a mass merchandising mentality. "We can't be all things to all people," he says.

Instead, he has built on Miss Jackson's tradition of being all things to a select group of patrons—about 2,000 in number—who have developed working and personal relationships with specific sales associates. These individuals are Fisher's bread and butter, and he recites a characterization so poetic one might think he's used it a few times before.

"They are rich people," he begins. "They can shop anywhere in the world. They don't need anything. They live a very fast-paced life. They're here today and gone tomorrow. They leave on a moment's notice. They deplore polyester. They are the wives of, or the entrepreneurs themselves. We have very few publicly held corporation executives or their wives.". . .

His sales associates keep personal histories of each patron, an invaluable tool that puts Miss Jackson's a step ahead of any competitor. "That's the difference between clerking and serving. Clerks are baggers and sackers," Fisher, 44, philosophizes. "Servers keep black books that have the name, address, daughter's name, son's name, husband's name, husband's secretary's name, husband's private telephone line. You build a history. The shrewder the sales associate, the better history you build, succinctly, quietly, secretly. The better history you build, the better business you build."

store selling expensive merchandise is expected to have well-dressed personnel who move gracefully and speak confidently, using correct grammar. The helpfulness and courtesy of personnel also affect store image. Customer judgments of the helpfulness or attentiveness of store personnel influence purchase behavior. In a recent study, 55% of 2600 women in a national sample said that they buy less apparel in a store when store personnel are not helpful.[5]

Selling as Communication

Selling is making it easy for the customer to buy. Effective selling is a "direct face-to-face, seller-to-buyer relationship which can communicate the facts necessary for making a buying decision; or it can utilize the psychology of persuasion to encourage the formation of a buying decision."[6] The function of a salesperson is to match merchandise and services with customer needs. This match can create sales, customer satisfaction, and store loyalty. For example, if the customer wants to be warm and look attractive while walking to work, the salesperson might suggest a stylish wool coat. On the other hand, if the customer wants to be inconspicuous and avoid pickpockets while riding to work on overheated public transportation, the salesperson might suggest a lightweight, plain, washable coat.

The communication between salesperson and customer follows the general communications model.[7] First, the salesperson learns the customer's wants, needs, attitudes, values, and buying motives. Different people make buying decisions in various ways and for different reasons. Self-esteem and self-fulfillment are some reasons for making purchases; an interest in economy or saving time are others. From training and experience, salespeople can learn to recognize and communicate merchandise information to these different types, either in person or by telephone.

Feedback from the customer helps the salesperson modify the communication to suit the customer's present state of mind. Interference with communications can obscure or alter both message and feedback.[8] This noise is especially confusing when the customer and salesperson associate different meanings with the same words. For example, *warm* to the salesperson may mean a heavy coat, while *warm* to the customer may mean a light coat which, when worn with a jacket, provides protection from wind and rain.

Importance and Availability of Training

Sales training can be viewed as an agent of change that helps people sell better than they have done before. This training can be done by owners, managers, and experienced salespeople in small firms, by the personnel department in larger firms, or by outside firms who specialize in sales training. In a good training program, trainers observe what trainees are doing right and build on that by helping them do the right thing more often. Discussions with trainees are an important part of training sessions. Feedback tells trainees how they are progressing.[9]

Sales training firms often use behavior modelling. Some training sessions last two or three days. Trainees generally watch selling demonstrations on videotapes or film, and discuss these examples. Trainees themselves are videotaped working in sales situations. There are training programs both for supervisors and salespeople. The purpose of the Mandev training program is to move some salespeople from the middle-sales-producers into the high-sales-producers category.[10] The chart in Exhibit 13-4 shows the productivity shift that Mandev associates with training.

Mohr offers a training program in one-hour modules for different merchandise categories. Grid offers three-day seminars that separate customers and salespersons into five distinct types and explains how to match them. Xerox has a two-and-one-half day program that uses one-hour laser videodiscs. The instructor can vary the order of discs or skip some and repeat others. Some stores also have training programs. J.C. Penney has several interactive management and retail training programs offered through public seminars or in-house seminars with videotape support. These programs cover time management, performance appraisal, conducting meetings, conducting group training, limited-service and full-service sales, and small store management. Literature from the Small

EXHIBIT 13-4 **Distribution of High, Medium, and Low Producers in a Typical Sales Force, and the Shift Achieved by Effective Training**

Source: Ten Sure-Fire Ways to Increase Retail Profits (North Miami Beach: Mandev, 1980), p. 4.

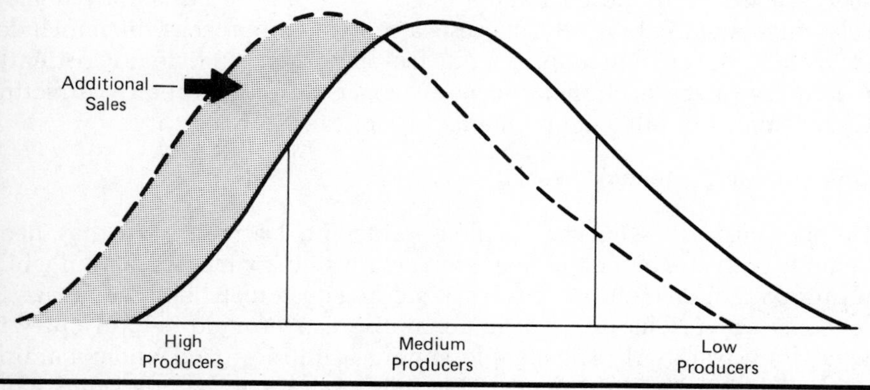

Business Administration and the National Retail Merchants Association is also available to teach salespeople how to sell.[11]

Is sales training really as effective as training firms suggest? One sales-training firm did an experiment to find out. The goal was a sales increase of 15% above trend in test stores in a six-month period. Eight test stores and eight control stores were matched on sales volume, staff, location type, store hours, advertising, promotions, and merchandise. Sales in the test stores rose when sales effort was reinforced, and dropped otherwise; the sales increases paid for the training program in less than five weeks.[12] However, prospective customers for sales training programs should realize that training-firm performance reports, like media performance reports, are marketing communications that, understandably, present their services in the best possible light.

THE ART AND SCIENCE OF PERSONAL SELLING

The selling encounter includes several stages which are similar to the steps in advertising. The *approach* is the salesperson's method of attracting the customer's attention. Determining customer wants and demonstrating merchandise are methods of *arousing interest* and *creating desire*. The closing is designed to *stimulate* the purchase action. The *follow-up* serves as a reminder to come again for more purchases.

Approach

The *approach* lets customers know that the salesperson is aware of their presence and also notifies prospective shoplifters that they have been noticed. A smiling salesperson should greet customers with a statement that cannot be answered in the negative. "This comes in white, yellow and green." "These are on sale this week." "This just arrived today." The greeting, "May I help you?" and others like it that can be answered in the negative invite customers to say "no" and terminate a potential sales encounter. Exhibit 13-5 suggests a courteous approach which includes (1) making the customer and friends feel important, (2) listening patiently regardless of the customer's haste or anger, and (3) explicitly directing the customer to other departments or facilities, if necessary.

Determining Customers' Wants

Helping customers determine their wants and learning what they need benefits both customer and marketer, creating customer satisfaction while minimizing merchandise returns. Watching customers' body language in response to various items of merchandise can provide helpful clues to what they want. All salespeople should acquire a good understanding of the firm's target customers. This helps salespeople understand what

EXHIBIT 13-5 **Suggestions for Courteous Treatment of Customers**

Source: Checklist on Customer Service—The Salesperson As A Key To The Store's Success (New York: National Retail Merchant's Association, 1977), p. 2.

Treatment Of Customers—Do You:

— Have an overall concept that customers are very important—that their actions will make or break the store?
— Avoid assuming preconceived ideas on who will buy and who won't buy? (Stories are told of the barefoot oil heiress who was turned away from one store and spent thousands in the store of a competitor.)
— Have patience with an irate customer? Do you react quickly in anger or do you respond quietly and calmly until the problem is settled?
— Avoid talking to your friends while the customer waits impatiently?
— Extend other courtesies such as explicit directions as to how to reach other departments or facilities?
— Avoid being impatient on returns? Direct the person to where you know he/she will really be helped?
— Avoid acting hurriedly and impolitely when closing time is near and perhaps lose the last big sale of the day?
— Listen carefully to what the customer really wants?

the customers may want even when the customers themselves are not sure.

Different categories of customers have different types of needs. For example, an *arguer* disbelieves claims in ads and on tags, and needs to have the saleperson show product knowledge. An *impulsive* customer lacks patience and wants a quick summary of key points with no oversell, while a *look-around* wants to take in information but needs to have the salesperson respond to buying signals.[13]

Merchandise Demonstration

Salespeople need to know how to demonstrate merchandise and to point out advantages, characteristics, and directions for cleaning and using, if these are not obvious. In this time of presold brands and self-service, many customers already have this information for familiar merchandise. A growing service in some stores is to help customers fit new merchandise into their existing stock of belongings. Therefore, customers are encouraged to bring in their own belongings, color samples, or swatches, and then buy additional items that they need. This trend of adding to an existng stock instead of replacing everything is a byproduct of inflationary times when customers need to economize on some items in order to afford others. However, when customers are not familiar with new merchandise, salespeople can be informative sources. Exhibit 13-6 shows helpful information about the care and cleaning of sweaters, provided by the Wool Bureau to help salespeople. In this era of synthetics, wool is not necessarily a familiar item to all customers.

EXHIBIT 13-6 Excerpts from Wool Bureau's Information for Salespeople about Merchandise Content and Care

Source: "How to Care for Wool Sweaters," New York: The Wool Bureau, pp. 1–2.

The Sweater

Guidelines for Care, Handling and Storage

Fine wool knitwear asks very little in terms of care and maintenance. By following a few simple procedures, your wool sweaters will be around for you to enjoy for many years. Remember, with wool you're investing in the best…doesn't it make sense to protect your investment properly.

STORAGE: Knits should be folded flat—not put on hangers—in order to guard against shape distortion. Wool takes to folding easily, and because of its remarkable resilience will bounce right into shape when you're ready to wear it again.

WASHING WOOL: Through the wonders of modern technology, some wools are now being treated to make them *machine washable* and *machine dryable*. This is accomplished with a remarkable process called SUPERWASH. . It actually eliminates wool's natural tendency to shrink or felt. So you get a garment that's virtually care free!

But most important, is the fact that none of wool's wonderful qualities are sacrificed after the SUPERWASH. process. Its remarkable hand, resilience and outstanding performance remain constant. Even after repeated washing and drying the natural beauty of the garment shines through.

Before washing any wool garment it is best to read the care instructions…following labels is the key to protecting the beauty of your fine wool sweaters.

For the washing process itself, a gentle cycle and warm water is generally recommended. Because wool cleans so easily, it is not necessary to subject the garment to the pounding caused by heavy agitation. In most cases, it is the intense agitation that contributes to shortening the life and overall look of the garment.

HAND WASHING: Use a mild detergent in lukewarm water, soaking the garment for several minutes. Swish gently and rinse clean. Be sure to eliminate all suds. Do not wring or twist. Instead, we suggest using the towel method to eliminate excess water. After rinsing, simply place garment in an absorbent towel and roll up. Gently wring the towel. Finally, remove the garment and lay flat to dry. Using these simple steps your sweater will look fresh and clean.

DRY CLEANING: Because wool cleans so easily, it does not require dry cleaning as often as other fabrics. In most cases, the dirt can be brushed off or spot cleaned with a little cool water. When dry cleaning is necessary, it's best to use the services of a reputable cleaner rather than the coin operated method.

STAIN REMOVAL: Taking quick action will often remove a stain before it has time to set. With any type of stain it's best not to let the garment go unattended for a long period of time. Rinse the stain immediately in *cold water*. Avoid hot water as it may set the stain.

For additional information on removing stubborn stains, refer to the enclosed Fact Chart.

Salespeople also perform a diplomatic function when customers shop accompanied by friends with diverse opinions. Feedback from friends indicates what merchandise to suggest initially, what additional merchandise to show, and how to answer objections. Training in anticipating and answering objections enables a salesperson to point out special merchandise qualities and to discuss price and other terms without being defensive.[14]

Customers buy benefits and satisfaction when they buy merchandise. The same merchandise may satisfy different needs for different consumers. The well-instructed salesperson should be able to sort out different customers' needs. The *need-driven* customer wants durability; the *belonger* wants the merchandise to look right; the *achiever* wants to buy the best; and the *inner-directed* customer wants to look good without effort in order to devote time to worthwhile causes.[15] Informed salespeople can use this information to decide which merchandise to suggest and what to do to make sales that satisfy customers.

Helping Customers Make Decisions

The salesperson needs to observe carefully to assist customers in their decision-making and to know when customers are ready to decide. The following example shows the influence of a salesperson during the decision-making phase. A customer who intended to buy both a wool coat and a car with her savings entered the fur department with her husband, and tried on some fur coats. The couple liked one coat, but the wife suggested that they look at wool coats. The salesperson mentioned that the fur coat they liked was the last one in the wife's size. The husband responded with the headline he remembered from a Blackglama advertisement: "What becomes a legend most?" The alert and responsive salesperson nodded her approval of this statement. The couple bought the fur coat.[16]

Selling by suggestion is effective in the decision-making stage. By this time in the sales transaction, the salesperson has enough feedback to know what related merchandise the customer might want, and can suggest it. For example, one salesperson wrote up a tie sale, then suggested and sold shirts to go with the tie, a robe, and pajamas and slippers to go with the robe. When his supervisor asked why he had not suggested socks, the salesperson phoned the customer, suggested socks, sold them, and received enthusiastic thanks for being so helpful. In another example, salespeople in the Home Depot store help the do-it-yourselfers, and suggest complementary merchandise. If the customer buys a door, they suggest locks, hinges, and a sill.[17]

Closing a Sale

After making the *purchase decision,* a customer may need help in recognizing that fact and in implementing the decision. At that point, the salesperson should not confuse the customer by introducing still other merchandise or talking about unrelated subjects. The salesperson can help by removing unwanted merchandise, and by changing the buy–no buy decision into a choice between limited alternatives. By asking which remaining merchandise is preferred, and whether the purchase will be a charge or cash transaction, taken or sent, the salesperson asks questions which cannot be answered with a "yes" or "no." However, no customer should be persuaded to buy unsuitable merchandise. This may result in a merchandise return and a lost customer. Effective selling at the closing can increase the proportion of shoppers who make purchases, increase the transaction size through selling by suggestion, and develop the customers' loyalty to the firm.[18]

Follow-Up

If the customer does not buy at this point, the decision is not necessarily a no-buy decision. Lack of funds, a desire to defer satisfaction, or the need to think about the decision may cause the customer to leave without purchasing. Some customers return later to close the sale. Therefore, salespeople should thank customers for coming and invite them to return. In addition, salespeople should offer to inform the customers about the arrival of new merchandise.

OTHER TRAINING

The training described in Appendix 13-A teaches new employees about a business and its customers, and how employees fit into the internal environment. The training described in this section informs employees about changes in policies, layout, advertising, special promotions, and selling techniques. This training should occur frequently. Studies have found that a large percentage of new training skills can be lost without reinforcement on the job. Sometimes, overloading trainees in the classroom can be less effective than reducing the amount of classroom information and developing some selling skills on the job. Ongoing training can reinforce selling skills, improve productivity, reduce employee turnover, and prevent sales losses which result from lack of employee information. If employees are not sure they have enough information, they should make no promises without checking with their managers. Customers interpret employees' promises as the firm's promises.[19]

Special situations encountered by salespeople include handling more than one customer at a time, handling problem returns or exchanges, satisfying a customer when the demand for advertised merchandise exceeds the supply, especially on the first day of a sale, and satisfying angry or impatient customers. Also, salespeople need to know how to work with personal shoppers who do the shopping for busy customers.[20]

Special attention should be given to such situations during training. If salespeople are not to be responsible for handling any of these situations, they should be told who will handle them. Also, trainers should make very clear the store's policy concerning certain ethically troublesome situations, so that the salesperson does not have the responsibility for making ethical judgments for the firm.[21]

In one study, department and specialty chain store salespeople were asked about 31 potentially troublesome situations. Salespersons suggested that the most important situations to be addressed by policy were as follows: pressuring customers into making purchases, giving markdowns for merchandise damaged by customers in the store, giving incorrect change on purpose, charging full price for a sales item without the customer's knowledge, charging the markdown price for full-price merchandise, and taking returns that should not be accepted.[22]

Some customers who use brand names to communicate desired quality do not necessarily prefer that brand. Offering a substitute for the brand should be done only after the salesperson shows the merchandise requested by the customer, or if the requested merchandise is not in stock. By highlighting first the points of similarity between the preferred brand and the substitute, and then the points of each product's superiority, the salesperson can help customers buy the desired benefit.

EMPLOYEE INFORMATION SYSTEMS

To reduce time and expense of ongoing training, management needs to develop simple information systems that employees can use to get current information about store policies and merchandise. Sales employees need to know how to use, stock, and care for merchandise they sell, and where other categories of merchandise are located in the store. This is especially true if substitutes and complements are carried in different parts of the store, requiring customers to travel to many locations to assemble an outfit, a room, or food for a recipe. User-friendly computer terminals and even bulletin boards posted currently can be used to pass on this information to employees.

If used properly, an information system can substitute for some of the training sessions that otherwise would be needed to communicate this information. Supervisors should encourage employees to ask questions and use the information system instead of making up erroneous information that deceives customers. Such deceptive sales communication is similar to deceptive advertising, a detriment to good company image.

An information system should include facts about current advertising, special events, and new selling techniques. When a potential customer makes a special trip to a store for a special event, employees must be able to direct the customer to the event. It detracts from the firm's image and wastes company time when employees try to get this information from other employees who do not know either. This, in turn, wastes customer time and increases the probability of losing not only that customer but also several others to whom the inconvenienced customer complains.[23]

SALES-FORCE MANAGEMENT

Sales-force management includes supervisory training, motivation and compensation for goal-attainment, productivity, and performance evaluation. Determining sales-force size, allocation, and scheduling are also involved. An important consideration in scheduling is managing part-time workers. Management goals for salespeople include coming to wor when scheduled, arriving on time, taking only the permitted break interacting with customers instead of socializing with other employee and meeting sales quotas.

Effective motivation exists (1) in the day-to-day example of supervisor and coworkers who are proud of the job they do, (2) in praise for a jo well done,[24] and (3) in adequate monetary rewards and incentives. Eval uation provides feedback to employees which explains compensatior promotion, termination, and transfers. Proper scheduling ensures tha employees are not underworked (too many employees for too few cus tomers) or overworked (not enough employees to handle the customers and that sales-per-employee goals are attainable.

Supervisory Training Recruiting and training effective supervisor are essential for having a productive sales force. Supervisors can b trained by the firm, or experienced supervisors can be hired from othe firms. Recently, a retailer took a full-page ad in the first section of th Sunday *New York Times* to recruit executives. Specialized agencies recrui and train sales managers.[25] Training includes learning how to listen maintain employee self-esteem, set goals, offer reinforcement, and coac sales performances.

Motivation and Compensation for Reaching Sales Goals

Through reading, listening, and observation, supervisors can discove what motivates salespeople to sell more merchandise. They can use thi information to plan incentives to increase productivity without increasin the number of salespeople. Management needs to convince salespeopl that achieving company goals brings them benefits in the form of money praise, or promotion.

According to organizational behavior theory, achievement is accom plished by the product of ability and effort. Both ability and effort ar necessary for success.[26] Thus employees with ability to succeed must b recruited, trained to get the knowledge to succeed, and motivated t succeed. Successful salespersons are people who have internal needs t persuade, and/or to earn recognition, commissions, advancement. Thes internal needs motivate employees to increase sales for their own self satisfaction. Individual motives of competence (a drive to master th environment for its own sake), achievement, status, and belonging als affect employee performance. The store can train its own managers t motivate salespersons, or hire training firms.[27]

Contests with recognition and prizes as rewards can motivate thos who want to achieve and gain status. However, Vroom's expectanc theory[28] implies that the motivating power of a reward is affected by th probability that the employee assigns to receiving a reward. This probabilit affects the expected value of the reward. For example, if winning a sale ontest has a prize of $10 and a probability of .1, the expected value is 1 × $10 or $1. Similarly, the expected value of getting a $100 commission vith a .03 probability is $3, and the expected value of getting a $5 ommission with .8 probability is $4. With this reward scheme, working or sales with the $5 commission has the highest expected value, and vinning the contest has the lowest expected monetary reward. Restructuring he reward system can change the expected values and can be used to hange employee motivation and priorities. Psychological rewards for vinning the contest, like a plaque or an article in the firm's newsletter, an be added to or substituted for monetary rewards.

A recent study showed that employee participation in decision-naking, provision of performance feedback, and job enrichment may be ositively related to retail salespersons' beliefs that performance will be ewarded. Employees who thought they had control of life's events were nore likely to connect rewards with performance.[29] The reward structure hould take into account such factors as selling, stock work, returns, and ther non-sales activities such as helping to create loyal customers. Em-loyees should perceive the reward system—regular pay, bonuses, pro-notion, praise—as fair.

Payment plans range from commission only to salary only. Com-nission is most effective when it is possible to tell who is responsible or a sale. A disadvantage of commission is that sometimes salespeople ght over customers, or hard-sell merchandise that the customer does ot want in order to complete a sale. This inconveniences the customer, ncreases the amount of returned merchandise, and harms the firm's nage. Taking turns, which is known as the *up system*, solves the problem f who gets the next customer. If this does not please customers who ave favorite salespersons, the system can be waived temporarily.[30]

alesperson Productivity and Company Goals

nproving productivity is especially important when costs of energy, upplies, and personnel are increasing rapidly. Productivity was originally efined by the federal government as output per manhour, and more ecently as output per person-hour. *Retail productivity* is often measured n dollar sales per square foot. Properly selected, trained, and motivated ales personnel can increase productivity and work toward profit goals y helping each customer buy more merchandise, by selling to more ustomers, and by making the purchasing experience so rewarding that ustomers will return in the future and urge others to come also. Increases n salesperson productivity help to offset the high per-customer cost of ersonal selling compared with nonpersonal selling alternatives of ad-ertising, sales promotions, and visual merchandising.[31]

Proper management of the selling function requires measuring and educing the cost of lost sales. A rough estimate of lost sales can be made by dividing the number of customers who make purchases by the numbe contacted. Information on which salespersons lose sales can be obtainec from the following exercise. Compute the average sales per salespersor by dividing *daily sales volume* by the *number of sales* made by eac salesperson. Use these average sales figures to separate salespeople intc high, medium, and low producers.

Exhibit 13-4 showed the distribution of high, medium, and lov producers in a typical sales force and the shift in this distribution achievec by effective training. Alternate these three groups for several weeks or typical business days, eliminating Saturdays and any special sales days For example, only high producers work on one Tuesday; only mediun producers work on another day comparable to Tuesday, and so on. Ther compare average sales per salesperson and annual gross margin of th high, medium, and low groups to see how much you gain from usin the high producers, and lose from using the low producers, comparec with the middle group. Consulting firms are available to help manager learn appropriate skills for hiring, training, and motivating high producers In evaluating this information for a large firm that has both *big-ticke* departments or merchandise areas, and *small-ticket* areas, allowance must be made for comparing these different types.

Performance Evaluation

Regular personnel evaluations, which influence salesperson productivity have both subjective and objective data. *Subjective data* include neatnes in appearance and behavior, fit with the firm's image, ability to follov directions, initiative, responsibility, courtesy, cooperation, and a positiv attitude toward customers, coworkers, and supervisors. *Objective datc* include attendance, punctuality, net sales (gross sales minus returns) sales per employee, and number of transactions.

A one-page evaluation form should include (1) a scale for subjective ratings: outstanding, above average, average, below average. It should also include (2) a place to indicate strengths, weaknesses, promotability and comments and (3) *spaces for the rater and employee to sign*. Managers and employees compare present with past ratings. Setting goals to achieve in the next rating period should be part of the evaluation process. A sample evaluation form is shown in Exhibit 13-7.

Information about performance evaluation should include causes for discharge: refusal to serve a customer, stealing, insubordination, and failure to notify the department about inability to report for work.

Sales Force Size and Scheduling

Computer-Aided Schedules Computer-processed information from point of sale (POS) registers can help retail managers plan effective employee coverage and scheduling in various areas of the store.[32] Exhibit 13-8

XHIBIT 13-7 **Content of a Performance Rating Form for Sales Personnel**
ource: Bloomingdale's, New York, NY.

Ratings of the employee's actual performance:

1. Knowledge of Merchandise
2. Knowledge of Systems
3. Customer Service
4. Ability to Work Well With Others
5. Ability to Accept Criticism
6. Initiative
7. Interest
8. Appearance and Behavior
9. Character
10. Attendance (Check Late & Absence Report)
11. Punctuality—Latenesses; punctual in maintaining lunch and relief schedules.
12. Productivity—based on actual sales production records. (Check commission Report).

'he form also includes spaces for indicating the following: strengths, veaknesses, general comments, summary rating, statement of promotability, oworker's comments, and interviewer's comments. A four-point scale excellent, above standard, meets standard, and below standard) is used or items 1–12 and the summary rating.

hows the output of a computer scheduling program. Line A is the customer ount, every half-hour, on four of the weekdays. Line B shows that the vailable salespeople were usually too few or too many to handle customers. Line C is the new scheduling for salespeople which provides more salespeople at times when there are more customers. This schedule will be mproved as some salespeople leave and others are hired to achieve the lesired schedule, line D. Using a base of full-time employees and adding part-time employees during peak customer activity, the salesperson chedule can be adjusted for peaks and slumps in customer counts. Another way to approach these peaks and slumps is to use marketing ommunications tools to get more customers into the store during normally low periods, like Tuesdays and early mornings.

Changes in the lifestyles of customers have changed store hours nd days, and tend to change employee schedules. Computers can be used to plan a variety of scheduling alternatives. For example, flex-time ccommodates employee preferences for evening or weekend work. By dvertising flexible schedules, a firm might attract more suitable applicants.

Part-Time Employees Retail work is perceived as a low-paying job done at inconvenient hours including holidays, evenings, and weekends. An important personnel factor for the rest of this century is conducting

EXHIBIT 13-8 **Example of Sales-Force Management before and after Scheduling**
Source: L. Spalding, "Better Service," *Stores,* 66 (January 1984), p. 74. Reprinted from *Stores,* copyright National Merchants Association.

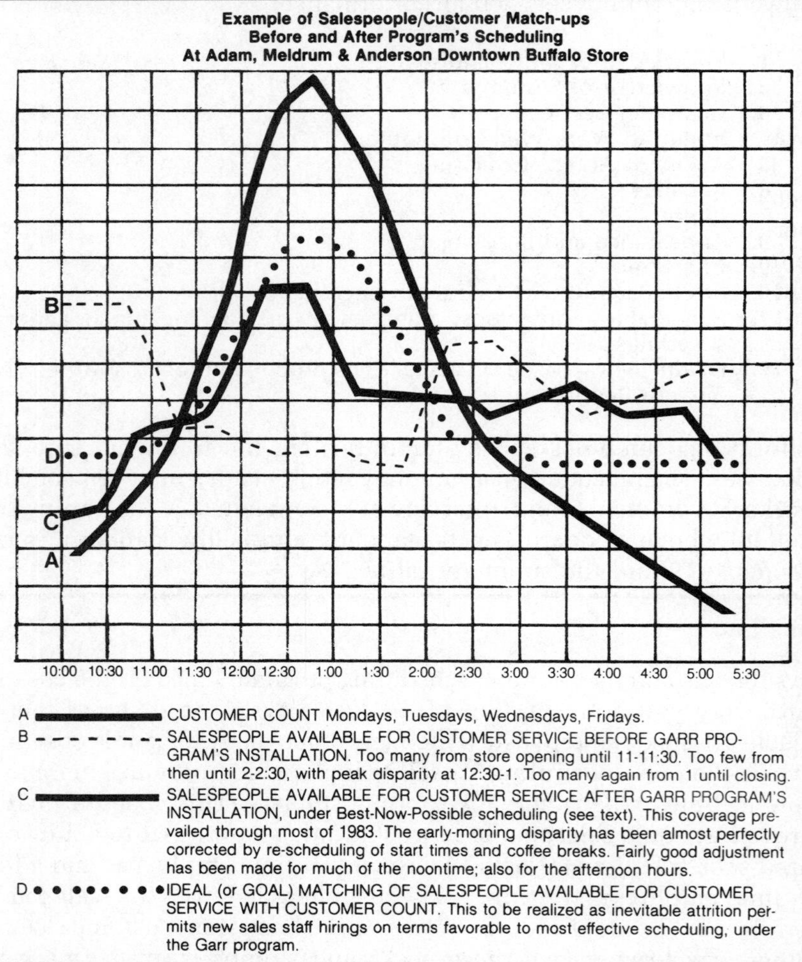

retail work with a growing ratio of part-timers to full-timers. In 1960 80% to 90% of retail salespeople worked full-time. In 1980, only about 40% to 50% were full-time employees.[33]

Potential part-time workers are people who need additional income and who are available for periods other than from nine in the morning to five in the evening. College students, mothers who wish to be home when the children get home from school, high school students who can work late afternoons, evenings and weekends, people who need time to paint or write, or people who need a second job may find that part-time work at "inconvenient hours" fits into their schedules.

Exhibit 13-8 shows that the number of salespeople needed varies from hour to hour. More are needed between noon and two o'clock than earlier or later. Part-time salespeople can be hired to augment the regular staff during busy periods. This accomplishes a marketing communications objective of having enough salespeople so that customers will not have to wait during busy times.

Research about part-time workers shows that they had a positive effect on productivity in Dutch clothing stores and French self-service supermarkets. Female part-time workers, during their first four months of employment for large Australian retailers, showed little difference in commitment to the organization compared with full timers, were happier about pay, and less happy about job security. The expectation that part-timers know about products, procedures, customers, and order history, even when frequently transferred from department to department, was considered unrealistic by the researchers in the last study. This situation might be alleviated by restricting the number of departments in which part-timers are placed.[34] More research is needed about the effect of part-timers on productivity.

From a marketing communications points of view, the advantage of part-timers is that they facilitate communications with customers by making it easier to schedule more salespeople at times when there are more customers. Whether or not these employees facilitate communications by creating good will and continuing sales depends on the selection process, described in Appendix 13-B; on their initial training, described in Appendix 13-A; and on the continuous motivation, reinforcement, and effective scheduling described earlier in this chapter.

Manufacturers' Salespeople Almost everything said about retail salespeople applies to salespeople who work for manufacturers. However, instead of selling directly to the consumer, they sell to other firms. All the reasons that would interest a consumer in a product also interest the firms' buyers', because consumer motivation is what sells the merchandise. Also, the manufacturers' salesperson must help retailers become informed about the merchandise so that information can be passed on to the consumer.

The manufacturers' salesperson must be aware of competition in the same sense that a retail salesperson is aware of both competitive products and other retailers. The one major difference between the retail salesperson and the manufacturers' representative is that the latter has only the clients' brands to sell and must stress those brands and their advantages. The retail salesperson often has several manufacturers' competing brands that can be offered to the consumer.

Usually both manufacturers' and retailers' salespeople are supported by advertising and promotion. These marketing communications tools are both consumer-oriented. The manufacturer should tell the retailer how the consumer is being presold and the retailer should tell the manufacturer how the product will be promoted by the store's personnel.

SUMMARY

Because satisfied, motivated personnel are a powerful and effective public relations tool, every effort must be made towards keeping personnel happy and competent. It has been said that a firm is just a building and the products are inanimate objects, but "the personnel are the firm." Customers interpret employees' actions as the firm's actions. By selecting employees who clearly communicate an appropriate image, and by training and motivating salespeople to sell effectively, firms can keep customers coming back and the merchandise going out.

Regardless of company size, salespeople need to learn about target customers, physical layout, merchandise, and competitors as well as company policies and sales transactions. They need guidance in how to approach customers, determine their needs, show appropriate merchandise, assist in a decision to buy, and encourage customers to return. Employee information systems can be used to inform salespeople about current advertising, merchandise location and features, and selling strategies that encourage more customers to buy more. Point-of-sale computer terminals can be programmed to inform employees about current merchandise and policies.

Motivation, compensation, on-the-job reinforcement, evaluation, and proper scheduling inspire and enable employees to continue to play an important part in the marketing mix. Productivity can be increased through (1) motivation with monetary and psychological rewards, (2) evaluation processes accompanied by promotions and terminations, and (3) effective scheduling of both full-time and part-time employees.

QUESTIONS

1. Explain the marketing communications problem created by a poorly trained salesperson.
2. Describe how the selling encounter follows the general communications model.
3. Specify a merchandise item such as a bed, shoes, or a stereo, and explain how personal selling is similar to and different from (a) advertising, and (b) display. Also, explain how advertising, display, and selling can work together to sell this merchandise.
4. Explain what types of merchandise benefit more from personal selling and what types tend not to need it.

5. Describe the stages in the selling encounter for (a) a car and (b) an expensive suit, and explain what part each stage plays in influencing the sale. Explain similarities and differences in the two situations.
6. Describe a previous shopping trip in which you interacted with a salesperson. Evaluate to what extent what the salesperson's words and actions influenced your buying or not buying the merchandise. If you were the salesperson's manager, what suggestions would you make to improve the salesperson's effectiveness?
7. Choose a merchandise category, like carpeting or cameras, and compare salary with commission methods of motivating salespersons to reach sales goals. Explain how non-monetary motivation can be used to help reach goals.
8. What criteria would you use to evaluate salespersons and why? What information input would you use and why? If you have been a salesperson and have been evaluated, how was your evaluation like or unlike your criteria?
9. Explain how you would use current computer technology to facilitate (1) scheduling of salespeople in (a) active sportswear, and (b) toys; and (c) keeping salespeople informed about new store merchandise and policies.

NOTES

1. R. Stanley, *Promotion,* 2nd ed. (Englewood Cliffs, NJ: Prentice-Hall, 82), p. 263. Because many excellent texts specialize in sales force management r manufacturers, this chapter looks at the retail aspect, and the manufacturer-tailer interface. However, most of the information in this chapter is of general terest for sales force management.

2. I. Barmash, "Selling, Retailing's Lost Art," *The New York Times* (March , 1983), p. D1.

3. Store image is covered more thoroughly in other chapters.

4. L. Blum, "Customer Response to Sales Personnel," *Personnel News d Views* (Spring-Summer, 1980), pp. 28–35; J. Burnett, R. Amanson, and S. unt, "Feminism: Implications for Department Store Strategy and Salesclerk ehavior," *Journal of Retailing,* 57 (Winter 1981), pp. 71–85; L. Rosenberg and Matsuoka, "Personal Service in Retailing: A Comparison of the United States d Japan," paper, University of Massachusetts, Amherst, 1985.

5. *Women's Wear Daily* (December 6, 1979), p. 17, Table 1.

6. T. Stroh, *Techniques of Practical Selling* (Homewood, IL: Irwin, 1966), 7.

7. See Chapters 1 and 3. The communications model is in Exhibit 1-8.

8. See J. Engle, M. Warshaw, and T. Kinnear, *Promotional Strategy* Homewood, IL: Irwin, 1979), p. 472; J. Evans and B. Berman, *Marketing* (New ork: Macmillan, 1982), p. 417; and M. Mandell and L. Rosenberg, *Marketing* nglewood Cliffs, NJ: Prentice-Hall, 1981), p. 496.

9. M. Elliott, "Sales Training: Hidden Persuader," *Advertising Age,* 51 uly 14, 1980), p. 56.

10. The Mandev, North Miami Beach, FL, training program has been used y Montgomery Ward, J.C. Penney, Macy's New York, Pizitz and The Parisian Birmingham, AL, Nordstrom in Seattle, WA and other stores. See also Exhibit 3-4.

11. "A new Realistic Approach to Training Sales Personnel," *Retail Week* (September 1, 1981), pp. 15–21; "Control Pace of Sales Class with Laser Videodiscs," *Marketing News,* 17 (November 25, 1983), p. 22; *J.C. Penney Programs for Management Excellence,* J.C. Penney, 1301 Avenue of the Americas, NY 10019, 1985. Clients include Ethan Allen Inc., and State Farm Insurance.

See also L. Moseson, *Unique and Successful Selling Techniques* (New York: National Retail Merchants Association, 1983); "Rebirth of a Salesman: Willy Loman Goes Electronic," *Business Week* (February 27, 1984), pp. 103–104; "Retailers Discover an Old Tool: Sales Training," *Business Week* (December 22, 1980), pp. 51–52; B. Rosenbloom, *Improving Personal Selling,* SMA No. 159, (Washington DC: Small Business Administration, 1976); *Sales Grid Seminars* (Austin, TX: Scientific Methods, Inc.).

Another training program is *The Retail Selling Skills Series: A System Overview,* Mediatec, 1150 Foothill Boulevard, La Canada, CA 91011. Clients include Burdines, Miami, FL; Dayton's, Minneapolis MN; I. Magnin, San Francisco, CA; Thom McAn, Worcester, MA; The Fair, Beaumont, TX.

The Mohr program has been used by Wanamaker in Philadelphia and G. Fox in Hartford, CT. Finally, see "The Science of Selling," *The Royal Bank Letter* (November-December, 1983), p. 1.

12. M. Lercel, "Canadian Clothing Chain Tests ABC of Selling Under Stringent Controls," *Mandev Reports,* (North Miami Beach: Mandev, 1982). FPR 01/2.

13. National Advertising Bureau.

14. See *Retail Selling Skills Series,* Mediatec.

15. "SRI International Recognizes MANDEV," *Mandev Training News* (January-February, 1979), p. 3.

16. M. Weisman, "What Do You Say When a Man Offers You a Fur Coat?" *Vogue,* 168 (December, 1978), p. 312.

17. S. Marcus, *Quest for the Best* (New York: Viking, 1979); "Retailing 1984 Awards," *Sales and Marketing Management,* 132 (January 16, 1984), pp. 23-24.

18. See: *Closing a Sale (Sales and Marketing Management* Special Report, 1977), pp. 29–31; K. Mills and J. Paul, *Successful Retail Sales* (Englewood Cliffs, NJ: Prentice-Hall, 1979); H. Mosley, "At Patricia's the Customer is Always Right," *Women's Wear Daily,* 139 (April 15, 1979), p. 42; B. Rosenbloom, *Retail Marketing* (New York: Random House, 1981), p. 308–311.

19. N. Rackham, "The Coaching Controversy," *Mandev Reports,* MR02/2, reprinted from the *Training and Development Journal* (November 1979).

20. "A Bullish Campaign for Understated Elegance," *Retail Week,* (July 1, 1981), pp. 36–37; "At His Service: How Bloomies Caters to Male Customers," *Stores* 61 (November, 1979), p. 43; R. DiGennaro, "Pressed into Personal Service," *New York Times Magazine* (November 28, 1982), p. 28; F. Russell, F. Beach and R. Buskirk, *Selling,* 11th ed. (New York: McGraw-Hill, 1982); "Shopping Services for Working Women," *Stores,* 61 (November 1979), p. 44; *RSS Retail Selling System* (Stamford, CT: MOHR, 1983).

21. M. Levy and A. Dubinsky, "Identifying and Addressing Retail Salespeople's Ethical Problems: A Method and Application," *Journal of Retailing,* 59 (Spring, 1983), pp. 47–66.

22. Ibid.

23. There is more about information systems in Chapter 4.

24. L. Chick, "Employee Productivity—Key to Profits," *Retail Operations 'ews Bulletin,* 8 (June 1980), pp. 3–8.

25. Lord & Taylor ad in *The New York Times,* (January 13, 1985), p. 7.
See also Kenzer Corp., Executive Recruitment, 777 Third Ave., NY)017; Mandev, Retail Management Skills, 17971 Biscayne Blvd., North Miami each, FL 33160; MOHR, Management of Human Resources, 30 Oak St., Stamford, T 06905.

26. T. Mitchell, *People in Organizations* (New York: McGraw-Hill, 1978).

27. *Retail Supervisory Training* (Stamford, Ct: MOHR, 1983).

28. T. Mitchell, *People in Organizations.*

29. R. Teas, "Performance-Reward Instrumentalities and the Motivation f Retail Salespeople," *Journal of Retailing,* 58 (Fall 1982), pp. 4–26.

30. "With Commission Programs, Selling is its Own Reward," *Chain Store ge Executive,* 60 (March 1984), pp. 29–30.

31. D. Friedland, *Ten Sure-Fire Ways to Increase Retail Profits,* (North iami Beach, FL: MANDEV, 1980); S. Gellerman, "Who's Against Productivity," *rsonnel News and Views* (Spring-Summer, 1980), pp. 16–27; "Lord & Taylor nters Equal Pay Consent Agreements," *Employee Relations Bulletin* (February 80), pp. 1–2; "Retail Clerks' Union: High Hopes," *Retail Week* (July 15, 1979), ɔ. 50–55.

32. See S. Sarle, "Effective Staff Planning," *Retail Control,* 48 (October 79), pp. 58–63.

33. L. Rubin, research for "World of Fashion" lecture to Advertising Club, Y, April 1983.

34. Leonie Still, "Part-Time Versus Full-Time Salespeople: Individual Atibutes, Organizational Commitment, and Work Attitudes," *Journal of Retailing,* (Summer 1983), pp. 55–79; Roy Thurik and Nico van der Wijst, "Part-Time bor in Retailing," *Journal of Retailing,* 60 (Fall, 1984), pp. 62–80.

APPENDIX 13-A

NON-SALES TRAINING

ontent

mployees need to learn about the firm's history, environment, position, rget customers, image, merchandise, layout, and all features that make e employer unique. Large suburban families may be the major target one firm, while urban singles aged 18–45 are the target of another; nployees need to know this type of information. Awareness of their rm's position, target, and image will help salespeople understand the ress code and behavior expected of them. Salespeople who do not know hat is expected tend to be unhappy and unproductive.[1]

Employees also need to know where they fit into the organization, id who are their supervisors and subordinates. They need to know the

[1] A. Dubinsky and B. Mattson, "Consequences of Role Conflict and Ambiguity Exerienced by Retail Salespeople," *Journal of Retailing,* 55 (Winter 1979), pp. 70–86.

role of the personnel department and union, if any. A simple organization chart can be used to communicate this information.

An important part of initial retail training is a tour of selling and non-selling areas. This tour enables employees to help customers locate merchandise and find exits, escalators, and elevators. Observation of receiving and marking, shipping, credit, data processing, merchandise location, customer service areas, and employee areas gives employees a general idea of how the firm operates. Customer service areas might include credit, repairs, alterations, returns, gift wrapping, delivery, restaurants and restrooms.

Information received on the tour, as well as updates, should be available in printed form at employees' work stations. If the store has a computer information system available to employees, this information can be in the information system. Employees who cannot guide customers to merchandise and service areas communicate that the business is not well managed. Customers who come into a store with store ads and cannot find the advertised merchandise, tend to buy the advertised merchandise from competitors instead.

Policies concerning absence, tardiness, and discipline for infractions of rules should be made clear to employees. The policy concerning absence and tardiness is especially important for employees whom customers encounter at the store. At all times, enough salespeople and supporting services must be available to transact sales and discourage theft of merchandise.

Training Process

Film strips, television cassettes, lectures, group discussions, role playing, and employee manuals facilitate training. A manual should summarize information communicated in training so as to serve as a reference at employees' work stations. At stores with computerized terminals, printed manuals can be replaced by continuously updated computer manuals. When computer terminals are available to display store policies, both salesperson and customers can read the current policy from the display screen. Role-playing helps trainees learn from their mistakes and the mistakes of others without losing sales and harming the firm's image.

Much of the training time for retail salespeople has been used to explain how to fill out forms for various transactions. However, transactions occur after merchandise is sold. It is important to include pre-sale training as well.

When computerized registers are used, salespeople need not hand-tally sales at the end of each day, or use sales tickets in unit control. Computer monitors (screens) can also guide salespeople in making transactions by displaying such cues as "Will you want anything else?" "Thank you and come again." When computers are used, salespeople need to earn what to do when the electric power is off or the computer breaks own. This includes dealing with irate customers who may have to wait much longer than usual to complete a purchase transaction.

Effective training teaches new employees to be good ambassadors nd communicate a positive image while increasing sales. While this raining entails a cost, it is less expensive than bad word-of-mouth customer-o-customer communication and extensive employee turnover. By their ppearance and actions, employees help sell or discredit a business and ts merchandise.

APPENDIX 13-B

SELECTING PERSONNEL

ecruiting

clear description of duties and hours, a clear specification of the type f person needed, and a consistent image of the firm as a good place to vork, facilitates attracting, hiring, and keeping potentially effective per-onnel. Analysing the selling job and breaking it down into duties and ctivities yield a job description. This specifies which qualifications the pplicant should have in order to do the job successfully.[1]

The following questions help define the job: Is this position a step owards higher management, or a dead-end job? Is stock work expected? s telephone work included? Are salespeople expected to do clerical vork, work with inventory, carry heavy loads, stand all day? Will they se electronic point-of-sale registers, or do many calculations by hand? Are night and weekend work optional or mandatory?

Because people tend to be uncomfortable when reality is inconsistent vith expectations,[2] new employees who find that reality does not fit xpectations tend to leave. This necessitates more recruiting and training xpense. A match between reality and expectations reduces turnover, esulting in a more experienced work force and potentially higher roductivity.

Sources of applicants include those who respond to signs, brochures, nd classified newspaper advertisements. Other sources are customers, riends and acquaintances of present employees, and college students vho are considering a marketing career. Employment agencies can be sed when these sources do not generate enough qualified applicants. A consistent, positive image projected by advertising, display, and personal elling tends to attract applicants who fit this image.

[1] R. Stanley, *Promotion*, 2nd ed. (Englewood Cliffs, NJ: Prentice-Hall, 1982), p. 273.

[2] A. Dubinsky and B. Mattson, "Consequences of Role Conflict and Ambiguity Ex-erienced by Retail Salespeople," *Journal of Retailing*, 55 (Winter 1979), pp. 70–86.

Just as the job-seeker has the right to know what to expect of the position, so does the employer have the right to know what to expect of an employee. If the appearance of the employee will communicate store image, as in a selling position, employees who look and act in a way that fits the firm's image are preferable, Equal Economic Opportunity Commission (EEOC) guidelines permitting and other things being equal.[3] However, employers should keep in mind that EEOC guidelines do make it illegal to discriminate on the basis of race, sex, or age.

Selection Criteria

Prospective employees should look neat and clean at an employment interview. If the customary appearance of the firm's salespeople is conservative, then the prospective employee should know enough about the firm to dress conservatively. Applicants in flamboyant dress or tattered jeans make it clear that they are not interested in complying with the firm's appearance guidelines.

Personal history data offered by applicants can be compared with data for the firm's successful and unsuccessful salespeople.[4] Experience with or interest in working with people is useful for personnel who spend much of their time working with customers. Camp counselling, waiter/waitress work, parenting, and volunteer work in the applicant's personal history provide experience in working with people. Books and other instructional aids are available for training interviewers to select appropriate candidates and to screen out those who might steal.[5]

A phone call to personal references and former employers, a credit check, and a physical examination serve to verify and augment the information on the application. Applicants should be ranked in order of desirability, and given a time limit to accept. If those with the highest ranks do not accept employment, the next-ranked acceptable applicants can be offered the position.

Desirable personality characteristics for employees who work with customers are sincerity, enthusiasm, friendliness, cooperativeness, and reliability. An effective salesperson should perceive accurately the customers' feelings, and use this information to sell the merchandise. Motivation to persuade can come from an internal need to persuade or from

[3] See Chapter 3.

[4] L. Blum, "Customer Response to Sales Personnel," *Personnel News and Views* (Spring-Summer, 1980), pp. 28–35. J. Burnett, R. Amanson, and S. Hunt, "Feminism Implications for Department Store Strategy and Salesclerk Behavior," *Journal of Retail Selling*, 57 (Winter 1981), pp. 71–85, Stanley, *Promotion*, p. 275.

[5] Blum, "Customer Response," pp. 28–35; Burnett, Amanson, and Hunt, "Feminism Implications," pp. 71–85; "Are You Hiring the Problem Employee?" Reid Psychological Systems, 233 North Michigan Avenue, Chicago, IL 60601.

the external motivations of recognition, commissions, or advancement. An effective salesperson needs to be able to take rejection from those customers who do not make a purchase.[6] Salespersons who like people, wish to persuade, and can tolerate rejection tend to stay at their jobs, helping the firm to achieve its goals of reduced turnover and lower hiring and training expense. Finding applicants with these characteristics is more of a challenge when applicants are scarce than when jobs are scarce.

[6] R. Buskirk, *Retail Selling* (San Francisco: Canfield, 1975); H. Greenberg and J. Greenberg, "The Dynamics of a Successful Salesperson," *Personnel News and Views* (Winter, 1978-1979), pp. 4-10; E. Randall, E. Cooke and R. Jefferies, "Can Assessment Centers be Used to Improve the Salesperson Selection Process?" *The Journal of Personal Selling and Sales Management*, 2 (Fall-Winter, 1981-82), p. 54.

14
PUBLIC RELATIONS AND PUBLICITY

INTRODUCTION

Corporations are impersonal organizations; public relations must constantly humanize them and make them friends of the public. *Public relations* is the organized effort to deal with various publics including the press. It has been said that the press has the power to make or break an individual or firm. Publicity, good and bad, affects a firm's public image, and calls attention to its social and economic responsibility. In the past, publicity and public relations (PR) have been managed separately from other marketing communications efforts. Recently, most organizations have realized that publicity about a firm's activities influences public opinion and the firm's image, so PR has been integrated with marketing communications. Although many examples in this chapter refer to large firms, publicity and PR functions are similar for smaller firms.

A simple publicity release concerning the appointment of an executive might read in part, "Leslie Smith, President of Smith's, announced the appointment of Jan Smart as Vice President and Treasurer, effective March 1." Exhibit 14-1 has two published notices of this type. These reflect the changes that occur in retailing as managers move from job to job, and as parent firms acquire businesses.

EXHIBIT 14-1 Publicity in Newspapers Announcing Retail Management Appointments

Source: *Women's Wear Daily* (February 2, 1984), p. 2.

Seeherman appointed ceo, Clarke chairman of Venture

NEW YORK — Julian M. Seeherman, president of the St. Louis-based Venture Stores division of May Department Stores, Inc., has been named to the additional post of chief executive officer, effective Feb. 15.

Meanwhile, Don R. Clarke has been promoted from vice chairman to chairman of Venture, reporting to Seeherman.

Thomas A. Mays, who had been chairman and ceo, will continue as vice chairman of the parent firm, a post he has occupied since 1980.

Seeherman has been with Venture since 1978, when he was named vice chairman of merchandising and sales promotion. He moved up to president in 1982. Clarke joined the Famous Barr Co. division in 1977 and rose to vice president of administration in 1979. In 1982, he was named senior vice president and chief financial officer and in 1983, became executive vice president. Last October, he moved to Venture as vice chairman.

Passow named president of Stix, succeeding Ray

NEW YORK — Harry W. Passow has been named president of Stix, Baer & Fuller in St. Louis, which was acquired Monday by Dillard Department Stores, Inc., from Associated Dry Goods Corp.

He succeeds Donald E. Ray, who as reported has been appointed president and chief executive officer of ADG's Sibley, Lindsay & Curr division in Rochester, N.Y.

Passow was general merchandise manager of ready-to-wear in Dillard's Fort Worth-based central division, reporting to Jim W. Sherburne, divisional chairman. Passow now reports to William Dillard 2nd, chief operating officer of Dillard's.

Passow came into the company in 1974, when Dillard's bought the Leonard Co. of Fort Worth, where he was divisional merchandise manager of ready-to-wear. He moved up to general merchandise manager in 1981.

PUBLIC RELATIONS AND THE PUBLIC RELATIONS DEPARTMENT

Definitions of Public Relations and Publicity

Public relations is a distinct management function which helps establish and maintain mutual lines of communication, understanding, acceptance and cooperation between an organization and its publics; involves the management of problems or issues; helps management to keep informed on and responsive to public opinion; defines and emphasizes the responsibility of management to serve the public interest; helps management to keep abreast of and effectively utilize changes serving as an early warning system to help anticipate trends; and uses research and sound and ethical communication techniques as its principal tools.[1]

Public Relations is the deliberate overall effort to create and maintain a firm's good image in the eyes of the various publics with whom it deals. *Publicity* is what appears in print or broadcast media as the result of this effort.[2] Publicity also can occur without any effort on the part of the marketer. For example, if a firm has a fire or an accident occurs on its premises, the press may cover these events. Fire and accident news are potential *unfavorable publicity*. Two unfavorable news stories, one reporting a Macy's fire and the other objecting to a gentlemen's night at a lingerie store, are shown in Exhibit 14-2.

When publicity is unfavorable, public relations personnel should contact the media and try to put the best possible face on the unfavorable events, although no amount of good public relations will cover up poor management or lack of quality and service. This is usually done by reaching the reporter who covered the story as soon as possible and explaining. For example, "The fire did little damage, no one was hurt, and we are open for business as usual. The merchandise in the area where the fire occurred has been moved to an adjacent department." In the case of an accident, the response might be, "The people involved in the accident were only slightly injured and will be discharged from the hospital shortly." In the same issue of a newspaper, page 1 had publicity about an employee strike and page 8 had news photos of pickets and the empty store. In the last photo was a large sign telling customers that the store was open. Ads on pages 5 and 6 announced that the store was open and hiring.[3]

Publicity differs from *advertising; it is not free advertising*. Advertising is controlled by the advertiser who works with media advertising departments and pays for space or broadcast time in which the ad is placed. Publicity is controlled by the media vehicles which do not charge marketers for publicity space or time, but which do decide whether or not to print or broadcast press releases or run news stories about fires or accidents. News editors also decide how to edit releases for print or broadcast. Publicity gets into media vehicles only when it is *newsworthy* such as when Bloomingdale's sold bags of ice chips from a Greenland glacier, the "oldest and purest ice on earth."[4] Another newsworthy event was the Lord & Taylor preview party for its New Orleans promotion, reported in Exhibit 14-3. Auto makers' new models are newsworthy as are leading fashion designers' new collections, new grocery products and product reformulations like the new Coca Cola formula.

Media will not print or broadcast press releases from advertisers if they contain no news or are merely self-serving. The statement of principles of the American Society of Newspaper Editors states that every effort should be made to make news content accurate, free of bias, and in context. If content is controversial, all sides should be presented fairly. When significant errors of fact and omission occur, they should be corrected

EXHIBIT 14-2 Excerpts from Unsolicited Newspaper Publicity about Fire and Protest

Source: Macy's: *The Morning Union*, Springfield, MA (January 30, 1984), p. 2; Lingerie Protest: *The Morning Union*, Springfield, MA (February 10, 1984), p. 15.

The nation

Hundreds flee Macy's fire

NEW YORK (AP) — Heavy smoke from a roof fire spread down an elevator shaft and through part of Macy's department store in downtown Manhattan Sunday, forcing hundreds of customers and employees to flee, officials said. Deputy Commissioner James Harding said the fire was reported at about 12:51 p.m. The store reopened about 3 p.m.

Lingerie triggers protest

By SARAH VAN ARSDALE
Union correspondent

NORTHAMPTON — About 15 demonstrators gathered outside a lingerie shop on Center Street here Thursday night to protest what they called the "objectification of women."

The protest, organized by two groups, was called in response to a "gentlemen's night" which had been advertised by Judith Fine, owner of the Gazebo.

The special night had been planned to help men "who otherwise would be intimidated to come in here," select lingerie gifts for St. Valentine's Day, Ms. Fine said.

One group of protestors called themselves "Revolutionary Women for Self-Defense," and handed out literature saying the store "decorates women for men's use and promotes male violence against women on gentlemen's night.' "

"I thought it was totally objectifying to have a night when men can think of what they want to use to decorate their women," one protestor, who asked not to be named, said.

□ □ □

The demonstrators said that while lingerie is seen as harmless by most people, it actually reinforces attitudes which lead to the objectification and therefore the abuse of women.

"Once women are seen as playthings to be decorated, men think its OK to beat them, rape them, and sexually abuse them," a demonstrator said.

Members of the other group, which included men, said their part of the demonstration was organized by an ad-hoc group.

"We felt that having a men's night is inviting men to take their fantasies and project them on the women they know, and that is objectifying women. It is important that men protest so that other men will see that a higher consciousness about sexual oppression is something both men and women have to work on," protestor Richard Ware said.

□ □ □

Ms. Fine said that she designs and sells the clothing so the women can treat themselves to something soft and feminine to wear under their work-clothes.

"It glorifies a woman, it doesn't objectify her. My philosophy is that I am a working woman and when I go out into the cold hard world I deserve to wear a silk camisole under my career clothes," she said.

The men attending the "gentlemen's night" were buying the lingerie "because they love their women, not because they hate them," she said.

Ms. Fine said she makes the lingerie so women can "be beautiful for themselves," and the only "racy" item she sells is most often bought by women for their women friends for birthdays she said.

EXHIBIT 14-3 A Newsworthy Event
Source: Excerpts from report by Mary Merris, "EYE Taylor-Made New Orleans," *Women's Wear Daily* (April 6, 1984), p. 6.

NEW YORK—From the jazz to the jambalaya, Lord & Taylor's preview party Wednesday for its Focus America: New Orleans promotion brought a touch of Dixieland to the rain-drenched city.

L&T provided plenty of ambience with banjos, giant framed photos of old New Orleans homes and a talkative contingent from that city. **Muriel Francis** reminisced about Tennessee Williams who, she said, modeled the home in "Suddenly Last Summer" after her family residence, while **Larry Hill,** a doctor who also owns the New Orleans restaurant, Sbisa, said, "In New Orleans, there are only two kinds of food—good and bad. We try for the good and have brought back open-hearth grilling."—Mary Merris

promptly and prominently.[5] PR managers must be aware of these guidelines so that they can work well with news editors.

Press releases should be presented as news stories written in the style of each medium, printed on the letterhead of the store, firm, or person involved, and marked with a heading like "News Release," or "Special Report from (firm name)." They should be marked "for immediate release" or "for release on (date)." These communications are also called *news releases*. Occasionally, a special caption—"Exclusive for the *Sun Times*"—is used. An example of a press release packet is shown in Exhibit 14-4.

Agency versus In-House Public Relations

Large firms that play an important role in their communities and interact constantly with media tend to have their own internal public relations departments. Smaller firms usually hire a public relations agency if paying an agency fee is less expensive than maintaining a full-time internal staff. In very small operations, the public relations function is generally handled

EXHIBIT 14-4 **Excerpts from a Press Release Packet**
Source: Macy's, New York, NY.

MACY'S 4TH OF JULY FIREWORKS ON THE EAST RIVER

MACY*S TENTH ANNUAL FOURTH OF JULY FIREWORKS

On Thursday, July 4th at precisely 9:20 PM, as night casts its shadow over New York City, the sky will suddenly erupt in a breathtaking burst of colors. Patriotic music will fill the air as Macy*s Tenth Annual pyro-spectacular "parade-in-the sky" begins.

Millions of spectators will view this dramatic display taking place on the East River covering the New York area from 23rd to 42nd Streets. The FDR Drive from 14th to 51st Streets will be closed for spectator viewing from 8 P.M. to 10:00 PM and will reopen to vehicle traffic at approximately 1:00 A.M.

To salute America's 209th birthday, a shell-shower of glittering gems, butterflies, chrysanthemums, silver swallows, multicolored peonies, rockets, and streamers will be launched into the night creating "Star Spangled Skies." Beams from 14 giant searchlights and 2 sky trackers will sweep the heavens spreading their rainbow of color twenty miles into the night skies.

by owners or managers. They telephone the newspapers and broadcasting stations to inform them of newsworthy events, or they teach an employee to write press releases and handle contacts with media. Some firms pay to send an employee to local classes in publicity or public relations. There are also numerous books and publications on the subject.[6]

When possible, it is better to handle routine publicity and public relations internally, and to use an agency only for those special matters for which the firm has inadequate resources or experience. A firm's public relations department specializes in the firm's own activities, whereas a public relations agency usually has a number of different accounts with different businesses.

Organization

The public relations department, occasionally called the "publicity department," usually has a public relations director or manager and a number of writers, depending on the size of the operation. In addition, it may have its own staff photographer or hire a free-lance photographer to be on call. In some cases, if the firm uses photography for its advertising, staff photographers may double as publicity photographers.

The several writers are usually assigned to specific areas of the store's operations. For example, there may be a fashion writer, a business and financial writer, and a hard lines and home furnishings writer. If a store has many special events, a writer may be assigned to this phase of the operation. In addition to writing releases for their particular areas, writers may become publicity managers or public relations managers for these specific areas. For example, if a store has a fashion show, fashion writers may play a key role in this event, not only writing the commentary for the show but actually doing the commentary. In addition, they may help organize the entire show and, of course, they will write the press releases.

In smaller operations, advertising copywriters may double as publicity writers. However, there is a distinct difference between the two types of writing. Publicity writing is journalism, as similar as possible to the way a news reporter writes a story. Copywriting describes an article and attempts to "sell" it to the reader. It takes a skillful writer to adapt to both styles.

Public relations managers supervise and may edit the writers' work, and they represent the firm at important meetings and events. They act as spokespeople for their firms and write speeches for top management to present at corporate meetings and other functions. The public relations department cooperates with the sales promotion manager to get maximum news exposure for sales promotion events.[7] Public relations executives should make a point of wandering around and noting people and activities. This should be done frequently.

Writing

The public relations department writes releases for all departments of the firm. These reports cover the firm's many and varied activities during a typical month. Here are some typical stories for which news releases would be appropriate:

1. For "Italian Weeks," merchandise from Italy is featured and the Italian Consul-General will open the event.
2. A famous Italian chef will appear in the housewares department and demonstrate his techniques in conjunction with "Italian Weeks."
3. The firm is sponsoring a bowling contest and giving prizes to the top bowlers.
4. The firm has appointed a new vice president and merchandise manager.
5. Jo Green, an employee, was the winner of the local amateur golf match at the Wynmoor Country Club.
6. The firm will sponsor a Scout Outing on May 16 to visit the state park and camp overnight.
7. The firm is planning to open a new branch store in the Bellaire Shopping Center in 1986.
8. Francis Jones, the president of the firm, will be the principal speaker at the annual dinner of the 110-year-old Humanitarian Club.
9. The firm has announced the dates for its annual art exhibit for local artists. There will be over 300 entries, a spokesperson said.
10. The unique and valuable china of the former Royal Family of Italy will be exhibited in the china department in conjunction with "Italian Weeks."
11. There will be a fashion show Friday evening, featuring an Italian couture collection in connection with "Italian Weeks."
12. Mar Marton, the author of *Wild West,* will be in the book department on May 28 to autograph copies of this new book.

These stories will be written in the style of news reports and timed properly. For example, if the newspaper has a weekly food page, the release about the Italian chef should be submitted for that page in time for a reporter to be assigned. If the paper has a weekly art column, the release about the art exhibit must be timed to make the deadline for that column. Well-written releases should require only a minimum of rewriting by the news or broadcast editor. This is important because busy editors, with deadlines to meet, welcome reports that require little attention.

A press release must have the name and telephone number of a person to contact for clarification or for more information, and a release date that tells when the information can be used. The release should conform to the format rules of the media vehicles. For example, the headline should be short and capitalized. It should be surrounded by ample white space so that the paper can write its own headline and include typesetting information. The text of the release should be double-spaced, with short paragraphs going from the most important to the least important news. If an additional page is needed, the word "MORE" should be at the bottom of a page in parentheses or dashes. A paragraph should not be split between two pages. The second and following pages should contain the page number and the firm's name. The symbol "--30--" should appear at the end of the story to denote the end. The date the press release was written should be included for the firm's records.[8]

Photography

A large public relations department has a staff or free-lance photographer who covers events on short notice. Typical stories taken from the list given earlier will need coverage. For example, the writer of the "Italian chef" story will advise a photographer that Gabriel Antonelli will be available at the Hilton Hotel Tuesday afternoon. The writer must have Antonelli's photograph by Wednesday, as Thursday is the deadline for the Food page. Or the dress rehearsal of the fashion show will be Monday night; the photographer must be there and take several pictures so that different photographs can be sent to all the town's publications and broadcasters. Of course, the photographer must check with the coordinator of the show to make certain the most important items in the collection have been photographed.

Publicity photographs in most cases must be taken at the location of the event. These pictures must look like a news photographer's work, which means *in action*. Photographs of fashions can be posed more carefully as it is understood that such pictures are *posed*. Generally, however, good news photos used in publicity must not look contrived. When possible, they must have a sense of immediacy. Photographs of a governor cutting the ribbon to open a shopping center and of a store employee helping customers on opening day accompanied the news article shown in Exhibit 14-5.

Coordination with Other Marketing Communications Functions

In many cases, large retail operations have a permanent marketing committee. This group is headed by the vice president of marketing or the equivalent and has as members the advertising director, the sales promotion director, the publicity director, and the display director. In situations where some of the above duties are combined in one position, subordinates such as the sales promotion manager, or the senior publicity person, may be included as well.

The following is an example of the teamwork required for a publicity event like a fashion show. The advertising department prepares an ad-

EXHIBIT 14-5 **News Story of Governor and Mayor Cutting Ribbon to Open Shopping Center**

Source: The Morning Union, Springfield, MA (July 6, 1979), p. 1.

Holyoke Mall Launched in Style

By Robert S. Perkins, Union Bureau Chief

HOLYOKE—Shoppers by the hundreds poured through the doors of the new Holyoke Mall at Ingleside Thursday, seven years after the complex was proposed and 14 months after groundbreaking for the $25 million window shopper's dream come true.

Shortly after Gov. Edward J. King cut the ribbon marking the official opening of the mall, Western Massachusetts shoppers were crowding the 80 specialty shops and one anchor store that opened Thursday.

Another 80 specialty shops and two more anchor stores are scheduled to open by Aug. 8 and, when fully occupied, the mall will have 180 specialty shops and restaurants with four anchor stores and a possibility of an additional two anchor stores.

Joining Gov. King in the opening ceremonies were U.S. Rep. Silvio O. Conte, Holyoke Mayor Ernest E. Proulx, representatives of The Pyramid Companies of DeWitt, N.Y., which developed the mall and a host of business and municipal officials.

King told those who assembled for the opening that the mall fell in line with his administration's view of the free enterprise system.

"When we stress the absolutely essential nature of the free enterprise system, we are saying we want you to be happy," the Governor said.

The free enterprise system provides people with jobs and helps protect them from the temptations of drugs and alcohol . . .

vertisement stating the date, time, and place of the show and perhaps a sketch or photo of one of the garments to be shown. The sales promotion department stages the show, hires the models, sets up the stage and runways, arranges the lighting, installs microphones, prepares the auditorium with chairs, arranges for the printing of the programs, and handles all related details. The public relations department writes the story in advance so that the papers and broadcasters can use the story and photographs in a timely manner while it is still news. Meanwhile, the merchandising department is putting together the apparel to be shown.

PUBLIC RELATIONS AND THE FIRM'S VARIOUS PUBLICS

The public relations personnel are responsible for initiating and maintaining good relations with various publics.

The Usual Publics
- *Personnel*
- *Unions*
- *Consumers*
- *Media*
- *The Trading-Area Publics, such as Charities and Schools*
- *Stockholders and the Financial Community*
- *Governments: Local, State, Federal*

Special Publics for Retailers
- *Vendors*
- *Local Merchants' Groups*

Personnel

One of the most important areas of public relations is the management-employee relationship. There are instances of poor internal public relations that remind one of the fable of the ill-shod shoemaker's children. Some firms with great public recognition and acceptance have poor or indifferent employee relations. Most Japanese firms are very conscious of the power of good employee morale and enthusiasm. These companies work hard to create a strong team spirit and as a result, Japanese productivity per worker is very high.

We can learn from this deliberately cultivated good relationship and high *espirit de corps*. Employee communications can run the gamut from regular short meetings, contests, simple weekly or monthly house bulletins to elaborate house organ magazines. Some of the latter are so well done that they are also circulated to customers.

The most successful company-employee relationships exist when firms have many levels of communication. Their weekly, biweekly, or monthly bulletins have mostly employee personal notes or articles covering births, deaths, marriages, anniversaries, graduations, birthdays, and perhaps congratulatory letters. There may also be reports of sports activities and company team events. Company magazines generally discuss larger issues than do bulletins, such as the business of the company, public issues, and the firm's position on important pending legislation.

Companies with good employee relations plan numerous social events involving the entire families of employees—picnics, Halloween parties, Fourth of July events, and Christmas parties. Birthdays are recognized and sometimes a day off given, small gifts presented, or cards sent. Good employee-employer relations are no accident. This happens because management tries on many levels to make all people in the company feel they are an important part of a successful team and an organization that cares. Good relationships pay off in terms of lower absenteeism, higher productivity, lower pilferage, more cooperation, better customer relationships, and community good will due to the complimentary word-of-mouth comments of employees.

A firm's public image is strongly influenced by its personnel, especially the salespeople, cashiers, checkout clerks, information people, receptionists, and service department people. The best merchandising, buying, and display skills are lost if the personnel with whom the public has direct contact are inefficient, incompetent, or indifferent.

Those employees unseen by the customer can often be just as important as those who meet the customer. For example, a shipping clerk who misdirects a package or a billing clerk who makes a wrong entry of customer data can infuriate a customer. Erroneous billings that remain on the customer's invoice for months after having been called to the attention of the firm, have lost many charge accounts. An infuriated customer can do the firm a great deal of harm by telling friends, "I will never do business with that firm again!"

It is the responsibility of the personnel department, working with the public relations people in charge of personnel relations, to screen personnel regularly and eliminate those who by their nature would alienate the customer public. This same team should make every effort to make the work life of employees pleasant, to listen to all gripes, and to make corrections in response to all legitimate complaints.

Unions and Labor Relations

The public relations director and the personnel director are usually charged with the duty of liaison to labor unions and their shop stewards and officers. Because the firm's image is very much affected by the public's perception of how the firm treats its employees, good union relationships are crucial. This is a major public relations function. A firm with constant labor-union friction and strikes with picketing will have a poor image in the community. Confrontation should be avoided and negotiations with the union begun long before contracts are to be renewed. Customers do not like to cross picket lines and face disgruntled employees.

However, in situations where the union demands seem unrealistic or excessive, the public relations department must make an effort to put its position before the public in a favorable light without resorting to name-calling or vindictiveness. After all, union and management will have to work together after the strike or confrontation. There have been cases where the public believed the firm was wrong and began boycotting it until the labor difficulties were settled. In such cases both the union and the firm may buy space in the local newspapers to state their case. Here again, the public relations department plays a crucial role in working with the advertising department on the copy that will appear in the ad to state the firm's position. The union also has its public relations department. There may be a battle of public relations departments to capture the good will of the public and the firm's customers.

When a firm is important to the community, its labor disputes are very visible. The media may send reporters to interview management and union executives to get both sides of the story. The firm's public relations personnel must prepare carefully for these interviews. The management position must seem reasonable. When both sides handle these matters well, the public usually calls it a "stand-off," feeling that there is something to be said for both sides. A skillful public relations director will agree to a joint interview in a television studio, realizing that a street interview, with the labor union official and pickets in front of the store, would be far more harmful to the store's position.

Good public relations calls for a continuing dialog with both unions and the employees themselves to avoid serious confrontations. The people in the personnel departments and labor relations departments should be available on short notice to hear complaints. Gripes should not be allowed to fester. Hundreds of employees with different needs and backgrounds make employee relations a demanding job. As retailers have more and more part-time help, the number of employees for most stores has increased markedly in the last few years. The time may come when a store's staff is almost doubled as two people, each working four hours, take the place of one full-time employee.

The public relations department together with the personnel department must evaluate fringe benefits very carefully. Blue Cross, Blue Shield, and medical coverage together with accident policies may play an important role in labor relations. Some firms have an internal medical staff, or they work out agreements with small clinics or health centers. Others have a full-time in-house nurse and an agreement with a doctor to be a full-time outside emergency resource. In any case, successful firms do not underestimate the total impact of the employer-employee relationship. They make certain that labor relations have a high priority in the firm's overall planning.

Consumers

It is obvious that the customers pay the bills and make the firm a success. Alienating customers for any reason will influence present and future sales. With this in mind, firms must give customer relations their top and continuing priority. The public relations department devotes a major part of its time to this area. An organization can survive many mistakes, but the one mistake it cannot survive is the alienation of its customers. In recent years, one of the most important phases of the public relations area is "keeping an ear to the ground." This means the department must make constant inquiries of consumers. Trained employees, students, or representatives of a research agency can interview customers using a prepared questionnaire to help the firm better understand its customers.

Another method of finding out who a store's customers are is to send questionnaires both to charge customers and to a group selected from ZIP-code mailing lists in particular areas, perhaps from subscription lists of magazines mailed to ZIP-code areas near the store. Such ear-to-the-ground tactics serve two major purposes. They provide the store with information about overall acceptance and negative reactions, and they help the store to update its demographic data.[9]

A number of the most successful firms attribute their success to understanding just who their customers are. It is the responsibility of the public relations department to find out customers' images of the firm and to report these findings to the various mangers and the advertising department. This will insure that the day-to-day operation keeps in line with overall company objectives, and communicates the proper image to the customers.

In the public relations department, the person in charge of customer relations must continually be aware of internal operations, reexamining policies from time to time. The public relations group should work with the personnel department to correct lack of employee knowledge about merchandise, department locations, or store policies. For example, are there long lines of customers at certain service desks or checkout counters? Should there be an information desk for customers even though there is a directory posted in a prominent place?

Credit department personnel who take care of customer's billing and credit complaints should be pleasant, firm, and not defensive. Employees who move into various jobs on short notice when such departments are busier than expected should be comfortable with this flexibility and informed about the various categories of merchandise and their locations. All salespeople should know how to find the locations of all departments with the help of a quick reference sheet in their sales books.

Firms must keep on top of many seemingly trivial details. Are salespeople poorly or inappropriately dressed so that they give a poor impression of the firm? Are many salespeople gruff and impolite with the customers? Has a store, in its cost-cutting efforts, eliminated so many salespeople that customers cannot get waited on? Is merchandise properly marked and easy to find? Some stores hire "shoppers" to act as customers and report on the salespeople who wait on them. Salespeople often call them "spies" and deeply resent this practice. However, a competent salesperson has nothing to fear from these observers, and can benefit from a good report.

The public relations department must share its information with the personnel department and other marketing groups. All departments share the responsibility of maintaining the firm's image. Questions relating to personnel and customer relations should receive proper attention through the research done by the customer relations section of the public relations department. Many firms believe customer relations to be so important that they make it the joint responsibility of the public relations director, the vice president of marketing, and the personnel director. Sometimes this area of public relations is called "consumer affairs." Whatever the title, the purpose is the same: to keep the customers happy.

Media

Customers have a reasonable expectation that if they respond to advertising, the advertised merchandise will be available, particularly on the first morning of an announced sale. If it is not, the customer has a legitimate complaint and must be satisfied. The expense of bad public relations can far exceed the expense of satisfying those customers with legitimate complaints.

If there is an information desk, it is imperative that the employees there know the answers to all questions about products and their locations, especially for advertised products and promotions. Such employees should have copies of all advertisements to keep on file, as most ads are supposed to be applied for at least a week. If advertisements refer to store department numbers instead of locations, people at the information desk must be able to translate the numbers into department locations and vice versa.

If a typographical error has been made in an ad so that consumers expect to pay a lower price than is correct, the correction should be published in the same media vehicle, if possible, and also shown to customers. Generally, a publication will print a letter apologizing for typographical errors. For relatively small price differentials, for example, $89 instead of $98, it may cost less in time and good will to sell at the incorrect $89 price.

Retailers must back up money-back guarantees advertised by manufacturers, and then settle with the manufacturers. Although customers may be exposed to manufacturers' ads, they have bought the merchandise at a store, and so expect the store to handle returns. The store's reputation is thus at stake in this situation, even if the problem was caused by the manufacturer. All good retailers stand behind the merchandise they sell.

In the long run, a firm cannot survive without consumer confidence and credibility. It is the duty of the public relations department to help build this reputation for integrity, policing the firm's claims in advertising, signs, and posters. Some vendors show excellent samples to buyers and send inferior merchandise to fill the order. The public relations department, speaking for the buying and merchandising staff, can insist that manufacturers assume full responsibility for delivering merchandise as per sample and specifications.

Some stores have set up their own bureau of standards to test merchandise, or they have outside laboratories or agencies check certain manufacturers' claims. For example, if a manufacturer claims that a particular product will "last through fifty washings or launderings," Sears will wash the product fifty times to check this claim. Sears believes when it tells its customers about the merchandise it sells, it must be absolutely truthful. Sears won an American Marketing Association achievement award and favorable publicity for its merchandise testing, its development of new products, and for avoiding placing commercials on television programs with excessive violent or antisocial behavior.[10]

The Trading-Area Publics—Charities, Schools, and Other

A firm should enjoy a good relationship with the people and institutions in its neighborhood. Because stores tend to be in a part of the community where they have high visibility, they are noticed. Hence, store representatives must participate in community affairs, serve on the boards of community enterprises and charitable organizations, and support causes that advance the good of the community.

Many firms have a policy that encourages employees, including managers, to be on the boards of such groups as the Red Cross, Scouts, Community Fund, Library Committee, Police and Fire Funds, Parks Commission, Salvation Army, League of Women Voters, Hospital Boards, Public School Boards, Little League, or Protestant, Catholic, and Jewish Charities. The employer allows time off to employees who participate in these activities. This participation helps the firm become known as a friendly organization that participates in good causes and community affairs without regard to race, creed, or color. The public relations department often supervises these activities.

Often, too, the firm's premises are offered to various groups for exhibits and public meetings. Because participation goes beyond mere monetary contributions, firms generally have a policy of active involvement. While a firm participates in all these activities for business reasons, the activity is not only self-serving. By being a genuine part of the community, the firm earns its place in that community and becomes known as a good neighbor. Also, in doing these community activities, businesspeople become better acquainted with their customers, which helps them to improve their marketing communications.

Sometimes it is helpful to build an image not just in the trading area, but on a larger scale. When a firm is known on a regional basis or even nationally, a number of benefits tend to accrue. Certain retail organizations are known coast to coast, from their activities, and so do a large business with tourists.

Smaller firms and groups of stores can build a reputation in their communities so that when visitors come to their town, local people will say, "You must visit the Jones Place" or "Be sure to shop downtown." Here again, the people in charge of public relations must send a positive image beyond the immediate area. Image-building might include creating a reputation as "ski experts" or "craft experts," or as offering the convenience of having small related shops in an area near parking. Exhibit 14-6 shows a press release from a Chamber of Commerce that tells of the creation of a tourism committee to cooperate with a local university. The Chamber will work with other towns to interest tour operators in making the area a stopover place for tour groups.

Managers of shopping centers seek publicity for their tenant retailers. One shopping center was featured on a CBS documentary television show which described the center as a safe, temperature-controlled, entertainment environment in which customers could socialize as well as shop. The television show was reported as news in the newspapers. Another shopping center was featured in a story in a local free weekly newspaper.[11]

Firms help both themselves and their publics by advertising in programs of community events staged by service organizations, and by sponsoring community events. Appropriate support can be given to football programs, programs for musical or dramatic entertainments, and regional art exhibits with prizes that attract contestants from nearby states.

EXHIBIT 14-6 **Excerpts from a Press Release for a Joint Downtown Effort to Attract Touritsts**

Source: Chamber of Commerce, Amherst, MA.

PRESS RELEASE: IMMEDIATE

CONTACT: Ann Campney, 253-9666 or Duncan Fraser, 586-2717

The Amherst Chamber of Commerce has created a new committee to encourage the growth of tourism.

Citing the growth of the tourist industry in New England, Chamber President William V. Gillen said that Amherst businesses that cater to seasonal visitors should be represented by a division of the chamber in the same manner that retailers are represented by the Amherst Downtown Council, a chamber arm formed several years ago.

The creation of a tourism committee was voted by chamber directors. . . .

Named to the committee so far are David A. Nichols, manager of the Lord Jeffery Inn, and Prue H. Arbib, community and public relations director of the University of Massachusetts Fine Arts Center. Others are expected to be named to the committee as the scope of its work expands, Fraser said.

The committee has mapped out as its first objective trying to interest more tour operators in making Amherst a stopping-over place for groups coming to visit the unique five-college area.

Fraser said his group will work closely with a recently formed Tourism Promotion Group which has representation from the greater Northampton-Amherst area. This group, with Marcia Burick of Northampton as chairman, was formed in response to a request by Northampton Mayor David Musanto that a special effort be made to promote the growing tourist industry in the Pioneer Valley.

However, there are also more frequent problems of a day-to-day nature that must be skillfully handled by a community affairs division. For example, a person is arrested in a store for shoplifting and turned over to the local police. The firm's attorney is told to prosecute the offender. Public relations alternatives are to release the story to the local press in order to discourage other would-be shoplifters, or to keep this bad publicity quiet. On the one hand, reading about the arrest and prosecution of a shoplifter may discourage other shoplifters from attempting the same act. On the other hand, publicity might suggest shoplifting ideas to people who had not previously thought about shoplifting.

Local Charities and Causes Organizations in the areas where firms do business tend to expect charitable contributions from them. However, such contributions can become a problem, for there are hundreds and hundreds of good causes. Under direction of top management, the PR department should set up policies governing charitable contributions. For example, some firms tell all who request money that they give only to certain specific organizations.

Retailers may cooperate with good cause in a number of other ways than by giving money, such as lending store premises and windows for shows and exhibits, or doing a fashion show with store merchandise for which the admission charge goes to charity. Many firms have allowed their parking lots to be used after work hours for fund-raising events. Filene's and Jordan Marsh department stores in Boston attracted publicity by hosting a benefit for a non-profit group and doing displays and events to tie in with this benefit. The Price Chopper supermarket in Hadley, MA, regularly contributed food and supplies to a Survival Center, thereby receiving a certificate of appreciation and accompanying publicity. Saks Fifth Avenue in New York City treated a terminally ill teenager to a shopping spree for a designer wardrobe, which was described in a syndicated newspaper article. A mass merchandiser, J.C. Penney, underwrote a public television program, gaining a newspaper article about this action. Firms that contribute to the expense of public television programs are mentioned on television before and after these programs.[12] Some organizations encourage employees to work on fund-raising for public radio and televison stations by offering time off to every employee who puts in a certain number of volunteer hours.

Local Schools Local firms are expected to support public and private schools and colleges in their community. This can be done in a number of ways. Firms can arrange tours of their premises for school groups, explaining operations and encouraging interest in their business. They can work with high schools and colleges to recruit personnel for full or part-time jobs. Some stores have "college boards" of students who help customers plan college wardrobes. Firms can sponsor special courses in local colleges and evening education programs, offering executives as speakers for such courses. Firms may even endow a chair in marketin or make other such direct contributions to the educational institutions It is the duty of the public relations department to encourage and maintai these relationships.

Other Community Groups In many communities there may be number of special groups that a firm feels it is necessary to support. Fo example, a group may have organized to buy additional land for a park playground, or swimming pool. Because it is a good community cause the firm may cooperate, offering its PR department to work for the group If the town sponsors a Santa Claus at Christmas, the firm should suppor the town's Santa and help publicize the event. It might also help witl the local Fourth of July celebration or parades on special occasions Because retailers are leading citizens, they, represented by their publi relations personnel, must be in the forefront of such activities.

Stockholders and the Financial Community

Stockholders Firms that issue stocks or debentures must prepar annual reports. The public relations department creates these and interin reports. Reports for large firms are elaborate, presenting the firm's genera and financial position in a visual and interesting manner. The publi relations department is also involved in preparing the annual meeting for stockholders, writing speeches for top management to present at th meeting and release to the press. The business, with the help of its publi relations personnel, must continuously interpret its financial positio and decisions to its stockholders and to the financial community at large

Financial Community Although stockholders and the financial com munity may overlap, they are really separate publics. Because many firm have financed their operation by issuing stock or debentures, they mus have a continuing relationship with the financial community: banks stockholders, business journalists, other businesses, and the firm's boar of directors. Periodic reports stating the financial position of the compan are required. A public corporation's sales volume, profits, and losses ar all a matter of interest to financial circles. Such reports usually nee interpretation, which is another function of the PR Department. Ther are periodic meetings with bankers, brokers, real estate people, and o course, the board of directors. Comparative statements are expected a intervals; for example: "Sales for (firm name) hit an all-time peak for th first quarter of 19--," or "Severe winter storms and bad weather hav reduced sales for January below last year's level . . ."

Because retail sales are a barometer of all business, retailers ar constantly asked, "How's business?" If a retail store does well, its suppliers the manufacturers, do well. If manufacturers have strong sales, the deman or the raw materials they use remains strong. It is clear that the retail icture is important to the financial community and to economists as vell. It might be said that as retailing goes, so goes the entire economy. 'his means that the public relations departments of retail stores must ssue periodic reports on the status of business and the expected outlook. 'his is generally in the form of a statement by the president or one of ie top executives.

When firms are doing well, they hire more personnel. This helps ie community at large. When local businesses prosper, the entire community feels at ease. If a firm's stock goes up or down excessively, a ianagement spokesperson should explain the cause for this change or iovement. Firms have a continuing obligation to keep the financial comunity abreast of their fiscal situation. The relationship with the financial ector is very important as it may affect the company's ability to borrow ioney at a favorable rate and to maintain a prefered position with its anks. Also, if the corporation needs to float a new stock or bond issue, s standing in the financial community will be a major factor in the uccess of these endeavors.

iovernments: Local, State, Federal

ll business firms have important relationships with city, state, and ederal governments. The larger the firm, the more its involvement with arious government agencies. Because of its visibility in the community, retail firm must go beyond the average business firm in its relationship vith each level of government. The public relations department must set p and maintain relationships with numerous governmental organizations.

The relationship with local government is particularly important. 'here should be a constant flow of information to the mayor's office, the ity, county or town planning commission, the parks department, the epartment of streets and highways, the fire department, the police deartment, the traffic department, and other relevant departments. Each f these departments can help a firm in various ways, and the firm must om time to time help these groups. For example, one or more firms hould spearhead campaigns for "A Better City," hold exhibits for the arks, fire, and police departments, work with the traffic department on arking and traffic problems, and help with special holidays and city vents.

Publicity about Worcester, MA firms' involvement with local govrnment in downtown revitalization is described in Appendix 14. Vorcester's redevelopment authority, backed by its business community, ity manager, and a majority of the city council, erected a shopping enter, hotel, heliport, bus terminal, two office towers, a theater, and a parking garage in Worcester's central business district. Shopping center management then provided a tenant mix of stores and restaurants custom tailored to the needs of county residents.

It is in retailers' interests to improve the communities in which they have stores. The police can be helpful with customers' parking problems and in setting up traffic patterns that may help the store. Better street lighting and streets in good repair also help retailers because these encourage more shopping, particularly during evening hours. Public transportation is also very important to a store, for if it is easy to get to a store, there will be more shoppers and shopping at all hours. Sidewalks, malls, planting of flowers, trees, and shrubbery, and the installation of fountains all add to the ambiance of the city. The ambiance helps all city businesses and the city itself by attracting people from the large area around the metropolitan area.

It is easy to see why a firm must make special and continuing efforts in all these areas. Owners and executives must be ready to serve on committees and governmental boards. Taking the larger view of "what's good for the community is good for the firm" serves both store and community. Retailers' cooperation tends to make the mayor more willing to officiate at branch store openings, the police more interested in taking care of stores' numerous traffic and parking problems, and the park department willing to help with special events for children and holidays.

While the relationship with the state government may not be as close as that with the local government, it too can be important. There are numerous cases where branches are located across state lines and the firm is actually based in two states. Even if this is rarely true, it is good for a firm to have a good relationship with the state or states in which it does business. In some cases the governor as well as the mayor is invited to important functions, such as the shopping center opening mentioned earlier in Exhibit 14-5. It is the job of public relations personnel to understand the rules and regulations of various governments and their agencies so that the firm can comply with them and be a good citizen.

SPECIAL PUBLICS FOR RETAILERS

In addition to the publics mentioned above, retailers have two additional special publics—vendors and merchants.

Vendors

Vendors are important special publics; they sell merchandise to the store. Without vendors, the store has nothing to sell. Most retailers realize this nd try to maintain good relations with vendors. Some stores have prepared olicy guidelines for dealing with vendors so that all retail personnel an follow a consistent policy. One important policy is that of minimizing he value of gifts from vendors to buyers and purchasing agents in order) minimize gift-induced bias.

Some retailers who think they have greater power than do vendors reat them with some disdain, often keeping their representatives waiting fter making appointments and giving them little time after they have ome a long distance to see the buyer or merchandise manager. The ublic relations department should discourage this policy and make special fforts to foster good relationships with suppliers. Efforts might include ne following: Encourage buyers to write a letter at least once a year elling vendors that their cooperation is appreciated and that future co-peration and role in the continuing success of the store will be valued. end the store's annual report to all important suppliers even though ney are not stockholders. Send suppliers a copy of the store's philosophy f maintaining standards and guaranteeing customer satisfaction, and opies of advertisements in which the supplier's merchandise appears. Vhen a manufacturer has had a long and successful relationship with a etailer, send a Certificate of Appreciation: "In appreciation of your valuable ontribution to Beach's Store for the past ____ years." This certificate hould be attractively executed, framed or suitable for framing, so that ne proud supplier can hang it in a prominent place in office or showroom.

ocal Merchants' Groups

Most towns and cities have a local merchants' group. It is important for ll retailers to work with such groups. A strong merchants' group has n important influence in community affairs. Such groups can set store ours on specific days and during the holiday season, and determine ight openings. They can also work out parking discounts and even free arking which they can subsidize as a group. They can agree on certain romotional events and sales days and cooperate on such events as a hristmas parade. They can also hire entertainment groups to focus at-ention on downtown shopping areas or shopping centers. Exhibit 14-6 howed an example of joint effort.

While the public relations department spearheads these efforts, the dvertising and sales promotion departments also play an important role. n some cases the larger store's PR department may act as liaison for the ntire merchants group. In some instances the merchants group publishes weekly shopping newsletter in which each store buys advertising so nat the paper is self-supporting. A store's PR department may take re-ponsibility for the editorial columns of such a publication.

PUBLIC RELATIONS' PART IN MAINTAINING IMAGE

Research, Planning, Evaluation, and Counselling

One of the responsibilities of the PR department is to find out what the media are saying about the firm, and to keep files of clippings. Analysing mail, sales records, speeches by opinion leaders, requests for interviews, media attendance at press conferences, relevant new legislation, personnel turnover, speech requests, the tone of questions at annual meetings, and information from personal contacts and opinion polls is another huge responsibility. Information acquired while attending seminars, conferences, and workshops should also enter the analysis. Publicity plans based on this analysis can be used to make long-term strategies, to anticipate problems and put out potential "fires" before they start. An evaluation of information sources, and of public response to publicity and PR efforts should also guide planning. PR managers should of course share relevant information with appropriate managers so that they can adjust their marketing communications where needed.[13]

Public Relations as a Coordination Function

Although all marketing efforts contribute to image and personality, the marketing and public relations managers have the responsibility of evaluating and maintaining a firm's personality and image on a continuing basis. Some firms are "good old reliable institutions," others are on the frontier of change. A new method of finding out how well a business communicates to its various publics is a *communications audit*. Such an audit can include computer analysis of press clippings.[14]

A store team supervised by the marketing vice president with the public relations department as the leader, and advertising and promotion as the support team, can plan and maintain store image on a daily basis. A store's displays, special events, celebrity visitors, advertising copy, art work and photography must always be in keeping with the image it wants to portray. Nothing a firm does should ever be out of character. If an individual does unusual or strange things, he or she is called eccentric. A firm can never afford to be eccentric, although it can be imaginative. Still, in the total picture, it must have a unity and consistency that the public likes and understands. All the various publics enumerated earlier must always know what to expect.

An example of coordination is an opening night party for a new store or branch. Such an event can generate much word-of-mouth publicity which builds traffic. Therefore, the opening maximizes customer quality to build community awareness, especially among such groups as business leaders, members of important private clubs, the Chamber of Commerce, overnment officials, vendors, relevant consumer groups, and prominent ›rofessionals from relevant fields. These people can be reached through press release sent to them two weeks in advance of the opening. An gency can do the mailing. An event, like a ribbon-cutting, a new product emonstration with vendor representatives present for discussion, or a peech by a newsworthy person will encourage invitees to attend and ttract others. Fliers should be passed out to the general public one day efore the event. Earlier, of course, ads with photos should be placed in ewspapers and several spot announcements put on radio. If some percentage of opening day sales has been donated to charity, that too can e publicized. Store representatives can appear on local television talk hows. Finally, thank you notes and discount coupons can be sent to all vho were invited, whether or not they came.[15]

ress Conferences and Press Parties

'ress conferences and press parties are among PR's most powerful tools. 'hey should be used only when a firm has an important statement to nake about a newsworthy event. In these cases, a statement should be ssued to the entire press by the public relations office. The statement hould make clear just what will take place, when, where, and with vhom. An NRMA press conference announcement is shown in Exhibit 4-7.

Like other marketing communications, meeting the press and publics equires both art and science. A good reason for calling the press conference, sincere approach, a brief statement prepared in advance followed by uestions, and no answers off the record will make for a good press onference. Communications firms are available to polish skills for managers' being interviewed by the broadcast and other media.[16]

Press conferences must be newsworthy enough to warrant media overage. Nothing is worse from a PR point of view than giving a press onference that no one attends. Press events can be either straight affairs vith no frills, or partly social with cocktails or buffet for the press. They an also at times be a kind of show, such as the unveiling of a new roduct, the opening of a new department or remodeled section, a fashion how, or an exhibit.

As a backup, the PR department must write up the entire event in ne past tense, suitable for pickup by the media, and have photographs or media vehicles whose own photographers cover the event. Reporters nay adapt such material for their own use, or use the release virtually ntact. In addition to sending the written release, it is a good practice to elephone all reporters to make certain they will attend. This personal ouch is appreciated by media people. Because press conferences are sed only for important announcements, no stone must be left unturned

EXHIBIT 14-7 **Announcement for NRMA Press Conference**
Source: National Retail Merchants Association.

National Retail Merchants Association • 100 W. 31 St., New York, N. Y. 10001 • 212—244-8780

TELEX — INT'L. 220 - 883 - TAUR TWX — DOMESTIC 710 - 581 - 5380 TPNYK

NRMA PRESS CONFERENCE

Wednesday, January 11, 1984 -- 2:30 p.m.

Rendezvous Room -- Hilton Hotel, Third Floor

Mr. William P. Arnold
Chairman and Chief Executive Officer
Associated Dry Goods Corporation, New York, N.Y.
Chairman of the Board and Chairman of the Executive Committee of NRMA

Mr. James R. Williams
President, NRMA

Mr. Verrick O. French
Sr. Vice President, NRMA Governmental Affairs

Mr. Charles A. Binder
Executive Vice President, NRMA

to assure their success. If top executives of a firm will be present, top executives of the media may be invited as well as the reporters who would normally cover the story. In that case it is usual to serve beverages and snacks, or perhaps more elaborate fare.

SUMMARY

The public relations function is to coordinate marketing communications efforts to achieve the best possible relations with internal and xternal publics. This effort continually projects image and personality) *communicate the firm* to these publics, while always evaluating feedback. ollowing the marketing concept, the PR manager must create and meet ie expectations of the firm's various publics: personnel, unions, consumers, edia, community, stockholders, financiers, governments, vendors, and)cal merchants' groups.

Public relations tools include press releases, events, photographs, lms, tapes, speeches, annual reports, company brochures, and training aterials. The PR department needs people who can *create newsworthy vents* to generate publicity, using the advertising, sales promotion, visual erchandising, and personnel departments. No marketing effort can be solo performance; PR coordinates the players.

Firms that have succeeded through the efforts of a single dynamic, iarismatic, newsmaking individual are exceptions. Only with the continuing effort of a good team of marketers, personnel and operations anagers does a firm achieve and maintain a great public image for the R department to project. Successful operations are created by many ipable people by means of accurate information, careful analysis, skillful lanning, and effective execution. This success must be constantly brought the attention of the public.

QUESTIONS

1. Explain the difference between publicity and advertising.
2. Why is public relations important to a firm?
3. Give reasons for and examples of good public relations for each of these internal publics: personnel, union, customers.
4. Give reasons for and examples of good public relations for each of these external publics: trading area public (charities, schools, other), stockholders and the financial community, governments.
5. Explain why a retailer must also have good public relations with vendors and merchants' groups.
6. Using some examples based on publics listed in questions 3, 4, and 5 above, explain how a firm can coordinate publicity, public relations, and advertising to create a consistent image.
7. Bring to class an example of (a) a news article about a recent event staged by or for a firm, (b) a news article about a firm which has done something newsworthy other than an event. Explain why these examples are newsworthy.
8. After reading this chapter, what skills would you suggest that a person needs for success in a publicity or publications career? Are you interested in a publicity or publications career? Why or why not?

NOTES

1. Definition given by Dr. Rex F. Harlow, of the Foundation for Public elations Research and Education, in S. Cutlip and A. Center, *Effective Public elations*, 5th ed. (Englewood Cliffs, NJ: Prentice-Hall, 1982).

2. Ibid. See also: R. Cole, *The Practical Handbook of Public Relations,* (Englewood Cliffs, NJ: Prentice-Hall, 1981).

3. W. Fox and L. Gorov "Filene's Workers Stage First Strike," *Boston Globe* 227 (February 28, 1985) pp. 1, 8.

4. "Store's Newest Item is Really Quite Old," *The Morning Union,* Springfield, MA (May 12, 1984), p. 2.

5. "Statement of Principles," American Society of Newspaper Editors, adopted October 23, 1975.

6. Harlow in Cutlip and Center, *Effective Public Relations;* Cole, *Handbook of Public Relations; J. Donohue, Your Career in Public Relations (New York: Messner, 1967); E. Gottleig and P. Klarnet, Successful Publicity* (New York: Gossett & Dunlap, 1964); W. Lippman, *Public Opinion* (New York: Macmillan, 1950); R. Reilly, *Public Relations in Action* (Englewood Cliffs, NJ: Prentice-Hall, 1981); L. Rubin, *World of Fashion* (New York: Harper & Row, Pub., 1976); J. Schwaninger and J. Aaron, *Tooting Your Own Horn* (New York: National Retail Merchants Association, 1978); J. Schwartz, *The Publicity Process* (Iowa City: Iowa State University Press, 1968); B. G. Yovovich, "Public Relations," *Advertising Age,* 52 (January 5, 1981), pp. S-1, S-4.

7. See Chapter 11.

8. Schwaninger and Aaron, *Tooting Your Own Horn* pp. 46–47.

9. Demographics are discussed in more detail in Chapter 3.

10. "Sears Buyer is Now Product Marketing Manager," *Marketing News,* 11 (June 30, 1978), pp. 1, 6.

11. "CBS Documentary Focuses on Shopping Malls Tonight," *Daily Hampshire Gazette,* Northampton, MA (August 4, 1982), p. 27; "The Malls," *Amherst Bulletin,* Amherst, MA (February 24, 1982), p. 3.

12. Ellen LaFleche, "Price Chopper Praised for Support of the Amherst Survival Center," *Amherst Record* (January 20, 1982), p. 13; "Stores Try Cultural Tack," *Advertising Age,* 53 (Febuary 8, 1982), p. 34E; "Teen Patient Treated to Shopping Spree," *The Morning Union,* Springfield, MA, (June 25, 1984), p. 5; Arthur Unger, "Why It's a Good Idea to Underwrite PBS—the Companies' View," *The Christian Science Monitor* (November 7, 1983), p. B20.

13. This paragraph is a brief summary of Chapter 2 in Cole, *Handbook of Public Relations.*

14. J. Weiss, "PR Industry, Looking Past 'Publicity,' Seeks Clearer Role in Improving Business Ties," *The Christian Science Monitor* (January 11, 1984), p. 11.

The Public Relations Society of America sponsors seminars and conferences which include public relations audits.

15. Robert R. Robichaud, "How to Milk a Store Opening for all it's Worth," *Marketing News* (March 16, 1984), Section 2, p. 8. The store in the example is Computerland in Boston, MA.

16. R. Douglas, "How to Take The Panic Out of Meeting Press," *Advertising Age,* 51 (February 18, 1980), p. 48; "Learning to Shine on TV," *Business Week,* (January 19, 1981), pp. 114–116.

APPENDIX 14

VARIOUS GROUPS WORK TOGETHER FOR MUTUAL BENEFIT: DOWNTOWN REVITALIZATION

xcerpts from a Guide to Downtown Worcester

Erecting a $80 million shopping center replete with 85 stores, a 300-room hotel, a heliport, bus terminal, two high-se office towers, a fine arts civic heater and a 4,000-car parking gaage smack in the middle of the ity's central business district may ave seemed preposterous to Vorcester dwellers in the late 50s—but not to the Worcester Reevelopment Authority.

Edward C. Maher, chairman f the Worcester Civic Center ommission, served as chairman f the Worcester Redevelopment uthority from 1963 through 1969. hough he cites "severe differences f opinion" during the planning f Worcester Center, he says that n the long run, the WRA had "the omplete cooperation of the busiess community of Worcester, as ell as backing by the city manager nd a solid majority of the city council." . . .

Traditions are often hard to relinquish, but as Worcester Center General Manager Karl Augenstein says, "Something had to be done to revitalize the downtown shopping area, or we would have lost all of the retail market to the suburbs where shopping malls were being built." . . .

While the present-day Worcester Center may have strayed slightly from the original plans, there is little doubt in the minds of most businessmen about just how important the shopping mall has been as a catalyst for downtown revitalization. . . .

Augenstein and Marketing Director Carolyn Kennedy readily admit that the Center is only now beginning to "come of age"—providing a tenant mix which complies to industry standards (there must be so many men's stores, women's stores, mixed-merchandise establishments and restaurants in a shopping mall) yet is "custom-tailored" to the needs of Worcester County residents. . . .

Source: This article was in an insert to the *Worcester Magazine,* a free weekly ewspaper published by Central Mass Media, Inc., in Worcester, MA, November 16, 1983, 1.

PART IV

Integrating a Perspective: Managing Marketing Communications

The test of excellent management is excellent results.—L. Rubin

15
PLANNING AND BUDGETING

INTRODUCTION

The marketing communications budget has two major components: the *total* amount that can be spent in a specific time period, for example, a year; and the *allocation* of this total amount across media, specific days, products, and institutional advertising. This budget must be sufficient for carrying out plans of the firm to meet overall company goals as well as marketing communications goals. A given dollar amount can be spent creatively or ineffectively, depending on management knowledge and information about the current and anticipated environment. One way to extend the budget is to coordinate all internal marketing efforts so that the sum of the effort is greater than it would be if the parts worked independently of one another. Another way to extend the budget is to cooperate externally with retailers (if a vendor) and with vendors (if a retailer) to promote, advertise, and sell products through stores.[1]

BUDGETS, PLANS, AND STRATEGIES

The marketing communications budget plan must be consistent with the marketing plan and other plans of the firm. The plan should enable the rm to reach marketing communications and other goals. Before planning ie firm's future, management must analyse where the firm is at present. hen strategies for achieving future goals can be chosen. Both long and hort-term planning are needed for proper timing: when should each goal e achieved? Finally, an evaluation process must be planned to see if ie firm is in fact reaching marketing communications and company oals.

To review, marketing communications goals generally include *wareness*, and *interest* in the firm and its products, desire for these roducts, and finally, the *action* of purchasing them. *AIDA* is one acronym or these goals. Another goal is consumer recognition of products, firms, r messages after exposure to advertisements. Related company goals iclude: having the largest sales in the industry, having larger sales than pecified competitors, increasing or maintaining market share, increasing ales by a specific dollar amount or percentage over last year's sales, emaining in business, and being purchased by a larger firm. Individual oals might include being promoted to a higher position, and not being red.

There seems to be a general consensus on what items should be in n *advertising* budget. The following items should *always* be included n the advertising budget[2]:

Paid advertising space and time in all print and broadcast media

Catalogs and other printed materials, signs for window displays

Administrative salaries, consulting fees, travel expenses of salespersons and others when on work for the advertising department, and office supplies used exclusively in advertising

Production supplies and expenses: art, photos, broadcast production, display installation

hese items *sometimes* belong in advertising accounts: overhead expenses uch as rent, heat, light, and phone; depreciation; research; samples; remiums; and cooperative fund allowances. And these items *never* belong n the advertising account: package manufacture, salespersons' cars and ther expenses, showrooms, annual reports, and charitable donations.

These lists, which apparently originated about 1960 in *Printers Ink*, ontain many "sometimes" and "never" items which are now considered art of marketing communications.[3] Marketing communications is a broader rea than advertising; its components are mentioned here and in other hapters in this book. Therefore, while using these lists as a reminder f what expenses are involved in marketing communications, the individual rm should budget communications into whatever account that reveals learly what is being spent for communications as opposed to other xpenses. A budget is a guide, planned in advance.

The marketing communications budget would also include:

Sales promotion expenditures including special events
Visual merchandising costs
Costs for public relations and publicity
Payroll costs and overhead for all the above categories
Note: *Salespersons' salaries are usually in a separate account.*

Two areas that some firms include in this budget are (1) boxes shopping bags, printed wrapping paper, and gift certificates, and (2 marketing communications research and development. Some firms charge packaging and stationery to a "supplies" category that also includes pens gummed labels, and other such supplies. Others reason that wrapping printed with a store name constitute a form of advertising. Manufacturer tend to charge packaging design to marketing budgets, and packaging itself to product costs.

Some believe that marketing communications research and devel opment is an overall management cost. As such, it should be charged to general overhead because it supports a broad range of decision-making It also helps maintain the firm's position in the community and among competitors. Others believe that this research is directly related to marketing communications. Allocating packaging and research costs is an admin istrative and accounting problem.

VARIOUS APPROACHES TO BUDGETING

The many approaches to budgeting can be arranged into these categories percentage of sales, adjustment for inflation, competitive parity, affordable residual, objective and task, and modeling. The actual names used for these categories sometimes vary, but the concepts do not. Because each category has advantages and disadvantages, it is advisable to use whatever mixture of categories will best help a firm to achieve its marketing com munications goals. Consultants and advertising agencies are available to offer advice about setting budget amounts. Some money can be set aside to use in experiments for getting information about advertising effectiveness of new and untried ideas. Some money should be set aside for contingencies.

Percentage of Sales

A widely used advertising budgeting device is to use some percentage of past or anticipated sales for the marketing communications or advertising budget. This is a very simple device, and enables marketers to compare their percentages with industry percentages. The problem with this ap proach is that a particular firm at a particular point in time may not ısemble the average firm. For example, a new firm or product may need dditional advertising, while a mature firm or product might need less dvertising than does the average. Promotional stores do more advertising nd sales promotions and thus need to spend a higher percentage of ıeir total sales on marketing communications (about 10%; 5% on adertising) than do conventional stores (about 7%, 3% on advertising). tores that have several branches in one area tend to have relatively ɔwer ad/sales percentages because all branches can benefit from the same dvertising.

Results of recent research about how much to spend on advertising eveals some guidelines related to the percent-of-total-sales approach. irms should spend more than the normal percent-of-sales allocation to ıaintain a higher market share, to advertise new products, to compete ı fast-growing markets, to utilize unused plant capacity, when the unit rice of the product is low or when price is an important factor in the urchase decision, for higher quality products, for standardized products, nd for a broad product line.[4]

Advertising/sales and advertising/margin ratios for selected industries re shown in Exhibit 15-1.[5] The exhibit shows that phonograph records, ıail-order houses, perfumes, drugs, soaps, and toys had the largest adertising/sales ratios for 1984. The lowest advertising/sales ratios were ɔr grocery, auto, and drug retailers; jewelry; and auto manufacturers. *Margin* is defined as *net sales minus cost of goods sold*. Phonograph ecord, perfume, toy, and soap manufacturers, mail-order houses, and ousehold appliance and furniture stores had the largest advertising-to-ıargin ratios in 1984.

These advertising-to-sales ratios are convenient yardstick figures. Iowever, there is no magic budget percentage that works for all firms, ven all of a given type, for three major reasons: cost and frequency of ommunication, quality of allocation among media, and competition and ppropriateness to the environment.

It is easy, but dangerous, to infer that the advertising to sales ratio ɔr a given industry always affords enough advertising to insure meeting he sales goals of a particular firm at a particular time. But sales also espond to other factors than advertising, such as how merchandise price nd quality compares to competitors', other marketing communications elative to competitors, immigration and emigration of customers from he market area, favorable or unfavorable publicity, weather, and non-ecurring events such as road construction, or strikes in trucking, transortation, or newspaper. Further, when an ad budget is determined as set percentage of sales, past sales are in effect determining present dvertising budgets.

Different stages in the advertising life cycle for different products equire different amounts of advertising. Stages include: the *unadvertised*

EXHIBIT 15-1 Selected Industry Ad/Sales and Ad/Margin Ratios

Source: Computed from 10-K reports filed by publicly owned companies with SEC, these figures include media and non-media spending (production and collateral literature). Schonfeld and Associates, management consultants in Evanston, IL 60201, *Advertising Age*, 56 (July 15, 1985), p. 39, and 55 (August 13, 1984), p. 44. Reprinted with permission from the July 15, 1985, and August 13, 1984, issues of *Advertising Age*. Copyright 1985 and 1984 by Crain Communications, Inc.

		PERCENTAGES			
		AD EXPENDITURE/NET SALES		AD EXPENDITURE/(NS − CGS)	
SIC CODE	FOUR-DIGIT SIC INDUSTRY	'83	'84	'83	'84
2065	Candy and other confectionary	6.9	6.6	17.5	17.1
2086	Bottled/canned soft drinks	5.9	6.5	11.9	12.5
2300	Apparel and other finished products	3.5	3.8	10.8	11.9
2510	Household furniture	1.9	2.1	6.5	6.9
2830	Drugs	8.4	8.9	14.0	14.6
2841	Soap and other detergents	7.4	7.5	17.9	18.9
2844	Perfumes, cosmetics, toiletries	9.0	11.5	15.2	19.3
3630	Household appliances	2.5	2.9	9.6	10.3
3652	Phonograph records	21.1	22.5	46.5	50.7
3711	Motor vehicles and car bodies	1.6	1.9	8.8	10.7
3911	Jewelry/precious metals	3.5	.7	9.3	3.9
3940	Toys and amusement sport goods	6.7	7.3	16.7	18.0
5311	Department stores	3.1	3.3	13.1	13.5
5331	Variety stores	2.1	2.2	7.2	8.0
5411	Grocery stores	1.3	1.4	5.8	6.0
5500	Auto dealers and gas stations	1.4	1.6	5.8	5.7
5600	Apparel and accessories stores	2.4	2.0	6.1	5.2
5621	Womens ready-to-wear stores	2.1	2.0	6.3	6.1
5661	Shoe stores	1.6	2.0	4.0	5.5
5712	Furniture stores	6.8	7.1	17.0	18.2
5722	Household appliance stores	5.4	5.7	19.3	19.0
5812	Eating places	3.2	3.7	15.4	15.8
5912	Drug and proprietary stores	1.8	1.6	6.9	6.1
5944	Jewelry stores	5.8	6.2	15.1	15.9
5949	Sewing and needlework stores	4.4	4.0	8.6	7.9
5691	Mail order houses	17.1	15.3	39.7	38.8
5995	Retail computer stores	2.8	3.7	10.6	12.6
7011	Hotels/motels	2.6	2.6	10.0	9.7
7990	Service/miscellaneous amusement/recreation	4.4	4.4	14.5	15.7

Note: NS − CGS is margin, i.e., net sales minus cost of goods sold.

stage where profit margins are high, the *initial* advertising stage where the margin is medium, the *growth* stage where the margin is low, and the *maturity* stage where the margin varies with the type of merchandise. At the maturity stage, the margin can occasionally be very low for manufacturers' brands, and high for private-label merchandise.[6] At each stage, the retailer and the manufacturer may have different advertising tasks.

he extent of the retailer's budget in part depends on how effective the ıanufacturer's advertising is for a particular product.

djustments for Inflation

nother part of setting a budget is to adjust for changes in inflation. oing so assumes that the marketer wants to stay even with previous ears' accomplishments. One problem with this approach is deciding hat index to use to measure inflation. Media and other costs do not ecessarily keep pace with aggregate indices. For example, the consumer rice index is expected to be up 5.2% in 198X, and the gross national roduct is expected to be up 4.9%. In 198X, media costs per thousand ersons reached (cpm) are expected to increase 8% for network television nd newspapers and 6% for spot TV and magazines. Trends in cpm since 967 show that network television, newspapers, outdoor media, direct ıail, and spot TV costs have increased more than have network radio, ıagazine, and spot radio costs. To afford the advertising that a nationally istributed grocery package product firm bought for $5 million in 1974, firm would have to spend $14.7 million in 198X.[7]

ompetitive Parity

he *competitive parity* method of setting advertising budgets is to do hat the competition is doing. Advertising spending in *measured* media published so that competitors can monitor each other's spending in ıeasured media. A variation of this technique is to aim at only a certain ercentage of total competitive spending for a particular product. However, umerical information about advertising expenditures carries no information about creativity and effectiveness. It does not tell whether comıercials, time slots, or media are effective. Also, it does not tell what ompetitors are planning to do in the future.

ffordable Residual

he *affordable residual* is to find out how much money is left after llocating all other expenditures for the firm, to reserve some funds for profit contribution, and to allocate the remaining funds to advertising. his is sometimes called the *all-we-can-afford* method. This method nplies that advertising is not very important and that it deserves only ıe leftovers. On the other hand, the affordable approach, when applied) an entire budget of which advertising is a part, forces one to set riorities and to do the most important tasks first.

bjective and Task Method, and Some Models

he *objective and task* method begins with deciding on what has to be one and then identifies how much that job will cost. This is the reverse of deciding how much you have to spend and then deciding what jobs to do. A problem with this method is that one might lose sight of coordinating specific tasks within the overall strategy of the firm.

Various quantitative models of response to advertising are available to determine estimates of advertising effectiveness. These models include sales forecasting models, game theory models, dynamic models of sales response to advertising, which are modifications of the Vidale-Wolfe model and consider advertising decay over time; and marginal cost/marginal revenue models. In the marginal models, an additional dollar budgeted for advertising is supposed to generate at least an additional dollar of effectiveness. This concept is attractive in theory; however, measuring the effect of an extra dollar is difficult in practice.[8]

ALLOCATING THE BUDGET

Individual media-advertising budgets can be broken down in completely different ways for different types of firms. Allocations can be divided by products, geographic regions, time, or media. For example, some firms might spend as much as 85% of their advertising appropriation for newspapers if that medium produces the best results for them. Others, who use radio and television effectively, might reduce the share of the advertising budget allocated to newspapers. Still others may discover after trial and error, or marketing research, that direct mail is the most efficient for them, so that they spend the largest share of their advertising budget for this category. There is no one absolute marketing rule that covers all situations, except that messages should be placed in media vehicles to which target customers respond.[9] Successful firms have always adapted their budget allocations to their specific environments, needs, times, and competitive situations.

Allocations may differ for departments within a store and for different store sizes. Exhibit 15-2 shows sales promotion costs as a percentage of sales for selected departments in department stores. These percentages range from a median of 1.7% for women's and misses sportswear in the larger stores to 6.3% for furs and fur garments in the smaller stores. The figures are sent in by participating stores and are subject to definitions of "sales promotion" used by these stores. The National Retail Merchants Association suggests that these figures probably include advertising and special promotions.

Median and *superior* percentages are included in Exhibit 15-2 for comparison. A store having the *median* percentage or above is in the top half of the reporting stores. A store having the *superior* percentage or above is in the top quarter of the reporting stores. The *superior* percentages are 1.1% and 2.8% for sportwear and fur departments respectively.

EXHIBIT 15-2 Sales Promotion Costs and Selling Salaries as Percentage of Sales for Department Stores by Selected Classifications

Source: *MOR 1983 Merchandising and Operating Results* (New York: National Retail Merchants Association, 1983), pp. 5, 29, 89.

Departmental Merchandising and Operating Results of 1982
Summary of All Department Stores—Sales Over $1 Million

DEPT. OR DEMAND CENTER OR SUB CENTER	DESCRIPTION	NO. RPTG CO'S	SALES PROMOTION COSTS (NET) % OF SALES		SELLING SALARIES % OF SALES (MAIN OR LARGEST SELLING UNIT)		
			Median	Superior	Median	Superior	
	UPSTAIRS DEPARTMENTS						
0100	TOTAL ALL SHOES	47	3.3	2.3	10.2	7.3	
1000	TOTAL ADULT FEMALE APPAREL	101	3.3	2.4	7.2	5.9	
1101	SUMMARY WOMENS & MISSES COATS & SUITS	84	3.8	2.9	7.0	5.8	
1110	WOMENS & MISSES DRESSY & TAILORED COATS	69	3.7	2.6	6.7	5.8	
1210	WOMENS & MISSES JACKETS, CASUAL & ALL WEATHER COATS	55	3.8	2.7	6.4	5.1	
1310	WOMENS & MISSES SUITS	40	4.7	3.3	7.5	5.6	
1401	FURS AND FUR GARMENTS	32	6.3	2.8	8.3	6.2	
1501	SUMMARY ALL DRESSES-EXCEPT JUNIORS	91	3.4	2.3	8.1	6.6	
1601	SUMMARY WOMENS & MISSES SPORTSWEAR	101	2.6	2.0	6.9	5.4	
1620	WOMENS & MISSES SPECTATOR SPORTSWEAR	48	3.7	3.0	7.3	5.1	
1630	WOMENS & MISSES ACTIVE SPORTSWEAR	47	2.8	1.9	6.0	5.1	
7610	CHINA	59	4.9	3.3	9.0	7.6	
7660	GLASSWARE	57	4.4	2.8	9.0	7.5	
7700	SILVERWARE	68	3.9	2.5	8.9	7.8	
7800	LAMPS & LIGHTING FIXTURES	68	4.7	3.3	8.6	7.3	
7801	SUMMARY—PICTURES, MIRRORS, CLOCKS & MISCELL DECORATIONS	42	3.5	2.0	9.8	7.7	
8000	TOTAL—HOME FURNISHINGS: APPLIANCES & UTILITY EQUIPMENT	97	3.8	2.7	8.3	7.0	
9000	TOTAL—DOMESTICS, DRAPERIES & HOME GOODS	99	4.1	3.0	8.7	7.7	

Departmental Merchandising and Operating Results of 1982
Department Stores—Sales $5-10 Million

	UPSTAIRS DEPARTMENTS						
1000	TOTAL ADULT FEMALE APPAREL	14	2.1	1.7	8.9	7.2	
1101	SUMMARY WOMENS & MISSES COATS & SUITS	10	2.8	1.8	9.7	6.3	
1501	SUMMARY ALL DRESSES—EXCEPT JUNIORS	14	1.9	1.5	10.2	6.6	
1530	ALL WOMENS DRESSES	7					
1540	ALL MISSES DRESSES	6					
1601	SUMMARY WOMENS & MISSES SPORTSWEAR	14	1.7	1.1	8.2	7.7	
1701	SUMMARY JUNIOR COATS & SUITS	7					
1801	ALL JUNIOR DRESSES	10	2.5	1.9	6.6	5.2	
1901	SUMMARY JUNIOR SPORTSWEAR	10	2.4	1.6	7.8	6.5	

Generally, the superior percentages are about 2% and 3% for the smaller stores and slightly under 2% for the larger stores shown in this exhibit.

These percentages are affected by both the advertising numerator and the sales denominator of the ad/sales ratio. If sales are large, the denominator is large, so that a small ratio can still yield a large sum for advertising. For example, if annual sales are $8 million and the budgeted amount is 1%, $80,000 is available for advertising. This may be too much. On the other hand, if sales are $80,000, a 1% budget allocation would allow only $8,000 for annual advertising, which may be too little. As does a financial investor, the marketing manager might have a portfolio of budgeted percentages for various merchandise categories, increasing or decreasing absolute dollar budgets in each category as needed.

Exhibit 15-2 also provides information about median and superior *selling salaries* as a percentage of sales. These percentages are much higher than the sales promotion percentages. The fact that selling salaries/sales is a larger ratio than promotion/sales emphasizes the importance of using retail sales personnel effectively. In department and specialty stores of both sizes in Exhibit 15-2, medians for selling expense/sales range from 6% to 10%; superior percentages range from 5% to 7%.

Exhibit 15-3 shows the sales promotion/sales ratios for five department-store and two specialty-store size categories for which merchandising and operating (MOR) information is available. The only categories comparable over all store sizes and types are total adult female apparel (A) and total adult female intimate apparel (B), as shown in Exhibit 15-3. These and other merchandise categories are listed in Exhibit 15-2. Medians range from 2.7% to 3.5% over all stores, with the superior

EXHIBIT 15-3 **"Sales Promotion"* Costs as Percent of Sales, in Selected Stores.**
Source: MOR 1983 Merchandising and Operating Results (New York: National Retail Merchants Association, 1983), pp. ix, x, 5, 9, 55, 59, 89. 107, 121, 143, 169, 225.

MERCHANDISE CODE	*DEPARTMENT STORES IN SALES CATEGORY*										*SPECIALTY STORES IN SALES CATEGORY*			
	OVER $1 MILLION		*$10–$20 MILLION*		*$20–$50 MILLION*		*$50–$100 MILLION*		*OVER $100 MILLION*		*OVER $1 MILLION*		*OVER $500 MILLION*	
TYPE	*M*	*S*	*M*	*S*	*M*	*S*	*M*	*S*	*M*	*S*	*M*	*S*	*M*	*S*
A	3.3	2.4	3.0	3.2	2.7	2.3	3.3	2.8	3.9	3.4	2.7	1.9	2.8	2.3
B	3.0	2.2	3.0	2.6	3.1	2.2	3.5	3.0	3.5	2.9	3.5	2.4	na	na

M = median; S = superior. Stores above median are those in the top half of the total stores reporting; stores above superior are those in the top quarter.
A = Total Adult Female Apparel, category 1000; B = Total Adult Female Intimate Apparel and Accessories, category 2000.

Note: Breakdowns are available for certain store types and sizes shown in Exhibits 15-1 and 15-2; however, the above are the only figures comparable over all store sizes and types for sales promotion. The ratios in the table above represent the net cost of sales promotion expense as a percentage of net sales. Net sales are gross sales less customer returns and allowances.

** Sales promotion is not defined, but probably includes advertising and special promotions.*

percentages ranging from 1.9% to 3.2%. These figures are only guides to indicate some general tendency of what responding stores are doing, not necessarily what they should be doing. Imaginative budgeting calls for occasional experimentation. Appendix 15 has a sample store budget allocation plan.

Allocation Concepts in Budgeting

Money does not talk; it helps marketing communications to talk. The National Retail Merchants Association has developed various budget planning charts, explanations, publications, and software directories to help retailers with budget allocations. Media and the Small Business Association also offer advice.[10]

Many department and specialty store retailers have defined and numbered their departments to correspond to the MOR (Merchandising Operating Results) categories discussed earlier. This allows them to make detailed comparisons of their own percentages with the median and superior percentages published by MOR for particular store sizes and types.

An *allocation-over-time* (or *product*) concept works on a seasonal (or merchandise) basis. For example, if the month of May produces 17% of annual sales for a store, then May receives 17% of the year's advertising budget. If apparel accounts for 50% of sales, then apparel gets 50% of the advertising budget. An allocation criterion for space in catalogs would require profit per inch to be the same for all merchandise.[11]

A related approach is that the advertising money should be spent on the merchandise that has the best chance of being sold at a particular time of year. As a result of this system, definite patterns develop and often continue. Therefore, results can be compared from year to year. For example, most Northern stores that sell apparel have run coat sales during the month of October, taking advantage of the Columbus Day holiday and the approach of cold weather. This allows them to evaluate and compare Columbus Day coat sales figures over a period of years and to determine if there are long-range trends in this category of merchandise. It also allows the stores to compare their sales with other stores that also run these annual events. Recently, some stores have had coat sales in June to reduce inventories and acquire cash.

Innovative versus Habitual Budget Allocations

If innovation gets better results, it makes no sense to continue past patterns. Because marketers tend to use preceding years' patterns as guidelines, it takes conscious effort to change. For example, alert managers may notice that the young families living in the area have grown older, or children have left to form their own households elsewhere. This means that the number of persons in each age category has changed. The biggest age category to watch is the Baby Boomer category of persons born immediately after World War II. As the age distribution of the population changes, merchandise and advertising allocations need to be shifted from toys and teen products to middle-aged adult needs. Other causes of changed allocations include less building of new housing in the relevant area and fewer people moving in. These changes may reduce customer interest in basic furnishings and appliances for homes. New celebrities, new movies, and new technology generate new products, such as personal home computers, which can be advertised, and which should be displayed and promoted. New technology makes some media vehicles less expensive than they have been, thus stretching the advertising dollar in one direction as inflation shrinks it in another.

When firms believe in holding pretty strictly to planned budget totals, the marketing manager can still shift expenditures from one category to another within the overall budget. In larger firms, budgets can become a matter of in-house politics as divisional and departmental managers fight to retain their share of the pie even when the situation indicates that relative shares should change. What may have been an important seller a year ago may be a poor advertising investment this year.

Unfortunately, retailing has been one of the most conservative of all businesses. Generally, stores shoot for last year's sales and figures, repeating whatever was done last year with some slight variations in the hope that the figures can somehow be improved. Each department is run on the basis of last year's sales. "Beat last year's figure" is the Bible of these retailers, and the way to do it is to do what you did last year, only better. Thus many retailers get into a rut, repeating the same pattern year after year, even when a change would improve sales. This concept goes so far as to virtually match ad for ad in the same media vehicles as were used the prior year. If the advertising rate for a media vehicle has increased from a year ago, the tendency is to cut the size of the ad slightly to stay within the budget. Keeping a budget allocation pattern when it needs to be changed to meet the demands of a new situation can interfere with achieving objectives.

Only by watching current trends and competitors' actions, and by budgeting a speculative amount for innovations will marketers discover new opportunities to feature new items in different media and so increase their sales. By creative allocation of marketing communications dollars through experimentation and testing, marketers can gain momentum over their competitors. Economists and marketing research firms have developed sophisticated models for these relationships. A good general approach is a heuristic, pragmatic, seat-of-the-pants approach: keep what works and replace what does not work through educated trial and error.[12] Strategic use of the publicity generated through press releases and newsworthy actions can make advertising more effective. Often the only cost of creativity is the imagination of existing personnel.

Category Interactions

A budget, like a consumer's perception of a firm, is a gestalt. It is a sum total of what is available for spending. Within the total are various interactions. There are many situations in which advertising a particular promotion and providing supporting displays and press releases for it can create a great deal of traffic and generate sales. When sales promotion is teamed with advertising, it is especially strong. The *interactions* achieved here, if they do not require resources beyond the separate efforts, are like free bonuses, sometimes called *synergistic*. The whole communications effect becomes greater than the effect of uncoordinated separate efforts—but costs no more than the separate efforts.

However, management must implement the coordination effectively—the whole can also be *less* effective than the separate efforts. For example, if advertising brings customers into a store, but uninformed, unmotivated salespeople send them away frustrated, the advertising money is in effect wasted. For manufacturers, advertising can get people to try a product, but if product quality is unacceptable, or if the advertising induces people who will not like the product to buy it anyway, there will be few repeat purchases, regardless of future advertising. Expectations generated by advertising about service, image, and product quality must be met. Advertising and other marketing communications must convey appropriate messages to appropriate targets.

Budgeting Steps[13]

The National Retail Merchants Association has developed a master budget planning chart. This chart has room for last year's percentage-of-sale allocations by media, materials, and payroll categories; for past and projected sales; and for this year's plans for each month. Exhibit 15-4 shows excerpts from this chart. The first step in budgeting is to enter last year's figures in the chart, as well as six-month and yearly totals. A record of past experience can be accumulated by saving these charts from year to year. With modern microcomputers, this information can be saved and used to generate averages and charts to depict past experience, helping to guide managers in making future plans. For example, annual salaries, newspaper space costs, direct mail, and other categories in the chart can be plotted over time to see which are increasing more than others. Management can then decide how to adjust for the differences.

The next step is to enter the six-month and annual sales goals for the planning year on the chart—in pencil, if they are to be revised during the planning process. National and regional monthly sales as percentages

EXHIBIT 15-4 Monthly Planning Chart for Budgeting Marketing Communications

Source: *Marketing–Sales Promotion–Advertising Planbook* (New York: National Retail Merchants Association, 1984), pp. 10–11.

MASTER BUDGET

		Salaries	Newspapers	Periodicals & Programs	Shows & Exhibits	Supplies	Cuts, Art, & Mats	Television	Radio	Direct Mail	Display Supplies	Display Payroll	Reserve	Total Publicity Expense	SALES
JAN	1983														
	%														
	1984														
	%														
FEB	1983														
	%														
	1984														
	%														
MARCH	1983														
	%														
	1984														
	%														
APRIL	1983														
	%														
	1984														
	%														

of annual sales are available for the following types of stores: durable goods stores, non-durable goods stores, department stores, apparel stores, furniture stores, furniture and appliance stores, and drug and proprietary stores. This information is also available for other store types on the national level, and for specified large states and standard metropolitan statistical areas. Examples of charts with monthly sales percentages for some store types are in Exhibit 15-5.

Having decided on allocations per month, managers now need to decide how much and what kinds of marketing communications are needed to reach the sales goals each month. This is the objective and task concept mentioned above. Managers should allocate the funds available for communications in a six-month period over the categories in Exhibit 15-5.

Then the six-month total store budget must be broken into individual months, keeping in mind that some months have higher sales than others. NRMA points out that retailers spend slightly less than some aggregate percentage of sales in December and slightly more in January, February,

EXHIBIT 15-4 **(continued)**

PLANNING CHART

Month	Year	Salaries	Newspapers	Periodicals & Programs	Shows & Exhibits	Supplies	Cuts, Art, & Mats	Television	Radio	Direct Mail	Display Supplies	Display Payroll	Reserve	Total Publicity Expense	SALES
JULY	1983														
	%														
	1984														
	%														
AUG	1983														
	%														
	1984														
	%														
SEPT	1983														
	%														
	1984														
	%														
OCT	1983														
	%														
	1984														
	%														
NOV	1983														
	%														
	1984														
	%														
DEC	1983														
	%														
	1984														
	%														

and July. This may mean that since sales in December are high, a relatively smaller percentage of sales yields a relatively large amount of dollars for marketing communications. On the other hand, in months of low sales, the standard percentage might not yield sufficient dollars to accomplish even a minimal marketing communications task effectively. However, as mentioned previously, the best returns are achieved when money is spent at a time when sales expectations are the greatest.

Since it is difficult to predict marketing communications costs as much as a year ahead, budgeters should have a reserve for contingencies: new merchandise that may need promoting, special institutional advertising, new special events, and unexpected community contributions.

EXHIBIT 15-5 Graphs of Retail Sales by Month and Type of Store (Percent of the Year's Total Sales Done Each Month)

Source: Marketing–Sales Promotion–Advertising Planbook (New York: National Retail Merchants Association, 1984), p. 54.

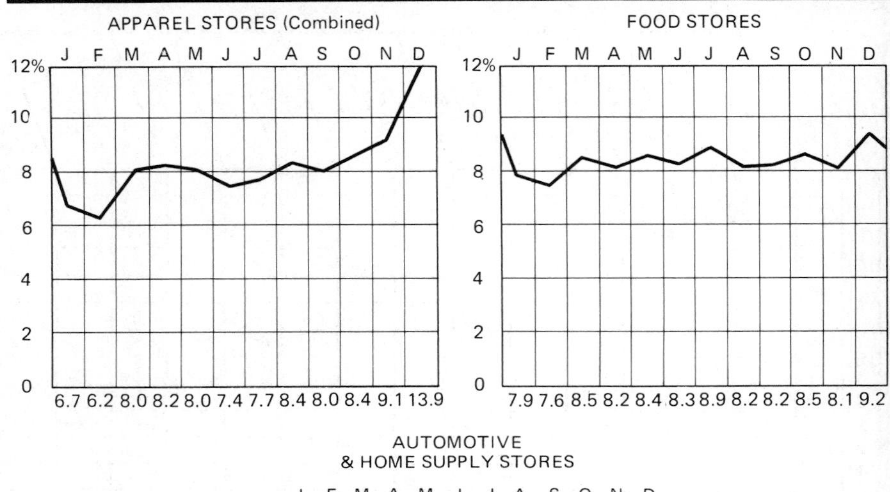

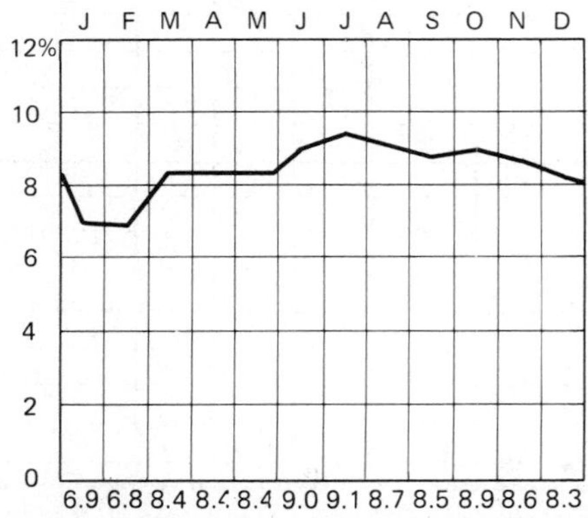

Some budgets have a contingency reserve from 10% to 20% of estimated budgets.

Six-month appropriations should then be allocated by department or merchandise categories, with the intention of promoting the healthy departments and hot categories most; weak ones less; sick ones least. Then budgeters should compare advertising expenditures as a percentage of sales with the percentages shown in Exhibits 15-1, 15-2, 15-3, and 15-5. In making these comparisons, budgeters should analyse to what extent a particular operation is "comparable," to explain why a particular firm's percentages do or do not match industry percentages.

Major promotions for each month should be planned six months in advance. A balanced overall portfolio approach is desirable. This includes prestige promotions like fashion shows and store brand promotions, sales of subsets of the store merchandise, and storewide events like anniversary sales, dollar days, and storewide clearances. About six to eight weeks in advance, managers should enter on the monthly calendar the specific advertising plans for all media vehicles, including the costs and the times of ads.[14] Plans for coordinating window displays and other special displays should also be entered, leaving room for the unexpected—special purchases or tie-ins with unexpected local events. Finally, the daily advertising should be prepared.

Buyers and merchandise managers should always make sure that there will be enough advertised merchandise to cover the ads. Advertising and other marketing communications cannot sell merchandise unless the merchandise is available when the customer responds. If for any reason the merchandise will not be on hand on the advertised date, that advertisement should be cancelled.

COOPERATIVE ADVERTISING

One way to extend an advertising budget is through cooperative advertising, in which vendors reimburse retailers for some expense of advertising brand-name products, usually media time and space. Such funding can help both parties, depending on how creatively each party uses it. The primary purpose of cooperative advertising is to sell the merchandise, but of course, retailers want the merchandise sold in *their* stores, not in those of competitors. This involves effectively communicating and emphasizing store name, location, and hours while also presenting the vendor's strong product offers. But retailers should remember that manufacturers offer cooperative funds to move their merchandise, and both parties share the retail advertising cost to accomplish that mutual goal.[15]

The question of whether or not to use cooperative funds has generated much literature. The literature points out that vendors are interested in having retailers order their products, stock them heavily in inventory, promote, advertise, display, and sell them. Once the retailer has the vendor's brand in inventory, the retailer has incentive to sell the brand to get funds to buy still more merchandise. Thus cooperative funds are an incentive that manufacturers and wholesalers use to induce retailers to stock vendor brands. Because manufacturers and retailers do have somewhat different objectives, it is important for each party to make objectives clear to the other party, and for each party to understand the others' needs and goals.[16]

Vendors and Cooperative Funding[17]

Manufacturers who want brand recognition promote their merchandise through strong national advertising so that potential customers recognize these brands when they are featured by a store. Manufacturers must treat budget decisions for *national* advertising and for *cooperative* advertising separately. The former builds the brand image and tells about the product; the latter tells where and when the branded merchandise is available. The more the sale of a product depends on the retailers' marketing communications, image, and in-store activities, the more cooperative funding incentives should be given to retailers by manufacturers. These funds are usually allocated according to the amount of brand-name merchandise retailers buy for resale. Therefore, retailers should use this funding only when the total amount available for advertising a brand is adequate for effective retail advertising.[18]

To get the cooperation of busy retailers, vendors need simple, flexible cooperative funding programs. Getting the retailer to spend even two-thirds of a co-op allowance is rare for a first-time cooperation. By law all retailer customers of a vendor must be notified if a co-op program is available. But this does not mean that all relevant retailers understand the program's rules and benefits. If retailers fully understood cooperative funding, there would be no need for NRMA to include co-op advertising information in its *Sales Promotion Planbook*, or to suggest questions for retailers to ask manufacturers about cooperative funding.[19] These questions are in Exhibit 15-6.

Getting retailers to use co-op funds effectively involves education, simple rules, and a user-friendly reporting system. NRMA suggests that retailers send a request like that in Exhibit 15-6 to their leading suppliers or ask their sales representatives to get the information requested. This information includes (1) the percentage of net purchases available for cooperative funding and the period in which this percentage is effective, for example, ("3% of net purchases in the last calendar year"); (2) the amount of the advertising allowance; (3) whether the manufacturer pays 50%, 75%, or 100% of media time and space, (4) the time limits in which the ad should appear, (5) the proof of performance required and when the proof is due, and (6) restrictions, if any.[20]

After receiving this information, retailers can calculate how much co-op money is available per product and total, and the matching retail funds required. Then retailers can allocate co-op dollars on a monthly basis, in rough proportion to sales of that product each month. By submitting invoices and proof of advertising promptly, the retailer should receive prompt payment. A co-op claim form suggested by a manufacturer for ads in newspapers and tabloids is shown in Exhibit 15-7. This claim form saves retailers the time and trouble of filling out a separate form

EXHIBIT 15-6 Request Form for Co-op Advertising Information
Source: *Marketing–Sales Promotion–Advertising Planbook* (New York: National Retail Merchants Association, 1984), p. 68.

Co-op Advertising Information Request

Date

Manufacturer's Name

Home Office Address

I am budgeting a yearly advertising program for my store. In order to take advantage of any Co-op Advertising allowances offered by vendors supplying me, I would appreciate your filling out the following information and returning it to me by

Date

Cordially,

1. Does your company offer a co-op allowance that I qualify for? YES NO
2. If answer to question #1 is YES, and your company has a printed Co-op Program, simply send the program and answer only those questions *not* covered in your printed plan. If NO, please return the entire form to me in the enclosed envelope.
3. What is the basis of accrual of co-op funds? (Example: 3% of net purchases, 5% of net purchases, open end or 50¢ per unit, etc.)
4. What is the time period that the accrual is based on? (Example: based on last calendar year's purchases.)
5. How much ad allowances, based on my purchases, have I available to spend?
6. Please stipulate whether your Co-op Program is on a 50/50 — 75/25 — 100% paid, or a fixed rate basis.
7. What are the time limits in which the Co-op must appear in radio, television, or newspapers, to insure your company's participation?
8. What "proof of performance" does your co-op plan require?
9. How soon after an ad is published or broadcast must we submit "proof of performance" to your company and whom do we mail it to in order to get paid?
10. What requirements does your company have in order for us to comply with their co-op plan.
11. Are there any restrictions in your co-op plan?

If your company has a printed Co-Op Plan and/or retail advertising kit, will you please enclose it with this form and mail it to me today.

for each newspaper and tabloid, and reminds them of the information required for reimbursement.[21]

Co-op Jargon and Rules

Some co-op jargon is shown in Exhibit 15-8. Here are some of the most important phrases: *Clear separation* is a layout specification which requires a clear separating line between the different brands shown in an ad. Using *competing merchandise* from different manufacturers in one ad must follow the manufacturers' guidelines to qualify for co-op funds. *Graduated percent participation* means that as the number of ads increase, the manufacturer increases the percentage reimbursed. For example, 50% is paid for the first ad, 75% for the second, and 100% for the third. *Unlimited accrual plans,* also called *unlimited co-op plans,* reimburse retailers for a fixed percentage of the cost no matter how little merchandise is purchased from the manufacturer or how many of the retailer's ads feature this merchandise. *Accrual* plans require specified merchandise sales amounts; *participation* is the percentage of ad cost that the manufacturer will reimburse.[22]

Vendors pay co-op allowances to retailers, and the retailers pay the media bills. By law, manufacturers' co-op programs must be in writing,

EXHIBIT 15-7 **Co-op Claim Form for Print Ads**

Source: Robert D. Wilcox, Account Services Manager, Retail Merchandising Services, Armstrong World Industries, Inc., P.O. Box 3001, Lancaster, PA 17604

(NAME OF RETAILER)

Claim #

Date:

CO-OP CLAIM FOR TABLOID OR MULTIPLE NEWSPAPER ROP ADVERTISING

NOTE ON USE OF THIS FORM: The information on this form permits you to reimburse our claim by showing you what advertising we did. . .the net amount we paid. . .and how we compute the portion owed by you.

1. This is to claim the advertising checked below:

_______ Tabloid newspaper insertion. The attached tabloid, in the same size and with the same content, was inserted on the dates shown, in the newspapers listed on the attached sheet(s). We have totaled the charges made to us by the newspapers used, and we have attached the invoice from each newspaper to support that charge. We have attached the printer's invoice which establishes our printing cost.

_______ Tabloid direct mail or other delivery. The attached tabloid, in the same size and with the same content, was distributed in the quantities and on the dates shown on the attached sheet. We have attached the printer's invoice which establishes our printing cost. We have attached the postal receipts and/or distribution invoices which establish our cost of distribution.

_______ ROP newspaper advertising. Our advertising shown on the attached tear sheet ran on the dates shown, in the newspapers listed on the attached sheet(s). It ran in the same proportion and with the same content in each newspaper shown. We have totaled the charges made to us by the newspapers used, and we have attached the invoice from each newspaper to support that charge.

2. The identity of the tabloid or ROP ad claimed on this form is as follows:

____

3. Our cost for printing and/or distribution was:

a. If tabloid advertising is claimed:

(1) The amount we paid to distribute the tabloid was:

Newspaper insertion: $ __________

Mail distribution: $ __________

Other distribution: $ __________

Total distribution: $ __________

(2) The amount we paid to print the tabloid was: $ __________

Total cost: $ __________

(3) Total pages in the tabloid were __________

(4) Cost per page, therefore, was: $ __________

b. If ROP advertising is claimed, space charges made to us by newspapers for this advertising were:

Total: $ __________

(OVER)

EXHIBIT 15-7 (continued)

4. Our co-op reimbursement claimed is: $ ____________
   Shown below is our computation of your share of space in the tabloid or ROP ad claimed.

5. This is how we compute your share of tabloid page or ROP ad claimed:
   a. Size of your product portion: _____ inches by _____ inches equals _____ sq. in.

   b. Size of total product portion: _____ inches by _____ inches equals _____ sq. in.

   c. Your product's share of product portion (a divided by b): _____%
   d. Cost of tabloid page or ROP ad (as shown on reverse side): $ ____________
   e. Cost of your portion (c times d): $ ____________
   f. Our co-op reimbursement (_____ % times e): $ ____________

____
Signature

____
Typed name and title

EXHIBIT 15-8 Definitions of Selected Terms Used in Co-op Advertising

Source: "Unraveling the Mystery," *Advertising Age*, 52 (August 17, 1981), p. S-2. Reprinted with permission from the August 17, 1981, issue of *Advertising Age*. Copyright 1981 by Crain Communications, Inc.

audit services: *Companies that specialize in auditing co-op ads on behalf of manufacturers; the largest of these is Advertising Checking Bureau, known as ACB. Others are Pinpoint Marketing and Advertising Audit Services.*

barter co-op: *The use of an exchange of merchandise from the manufacturer as barter for using the funds earned from that merchandise to pay for advertising; usually a process used by companies that do not have regular co-op plans.*

co-op action plan (CAP): *A program developed by the Newspaper Advertising Bureau to facilitate handling of newspaper co-op.*

claim period: *The period of time allowed after advertising has been run or a deadline date after which claims cannot be filed; usually 30, 60 or 90 days after ad date.*

clear separation: *A layout specification that requires a clear separating line between products.*

competing merchandise: *Products that directly compete; for example, two different types of men's shirts or two types of motor oil; manufacturers may specify that ads containing competing merchandise do not qualify for co-op reimbursement.*

co-op accrual script: *A process some companies use to notify their retailers of how much money is accrued, either under a bonus plan or their regular co-op plan; usually a small certificate (somewhat like a dollar bill) that states an assigned amount of funds and must be returned with the claim is used.*

electronic tear sheet: *In broadcast, a statement placed on a script telling when and at what cost a commercial was aired. The concept was developed by the Assn. of National Advertisers, in cooperation with the Radio Advertising Bureau and the Television Bureau of Advertising.*

format: *A border or logo design not usin[g] more than 19% of the ad space, whic[h] allows for product art drop-in and th[e] effective use of co-op funds withou[t] losing the retailer's store identity.*

Fred Meyer Corollary: *A court decisio[n] that requires manufacturers an[d] wholesalers to offer the same plan t[o] all advertisers within a market area. [It] also requires that they notify all the[ir] known outlets that the plan is available. They must also provide supportin[g] documentation for reasonable oppor[tunity] to use those co-op funds.*

front-ending: *The process of contactin[g] the manufacturer before an ad is ru[n] and to make sure that the co-op al[lowance] will be paid.*

FTC: *The Federal Trade Commissio[n] competition division is the regulatin[g] agency for co-op.*

graduated percent participation: *A par[ticipation] plan based on the numbe[r] of ads that the advertiser runs; for in[stance], the first ad may be 50% paid[;] second ad 75% paid; third ad 100% paid.*

multiple listing ads: *A single ad with [a] number of dealers or retailers listed a[s] purchase points for consumers to bu[y] the product; this requires those adver[tisers] to use co-op funds jointly to pa[y] for the ad.*

omnibus ad: *An ad format that contain[s] more than one product—usually a stac[k] ad or full-page ad containing a numbe[r] of product elements; this is commo[n] in the drugstore and discount store typ[e] of advertising.*

open-ended: *A method of accrual tha[t] allows for a specific amount of dollar[s] to be accrued with the first purchas[e] of product; for instance, an open-ende[d] plan may provide for a specific dolla[r] allowance per store based on any pur[chase] of a certain product.*

EXHIBIT 15-8 (continued)

participation: *A basic part of a co-op plan that defines the percentage of a specific ad the manufacturer will reimburse so long as the advertiser has sufficient accrual to cover that amount of money.*

qualifying media: *Those media listed in the plan that require no specific approval of their status; normally media that have some type of outside audit.*

rate-based accrual: *A method of determining accrual based on the prevailing media rate; for instance, a plan may allow for 100 in. of advertising at the local earned rate—that amount of money would be available for any media.*

Robinson-Patman Act: *The basic regulatory act covering co-op; outlines the responsibilities of all parties in the process of using co-op funds.*

tear sheet: *In the print media, this is an actual copy of the full page on which the ad appeared and must include the name of the medium and the date of publication.*

tie-in ads: *Co-op ads designed to tie in with national advertising that has been placed in the media by the manufacturer; these ads use local co-op funds to indentify, in separate ads (usually in the same issue), where these products can be purchased.*

unlimited accrual: *A plan that offers unlimited payment of ads at a specific participation percentage no matter how many ads the advertiser wishes to run.*

---

and all retail customers must be treated proportionally equally. Media-vehicle sales representatives often encourage groups of non-competing retailers to pool their co-op allowances and run larger ads for more impact. Vendors tend to resist pooling because while they want their offer of co-op dollars to attract sales of merchandise, they may not always want the retailer to use all available co-op funds. For example, a vendor offers 3% co-op and expects that 2% of the total amount actually will be spent; the larger retailers will spend 3% and many small retailers won't use co-op because the media acceptable to the manufacturers have too much wasted circulation for their stores. The vendor decides what media vehicles are acceptable for co-op. When the cost of newspapers and broadcast media is very high and there is substantial wasted circulation, many vendors allow retailers to use equivalent co-op funds for direct mail or other alternatives. The retailer should get the vendor's co-op agreement in writing as protection in case the vendor's salesperson or contact is transferred or leaves the company.[23]

A manufacturer must offer co-op funds to all retailers who carry a brand in the same area. Unless these retailers differentiate themselves from each other, their advertising mainly supports the manufacturer. However, if the retailer can achieve a differentiation while at the same time following the manufacturers' guidelines, then the co-op funds and other aids extend the retailers' marketing communications budget effectively.

In billing manufacturers for co-op costs, retailers should include (1) publications' invoices for a tabloid insert, (2) postal receipts and copies for mailed tabloids, (3) printers' invoices, copies of direct-mail advertisements, and newspaper and broadcast invoices, (4) tearsheets of print ads and electronic tearsheets which prove the existence of broadcast ads. Retailers may charge vendors for their proportional share of the store headline and logo in a print ad. For example, if an ad measures 100 square inches, six vendors take ten square inches each, and the headline and logo take 40 square inches, then each vendor pays for ten square inches plus 1/6 of the 40 square inches. Vendors should be charged similarly for broadcast mention of store name, location, and image. NRMA suggests a format, shown in Exhibit 15-9, to keep track of co-op dollars owed by vendors for the various media categories.

Not all co-op funds must go to advertising. Some are used for special events and promotions.[24] When the retailer and manufacturer cooperate on a sales promotion event, the event can be integrated with advertising display, publicity, or personal selling. This integrated, cooperative effort tends to build image, position, and traffic, all of which helps both retailer and vendor sell merchandise and develop loyal customers. Funds for such efforts should be agreed upon in advance and in writing.

While some co-op ads are designed by retailers to include the brands of several vendors, other ads are made by vendors and include the names of several retailers. These vendor-generated ads should list cooperating stores by location so that prospective customers easily can find out where to buy the merchandise. On one hand, a retailer may wonder what good it does to be one of a long list of stores in a vendor ad. On the other hand, for a relatively small investment, the retailers listed in these ads communicate that their stores have the advertised merchandise. They also gain from the image generated by the other stores listed in the ad if the other stores have a comparable image. The impact of the larger ad and of the prestige of being associated with other prestige retailers may benefit a retailer more than a small, one-retailer ad.[25]

Being listed in a vendor's ad should be tested to see if it is a good use of the advertising dollar.[26] One way to test the effectiveness of this listing is to have salespeople ask customers who buy the advertised brands if they have seen the ad. Another way is to ask the manufacturer to have a coupon in the ad which can be turned in at cooperating stores for a small discount on the advertised merchandise. Retailers who tend not to use the manufacturer's suggested price should make sure that the manufacturer's ad has a disclaimer which states that price may vary with retailers.

SUMMARY

The marketing communications budget can include appropriations for advertising, sales promotions, visual merchandising, public relations and publicity, including appropriate payroll and overhead. Salespeople's

XHIBIT 15-9 NRMA Form for Posting Co-op Ad Dollars by Vendor and Media
ource: Marketing–Sales Promotion–Advertising Planbook (New York: National Retail Ierchants Association, 1984), p. 69.

Co-operative Advertising Dollars

VENDOR	DOLLARS	MEDIA USAGE				
		NEWS PAPERS	RADIO	DIRECT MAIL	TV	OTHER

ayroll costs are usually in a separate account. A given dollar amount an be spent creatively or ineffectively, depending on a good fit with the xternal environment, and coordination of all internal marketing efforts.

Various approaches to setting the total budget amount include per- entage of sales, adjustment for inflation, competitive parity, affordable esidual, objective and task, and models including the marginal cost- 1arginal revenue model. Because each approach has limitations, a com- ination is recommended for reaching marketing communications goals.

Creative, innovative budgeting allows room for dealing with unexpected threats and taking advantage of opportunities, by reserving funds to try the new and risky, and to deal with contingencies.

The overall budget amount must be allocated over products, over geographic regions, over time periods, and over media and media vehicles. Continuing changes in the environment require managers to reexamine budget amounts and allocations frequently. What succeeded in the past may not be relevant for present and future. A budget advantage of coordinated communications effort is that interactions among advertising, display, sales promotion, publicity, and personal selling create a whole effect that is greater than the sum of the separate effects. When uncoordinated communications tend to work against each other, they waste the time and money spent for them.

Manufacturers and retailers can usually benefit from cooperative advertising if both understand how to use this form of funding. By law, manufacturers must provide written information about their cooperative funding arrangements. Retailers should estimate the potential effect of each vendor's co-op contribution on their sales before participating. An alternative is to participate on a trial basis and then evaluate what happens to sales as a result of this participation. A retailer can be listed as a cooperating store in a vendor ad, can list vendor products in a store ad, or both. The former involves evaluating the pros and cons of being with the other stores on the vendor's list. The latter involves deciding how much help to accept from vendors while maintaining store identity.

QUESTIONS

1. You have a small, independent store in a shopping center. What major items will be in your marketing communications budget? Your neighbor has a small manufacturing firm which sells toys to mass merchandisers. What major items will be in your neighbor's marketing communication budget?
2. Consider the various approaches to budgeting discussed in this chapter: percentage of sales, adjustments for inflation, etc., and suggest a combination of these approaches for (a) a candy manufacturer, (b) a supermarket chain, (c) an apparel store.
3. MOR lists both *median* and *superior* percentages for sales promotion costs and selling salaries as a percentage of sales. How would you use these median and superior percentages to guide your budget planning? Explain.
4. What problems might you face if you planned a marketing communications budget based on quantitative factors only?
5. Explain why innovative budgeting is potentially more profitable than habitual budgeting.
6. Explain why it is important for retailers to plan six-month and monthly budgets instead of weekly or annual budgets.

7. Explain co-op advertising goals from (a) a household appliance manufacturer's point of view, and (b) from a household appliance retailer's point of view.
8. What are the potential dangers for retailers and manufacturers who use co-op advertising, and how can each party avoid the dangers?
9. Your store is one of four in a shopping center that buy the same brand-name merchandise from the Shoretown vendor. Shoretown offers co-op funds for advertising. What can you infer about what co-op support Shoretown offers your competitors in this shopping center? How might you differentiate your store from competitors' stores in the shopping center and still respect Shoretown's guidelines for using the Shoretown co-op funds?

NOTES

1. Herb Zeltner, "Media Budgeting Needs Creative Touch," *Advertising ge,* 55 (November 29, 1984), pp. 3, 46.

2. William H. Bolen, *Advertising,* 2nd ed. (New York: John Wiley, 1984), p. 452–453; Christopher Gilson and Harold W. Berkman, *Advertising Concepts nd Strategies* (New York: Random House, 1980), p. 194; Phillip Kotler, *Marketing lanagement,* 5th ed. (Englewood Cliffs, NJ: Prentice-Hall, 1984), pp. 621–622; enneth E. Runyon, *Advertising,* 2nd ed. (Columbus, OH: Chas. E. Merrill, 1984), . 52.

3. See Bolen, *Advertising,* pp. 452–453.

4. "PIMS Research Answers Question: How Much Should We Spend on dvertising," *Marketing News,* 18 (September 14, 1984), p. 14.

5. See also Exhibit 1-7 in Chapter 1 for Standard Industrial Classifications.

6. Steiner model in Mark S. Albion and Paul W. Farris, The *Advertising ontroversy* (Boston: Auburn House, 1981), p. 146.

7. Robert J. Coen, "Price Increases to Moderate in 1985," *Advertising Age,* 5 (November 29, 1984), pp. 11–13.

See also Zeltner, "Media Budgeting," pp. 3, 46.

8. Gary L. Lilien & Phillip Kotler, *Marketing Decision Making, A Model-uilding Approach* (New York: Harper & Row, 1983).

9. James F. Engel, Hugh G. Wales, and Martin R. Warshaw, *Promotional trategy,* 3rd ed. (Homewood, IL: Irwin, 1975), pp. 218–221; Michael L. Ray, *dvertising and Communication Management* (Englewood Cliffs, NJ: Prentice-all, 1982), p. 165.

See also Chapter 10.

10. *How Do You Plan an Advertising Budget* (Salem, MA: New England ewspaper Association, 1984); *Directory of Retail Software* (New York: National etail Merchants Association, 1984), and software updates in current issues of *larketing News; Marketing–Sales Promotion–Advertising Planbook* (New York: ational Retail Merchants Association, 1984) and annually; Joseph R. Rowen, *'anning and Budgeting Retail Marketing Communications* (New York: National etail Merchants Association, 1981).

11. Vithala Rao and Julian Simon, "Optimal Allocation of Space in Retail dvertisements and Mail Order Catalogs," *International Journal of Advertising,* (April–June, 1983), pp. 123–129.

12. Gary L. Lilien and Philip Kotler, *Marketing Decision Making, A Model Building Approach* (New York: Harper & Row Pub., 1983); Publications of the Marketing Science Institute, Cambridge, MA.

See also Chapter 4 of this book.

13. "Take These Ten Steps to Better Sales Promotion Planning," *Marketing–Sales Promotion–Advertising Planbook,* note 5, pp. 2–3.

14. Monthly calendars in the *Planbook* suggest ideas and dates for promotions. See Exhibit 6-9 in Chapter 6 and Exhibit 11-1 in Chapter 11.

15. R. D. Wilcox, "Co-op Hikes Ad Value for Retailer, Manufacturer," *Advertising Age,* 55 (September 20, 1984), p. 45.

16. Tom Bayer, "Co-op Angering Retailers," *Advertising Age,* 54 (February 7, 1983), p. 58.

See also Chapter 5 of this book.

17. Ed Crimmins, Cooperative Advertising, *Sales & Marketing Management,* 128 (August 16, 1982), pp. 65–68; "Free Suburb Papers Get Co-op Break from FTC," *Advertising Age,* 51 (August 4, 1980), p. 64; Stephen A. Greyser and Robert F. Young, "Follow 11 Guidelines to Strategically Manage Co-op Advertising Program," *Marketing News* 17 (September 16, 1983) 17, Section 1, p. 5; Carroll Shelton, "Watching Out for the Regulations," *Advertising Age,* 52 (August 17, 1981), p. S14.

18. Ann Helming, "Co-op Is No Four-Letter Word to This Agency," *Advertising Age,* 54 (March 7, 1983), pp. M20–M22; "Advertisers Give High Grades to Their Co-op Programs," *Marketing News,* 19 (February 15, 1985), p. 15.

19. Renee Blakkan, "Savory Deals Tempt Hungry Retailers," *Advertising Age,* 54 (March 7, 1983), pp. M9–M11. The Radio Advertising Bureau, Television Bureau of Advertising, and Newspaper Ad Bureau report that co-op funds are used increasingly by retailers but are still relatively unused. These bureaus collect and provide information about cooperative funds.

20. See Exhibit 15-6.

21. Wilcox, "Co-op Hikes Ad Value"; Robert D. Wilcox, "Co-op Advertising," *Advertising Age,* 55 (January 9, 1984), p. M31; Wilcox, "When the Shoe's on the Other Foot," *Advertising Age,* 54 (March 17, 1983), pp. M14–M16.

22. Blakkan, "Savory Deals," and letter from Robert D. Wilcox, Armstrong World Industries, PO Box 3001, Lancaster, PA 17604 to Patricia M. Anderson.

23. *The Co-op Source Directory* (New York: Standard Rate and Data, annual), mentioned in Robert D. Wilcox, "Co-op Ads Raise Many Questions," *Advertising Age,* 55 (May 24, 1984), p. 14.

24. Morris Saffer, "Selling Is the Main Event," *Advertising Age,* 54 (November 14, 1983), p. M48.

25. Wilcox, "Co-op Hikes Ad Value."

26. See Exhibit 5-4 for vendor ad listing stores, and Exhibit 5-6 for store ad listing vendors, in Chapter 5 of this book. Saffer, "Selling Is the Main Event," p. 48.

APPENDIX 15

A SAMPLE STORE BUDGET ALLOCATION PLAN

Allocations for a sample annual advertising budget of $500,000 for a ypical department store located in the center of a city with outlying ranches might be as follows:

Newspaper daily and Sunday ad space	36%
Radio advertising time	9
Television advertising time	5
Direct mail	5
Advertising personnel payroll	30
Operations and production	10

f billboards, transportation ads, and circulars are used, the above figures hould be adjusted. Overhead would be covered in the general store verhead account. To save money, some run of press advertising (ROP) n newspapers or some run of schedule (ROS) in broadcast advertising an be used, but not when it is important to advertise a sale *before* the ale.[1]

Smaller firms that do not have their own internal staffs would charge he cost of outside advertising agencies, display people, and public relations gencies to their marketing communications budgets. Somewhat larger tores with an advertising staff but no public relations people would nclude the cost of an outside public relations firm in the budget. Firms hat require photography and do not have a full-time staff photographer vould charge the services of an outside photographer to the marketing ommunications budget.

Photographers' fees cover their studio space, cameras, lighting quipment, and other overhead. Agencies charge either fees or a set ommission of up to 15% for national advertising. Generally, 15% is onsidered high for retailers because of wasted circulation. *Commission* s a percentage of the media billing for time or space used. The less time r space used, the less money the agency has available to spend on a etailer's work. For example, 10% commission on a billing of $90,000 is 9,000, but 10% commission on a charge of $8000 is only $800. There s an ongoing debate as to whether commission or fee is preferable. There s a growing tendency toward the more flexible fee which allows agency ffort to match the advertising task. Another alternative is a variable narkup formula in which the markup percentage is reduced by 1% for

[1] *Ad Dollar Summary* (New York: Leading National Advertisers, 1984 and annual pdates); "Local Bumping," case in Gilson and Berkman, *Advertising* (New York: Random Iouse, 1981), p. 351.

every $10,000 increase in the total net cost of a commercial between $30,000 and $120,000 or more. For example, the markup percentage is 35% for the $30,000 cost and 25% for a cost of $120,000 or more.[2]

[2] Lincoln Diamant, "Formula Trims Production Costs," *Advertising Age*, 55 (May 10, 1984), p. M-10; Robert C. Isham, "Stability on One Hand, Productivity on the Other," *Advertising Age*, 54 (May 23, 1983), p. M-36; Charles B. Jones, "Markups Mistaken for 'Commissions'," *Advertising Age*, 54 (April 25, 1983), p. 60; Harvey Lloyd, "In Defense of Photographers and Their Roles," *Advertising Age*, 54 (December 12, 1983), pp. M28, M30; Merle Kingman, "To Fee or Not to Fee," *Advertising Age*, 54 (August 29, 1983), p. M-24; Anna Sobczynski, "Industry Experts Read Between the Lines," *Advertising Age*, 55 (March 26, 1984), pp. M27–M29.

16
INTEGRATED COMMUNICATIONS STRATEGY

INTRODUCTION

o be in business in the year 2000, today's firms need to incorporate ıarketing communications into their strategic planning. Compartment- ized thinking, lack of attention to marketing concepts and philosophy, ıd single-approach, short-run, band-aid solutions to long-run problems ıcourage failure. Strategy involves understanding where you are in the ırrent environment and how you can get to where you want to be in ıe future.[1] Implementing strategy requires leadership and constant daptation.

Holistic thinking involves putting individual problems in a unified amework. This type of thinking is necessary for business success. The *hole* includes the physical, social, and technological environment; cus- ›mers and their life-styles; and changes in merchandise, marketing com- ıunications, and related policies. It includes paying attention to what nployees value and do best.[2] All too often, major efforts are made to atch up only a single area, neglecting the larger picture. For example, utstanding marketing communications will not work well if product uality is low compared to competitors' quality.

Tom Peters and Nancy Austin, in their best-seller, *A Passion for Excellence—The Leadership Experience*, point out that top management succeeds and communicates best by constantly getting out on retail-selling floors or plant-working areas. They call it MBWA—Managing by Wandering Around. Executives see, suggest, and participate on the spot, rather than sit in offices and dictate memos. Also important is the necessity for management to encourage constant innovation through small formal or informal groups known as "skunkworks," which are encouraged by management. Good ideas are always rewarded in some manner.

STRATEGIC PLANNING FOR THE LONG RUN

Product manufacturers who sell through retailers, as well as retailers themselves, suffer when they cannot plan for the future.[3] Managers with such uncertainty tend to blame poor performance on such things as "mediocre advertising," "image problems," "deteriorating locations," "tough competition," "wrong clientele," or "poorly utilized computers." Any or all of these problems may exist, but dealing with each of them should be part of a coordinated, long-range plan. Failure of a marketing communication to achieve desired results may not be entirely the fault of the communication. Other causes may exist elsewhere in the marketing mix.

Strategic Planning

Strategic planning concerns "efforts to keep the whole corporation optimally adapted to its best opportunities in the face of a constantly changing environment."[4] Strategic planning involves (1) setting long-run objectives for the business, and (2) analysing the competition, customers, and other relevant factors in the current situation. One environmental trend is the widespread use of music and television which break down cultural differences. With more variables, and awareness of different cultures, advertising can emphasize the underlying, general human condition, human emotions and values which transcend language and politics.[5]

Strategic planning also includes (3) formulating strategies that match strengths to opportunities and deal with weaknesses and threats, (4) evaluating strategies with respect to costs and benefits, (5) implementing the chosen strategy, and (6) evaluating that implementation. Strategic planning is an overall, not a piecemeal, approach. Therefore, advertising, visual merchandising, special promotions, publicity, and personal selling should be coordinated with other marketing efforts; and marketing efforts should be coordinated with accounting, finance, and other parts of the operation. This is a holistic approach.

An example of retail strategy is when we have a hypothetical store ı the high-rent district, Ultra's, provide many store services, use elaborate dvertising and fixtures, display little merchandise, and have a relatively ırge sales force. A contrasting strategy example is to have a store, in ıe low-rent district, Basic's, provide no free services, and have spartan xtures, price-oriented advertising, self-service, and crowded displays.[6] ommunications should be consistent with the firm's internal environment. or example, if the ads lead customers to expect that the store will be ke Ultra's, and the store is actually like Basic's, subsequent ads lose redibility and customers.

A creative strategy suggested for the highly competitive environment developing an *unfair advantage.* This unfair advantage is actually a ɔng-run, tactically integrated plan designed to anticipate environmental hange and achieve high growth and profit levels by establishing a position ı consumer markets so powerful that competitors can retaliate only in n extended period of time and at *prohibitive cost.* This strategy is based n a marketing concept, on an understanding of the current and anticipated ıture environment, including competitors and customers. It is different om "beating last year's figures".[7]

xamples of Integrated Solutions

ong-run holistic solutions that tackle the entire situation, may involve hanges in image and marketing communications accompanied by a back-p change in merchandise and decor. Two department stores that illustrate ıis point are Macy's and Bloomingdale's. The main stores of both of ıese retailers were located in New York City in an environment which ad changed rapidly since the end of World War II. It became obvious ıat if these retailers did not respond to these changes, their very survival ould be in serious doubt. Some stores that did not respond to the hanging times were no longer on the scene.[8] Step by step, department y department, Bloomingdale's and Macy's management not only changed ıeir merchandise policies but spent millions of dollars on new installations nd interior architecture. Macy's Cellar became a nationwide example f such compete changes. This basement area, a bargain budget apparel epartment, was eliminated entirely in favor of an upscale housewares nd food department. This department was in the form of stores along grand cobblestone street, including a grocery store, pasta center, candy ore, bakery shop, and delicatessen. The housewares section stocked ery expensive gadgets along with more conventional merchandise. To ɔp off these changes, Macy's invited P.J. Clarke, one of the popular estaurants in New York, to open a branch in the Cellar. Through the ears, this restaurant has attracted an Ivy League clientele.

This change of the use of the space in the basement typified the changes in other departments throughout the store. This same philosophy was used by Bloomingdale's to update many of its departments. The two stores' managements had the same general goal: to profit by making shopping in their stores an exciting and interesting experience.

With this as an introduction, let us examine the interrelationship of marketing communications strategic planning with theories, decision support systems and trends, and show how holistic thinking and strategic market planning can help make a firm more successful. As has often been said, "Nothing happens in a vacuum". Every change has feedbacks, spinoffs, interactions, and effects on image, goodwill, traffic, and purchases throughout the firm and its environment.

Strategic Planning with Theories and Paradigms

In order to take a holistic approach, it is helpful to get away from thinking about specific practical applications and to examine briefly some current thinking about marketing theories and paradigms. A *theory* is a systematically related set of statements that is empirically testable. *Paradigms* can be viewed as foundations of theories. A paradigm is a set of linked assumptions about the world, or any part of it, that is shared by a community of scientists investigating that world.[9]

Of interest to marketing communications is the *stimulus-response* paradigm which explains the reactions of customers to management actions. For example, the ad is a stimulus and the customer's purchase action is a response. The *dyadic exchange* paradigm sees a two-way transactional arrangement between seller and buyer in which the customers are more active than as mere respondents to stimuli. In this paradigm, the outcome depends on bargaining and on the relative power of buyer and seller. Both of these paradigms focus on the consumer and omit competition. They involve the questionable assumptions that customers know what they want, that research will find out what customers want, and that satisfied customers will make repeat purchases.

In contrast, strategic management focuses on sustaining a *competitive advantage*. Focusing on competitors includes both the element of customer satisfaction and the element of competition for differential advantage. This competition is the incentive for innovation. The focusing on competitors includes marketing communications.

Decision Support Systems and Strategy

Let us now look at marketing communications strategy from a *decision support system* (DSS) point of view. One current DSS is designed to help firms find out which consumer benefits give their firms a competitive advantage in the marketplace. This DSS uses a modification of the media-election method. It is broadened to be applicable to marketing communications strategy. Inputs into this DSS include up to 15 *bundles of benefits* that the firm might consider offering, up to five different *market segments* that the firm might consider as potential customers, the *desired features* in the benefit bundles, and the *demographic and psychographic characteristics* of the segments. Output includes descriptions of the types of customers whose wants match various benefits.[10]

rends and Strategy

o consider the big picture, marketers should look up from short-run etails and notice some emerging trends that will affect communications trategy in marketing. These trends include (1) time-poor and money-ich households with dual incomes; diverse individualistic lifestyles and nterest in high-margin premium products, (2) deregulation, which allows etailers to take on financial services and supermarkets to carry non-rocery products, and (3) dominance of wants over needs. The last trend neans shorter product life cycles because wants are more volatile than eeds. This means that firms must plan a shorter payback period.

Other trends include individual rather than household consumption, working and shopping from home, growing interest in one-stop, hassle-ree shopping, (2) nontraditional competition as retailers and merchandise ines and integrate backward towards manufacturing and manufacturers ntegrate forward into retailing. These trends suggest that firms need to edefine their businesses more broadly, which in turn affects their po-itioning strategy. Perhaps one way to redefine business will be to have portfolio of competing firms under one parent company. The firms ould have different positions, images, and marketing communications, ttracting different, sometimes overlapping, segments. With or without ackward or forward integration, both manufacturers and retailers need o understand how the other's marketing communications help both sell he merchandise.

Computer capability to report daily on profitability allows firms to eep track of which merchandise lines, which business units, and which narketing communications are profitable. To manage personnel costs ffectively and to make sure employees project a favorable image and lo not alienate customers, management needs to recruit selectively and o train and motivate the workforce.[11]

nvironmental Considerations

he communications model describes the process of communication. his process includes the encoding of the message by the marketer or n advertising agency, sending the message, and decoding and feedback y consumers—all modified by "noise" in the environment. When communications are considered as part of an information system, consumers may actually seek out and interact with marketing communications instead of being mere respondents to stimuli.

Retailers are often constrained by the local environment, and must fit into communities with unique customs, institutions and lifestyles, all of which tend to change over time. One current development is the urban shopping center which has a sizeable advertising budget and promotes the mall as an *experience*, using local newspapers, city magazine, ads in a magazine format, and broadcast media. Customers tend to be white-collar professionals who are not at home during the workday, but who can get to the mall for lunch and after work.[12]

As the environment changes, marketers must rethink their positioning. A firm must have a clear position in the minds of target consumers so that they know what the firm stands for. Marketing communications that tell consumers about a firm must be consistent with this position.

Because individuals perceive reality differently and see and hear advertising and displays selectively, the retailer must be particularly careful to project a consistent image. Good vendor resources help build store image. Attitudes towards a firm are influenced not only by marketing communications but also by past experience with a firm and its merchandise, and by the demographics and psychographics of the customers. A new market segment, the corporate woman, requires marketing communications and shopping options that save time. This segment is responsive to direct-mail advertising, clubs that for a membership fee offer individual wardrobe planning and other time-saving services, and ads in city business publications featuring profiles of high achievers.[13]

Marketing research and marketing information systems tell managers about the effectiveness of marketing communications. Research and decision support systems work on specific current problems. The information system provides ongoing information for routine decisions. Knowledge is power. A new development in computer software that will help marketing communicators analyse information is the *data massaging* approach. The "Cassandra system," owned by Nielsen, outputs selected data and reports from the Nielsen tapes in the format chosen by the client. "Apollo" reports on the cost of rating points that Nielsen and Arbitron determine by extrapolating and arranging the Nielsen and Arbitron information. Cassandra and Apollo seem to be more compatible than competitive.[14]

ADVERTISING, A MAJOR MARKETING COMMUNICATIONS TOOL

Advertising is the major marketing communications tool. It is expected to play a key role in strategic marketing. A major portion of many marketing communications budgets will continue to be spent for advertising unless there are major changes in marketing strategy.[15] Possible exceptions to his extensive use of advertising are the specialty retailers in shopping enters, both independents and chains, which tend to rely on traffic enerated by the shopping centers' strategic marketing communications.

dvertising Customs

n the normal course of events, the old method of determining how to dvertise was heavily influenced by last year's sales figures. Each product ategory expected to beat last year's sales figures. If the inflation factor was X% per year, then firms must increase sales by more than X% to xceed last year's sales figures in constant dollars, or dollars corrected or inflation.

Generally, sales follow a seasonal pattern. Each retail merchandise nanager and buyer follows a season of advertising designed to go against ast year's sales figures for a specific time period. This means that if the rst three weeks in May had high sales figures last year, advertising was cheduled for those weeks to attempt to better those figures. The higher ne past sales, the more total advertising money was budgeted. Over-pending was allowed in a particular week or month, but the annual dvertising expenditure was kept in line.

ew Concepts

ow the new concepts of strategic marketing have begun to challenge ne old routine as marketers realize the growing interdependence of ad-ertising and sales. However, even with a new, more sophisticated ap-roach, the seasons and consumer buying habits do not change rapidly. is clear that the advertising schedules must still consider customers' wn timing and the environment. What has changed is the way marketers pply the new concepts to the target consumers and seasonal demands.

Typical retailers and manufacturers of brand-name merchandise must ontinue to advertise spring merchandise, like bathing suits and lawn nowers, in the spring and fall merchandise, like coats and snowblowers, n the fall. A strategic marketing plan calls for treating the suit or coat d as part of a total picture, rather than as separate items. The suit and oat ads are building blocks that, when put together with other blocks, nake an important statement about firms and products. The marketing npact of the whole integrated marketing effort is then greater than the um of the parts. In other words, in addition to advertising suits and oats when consumers will buy them, the ads are also used to build store nd brand image and to take a position in the consumers' minds.

A parallel illustration might be of building a structure with blocks. ne block is not necessarily more important than another, but when the tructure is complete, it has a unity and design that has been put in lace block by block. Strategic marketing calls for each block to do a pecific task, such as selling suits or soups, yet at the same time these blocks must work at the general task of selling the firm or brand itself and communicating the image the firm is trying to create. This means that over a period of time, the advertising not only sells merchandise but also conveys to the public the firm's philosophy—what it stands for, the niche it expects to fill in its environment. The advertising also projects customers' lifestyles, pricing patterns, and approach to fashion, food, or whatever categories of merchandise a marketer sells.

All this calls for considerable overall planning and long-range thinking. Advertising is only part of a larger picture that can be created only through such thinking and planning. Marketer's must ask themselves where they want to be in five years, ten years. Are the current ads prophetic of the direction they wish to take for this long pull? As advertising is only one of the marketing communications tools, how should it support and be supported by the other tools: special promotions, visual merchandising, personal selling, and public relations? All of these tools need to be coordinated and timed so that they will work together to communicate the firm's position as well as to sell merchandise.

Consistency and Identity

Holistic thinking calls for an integrated approach. Advertising must reflect the current status of the firm, not the wishful thinking of the advertising people. For example, ultra-modern advertising confuses customers if a store's premises and merchandise look old-fashioned.

In most cases, the photography, layout, and artwork that make up an advertising message are as important as the copy. The illustrations and layout carry messages of their own. For example, there is *high-fashion* art or photography. Such art or photography should only be used if the products are in keeping with this philosophy, and the target includes high-fashion customers. The illustrations, print style, and logo must reflect the firm's philosophy and not feature the technique of a particular artist or photographer unless this is appropriate and related to company image.

Leading advertising experts have long maintained that a firm should build an identity through its advertising. These experts say the test of this identity is that when ads are shown to several hundred readers with the company's logo covered, target consumers can still recognize the firm. Such recognition means that the firm has built an identity and is advancing its interest on a day-to-day basis. If consumers' response is inconclusive, the firm should strive to integrate its advertising with its other marketing actions.

Advertising Forms and Media[16]

The combined efforts of art, copy, and production staff can create cost-effective and exciting advertising that pulls customers into stores to buy products. Print advertising in newspapers, magazines, outdoor billboards, nd transit, and in various forms mailed directly to customers, tells ustomers about merchandise. It also communicates what the customers' mage will be as a result of buying, giving, wearing, or using that merhandise. Such advertising should identify and sell the merchandise. ds should be focused, simple, and organized.

Direct-response advertising results in a measurable response or ansaction at any location. Customers can order by mail or phone, by omputer, or in person. Well-known forms of direct response print adertising are catalogs, letters, and newspaper tabloids. The table of contents f a new form of print advertising, the *catazine* or *magalog*, is shown n Exhibit 16-1. This print form is a retail catalog that has both feature rticles, as in magazines, and merchandise for sale, as in catalogs. Marketers ow are experimenting with binding mini-catalogs into mass circulation nagazines to increase awareness of the type and variety of merchandise ney sell.[17] Smaller, more local marketers can use smaller, more local nedia, such as programs for college football games. The ad shown in xhibit 16-2 was used in both a football program and a local newspaper.

Because media vehicles are the instruments through which advertising s communicated, media-selection decisions and timing are a very important omponent in advertising effectiveness. When the reach of a media vehicle loes not coincide with the geography of a trading area, a mix of media ehicles can be used. Radio advertising can be directed at specific, segnented, local audiences, and can reach mobile consumers. Network teleision can be used for national advertising and cable TV for more local, egmented advertising. A new medium targeted at high earning, high onsuming, seldom-at-home persons aged 18–34 is soundless "video vallpaper" on the walls of night clubs. Content includes old movies, ideo art, laser shows and ads.[18]

New technological developments are changing the relative costs and ffectiveness of broadcast advertising media. As technology develops to et consumers zap, or delete, TV commercials, producers must work hard o give commercials the quality of feature films to reward viewers for vatching. On the other hand, the color and graphics of videotex ads, hat supposedly would reward viewers for watching, have been used less han the black and white—and relatively inexpensive—text. Combinations f marketers like IBM, Sears, and CBS and Penney, RCA, and Citicorp ontinue to work to make videotex a mass medium.[19]

hilosophy of Advertising

Critics of advertising hold that advertising adds to the cost of products nd that in the long run, the consumer pays for it. It is claimed that were t not for the cost of advertising, the price of most advertised products vould be anywhere from 10% to 25% less. The answer to this criticism f advertising is that a *mass production* society must have *mass conumption*. The fact is that our highly automated industrial production

***EXHIBIT 16-1* Table of Contents of a Catazine**
Source: Jordan Marsh, Boston, MA.

This is the place to pick up your options and play out your fantasies. ★ It's you, center stage at the start of a new season, reel life meeting reality in the most sought-after looks. ★ JM at the movies, with the movie makers. ★ So you won't miss a beat, a pull-out guide in the centerfold. ★ Plus the on – and behind – the scenes coverage you've come to count on. You. Him. Kids. Home. ★ Now take a deep breath and on with the show!

Cover photograph by Hollywood legend, George Hurrell. "More by – and on – him," page 28 and insert. Stylist: Catherine Chamberet. Hair and Makeup: Susan Duffy.

Act boldly: the inspiration is Matsuda. He advances in the slouchy signature suit, $570, pure linen with a matching shirt. She demurs, propriety itself in double collars and long skirts. Or so it seems. Jacket, $295, skirt, $160, and blouse, $100. Shopping guide, see insert.

JM Magazine photographed on location at 20th Century-Fox Studios, Hollywood, California. Photographer: Robert Farber. Stylist: Perrine Anderson. Hair and Makeup: Bill Westmoreland

A JM Publication, 1984

EXHIBIT 16-2 Small-Town, Small Store Ad in College Football Program

Source: Webs, Amherst, MA. Size of original, $4\frac{7}{8} \times 4\frac{7}{8}''$.

with its sophisticated technology produces huge quantities of products more cheaply. When the same manufacturing tasks are done by hand or accomplished on a smaller scale, the cost of the products is higher.

Hence, mass production requires mass distribution and mass consumption. Mass consumption can only be obtained through marketing techniques, including the advertising that tells millions of people about a product. This philosophy also assumes a free-enterprise system where products compete with each other in the marketplace, and consumers determine how they will spend their discretionary income. An added criticism of our mass-marketing society is that many manufacturers deliberately build in artificial obsolescence and make products less durable than they should be. On the other hand, it can be said that the competitive aspects of a market-oriented society produce jobs for millions, achieve a high standard of living, and that in that system, only products made properly and priced fairly survive.

Perhaps both supporters and critics of our market-oriented society have valid points. As the public becomes increasingly well educated, it will make increasing demands for better quality merchandise that will last longer. Advertising will be read carefully and exaggerated claims easily recognized. There may be less of demand for unnecessary goods. The commercialized aspects of Christmas, Mother's Day, and Father's

Day will be more generally recognized and there will be less exploitation of such occasions. Ultimately, the public influences all commercial transactions by the manner in which it votes with its dollars.

OTHER MARKETING COMMUNICATIONS EFFORTS

Sales Promotion[20]

Sales promotion has been defined as marketing communications other than advertising, visual merchandising, personal selling, or publicity. It usually works best in combination with one or more of these other marketing communications tools. For example, sales promotion teamed with advertising, with displays, or both, has a synergistic effect which exceeds the sum of the separate effects, but incurs only the costs of the separate effects. Sales promotion includes special events, appearances, demonstrations, entertainments, exhibits, contests, seminars, sales, issuing coupons, and offering free samples.

The purpose of sales promotion is to help build image, to generate shopping traffic, and to sell merchandise. Sales promotion tends to be scheduled in a more irregular manner than advertising, which is usually done on a regular daily or weekly basis. Promotions can be used to generate traffic during slow seasons, months, days, and hours, and are important competitive tools in holiday seasons like Christmas.

The personal appearance of a rock star in the record department might sell hundreds of records, or a famous author in the book department can sell hundreds of books. A special exhibit or fashion show can attract hundreds of persons. With minimal expenditure and plenty of imagination and ingenuity, sales promotions can generate substantial sales. Exhibit 16-3 has advertisements for two such promotions: breakfast with an author, and breakfast with Peter Rabbit. Both require advance reservations and tickets, which help defray the costs of the promotion.

Visual Merchandising, Including Display[21]

Visual merchandising helps a store become a kind of theater, an exciting, entertaining place to shop, a place in which to spend recreational time and money. Visual merchandising should make customers want to return again and again. Store windows and interior store displays should have a unified look, presenting a clear image and identifiable product offers.

Effective displays sell by suggestion through showing customers how merchandise items can be used, worn, and combined, and how rooms might be furnished. For example, Gimbels, a department store in New York City, used stars from network soap operas as inspirations for several room displays of furniture and accessories. Photographs of the rooms and the stars were included in a newspaper ad, which also invited

EXHIBIT 16-3 **Advertisements for Breakfast Promotions**
Source: Macy's and B. Altman's, New York, NY. Appeared in *The New York Times* (March 1984). Sizes of originals, 4¼ × 6½″ and 2½ × 4¾″.

the public to visit the rooms and meet the stars, thus combining display, advertising, and special promotion.[22]

Aislevision is a new type of sign display that is suspended over supermarket aisles. On either end of the sign are listed the product categories shelved on the aisle below the sign and in the center is space for a manufacturer's ad. Aislevision was created by the firm that originated shopping-cart ads.[23]

Store logos on bags allow customers to display the store name as they carry the bags from the store and reuse them. Shopping bags can also carry messages. Some bags carry public-service messages with toll-free phone numbers for such services as reporting child abuse. The shopping bag in Exhibit 16-4 suggests delicious food products available at a farm market.

Personal Selling[24]

To many customers, the personnel are the firm. In doing the business of the firm, the employees can make customers feel pampered and important,

EXHIBIT 16-4 **Atkins Farms Market Shopping Bag with Product Suggestions**

Source: Atkins Farms Fruit Bowl, Amherst, MA.

or oppressed and inferior. Because employees can create effective public relations, every effort must be made to help them be happy, competent, and motivated. Regardless of firm size, salespeople need to learn about the firm's target customers, layout, merchandise, and competitors as well as policies and sales transactions. They also need to know how to approach customers effectively, determine their needs, show appropriate merchandise, assist in a decision to buy, and encourage customers to return. Education in the marketing concept, motivation, compensation, evaluation, and effective scheduling inspire employees and help them to produce sales and loyal customers.

Public Relations and Publicity[25]

Public relations is the effort, and favorable publicity is the desired result of activities that place firms in the news columns of newspapers and magazines or the news programs of broadcast media. Ineffective public relations can cause low visibility or generate an unfavorable company image. A firm must make efforts to earn a respected position in the community and to be newsworthy—the secret of receiving favorable publicity. Sales promotion activities, as well as unusually creative advertising, displays, and personal selling usually play a key role in attracting publicity by being newsworthy. Public relations personnel help coordinate these other marketing communications tools.

Publicity is a powerful marketing tool. What is read in the news columns or heard on the air has credibility because it is considered an objective point of view. The publicity in Exhibit 16-5 praises several firms for differentiating themselves from competitors by creating in-store and advertising environments in which target customers feel comfortable. This article also suggests that personnel be allowed to use their creative talents. Publicity is effective when it creates extensive and positive word-of-mouth communications.

Orchestration: Putting It All Together

It is up to the marketing executives in advertising, sales promotion, public relations, visual merchandising together with the merchandise managers and executives to present the entire firm with a unified position and image. Using all the marketing tools in a coordinated and meaningful way takes a great deal of cooperation, planning, and integration.

Planning and budgeting are important support functions for marketing communications. Creative, innovative budgeting is based on past experience, information about competitors and firm and product life cycles, the overall firm budget, and the task to be done. Budgeting should also allow room for dealing with unexpected contingencies. Continuing changes in the environment require management to reexamine budget allocations regularly, because what succeeded in the past may not be relevant for present and future. When retailers and manufacturers understand how to use effectively the cooperative funds for advertising and other marketing communications, they can stretch their budgets for mutual benefit.[26]

When properly done, the whole communications impact is greater than the sum of its parts. Communication is successful when the public becomes highly aware of the firm and what it stands for in the community. An example of store-wide cooperative effort through various marketing communications components is an anniversary sale. This might last as long as three or four weeks and is planned up to eight months in advance.

Achieving just the right atmosphere and tone and projecting the right image takes skill and imagination. The entire concept must be orchestrated so that the total effect is communicated exactly as the planners intended. These communications efforts cannot take place unless and until the firm develops a marketing philosophy.

***EXHIBIT 16-5* Publicity about Retailers Who Create Comfortable Environments**

Source: Samuel Feinberg, "From Where I Sit," *Women's Wear Daily* (July 25, 1984), Section 1, p. 14.

Aldo Papone, vice chairman of American Express Travel Related Services Co., and executive vice president of American Express Co., aligns himself with "*contextual management*" *against* "*people-proofing.*"

People-proofing, as he defined it in Tuesday's column, is *bureaucratic control.* In *contextual management,* on the other hand, "everyone carries out his or her responsibilities in relation to storewide concepts. Stores that harness the individual characteristics and capabilities of talented men and women, that allow their people to express themselves within the context of corporate rules and regulations, thereby encourage an all-important entrepreneurial spirit. Too many retailers set so many arbitrary controls it becomes impossible for a creative person to function."

Papone conceded that contextual management is "a long way from the old adage that success in retailing is based on three factors: location, location and location."

With few exceptions, Papone continued, "retailers are failing to differentiate themselves from competitors," adding, "Macy's, Bloomingdale's, Saks Fifth Avenue, Dayton's, Mervyn's, Barneys, Wal-Mart and Toys 'R Us are among the rare exceptions.

"Differentiation is not just related to merchandise content. It also means creating an environment in the store and in advertising with which target customers find themselves comfortable.

"At one time, Macy's New York, for one, thought of itself as being all things to all people. But when Ed Finkelstein returned from California in 1974 as president of the New York division and later as chairman of the parent corporation, he furthered a conception, begun by his predecessors, of concentrating on exciting lifestyle environments for the middle to upper-middle part of the marketplace. Management of this type does not manage to an economic cycle but, in good or bad times alike, offers merchandise in depth so as to avoid the risk of losing shoppers who could be storewide customers. That is why Macy's has been successful in transplanting its name and consumer franchise to Florida and why it will continue to provide both the steak and the sizzle in Texas.

. . .

The industry has not been able to put across as well as it should that one can go from an assistant buyer to a merchandise manager in a relatively short period and achieve major compensation. The reverse side of the coin is that upward mobility has created a lack of expertise that would be gained in a longer stay in many critical areas of the business. Retailing must find a way of compensating and otherwise motivating high-potential people so they will remain for a greater period in a given position."

MARKETING PHILOSOPHY

A marketing philosophy is a particular system of principles for the conduct of a firm's marketing activities. Such a philosophy vitally affects how a firm uses marketing communications. With their philosophies of mass marketing and related mass communications, giant firms like Sears, J.C. Penney, Levi Strauss, Lever Brothers and Procter and Gamble have allocated millions of dollars to spend annually on sales promotion, advertising, and publicity. If other firms simply try to follow suit, imitating this barrage of public exposure by the giants, smaller firms will soon be victims of reduced sales, less traffic, and lower profits.

In this environment of mass marketing, smaller marketers must strive to be different, to be "non-mass." Smaller firms need a niche. Their salvation lies in a philosophy of being different, in being somehow unique and special, and separating themselves from the giants. Small, independent firms are Davids faced with Goliaths. They can survive in the long run because their smaller size and smaller management enables them to be more flexible, to move and to innovate more quickly. They do not need to put out huge catalogs that must be planned a year in advance of the selling season. They can work closer to the selling seasons and closer to their own special customers, featuring more specialized, up-dated products.

Success in any business depends on imagination, thinking through what a firm's role and image should be. The French put it well with their phrase *raison d'être,* reason for being. If a business is "just another firm" and has no clear idea of what it stands for, it is in trouble because it does not know what to communicate! Successful businesses were started by people with ideas. They saw a need for their business and moved to fill that need. They had a philosophy. Examples of some successful philosophies are in Appendix 16. These include Filene's reduced-price philosophy, Macy's bigness philosophy, Neiman Marcus' special-quality philosophy, K mart's quantity/low price philosophy, and Levi Straus' durability philosophy.

Creating a Marketing Philosophy

What should be a firm's marketing philosophy? Why should anyone buy a particular brand, or shop in a particular store or shopping center? Just because it is there? There are firms and product brands that can succeed for a while just because they are there, especially when the economy is thriving and when competition is weak or nonexistent. However, this cannot last, for soon a competitor who does have a strong marketing philosophy will see the opportunity. Then the good old firm with no idea of the role it should have played will go down the drain.

A successful brand or store must not only have a philosophy and an image, but must also constantly reexamine that philosophy and image, keeping it up-to-date. Like people, firms and brands must have the kind of personality that attracts a following and makes customers like them. In addition to having a *good personality,* the firm through its advertising, sales promotion, and publicity must communicate its character to the community on a day-to-day basis. This might be done as follows.

First, management must ask such questions as: What do we want to stand for in the mind of the public? Quality merchandise? Bargains and Values? Reliability and Service? Big Assortments? Unusual Merchandise? First in Fashion? Regular Guys? Friendly? Easy Credit? Always thinking of the Public? or any possible combination of these? It is not always easy to come up with good answers or, having determined them, implement them and communicate them to potential customers.

Communicating a Philosophy

Second, once the matter of philosophy and image is settled positively, not by default, the firm must implement its marketing decision. From this point on, every dollar spent on merchandise, every ad run, every display and salesperson, every sales promotion event, and all public-related efforts should contribute to building that image. This is a decision that must stand the test of time, but can be constantly updated. It must be a deep commitment, not a superficial or cosmetic application. It can never be made only on the basis of transient value or current ideas. These, together with competition may change today, tomorrow, or next year. The philosophy must stand the test of time.

Third, management must make certain that the firm lives up to its philosophy, every day and every year, with no short cuts or temporary backtracking. In this effort, a firm can reach for the stars by making its advertising and sales promotion different, interesting, and exciting. In telling the day-to-day story through its advertising, sales promotion, and publicity, it can also tell the larger story of its philosophy and its commitment to the community. Advertising and sales promotion should not include ordinary sketches or photographs. Copy should not be run-of-the mill. It should be creative, attract attention, and be unlike other advertising in its competitive area. If the firm does not have staff with inspiration and imagination, these can be hired and rewarded. Target customers should be able to identify an advertiser, even without looking at the firm's name in an ad or on a building.

Next, such ideas and philosophies must become part of strategic marketing to target customers. Research keeps a firm up-to-date on customer characteristics. Keeping the characteristics of the target customers in mind, marketers must provide products and plan marketing communications for their customers.

Finally, it takes management ability to put the whole package together in an exciting manner. Today good communications is in part good show biz. Planning is essential to make any store or product entertaining and enjoyable. Creativity and innovation are essential and are fueled by recognition.[27] Buying merchandise can be made a rewarding experience if interesting and exciting environments make it fun. Even the Queen of England visited a store when she came to New York City. Visitors to any city should want to visit stores that are exciting and interesting; manufacturers can help stores create this excitement through display and promotion aids.

For example, hundreds of target customers in hypothetical firm Chu's geographic area should ask their neighbors, "Did you see Chu's displays this week? Did you see Chu's ad in this morning's paper? Did you hear Chu's spot on radio? Did you view Chu's television commercial?" When this happens, one knows a firm is on the right track. It is building an exciting image and getting its story across.

To sum up, successful marketers know how to use marketing communications to make their brands or firms a center of interest and excitement, with exhibits, new merchandise, unusual offerings, and entertainments for the children and adults in the target market. In an age of mass merchandising, it is important to be unusual and different, interesting and exciting, as well as important to the community. By being different from all the others, a firm or brand can succeed in an age of mass merchandising, mass communication and mass marketing.

Interdisciplinary Thinking and Evolutionary Pragmatism

A *pragmatist* tests the validity of concepts by their practical results. *Evolutionary marketing pragmatists* do research to find out who their customers are, where they buy merchandise, and why. The interdisciplinary thinking in this section is based on Charles Darwin's biological theory of evolution and the survival of the fittest, which as *social Darwinism*, has been transferred to other fields like management and sociology. As white rabbits survive in the Arctic by adapting to their environment, firms should survive competition by adapting to theirs. They should evaluate what works and what does not, repeating successes and dropping failures. Firms must set aside resources for taking risks and for trying new marketing communications ideas, and change when the change will bring the firm closer to long-run management goals.

SUMMARY

Sink or swim is the message of this chapter. Either develop a philosophy relevant for the environment and learn about target customers and the effectiveness of your marketing communications, or the firm won't be in business in the long run. Strategic planning and evolutionary pragmatism are phrases that mean to adapt the corporation to its best opportunities in a constantly changing environment. Plans must be implemented and implementations evaluated with respect to reaching goals. Marketing communications must be coordinated with one another, with other marketing, and with other strategic planning to work toward goals and toward integrated solutions to problems.

From the earlier emphasis on stimulus-response in communications, we move to strategic management that focuses on sustaining a competitive advantage. Advertising, special promotions, visual merchandising, personal selling, public relations, and publicity work to make a store or brand appear unique and special. This communications effort must be coordinated with the other parts of the marketing mix, product, price, and place.

Michael Becker, chief creative officer of Ted Bates Advertising, told the Federal Trade Commission recently that the future of advertising is found in the past. This means that the basic concepts will still apply, but changes in technology will modify details. For example, art directors can assemble mix-and-match commercials in their offices, commercials will reach consumers via lasers, satellites, and fiber optics, computer-controlled billboard ads will also report current road conditions—but human nature will remain the same.[28] As the saying goes, the only permanent thing is change. Successful marketing must be in the vanguard of the changing world.

QUESTIONS

1. Explain what strategic planning is and give an example related to marketing communications for a particular firm.
2. Explain why you think theory is or is not important in managing marketing communications. Of what use are paradigms?
3. Many firms operate marketing communications according to the stimulus-response theory. The dyadic exchange theory is a different theory. Explain which of these theories you prefer and why.
4. Why is competitive advantage important to firms, and how can marketing communications help sustain it?
5. Why is it necessary to use a holistic approach and to coordinate the various marketing communications tools? Describe a scenario in which this coordination does not occur for advertising, display, personal selling, and merchandise selection, and explain the problems this causes.
6. Explain what a marketing philosophy is and give a specific example.
7. Explain what evolutionary pragmatism is. What do marketers have in common with white rabbits in the Arctic?
8. Michael Becker told the Federal Trade Commission that the future of advertising is found in the past. Explain what this statement means to you.

NOTES

1. "The New Breed of Strategic Planner," *Business Week,* (September 17, 1984), p. 66.

2. "Who's Excellent Now," *Business Week,* (November 5, 1984), p. 77.

3. "Mass Merchandising News," *The Discount Merchandiser,* (August 1984), pp. 10–20, 110–119.

4. Phillip Kotler, *Marketing Management,* 5th ed. (Englewood Cliffs, NJ: Prentice-Hall, 1984), p. 279. For a fuller discussion, see pp. 34–75 and 279–80.

See also:

Alfred Eisenpreis, "A Guide to Effective Traffic Engineering," Newspaper Advertising Bureau, NRMA National convention speech, January 9, 1983, New York Hilton; Stanley Marcus, "Retailing's Urgent Need for Creativity," NRMA National convention speech, January 10, 1984, New York Hilton; Kurt Salmon & Associates, "Consumer Market Research Overview," report, 1981; E. B. Weiss, "Retail Trends That Will Shape Tomorrow's Marketing," Doyle, Dane & Bernbach, 1967; Ruth Ziff, "How American Consumers Expect to Live," Conference Board, 1980.

5. Jennifer Pendleton, "Technology Will Transform Advertising: Rosenshine," *Advertising Age,* 55 (March 19, 1984), p. 32. (Rosenshine is Allen Rosenshine, chairman-CEO, BBDO.)

See also, T. Levitt, "The Globalization of Markets," *Harvard Business Review,* 61 (May-June 1983), pp. 92–102.

6. Isadore Barmash, "How They Plan," *Stores,* (September 1983), pp. 7–15; B. Berman and J. Evans, *Retail Management* (New York: Macmillan, 1983).

7. *The Marketing-Driven Approach to Retail Management* (Columbus, OH: Management Horizons, Inc., 1985).

8. See Appendix 1 about Grant's and Korvette.

9. This section was based on articles in the *Journal of Marketing,* 47 (Fall 1983):

Rohit Deshpande, "'Paradigms Lost,' On Theory and Method in Research in Marketing," pp. 101–110; Shelby D. Hunt, "General Theories and the Fundamental Explananda of Marketing," p. 13; George S. Day and Robin Wensley, "Marketing Theory with a Strategic Orientation," p. 81; Johan Arndt, "The Political Economy Paradigm," p. 45.

10. Paul E. Green, Vijay Mahajan, Stephen M. Goldberg, and Pradeep K. Kedia, "A Decision Support System for Developing Retail Promotional Strategy," *Journal of Retailing,* 59 (Fall 1983), pp. 116–143.

11. This section is based on Jagdish N. Sheth, "Emerging Trends for the Retailing Industry," *Journal of Retailing,* 59 (Fall 1983), pp. 6–18.

12. "Urban Mall Ads Lure Shoppers," *Ad/Pro,* 1 (January 1985), p. 7.

13. See Chapters 1–5, and "How Szuba Is Shaping Carson's, Making It 'For Me'," *Ad/Pro,* 1 (January 1985), pp. 4–5.

14. See Chapter 4 and Anna Sobczynski, "Ratings Services Guide Sellers and Buyers," *Advertising Age,* 56 (January 10, 1985), pp. 27–30.

15. See Chapter 15.

16. See Chapters 6–10.

17. "Cutting Costs on Distribution," *Ad/Pro,* 1 (January 1985), pp. 1, 5.

18. L. Skehazy, "Ads against Wall in Video Background," *Advertising Age,* 56 (February 28, 1985), p. 6.

19. "For Videotex, the Big Time Is Still a Long Way Off," *Business Week,* (January 14, 1985), pp. 128–136; Felix Kessler, "In Search of Zap-Proof Commercials," *Fortune,* (January 21, 1985) Vol III, No. 2, pp. 68–70.

20. See Chapter 11.

21. See Chapter 12.

22. "Soap Stars—Star Rooms," Gimbels ad in *The New York Times* (January 13, 1985), p. 6.

23. "Supermarket Aisle Ads Provide Manufacturers a Cheap Medium," *Marketing News,* 19 (January 18, 1985), pp. 1, 4.

24. See Chapter 13.

25. See Chapter 14.

26. See Chapter 15.

27. Paul Harper, "Quality People Hold Key to Success," *Advertising Age,* 56 (March 18, 1985), p. 40.

28. "Future of Advertising Is Found in the Past," *Advertising Age,* 56 (January 14, 1985), p. 36.

APPENDIX 16

EXAMPLES OF MARKETING PHILOSOPHIES

Most executives haven't thought about the word *philosophy* since going to school, when they may have read about Socrates, Plato, and Aristotle. However, a firm should have a philosophy, and the public should know what it is. A few examples of successful philosophies follow.

Lincoln Filene decided that if new merchandise didn't sell quickly enough, it was because customers didn't think it was a good value at the price it was offered. It occurred to him that if he automatically reduced the price of that merchandise over a period of time, some customers would probably buy at the lower price level. It also occurred to him that unsold merchandise tied up cash that could be used to buy more merchandise. Therefore, he created the automatic markdown. If after several markdowns, there was still some merchandise left, it was given to charity organizations. Suddenly customers began pouring into Filene's department store in Boston. They became experts. If they saw little action on an item they wanted after its first markdown, they waited for the next one. That brought them into the store day after day, week after week, where they were exposed to and bought other bargains. Lincoln Filene's philosophy became a success story, which others have copied to some extent today.

Let us move to other retail philosophers, the Strauses of Macy's department store in New York City. These merchants realized that for a store located in a huge city of millions of people of all incomes, tastes, and backgrounds plus many thousands of visitors, a narrow philosophy would be difficult. The more they thought about this problem, the more certain they became that their situation dictated the philosophy for success. Macy's would be big, and try as nearly as possible be all things to all people. Their store must have merchandise to appeal to many different tastes and most pocketbooks. This concept demanded bigness—the world's biggest store! While no store can actually be all things to all people, Macy's came as close as possible to fulfilling that philosophy. They added to this idea the concept that people like to save money, so they offered merchandise that was cheaper when you paid cash, with the slogan, "It's smart to be thrifty." For many years Macy's built its success on selling for cash, pleasing millions of customers and saving them money at the same time. This philosophy of *Think Big* paid off handsomely. Even though today Macy's credit policy has changed, most other parts of the concept remain intact.

Let us now discuss another business philosopher, Stanley Marcus of Dallas' Neiman-Marcus. His philosophy suited a retailer in a prosperous city with a high per-capita income. Figuring that Dallas would have thousands of customers who would demand quality and some of the better things in life, why not cater to this group, offering expensive, up-to-the-minute fashion merchandise? At the same time the store would offer more moderately-priced merchandise for a large less affluent group who would be proud to buy at a store that catered to the successful. Then why not have such unusual merchandise that it might appeal to high-income people all over the United States? Why not become a national store? Soon Neiman-Marcus was communicating to affluent people everywhere through its advertising and its famous Christmas catalog, selling merchandise to many thousands who had never been to Dallas. The offerings of "his" and "her" airplanes, oil wells, robots, etc., became legendary. This philosophy was well thought-out and executed with unusual flair and panache.

The national K mart mass-marketing chain grew out of the Kresge bargain stores which had a philosophy of serving blue-collar customers with limited incomes. Their appeal was price, for the stores were able to save money on many categories of merchandise, which K mart bought in huge quantities at low prices. As inflationary pressures grew, K mart's sales grew also. However, even K mart seems subject to retailing changes. It is now upgrading some of its merchandise and interior decor as off-price and factory-outlet stores come in to compete for the low end of the market.[1]

We could mention other great retail philosophers such as Julius Rosenwald of Sears Roebuck and his "money-back guarantee," Marshall

[1] See Berman and Evans, *Retail Management*.

Field of the Chicago department store and his great import programs of exceptional values, and F. W. Woolworth and his idea that thousands of items could be purchased for five or ten cents. These and many other successful company leaders had strong ideas about why they should be in business and why they would succeed. They did not rest on their laurels but constantly made innovations.

On the other hand, Grant's lost its dry-goods philosophy, Korvette lost its discount hard-goods philosophy, and both went out of business.[2] Any change in response to changing environments needs to be clearly communicated to employees and customers. Without clear, consistent marketing communications, customers and employees get a confused image and perceive that the changed stores have no sense of direction.

Now the case of a manufacturer and a product. Levi Strauss is a good example of a company with a philosophy about its products. The original Strauss philosophy was to make the best possible men's work pants. They had to wear longer and take rough usage better than other pants then being sold. At points of stress they would have a metal rivet for reinforcement. They would be made of a strong durable fabric created by sailmakers in De Nîmes, France (hence the name denim). Seams would be double stitched and only metal buttons used.

These pants would be sold for prices that all could afford. Their trademark would be two horses pulling in opposite directions with a pair of pants in the middle attached, symbolizing great strength. These pants and their symbol became world-famous, first with miners in the West where they were first sold, then with farmers, and more lately with young people who made them a fad. Stories have been verified that visitors to Moscow wearing blue jeans have been offered as much as $100 in rubles for their jeans. "Levis" are a great success and an outstanding example of a good philosophy later augmented by marketing tools, advertising, publicity, and promotion.[3] However, the boom in blue jeans is over, and Levi must set itself for steady volume in the long run.

Management of 1100 convenience stores in the Sunbelt has a growth philosophy with a four-year plan. National Convenience Stores plans to reach sales goals by (1) increasing sales to the core target, males aged 18–34; (2) adding higher margin merchandise while concentrating on fast-food, nonfoods and gas; (3) adding at least 405 units, in existing markets only, by 1987, and (4) retaining its excellent management team. Marketing communications changes include new inside and outside store design, redesigned logo, and new emphasis on advertising.[4]

[2] See Appendix 1.

[3] See also "Levi's: The Jeans Giant Slipped as the Market Shifted," *Business Week* (November 5, 1984), pp. 79, 82.

[4] Jennifer Lawrence, "National on the Go in Convenience Market," *Advertising Age*, 55 (December 3, 1984), pp. 4, 82.

Entrepreneurs vs. Intrapreneurs[5]

There is a growing urge these days to go into business for oneself. People seem to believe that if they have skills and abilities plus ideas of providing new or better products or services, they should start businesses. Leading educational institutions report that enrollment in all types of entrepreneurial courses have increased tremendously since 1975. Each year since has seen rapid growth in attendance in courses for licensed real estate brokers, motion picture production, restaurant operation, franchise purchasing, hotel operation, and service business operation. Many leading firms report the loss of some of their most talented employees who leave top jobs to go into their own businesses.

To stem this tide a number of leading companies are allowing or encouraging employees with ideas for new products or services to present them to the firm. If the company believes that the ideas have merit, the employees are given financial support and helped to set up a business under the aegis of the company for which they work. It is agreed that if the enterprise is successful that the *intrapreneurs* will receive a good share of the profits and will manage the offshoot with no interference. If the concept fails, there are to be no recriminations but only encouragement to try again. It is believed that such policies will help keep the most talented people in the company and often start a new branch or subsidiary that can be very profitable and successful. Among the leading firms trying this concept are General Motors, Data General, Texas Instrument, AT&T, Minnesota Mining & Manufacturing, General Electric, IBM and Hewlett Packard.[6]

[5] "Intrapreneuring or Why You Don't Have to Leave the Corporation to Become an Entrepreneur," Gifford Pinchot III (New York: Harper & Row, Pub., 1985).

[6] *Time Magazine,* 125, No. 5 (February 4, 1985), p. 46.

INDEX

R

S